SHanson

Harson

Reading as Communication

**THIRD
EDITION**

Reading as Communication
An Interactive Approach

Frank B. May
Portland State University

Merrill, an imprint of
Macmillan Publishing Company
New York

Collier Macmillan Canada, Inc.
Toronto

Maxwell Macmillan International Publishing Group
New York   Oxford   Singapore   Sydney

Cover Photo: PhotoEdit, Tony Freeman

This book was set in Meridien.

Administrative Editor: Jeff Johnston
Developmental Editor: Linda James Scharp
Production Editor: Carol Sykes
Art Coordinator: Lorraine Woost
Cover Designer: Cathy Watterson
Photo Editor: Terry Tietz

Photo Credits: Andy Brunk/Merrill, pp. 4, 113, 121, 129, 154, 227, 235, 264, 299, 306, 402, 423, 437, 441, 449, 520; Frank May, pp. 8, 13, 19, 29, 37, 47, 62, 72, 148, 161, 178, 193, 205, 221, 256, 274, 290, 372, 381, 387, 410, 467, 477, 489, 506, 512; and Gale Zucker, p. 95.

Macmillan Publishing Company
866 Third Avenue, New York, NY 10022

Collier Macmillan Canada, Inc.

Library of Congress Catalog Card Number: 89–62393
International Standard Book Number: 0–675–21101–8
Printed in the United States of America
4 5 6 7 8 9—94 93 92 91 90

For my family
Amy, Dell, Kerry, Kelly
Ben, Katy, Keenan
and
Kay and Shirl
With intense love and appreciation

Preface

Reading is an interactive process—research, observation, and common sense show us that. Yet this idea of reading is only slowly entering the core of our educative process. I still see teachers who treat reading and reading instruction as either-or processes:

It's "either they get it or they don't. I can't take time to give every kid exactly the right background before he reads something." In some classrooms the chance for children to practice integrating their background with what they're reading is denied by teachers who seldom take the time for prereading "schemata enhancement."

It's either "Phonics *is* reading" or "Throw phonics out." In some classrooms there's little attempt to show children how decoding and comprehension processes interact to produce meaning.

It's either whole language as the new religion or subskill drill as the old religion. In some classrooms, to be doctrinaire is more important than being useful to a child.

Well, what can we do but *not* expect miracles? The good news is that many teachers *are* treating reading as an interactive process—between author and reader, between decoding and context, between words and schemata. Equally important, they're also treating reading *instruction* as an interactive process—one that occurs between teacher and child on an equal basis, between child and child on a cooperative basis, between reading and writing on a conceptual basis.

Furthermore, many teachers seem to be treating comprehension in ways that differ from those ways (or lack thereof) shown by Durkin's studies of the 1970s. Modeling is *in*—or at least it seems less foreign in elementary classrooms. I now can see teachers (often enough at least to give me encouragement) *showing* students how they go about comprehending text. Perhaps mere testing ("Answer the questions at the end of the story") is a dying form of reading instruction. I sincerely hope so.

I won't bore you about the contents of this third edition of *Reading as Communication*. That's what the table of contents is for. Nor will I insult your intelligence by telling you that this book is good for both undergraduate and graduate classes. Every college textbook author tells you *that*. This book is for those people who are either beginning or intermediate students of reading instruction.

vii

It's only for "advanced" students if they're very advanced in age (and forget what they learned three years ago), very advanced in wealth (and have no qualms about buying yet another textbook), or were once very advanced in opinion of their own knowledge but have discovered they know very little after all.

I'd like to thank a few caring people who made this book possible. First the people who gave up many hours to read and comment as official reviewers: Jerry Converse, of the California State University at Chico; Sarah Martin, of Eastern Michigan University; Sam Miller, of the University of North Carolina; Timothy Rasinski, of Kent State University; Sam Sebesta, of the University of Washington; Timothy Shanahan, of the University of Illinois at Chicago; and Sean Walmsley, of the State University of New York at Geneseo.

A special thanks to Jack Graves, of the California State University at Stanislaus, for being both a reviewer and a friend, and whose suggestions I enjoy and respect.

My thanks to Linda James Scharp, to Carol Sykes, to Jeff Johnston, and to other members of the Merrill Publishing staff for their warm cooperation and refined production skills.

Last, but definitely not least, I'd like to thank Dr. Amy Driscoll, a colleague of mine at Portland State University who has always been there for me when I needed someone—for inspiration, friendship, and advice. Thanks, Amy.

Contents

3

Emergent Literacy: The Interacting Language Arts at Home and School 57

Carol L. Peterman

4

Comprehension: Developing the Contextually Fluent Reader 109

5

Comprehension: Developing the Thoughtful Inferential Reader 141

6

Developing Your Students' Reading Vocabulary 173

Appendixes

Reading as Communication

The Battle over the Nature of Reading: What Kind of "ist" Are You?

━━━━━━━━ **CHAPTER PREVIEW*** ━━━━━━━━

What you think about the nature of the reading process will definitely influence the way you teach reading. This chapter can help you begin to think about where you stand. For instance, at this very moment are you more of a behaviorist or a Gestaltist in your ideas about learning and reading instruction? These ideas can make a real difference in the way you teach. Perhaps you're neither Gestaltist nor behaviorist but a cognitive psychologist instead. Or perhaps a cultural anthropologist. Do your assumptions about reading reflect a "top-down" or a "bottom-up" view of reading? Those assumptions can truly affect your teaching.

What about your concepts and attitudes toward writing and authors? These too can make a difference in how you teach reading. And what about the actual *process* of reading instruction? Should it be an intel-

---

*Research (Thomas & Robinson, 1977) shows that readers who read the subheadings and preview a chapter before they read it tend to understand a chapter better than those who skip these two steps.

lectual, mechanical operation of "Push-pull-click-click . . . Change kids that quick"? Or is it more of a social, cooperative learning process, involving children's *feelings*—about themselves, about school, and about reading?

Read on. We've much to think about together.

Thought is the seed of action.

—Ralph Waldo Emerson

All our knowledge has its origins in our perceptions.

—Leonardo da Vinci

Thought is the child of action.

—Benjamin Disraeli

Man is what he believes.

—Anton Chekhov

Behavioral psychology is the science of pulling habits out of rats.

—Douglas Busch

ARE YOU A BEHAVIORIST OR A GESTALTIST?

Teachers of reading, perhaps more than any other teachers, have daily, almost moment-by-moment decisions to make about learning. When Jodie makes a mistake reading a particular word in a sentence, should you interrupt her? Should you wait until she has read the entire sentence before discussing the word she has missed? Should you let the mistake go if she has substituted a word that means the same thing? Should you stop her immediately after the mistake and have her slowly "sound out" each letter? Or should you have her use a more visual approach of looking for familiar letter patterns? Or maybe you should have her pretend that the word she missed is a blank and ask her to think of all the words that might fit in the blank. I've given you five or six alternatives, all of which require you to make a decision based on your view of learning—as well as your view of the reading act.

According to research (Barr & Duffy, 1978; Bawden et al., 1979; Gove, 1983), the way you think learning takes place influences the way you teach. Not that we need research to tell us this. It's just common sense, isn't it? But perhaps you haven't had the chance yet to decide how *you* think learning takes place. Maybe on this topic you've only had the chance to tell a *professor* what you thought he or she wanted to hear; you've yet to decide how *you* think. For instance, do you think like a behaviorist or like a Gestaltist?

THE BEHAVIORIST VIEW OF LEARNING AND READING

The behaviorist view of learning and reading processes has been the most dominant view since the 1920s. Every now and then the Gestaltist view gets a foothold again, but until the early 1980s, it was not very popular. All the most influential behaviorist psychologists, such as Pavlov, Thorndike, and even Skinner, have relied on three variables to explain learning: stimulus, response, and reinforcement. Pavlov spent his free moments ringing chimes whenever he offered food to dogs. You remember, don't you? Before long the dogs would salivate not only when offered food but also when offered nothing more than the sound of a chime. (I do the same thing when it's not my turn to cook and my best friend says, "Okay, honey, dinner's ready.") At first the stimulus is the sight and smell of food, but eventually the stimulus becomes the sound of a chime (or a loved one's voice). The salivation (sorry about that repulsive word) becomes the response, and the actual food becomes the reinforcement. The more frequently such a chain of events occurs—stimulus, response, reinforcement—the more firmly established the learning becomes, according to behaviorist theory.

Thorndike liked cats better than dogs. No one knows why, but perhaps it was because cats are cheaper to feed. At any rate, as you remember, he locked them up in wooden boxes, put a catch on the door of the box, and placed a dish of food *outside* the door. (In all other respects, I understand, he was a nice man.) With the sight of the food as the stimulus, a cat thrashed about until eventually it accidentally opened the door (response) and got its reinforcement (the actual food). The next time, though, the cat usually took less time getting out of the box, and eventually it went straight for the latch and opened the door. The frequency of trials, Thorndike surmised, increased the chance that the learning would stick.

Skinner used pigeons. Cheaper yet? I don't know. At any rate, he would wait for one to move in the right direction, then reinforce it by punching a hand-held button that released a tasty pellet. Once, on national television, Skinner taught a pigeon, in less than two minutes, to spin around in a circle. As soon as a partial circular movement had been established, he waited until the pigeon moved even farther in a circular direction before rewarding it with a pellet. In other words, Skinner skipped the type of artificial stimulus used by Pavlov and Thorndike and relied on the pigeon's memory of its own movement (a more intrinsic, natural kind of stimulus). His method was very effective, but I hasten to add that he first starved the pigeon by one-third of its body weight before he trained it. (If I were that starved, I would not only spin around in a circle; I would recite the Gettysburg Address at the same time.)

So you see, Pavlov, Thorndike, and Skinner believed that the frequency of the stimulus, response, and reinforcement encouraged learning to take place. They also believed that complex behavior was nothing more than the adding up of numerous stimulus-response-reinforcement "bonds." If we apply this theory to reading instruction, we would want to teach the smallest, simplest behaviors

first and gradually build up to more complex behaviors. Right? We'd teach children letters like *a* and *p* first, wouldn't we, asking them to respond with the middle sound in *cat* every time they saw the stimulus letter *a* and to respond with the sound /p/ every time they saw the letter *p*. And of course we would reinforce them with a smile or a kind word every time they behaved correctly. When we wanted more complex behavior, we would teach them to "chain" the two bonds and respond with the sound /ap/ when they saw the letter *a* followed by *p*. And for even more complex behavior, we could eventually get them to respond correctly to *words* such as *cap, lap,* and *nap.*

Sounds simple, doesn't it? Teach children letters, then "phonograms" like *ap, ip,* or *ite,* then words like *cap, lip,* and *kite,* then phrases, then sentences. Thus, according to behavioristic thinking, learning to read becomes a problem of addition. We slowly add up the parts until we get the whole.

THE GESTALTIST VIEW OF LEARNING AND READING

Gestalt is a German word meaning a unified whole, pattern, or form. For Gestaltists, learning moves best from whole to parts rather than from parts to whole.

Gestaltists have done many experiments with human beings, but the best-known have been with ambiguous figures. Do you remember this one? What do you first see inside the rectangle in Figure 1.1?

Some people see a beautiful young woman looking to the left, some see an old woman with a huge nose and jutting chin. What we see is dependent not so much on the stimulus, say the Gestaltists, as it is on our *hypothesis* about the stimulus. And that hypothesis depends upon our background, needs, and interests. In other words, we have considerable control over the stimuli in our environment. We usually see what we need or want to see. Furthermore, we tend to perceive the "parts" on the basis of a "whole" (an expectation or theory) in our heads. And we perceive the whole suddenly, all at once, without adding up the parts.

But Gestaltists didn't limit themselves to mere humans in their studies. They went back and took a second look at some of the animal experiments the behaviorists had been doing. Kohler (1915) taught chickens to peck at the *darker* of two squares in order to get food. But after pecking the same square numerous times, the chickens switched suddenly to a new square. Why? Because the new square inserted in the cage was even darker than the *old* dark one. Hmmmm . . . what have we here? A thinking bird with a mind of its own? Here we thought the bird had formed a strong bond with a *particular* dark stimulus. Instead it had formed a kind of nonverbal hypothesis (minor though it may be): "Duh, let's see now. Whichever one is darker, I'm supposed to peck at that."

Koffka (1928) repeated some rat-maze experiments that had been performed by behaviorists. He noticed that the rats' solution to the maze was very sudden, as if they had suddenly caught on—as if a brand new, nonverbal hypoth-

FIGURE 1.1
An ambiguous figure

esis were tried and it worked! This observation seemed to conflict with the notion of frequency—that the more the rat tried the experiment, the faster it would get at reaching the food. Perhaps even rats form a kind of generalization (a whole) that influences the way they perceive the separate stimuli (the parts). Perhaps even rats are problem solvers.

ENTER, COGNITIVE PSYCHOLOGISTS
AND CULTURAL ANTHROPOLOGISTS

Yes, even rats, I said (with the emphasis on *even*), for I'm making the assumption that you agree with me about humans. They're the most intensive problem solvers in the world. If you're like me, you spend half your day solving problems: How to stagger from bed to bathroom without crashing into something very hard and hurting. How to make a good cup of coffee without forgetting to put the filter in the filter holder. How to get out the door without forgetting half the things you'll need in order to pretend competence, dignity, and sophistication all day long.

Part of problem solving, of course, is making predictions or hypotheses. As we move out into the world each morning, we're kept very busy making predictions and confirming their validity (or lack thereof). *Prediction:* "If I wear this beautiful red silk shirt, surely I'll be warm enough." *Confirmation:* "Ridiculous! You're now freezing for the sake of vanity. Next time wear wool." *Prediction:* "Interstate 5 will be the fastest way to get to work by 8:00." *Confirmation:* "Wrong! Next time take Old Harrison Road past Jack's meat market and cut through the service station without ringing their bell."

Dyson says approximately the same thing about humans, using the framework of "cognitive psychologists"—young friends and tennis buddies of Gestalt psychologists:

> From the point of view of cognitive learning theory, children have a strong desire to master their environment. . . . They select, interpret, and integrate information about the world in order to form a working model of that world. On the basis of their models, they make predictions about how the world works, and when those predictions do not work out, they attempt to solve the puzzlement. (1982, p. 831)

In his book *Joining the Literacy Club,* Frank Smith seems to agree with cognitive psychologists. But he suggests that we educators drop our love affair with experimental, behavioristic psychologists entirely. Better yet, he says, take up with cultural anthropologists—specifically with ethnographers, people who never overlook the *social* nature of learning.

> Unlike experimental psychologists, cultural anthropologists have long recognized that it is impossible to study a situation objectively if investigators intrude their own rules, desires, or frames of reference. . . . The participant-observer approach of reading and writing with children offers a way of learning [that] many teachers employ intuitively. . . . Learning is a social activity, and its most important aspects from the learner's point of view are the people in the "club" that the learner must join. (1988, pp. 120–122)

What Gestaltists, cognitive psychologists, and ethnography advocates seem to imply is that behavioristic, experimental psychologists, because of the *way* they've been investigating the learning process (in quiet, sterile labs instead of bustling, messy classrooms; and with rats, cats, and pigeons instead of girls, boys, and teachers) are, shall we say, slightly irrelevant.

Behaviorists, on the other hand, seem to imply that learning is learning. No matter what the context, if you can find the right reinforcement, learning will take place. Just provide that learner's particular reinforcement (praise, tokens, candy, money), and you can "get him to learn anything you want him to learn." Just break the learning process down into smaller and smaller parts and reinforce him for learning each part, step by step.

Well, what to do. When trying to apply these theories to the teaching of reading and writing, we're forced to make some philosophical decisions. Let's take an example. How would a human being deal with this reading situation. Which philosophy would you choose at this point in your thinking. One of them? More than one?

The _____ went sailing across the _____ .

Behaviorist: Given the proper reinforcement, the learner will fill in the blanks according to the specific *stimuli* provided in the letters, words, and blanks.

Gestaltist: The learners will fill in the blanks according to various *meanings* they have gathered in the past. These meanings coalesce into a unified theory, and the blanks can be readily filled in.

Cognitive psychologist: Children have already formed a working *model* of their world. There are things that go sailing across things. The learners will plug in those things that fit their individual models.

Ethnographer: Children differ according to their *interests* and sense of *relevance.* I have no idea how each child will read this sentence. I'll just have to observe to see the differences, which in past observations have depended so much on the individual's interests, and how relevant the information is to each individual's life.

So which one did you choose, and did your choice actually fit the way *you* read the sentence? When you get the chance, you might want to ask someone else to read the same sentence. The way another person fills in the blanks (and the reasons given for this) might surprise you. Meanwhile, let me introduce you to four philosophers from the planet Zania, who will help us see the complexity of this debate about the nature of reading.

FOUR PHILOSOPHERS FROM THE PLANET ZANIA DISCUSS READING

Four philosophers from the planet Zania were given permission by Mrs. Kelley, the elementary school principal, to visit a third-grade classroom to determine what Earthlings were talking about when they used the word *reading*. The four

philosophers stumbled down the corridor to room 18, Miss Jerinski's room. Neither their eyes nor their ears had become adjusted to the Earth's heavy atmosphere and pollution; consequently, they could see and hear very poorly. Yet they were determined to examine the phenomenon of reading that seemed to concern so many Earthlings.

Philosopher Alpha studied a child who was being taught by Mr. Blair, an aide to Miss Jerinski. Mr. Blair was showing Cindy that the words *dog, dig,* and *dive* all start with the same letter and that this letter represents the same sound in each word. "Aha," said Philosopher Alpha. "Reading is a decoding or deciphering process. When a child learns to read, she is learning to translate written symbols into spoken ones. Reading is nothing more than decoding."

Philosopher Beta examined a child who was being taught by Miss Jerinski. Miss Jerinski was asking Brad some questions before and after he silently stared at each page of a book. "Eureka," said Philosopher Beta. "Reading is a process of gathering meaning from written symbols. Reading is nothing more than comprehension."

Philosopher Omega scrutinized a "scope and sequence chart" that Miss Jerinski had presented to him. On this chart were "subskills" such as these:

____ Decoding the initial consonant letters *h, m,* and *p*
____ Decoding the final consonant clusters *st* and *nd*

_____ Selecting the topic sentence in an information paragraph
_____ Determining when words are used as metaphors

The phrases went on and on. There were handtoes and handtoes of them. (The term _handtoe,_ on the planet Zania, refers to a set of twenty.) There were so many different phrases that Philosopher Omega was at first quite confused as to the nature of reading. But suddenly it came to him. "I know exactly what reading is!" he exclaimed. "Reading is one gigantic skill that's made up of many, many tiny subskills. Put all those subskills together and what have you got? Reading!"

Meanwhile, Philosopher Theta was staring at a girl who was, in turn, staring at a book. Every now and then the girl let out a laugh or shook her head, as if disagreeing with someone. Once she even said out loud, "That's a bunch of malarkey!" Several times she wrote down some words that seemed to be similar to, but not the same as, the ones in the book. Philosopher Theta continued to watch in amazement. The girl was totally wrapped up in what she was doing. The book seemed to be entertaining her, sometimes annoying her, and perhaps informing her of something, since she often wrote things down. Theta decided to interrupt the girl and talk to her.

"What is it that you're doing?" he asked.

"I'm reading this book," she said.

Theta scratched his head. "Could you tell me who made that book?"

The girl shrugged her shoulders. "I don't know who made it, but a man named Butterworth wrote it."

Theta squinted at the girl. "Wrote it?"

"Yes," she said. "You know. He made up the story. It's called _The Enormous Egg._"

Theta nodded his head and stroked his beard. "I see. And when you're reading this story that Butterworth made up, are you talking with him?"

The girl giggled. "Well, not really," she said. "But in a way I guess I am. It's just as if Mr. Butterworth were telling the story to me."

Theta nodded. "Amazing!" he said. "Truly amazing. Can you read the book in such a way that I might hear what Mr. Butterworth is saying?"

The girl gave Theta a strange look and shrugged her shoulders. "Sure," she said. "I'll read you a little bit of it."

She proceeded to read a short part in which a scientist was explaining how a normal chicken could lay a dinosaur egg. The philosopher gasped and interrupted the girl again. "Are you reading exactly what Mr. Butterworth is saying to you?"

"Sure," she said.

"But how do you know?"

The girl shrugged her shoulders again. "It's right there," she said, pointing to the words on the page. "See these little words here? Mr. Butterworth wrote them down and I'm reading them just the way he wrote them."

Theta smiled. "That's really wonderful, isn't it?"

The girl smiled back. "Want me to read some more?"

Theta said, "Yes, please. But first tell me something. Before you read me more, do you have any idea what the words are going to say next?"

"Oh, sure," she said, and proceeded to predict the general nature of what the author then said. After listening to her read more and asking her more questions, Philosopher Theta walked out into the corridor to join his three companions. "Reading is a code-emphasis process!" one of them was shouting. "It's a meaning-emphasis process!" another one said. The third one replied mysteriously, his arms spread outward, as if holding a large globe. "Reading is huge," he said. "It's a gargantuan set of decoding and comprehension subskills!"

"Gentlemen," Theta said softly. "I know exactly what reading is." The others waited, staring at him hostilely. "Reading," Theta said, "is a game!"

"A game!" the others cried.

"A game," he said, with a twinkle in his eyes. "A kind of guessing game. In fact, Earthlings have developed a highly sophisticated set of rules for this game."

"Rules?"

"Yes," Theta replied, chuckling to himself. "Rules about how to think when you want to communicate with someone else. Rules on what sounds you have to make or what symbols you have to write or what order the word-noises have to be in. Rules for what the word-noises will mean."

"Are you saying . . . ," Alpha started to ask.

"I'm saying," said Theta, "that reading is a game that a reader plays with an author. It's a guessing game."

"A guessing game!" the other three shouted.

"Exactly," said Theta. "When Earthlings read, they are intelligently guessing what the author is going to say and then confirming their guesses by looking for special clues."

"Impossible," said Omega. "Reading is a vast set of tiny subskills. I can show you right here on this chart . . . "

"It's nothing more than cracking a code!" said Alpha. . . .

The four philosophers from Zania spent considerable time arguing over their isolated perspectives, then drove off in four rented cars to different schools and universities throughout the country. Several weeks later they met again at the International Airport in Chicago, where their spaceship had been guarded and studied by employees of the Chicago Museum of Science and Industry. I was fortunate enough to be allowed to interview three of the philosophers before they took off for Zania.

My first interview was with Philosophers Alpha and Beta and went something like this:

MAY: As I recall, Philosopher Alpha, you were convinced before you left Chicago that reading is more of a decoding process rather than one of gathering meaning. Do you still feel that way?

ALPHA: Yes, I do. To me, reading is primarily the translation of written symbols into speech sounds—a decoding process.

BETA: I beg to differ, Alpha. Reading is the process of getting meaning from those written symbols—it's a comprehension process.

ALPHA: [shaking his head] That doesn't come until the end.

BETA: What do you mean?

ALPHA: I mean, first an Earth child has to notice each letter in a word; then he has to figure out the meaning of that word; then he has to do that for each word in a sentence; and finally he has to figure out the meaning of the sentence. Decoding comes first—then comprehension.

BETA: An Earth child does not read one letter at a time, Alpha—any more than Zania children listen to one speech sound at a time.

ALPHA: Listen, Beta, I've been talking to some professors at the University of Aritexas, or something like that, and they've been using some pretty sophisticated timing devices and cameras. The professors *I* talked to say that Earth people read letter by letter from left to right. The meaning doesn't come until later. (Gough, 1972)

BETA: Well, I've been talking to some professors at the University of Illiana, and they've been using a pretty sophisticated method of studying Earth children's reading errors. It's called "miscue analysis," and what they say is, readers don't begin with letters and build up gradually to the sentence meaning. They start with an idea of what the author might say next and check their predictions by sampling from the print.

ALPHA: You mean Theta was right? That reading is a guessing game?

BETA: Well, yes, in a way. It's a very intelligent guessing game based on the Earth child's past experiences and on his ability to notice a variety of clues.

ALPHA: What kind of clues?

BETA: The way a word fits in with the meaning of the *rest* of the sentence. Or the order of the word in the sentence. Or the way the word is spelled.

ALPHA: [laughing] Nah. You've got it wrong. As usual, Beta, you're a romantic. A mystical thinker. It doesn't happen that way at all. Take it from me. The only Earth children who guess are the poor readers, not the good ones. A good reader systematically "plods through the sentence, letter by letter, word by word. . . ." (Gough, 1972, p. 335)

BETA: Until he finally reaches comprehension?

ALPHA: Until he finally reaches comprehension. But decoding is where all the work is—translating those symbols into sounds. Comprehension is secondary, I'm convinced of that.

BETA: Did your professor friends say that—that comprehension is secondary?

ALPHA: No, but I did.

MAY: Thank you gentlemen. This has been most interesting.

BETA: [smiling] You can call Alpha a gentleman if you want to, but I'm female.

MAY: Oh, I'm really sorry. I didn't realize . . .

BETA: [taking off her hat] Zanian females have hair; Zanian males lose theirs when they reach pubescence. That's the only way you can tell us apart.

Decoding: translating written words into spoken or subvocal words

After the embarrassing ending to the first interview, I proceeded with more caution in the interview with Omega, who unfortunately was wearing a helmet.

MAY: If you were living on the planet Earth, would they refer to you as Mr. Omega or Ms. Omega or something else?

OMEGA: Dr. Omega.

MAY: Uh, thank you. Tell me, Dr. Omega. Have you changed your mind about the reading process since you left Chicago?

OMEGA: No, I haven't.

MAY: I see. Well, as I recall, you left Chicago believing that reading is nothing more than a vast set of tiny subskills.

OMEGA: [beaming] Yes, vast indeed. Why, in one school system they were teaching children over 300 of these subskills in the first six grades!

MAY: Could you give me a few examples?

OMEGA: Oh, there was one I really liked. It's called "discrimination between the voiced and unvoiced *th* in words like *this* and *thin*." And another one I liked was called "pronouncing the /ō/ sound when it's represented by *oa* in words like *boat* and *oak*." Such precision is really quite beautiful, something I hadn't expected to see on Earth.

MAY: Hmmm. Any comprehension subskills?

OMEGA: Oh yes. Lots of those too . . . like "recognizing when a story is a fantasy and not a true story," and, let's see, like "recognizing the main idea in a nonfiction story."

MAY: You mentioned that this school system is teaching over 300 subskills. Is this a good thing, as far as you're concerned?

OMEGA: Certainly. The more subskills your Earth children learn, the more they learn how to read.

MAY: And you're convinced that this is the best kind of reading instruction.

OMEGA: Yes. It reminds me of a club I was in as a boy back in Zania. Every time I learned a new skill, you know, like projecting my voice for a hundred yards, I was given a badge I could wear on my zober-haired sweater.

MAY: [much more relaxed now that I knew what sex he was] What's a zober?

OMEGA: Oh, it's like one of your monkeys, I guess.

MAY: Interesting. So, you'd get a badge for each new skill?

OMEGA: Yes, it was like the way children in your schools get rewarded for passing a subskill test. If they get 80 percent correct, they get their card punched, or their checklist checked, or something definite like that. For example, if they pass a test on "reading words with the digraphs *th* or *sh* in them," they get punched or checked off. Some teachers give them little scratch-and-sniff stickers or maybe a token they can use for buying something later.

MAY: I see. And so you think that reading is a process of learning one little subskill after another until you accumulate enough to be called a reader.

OMEGA: [delighted] Yes, that's it. Like in the Yellow Zobers—that's the name of the boys' club I was in—we were called Banzoombles after we passed all the tests.

MAY: Banzoombles?

OMEGA: Something like your Eagle Scouts.

MAY: Right. And did you find any evidence during your travels that this procedure of teaching and testing subskills produces good readers?

OMEGA: Well, the principals of all the schools I visited were quite enthusiastic about it.

MAY: And the classroom teachers?

OMEGA: Oh, I'd say they believed in it pretty much, although I'd have to say that many of them thought they did things because the principals wanted them to do them.

MAY: How about the reading specialists?

OMEGA: They weren't quite as enthusiastic. Some of them didn't think the subskill method of teaching was all that effective.

MAY: What you've just said about teachers, principals, and reading specialists fits a survey I've seen. (Shannon, 1982)

OMEGA: [showing interest by raising his eyebrows] Yes?

MAY: The survey showed pretty much what you said. The reading specialists were not overly impressed with the validity of the commercial materials the class-

room teachers were using—the materials based on the subskill approach to instruction.

OMEGA: Oh?

MAY: But the principals were.

OMEGA: [satisfied] Ah.

MAY: And most of the teachers said they use the subskill materials because the administrators expected them to.

OMEGA: Rightly so.

MAY: Well, what about it, Dr. Omega. Do you think the subskill method is scientific?

OMEGA: What does that mean—*scientific?*

MAY: It means that a large group of children are taught using the subskill approach and their achievement is compared with a large group who did *not* use the subskill approach. It also means that someone can demonstrate that there are such things as subskills that good readers use as they read. John Downing, for example, says that the "so-called reading skills" are "largely mythical" and have "no basis in objective data from studies of actual reading behavior." (1982, p. 535)

OMEGA: [smiling] Your notion of *scientific* is amusing to me. On Zania we once had such a notion, but we gave it up.

MAY: Really? Why?

OMEGA: Because too few of us understood it. Oh, many Zanians pretended to understand. But for the most part, they just used the word *scientific* without *being* scientific. So we dropped the idea of *scientific* and went back to *logical.* That's why I'm so impressed with the subskill notion, because logically, every skill can be broken into subskills. And every subskill can be broken into even smaller subskills. If you break a skill down into fine enough subskills, you can gradually teach it to a very young Earth child. Maybe even to a—what do you call it here?—a rug rat.

MAY: No matter what the skill is?

OMEGA: Certainly.

MAY: I can tell you about studies that raise serious questions about the subskill approach to instruction. (Downing, 1982; Stennett et al., 1975)

OMEGA: [smiling] Are they based on your so-called scientific method?

MAY: Yes.

OMEGA: I think my spaceship is about to leave. I've enjoyed our little conversation.

BOTTOM-UP OR TOP-DOWN: WHAT VIEW DO YOU TAKE

The Michigan Institute for Research (Barr & Duffy, 1978; Bawden et al., 1979) conducted several studies to determine teachers' beliefs about the nature of the reading process. They found that their views fell into two major categories. The labels often given to these categories are both descriptive and amusing—"bottom-up" and "top-down." If a teacher indicates that her most important instructional goal is to get her students to "really know the sounds that the letters make," her view of reading would probably be placed in the bottom-up category, since the unit of language she emphasizes is at the "lowest" level. If a teacher says that her most important instructional goal is to get her students "to read more library books," her view would probably be placed in the top-down category, as her emphasis is on "higher" units of language.

Bottom-up approaches to reading include the assumption that reading begins with print and proceeds systematically from letters to words to phrases to sentences to meaning. Top-down approaches assume that reading begins with knowledge and hypotheses in the mind of the reader. You remember that sentence I gave you before: The _____ went sailing across the _____ . Now, suppose you were reading a story about a tennis match and you came to these two sentences: Jerry swung the racket. The _____ went sailing across the _____ . (I fooled you earlier, didn't I?) As I said before, because of your background knowledge and your ability to hypothesize, you would know right away what words to expect in the blank slots. To make sure of your predictions, however, you probably would sample a bit of the print, if it was available to you—something like this: The b‒ ‒l went sailing across the n‒ ‒. By checking the print in this way, you would confirm your predictions. This way of perceiving the reading process is called the top-down view.

The chart in Table 1.1 was developed by Mary Gove (1983) and published as part of an article in *The Reading Teacher*. By examining it, you can get some idea of where you presently stand on the important issue of what the reading process really is. I hope, though, you'll keep an open mind until you "hear me out" in Chapter 2.

WHAT ARE YOUR VIEWS ON WRITING AND AUTHORS?

Karen is a lucky six-year-old. From the age of one, her parents read books to her. They bought her books. They gave her paper and pencils. They encouraged her scribbling. They praised her when she first wrote her name. They read everything she wrote with eagerness. Without even trying they were teaching her that reading is a process of communicating with others. Without even trying they allowed her to discover the important connections that exist between learning to read and learning to write.

If her teachers continue to teach her these concepts, two things will probably happen: (1) She'll stay motivated toward learning to read, and (2) she'll develop the type of mental set that will cause her to read for meaning rather than merely for "sounding out the words" or for "getting the diggy-nabbed assignment done."

On the other hand, if Karen begins to perceive reading as nothing more than sounding out words, filling in blanks, and handing in assignments, you may have

TABLE 1.1
Conceptual framework of reading

| Concept Areas | Summary of Beliefs | |
	Bottom-Up Conceptual Framework of Reading	Top-Down Conceptual Framework of Reading
Relationship of word recognition to comprehension	Believe students must recognize each word in a selection to be able to comprehend the selection	Believe students can comprehend a selection even when they are not able to recognize each word
Use of information cues	Believe students should use word and sound-letter cues exclusively to determine unrecognized words	Believe students should use meaning and grammatical cues in addition to graphic cues to determine unrecognized words
View of reading acquisition	Believe reading acquisition requires mastering and integrating a series of word recognition skills	Believe students learn to read through meaningful activities in which they read, write, speak, and listen
Units of language emphasized instructionally	Letters, letter/sound relationships, and words	Sentences, paragraphs, and text selections
Where importance is placed instructionally	View accuracy in recognizing words as important	View reading for meaning as important
Student evaluation	Think students need to be tested on discrete subskills	Think students need to be tested on the amount and kind of information gained through reading

Source: Reprinted with permission from M. K. Gove and *The Reading Teacher*, 37 (1983): 261–268.

a "reluctant reader" on your hands—or at best one who thinks of "school reading" as entirely different from "real reading." From the very beginning of her school days, Karen needs to be helped to perceive reading as an enjoyable process of communicating with authors.

But let's talk about authors for a moment. You've seen many of them, no doubt, on television talk shows or in person. Perhaps you're an author yourself, or you know one personally. At any rate, you would probably agree that authors have very little in common as far as personality or physical characteristics go. But they do have one need in common. They all need to communicate. More specifically, they all need to entertain or inform.

As you could see from my account of four philosophers from Zania, I was trying both to entertain and to inform you and my other readers—as if I were a personal friend, telling you something I knew about reading in as interesting a way as I could. And this is the way most authors seem to look at their writing—

as a means of communicating with people by sharing ideas and feelings. This is true whether the author is trying to write a best-selling novel, a cookbook, or a ''Dick-and-Jane'' story designed to help first-graders learn to read. (Even with a ''Dick-and-Jane''-type story, created as a teaching device, the author does try to communicate some type of message.) Once teachers thoroughly grasp this point, some interesting things begin to happen: (1) They notice that they are more inclined to have children read to understand the author's message rather than merely to pronounce the words; (2) they find themselves asking children, ''What does the *author* say?'' rather than, ''What does the *book* say?''; and (3) they find themselves asking children fewer questions about the extraneous details in a reading passage and more questions about the important ideas or feelings the author wishes to share.

What I'd really like to persuade you to believe (and to pass on to children) is that authors and readers do communicate. You and I are having a form of conversation right now. It's true that we're missing an important ingredient in any good conversation—your ability to influence what I have to say directly. This is unfortunate. If you *could* influence me, I would then modify what I have to say in response to your ideas and questions—and even your facial expressions. But we *are* having a conversation. You're doing with me just what you do when you chat with other people. You're ''listening'' to my words; you're predicting what I'm going to say next; you're agreeing or disagreeing with me; and you're even having thoughts about me as a person—''he's nice,'' ''he's obnoxious,'' ''he's interesting,'' ''he's weird,'' and so on.

As a mature reader, you normally read as if some type of communication were actually taking place. Sometimes this may take the form of imagining yourself listening to the author speaking to you. At other times it may take the form of actually becoming the author—entertaining or informing yourself. This last form is particularly true when you're reading the fast-paced, exciting parts of a novel, devouring the words like popcorn. In either case, whether you're ''listening'' to the author or taking the author's place, you're engaged in real communication.

But what about writing itself? Do you think of this activity as something directly related to reading? Do we read when we write? Does writing help children learn to read better? Is an author, writing for children, better understood by children who write also? The answer to at least the last three questions seems to be a resounding ''Yes.'' In Chapters 4 and 8, I'll be talking to you about this.

CHOICES TEACHERS MAKE BEFORE READING INSTRUCTION BEGINS

During the weeks before school begins in the fall, and also during the first few weeks of school, teachers have to make many decisions about their program of reading instruction. In addition to deciding which definition of reading will most influence their instructional practices, they have many other types of decisions to make. Mrs. Blanchard, for instance, teaches in a first-grade, self-contained class-room. This is her second year of teaching, and she is trying to decide whether to continue using a basal reader program or to begin the year with a language experience approach—or even a whole language approach. With the basal reader program, as described in Chapter 10, she is provided with several basal readers, at various levels of reading difficulty, that are full of fictional stories, poems, informational articles, and plays. She has teacher guides and workbooks to go with each basal reader, and tests and other materials that correlate with each of the readers.

On the other hand, she's wondering if she might like to try a language experience approach, at least as a modification of the basal reader program. With this approach, as described in Chapter 8, children create much of their own reading material by dictating stories and ideas to the teacher or teaching aide. With this approach, children can more readily perceive reading as a communication process, rather than as a mere "sound-it-out" process.

She's even pondering whether to take the plunge and try a whole language program, one in which children make many of the decisions about how they will learn language skills; one in which writing and reading become inseparable parts of the learning process (as described in Chapter 8).

A second decision Mrs. Blanchard has to make is how to group her students for instruction. She knows that the experience of reading should be success-filled; therefore, she doesn't want to instruct her students with materials that are too difficult. So she ponders: "If I'm going to use basal readers, I may want to group the children into different basals. In that case, I'll need to use an informal reading inventory." With this technique, described in Chapter 11, each child reads a small portion from each of several of the basal readers. After listening to a child read and noting the types of errors he makes, Mrs. Blanchard decides which basal would be most appropriate for this child.

On the other hand, if she decides not to use basal readers and to use a language experience program (Chapter 8), or a whole language program (Chapter 8), or a literature program (Chapter 9), maybe she'll want to use both an informal inventory and miscue analysis—to determine each child's concept and strategies of reading (Chapter 11).

A third decision for Mrs. Blanchard, and one she must make continually throughout the year, is what specific help each child needs in becoming a better reader. This she decides to do through miscue analysis (Chapter 11), through observations of each child's reading and writing (Chapters 8 and 9), and through individual conferences (Chapter 9).

Mr. Nicholson and Miss Porter, a fifth-grade teaching team, have no fewer choices to make than does Mrs. Blanchard. Their biggest decision so far has been whether to use a personalized literature program (Chapter 9), a basal reader approach (Chapter 10), or a combination of these two plus a strong writing program that ties in directly with the reading program. They've heard a lot about "whole language" programs, and they wonder whether this type of program can really be appropriate for fifth-graders.

Mrs. Blanchard, the first-grade teacher, decides to go for a basal reader program this year, although she plans to incorporate some language experience approaches and other types of writing experiences. Mr. Nicholson and Miss Porter decide to skip basal readers this year and try out a combination literature/writing program. All three of the teachers are very excited about the new school year (although all three are experiencing butterflies).

READING AS A COOPERATIVE LEARNING PROCESS

Perhaps by now it goes without saying that reading is a social process. That is, it involves the willingness on the part of readers and authors to communicate with each other. The authors have to want to communicate their ideas so badly that they stay up late at night writing, revising, polishing, until the information or entertainment they need to provide seems clear or amusing or beautiful or exciting (or, perhaps, in the case of textbooks, not overly burdensome). The readers, on the other hand, have to want to communicate with the author so badly that they stay up late at night reading, studying, pondering (or, in the case of a good novel, gulping) until the information or entertainment they need also seems clear

or amusing or beautiful or exciting (or not overly burdensome). The process of reading is a social act, but the process of *learning* to read can be even more so. As I'll explain in later chapters, children can learn a great deal about writing and reading through working cooperatively with each other—helping each other get into the "literacy club," helping each other write, listening to each other read his own writing, reading each other's writing, listening to each other read good literature, conferencing each other on both writing and reading. Under the direction of a skillful teacher, the classroom can become an actual language lab.

But in addition to cooperative learning among peers, children need cooperative learning experiences directly with the teacher. Research (Bawden et al., 1979; Bond & Dykstra, 1967; Chall, 1967; Dykstra, 1968; Gove, 1981) shows us again and again that the teacher is a major variable in how well a child learns to read. The teacher's self-confidence (which comes partly through his or her knowledge of how to teach reading) seems to be an important factor. The teacher's enthusiasm is another. The teacher's organizational ability is a third. And the teacher's communication of warmth or caring is another.

In many cases, but not all, the teacher's ability to communicate with a child seems to be more important than the child's intelligence quotient, the state of his home life, or any other genetic or environmental factor. This presents a tremendous challenge to teachers—particularly in situations in which they do not get as much parental, societal, and administrative support and assistance as they need. But it appears to be a fact of life.

It's teachers who make the difference. It's their enthusiasm for reading good books to themselves and to their students. It's their awareness of instructional strategies—those that encourage children to look for ideas and feelings that authors wish to share and not just those that bind children to filling blanks with correct answers. It's their ability to organize the instructional time and materials in such a way that steady growth in reading ability can take place. It's their concern for children and their future. It's all these things and much more that cause teachers to make the difference. And teachers do make the difference.

SUMMARY OF MAIN IDEAS

☐ The way you think about the reading process will influence the way you teach reading.

☐ A "bottom-up" theory of reading encourages a teacher to emphasize decoding more than comprehension, to be concerned more with word accuracy than with understanding an author's message.

☐ A "top-down" theory of reading encourages more emphasis on comprehension, with less emphasis on subskill practice and tests and on word-by-word accuracy.

☐ Teachers must make many choices before (and during) instruction, and one is the choice of emphasis on units of language.

☐ Teachers make a major difference in children's success or failure to read well.

APPLICATION EXPERIENCES FOR
THE TEACHER EDUCATION CLASS

A. *What's You're Opinion?* Discuss why you agree or disagree with the following opinions. If you do this in a small group, compare your decisions with those of other groups. You are encouraged to use short quotations from the textbook, but most of your discussion should be in your own words. Use your own experiences and observations to help explain your point of view; this will help make the ideas *yours. Making inferences and value judgments is the goal in this experience rather than reciting correct answers.*

1. Teachers should teach according to their beliefs about learning.
2. The author, May, is obviously pushing the behaviorist view of learning and reading.
3. The subskill approach is a bottom-up, behaviorist view of reading.
4. Teaching and testing subskills is the only way to assure that children learn to read well.
5. The Gestaltist, top-down view of reading makes more sense than the behaviorist, bottom-up view.
6. The most important influence on the child's reading ability is the home.

B. *Miscue Analysis:* When a reader makes a mistake, it is often referred to as a *miscue.* Find Jennifer's miscues in the following passage. What can you tell about Jennifer's concepts of reading? Does she seem to perceive reading as mostly a decoding operation (translating written symbols into speech sounds), or does she appear to perceive it mostly as a comprehension operation (discovering the author's meaning)? Is reading, to Jennifer, like telling a story?

Author*	*Jennifer, 3rd Grade*
"I didn't hear you!" Walter said.	"I don't hear you!" Walter said.
"I called and called," his mother said.	"I cannot call," his mother said.
"I had the radio on," Walter said. "I couldn't hear you."	"I have a radio on," Walter said. "I cannot hear you."
"Well, you can now," his mother said.	"Will you come now?" his mother said.
"I want you to go to the store."	"I want you to go to the store."

C. *Scope and Sequence Charts:* Examine "scope and sequence" charts provided by publishers of basal readers and also available in many media centers or libraries. These charts describe in great detail the subskills that are emphasized at each grade level. You may also be able to find School System Curriculum Guides, which normally include the "performance objectives" for the reading program. These performance objectives are essentially a list of subskills the school system wants to have taught. After you examine these materials, you may wish to discuss the following question with others in your class: *If children do well on tests of these subskills, will they be able to read better?*

---

*Bank Street College of Education, "Walter's Walkie-Talkie Machine," *Green Light, Go,* Rev. Ed. (New York: Macmillan, 1972). Reprinted by permission of the publisher.

FIELD EXPERIENCES IN THE ELEMENTARY SCHOOL CLASSROOM

A. *Informally* interview several children, one at a time, to see if you can determine what their concepts of reading are. Ask them questions such as these:

1. What do you think reading is?
2. When you were younger, did you think reading was something else?
3. Do you think that reading is mainly pronouncing the words or understanding the words?
4. What is an author?
5. When you read, do you try to understand what the author is telling you?
6. Do you have a favorite author?
7. Do you think reading is like listening to someone tell you something?
8. When you read, do you ever pretend that *you* are telling the story?
9. Do you have a favorite book? Why is it your favorite?

After you have finished each interview, jot down what you think are the child's concepts of reading. If possible, share your results with others in your reading class.

B. As you watch another teacher teach reading, see if you can determine whether that teacher has more of a top-down or bottom-up view of reading. Use Table 1.1 as a guide to your observations. Keep records and compare your findings with others in your reading class.

REFERENCES AND SUGGESTED READING

Artley, A. S. (1980). Reading: Skills or competencies. *Language Arts, 57,* 546–549.

Barr, R., & Duffy, G. (1978). *Teachers' conceptions of reading: The evolution of a research study* (Research Series No. 17). East Lansing, MI: Michigan State University, Institute for Research on Teaching.

Bawden, R., Buike, S., & Duffy, G. (1979). *Teacher conceptions of reading and their influences on instruction* (Research Series No. 47). East Lansing, MI: Michigan State University, Institute for Research on Teaching.

Bond, G. L., & Dykstra, R. (1967). The cooperative research program in first-grade reading instruction. *Reading Research Quarterly, 1,* 5–142.

Chall, J. (1967). *Learning to read: The great debate.* New York: McGraw-Hill.

Downing, J. (1982). Reading—skill or skills? *The Reading Teacher, 35,* 534–537.

Dykstra, R. (1968). Summary of the second grade phase of the cooperative research program in primary instruction. *Reading Research Quarterly, 2,* 49–70.

Dyson, A. H. (1982). Reading, writing, and language: Young children solving the written language puzzle. *Language Arts, 59,* 829–839.

Goodman, K. (1971). Reading: A psycholinguistic guessing game. In H. Singer & R. Ruddell (Eds.), *Theoretical models and processes of reading* (pp. 259–271). Newark, DE: International Reading Association.

Gough, P. (1972). One second of reading. In J. Kavanagh & I. Mattingly (Eds.), *Language by ear and by eye* (pp. 331–358). Cambridge, MA: MIT Press.

Gove, M. K. (1981). *The influence of teachers' conceptual frameworks of reading on their instructional decision making.* Unpublished doctoral dissertation, Kent State University, Kent, Ohio.

Gove, M. K. (1983). Clarifying teachers' beliefs about reading. *The Reading Teacher, 37,* 216–268.

Harst, J., & Burke, C. (1977). A new hypothesis for reading teacher research: Both teaching and learning of reading are theoretically based. In P. D. Pearson & J. Hansen (Eds.), *Reading: Theory, research and practice,* Twenty-sixth Yearbook of the National Reading Conference. Clemson, S.C.: National Reading Conference.

Koffka, K. (1928). *The growth of mind: An introduction to child psychology.* London: Routledge and Kegan Paul.

Kohler, W. (1915). Opteshe untersuchungen am chimpanse rind am haushuh. *Abhandlungen preussicche physiche-mathematishe klasse. Akademic der wisenshaften,* M. 3.

Krechevsky, I. (1932). Hypotheses in rats. *Psychology Reviews, 39,* 516–532.

McNeil, J. D. (1974). False prerequisites in the teaching of reading. *Journal of Reading Behavior, 6,* 421–427.

Otto, W. (1982). The new debate in reading. *The Reading Teacher, 36,* 14–18.

Rumelhart, D. (1976). *Toward an interactive model of reading* (Technical Report No. 56). San Diego: Center for Human Information Processing.

Shannon, P. (1982). Some subjective reasons for teachers' reliance on commercial reading materials. *The Reading Teacher, 35,* 884–889.

Smith, F. (1971). *Understanding reading.* New York: Holt, Rinehart, & Winston.

Smith F. (1988). *Joining the literacy club.* Portsmouth, NH: Heinemann.

Stennett, R. G., Smythe, P. C., & Hardy, M. (1975). Hierarchical organization of reading subskills: Statistical approaches. *Journal of Reading Behavior, 7,* 223–238.

Thomas, E. L., & Robinson, H. A. (1977). *Improving reading in every class.* Boston: Allyn & Bacon.

Weaver, P. (1978). *Research within reach, a research-guided response to concerns of reading educators.* Washington, D.C.: National Institute of Education.

Wittrock, M. C. (1978). The cognitive movement in instruction. *Educational Psychologist, 13,* 15–30.

What Are Good and Poor Readers Like?
An Interactive View

━━━━━━━━━━ **CHAPTER PREVIEW*** ━━━━━━━━━━

When we teach reading, we need to keep models of good readers in mind. What do good readers do that makes them read with fluency and comprehension? In this way we can keep our goals as reading teachers clearly in mind. We also need to keep models of poor readers in mind. What do they do that makes them read poorly? In this way, too, we can keep our goals in mind—and avoid teaching children in such a way that we actually cause poor reader behavior.

We'll look at poor readers first in this chapter—to see what they actually do to manufacture this thing called poor reading. We won't think too much about causes in this chapter; that will come in Chapter 4. Instead we'll move right along to a comparison with good readers and what their behavior looks like—how they differ

---

*Just a reminder of what I said in Chapter 1, that research (Thomas & Robinson, 1977) shows that readers who read the subheadings and preview a chapter before they read it tend to understand a chapter better than those who skip these two steps.

from poor readers in their use of four cueing systems; in their decoding skill; and in their use of metacognition, inferences, and schemata. Again, we won't talk much about causes of good reading. This will come in Chapters 3 and 4.

Next we'll plunge right in to a discussion of the interactive theory of reading—a complex theory but one I think you'll find easy (and kind of fun) to understand. And finally we'll explore the brain a bit and what it has to do with interactive reading.

Chapter 1 was an adventure (a space adventure, if you will) in which we went back through time to see the effects on our pres-

ent-day thinking of behaviorists like Pavlov, Thorndike, and Skinner versus the effects of Gestaltists like Koffka, Kohler, and Krechevsky. Chapter 2 will be a different kind of adventure—an anthropological one rather than an historical or space adventure. We'll play the role of what anthropologists call "participant observers" in the subculture called "school kids," watching them read and jotting down our field notes on what they do to get through a page of print. As you read the quotations in the following section, keep in mind that although those people we visited from planet Zania were fictitious, *these* people are real kids.

1. ANTHROPOLOGICAL OBSERVER: *What do you think reading is?*
   NATHAN, a poor reader at the end of first grade: *Reading is something to help you learn words.*
   JOSHUA, a good reader at the end of first grade: *Reading is fun. It's like telling a story.*

2. ANTH: *When you were younger, did you think reading was something else?*
   NATHAN: *No, it's the same thing.*
   JOSHUA: *Yes, just a story.*

3. ANTH: *Do you think that reading is mainly sounding out words or is it* understanding *the words?*
   NATHAN: Sounding them out.
   JOSHUA: *It's understanding what it means. . . . You have to understand stuff.*

4. ANTH: *What is an author?*
   NATHAN: *I don't know.*
   JOSHUA: *Someone who is telling you a story . . . a person who writes books.*

5. ANTH: *Do you think reading is like listening to someone tell you something?*
   NATHAN: *No, it's not.*
   JOSHUA: *Yes, because sometimes it's like someone is telling you a story, but sometimes it's like a whole world you have to learn. I feel like you have to be a detective or something.*

6. ANTH: *Do you try to understand what the author is telling you?*
STEPHANIE, a poor reader in third grade: *No, I just read. . . . Reading is pronouncing the words.*
BRENDA, a good reader in third grade: *Yes, I do. I like to pretend I'm telling the story, because it helps me understand— and remember it better.*

7. ANTH: *What's it really like inside your head when you're reading?*
DAVID, a poor reader in fourth grade: *It's no fun in there. Reading's hard work.*
MARGARET, a good reader in fourth grade: *It's like the book is putting on a play and you picture it in your head.*
JAMES, a good reader in fourth grade: *Reading is when you fall into your imagination.*

8. ANTH: *Would you read this to me, Valerie?*
AUTHOR: *The ranger had marked off a place for people to cut trees.*
VALERIE, a poor reader in fourth grade: *The rangers had market of a plack for people to cut trees.*

A LOOK AT POOR READERS: OBSERVATIONS AND RESEARCH

The author I just quoted (Dunkeld, 1979, p. 5) is trying to tell Valerie (in written form) that the forest rangers had marked off a place for people to cut Christmas trees. Valerie, though, is content with her own rendition, that the rangers had *market of a plack* for people to cut trees. Why is she satisfied with *market* instead of *marked,* with *of* instead of *off,* with *plack* instead of *place?* Is this because she doesn't *know* the words she has missed? Or is it more complicated than that?

Let's look at her first two miscues, *market of* for *marked off.* "The ranger had *market* of'' doesn't make sense, does it? It doesn't sound right because *market of* doesn't fit the syntax (the order and types of words expected). Valerie would never *talk* this way, but she's content to *read* this way. Why is this? Maybe it's because of her concept of reading. Even though Valerie is only eight years old, perhaps she has already developed too much of a bottom-up view of reading. To her, reading may be a word-by-word operation—to read is to come up with a word for the next set of letters, then the next, and then the next. She doesn't seem to have developed the concept that reading is a process of *creating sense* out of what an author has written. She doesn't go back and correct any of her three mistakes. She just "plods" on, as Alpha put it, trying to come up with one word after the other, *market* for *marked*, *of* for *off*, and *plack* for *place*.

> **Miscue:** a reader's substitution, omission, insertion, or repetition of a word

Suppose we check our theory about Valerie's miscues by looking at Valerie's third miscue. Here she's content to read, "a *plack* for people to cut trees." But *plack* isn't even a word, you say. Well, actually, *plack* is what they used to call a small coin in Scotland back in the sixteenth century, but I doubt that Valerie had that in mind, don't you? So what does this new evidence tell us? Not only is she willing to substitute words that don't fit the syntax of the sentence, but she's also willing to substitute "nonsense" words (also referred to as "nonwords"). Her problem is worse than we thought, then; for her substitution of *plack* indicates that her concept of reading is quite far from the mark. To her, reading may be merely the process of making wordlike *sounds* in response to sets of letters. But perhaps she has learned to respond according to her training. Is it possible that she has actually been reinforced for coming up with word-noises and meaningless substitutions? If so, then how could such reinforcement possibly take place? In Chapter 4, we will spend a considerable amount of time discussing the answer to this question. For now, though, let's look at what research says about poor readers.

An award-winning study by Beebe (1979–80) shows that those children who are willing to make substitutions that don't fit the syntax of the sentence tend to score low on comprehension tests. Researchers Englert and Semmel (1981) found that the same was true for those willing to make *nonsense* substitutions. Valerie, you'll remember, made both types of substitutions. As these two studies show, poor readers usually concentrate more heavily on decoding (translating print into sound) than on understanding. Valerie, for example, is far less aware than good readers that the purpose of reading is to make sense of a passage.

But how else do poor readers differ from good readers? Let's look at another third-grader named Cora. (Lest you fear from my examples that most poor readers are girls, let me add that the vast majority are boys.) In the same story that Valerie read is this passage:

> "What do you mean?" said Pete. "They don't let you just go into the forest and cut trees."
> "Yes they do," said Cathy. "You have to buy a permit first."

Cora read the passage just fine until she got to the word *permit*. For *permit* she substituted the word *permanent*. Because of her particular background, perhaps,

Cora chose to talk about buying a permanent rather than a permit, even though the story was about cutting a Christmas tree in the forest. In other words, not only are poor readers willing to ignore the *syntactic* context; they are also willing to ignore the *semantic* context (meaning). In this particular case, the word *permanent* fits the syntactic context all right. "You have to buy a permanent first" *sounds* all right. But it doesn't fit the *semantic* context, since the author is not talking about *hair* at all. Like Valerie, Cora was willing to come up with a *word* she thought was correct even though the *meaning* couldn't be correct.

So, what do we have so far? Poor readers tend to make the kinds of substitutions when they read that they would never make when they speak. While they treat speaking and listening as meaningful communication processes, they treat reading as a meaningless word-calling task. Reading, to them, is a bottom-up view (of letters) without a top (message) in sight!

While part of poor readers' troubles seem to result from their wrong idea of what reading really is, another part often relates to the very thing they emphasize the most when they read—they concentrate on decoding, but their decoding skills are often weak. Travis, a second-grader, will now demonstrate this for us by reading a story designed for early first grade. Every time Travis defaults on a word for at least five seconds (doesn't say the word), the teacher tells him the word. A default is shown with a *d*.

     d
Mary has a dog. His name is Rex. He is little. He is brown. He likes to play. He
likes to run. He runs fast. Mary follows him. Then he stops. He can do tricks. He
sits up. He rolls over. He shakes hands. He can swim. He swims in the river. He
gets wet. Mary picks him up. Then she gets wet. She puts him down. He shakes
himself. Then he is dry. "Good dog," says Mary. She likes her dog.*

Although Travis is now in second grade, he has considerable trouble with this early first-grade story. Why? It's not because he's making unsuitable substitutions. He seems to lack the confidence even to *try* making substitutions. For instance, even after finding out that the dog can do tricks and can sit up, Travis doesn't try to complete this sentence: "He rolls _____." Travis just stares at the page until the teacher gives him the word. And when he finds out that the dog can swim, he confidently reads the next four words but stops on the fifth one: He swims in the r_____ .

So what's his problem, then? What is he afraid of? As you've probably guessed, Travis is afraid of making a mistake; he's afraid of predicting. But why? Well, for *some* poor readers, especially for those who are extrasensitive, it's because they've been *corrected* every time they've made a mistake. To them, a correction is like a rebuke. For other poor readers, their fear of making a mistake is caused by lack of enough sight words (words that are instantly recognizable). Their visual memory for words has not been sufficiently developed. (Chapter 6 shows how to use games, patterned books, and other activities to help this problem.) And for still others, their fear can be caused by their inability to notice common "phonics" patterns in words and syllables. (Chapter 7 provides ideas for dealing with this problem.)

A poor reader, then, ignores—or doesn't know how to use—one or more of the "cueing systems" that good readers use: *syntax* (the order and type of word expected next), *semantic cues* (the surrounding words that provide context and meaning to the unfamiliar words), and *graphophonic cues* (those cues obtained

*Colin Dunkeld, Portland Informal Reading Inventory, Form P. Unpublished manuscript, Portland State University, School of Education. Reprinted by permission of the author.

from spelling patterns and the sounds they represent). But a fourth cueing system is based on background experiences—with things, people, and oral language. The *poor* reader is often quite deficient in this respect. In the next two sections I'll explain these four cueing systems more thoroughly and show how good readers use them.

A LOOK AT GOOD READERS: OBSERVATIONS AND RESEARCH

Author	*Bobby*
The rangers had marked off	The rangers had market off—had marked off
a place for people to	the place for the people to
cut trees.	cut their trees.

Bobby is a good reader in the third grade. He enjoys reading, he reads with good intonation as if he were telling the story himself, and he scores high on reading comprehension tests. And yet a teacher with a strictly bottom-up view of reading (letters and words are the most important units) might consider Bobby a poor reader. After all, in a twelve-word sentence, he makes four "mistakes." He self-corrects *market* with *marked,* he says *the place* for *a place,* he inserts *the* before *people* and *their* before *trees.* Whew, that's a lot of mistakes. But rest assured that good readers don't miscue that often in every sentence. On the other hand, they do tend to make more "errors" than a teacher would like—if the teacher has word-accuracy as his major goal.

Why do they make such errors? Is it because they don't "know" the words? Let's look. At first Bobby says *market* for *marked.* Is this because he doesn't know the word *marked?* No, he knows it, all right. It's just that he allows himself to be fooled for a moment by the two words' great similarity in physical appearance. But only for a split second, and then he corrects himself, probably because *market* doesn't fit the syntactic cues in the passage. *The rangers had market off* simply doesn't sound right, for one thing. And a word like *market* doesn't go with a word like *had* unless you put the word *a* between them (had a market).

So let's look at his second "mistake": *the place* for *a place.* Does Bobby not know the word *a?* A reader with great comprehension and love of reading? Of course he knows it. But in this particular passage he predicts the word *the* will follow *marked off* and come before *place.* And since it works so well, he sticks with it (just the way you and I do when we read). But what about his last two miscues? What two words does he miss? Look back at his rendition and see if you can find the last two words he misses.

Couldn't find two misses, could you? That's right; rather than *miss* two words he *inserts* them—again, just as we do when we're "on a roll" and reading well. According to Bobby's version of the story, the rangers had marked off *the* place for *the* people to cut *their* trees. Did Bobby get the author's message? Was his comprehension good? Yes, on both counts. Otherwise he wouldn't have been able to make such meaningful miscues.

From a bottom-up point of view, Bobby was expected to respond correctly to each word in the sentence. He was not expected to make a self-correction, a substitution, and two insertions. I'm sorry, Bobby, but that's four strikes against you. You had a chance to make 12 points on that 12-word sentence, but you get only 8 points. Eight out of twelve is only 67 percent; not a very good score.

From a top-down point of view, Bobby was expected to make hypotheses about the author's *meaning* as he read the sentence. He was expected to confirm his hypotheses as he sampled from the print. He was expected to understand the author's message. Well, judging from the four meaningful miscues he made, he did make several hypotheses, he sampled enough of the print to confirm them, and he understood the author's message. Nice going, kid. (But then, you really don't need my praise, do you, since you were rewarded by your success in understanding the story.)

Now that we've had fun with Bobby, let's look at the research concerning good readers. Are these children the bright ones with high IQs? Not necessarily. There *is* a fairly strong relationship between IQ scores and reading comprehension scores, but there are many children with an average or below average IQ who read quite well—and many with a high IQ who read quite poorly. There are numerous things that differentiate good from poor readers, but one of the most important is that of "reading concept." Good readers perceive reading as a form of communication; that is, they sense that there's a story or message being presented to them, and they use searching-type behavior to "ferret out" what's happening or what's being said.

This kind of hunting behavior leads them to attack a reading passage as if it were a totality—a whole living animal, rather than a pile of separate lifeless bones. Good readers don't slowly pick up each bone, with much phonetic huffing and puffing, and toss it aside, one bone at a time, until they have no bones left. They attack it the way you do when you pick up a newspaper or magazine and read your favorite columnist. With hope! With an expectation of a successful hunt, a hunt that leads to entertainment, information, ideas, good feelings. Part of this expectation comes from things like their home background, intelligence, and personality characteristics, but a great deal of it comes from the concept of reading that *teachers* have helped them develop.

This point, about the importance of teachers, will come up again and again in this book. But for now, let's look at what these expectations on the part of good readers lead to. According to the study by Mona Beebe (1979–80) that I mentioned earlier, children who score high on reading comprehension tests tend to be those who are more willing to risk making a mistake. They'll say something like *market* for *marked,* but as soon as they realize it doesn't fit the context, they'll correct their mistake. In other words, they make plenty of self-corrections as they read, the way you and I do. In fact, they correct twice as many substitutions as do poor readers (Weber, 1970). They also make plenty of substitutions, the kind that don't really change the author's essential message: *this* for *that, a* for *the, what* for *which,* even *she* for *he,* if they think the subject is a female rather than a male. And, as you'll often see in the examples I use in this book, they also tend to use meaningful insertions and omissions of words. As Karen D'Angelo and Marc Mahlios (1983, p. 778) found in their study, very few insertions or omissions ever distort the author's message. "Omission miscues," they say, "are often deliberate and represent meaningful interaction between the reader and text. . . . As a reader develops proficiency, omissions tend to be well known words or redundancies. . . . *Insertions increase as a reader gains proficiency."* (Italics mine.)

THE FOUR CUEING SYSTEMS
USED BY THE GOOD READER

> As I mentioned, poor readers tend to ignore or have trouble with one or more of the cueing systems. They might pay attention to the letters but not the meaning. They might pay sufficient attention to the author's syntax and meaning but ignore a spelling pattern that would help them decode an unknown word. They may read something letter-perfect but, because of their insufficient background, not understand what it means. Good readers, on the other hand, allow the four cueing systems to interact as they read, thus providing themselves with four avenues of understanding at the same time.

Let's look once more at Bobby's way of describing what the forest ranger did. This time I'll give you a little more of the text and also show you a coding system that some researchers and teachers use:

> **Text:** a portion of a fiction or nonfiction selection

"We can go into the forest," said Cathy, "and cut our own tree." Next Saturday the whole family drove to the forest. They found the ranger station and bought a permit . . . The rangers had [market the the their off] a place for people to cut trees.

As this research code shows, Bobby read it this way: "The rangers had market off—marked off the place for the people to cut their trees." (The big C around *market* and extended under the word *off* tells you that Bobby substituted *market* for *marked* and went right on to read the next word *off;* he then corrected *market off* to read *marked off.* This is a code you'll become skilled in using as you read the next few chapters. It is summarized in Chapter 11.)

In reading this sentence, Bobby probably used all four cueing systems to deal with the word *marked.* At first he relied too much on graphophonic cues and substituted *market.* But immediately the syntax and semantic cues from the previous sentences and from the words surrounding *marked* told him to make a self-correction. Furthermore, his background experiences must have helped him recognize the need for a self-correction; forest rangers are normally not found in a market, for example. Also, the phrase *market off* is not one he is used to hearing, but *marked off* is one he may have heard in several different contexts. At any rate it is quite likely that Bobby used all of the following cueing systems to help him determine the author's message:

1. *Syntax cues:* those context hints provided by the *order* of the words in the sentence or by the *type* of word (noun, verb, adverb, or adjective) expected in the next "slot." For example, we intuitively expect to read first a noun then an adjective following the word *the* when we see "The candy is in the _____. It's in the _____ bowl." As another example, we intuitively *expect* to read a verb in the following slot: The car _____ fast!

2. *Semantic cues:* those context hints provided by the meaning of the surrounding words. For example, when we see "The car _____ fast," we expect to read a word such as *moved* rather than *munched.*

3. *Graphophonic cues:* single letters or sets of letters, particularly their positions in words, and the speech sounds they represent. For example, the letter *y* stands for a very different sound at the beginning of a word than it does at the end of a word. If authors use *y* at the beginning, as they would for *yellow, yeast,* and *yuck,* they're telling the reader to think of a certain beginning sound. But they don't want the reader to think of the same sound at the end of two-syllable words, as in *belly, funny,* and *Betty.* The *position* of a letter is a major phonographic cue. As another example, the letter *a* stands for a different sound in *plan* and *plane.* Confusing the two would certainly make a difference in this sentence: "It's my plan," Jim said, "to sail across the ocean." (Try substituting *plane* for *plan.*)

4. *Background cues:* memories, mental images, associations, or minitheories about the world that help the reader understand. These cues are based on past experiences and also on the language heard and spoken during those experiences. The word *plane,* for instance, can be read with meaning only after a child has seen a plane and heard the word applied to it: "My mom went on a plane to New York."

DO GOOD READERS DIFFER FROM POOR READERS IN THEIR DECODING SKILL?

There are still other ways that good readers differ from poor readers. A teacher who wishes to push for a heavy phonics approach to reading instruction can find plenty of studies to show that good readers tend to have better decoding skills than poor readers—for example, they have a better sight vocabulary, better recognition of graphophonic patterns (phonics), and better awareness of suffixes. "Therefore," say some teachers, "just concentrate on sight words, phonics, and suffixes and you'll produce good readers."

Now, there's something a bit tricky here—a little like the chicken and the egg question. Do good readers become good readers because they study phonics, sight words, and suffixes? Or do they pick up phonics, sight words, and suffixes intuitively as they read more and more and more? What is the cause, and what is the effect? At present, the evidence calls for an indefinite, mixed answer: Many children learn decoding (phonics, sight words, and suffixes) from reading a lot and asking interested adults lots of questions. Spending a lot of time teaching *these* children to decode is like teaching tadpoles to become frogs. On the other hand, many children, who seldom read on their own at home or school, do learn how to decode through intensive instruction. Whether this makes them better "readers" is a moot question since some of them are turned off in this way to reading.

It's true, on the other hand, that the majority of good readers do show a better awareness of graphophonic cues, but some of them have simply learned how to ignore them. They've become bluffers who plow through sentence after sentence, relying on background, syntax, and semantic cues, and using little more than first letters for their graphophonic cues. This works fine in the early grades, but later the bluffers get caught more and more in a game of wild guessing. By the time they reach high school, it becomes clear that they are not truly "good readers." A good reader learns to use all four cueing systems comfortably and confidently.

> From my own experience in working with children and teachers, I'd have to say that teaching "phonics," sight words, and suffixes can be important for many children, but it is definitely of secondary importance to helping them gain a love for reading and a concept of reading as a meaningful sharing of ideas and stories.

DIFFERENCES IN METACOGNITION, INFERENCES, AND SCHEMATA

The good reader is not a bluffer in another sense as well. A good reader tends to know what she knows and what she doesn't know. We've already seen how a good reader is willing to use substitutions but self-corrects those which violate syntactic or semantic cues. Self-correcting is an example of knowing what you do and don't know. Another example occurs when a good reader tells herself that she doesn't understand a sentence or paragraph she has just read, so she goes back and reads it again. This type of self-correction is called *comprehension moni-*

toring and is part of a process called *metacomprehension.* (The prefix ''meta'' means *after* or *along with*.) You, yourself, are undoubtedly good at metacomprehension or you wouldn't be so successful in understanding what you read. By the time good readers get into sixth grade, many of them are already experienced with this process. In Chapters 4 and 5, we'll talk about helping poor and average readers learn it too.

The good reader also tends to be better than poor readers in making inferences as he reads. Researchers Diane Lapp and James Flood (1984) have found, in fact, that a good reader processes *inferences in his head* even more than he processes sentences on paper. Let me give you an example of this from our now famous story of the forest ranger. When we last left Cathy and Pete, they had bought a permit and were ready to cut down their own Christmas tree.

> ''Look at that one,'' said Cathy. ''It's perfect.''
> ''No, it's not,'' said Pete. ''It's way too small.''

To understand these two sentences, the reader must make several inferences. You might infer, for example, that Cathy is pointing to some kind of evergreen tree when she says, ''Look at that one.'' When she says, ''It's perfect,'' you might infer that it has a conical shape, that its color is pleasing, that it's a good size for your living room, and so on. And when Pete says, ''It's way too small,'' you might infer that it's a ''baby tree'' or it's about three feet high or that Pete is just envious because Cathy found it first. At any rate, you would make numerous inferences just in understanding those two simple sentences. Not that you would make such inferences consciously. The good reader makes them instantaneously and intuitively (Lapp & Flood, 1984). Unfortunately, the poor reader often does not (Carr, 1983), although it is possible, as we'll see in Chapters 4 and 5, to do something about this problem.

Story and Informational Schemata

This leads us to one other way that good readers shine and poor readers don't. There's a special type of inferring that *you* do, I'm sure, whenever you read a story. You infer that it's going to follow some kind of pattern you've run across before—such as boy meets girl, they fall in love, boy loses girls, boy gets girl back again, and they live together happily ever after (even though sometimes they live together for only ten years and then get a divorce). In other words, in your head you carry around several outlines or organizations for stories. Reading researchers call a mental outline like this a *schema;* when they talk about more than one schema, they use the word *schemata,* the plural of schema. These schemata are minitheories that help us predict what is coming next when we listen to or read a story. At the beginning of a story we expect the main character or characters to appear in some kind of setting. We expect some kind of problem to arise before too long, and we expect the characters to react to the problem. As we read the written material (called *text* by researchers), we wait expectantly for our minitheories to be confirmed. As Marshall puts it, ''The closer the reader's organization is to that of the text, the greater comprehension is likely to be'' (1983, p. 616).

We use schemata when we read story text and when we read informational text. For purposes of reading a story, the schema in our head is a little like the outline or "query letter" an author sends to an editor to pique her interest. Whereas the outline provides the editor with descriptions of characters, setting, conflict, and resolution, a story schema provides the *reader* with *anticipations* of those story elements. For purposes of reading *informational* text, however, the schema in our heads is more like a page from a *College Outline* book, but with lots of "empty slots" for us to fill in. In other words, as we read more and more informational text, we get used to the ways authors describe or explain things to us. We wait with mild (perhaps meager) anticipation for the author to fill in those slots that lie empty in our schema.

But how *do* we expect informational authors to describe or explain things to us? Well, I mentioned that our "story schema" includes expectations that an author will give us a setting, main character, conflict, and resolution. But what does our "informational schema" include? Usually it includes expectations that an author will give us one or more of these:

A main idea and supporting details

A cause and the resulting effects

Some effects and a possible cause

Some steps to follow in sequence

A description of people, things, places, or events

A problem and some possible solutions

All right, but how good are good readers at using a story schema or informational schema to predict what the author is going to say? Lapp and Flood (1984) found that they're quite adept at this, whether an author is telling a story or providing information. Flood (1978) presented this sentence to good readers: "Christmas always meant going to Grandma's house," and asked them to write a second sentence to go with it. What do *you* think the second sentence should be like? Should it be like this: "There we ate turkey, pumpkin pie, and cranberry sauce, and played with all the farm animals"? If so, your schema for this scene would include the notion that grandmothers live on farms and love to stuff their guests with delicious food. Actually this is the *type* of sentence that Flood got from his subjects—a sentence that was highly descriptive "about the event of Christmas."

Then he asked his subjects to respond to this sentence: "One of the oldest drinks known to man is milk." What kind of second sentence do you think they wrote? Should it be like this: "Maybe this is because milk is so nutritious"? Flood found that all the subjects came up with an informative second sentence that tied in with the first, indicating that good readers can use their background schemata to anticipate the kind of text that will be coming—narrative, nonnarrative, formal, informal, humorous, serious. Again we see that good readers *attack* what they read, armed with schemata, with hypotheses to confirm or deny, with "empty slots" they expect the author to fill in with informational or story-type data. Good readers are active hunters and gatherers, with purposes of their own.

BUT HOW DO ALL READERS—BOTH GOOD AND POOR—LEARN?

There's an assumption that people sometimes make when they discover the differences between good and poor readers. This assumption is that all we have to do is show poor readers how to do exactly what good readers do. Well, there does seem to be some truth to this, as I'll show you in Chapters 4 and 5. But let me warn you that it's not that simple. You can sometimes teach a poor reader, for example, to do more self-correcting, like good readers do. But you may not be able to *directly teach* him to enjoy reading or perceive himself as a reader or select good books to read.

There are some things that seem to be important in the learning process for both our good and our poor readers. Such things we need to pay attention to— perhaps even more than we pay attention to how we can pass on good readers' habits to poor readers. I'm not going to present a barrage of research on this topic. Much of it you've probably picked up in "ed psych" or "psych" classes, or in helping to raise children, or through baby sitting. Let me just list some commonalities that seem to exist among children and see if they ring a bell for you.

1. Children are problem solvers. They need to be placed in nonthreatening, problem-solving situations in order for some kinds of learning to take place. Both poor and good readers can grow in their reading and writing abilities if this happens. Writing and reading about things they're inter-

ested in provides both poor and good readers a chance to solve real problems (and to learn how to read and write too). (See Chapters 8 and 9 for more.)

2. Children, whether good or poor readers, need plenty of opportunities for choice. Poor readers are often not given much choice, and this is where teachers make a big mistake. Instead of giving poor readers opportunities to choose from dozens of "delicious" and enticing books, they often provide them with round-the-circle oral reading and dozens of corrections per minute (Allington, 1980).

3. All children (and adults) are motivated through novelty, through having their basic needs for belonging and importance met, through chances to work at the appropriate level of difficulty, and through frequent, specific, and loving feedback. What we sometimes call poor reading is nothing more than poor, unmotivating teaching. (See Chapter 13.)

4. All children (and adults) retain information better if they are given a chance to master a few things well rather than covering a host of things poorly, to get emotionally involved in the learning process, to practice during the introduction of information and then later on at spaced intervals, and to receive instruction that is based on prior knowledge. And yet it is these kinds of things, especially prior knowledge, that are so often neglected in the teaching of reading (Durkin, 1978–79). (See Chapter 13.)

5. Both poor readers and good ones need *time* for learning: for reading real books instead of filling in worksheets; for writing about real concerns instead of filling in blanks. Time to think instead of being harassed by impatient teachers for one-second answers (Gambrell, 1980).

6. All children bring more than an empty shell to school. They are living, breathing, highly individual treasures of information, experiences, and feelings. Good teachers pay attention to these treasures; poor teachers don't.

AN INTERACTIVE THEORY OF READING

Tell me, I'll forget. Show me, I may remember. But involve me and I'll understand.

—Chinese Proverb

The schemata that help to guide us as we read are not limited to scenarios or outlines or expectations about the styles that authors will use. They seem to be much more pervasive than that. When a little girl says to her mother, "My legs are all out of breath," we know exactly what she means, don't we? And we know intuitively how she came up with her conclusion—her past experiences of "running out of breath" acted as a kind of filter for understanding the sensations in her legs. The phrase "out of breath" became part of a schema or minitheory for explaining what happens whenever she exerts herself.

This is the way many of our schemata form as we grow up and learn about the world. We put two and two together and sometimes, if we're lucky, it comes out four the first time. Other times it comes out five or three and we have to wait for other experiences to teach us that we were wrong. Bobby, the good reader who seemed to realize that a forest ranger would be more likely to *mark* something than to market it, must have already developed a schema related to "forest ranger." This schema might include the ideas that a forest ranger wears a khaki uniform, fights fires, collects money from campers, and even marks off a place for cutting Christmas trees. And with this "forest ranger" schema and other schemata (such as a minitheory on the nature of Christmas trees and where they might be found), he was able to predict what the author was going to say and to understand what he did say.

> **Schemata** (plural of **schema**): minitheories about things, people, language, places, and other phenomena in our background of experiences

Rumelhart (1984) has been engaged in schemata research for several years at the Center for Human Information Processing at the University of California at San Diego. Besides his contributions related to schemata, he has often been given credit for developing a major "interactive theory of reading." In this section of the chapter, I will explain this theory to you and invite you to consider it as a possible guide to your own teaching of reading. Actually, I've been explaining his interactive theory throughout the chapter, but now that we've talked about schemata, you'll be able to understand his theory even better. I like some of the examples Rumelhart uses. For instance, what schemata are set in motion in your head as you read these next two sentences?

"Mary heard the ice cream truck coming down the street. She remembered her birthday money and rushed into the house." (Rumelhart, 1984, p. 1)

All right, let's check your schemata. How old do you think Mary is? Jot down her age if you wish, and we'll see if you change your mind later. Okay, why do you think she rushed into the house? If you have your answer clearly in mind, then we're ready to move on to the next two sentences:

"Mary heard the bus coming down the street. She remembered her birthday money and rushed into the house." (Rumelhart, 1984, p. 1)

How old is the Mary in *this* scene? And why did this Mary rush into the house? Did your answers change? Did you find that Mary got older and that her reason for rushing into the house changed, even though we only changed *ice cream truck* to *bus?*

Let's try it again. Instead of changing the ice cream truck to a bus, we'll leave the ice cream truck alone. Here are the next two sentences.

''Mary heard the ice cream truck coming down the street. She remembered her gun and rushed into the house.'' (Rumelhart, 1984, p. 2)

How did your answers change this time? Did Mary's age change again? And what was she going to do that the other two Marys had no intention of doing? What really happened when we changed *birthday money* to *gun?*

Rumelhart feels that when we read something like these sentences, we put our schemata to work to help us make inferences about what's really happening. If we read that Mary heard the ice cream truck coming down the street, we immediately make inferences about her age, about the nature of the truck, and the nature of her desires. It's no surprise to read that she remembered her birthday money and rushed into the house. It's quite easy to infer that her birthday money is hers to spend any way she wishes and that she is about to make excellent use of it.

On the other hand, if we read that Mary heard the *bus* coming down the street, we make use of a different set of schemata. Now, instead of a little girl eager for sugary delights, we might infer things about an older girl or a woman waiting for the bus to take her to work. So we retrieve those schemata related to such things as waiting for buses, ignoring the stares of strangers, and so forth. But the author comes up with ''Mary remembered her birthday money. . . . '' Now we're forced to change our hypothesis and make new inferences. Maybe her decision to take a bus was a sudden one and she has no money with her. Maybe her birthday money is all she has to her name, poor soul.

In the third pair of sentences we read that Mary heard the ice cream truck coming down the street. So we get set with our schemata related to ice cream trucks and little children longing to dirty up their T-shirts. But the author comes up with ''She remembered her gun and rushed into the house.'' This requires a severe shift in our schemata, doesn't it? Instead of thinking about birthday money in a nice little girl's treasure box, we have to shift our thinking to something like a .25 automatic pistol in a not-so-nice older girl's bureau drawer. Having changed our schemata, we now change our inferences as well. Instead of inferring that Mary is merely going to *purchase* a creamsicle, we now infer she's going to steal one—along with all the money in the till.

From an interactive viewpoint, the words ''rushed into the house'' change in meaning as the author changes *ice cream truck* to *bus* or as he changes *birthday money* to *gun.* If you merely think about each *word* in the phrase ''rushed into the house,'' you can't arrive at the author's meaning. The author's meaning is *outside* the words. It's in your head, where you've stored those types of organized hunches we're calling schemata. There is an interaction between the words of the author and the schemata of the reader.

According to Rumelhart, a reader is "constantly evaluating hypotheses about the most plausible interpretation of the text. Readers are said to have understood the text when they are able to find a configuration of hypotheses which offer a coherent account for the various aspects of the text" (1984, p. 3).

Of course, if a reader's experiences have not yet resulted in schemata necessary for making the right inferences, she will fail to comprehend what the author has said. Nearly every experience we have as we grow up helps us to develop schemata. We create schemata about cars, for example—what they're for (to take daddies and mommies to work and children to the beach) and how they run (there's a big noisy gizmo under the hood that drinks gasoline and forces the wheels to go around). We create schemata about mommies too—what *they're* for (to take care of kids when they're lonely or hungry) and how *they* run (they have two fast-moving legs and a face that smiles or frowns at us, and they don't need help in getting dressed or parting their hair). We create thousands and thousands of schemata about things, people, actions, places, *and about language.* And as we grow older and wiser, we keep modifying those schemata to make them match the new information we receive. Then, when we read, we apply them to the written text. Our schemata help us to make inferences (about what's between the lines), to predict what the author is going to say next—even the order in which it will be said, and to understand the message (what the author means).

So by now you may comprehend better what I'm talking about when I say that reading is an interactive process. For one thing, an interaction takes place between the words we see in print and the way our mind has been storing and organizing our background of experiences. Earlier in the chapter I referred to this background as one of the four cueing systems. Now I think it would be more accurate to call this cueing system the *schematic cueing system.* We can say, then, that there's an interaction between the letters (graphophonic system) and the schematic system. But that's not all. Remember that we have two other systems—the syntactic and semantic systems. It is Rumelhart's belief, and that of many other researchers (Brewer, 1972; de Beaugrande, 1984; Englert & Semmel, 1981; Goodman, 1971; Jones, 1982; Smith, 1979), that all four systems are constantly interacting as good readers read.

I think the best way to complete my explanation is to use you, the reader, as an experimental subject. First, I'll give you a sentence, then I'll ask you to predict the next sentence—one word at a time. All right? Here's the first sentence:

Mary looked down the snowy hillside and saw a lake.

What do you think the first word of the next sentence will be? Jot down your answer, please, before reading any further. Some people say "She," some say "It," some say "The." The author used the word "Three."

What word do you think will follow "Three"? (You might jot the entire sentence down as you create it. So far you would have "Three _____ . . .") If you've written down your prediction for the second word, you're ready to read on. Some people predict *skaters,* some say *birds,* some predict *deer.* What did you say? What made you say it?

Okay, the second word is actually *ducks*. Now here we go with the third word, but this time I'll give you a hint from each of the four cueing systems before you make your prediction:

1. *Syntactic cue:* The author has already said, "Three ducks . . ." What kind of word would you intuitively expect next? A verb like *paddle?* A noun like *water?* An adjective like *pretty?* An adverb like *noisily?* If you decide on a verb, should it be in the present or past tense?
2. *Semantic cue:* What verb goes best with "Three ducks . . ."?
3. *Schematic cue:* What minitheories do you have about ducks, snow, and lakes that help you predict whether the verb will be *swam* or *waddled* or *slid* or *quacked?*
4. *Graphophonic cue:* Suppose I give you just the first letter. It's an *s.*

What do you think the third word is? "Three ducks s_____ . . ." Did you predict *skated?* Some people do. How about *slid* or *sat?* What if I give you a better graphophonic cue: The first *two* letters are *sw.* "Three ducks sw_____ . . ." You're right, the first three words are "Three ducks swam . . ." The fourth word is *in,* so what do you think the fifth word is? Both the semantic and syntactic cues would help you predict the word *the,* right?

So now we have, "Three ducks swam in the . . ." And I'll bet you predict that the next word is *water,* right? Sorry, not right. The next word starts with the letter i_____ . If you use your schematic cues, you'll come close, but let me give you a syntactic one as well. Here's the way the entire text looks so far:

Mary looked down the snowy hillside and saw a lake. Three ducks swam in
the i_____ _____ .

You're right. "Three ducks swam in the icy water." What you just demonstrated to yourself is the way a good reader must allow all four cueing systems to interact in order to read with accuracy and comprehension. In Figure 2.1 you can see how a child read the same two sentences. But she had it easier than you did, since both sentences were there to look at from the very beginning.

INTERACTIVE READING AND THE BRAIN

You are justified in asking how the human mind can possibly do so much as it helps us read. "To do all that," you might say, "would take a computer the size of a building." And you would be correct. It might take a computer that size to read with the intelligence that humans display when they read. Although computers have been "taught" to read (Dehn, 1984; Estes, 1983), they get pretty mixed up if you give them text that is not extremely predictable. You can program them ahead of time with "schemata," but it would be difficult to program them with as many as human beings carry around in their heads. Moreover, it would be difficult to program them to apply sufficient judgment as to which schemata really best fit the text.

FIGURE 2.1 A sample of interactive reading

Mary looked down the snowy hillside and saw a lake. Three ducks swam in the icy water.

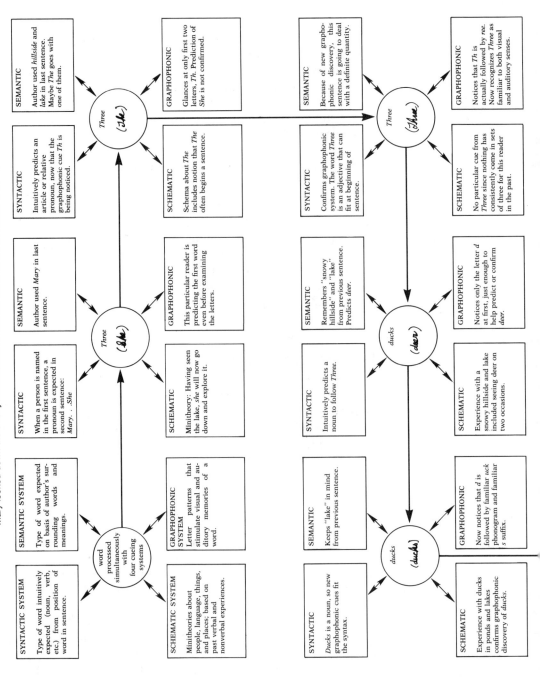

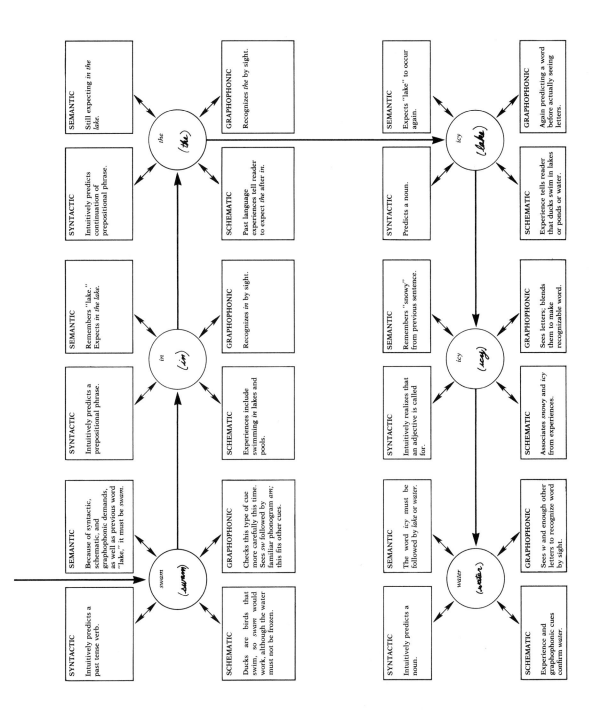

SYNTACTIC
Intuitively predicts a past tense verb.

SEMANTIC
Because of syntactic, schematic, and graphophonic demands, as well as previous word "lake," it must be *swam.*

GRAPHOPHONIC
Checks this type of cue more carefully this time. Sees *sw* followed by familiar phonogram *am*; this fits other cues.

SCHEMATIC
Ducks are birds that swim, so *swam* would work, although the water must not be frozen.

swam
(swam)

SYNTACTIC
Intuitively predicts a prepositional phrase.

SEMANTIC
Remembers "lake." Expects *in the lake.*

GRAPHOPHONIC
Recognizes *in* by sight.

SCHEMATIC
Experiences include swimming *in* lakes and pools.

in
(in)

SYNTACTIC
Intuitively predicts continuation of prepositional phrase.

SEMANTIC
Still expecting *in the lake.*

GRAPHOPHONIC
Recognizes *the* by sight.

SCHEMATIC
Past language experiences tell reader to expect *the* after *in.*

the
(the)

SYNTACTIC
Intuitively predicts a noun.

SEMANTIC
The word *icy* must be followed by *lake* or *water.*

GRAPHOPHONIC
Sees *w* and enough other letters to recognize word by sight.

SCHEMATIC
Experience and graphophonic cues confirm *water.*

water
(water)

SYNTACTIC
Intuitively realizes that an adjective is called for.

SEMANTIC
Remembers "snowy" from previous sentence.

GRAPHOPHONIC
Sees letters; blends them to make recognizable word.

SCHEMATIC
Associates *snowy* and *icy* from experiences.

icy
(icy)

SYNTACTIC
Predicts a noun.

SEMANTIC
Expects "lake" to occur again.

GRAPHOPHONIC
Again predicting a word before actually seeing letters.

SCHEMATIC
Experience tells reader that ducks swim in lakes or ponds or water.

icy
(lake)

Our brain, on the other hand, is quite capable of shifting gears numerous times as it helps us shift hypotheses, reminds us of previous experiences, feeds us ready-made schemata, and makes us pay attention to all four cueing systems *at the same time*. Our brains are much, much better in most respects than the best computers yet built and will probably outperform them indefinitely when it comes to creative thinking, judgment, and inferential thinking. It is now fairly well established that the human brain contains at least 100 billion neurons (nerve cells). That, in itself, is awe-inspiring, considering that this is one million times as many units as most computers have and that the brain weighs only about three pounds. Yet even more awe-inspiring is the idea that the number of interconnections among the brain's 100 billion neurons is, as Anthony Smith writes in *The Mind*, "about as infinite as anything we know" (1984, p. 6). "It is certainly larger than the number of atoms presumed to exist in the entire universe" (p. 4). But as a reading teacher, all you need to realize is that each one of those interconnections can provide the mind with another unit of information—a word, a memory, a speech sound. And several of these interconnections, probably working in concert, can provide us with an almost instantaneous schema.

Not that the brain is terribly fast. It's not as fast as electricity by any means, since the speed of transference between neurons is only around 200 miles per hour or roughly 300 feet per second. Is this really fast enough to do all the things I said a reader could do as she reads? Well, let's look at the brain a bit closer and see. When we get inside the brain, we find a scene not at all like you see when you examine a computer chip through a magnifying glass. The computer chip looks like a well-laid-out set of city streets. The brain looks more like a mass—in miniature—of hopelessly tangled spaghetti and broccoli florets and extremely elongated parsley leaves. Each neuron has hundreds of thousands of "fingers" (dendrites and axons) reaching out in all directions toward other neurons. Some of them fold back and forth and are extremely long. And each one carries nerve impulses that jump to other dendrites or axons and excite other nerve cells. Sometimes the nerve impulse travels only a few inches before connecting with another nerve cell; sometimes several feet!

Let's do some imagining together for a moment. Suppose that during each second of time we will permit only *one* isolated nerve cell to be stimulated through our senses (a ridiculously impossible limitation). But as this lonely nerve cell is stimulated, it sends out nerve impulses at 300 feet per second along thousands of dendrites and axons toward other nerve cells. Are you with me so far?

Now let's suppose that the average distance for a nerve impulse to travel before it connects with (and stimulates) another nerve cell is about one foot. This would mean, at 300 feet per second, that we would have time for 300 interconnections with other nerve cells during a period of one second. Still with me?

All right. Let's bring in a child to read for us. But first we'll give him some rules. "Sorry, Johnny, but for every second that you read, we'll permit you to have only one brain cell stimulated by your senses." Johnny, being a compliant child, agrees to our limitation. So we give him one more rule. "Furthermore, Johnny, it's all right for that one nerve cell to send out impulses that stimulate

other nerve cells, but no fair letting the other ones stimulate still other nerve cells." Johnny nods his head, and we're ready to begin.

Now, we know from research that the average elementary school child reads about two words per second (Sticht, 1984).* Can our subject, Johnny, maintain that reading rate with only 300 interconnections allowed per second? Well, it might be possible—since at two words per second he can *still* make 150 interconnections on each word that he reads. And with these 150 bits of information per word coming in, he might still get enough graphophonic, semantic, syntactic, and schematic cues to determine the pronunciation and meaning of the word.

We watch him with bated breath, our stopwatches poised to record his time. After five minutes we stop him and count the number of words he says he has read. *Voilà!* Still two words per second!

We're impressed, but the look in Johnny's eyes tells us that maybe he cheated. Maybe he didn't really restrict his senses from stimulating only one nerve cell per second. Maybe he didn't really restrict all those nerve cells from interacting with each other.

After reading up on this subject a little more, we decide to forgive Johnny. He couldn't really help himself from cheating. He might have *tried* to limit himself, but he had many, many more than 150 bits of information to work with on

---

*Average high school student, three words; average college student, four words.

each word. For, with two words per second stimulating his mind, it's obvious that more than one nerve cell would be stimulated by the senses each second. More likely, thousands of cells would each be stimulating thousands of others during a one-second interval. Research on the retina of the eye shows that the amount of information our brain can generate in one second is indeed quite massive. Jeanne McDermott, in the April 1985 issue of the *Smithsonian,* reports that the retina (working with the brain) performs the equivalent of 10 billion calculations per second!

Are you convinced, then, that our brain, with the help of our eyes, has the capacity to carry on interactive reading? Naturally, I hope so. But to me the rapid operation of the brain is only the tip of the iceberg. It is just one aspect of the total entity we call a human being. And the interactive nature of the reading process, as marvelous as it is, is just one example of the potentially incredible capabilities of the learner.

SUMMARY OF MAIN IDEAS

☐ Poor readers, on the average, tend to view reading incorrectly as primarily a decoding, word-calling process.

☐ Poor readers are generally deficient in their concept of reading, their ability to use all four cueing systems in an interactive way, their visual memory of sight words, and their recognition of graphophonic patterns.

☐ Good readers tend to view reading as a communication process between author and reader.

☐ Good readers score high on comprehension tests, but in the process of comprehending a passage, they often make meaningful substitutions, self-corrections, omissions, and insertions. Teachers with a bottom-up theory of reading tend to view these miscues mistakenly as reading errors.

☐ Good readers allow four types of cues to interact as they read: syntax cues, semantic cues, graphophonic cues, and schematic cues.

☐ Poor readers and good readers have common learning needs that teachers need to pay attention to. What we sometimes label as poor reading is actually poor teaching.

☐ Schemata are minitheories of how our world—and all the ingredients important to us—operate. These schemata interact with the cues from the author's text to help the reader make hypotheses, inferences, and predictions.

☐ The human brain permits so many interconnections per second among its nerve cells that it is easy for a good reader to pay attention to all four cueing systems in a way that seems simultaneous.

APPLICATION EXPERIENCES
FOR THE TEACHER EDUCATION CLASS

A. *What's Your Opinion?* Discuss why you agree and/or disagree with the following opinions. If you do this in a small group, compare your decisions with those of other groups. You are encouraged to use short quotations from the textbook, but much of your discussion should be in your own words. Use your own experiences and observations to help you explain your point of view; this will help make the ideas *yours*. *Making inferences and value judgments is the goal in this experience rather than reciting correct answers.*

1. More than anything else, poor readers need to learn more sight words and phonics.
2. Good readers would tend to treat reading situations in about the same way they would treat listening situations.
3. Children should be encouraged to make any substitutions they wish.
4. Semantic cues are the most important cues for the reader.
5. Good readers are good simply because they've learned more words and more phonics.
6. The interactive theory of reading means that good readers just mix phonics with their background of experience and whiz right along.
7. Those schemata things are nothing more than our past experiences.

B. *Miscue Analysis:* With at least one other person, find the different ways Amy miscues in the following "text."

Author's Text	*Fifth-Grader Amy's Miscues*
One cold (winter) day, a friend	Omitted *winter*
went into Dr. Jenner's small	No miscues in this line
office to talk over a problem. He	No miscues in this line
found the young scientist busy at *(that)* *(science)*	Substituted *that* for *the* and *science* for *scientist*
his desk, working in his overcoat, *(as)*	Substituted *as* for *in*
gloves and boots, his nose red with *(He had)*	Treated comma as period, then inserted *He had*
the chill. Dr. Jenner's friend	No miscues in this line
could not resist the temptation *(R)* *(rest)*	Repeated *could* and substituted *rest* for *resist*
to laugh. *(R)*	Repeated *to*

Do you think Amy repeats a word so as to give herself more time to think? Which of Amy's substitutions didn't change the author's meaning? How did the other three substitutions fit the syntax cues but not the semantic cues? Did Amy's omission and insertion change the author's meaning? Is Amy's concept of reading that reading is a process of getting an author's meaning? What do you think her concept is?

C. *Reading a Story Written in Applebet:* With the entire class or a small group, try reading the first three pages of the story in Figure 2.2 (on pages 50–53) called "The Sam Trap."

1. Notice that you can read much of this story without using the graphophonic system. That is, you can predict many of the words by relying on the syntax patterns of the language, on the semantic clues offered by the words in English (consider them your sight words), and by your own schematic clues related to similar stories. Discuss with others in your group how you are "figuring out" the message of the author.

FIGURE 2.2
"The Sam Trap" (a primer in Applebet)

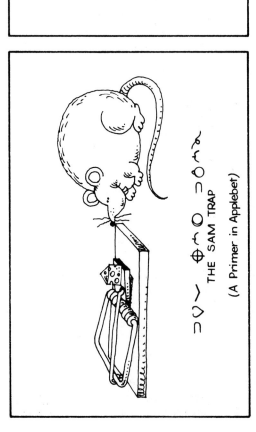

THE SAM TRAP

(A Primer in Applebet)

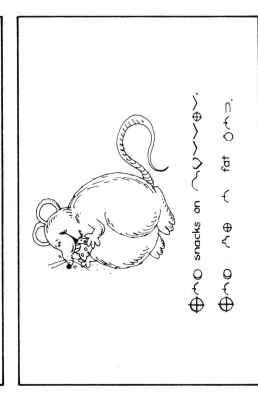

This is ⊕⌒◯.

⊕⌒◯ ⌒⊕ ⋏ ◯⌒⊃.

⊕⌒◯ snacks on ⌒⋁⋁⋁.

⊕⌒◯ ⌒⊕ ⋏ fat ◯⌒⊃.

50

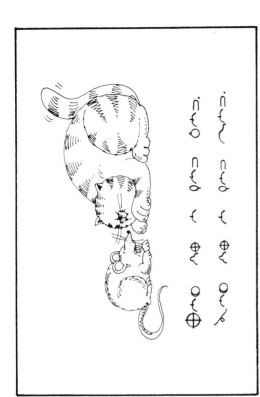

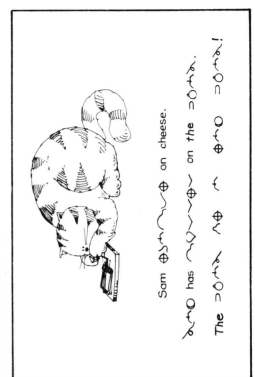

Sam ⊕ on cheese.

has on the .

The ⊕ !

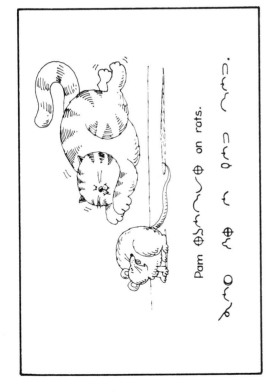

Pam ⊕ on rats.

Pam ,the , has a .

The is rat .

51

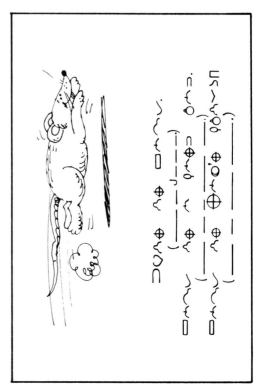

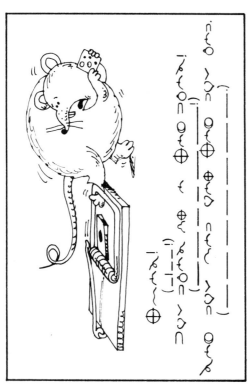

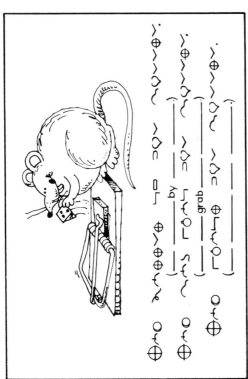

by

grab

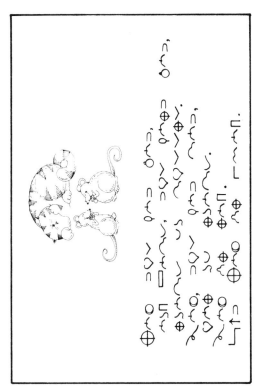

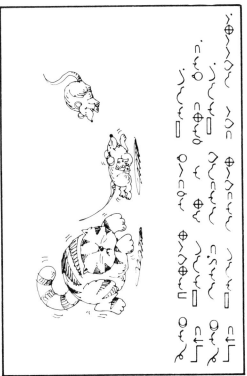

53

2. Before going on with the story, study the strange alphabet shown in Figure 2.3 called "Applebet." Try writing your own first and last name in this alphabet, then have at least three other people spell and read your name, using Applebet only (for example, "Your first name is bed-ox-bed. Oh, your first name is Bob.") Discuss the Applebet with others: How is it similar to and different from our regular alphabet?

3. Now return to the first page of "The Sam Trap" and use all four cueing systems to read the story to the end. Notice and discuss how the graphophonic system sometimes allows you to predict the next word and how sometimes it merely confirms a prediction you've already made from the other three cueing systems. Finish by talking about the interactive theory that readers and authors interact and so do the four cueing systems.

D. *Discussing the Problems of a Beginning Reader:* Discuss the frustrations and feelings you had as you were reading "The Sam Trap." How might they be similar to or different from beginning readers' experiences? Now discuss how you used the four cueing systems as you read. Share your examples with other people in the class.

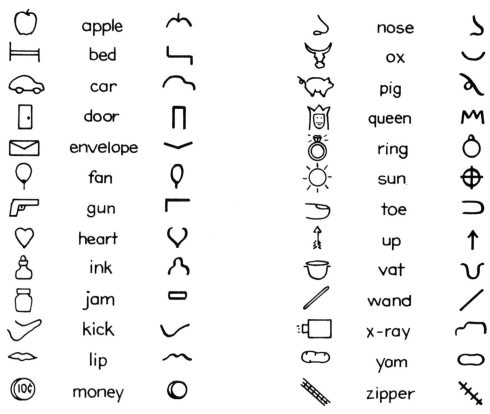

FIGURE 2.3
An Applebet

FIELD EXPERIENCES IN THE ELEMENTARY SCHOOL CLASSROOM

A. Listen to one or more children read who are above their grade level in general reading ability. Then listen to one or more children read who are below their grade level in general reading ability. Compare the types of miscues they make. Do the high-level readers make meaningful substitutions and self-corrections? What kinds of substitutions do the lower-level readers make? If possible, use a tape recorder for this experience.

B. Informally interview several children to determine the development of their schemata and how their level of schemata development might interfere with reading comprehension. For instance, you might ask them about people of different occupations: What is a farmer? What do farmers do? What is a secretary? What do secretaries do? What is a housewife? A teacher? A jockey?

Try other categories of schemata such as *wearing apparel* (Why do people wear different kinds of hats?) or the *transportation* category (Why do some people drive to work and others take a bus or a train?). Try the *time* category. For example, How long is a moment? A generation? A while?

REFERENCES AND SUGGESTED READING

Allington, R. L. (1980). Poor readers don't get to read much in reading groups. *Language Arts, 57,* 872–876.

Beebe, M. J. (1979–80). The effect of different types of substitution miscues on reading. *Reading Research Quarterly, 15,* 124–136.

Brewer, W. F. (1972). Is reading a letter-by-letter process? In J. Kavanagh & I. Mattingly (Eds.), *Language by ear and by eye* (pp. 359–365). Cambridge, MA: MIT Press.

Carr, K. S. (1983). The importance of inference skills in the primary grades. *The Reading Teacher, 36,* 518–522.

D'Angelo, K., & Mahlios, M. (1983). Insertion and omission miscues of good and poor readers. *The Reading Teacher, 36,* 778–782.

de Beaugrande, R. (1984). The literacy of reading: Fact, fiction or frontier? In J. Flood (Ed.), *Understanding reading comprehension* (pp. 45–74). Newark, DE: International Reading Association.

Dehn, M. (1984). An AI perspective on reading comprehension. In J. Flood (Ed.), *Understanding reading comprehension* (pp. 82–100). Newark, DE: International Reading Association.

Dunkeld, C. (1979). Portland informal reading inventory, Form P. Unpublished manuscript, Portland State University, School of Education.

Durkin, D. (1978–79). What classroom observations reveal about reading comprehension instruction. *Reading Research Quarterly, 14,* 481–533.

Englert, C. S., & Semmel, M. I. (1981). The relationship of oral reading substitution miscues to comprehension. *The Reading Teacher, 35,* 273–280.

Estes, T. H. (1983). A commentary on *Reading and Understanding: Teaching from the perspective of artificial intelligence. The Reading Teacher, 36,* 483–490.

Flavel, J. H. (1979). Metacognition and cognitive monitoring: A new area of cognitive-developmental inquiry. *American Psychologist, 34,* 906–911.

Flood, J. E. (1978). The influence of first sentences on reader expectations within prose passages. *Reading World, 17,* 306–315.

Gambrell, L. B. (1980). Think-time: Implications for reading instruction. *The Reading Teacher, 34,* 143–146.

Goodman, K. (1971). Reading: A psycholinguistic guessing game. In H. Singer & R. Ruddell (Eds.), *Theoretical models and processes of reading*. Newark, DE: International Reading Association.

Herrmann, B. A. (1988). Two approaches for helping poor readers become more strategic. *The Reading Teacher, 42*, 24–29.

Jones, L. L. (1982). An interactive view of reading: Implications for the classroom. *The Reading Teacher, 35*, 772–777.

Lapp, D., & Flood, J. (1984). Promoting reading comprehension: Instruction which insures continuous reader growth. In J. Flood (Ed.), *Promoting reading comprehension* (pp. 273–288). Newark, DE: International Reading Association.

Marshall, N. (1983). Using story grammar to assess reading comprehension. *The Reading Teacher, 36*, 616–628.

Rumelhart, D. D. (1984). Understanding understanding. In J. Flood (Ed.), *Understanding reading comprehension* (pp. 1–20). Newark, DE: International Reading Association.

Smith, A. (1984). *The mind*. New York: Viking.

Smith, F. (1979). *Reading*. Cambridge: Cambridge University Press.

Sticht, T. G. (1984). Rate of comprehension by listening or reading. In J. Flood (Ed.), *Understanding reading comprehension* (pp. 140–160). Newark, DE: International Reading Association.

Thomas, E. L., & Robinson, H. A. (1977). *Improving reading in every class*. Boston: Allyn & Bacon.

Weber, R. M. (1970). First graders' use of grammatical context in reading. In H. D. Levin & J. P. Williams (Eds.), *Basic studies in reading* (pp. 147–163). New York: Basic Books.

Emergent Literacy: The Interacting Language Arts at Home and School

Carol L. Peterman
Portland State University

CHAPTER OUTLINE

CHAPTER PREVIEW

Remember Karen, the lucky six-year-old from Chapter 1 whose parents read to her often, provided her with books, and encouraged her to explore written language through her "pretend writing"? No doubt Karen is ready to learn how to read and write. In fact, in many ways she's already begun the process of becoming literate. Because of her early experiences with language, Karen is also ready for many of the lessons that will occur in primary classrooms.

This chapter is about children like Karen—children who are eager to start school so that they can learn more about becoming members of the literacy club, just like their parents and older brothers and sisters. It's about the home and school factors that contribute to success in learning about language. You'll discover that, as teachers, you don't have to wait for a magical age or grade level in order to provide literacy lessons, even though tradition dictates that reading and writing are taught during certain grades.

In this chapter we'll discuss the importance of reading stories to children. Being read to at home provides a natural bridge to learning about literacy at school. We'll look at the benefits of story reading and discuss recommended techniques for presenting stories based on those used by parents and teachers alike.

You'll see examples of children's development in early reading, writing, and other related literacy skills, such as "phonological and metalinguistic awareness." These examples illustrate the natural, yet untimed, progression toward conventional literacy.

Understanding individual children's approaches to literacy will influence your decisions about the types of experiences you, as a teacher, will provide. This means that we need to discuss ways of evaluating what children already know about reading, writing, and other language skills. In a sense, teachers become astute observers and researchers who gather information about children's strengths. These data provide the rationale and guidelines for designing an appropriate curriculum.

By the end of the chapter you'll be able to make decisions about your classroom environment and the kinds of literacy events you'll want to provide. These activities and lessons should help children explore and expand their existing language base. My goal is to convince you that your literacy program should capitalize on the abilities and interests of the children rather than expecting them to fit into a predetermined program—especially if it fails to recognize the importance of children's experience with, and proficiency in, the use of the four cueing systems.

Pretty soon I will be going into kindergarten. I think it will be great! I want to learn how to read, but I already started learning. I can read my name because I write it myself. And this is my name:

LAuRA

—B. Daviess

THE PROCESS OF LEARNING ABOUT LANGUAGE: EMERGENT LITERACY

A Current Definition of Readiness

Perhaps you can recall a time when you felt you weren't ready for an exam. Or perhaps you didn't think you were ready to teach that first lesson. Maybe you weren't ready to learn to swim. I'm sure you'd agree that readiness for any task or experience is important if success is the goal.

But what is readiness for any given task? Is it something that simply develops over time, without experience or training? Is it a set of subskills that people learn one at a time until they're suddenly ready? Or maybe there's more to being ready than simply learning a series of prerequisite skills. Perhaps experience (or schema development) contributes to readiness as well. Let me give you an example from my own experience.

Last winter, a group of my colleagues and I embarked on a trip to the mountains to go skiing for the weekend. Although not a skier myself, I decided to go along just for fun. My friends encouraged me to take a lesson, but my definitive response was, "Maybe next time. I'm just not ready."

Now, was it the case that I didn't have the specific skills needed for skiing? Were my muscles not yet developed? Perhaps my physical coordination wasn't adequate. Or maybe I just didn't have the adequate mental set (or schema) to try this new activity. My solution was to wait until I had more confidence in my ability to be successful. But was waiting the answer to my lack of readiness for learning to ski? In retrospect, I'd say that waiting did little but raise my anxiety level on the next trip.

Even though I felt I wasn't ready to learn to ski, it turns out that I *was* ready to consider the process of learning to ski. I was ready to watch other skiers, to consider the skills I'd need to be a good skier, to think about the equipment I'd need, and at the same time to develop my schema for joining the club of those not restricted to the warmth and comfort of the ski lodge. I knew that learning to ski was a risk, yet I had to be willing to try it before I'd make any progress. I'd need to gain proficiency through direct instruction and, equally important, through practice. Ultimately, the more experience I had with learning to ski, the more I was able to draw on other skills and abilities even remotely related to skiing, such as roller skating and water skiing. In fact, the wise advice of my good-looking ski instructor was not to overanalyze the task but to "Just do it, Carol!" It was only then that I got a feel for what it was like to ski down a (small) mountain, to feel like a skier.

The same is true of literacy learning. Children are ready to learn about certain aspects of language and literacy based on what they already know about these concepts. They come to view themselves as successful club members and are usually willing to take risks in order to learn more about the process. The more they experiment with language, the more they are able to test their hypotheses about language. The more they test their hypotheses, the more they add to or otherwise modify their schema about language. Their explorations are more than simply precursors of conventional literacy—they are "legitimate aspects of the ontogeny [the entire development] of literacy" (Teale, 1988, p. 46, parenthetical mine). More simply, through their attempts to read and write, we see evidence of "emergent literacy."

What Is Emergent Literacy?

> **Emergent literacy:** the *process* of learning about language. It is a *product* of children's explorations with concepts and conventions about language with which they are already familiar.

Children use and explore language long before their products sound or look conventional. In other words, children may not be able to read a text word for word, or write using conventional spelling. Instead, they engage in what might be called "pretend" reading and writing. Yet these attempts to read and write show evidence of their readiness to learn more about conventional language, especially if they learn through their own process of trial and error.

Here's an example. When a child discovers that his parents can't read his "writing," he gradually becomes aware of the various cueing systems that make language readable to literacy club members. He begins to attend more closely to his parents as they engage in literacy activities. He asks questions about signs and labels in the environment. He begins to "read" stories that have been read to him by his parents. He modifies his writing attempts to integrate what he's learned through his interactions during storytime and from his observations of literate others. With each event, he experiments with language and gradually learns about the conventions of literacy.

What are the implications for teachers, you ask? Well, if we judge children's readiness for learning about language by their products alone, say, their "scribblings" or their score on traditional readiness tests, we might come to the conclusion that they know very little about conventional literacy. However, if we observe and explore their *process* of literacy learning, we'll understand that their attempts to construct meaning from language are signs of readiness to move toward conventional literacy.

A definition of readiness for learning, then, might be the child's interest in exploring literacy from his own level of understanding while moving toward conventional literacy. This involvement helps children feel like successful language users rather than like outsiders who are excluded from this very important club (Dyson, 1984; Smith, 1984). Excluding them from the reading and writing club simply because they don't know conventional spellings, for example, would be like banning me from the ski slopes because I hadn't mastered the more conventional ways of slowing down and stopping. Frankly, just sitting down often works quite well for me, though it's hardly conventional.

Examples of Emergent Literacy at Home and in School

At home, parents from various cultures with different uses for literacy seem to intuitively provide the kind of supportive, nonthreatening environment children need in order to feel included in the literacy club and to develop their schema for learning about written language. Let me explain further; then I'll give you an example of a child's perception of the process of learning to read.

By the time their formal education begins, most children today have been exposed to a variety of literacy events. In fact, their parents or other family members have encouraged, modeled, and sometimes even provided direct instruction in certain aspects of language and literacy concepts. One of the most powerful ways children can learn about language is through participation in the story-reading event. Most parents seem to naturally know how to identify their child's level of understanding and simplify the story-reading process, if necessary, so that learning is taking place. Taylor and Strickland express it this way:

Parents . . . read books with children for the sheer pleasure it brings and the relationship it binds among their loved ones. . . . They do not deliberately set out to give language lessons. Nonetheless, all kinds of lessons about language do occur. (Taylor & Strickland, 1986, p. x)

Mitchell, a four-year-old I interviewed, reveals some of these language lessons. Here are his responses to questions designed to learn more about children's perceptions of the reading process:

INTERVIEWER: Tell me, Mitchell, are you learning to read?
MITCHELL: Yes!
INTERVIEWER: How are you learning to read?
MITCHELL: I heard my mom read the book before and now I know.
INTERVIEWER: Is anyone helping you learn to read?
MITCHELL: My sister.
INTERVIEWER: How is she helping you?
MITCHELL: She tells me what the words say.
INTERVIEWER: Is anyone else helping you?
MITCHELL: My mom and dad.
INTERVIEWER: How are they helping?
MITCHELL: They show me what the words are. (Peterman, Greer, & Turnipseed, 1984)

Through this discussion with Mitchell, we can see that he knows he's learning to read. He knows that in listening to his mom read and by having people "tell" him "what the words say" and "show" him "what the words are," he'll learn how to read. Mitchell seems to have developed a schema for reading that includes a desire to learn how to read, knowing that others can help him learn to read, knowing *how* others can help him learn to read, and knowing that words "say" something when he knows "what the words are." We can infer that Mitchell is aware of at least three of the four cueing systems: the schematic, or use of experiential cues and/or background knowledge; the syntactic, or use of the order of the words read to him by his mother; and the semantic, or use of his knowledge that words have to make sense in order for him to read the story like his mom does. Mitchell seems relatively unaware of the fourth system, the graphophonic system. Ironically, the graphophonic system is one that many kindergarten and first-grade classrooms emphasize.

If Mitchell were in your kindergarten or first-grade classroom, would you say that he's ready to learn to read?

As a former first-grade teacher, I can remember having discussions with my colleagues about literacy activities that I promoted in my classroom. Many of these activities might have been considered to be beyond the typical first-grade level. For example, children wrote about authors and presented reports on their works. Often, my colleagues would say, "That must be fun, but, you know, my kids just aren't ready for that yet." Or "Well, I'm going to wait until around

February before I try that, then they'll be ready." Or "They don't know all of the letters and their sounds so they're not ready to write yet."

The point is that we should give children the opportunity to show us what they're ready to experience. By giving children the opportunities to explore language at their own level of understanding, we give them the message that it's all right to take risks and explore their own hypotheses about written language. By doing so, they'll begin to see themselves as successful members of the literacy club.

So rather than asking, "Are children ready to learn to read and write?" or, "When should formal instruction in reading and writing begin?" we should be asking questions like, "What do children already know about reading and writing?" and "What can I do to help them want to learn more?"

The last two questions will be addressed in later sections of this chapter. But for now, let's take a look at reasons why the first two questions are still asked by some primary-grade teachers.

The Influence of History on Our Attitudes about Readiness

In her reading methodology textbook, Dolores Durkin (1989) explains that readiness programs were created in the 1930s to fill the void between the time that children entered first grade and the time that "neural ripening" occurred. But in order to understand why this was the popular opinion at that time, we need to turn back the clock another decade or so.

Historically, learning to read has been linked with the beginning of formal education, usually occurring in first-grade classrooms, when children are between the ages of five and seven. It seems that little thought was given to the reasons for this tradition until the 1920s, when school surveys were developed and administered as a result of a growing interest in the scientific measurement of children's behavior. Of the significant findings, the most relevant to this discussion is the fact that large numbers of children were failing first grade during this time period.

A logical explanation was proposed by educators who were familiar with the theory of recapitulation, posited by the famous turn-of-the-century psychologist G. Stanley Hall and supported by his followers Arnold Gesell and Lewis Terman. This theory (which Hall labeled a *law*) states that development takes place in stages following a natural, logical order. Growth, or the passing from one stage to the next, occurs as a result of simple maturation.

Educators took this theory and applied it to the concept of readiness for learning to read, arguing that learning to read occurs at one of these predetermined stages. If children were failing to learn to read, it must be because they weren't at the stage of development necessary for success; they weren't "neurally ripe" (Gesell, 1925). In short, they weren't *ready* to learn to read.

Is There a "Magical Moment" When Children Are Ready?

The logical solution was to wait for the passage of time. But how long should one wait for that magical moment? As a result of the technological advances of the Testing Movement, could educators determine the necessary mental age for this stage of development?

Mabel Morphett and Carleton Washburne (1931) set out to answer these questions in what later became a highly influential study. Looking at only one method of instruction in a single, yet large and progressive, school district, they determined that children needed a mental age of 6½ years in order to be successful with reading in first grade.

This presented somewhat of a problem for teachers who had been accustomed to starting their reading instruction at the beginning of first grade. Many of their children wouldn't reach the necessary mental age until well into the school year. Teachers asked, "What do we do with the children while we're waiting for them to develop?" The solution this time came in the form of reading readiness programs.

You may have seen these programs in your observations of kindergarten classrooms today, even though they were designed for use in first-grade classrooms in the 1930s. These programs usually provide practice in skills such as visual discrimination of pictures and letters, but sometimes geometric shapes. They also provide practice in auditory discrimination, including initial consonants and rhyming words. The better ones also provide instruction in vocabulary development. Figure 3.1 gives you an example of a page from one kindergarten readiness (K-R) program with a publication date of 1986. Later we'll take a closer look at the effectiveness of these programs.

At this point you may be asking yourself, "Why are these programs now being used with younger children? Are children simply ready at an earlier age? Given the theory of recapitulation, how is this possible?"

The launching of *Sputnik* by the Soviet Union in 1957 resulted in a sense of urgency about the quality and content of the American educational system. Suddenly, the emphasis was on teaching more—and teaching it earlier—which

From K-R.

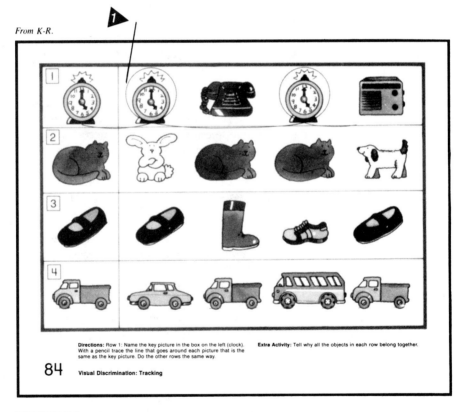

FIGURE 3.1
Visual discrimination of pictures: K-R workbook page from a 1986 basal series. From *Scribner Reading Series,* Charles Scribner's Sons, Macmillan Publishing Co.

meant that the philosophy of waiting for the moment of "neural ripening" was no longer acceptable. Obviously, educators would have to consider other factors that might contribute to a child's readiness for learning to read. Some of these possibilities are discussed in the next section.

Factors That Contribute to Success

A few years after Morphett and Washburne published their findings, a scholar by the name of Arthur Gates (1937) conducted his own study with the same goal of determining the appropriate mental age required for success in beginning reading. Unlike Morphett and Washburne, Gates looked at different types of instruction as a possible factor influencing children's success or failure. He found that children with different mental ages could be successful in programs with different instructional methods and materials. Although his ideas were largely ignored in the 1930s, due to the controversial findings, people in the late 1950s were willing to give them more credence. After all, Gates's findings provided a rationale for giving children an earlier start at reading by simply modifying the instructional methods or the materials.

More current evidence was also available. Through reexaminations of studies conducted in the 1930s, J. McVicker Hunt (1961) concluded that experience and training have much to do with success at a given skill or activity, while Benjamin Bloom (1964) stressed the importance of the first five years of life in a child's intellectual development. Of course, Jerome Bruner's famous words couldn't have been more timely. He wrote, "We begin with the hypothesis that any subject can be taught effectively in some intellectually honest form to any child at any stage of development" (1960, p. 33).

So you see, by the end of the 1960s there were at least three factors to consider in determining readiness or potential for success: the intellectual development of the child; the type and quality of instruction; and the environment for learning, especially during the first five years of life.

But what factors will contribute to success in reading and writing in the 1990s? What experiences in the home environment are related to later achievement in school?

The Role of the Home Environment

Several case studies and diary accounts of parent-child interactions, especially those occurring during literacy events, have shed light on these questions. Not surprisingly, the way parents interact with books—their behaviors with these and other literacy materials—provides children with a model of the importance of literacy in everyday life (Hiebert, 1978). It seems that the number of books in the home, including those checked out from the local library, is an indication of the importance of literacy in the home environment (Clark, 1976; Mason & Dunning, 1986).

Equally important are the uses of literacy in the everyday lives of family members. For example, in a case study of Corey, a three-year-old boy, one of my graduate students explains the uses of literacy in this child's family:

> Reading for a variety of purposes is modeled at Corey's home. Home decorating magazines, novels, cookbooks, recipes, newspapers and "how-to" manuals are all often referred to. Corey undoubtedly observes his mother, Jan, write more frequently than his father, Greg. He sees Jan write grocery lists, checks, letters, poems, draw up plans and design greeting cards. Greg spends a great deal of time at a word processor at work.
>
> Indeed Corey has observed his parents' use of reading for pleasure and purpose throughout his life. Recently, prior to the kitchen remodeling, Greg borrowed a number of architectural books to read about structural supports, as he planned to remove a wall. As Greg was climbing up into the attic, Corey inquired, "You going in the attic?"
>
> GREG: Yep. I need to check the beams that make the ceiling.
> COREY: How come?
> GREG: The book Bob gave me told me how to remove the kitchen wall. The beams up here hold the ceiling up. When I take the wall out, I want to be sure the ceiling stays up.
> COREY: When are we taking out the wall?
>
> The reference Greg made to Bob's book validated his use of getting information from books. (Daviess, 1988, p. 2)

The development of literacy through the home environment has been documented in other studies around the country. In her ethnographic study of families in various suburbs of New York City, Denny Taylor (1983) discovered that reading and writing are used to solve practical problems and maintain social relationships. In a later study, she found that black urban families living in poverty also had their own uses for reading and writing (Taylor & Dorsey-Gaines, 1987) similar to those found among black and white communities of the Carolina Piedmonts (Heath, 1983).

Some of these uses were categorized by William Teale (1986) in his study of the literacy activities found among low-income white, black, and Mexican American families. Reading and writing were used in daily living activities, entertainment, school-related work, religion, interpersonal communication, information networks, storybook time, and teaching and/or learning literacy. He concluded that the process of becoming literate is inextricably linked with our families' social and cultural traditions, which define who and what we are. Thus, the study of "literacy development is basically an investigation of the acquisition of culture" (Teale, 1988, p. 49).

Just as a person's cultural upbringing affects his literacy learning, the reverse can also be the case. Many parents read to their children in order to pass along cultural stories and lessons. During these events, parents assist in the process of learning to read by listening to children, by answering their questions, by providing them with opportunities to explore written language and their own writing, and perhaps most importantly by reading to them.

> The importance of adult-child interactions is highlighted in what Teale (1988) calls "the early reader studies." These studies are "important to emergent literacy research because they . . . give strong indications of the significance of reading to children and providing a literacy-rich environment in which materials and adults are available to the child to assist in literacy development" (Teale, 1988, p. 51). (For more on this, see Clark, 1976; Durkin, 1966; and Torrey, 1969.)

As you probably already know, reading to children has long been considered an important event in the literacy development of children. Perhaps you recall times when your parents read to you at bedtime, or maybe you read to your own children. Not surprisingly, in an important study of the relationship between preschool literacy-related activities and success in school, Gordon Wells found that reading stories to children has numerous benefits that help them "cope with the more disembedded uses of spoken language that the school curriculum demands" (1985, p. 253).

In fact, the past decade has given us many studies that highlight the positive effects story reading can have on children's language development, their interest in books, their academic readiness for school-related tasks, and their social attitude (S. McCormick, 1983). In the next section, you'll see how the story-reading event can be the pivotal point for making the connection between early language development and the emergence of conventional reading and writing. You'll discover that children's self-initiated explorations with written language help them develop print awareness, phonological awareness, and early writing strategies. Perhaps most important is the development of a story schema, which helps children see how the schematic cueing system combines with the graphophonic, syntactic, and semantic systems. Once they have developed this schema, children are well on their way toward developing effective, interactive reading strategies.

CHILDREN'S EXPLORATION OF LANGUAGE

The Importance of Reading to Children: Language

Let's talk for a while about one of the main reasons why reading to children is so important. Not only is the experience usually a warm and loving one, in which significant bonding occurs between parent and child, but it also allows for what linguists call the *input* of language and language concepts.

Input of language occurs as a result of the "communication environment" in which the child interacts. Typically we think of the home environment and the interaction between parents and their children as having the most impact on the acquisition of language (Menyuk, 1988). Later, teachers and other care-givers contribute to the child's language development.

But what do parents do to help children acquire language? How do they help children learn the conventions of language? Do they modify their speech patterns as a function of their child's age and linguistic ability?

Ironically, parents often provide children with insufficient models of oral language when they attempt to simplify their own speech. Researchers have noted that some parents from different cultures speak "motherese" (Gleitman, Newport, & Gleitman, 1984) to their children, very much like some people speak to "foreigners, the hard-of-hearing, and the very elderly—people who, the speaker assumes, might have difficulty in understanding what was being said" (Menyuk, 1988, p. 92). Perhaps this type of speech makes it difficult for children to make connections between these utterances and conventional language.

On the other side of the coin is the argument that parents modify their language to more closely match the ability of the child, then extend his language by repeating and expanding the utterances. This "scaffolding," an analogy used by Bruner (1976), serves to provide children with "temporary language platforms that support and encourage children's language development to more complex levels" (Hoskisson & Tompkins, 1987, p. 24).

"Language development grows out of a series of rich interactions with parents and other speakers of the language. But the child's learning of language is not merely a process of imitation. The child's use of linguistic "input" is selective, thereby demonstrating his/her active role in learning. Thus, the child is said to be constructing language. However, this construction is a social rather than a one-way process. Parents respond to their child's utterances by expanding and recasting them, by displaying their comprehension or misunderstanding of them, and by giving feedback as to their truth. In the give and take of daily "conversation" the child learns how to structure language, how to mean in language, and how to be communicatively competent" (Teale, 1988, p. 12).

Evidence of parents' attempts to accommodate the child's level of learning can be seen in the story-reading event. Jerome Bruner (1976), for example, pointed out that a child's language learning can be affected by the mother's interactional style when looking at picture books with her child. The mother typically asks, "What's that?" and the child almost always responds. "She is constantly establishing linguistic distinctions between the given and the new, the familiar and the unfamiliar" (Bruner, 1976, p. 210). This routine, which the child begins to predict, is the product of many interactions of this nature.

In a follow-up study, Ninio and Bruner (1978) found that in addition to labeling pictured objects, mothers often direct their child's attention to important features, ask them to talk about the ideas in the book, and give them feedback that will help them better understand the book. With older children, the labeling procedure is often replaced with questions and answers about the story (De-Loache & DeMendoza, 1986; Harkness & Miller, 1982; Pellegrini, Brody, & Sigel, 1985; and others). As children become more competent, they initiate more interactions, while adults become less directive yet more demanding (Pellegrini, Brody, & Sigel, 1985).

So it appears that parents are aware of the linguistic competence of their children and can design interactions to support and expand their children's language abilities. Now, whether or not parents are fully aware of what they're doing, it seems that they're quite capable of effectively presenting stories. And at the same time it seems that children are aware of what they're learning from their parents.

For example, take Wally, a child in Vivian Paley's kindergarten classroom, who tells a delightful story about the importance of learning language from adult models.

> A little boy lived all alone in a deep forest. When he wanted to know a word he asked lions and tigers and wolves. They told him pretend words because he couldn't speak animal language. One day he saw a lady and a man who didn't have a little boy.
> "What language do you talk?"
> "Animal pretend talk."
> "That's okay because we can teach you people's language. Which one do you want to learn?"
> "English."
> "Good, because that's our language. What words do you want to know?"
> "Lion, tiger, and wolf."
> "You already know them. You just said them."
> "Then animal pretend talk must be English."
> So they lived happily ever after. But the man and lady knew some words the boy didn't know, so they did have a lot to teach him. (Paley, 1981, pp. 120-121).

The Importance of Reading to Children: Conventions

In the past decade we've learned a great deal about how parents and teachers read to their children. We've learned that when story reading is included as a natural extension of children's exploration of written language, it can result in the following language and literacy benefits:

1. Concept development, vocabulary development, and linguistic competence
2. Knowledge of the content, structure, and conventions of written language
3. Academic readiness
4. Word recognition skills
5. Later achievement in reading

Concept development, vocabulary development, and linguistic competence. During story reading, children hear specific linguistic forms, including dialogue and narrative structures. They are also exposed to specific vocabulary items (DeLoache and DeMendoza, 1986). As a result, they begin to display literacy skills and uses of language which they had encountered in the stories (Teale, 1984, 1988).

> ''Reading to children may provide a specific, recurrent context in which previous conversations can be remembered and used by children to extend and elaborate their own conversational repertoire'' (Goldfield & Snow, 1984, p. 209).

Knowledge of the content, structure, and conventions of written language. Given lots of story-reading experience, children begin to understand that books are for reading, not just for manipulating. Eventually they realize that the print carries the storyline, and the pictures are only representations of real objects. These pictures, though static in nature, can also represent events that occur outside real time. As a result of these realizations, children begin to experience the vicarious nature of the story-reading event (Snow & Ninio, 1986).

Research also shows that by listening to stories, children can better understand how written language compares to oral language (Mason et al., 1988). Children begin to understand how authors convey ideas in stories and how stories are constructed. Discussing a story clarifies its meaning while enhancing children's listening comprehension and oral language ability (Mason, 1985a; Walker & Kuerbitz, 1979).

The mechanics of reading are also demonstrated during story reading. Children begin to understand the relationship between the written symbols and their sounds. Conventions, such as the left-to-right sequence of words on a page and the front-to-back sequence of pages in the book, are demonstrated through story reading (Anderson, Teale, & Estrada, 1980).

Academic readiness. Reading aloud to preschoolers can instill a love of books that will spark their interest in learning to read (S. McCormick, 1983). This interest in the written word ''will help to develop readiness for successful first grade participation'' (Walker & Kuerbitz, 1979, p. 149).

Word recognition skills. Various word recognition skills can be introduced during story reading. For example, understanding the main parts of a story helps children learn to match the words on the page with the story events (Peterman et al., 1987), especially if the same story is presented on numerous occasions (Schickendanz, 1978). Clay (1979b) proposes that through story reading, children learn that print can be turned into speech, that the print will make sense, that there is a message recorded in the print, and that some language units are more likely to occur over and over again in writing. Children can begin to collect a

"It was of the utmost importance for me to learn to read for many reasons. One being that as far back as I could remember, my mother read aloud to my older brother and me and I just knew that all kinds of wonderful stories and interesting things were there for the taking between the covers of books. What I didn't like, however, was always being at the mercy of my mother's timetable for the daily read aloud session. I wanted to find out all this stuff when *I* wanted to find it out" (reflections of Tomie de Paola in the foreword to Cullinan, 1987, p. v).

store of sight words by listening to and watching others read to them. "Because the children can predict what is printed on the page, they can 'read' the lines even though they might not be able to recognize the individual words in isolation or in other contexts" (Bridge, 1986).

Later achievement in reading. Marilyn Cochran-Smith suggests that children's experiences with stories may have an important influence on their later achievement in school, namely, on their reading and writing performances, their "language acquisition and development, and their imaginative and creative growth" (1983, p. 197). The more children are exposed to story time, the more likely they are to experience related gains in reading achievement (Walker & Kuerbitz, 1979). It just may be that reading and discussing stories with children help them "cope with the more disembedded uses of spoken language that the school curriculum demands" (Wells, 1985, p. 253).

I hope you're convinced of the importance of reading to young children and encouraging parents to do the same at home. But equally important for the development of literacy are children's self-initiated explorations of language. Initially, these might occur as children begin to notice print in their environment and begin to ask questions about written language. Let's talk now about how children develop awareness of printed language.

Children's Developing Print Awareness

Those of you who have had contact with young children probably know something about their awareness of print in the environment. Almost as a matter of course, when adults take children on errands, they tend to point out significant or highly interesting words, road signs, and "environmental print." Now, whether this routine is child-initiated or is a strategy on the part of the parent to make the trip more interesting, children begin to label many print-carrying symbols with which they come into contact. No doubt many children will recognize something that's of interest in their environment, even if it's simply the omnipresent McDonald's sign.

Of course, there are those who'd say that recognizing the McDonald's sign, for example, is not an indication that the child can actually read. And perhaps, in a conventional sense, the child isn't reading. On the other hand, this awareness of print in the environment reveals the beginnings of literacy that lead to what researchers call "metalinguistic awareness," or the child's intuitive knowledge about language and his ability to reflect on, and express, this awareness.

Here's an example of a family literacy event, in which the child's interaction with print reveals an awareness that words are spelled a certain way and that the spelling is revealed on the object itself.

> I told Michael I was making a grocery list and asked if he would like to make his own. He started to write grapefruit on his own, without asking for help. Then he asked,
>
> MICHAEL: How many grapefruit can I get with a dollar?
> MOM: Oh, probably three.
> MICHAEL: (Finished writing GRAPFRT.) How do you spell red grapes?—Wait, never mind.
>
> At this point he began searching through his crayons looking for a *red* crayon. I realized he was going to copy "red" off the label! The label had been peeled off— and then he was frustrated.

MICHAEL: Mom, how do you spell "red"?
MOM: Guess and go, honey.
MICHAEL: I want to spell "red" the *right* way. Maegan, how do you spell "red"?

His two-year-old sister was sitting next to him. He sounded out "er," "eh," "du."

MICHAEL: I got it! R-A-D, right, Mom?
MOM: Right! (I felt a twinge of guilt for not being truthful.)
MICHAEL: How much does Captain Crunch cost?
MOM: Probably about three dollars.
MICHAEL: Oh good! I have enough for Captain Crunch! Mom, does it start with C or K? Please tell me, 'cause I can't figure it out. C and K both say the Kuh sound. Just write the *real* answer for me.

I pretended to be busy writing my list and didn't respond so he wrote CAPTON.

MICHAEL: Hey, does captain have "on" in it?
MOM: Captain—sounds like it!
MICHAEL: No it doesn't, does it? Tell me, 'cause I'll see it on the box when we buy it. So you better tell me!

Now *I'm* frustrated. I don't want to lie to him.

MOM: OK—instead of O-N it's actually A-I-N. There's no way you could figure that out, honey. It's just one of those spellings we have to learn. (Barnes, 1988, pp. 12–132)

Some researchers say that younger children, who are less aware of the graph-ophonic system, may be reading simply the environment rather than the actual print (Mason, 1980). Others suggest that as children become aware of print in the environment, they're not only developing knowledge of the functions and uses of print and their metalinguistic awareness, but they're also beginning to learn about the phonological or graphophonic system of written language (Hiebert, 1986).

"The environmental print studies suggest that children do develop concepts about the functions and uses of written language through contact with print in the everyday environment. They also suggest that knowledge of environmental print provides the foundation which enables children to begin learning about the graphic system" (Teale, 1988, p. 52).

I have a nephew who is now quite a proficient reader. But when he was about four years old, he could recognize a particular pizza sign (or perhaps it was the particular restaurant he recognized). In any case, whenever my sister drove by this particular pizza parlor, Philip would excitedly announce, "pizza!" Well, my sister didn't think too much about it until a few weeks later when Philip was "reading" the newspaper with his father. That evening Philip announced that he could read the word *pizza*. Kathy checked to see what he was "reading," assuming that he had seen an advertisement for his favorite restaurant. This would have been quite exciting in itself, since it would demonstrate Philip's ability to transfer the logo from the actual restaurant to the written form in a newspaper ad. But what Kathy found was that Philip was now able to read the word *pizza* outside the context of the restaurant itself or the logo that contained the word. He had learned to recognize a word that was of great interest to him, and—just as important—he was aware that he was able to read the word.

Philip had learned a sight word, one he could recognize as a whole without breaking it down by the sounds of the letters. In time, Philip began to collect a store of sight words that perhaps helped him "crack the code" of the alphabetic system. You see, since our English orthography is alphabetic, the letters represent fairly distinct sounds. These letter-sound correspondences are consistent enough that children can begin to intuitively make connections among words that begin with the same letter (and thus the same sound) or among words that have the same or similar patterns. We might say, then, that environmental print has the potential for increasing children's phonological awareness.

Children's Writing Development

Children's phonological awareness is also developed through their early writing attempts. Carol Chomsky (1971, 1979) believes that children learn how to read by first exploring their own invented spellings (such as Michael's spelling, GRAPFRT for *grapefruit*). These spellings, although often unconventional, show evidence of a child's phonological development, which is said to have "reciprocal gains" in reading (Clay, 1975, 1984). This means that as the child becomes aware of the graphophonic principles used in writing, he begins to notice these principles in his reading. By noticing words and phonics generalizations in his reading, he achieves closer approximations in his writing. Because the reading process is so closely linked with the writing process, the child begins to "read like a writer" (Smith, 1984). (For two very interesting articles on this topic, see Squire, 1984, and Tierney & Pearson, 1984.)

> "The young child's reading and writing abilities mutually reinforce each other, developing concurrently and interrelatedly rather than sequentially. The child develops as a reader/writer; therefore, it is more appropriate to speak of *literacy* development rather than reading readiness or reading development. Furthermore, reading and writing have intimate connections with oral language. Truly, the child develops as a speaker/reader/writer with each role supporting the other" (Teale, 1986, p. 5).

Identifying Writing Stages

Let's look at some examples of children's development in writing. At first, their writing products appear to be mere squiggles, lines, and circles created through the process of what many adults would call "scribbling." However, thanks to several early-literacy researchers, we now know that these early explorations are in fact quite sophisticated (Bissex, 1980; Chomsky, 1979; Clay, 1984; Harste, Woodward, & Burke, 1984; Henderson & Beers, 1980; Read, 1971; Temple, Nathan, & Burris, 1982).

At this stage of development, children emulate the shapes, circles, lines, dots, or other distinctive features of written language. In English, children often use letterlike shapes, letters, and sometimes numbers to represent a message. They may write from left to right, from top to bottom, or randomly on the page, and their letters may appear to be backwards or upside down. Their writing shows no apparent understanding of the graphophonic system, and therefore the message is not stable or permanent. Since there is no systematic sound-symbol relationship, the child simply has to remember what he wrote.

In the writing samples of Figure 3.2, you'll notice that these children's "scribbles" contain features of the writing system in their cultural environment. Dawn's writing looks very much like cursive English, while Najeeba's writing shows the characteristic symbols and dots of Arabic. Similarly, Ofer's writing shows the recognizable elements of the Hebrew writing system.

Most children, however, will tell you that what they wrote does have meaning and is a written representation of an oral message. For example, when asked what she wrote in Figure 3.3, Julia confidently read her message, "I'm going swimming after school with my mom."

Although Gentry (1982) calls this stage "Precommunicative Spelling," I prefer to call it *featural spelling* since it appears that these children are involved in the exploration of the features of written language. Since the message can be decoded by the child (at least temporarily), it therefore qualifies as spelling. The term *precommunicative spelling* seems inappropriate since these products do, in fact, communicate to the reader, even if the reader is solely the writer. Furthermore, these products reveal much about the child's knowledge of writing; thus they become communications with knowledgeable and sensitive teachers.

As children move closer to conventional spelling, they begin to use what Gentry calls "Semiphonetic Spelling." During this stage they become aware of the alphabetic principle—that letters are used to represent the sounds in oral language. They may not understand that these sounds should be written as distinct units (what we call *written words*). They believe that just as their spoken messages are a string of sounds, their written messages should be a string of letters. At this stage their spellings are very economical: Words are sometimes limited to letter names (R for *are*, U for *you*) and are often abbreviated (MT for *empty*, SM for *swimming*). These features are present in Eric's writing in Figure 3.4.

When children begin to represent, in writing, all the sounds that are present in the spoken words of the message, we can consider them to be "phonetic spell-

Dawn, a 4-year-old from the United States, writes in unconventional script using a series of wavy lines. Each line is written from left-to-right. Dawn creates a page of such lines starting at the top of her page and finishing at the bottom of her page.

Najeeba, a 4-year-old from Saudi Arabia, writes in unconventional script using a series of very intricate curlicue formations with lots of "dots" over the script. When she completes her story she says, "Here, but you can't read it, cause I wrote it in Arabic and in Arabic we use a lot more dots than you do in English!"

Ofer, a 4-year-old from Israel, prints, first right-to-left, then left-to-right, using a series of rectangular and triangular shapes to create his story, which his grandmother says, ". . . looks like Hebrew, but it's not." Her concern because he sometimes writes "backwards" sound like the concerns of many parents and teachers in the U.S., with the difference being that left-to-right is "backwards" in Hebrew, and right-to-left "backwards" in English.

FIGURE 3.2
Early writing attempts of four-year-olds. From J. C. Harste, V. A. Woodward, and C. L. Burke, *Language Stories and Literacy Lessons* (p. 82). Portsmouth, NH: Heinemann Educational Books, Inc., 1984.

FIGURE 3.3
Julia's featural spelling: "I'm going swimming after school with my mom."

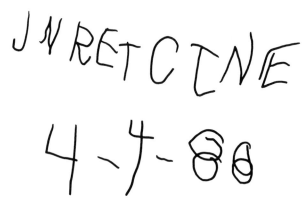

FIGURE 3.4
Eric's semiphonetic spelling: "I went into my classroom and everyone was there."

ers." At this stage the words they spell might not look like English words (that is, they might not be spelled conventionally), but you can decipher their writing by using the letter-sound correspondences. For example, take the invented spelling HLDRN. Think about the sound you hear when you say the name of the letter H and you'll see how this logically spells *children.*

Brian's spellings, shown in Figure 3.5, include all of the essential sound features of the words—he chooses letters on the basis of their sound—and we can read his message with relative ease. It's interesting to note his spelling of *my* (maie), which includes all the sounds of this diphthong (even though he's still working on some of the spellings for these vowel sounds). As adults, we should accept these spellings as correct, just as we would accept their overgeneralizations in oral language: He will mow the lawn. He mowed the lawn. He will go to the store. He goed to the store. Both in their writing and in their oral language, these children are demonstrating a real awareness of the rule-governed nature of their language.

Before children achieve proficiency at conventional spelling, they will use transitional spellings. At this stage children follow most of the basic conventions but might reverse the order of some of the letters (HUOSE for *house,* RAOD for *road*). Vowel generalizations are used according to the child's rule knowledge rather than according to convention (SKAET for *skate,* GROWND for *ground*). These spellings look more like English orthography since more of the features are

FIGURE 3.5
Brian's phonetic spelling:
"I looked for my Easter
basket."

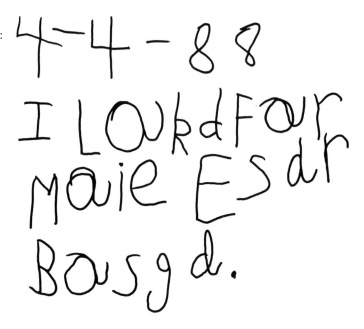

present. In some cases, children show their knowledge of irregularly spelled words (words that don't follow phonics generalizations) by including them in their products (YOUNIGHTED for *united*). Holly's product, shown in Figure 3.6, shows many of these features.

    The stage in which children consistently apply the basic rules of English orthography is called "Correct Spelling," according to Gentry (1982). I prefer to call this *conventional spelling* since Gentry's term implies that the other stages are incorrect. In any case, at this stage the child knows how to spell a large number of words and seems to know when a word doesn't "look right." He can consider alternate spellings which might include silent letters and irregular spelling patterns.

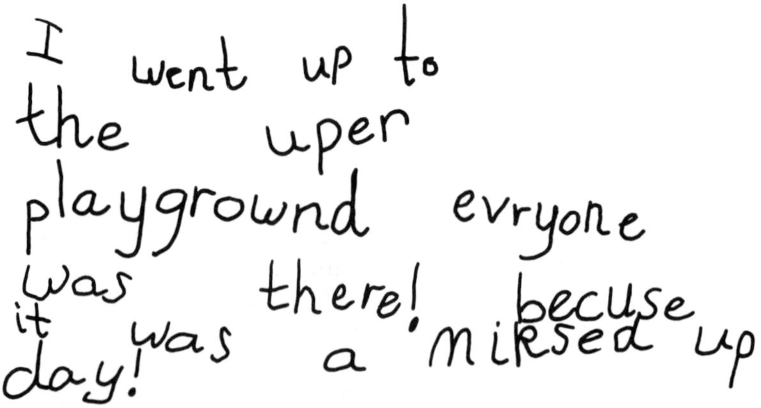

FIGURE 3.6
Holly's transitional spelling: "I went up to the upper playground. Everyone
was there! Because it was
a mixed up day!"

I went up to the uper playgrownd evryone was there! becuse it was a mixed up day!

How Children "Move" through Writing Stages

Now that you've seen examples of children's writing, let's talk about how children move through these stages. This concept is important since children move through the stages at different times and rates—there is no particular time or grade-level designation for each writing stage.

The samples you've just studied were collected by a group of my student teachers who were placed in kindergarten, first-, and second-grade classrooms. For one of our weekly seminars, I'd asked them to bring two samples of writing from children who represented the lowest and highest ability in their classroom. Table 3.1 shows each child's level of development, his grade, and a sample of his writing.

Notice that Brian, the kindergartner, has learned more of the conventions of writing than his classmate, Julia. Although Eric is older than Brian, he is still discovering the graphophonic system. Eric's second-grade classmate, Holly, seems well on her way to using conventional spellings. So it seems that children's writing development doesn't happen at the same time for all children. Their progress seems to be more than a function of age or grade level.

But what are the reasons why Brian is at the stage he is? Was it the support of the home literacy environment? What did his parents do to encourage and promote his explorations of writing?

We've already discussed the idea of scaffolding, but let's review that concept briefly. As parents and children engage in social interactions that are commonplace in the home environment, parents modify their speech patterns to allow children to be successful language users. Parents label signs, read stories, model adult literacy events, and actively engage children in conversations. Eventually, children become aware of the print in their environment, both inside and outside their home. As they see their parents engaging in adult literacy events, they too want to participate in the activities that help them become members of the literacy club. They become increasingly interested in attempting to read and write. They learn that they can read print in the environment and that their oral language can be turned into print. Through their writing attempts they learn certain phonological rules and procedures. In reading their writing they begin to grasp

TABLE 3.1
The writing stages and grade levels of four children

Writing Stage	Name	Grade	Example
Featural speller (Precommunicative)	Julia	Kindergarten	JNRETC
Semiphonetic speller	Eric	Second grade	kasrm
Phonetic speller	Brian	Kindergarten	Esdr Basgd
Transitional speller	Holly	Second grade	playgrownd

the connection between the two processes. Through their success in reading and writing children begin to intuitively learn the rules or conventions of language.

> "As children attempt to read their own writing, they may come face to face with contradictions between what they are attempting to write [the sound combinations of the words they are trying to encode in graphic symbols] and what is actually on the page. The contradictions result in cognitive conflicts [which the child must resolve] that promote learning" (Teale, 1988, p. 6: parenthetical mine).

Putting It All Together: The Development of Story Schema

We've seen that the reading/writing connection can be observed in children's attempts to read their own writing. But it can also be seen in their attempts to read their favorite storybooks. Children are able to compose a text based on their recall of the events and the basic elements of the story. At this stage they tell the story in their own words, demonstrating their awareness that a story that has been read to them can be "reread" using their oral language.

After many interactions with the same book, children begin to realize that there's something stable about the way the story is presented. They begin to memorize actual words used when the book is read to them. Their attempts to reread the story reflect this knowledge. Later, as they begin to collect a store of sight words, and as their phonological awareness develops, their "reading" of the text becomes closer to the actual print.

As a result of exposure to a number of different stories which may be read repeatedly at the request of the child, a "concept of story" is developed (Applebee, 1978). We can think of a concept of story as part of the schematic cueing system for approaching narratives, and we can note this concept in children's attempts to read their favorite storybooks. Children begin to predict that the story will include a main character who will encounter a problem, set a goal (usually to solve the problem), attempt to solve the problem, and ultimately reach a resolution. Since many stories help children learn life lessons about how the world works, we could consider stories to be a vehicle for helping children gain general knowledge and develop cognitive structures and schemata for how they'll ultimately interact with the world.

You can determine a child's developing story schema by listening to him reread his favorite books or, more simply, by listening to him retell stories that have been read to him. As a teacher, you can promote children's story schema by focusing your questions and discussions on the "story grammar" components (the problem, goal, and resolution). In fact, in my own study of how teachers' story presentation techniques affect children's literacy learning, I found that listening comprehension improved over a period of four weeks when teachers focused on story grammar components, especially when drawing on the children's own related experiences (Dunning & Mason, 1984; Peterman, 1988; Peterman, Dunning, & Mason, 1985). As a measure of listening comprehension, we analyzed children's retellings and their answers to questions that probed the story grammar components.

One particular kindergartner stands out as making quite notable improvements in his listening comprehension and concept of story. In fact, his retelling of *The Wobbly Tooth* (Cooney, 1978) was so amazing that I had to verify that he hadn't heard the story before. He started out by telling me "one part" he remembered:

> I'll tell you one part I remember. Her friend came over and asked to play baseball and she said, "Great!" And so they played baseball and it was a hard team to play and her hits weren't good very much. And then when it was her turn and her team was losing a lot—just by one point—.

The child paused, so I asked, "What else do you remember?"

> The ball went real fast and she couldn't hit it. And when the next ball was gonna come, she was ready. And then she hold the bat up and she hit it. And then she tried to run to home plate but the ball was going fast and she tried to make it to home plate and then the ball was already at home plate. And she slid in a pile of dust and she was dusty. And then one of the boys said, "Hey, look!" and she looked at her teammates and they were looking at her and I think one of them said, "Hey, I think her tooth is finally coming out!" And then she, her tongue reached over and all she could feel was a little hole. And that's the end of the story.

Feeling quite content that the child had so accurately described the resolution to the girl's problem (her tooth had finally come out when she forgot about it), and that he had included so much of the dialogue, I hesitated to probe further. But since this was the procedure I used for collecting consistent data, I asked again, "What else do you remember?"

> Before that she tried to—the first part of the story—she felt her tooth that was loose. And she tried to use her dad's electric toothbrush with extra stiff bristles and that didn't work. And then she tried to jump up and down with stiff knees and that didn't work. And then she tried to look at her favorite book about horses and then—and that didn't work. And then she tried to go on her roller skates and then she singed her song and then that didn't work. And that's when the boy came over to see if she wanted to play baseball. I told you about the baseball. And after that is the end of the story.

Pretty amazing, wouldn't you say? But wait, there's more. The child had previously described the resolution, and after further probing, he described the events leading up to the resolution. What was left to tell? The setting, right? So I asked again, "What else do you remember?"

> Well, at the *very* beginning she woke up and put her tongue under her loose tooth and I don't remember anything else.

Children need to realize that relying on their story schema can be a useful strategy for attempting to read stories. In fact, they should be made aware of the four cueing systems available for constructing a text. By using their knowledge of the syntactic and semantic rules of their oral language, their graphophonic knowledge, their background knowledge about the events of the story (their event schemata), and their story schema, children can construct a text that is very close to the actual print. We could say that the process of learning to read is one of constructing meaning based on the child's ability to use all of the available cueing systems. Tierney and Pearson (1984) compare this process with the process used to construct text during writing, once again emphasizing the symbiotic relationship between reading and writing.

Children's Early Reading Development

Not unlike children's early writing behavior, their early reading behavior follows a natural development. In her research with preschool children, Jana Mason (1984) found that in the beginning stages, children formulate certain hypotheses about written language, beginning with knowledge about the function of print. They recognize the intent of print—to provide a message. With words in their environment, children begin to associate print with the names of the objects. For example, the child might read "Kroger milk" as "milk" or "a milk box." What the print says is less important than what the print means according to the child's previous experience with the print-carrying object. If family members call the carton of milk in the refrigerator "a milk box," then children are likely to "read" "Kroger milk" as "a milk box" (Harste, Woodward, & Burke, 1984).

In storybooks, children realize that the story is contained within the pages of the book and that they can tell the story. They might use different words to tell the story each time they "read" the book. But the meaning (or the storyline) is dependent on the events portrayed when it was shared. If the parent highlighted a particular story event through discussion, especially if it was shared by the parent and child in "real life," then the child is likely to "read" the story from this point of view.

At the next level, children become knowledgeable about the form and structure of print. They are aware that letters have distinct forms and that these forms can be related to speech sounds. When attempting to read stories, children at this level struggle to reconcile the fact that they know the story and can retell it in their own words with the fact that specific words are represented with specific letters.

Finally, children acquire knowledge about the conventions of print—the terminology used to talk about reading, such as "sentence," "word," and "top of the page," for example. At this point, children are almost constrained by the fact that they "know what they don't know" about written language. They become less willing to explore written language because they realize it's the print that dictates the sequence of events and the outcomes of the story. They sometimes refuse to write, saying that they don't know the letters.

"Michael knows that there is a *real* way to spell words—that "kids' guess and go" spelling is not the *real* way. He wants his mother to "just write the *real* answer—not the kids' spelling it out." The times that Michael shows a clear *lack* of constraint about what he doesn't know is when he is role-playing or writing for his own purposes" (Barnes, 1988, p. 13).

We can see these developing "knowledge strands" in children's attempts to read labeled pictures and photocopied pages taken from a storybook that has been read to them. Modeling after the research of Emilia Ferreiro and Ana Teberosky (1982), Jana Mason and I (Peterman & Mason, 1984) designed these tasks with the intent of probing the child's *process* for approaching print while also looking at their actual responses, or *products*. Eight labeled pictures from children's books were presented on cards to children using the following procedure:

1. Show me where there's something to read.
2. What do you think it says?
3. Where does it say _____ ? (The child's exact words from step 2 were repeated in the blank.)
4. How do you know? or How can you tell?

Four of these cards included predictable text in which the child could hypothetically "read" the picture. For example, the picture shows a train, and the text or label is *train*. The remaining four cards included nonpredictable text. For example, the picture shows a car, and the text or label is *wheel*. For these, the child would have to rely on information other than the picture in order to successfully read the words.

Figure 3.7 shows a child's responses in March of his kindergarten year (the top line) and in September of his first-grade year (the bottom line). Notice that in March the child appears to be predicting what the print says solely by "reading" the picture: "truck" for *wheel* and "house" for *door*. In September the child begins to incorporate his knowledge of the graphophonic system while retaining the quest for meaning. This is especially noticeable in his response, "wheel. It might say *we will* go in a car." Although the child appears unable to read the entire word, he constructs an appropriate text based on his knowledge that he must consider the initial consonant and still come up with a meaningful response. Notice his response to the word *door*, indicating the same considerations: "Is that a *b* or *d*? Du, ah, ah, like dopen, cause it might be opening the door."

When we asked children to read photocopied pages taken from a storybook that had previously been read to them, they had the option of using their memory of the story as well as their syntactic and semantic knowledge. In Figure 3.8, notice the child's use of (1) picture cues, (2) memory of the story, and (3) beginning consonants.

Procedure: Show the child each labeled picture. Say, "Can you read this for me? What do you think it says?" If they say they can't read, say, "It's all right to pretend to read. What do you think it says?"

 bear	 wheel	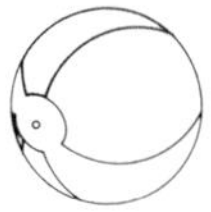 ball	 rag dolls
"bear" (March) ↓ "bear" (September)	"truck" ↓ "wheel. It may say we will go in a car."	"ball" ↓ "ball"	"doll" ↓ "dolls"

 train	 door	 boat	 wood blocks
"train" ↓ "toot"	"house" "Is that a b or d? Du au - au, like dopen, cause it might be opening the door."	"boat" ↓ "boat"	"blocks" ↓ woo-t

FIGURE 3.7
Word reading responses in March and September

Procedure: "Now, I want to see if you can read these pages from the story that your teacher just read to you. What do you think it says here?" Ask this same question for all of the photocopied pages.

the baby will cry

Bubble: "waa"
(How do you know?)
"Because I see her mouth open and tears are right here falling down."
Phrase: "The baby's crying."

the dogs will bark

Bubble: "ruff, ruff"
(How do you know?)
"Cause they're growling."
Phrase: "The dogs are barking and it says *bark* right there" (points to phrase).

the owl will shiver

Bubble: "owl"
Phrase: "The owl is shivering."

the magpie will call

Bubble: "bell"
(How do you know?)
"Because it starts with a *b* and he heard the bell ring."
Phrase: "Mockingbird...I don't know the rest of it."

FIGURE 3.8
Story-reading responses

Notice the child's explanations of how he knows the speech bubble said "waa" or "ruff ruff": "because I see her mouth open and tears are right here falling down" and "'cause they're growling." This shows the importance of the picture in his responses. Yet he's also using his memory of the story and beginning consonants when he says he knows the speech bubble says "bell, because it starts with a *b* and he heard the bell ring." (The bell ringing is an important event in this story.) Also notice his use of beginning consonant and picture in his response, "mockingbird . . . I don't know the rest of it."

In this section you've seen examples of children's developing knowledge in the use of the four cueing systems through their attempts to read and write. Next we'll talk about the importance of observing and noting children's behaviors during these attempts.

LEARNING WHAT CHILDREN ALREADY KNOW ABOUT LANGUAGE

Teachers as Observers/Researchers

In a compilation of two final reports to the National Institute of Education, Harste, Woodward, and Burke (1984) offer *Language Stories and Literacy Lessons* which represent their latest insights on the overlapping roles of teachers and researchers alike. They submit that we can learn much about the process of literacy learning by using the child as informant. For example, we can observe children's behavior while they're engaging in literacy events. At the same time, we can discuss the process with them, making literacy learning a social experience. Through these observations and interactions, we can learn much about what children already know about language and literacy. Once we understand the process of literacy learning, we can begin to provide appropriate experiences that will allow children to explore and test their hypotheses about language.

> "What educators need to know, we think, is how written language users come to experience and value the strategies involved in successful written language use and learning and how such knowledge can lead to further exploration and expansion of the human potential. . . . By comparing, contrasting, and evaluating the strategies involved in children's literacy learning prior to their going to school, we can evaluate the adequacy of current instruction procedures, as well as adduce directions for the future" (Harste, Woodward, & Burke, 1984, p. xvii).

So, as teachers, we must use our observations in deciding how to set up our classroom environment. These observations can also be important evaluations of the effectiveness of our literacy programs based on the children's progress. But can we measure progress simply by looking at scores on a readiness test or by the "mistakes" on a worksheet? Let's take a look at this question.

Evaluation: Products or Process?

For many years reading readiness tests were provided to determine whether children were ready to learn to read. To test listening comprehension, the teacher read a sentence and asked the children to circle a picture that matched the sentence. To test visual discrimination, the teacher asked the children to circle the shape, number, or letter that matched the one at the beginning of the row. To determine auditory discrimination, the teacher asked the children to draw circles around pictures that begin with the same sound as (or rhyme with) pictures at the beginning of the row. If a child scored below a certain point, he was diagnosed as being unready to learn to read.

Often, teachers failed to use these tests diagnostically. That is, rather than studying test results to determine children's strengths and weaknesses in a particular area, they (too often) used the tests to label children as either "ready" or "unready," similar to assigning a letter grade of A or F on students' permanent records. If children were identified as "unready to learn to read," they would receive instruction at the lowest level, beginning with letter names and their corresponding sounds, regardless of what they actually knew about the process of literacy.

In fact, when I was teaching first grade in 1980, I had a conversation with one of the kindergarten teachers about the children in her classroom who would be in mine the following year. She wanted me to know which children would be in my low, average, and high reading groups. Her source of information: Metropolitan Readiness Test scores, a test similar to the one I described above.

I'll never forget Aaron, who was placed in my low reading group. Granted, he didn't have a clue about the sound the letter *B* makes. He didn't even know what it meant to "draw a line around" his answer on the test. But after the first few days of school, I noticed that he could read just about anything I put in front of him. I started thinking about his Metropolitan test scores and decided I should give him the test again since, obviously, his test scores had to be inaccurate. He must have just been tired, or maybe he missed the directions on a certain portion. I never thought the test might be invalid.

After administering the test again and coming up with basically the same results, I decided to take a closer look at the test and, more importantly, to take a closer look at what Aaron knew about the process of reading. Aaron wasn't able to tell me the sounds that individual letters record even though he could read nonsense words (such as *gat, darch, lipe,* and so on). He had trouble answering questions about stories that I read to him, yet he could read and retell stories that he was interested in.

I came to the conclusion that the readiness test was a measure of knowledge in specific subskills associated with reading, but it wasn't a measure of the process of reading. The isolated subskills didn't make sense to Aaron. He wasn't able to use his knowledge of all four cueing systems to produce a correct response on the test.

You see, when Aaron reads, he uses graphophonic cues to *verify* the text he has constructed based on predictions he makes about what he'll be reading. It's his success in reading that makes the graphophonic cues make sense, not the other way around. His oral language proficiency allows him to use the syntactic and semantic cueing systems as well. All of these strategies fit together to help Aaron construct something meaningful in his reading. As Anne Dyson says, "The written language puzzle is a complex one. And, as with most puzzles, children cannot solve it by being given only one piece at a time" (1984, p. 174). Thus, the readiness test was not designed to test the process of reading—instead it merely isolated products that made no sense to Aaron. You'll hear more about the processes versus the products of reading from Frank May in the next chapter. For now, though, we have to consider how we can evaluate children's *process* of reading with the idea of using this information to design our literacy program.

There are some published tests I can recommend. Researchers designed these tests to gain information about children's development in literacy and to compare children on certain conventions of literacy learning. In all of their studies, the researchers found that "children learn these conventions through interacting with print, not by teaching them in isolation or by *waiting* until the child is mature enough to learn them" (Teale, 1988, p. 54). These tests include the *Sand* and *Stones* (Clay, 1972, 1979c), *The Linguistic Awareness in Reading Readiness Test* (Downing, Ayers, & Schaefer, 1986), and *The Written Language Awareness Test* (Taylor & Blum, 1981). Jana Mason is currently working on *The Early Reading Test*, which will soon be published by Testronics, so be looking for that one in the near future. In the meantime, let me describe some other, less formal ways for you to collect information about what your children already know about literacy.

Activities That Evaluate Process

When reading stories to children, you can ask them to predict what the main character in the story will do to solve his problem and then ask the children what they have done or would do in a similar situation. Or you can simply ask them story grammar questions to evaluate their concept of story. You can also have them retell the story, dramatize the story, reread or attempt to read the story, or write what they remember or enjoyed from the story. Their products will, of course, be revealing of what they know, and you can begin to identify the various stages represented among the children in your classroom. But equally important are your observations of the processes of literacy learning. During the story reading does the child participate in the discussions? Does he make predictions based on the available evidence? What cueing systems does he use when attempting to write about and read the story? Keeping ongoing records of answers to these questions will help you map children's progress as they move toward conventional literacy.

To tap children's knowledge of the phonological system, you can ask them to read print in their environment. You can do this on field trips, on the playground, during neighborhood walks, and in the classroom. You can create flashcards that include pictures containing print from their environment. On the reverse side of the cards, include the print alone to see if they can apply graphophonic cues.

Ask children to spell words using magnetic letters. Many will have these at home on their refrigerator, so they'll be used to working with them. See if they can spell highly interesting words (*mom, play, rain,* and so on); then try equivalent nonsense words (*jom, dray, tain,* and so on). While they're manipulating the letters, ask them to tell you the names of the letters. You can assess their knowledge of the conventions of written language by noting whether they work from left to right and top to bottom. You can check their visual discrimination of letters like *b, d, p,* and *q.* You can probe their metalinguistic awareness by having them tell you how they knew the spellings of these words (and remember to ask this even if they use invented spellings). Ask them to point to a word, then a letter, to see if they know these important instructional terms.

Next, you might want to see if they can *read* these words, by either using the magnetic letters or presenting word cards. Note the differences between their responses and the actual print. Again, ask them *how they know* what the word says. You can create your own labeled pictures that contain predictable and nonpredictable print. See whether they reconcile the difference between the picture and the print. Have them read predictable books such as *Brown Bear, Brown Bear,* by Bill Martin (1983), or *The Very Hungry Caterpillar,* by Eric Carle (1969), to see which cueing systems they use.

You shouldn't overlook having children write something for you. They can write anything they remember from a story that was read to them. They can write grocery lists when playing in the housekeeping center. They can write nonsense words for you to see if they can make up their own words that "sound and look funny." Watch them closely while they're writing. When they pause, ask them what they've written for you. See if they can tell you how they knew what to write. Finally, analyze their product to determine their writing level.

Monitoring and recording this type of information can be time-consuming if your classroom is not set up for language exploration. But you'll need to remember that these observations will be ongoing throughout the year. If your classroom is one in which children can naturally explore language, then these observations can occur over the course of the day. Most importantly, these tasks should come out of the need for children to interact with written language. In other words, they should write what they remember from the story they've listened to because they know it will help them remember the story. Or maybe they want to write their own version of the story to share with a parent or classmate. Perhaps they need to sign an attendance sheet that lets the classroom helper know how many white milks and chocolate milks the class needs for their midmorning snack. In any case, they should see any literacy activity as something useful, something that will help them "get things done" (Teale, 1986, p. 9).

> "Literacy develops out of real life settings in which reading and writing are used to 'get things done.' Therefore, the functions of literacy are as much a part of learning to read and write as are the formal aspects of written language" (Teale, 1986, p. 9).

Gathering Information from Home: Family Literacy

You can make literacy events more meaningful to children at school by understanding the functions of literacy in their own home environment. So, at the beginning of the school year, you may want to gather information about the child's home literacy environment. Such information will help you establish classroom activities, events, and interactions that will be familiar to the child. Let me give you an example from one of my students.

In Gene's family, important messages were left on the floor by the front door. When Gene came home, he knew where to look for messages, and if one was there, it was likely to be very important. This was a family-specific literacy activity that had a very definite and important function. But it's also one that could be easily modified and implemented in the classroom.

But short of visiting your children's home environments, how can you gather this kind of information—especially when you'll probably have at least 25 children in your classroom?

One way is to send home an informal questionnaire for parents to fill out and send back to school with their child. Or you could have parents fill out these forms on the first day of school when they bring their child to your classroom. This is probably a better idea, since it will allow you to explain why you'd like to have this kind of information. Questions you might include are listed in Table 3.2.

Sometimes parents are reluctant to talk about their home environment, and we need to respect their wishes. However, it's still possible to gain information through an informal interview with the child, using the questions on the questionnaire. Or you can gather information about how the child thinks he is learning to read and write. Here's an example from one of my graduate students:

Q: How are you learning to read and write at school?
A: At school I do—well, *all* the kids do "guess and go" at the table with Mrs. Mogul and sometimes a parent helper. Or there is a playdough table. And cross-age tutors—two always. And we read our little books, you know, the nursery rhymes I read to Maegan.
Q: Good. What do you do at home?
A: I write on paper a lot, and read to Maegan.
Q: Is it important to know how to read?
A: Well—so you can read "Danger" signs—you know, like "slippery" and things.
Q: Is it important to know how to write?
A: Yeah, then I can write my book, like Steven Kellogg's. (Barnes, 1988, p. 7)

TABLE 3.2
Parent questionnaire items

Directions: For each item, circle the choice that best describes the events in your home.

Child's name: _____

Birthdate: _____

Today's date: _____

5 =	More than once a day
4 =	Once a day
3 =	Two or three times a week
2 =	Once a week
1 =	Occasionally
0 =	Never

 1. How often do you read to your child? 5 4 3 2 1 0
 2. How often does your child try to read? 5 4 3 2 1 0
 3. How often does your child check out
    books from the library? 5 4 3 2 1 0
 4. How often do you discuss stories you
    read aloud to your child? 5 4 3 2 1 0
 5. How often does your child listen to
    stories on tapes and/or records? 5 4 3 2 1 0
 6. How often does storytelling without
    a book occur in your family? .5 4 3 2 1 0
 7. How often do family members help
    your child print? 5 4 3 2 1 0
 8. How often does your child try to
    print letters, words, or stories? 5 4 3 2 1 0
 9. How often does your child watch
    Sesame Street? 5 4 3 2 1 0
10. How often does your child talk to
    you about TV programs? 5 4 3 2 1 0
11. In what ways does your family use/enjoy reading?

12. In what ways does your family use/enjoy writing?

13. Describe one family routine in which reading and/or writing are used.

Source: Adapted from Mason & Dunning, 1986.

But even some children are reluctant to talk about their home environment, or maybe they aren't able to verbalize family events or routines. In this case, you might try a modeling activity. Collect several stuffed dolls or animals for the child to select as their "friend" or "pretend brother or sister." Then have them show you how their "friend" is learning to read. This role playing is often quite natural for children who "play school" with siblings and neighborhood friends.

Now that you have some specific activities to try, let me give you some general guidelines for evaluating what children know about literacy and for mapping their progress. These suggestions are adapted from those used by actual practicing teachers (Fields & Lee, 1987).

General Guidelines for Evaluating Literacy Learning

First of all, as I've already indicated, evaluation should be ongoing. At least once a month, collect samples of children's writing, listen to their reading, and record evidence of their developing oral language. Keep this information in a folder, refer to it frequently, and show it to the child and his parents so that they too can see his progress.

Second, ask the child to talk about his own progress. He can tell you whether he put forth a good effort on a particular activity, or whether he thought the activity was too difficult. Sometimes what we'll learn is that children weren't interested in the activity and completed it simply to please you. If children are interested and excited about literacy, they'll naturally want to share it with you.

> "*Evaluation is the basis of planning future learning.* Feedback from evaluation should be used by both teacher and learner as they mutually determine the next steps in the learning process" (Fields & Lee, 1987, p. 187).

The next two guidelines go hand in hand. Let me quote from Fields and Lee: (1) "Evaluation must be related to long-term goals" and (2) "Progress is shown by accomplishments in the real world" (1987, p. 187). In other words, children learn best by exploring literacy from their own perspective—through their own attempts to read and write print that is interesting and functional to them. As a result, we need to remember that evaluating the conventions of reading and writing is secondary to evaluating their progress toward these conventions. Our goal as teachers is for children to experience the love of reading and writing and to see how their literacy experiences are related to the "real world." "Too often school learning does not relate to life-long skills, but only to contrived school situations" (Fields & Lee, 1987, p. 187).

Perhaps the most important point to be made about evaluation is that it should be the basis for making decisions about your literacy program. So, in order to design and implement an appropriate curriculum, you must ask yourself the following questions: "What do the children already know about language?" and "How can I encourage them to draw on what they already know in order to promote further learning?" In answering the first question, teachers will be able to provide scaffolds similar to those provided by the child's parents. In the next section we'll address the second question.

BASING YOUR LITERACY PROGRAM ON WHAT CHILDREN ALREADY KNOW

From Home to School: Fostering Story Understanding

Because of their experience with stories read to them at home, many children have expectations about story reading in school. Many teachers realize this and have made the story-reading event a central component in their literacy programs. Let's see how teachers can capitalize on children's experience with stories.

Many of the story-reading techniques found in the literature deal with the interactions between parents and their children and with the active participation of the child with the adult and the text (Harkness & Miller, 1982; Pelligrini, Brody, & Sigel, 1985; and others). Teachers can also promote this type of verbal give-and-take during school story-reading experiences by asking children to predict what will happen in the story, by linking the child's experiences with those of the main character, and by discussing the central events in the story. In fact, these techniques are suggested in reading methodology textbooks, with the exception that the children will be doing the reading (Durkin, 1989; Mason & Au, 1986; Pearson, 1982).

Story-reading techniques implemented in classrooms should not only maintain children's interest but should also include as many children in the discussion as possible. These discussions should provide "more elaborate ways for children to react to the text" (Mason, 1985b, p. 16). The following recommendations have been suggested in the literature and fall easily into three categories:

1. Prereading techniques
2. Guided reading techniques
3. Postreading techniques

Prereading techniques. Based on findings from a study of home and school story reading, Christine McCormick and Jana Mason (1986) suggest that parents and teachers show children the cover of the book to be read and say, "Here's a book we will read. Look at the title on the front cover. It says _____. What do you think this book will be about?" The adult might show children the illustrations and ask them what they think will happen.

Adults should foster ties between text events and children's experiences (DeLoache & DeMendoza, 1986; Snow & Ninio, 1986). Ask questions about or focus discussion on appropriate background experiences related to the story; ask questions and elicit statements from the children about what they would do in a

"An important aspect of learning to read involves an expectation on the part of children that the texts they encounter will make sense and have some kind of predictable structure. Making sense of a text is no less important for children learning to read than are the word, letter, and letter-sound recognition skills which are usually taught. This view of the beginning stages of reading acquisition as a blend of word recognition and comprehension skills has implications for the way teachers present texts to children before they are able to read the texts themselves. One implication is that teachers should help young children experience the process of text comprehension as part of the learning-to-read process. Since independent reading skills are not yet developed, the process might be experienced through story listening" (Mason, Peterman, & Kerr, 1988, p. 2).

particular situation (one the main character in the story will encounter); tell the students that the main character in the story will have to face a similar problem; and ask them to predict what the main character will do (Pearson, Hansen, & Gordon, 1979). Taking this directed reading approach one step further, the adult should ask children to listen for a purpose—for example, to find out how the main character attempts to solve the problem, to see if their predictions about what the main character will do are correct, and so on.

Guided reading techniques. McCormick and Mason (1986) suggest that the story reader be dramatic or enthusiastic, emphasizing important words and pausing to allow children to talk about the pictures or the story. They recommend holding the book so that the pictures and words are clearly visible to the children. Occasionally, you might follow the important words with your finger when you want to highlight certain conventions of reading (such as top-to-bottom or left-to-right directionality). They also suggest that you point out how the pictures sometimes help you understand the story. Highlight the important parts of the book by asking prediction questions related to the "story grammar components," such as the setting, the problem, the goal or attempt to resolve the problem, and the resolution (Beck et al., 1979).

Postreading techniques. In her reading methodology textbook, Dolores Durkin (1983) urges teachers to follow through on purpose-setting questions by restating them and discussing possible answers. This technique is important because it establishes a useful routine that children can begin to predict. In your discussion, refer to the prereading discussion, tying in the children's comments about events in their lives that were included in the story. Discuss the main character's solution to the problem, and then compare it to the children's predictions. Ask them what they would do (or have done) in the same situation (Pearson, Hansen, & Gordon, 1979).

As a way of promoting active participation with the story, you can encourage children to retell, dramatize, or write about the story (Galda, 1982; Morrow, 1984). You might need to coach them on how to retell the story while showing the pictures. Leslie Morrow (1984) suggests that you have them start with "Once upon a time" or "Once there was," followed by an introduction of the characters and a description of the setting. Next, ask them to describe the main character's problem and how he or she tried to solve the problem.

Finally, you should encourage children to reread books on their own that you've read aloud to them. Because these books have been shared in a positive social setting, they have special significance to the children. The children have incentive to read these in order to "show off" their accomplishments in learning to read. Table 3.3 shows a sample plan for reading a story using some of these recommended techniques.

Story-reading episodes can significantly contribute to children's early literacy development at home and at school. As teachers you can prepare discussions and questions that will help children attend to the most important parts of the story (Peterman, 1988). If, over repeated readings, you relate these parts of the story to the accompanying pictures, you'll help them realize the stability of the print with the storyline. By presenting stories in this way, you'll be giving children the important message that reading is more than merely sounding out the

TABLE 3.3
Story synopsis and possible discussion/questioning techniques: *The Wobbly Tooth,* by Nancy Evans Cooney

Story Synopsis

The story takes place at Elizabeth Ann's home and, later on, at a baseball field. A problem occurs when she wakes up with a wobbly tooth, a stubborn tooth that won't come out and bothers Elizabeth Ann. She decides to get rid of it. After many unsuccessful attempts to get rid of it, she decides to just forget about it, since maybe her mother is right in that it just isn't ready to come out yet. But even trying to forget about it is difficult. So when her friend invites her to join in a baseball game, Elizabeth Ann is delighted. During this close game, Elizabeth Ann has a hard time doing anything right. When Elizabeth Ann is up to bat, her team is one run behind. Surely she can get that run! Unfortunately, the ball wins the race and Elizabeth Ann is out. But that is not all that is out: Elizabeth Ann had lost her tooth. Her problem is solved when she forgot all about the tooth and let it come out when it was ready.

Prereading Techniques

1. Show the cover of the book, read the title, and ask children to notice that Elizabeth Ann's tooth is missing. Say, "If the story is called *The Wobbly Tooth,* what do you think the problem is?"
2. Stimulate a discussion about when children have had wobbly teeth of their own and ways that they have lost them. Ask if they had a problem with their teeth when they were coming out.
3. Link children's experiences with those in the book by telling children to listen to the story to see what the problem is and if Elizabeth Ann solves it the same way they would.

Techniques to Implement during the Story Reading

1. After reading about Elizabeth Ann's unsuccessful attempts to force the tooth to come out and her decision to just forget about the tooth, ask children to predict what she'll do next and what will happen.
2. After reading about Elizabeth Ann's attempted home run, ask children to predict what has happened to cause the children to stare at her.

Postreading Techniques

1. Ask children what Elizabeth Ann's problem was and how she solved it. Compare her actions with what they have/would have done in their own lives.
2. Discuss children's predictions about questions asked during the story reading.
3. Have children retell the story in their own words.

printed letters on the page (the graphophonic system). They'll realize that they can rely on their understanding of the important aspects of the story to help them read the print (schematic system). Hearing written language presented orally helps them focus on the syntactic and semantic systems as well.

Making Decisions about Your Literacy Program

Just as very young children notice print in their home and community environment, children in the early primary grades are aware of the literacy environment of their classroom. I've come to the conclusion that most children are especially aware of print that's of interest to them. They're constantly asking, "What does that say?" or "What does that mean?" Even when children are in a new and potentially strange environment, they seek out print that is familiar to them.

I've observed this awareness many times when my college students bring their children with them to my office for a scheduled meeting. Most of the books in my office are college textbooks or instructional materials. But on one of the bottom shelves are children's books. While I'm advising the parent, it takes the child about five minutes to find these books and another minute or two to select one of interest. The children know which books are written for them because they've seen them in other environments.

Because children are so aware of print in their environment, it's important to provide an appropriate, "literacy-rich environment" (Mason, 1986, p. 58). But what else should we consider when planning literacy programs?

In a chapter on kindergarten reading programs, Jana Mason discusses the need for a "literacy-rich classroom, a multifaceted program, and active processing" by the child (1986, p. 58). She makes these recommendations based on her observations of actual kindergarten classrooms. But what does a "literacy-rich classroom" look like? What are the components of a "multifaceted program"? And how do you encourage "active processing" by the child? Let's look at these questions one at a time.

What Does a Literacy-Rich Classroom Look Like?

A literacy-rich environment is one in which children understand and experience the purposes for learning to read and write. In this environment children have access to paper and writing utensils, and they participate in functional print activities. Children can be responsible for taking attendance by signing their names when they walk in the door. They can rotate their names on a chart showing the helpers of the day (the line leader, the door holder, the paper passer, and so on). Hall passes can be used for monitoring the use of the restrooms.

> "Learning about reading and writing ought to occur in situations where written language serves functions such as to entertain (as in books), to inform (as in instructions on packages), or to direct (as on traffic signs)" (Anderson et al., 1985, p. 32).

One of my favorite, and most successful, ideas was to make mailboxes for each child constructed out of cardboard milk cartons. These cartons were stapled together to look like post-office boxes with each child's name on the flap. Throughout the day, the children were allowed to write messages to anyone in the classroom. Of course, at the beginning of the year, many of the children were at the featural or semiphonetic writing stage and needed some encouragement to write to each other. I usually got them started by writing a short message to each of them, using their names and a few sight words they'd learned—for example, "Hi, Jennifer. I like your mom." I told them they could "pretend write" or write any way they knew how. (Some teachers tell children to "guess and go.")

During the first week or so, I often wondered why I'd started this routine. There were so many who said, "Teacher, I can't read this. What does it say?" But I simply told them they'd have to go ask the person who wrote the letter to read it for them. When the writer realized that he wasn't communicating with his audience, he searched for a way to make his writing more readable. The children realized there was a way to communicate with others using a system that everyone could read (what we call the *graphophonic* system). This activity brought the children's attention to the graphophonic system in a much more relevant way than through the readiness workbooks my school district had ordered. Of course, those same workbooks were great review for letters that they were exploring on their own.

I also had children collect their own set of personal word cards, which they kept in a three-by-five file box. These cards included high-interest words that the children learned to identify on sight. They could use these words to help them write notes or stories. As their store of sight words increased, I had them begin to alphabetize the word cards and make sentences with them. This activity allowed them to experiment with words and sentences without having to worry about the mechanics of writing using a pencil.

Other materials you'll find in a literacy-rich environment include newspapers, children's magazines, comic strips, word games and other literacy-related games, and books of all sorts—books from the library, books the children bring from home to share, books related to a unit of study, and books made by the teacher, the children, and authors who have visited the area.

Environmental print in a literacy-rich classroom includes posters on topical subjects, displays of numbers and their meaning, color charts, the alphabet, a list of classroom rules, the children's art work, stories the children have dictated to the teacher, and plenty of labels. These labels might include objects you want the children to notice and might change throughout the year (exit, drinking fountain, desk, clock, door, and so on). Although it may not be as aesthetically pleasing to teachers (or perhaps to other adults), the children can create their own bulletin boards around a topic of interest. Just turn them loose in the art center and let them go to work. My students once created a great collage of words they noticed on one of our weekly neighborhood walks. Of course, the bulletin board was at *their* eye level, not mine. And remember, those lists, posters, and labels should also be displayed so that the children can appreciate them, even if they look odd to our eyes.

The physical layout of the classroom is also important in a literacy-rich environment. Learning centers are prominent in classrooms where children are actively exploring language. Centers for art, writing, and role playing are among the favorites of teachers and children alike. These centers can revolve around a social studies or science theme and can be rotated with those from the other teachers at your grade level. Listening stations, which include tape recordings of favorite storybooks, are especially important. In addition to listening to these stories, children can record their own retelling of these books or practice their oral reading into the tape recorder. Drama centers with puppets and other props allow children to explore oral language creatively. And, of course, a quiet and comfortable place for children to read silently is essential.

> "The classroom environment should support literacy and serve as a bridge between home experiences and the more demanding work of first grade" (Mason, 1986, p. 59).

What Are the Components of a Multifaceted Approach?

Remember the readiness programs I mentioned earlier—the ones with the visual discrimination of pictures, letters, or geometric shapes? How effective are these programs for children who are beginning to explore the relationship between oral and written language or, better yet, for those who are already reading?

My experience with Aaron and his readiness test helped convince me that there was something missing from a program that taught reading as if it were an accumulation of a series of subskills. You see, the creation of readiness tests in the 1930s resulted in the opinion that if children weren't ready for formal instruction in reading, they needed to work on the skills presented in the readiness test itself. Perhaps this was the beginning of the "teaching to the test" controversy.

But, ironically, children who are least familiar with the conventions of reading and writing (and who would undoubtedly do poorly on a traditional readiness test) *and* those who are already reading (like Aaron) need to explore language as a process of using all of the available cueing systems. This approach allows them to use all the pieces of the language puzzle in order to construct a complete picture. To focus strictly on the names and sounds of the letters of the alphabet, for example, would be to impose what is called an *instructional constraint* on children. (You'll hear more about this in Chapter 4.) It would be like asking children to wear blinders and focus on only one of the four cueing systems, the graphophonic, which is probably the least efficient. It gives children the message that they can't read or write yet because they haven't been taught all the sounds of the letters. It trains then, unfortunately, to ignore their already existing proficiencies in the other cueing systems. Without the integration of the four cueing systems, children are left with an inaccurate, incomplete picture of what it means to be a reader.

> "What the child who is least ready for systematic reading instruction needs most is ample experience with oral and printed language, and early opportunities to begin to write" (Anderson et al., 1985, p. 29).

So, how can you present literacy lessons in a way that helps children use their oral language (syntactic and semantic cueing systems), their background knowledge of events and texts (schemata, event schemata, and story schema), and their awareness of phonology (graphophonic cueing system)?

Many of the activities that were suggested for gathering information about children's approaches to literacy also work well for extending their knowledge. You might want to reread the section "Activities That Evaluate Process" (p. 88–90) and consider how you would use these activities as part of your curriculum while also gathering information about children's ongoing progress.

Reading good literature to children, discussing their related background experiences, letting them predict story events, and having them retell or dramatize the story helps children realize that reading (and learning to read) is a constructive search for personal meaning. Children love to tell their own stories, which they can dictate to you while you write them down. Later, they can reread these stories. They can also write their own stories using invented spellings. Frankly, any activity that involves children in reading, writing, speaking, and listening processes will help them see the interrelatedness of these processes for learning about literacy. In Chapter 8, you'll learn more about how children's writing and the language experience approach can be used with children of all ages.

Finally, exposing children to poetry, alphabet books, wordless picture books, and informational texts will help them see that language comes in different forms.

How Do You Encourage Active Processing by the Child?

> "Since learning to read is largely intuitive, as most learning is at this age, explanations, directions, and direct teaching may do more to confuse than to help. After children have established successful reading processes, they can discuss ways to gain greater depth and evaluative ability" (Fields & Lee, 1987, p. 172).

Perhaps the most important guideline for encouraging active processing is to provide children with materials and activities that are interesting and challenging to them. They'll naturally want to explore language when they're given the freedom to select their own writing topics, choose the books they wish to read, and express their thoughts in any appropriate mode. When they view the learning-to-read process as an outgrowth of their own questions and hypotheses, they will be apt to consciously attempt to solve the written language puzzle.

SUMMARY OF MAIN IDEAS: MESSAGES FOR TEACHERS FROM TEACHERS

As a way of reviewing some of the main ideas from the chapter, I'd like to share some concerns, attitudes, insights, and suggestions of practicing teachers. These teachers were students in my courses over the past year or so. I'd like to thank them for their contributions.

☐ "Children already know a lot about reading and writing before they come to school. This is because they have a desire and/or a need to do so. This motivation results in attempts to read and write which are initiated by the child."

☐ "Parents model reading and writing functions in the home environment. Children will work hard at joining this literacy club, which includes social and functional activities."

☐ "Parents help children learn about language by modifying their speech, engaging in literacy routines with their child, and especially by reading to them."

☐ "Reading to children helps develop their listening comprehension, thus their later reading comprehension. This happens because it allows children to see that reading includes predictions about story events, which stems from a discussion of the story. Children see that the language of books is similar to oral language. They also learn how to apply their own background knowledge to the story, they learn the conventions of reading, including phonological underpinnings, but mostly they learn the love of reading."

☐ "The children themselves should dictate what the primary grade curriculum should look like. It should be based on what the children already know about literacy and what they need and want to learn."

☐ "We can learn what children know about language by providing experiences for their interaction with language. We can evaluate the product but also explore their process of learning."

☐ "The teacher's role is to mold the environment so that children can explore their existing knowledge about language. Direct instruction in concepts that they don't understand will probably not be effective. Children learn best in a nonthreatening, supportive environment where the children are free to make mistakes, try new ideas."

☐ "Just as you encourage oral language development and praise their efforts in that area, do so with their written language development. Reconsider what 'mistakes' are."

☐ "We would do well to try to create more natural settings in our day care centers, preschools, and kindergartens—settings where children and adults are interacting in more natural, familylike ways instead of the old classroom model of teacher instructing students. Reading and writing need not be taught as a series of skills but can be thought of as a child's natural interaction with her entire environment."

APPLICATION EXPERIENCES FOR THE TEACHER EDUCATION CLASS

A. *What's Your Opinion?* Discuss your feelings about the following statements. Use both the textbook and your own experiences to back up your beliefs.
   1. Children need to know the names of the letters of the alphabet and their corresponding sounds before they can learn to read.
   2. If children can sound out the letters in words, then they can use their oral language to determine meaning.
   3. As soon as children attempt to write, we should encourage correct spelling.
   4. Parents should encourage children to participate in family literacy events even before they can read or write conventionally.
   5. One of the goals of the kindergarten teacher should be to make sure all of the children know the same conventions of language so that the first-grade teacher can use a standard curriculum.
   6. Traditional readiness skills such as auditory and visual discrimination can be taught through children's attempts to read and write. This method will be more effective than the use of worksheets.
   7. Readiness tests can give us important information about what children know about language and literacy.
   8. A first-grade teacher does not have time to read stories to children. They have more important things to do.

B. Analyze the child's responses in Figure 3.9 in terms of the cueing systems he used. Make a statement about his print awareness, his metalinguistic awareness, his knowledge of phonology, and his decoding strategies.

FIELD EXPERIENCES IN THE ELEMENTARY SCHOOL CLASSROOM

A. Spend a morning in a kindergarten or first-grade classroom. Use your observations to answer the following questions about the literacy environment:
   1. Do the children have an opportunity to use reading and writing for their own purposes?
   2. Is the environment filled with opportunities for the children to interact with print?
   3. Is the environment one in which the children are free to take risks in their exploration of language?
   4. Does the teacher provide activities that allow children to take advantage of what they already know about language?

B. Observe a child who is engaging in an unstructured writing activity. While he's working, be thinking about questions you'll want to ask him about his product as well as his process of writing. Later, analyze his answers and make a judgment about his writing development.

 bear	 wheel	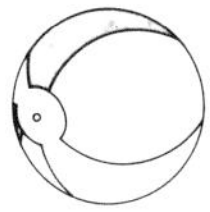 ball	 rag dolls
"bear"	*"I don't know, can I sound it out? Wu- hu-ch-ul, huweel."* *(Never recognized Wheel.)*	*"ball"*	*"er-aa-gu.* *The first one says rag. Is that a b or d? Bu-au- ulz, balls, dolls, rag- gedy dolls!"*
 train	 door	 boat	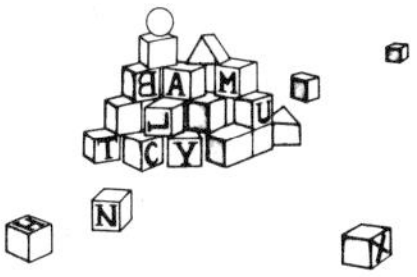 wood blocks
"train"	*"dollhouse"* *(Does it say all that?)* *"No, du-au- ru, daur."*	*"boat"*	*"bulocks"*

FIGURE 3.9

C. Interview a child about the ways he is learning to read and write at home and at school. Later, be prepared to discuss what you learned from his answers.

D. Observe a story-reading session. Note the techniques used by the teacher and make a judgment about the children's developing concept of story.

REFERENCES AND SUGGESTED READING

Anderson, A. B., Teale, W. H., & Estrada, E. (1980). Low income children's preschool literacy experiences: Some naturalistic observations. *The Quarterly Newsletter of the Laboratory of Comparative Human Cognition, 2,* 59–65.

Anderson, R. C., Hiebert, E., Scott, J., & Wilkinson, I. (1985). *Becoming a nation of readers.* Urbana: University of Illinois, Center for the Study of Reading.

Applebee, A. N. (1978). *The child's concept of story: Ages two to seventeen.* Chicago: The University of Chicago Press.

Barnes, M. (1988). *Mom, please tell me, 'cause I can't figure it out!* Unpublished manuscript, Portland State University, School of Education.

Beck, I. L., McKeown, M. B., McCaslin, E. S., & Burkes, A. M. (1979). *Instructional dimensions that may affect reading comprehension: Examples from two commercial reading programs.* Pittsburgh: University of Pittsburgh, Learning Research and Development Center.

Bissex, G. L. (1980). *GNYS AT WRK: A child learns to write and read.* Cambridge, MA: Harvard University Press.

Bloom, B. (1964). *Stability and change in human characteristics.* NY: Wiley.

Bridge, C. (1986). Predictable books for beginning readers and writers. In M. Sampson (Ed.), *The pursuit of literacy: Early reading and writing* (pp. 81–96). Dubuque, IA: Kendall/Hunt.

Bruner, J. (1960). *The process of education.* Cambridge: Harvard University Press.

Bruner, J. (1976). On prelinguistic prerequisites of speech. In R. Campbell & P. Smith (Eds.), *Recent advances in the psychology of language.* NY: Plenum Press.

Carle, E. (1969). *The very hungry caterpillar.* Cleveland: Collins-World.

Chomsky, C. (1971). Write first, read later. *Childhood Education, 47,* pp. 296–299.

Chomsky, C. (1979). Approaching reading through invented spelling. In L. Resnick & P. Weaver (Eds.), *Theory and practice of early reading* (Vol. 2). Hillsdale, NJ: Erlbaum.

Clark M. (1976). *Young fluent readers.* London: Heinemann.

Clay, M. (1972). *Sand: Test Booklet.* Auckland: Heinemann Educational Books.

Clay, M. (1975). *What did I write?* Exeter, NH: Heinemann.

Clay, M. (1979a). *The early detection of reading difficulties.* Auckland: Heinemann.

Clay, M. (1979b). *Reading: The patterning of complex behavior.* Portsmouth, NH: Heinemann.

Clay, M. (1979c). *Stones: Test Booklet.* Auckland: Heinemann Educational Books.

Clay, M. (1984). *Observing young readers.* Exeter, NH: Heinemann.

Cochran-Smith, M. (1983). Reading stories to children: A review critique. In B. Hutson (Ed.), *Advances in reading/ language research: A research annual* (Vol. 2, pp. 197–229). Greenwich, CT: JAI Press.

Cooney, N. (1978). *The wobbly tooth.* NY: Greenwillow Press.

Cullinan, B. (Ed.). (1987). *Children's literature in the reading program.* Newark, DE: International Reading Association.

Daviess, B. (1988). *Right from the mouths of babes.* Unpublished manuscript, Portland State University, School of Education.

DeLoache, J., & DeMendoza, O. (1986). *Joint picturebook reading of mothers and one-year-old children.* Unpublished manuscript, University of Illinois at Urbana-Champaign.

Downing, J., Ayers, D., & Schaefer, B. (1986).

The linguistic awareness in reading readiness test. Slough, England: NFER-Nelson.

Dunning, D., & Mason, J. (1984). *An investigation of kindergarten children's expressions of story characters' intentions.* Paper presented at the National Reading Conference, St. Petersburg Beach, FL.

Durkin, D. (1966). *Children who read early.* New York: Teachers College Press.

Durkin, D. (1989). *Teaching them to read* (5th ed.). Boston: Allyn & Bacon.

Dyson, A. (1984). Reading, writing, and language: Young children solving the written language puzzle. In J. Jensen (Ed.), *Composing and comprehending.* Urbana, IL: ERIC Clearinghouse on Reading and Communication Skills.

Ferreiro, E., & Teberosky, A. (1982). *Literacy before schooling.* Portsmouth.

Fields, M. V., & Lee, D. (1987). *Let's begin reading right: A developmental approach to beginning literacy.* Columbus, OH: Merrill.

Galda, L. (1982). Playing about a story: Its impact on comprehension. *The Reading Teacher, 36,* 52–55.

Gates, A. I. (1937). The necessary mental age for beginning reading. *Elementary School Journal, 37,* 497–508.

Gentry, J. R. (1982). An analysis of developmental writing in *Gnys at wrk. The Reading Teacher, 34,* 378–381.

Gesell, A. L. (1925). *The mental growth of the preschool child.* NY: Macmillan.

Gleitman, L., Newport, E., & Gleitman, H. (1984). The current status of the motherese hypothesis. *Journal of Child Language, 11,* 43–79.

Goldfield, B., & Snow, C. (1984). Reading books with children: The mechanics of parental influence on children's reading achievement. In J. Flood (Ed.), *Promoting reading comprehension* (pp. 204–215). Newark, DE: International Reading Association.

Harkness, F., & Miller, L. (1982). *A description of the interaction among mother, child and books in a bedtime reading situation.* Paper presented at the seventh annual Boston Conference on Language Development, Boston, MA.

Harste, J. C., Woodward, V. A., & Burke, C. L. (1984). *Language stories and literacy lessons.* Portsmouth, NH: Heinemann.

Heath, S. B. (1983). *Ways with words: Language, life and work in communities and classrooms.* New York: Cambridge University Press.

Henderson, E. H., & Beers, J. (Eds.). (1980). *Developmental and cognitive aspects of learning to spell.* Newark, DE: International Reading Association.

Hiebert, E. (1978). Preschool children's understanding of written language. *Child Development, 49,* 1231–1234.

Hiebert, E. (1986). Using environmental print in beginning reading instruction. In M. Sampson (Ed.), *The pursuit of literacy: Early reading and writing* (pp. 73–80). Dubuque, IA: Kendall/Hunt.

Hoskisson, K., & Tompkins, G. (1987). Writers' tools: Spelling. In K. Hoskisson & G. Tompkins (Eds.), *Language arts: Content and teaching strategies* (pp. 401–438). Columbus, OH: Merrill.

Hunt, J. McVicker. (1961). *Intelligence and experience.* NY: Ronald Press.

Martin, B. (1983). *Brown bear, brown bear, what do you see?* NY: Holt.

Mason, J. (1980). When do children begin to read: An exploration of children's letter and word reading competencies. *Reading Research Quarterly, 15,* 203–227.

Mason, J. (1984). Early reading from a developmental perspective. In Pearson, P. D. (Ed.). *The handbook of reading research.* NY: Longman.

Mason, J. (1985a). Cognitive monitoring and early reading: A proposed model. In D. Forrest, G. MacKinnon, & T. Waller (Eds.), *Metacognition, cognition, and human performance* (pp. 77–101). New York: Academic Press.

Mason, J. (1985b). *How the development of literacy takes place: Contrasts made among three approaches to learning, namely, maturation, skill learning, and problem solving.* Unpublished synthesis of existing studies/reviews, University of Illinois.

Mason, J. (1986). Kindergarten reading: A proposal for a problem-solving approach. In B.

Spodek (Ed.), *Today's kindergarten* (pp. 48–66). NY: Teachers College Press.

Mason, J., & Au, K. (1986). *Reading instruction for today.* Glenview, IL: Scott, Foresman and Company.

Mason, J., & Dunning, D. (1986). *Proposing a model to relate preschool home literacy with beginning reading achievement.* Paper presented at the American Educational Research Association Annual Meeting, San Francisco, CA.

Mason, J., Peterman, C. L., & Kerr, B. (1988, April). *Fostering comprehension by reading books to kindergarten children* (Technical Report No. 426). Urbana: University of Illinois, Center for the Study of Reading.

Mason, J., Peterman, C. L., & Kerr, B. (in press). Reading to kindergarten children: How teachers present stories, informational texts, and picture-phrase books. In D. Strickland & L. M. Morrow (Eds.), *Emerging literacy: Young children learn to read and write.* Newark, DE: IRA.

Mason, J., Peterman, C. L., Powell, B., & Kerr, B. (in press). Reading to kindergarten children: An analysis of contrasting instructional techniques. In J. Mason (Ed.), *Reading and writing connections.* Boston: Allyn & Bacon.

Mason, J., Stewart, J., & Dunning, D. (1986). What kindergarten children know about reading. In T. Rapheal (Ed.), *The context of school-based literacy* (pp. 97–114). NY: Random House.

McCormick, C., & Mason, J. (1986). Intervention procedures for increasing preschool children's interest in and knowledge about reading. In W. Teale & E. Sulzby (Eds.), *Emergent literacy: Writing and reading* (pp. 90–115). Norwood, NJ: Ablex.

McCormick, S. (1983). Reading aloud to preschoolers age 3–6: A review of the research. *Reading Horizons, 24,* 7–12.

Menyuk, P. (1988). *Language development: Knowledge and use.* Glenview, IL: Scott, Foresman and Company.

Morphett, M. V., & Washburne, C. (1931). When should children begin to read? *Elementary School Journal, 31,* 496–503.

Morrow, L. (1984). Reading stories to young children: Effects of story structure and traditional questioning strategies on comprehension. *Journal of Reading Behavior, 16*(4), 273–288.

Ninio, A., & Bruner, J. (1978). The achievement and antecedents of labelling. *Journal of Child Language, 5,* 5–15.

Paley, V. G. (1981). *Wally's stories.* Cambridge, MA: Harvard University Press.

Pearson, P. D. (1982). Asking questions about stories. *Occasional Paper #15.* Boston: Ginn.

Pearson, P. D., Hansen, J., & Gordon, C. (1979). The effect of background knowledge on young children's comprehension of explicit and implicit information. *Journal of Reading Behavior, 11,* 201–209.

Pellegrini, A., Brody, G., & Sigel, I. (1985). Parents' bookreading habits with their children. *Journal of Educational Psychology, 77*(3), 332–340.

Peterman, C. L. (1988). *The effects of storyreading procedures collaboratively designed by teachers and researcher on kindergarteners' literacy learning.* Unpublished doctoral dissertation, University of Illinois, Champaign-Urbana, IL.

Peterman, C. L., Dunning, D., Eckerty, C., & Mason, J. (1987). *The effects of storyreading procedures collaboratively designed by teacher and researcher on kindergartners' literacy learning.* Paper presented at the American Educational Research Association Conference, Washington, DC.

Peterman, C. L., Dunning, D., & Mason, J. (1985). *The storyreading event: How a teacher's presentation affects kindergarten children's attempts to read.* Paper presented at the National Reading Conference, San Diego, CA.

Peterman, C. L., Greer, E. A., & Turnipseed, M. (1984). *Exploring children's perceptions of the learning to read process: Interviews, observations, and literacy tasks.* Unpublished manuscript, University of Illinois.

Peterman, C. L., & Mason, J. (1984). *Kindergarten children's perceptions of the form of print in labelled pictures and stories.* Paper presented at the National Reading Conference, St. Petersburg, FL.

Prescott, G. A., Balow, I. H., Hogan, T. P., & Farr, R. C. (1977). *Metropolitan Achievement Test* (Survey Battery, Preprimer Form JS). NY: Harcourt Brace Jovanovich.

Read, C. (1971). Pre-school children's knowledge of English phonology. *Harvard Educational Review, 41,* 1–34.

Schickedanz, J. (1978). "Please read that story again!" Exploring relationships between reading and learning to read. *Young Children, 33,* 48–55.

Smith, F. (1984). Reading like a writer. In J. Jensen (Ed.), *Composing and comprehending* (pp. 47–56). Urbana, IL: ERIC Clearinghouse on Reading and Communication Skills.

Snow, C., & Ninio, A. (1986). The contracts of illiteracy: What children learn from learning to read books. In W. Teale & E. Sulzby (Eds.), *Emergent literacy: Writing and reading* (pp. 116–138). Norwood, NJ: Ablex.

Squire, J. (1984). Composing and comprehending: Two sides of the same basic process. In J. Jensen (Ed.), *Composing and comprehending* (pp. 23–32). Urbana, IL: ERIC Clearinghouse on Reading and Communication Skills.

Taylor, D. (1983). *Family literacy: Young children learning to read and write.* Exeter, NH: Heinemann.

Taylor, D., & Dorsey-Gaines, C. (1987). *Growing up literate: Learning from inner city families.* Portsmouth, NH: Heinemann.

Taylor, D., & Strickland, D. (1986). *Family storybook reading.* Portsmouth, NH: Heinemann.

Taylor, N. E., & Blum, I. H. (1981, April). *The effects of written language awareness on first grade reading achievement.* Paper presented at the annual meeting of the American Educational Research Association, Los Angeles, CA.

Teale, W. (1984). Reading to young children: Its significance for literacy development. In H. Goelman, A. Oberg, & F. Smith (Eds.), *Awakening to literacy* (pp. 110–121). Exeter, NH: Heinemann.

Teale, W. H. (1986). The beginnings of reading and writing: Written language development during the preschool and kindergarten years. In M. Sampson (Ed.), *The pursuit of literacy: Early reading and writing* (pp. 1–29). Dubuque, IA: Kendall/Hunt.

Teale, W. (1988). Emergent literacy: Reading and writing development in early childhood. In J. E. Readence & R. S. Baldwin (Eds.), *Research in literacy: Merging perspectives* (pp. 45–74). Thirty-sixth Yearbook of the National Reading Conference. Rochester, NY: National Reading Conference.

Temple, C. A., Nathan, R. G., & Burris, N. A. (1982). *The beginning of writing.* Boston, MA: Allyn & Bacon.

Tierney, R., & Pearson, P. D. (1984). Toward a composing model of reading. In J. Jensen (Ed.), *Composing and comprehending* (pp. 33–46). Urbana, IL: ERIC Clearinghouse on Reading and Communication Skills.

Torrey, J. W. (1969). Learning to read without a teacher: A case study. *Elementary English, 46,* 550–556.

Walker, G., & Kuerbitz, I. (1979). Reading to preschoolers as an aid to successful beginning reading. *Reading Improvement, 16*(2), 149–154.

Wells, G. (1985). Preschool literacy-related activities and success in school. In D. Olson, N. Torrance, & A. Hilyard (Eds.), *Literacy, language, and learning: The nature and consequences of reading and writing* (pp. 229–255). New York: Cambridge University Press.

Comprehension: Developing the Contextually Fluent Reader

━━━━━━━━━━━━━ **CHAPTER PREVIEW** ━━━━━━━━━━━━━

Teachers, and the environment they create, have a lot to do with how well children comprehend what they read. In this chapter we'll discuss the constraints that teachers can unconsciously place upon children's comprehension—such as by testing children rather than teaching them. Then we'll move on to the important role that teachers have in developing children's concepts of reading—what they think reading really is. As Dr. Peterman explained in Chapter 3, children's notions of what reading is begin very early in life. And once children move into a school environment, these notions can be either enhanced or changed—hopefully for the better, but not always. In addition to reading *concepts,* you and I will talk about the importance of children's *strategies* of reading—how these strategies are influenced by their concepts and how concepts and strategies affect comprehension.

Finally, we'll discuss fluency and what it has to do with comprehension—how *fluent,* natural reading, rather than stumbling, "sounding-it-out" reading, can be a reasonable goal of your instruction from the very first day of each school year.

The child should never be permitted to read for the sake of reading as a formal process or end in itself. . . . Word pronouncing will therefore always be secondary to getting whole sentence meanings, and this from the very first.

—A teachers' guide in 1895

Fluency comes not from accumulating vocabulary. It comes from accumulating thoughts.

—Brad Eliot

Patience . . . In time the grass becomes milk.

—Somebody's mother

READING COMPREHENSION: PRODUCT OR PROCESS?

Let's take a "hard-headed" business viewpoint of reading for a moment and ask a light-hearted question: Is reading a product or a service? I mean, in dollars and cents, what do you produce when you have a good student read five pages? Do you produce, say, five dollars worth of comprehension which the student can distribute back to you in the form of answers to your questions? If he gets four out of five questions right, do you now have a product worth some symbolic value, such as $4.00 or 80 percent? And should you pay your student for his product by passing out so many dollars worth of praise? A far-fetched and facetious analogy, I'll agree, but perhaps you know of teachers who try to teach reading comprehension in essentially the same manner: "Read this much, boys and girls. Then I'll ask you some questions and find out how well you read it."

All right, suppose we admit that reading does result in some kind of product, at least in the mind of the reader—a flock of facts, a herd of skills, a gaggle of attitudes. Doesn't it also result in a process—a service of some kind? And if so, who *does* the serving and who gets served?

Wittrock suggests that many teachers think of reading as not producing a thing, either product or service. That is, they think of reading as a "passive, receptive process . . . consumptive" rather than productive. But reading comprehension, Wittrock says, is not passive. It's a "generative process" similar to writing. Unlike writing, it "does not involve the construction of sentences to guide the thoughts of others. But it does involve using sentences written by others to guide one's thoughts to relevant experiences, principles, and knowledge" (1983, p. 7).

To carry my business analogy a little further, reading should probably be thought of more as a service than as a product. To read with comprehension, you have to serve both yourself and the author. And this requires interacting with the author by relating the author's statements to your own schemata. Such interaction often takes the form of subconsciously asking yourself questions. Take the following situation as an example:

> *Author:* The teller at First National Bank was very worried about the run.
>
> *Reader:* Is this about a run in her stocking or a run on the bank?

In other words, reading comprehension becomes a process of thinking. But this thinking is based not on the words themselves but rather on the *stimulation of schemata* provided by the words. (The reader must refer to his schemata in order to think about the word *run.*) A true communication process is taking place— serving both the author, who wants to communicate with the reader, and the reader, who normally prefers to *understand* what the author has to say. (At least it's less painful that way.)

Now, what are the implications of this process-service view of reading comprehension rather than a product-evaluation view? Just this: If you, the teacher, have a product-evaluation belief, you'll probably be spending a lot of time teaching comprehension by essentially testing your students. The following statement may be perceived by the teacher as teaching, but it's really testing: "Here's something to read, girls and boys. You have ten minutes to read it, and then I'll ask you some questions."

If, on the other hand, you have a process-service belief about reading comprehension, you'll probably spend a lot of time *preparing* your students for the reading process, getting them interested in the topic, building their schemata before they read, and modeling your own thought processes for them. In other words, you'll spend a considerable amount of time teaching them *how* to comprehend rather than merely testing their memory.

Let me suggest that you concentrate on two ideas as you continue this chapter and move into the next one. One of them you and I have already talked about in Chapter 1: how teachers' beliefs about reading influence the way they teach reading. The other one is how you can *teach*—rather than test—reading comprehension.

TEACHER-MADE CONSTRAINTS ON READING COMPREHENSION

In Chapter 2, we saw that Valerie was content to read that "the rangers had *market of a plack* [instead of marked off a place] for people to cut trees." We left our study of Valerie by asking a question: "Is it possible that she's been actually reinforced for coming up with word-noises and meaningless substitutions? If so, then how could such reinforcement possibly take place?"

Let's see if we can answer that question right now. As Jerome Harste and Robert Carey have confirmed through their research (1984, p. 32), what the teacher believes (or consents to believe) about the process of learning to read "strongly affects what instructional strategies are employed." For example, if the teacher believes that learning to read requires correction of each word that a child reads "wrong," she will probably emphasize *word* correction more than *meaning* correction. This emphasis will in turn produce what Harste and Carey refer to as an "instructional constraint." An instructional constraint is something in the teaching-learning environment that limits what is learned. For example, the teacher we just mentioned will probably have students who will learn to concentrate more on one word at a time rather than the author's message. A child like Valerie, then, becomes *willing* to plug in *market* for *marked, of* for *off,* and even *plack* for *place,* since *plack,* after all, *sounds* like a word.

But why are children, especially young children, so eager to concentrate on what they think the teacher wants? You probably know the answer to this question already. All of us, starting at birth, are placed in situations in which we're dependent upon another person for affection, for a sense of belonging, for a feeling of importance. In the classroom, the teacher is usually the major "giver"— the major person to meet children's needs. Is it any wonder that children try to please the teacher? Not that there's anything wrong with trying to please. Even as adults we keep right on trying. (I like to please a special friend of mine, for example, by bringing her coffee in the morning.)

Now back to Valerie. It is quite possible that Valerie's main problem is highly related to—although not necessarily caused by—her past teachers' emphasis on words rather than meanings. A word emphasis by the teacher seems to be a particularly damaging kind of instructional constraint, one that encourages what Frank Smith refers to as "tunnel vision" (1979). The children learn to concentrate so hard on each word, they ignore the rich matrix of surrounding words that provide semantic and syntactic cues to meaning. They become, as Dasch puts it, "overly concerned with the visual information . . . and try to decode letters and words rather than process units of meanings. They [fail] . . . to use prior knowledge to make sense of the text" (1983, p. 428).

You may be wondering if it's possible to stop such word correction in a "real" classroom. "After all," as some teachers tell me, "the children will correct each other, even if I don't." "True," I usually say, "if you let them." As a classroom teacher myself, I had to explain to my students why I did not want them to correct each other and why we needed to concentrate on the author's meaning rather than every single word. It was also necessary, of course, to let each child correct himself whenever the author's meaning was missed by a particular miscue. (Even with all this explanation, however, I sometimes had to provide a firm reminder to one or two children who considered themselves professional critics for *The New York Times.*)

Perhaps the worst case of peer-critic behavior I've ever seen was in a third-grade classroom I visited. The "correctional system" there was something to behold. Every time a child corrected another child for his "mistakes," the critic was handed a token by the teacher. When said critic had accumulated enough tokens, he would actually receive a prize!

Instead of encouraging such negative bee stings of "correction," I would recommend developing a positive esprit de corps (call it "cooperative education" if you will) with teacher comments like these:

"I enjoyed that, Ben! You read it as though you were telling it to me."

Or how about:

"I could almost hear the author talking when you read that!"

Or:

"I'll bet the author would be pleased if she heard the way you read that!"

Other Teacher-Made Constraints

What are some other teacher-made constraints on reading comprehension? One of them is the *timing* of teachers in asking "comprehension" questions. Many teachers ask no questions until *after* the children have read an entire selection. This approach is fine if you want to see what they *remember*, but memory and comprehension are not the same thing (Smith, 1979; Farr & Carey, 1986). Andy might have good comprehension of a story but a poor memory of it. Robert may have both poor comprehension and poor memory of the story. If you, the teacher, check only on memory, how will you know how to help Andy and Robert? With Andy, you'll want to help him learn how to retain key features of a story so that he can talk about them later. With Robert, you'll want to concentrate first on helping him *comprehend* what he reads; then you can concentrate later on improving his ability to remember what he reads.

However, unless you check on comprehension *while Andy and Robert read* you won't know how to help either one of them. Nor will you be able to help Robert use all four cueing systems and thus read interactively. Not every selection they read should be handled this way, of course, but you'll need to use the "before and during approach" enough to allow you to *teach comprehension*—rather than merely testing memory after they read. So you see, the *timing* of your questions is another constraint—another influence on how well students learn to comprehend what they read.

Still another instructional restraint would be the *audience* Andy or Robert would be expected to read *to*—to themselves, to the teacher, to their peers? Andy might comprehend equally well in all three situations. Robert, on the other hand, might comprehend nothing if he has to read in front of his peers. It is not unusual for a child to do poorly with his peers and teacher, yet comprehend quite well when reading silently or out in the hall with a teacher's aide.

Another constraint is the *interrogation manner* some teachers use. If they ask questions as if they're administering an oral examination, some children comprehend, or remember, nothing more than the intensity of the teacher's voice or the impatience in her eyes. If, however, teachers use questions in an informal way, and in a manner designed to stimulate children's thinking, both Robert and Andy might do quite well.

But equally important is the *type* of questions teachers ask. If they ask only *literal* questions rather than questions that require inferential (interpretive) thinking, students "become adept at searching for the correct answer and ignore the whole story" (Swaby, 1982).

The point of all this, of course, is that comprehension can't be thought of as something isolated from what teachers do in the classroom. I may have given you the false impression in Chapter 2 that interactive reading is a *natural* process that good readers engage in and poor readers don't . . . period. But as you can see, teachers have a great deal to do with how "natural" it is. As Peter Mosenthal put it, "The most important context influencing reading comprehension in classroom lessons may be the interaction between the teacher and the students" (1984, p. 17).

CONCEPT OF READING: A MAJOR VARIABLE OF COMPREHENSION

Each child develops a theory or schema about reading—what it is, what you're supposed to do when you read, what "big people" do when they read. Some get the idea, because they've been read to a lot, that "reading is telling a story that's in the book," and this, of course, is a useful concept for someone just learning to read. Some children get the idea that reading is "saying the words exactly the way they are on the page," and this may or may not be such a good concept. It depends on whether they're keyed in to the words themselves or to the author's larger meaning.

Perhaps the worst side effect of the word-emphasis instructional contraint is the erroneous concept of reading that children can develop as a result. In the process of trying to please the teacher, they can gradually come up with a schema about reading that may slow down their growth in reading ability for years. Once they get the notion that reading is a process of correct word calling rather than a search for meaning, it may take a great deal of time and effort (usually by a special reading teacher) to undo the damage—and it can't always be undone.

As I mentioned, one way that teachers reinforce this wrong concept is by correcting children for each word "error," even when their substitutions, insertions, and omissions are completely in line with the author's meaning! Given half a chance, and given a teacher who emphasizes meaning, they will usually go back and self-correct miscues that don't make sense!

Let's see what you would do in the following situation in which Melody is reading to you:

Author	*Melody*
"Walter!" Walter's mother called again."	"Walter!" Walter's mother called again.
Walter did not answer.	Walter *didn't* answer.
"Walter!"	"Walter!"
Still no answer.	*He* still *didn't* answer.

What do you think you would do in this situation? Would you be tempted to stop and correct her? If so, don't feel bad. Experienced teachers I've worked with tell me it has taken them a while to break an old habit. (After all, how many times were *they* corrected for a "wrong word" when they were learning to read?)

Now let's see what you would do with Dena.

Author	*Dena*
Next Saturday the whole	Next Saturday the whole
family drove to the	family *droove* to the
forest. They found the	forest. They found the
ranger station and	ranger station and
bought a permit.	*brought* a permit.

What should you do this time? Should you stop her at the end of the first sentence? At the end of the paragraph? Anytime? Should you say something gently, such as, "Okay, Dena, what do think the first sentence is about?" (If she says, "I don't know," what might you say that would help her understand the first sentence?) What would you do about the second sentence?

STRATEGIES FOR READING: ONE-CUED READING DOESN'T WORK

Matt was a fifth-grader when he was tape recorded reading a fifth-grade selection from an informal reading inventory (Silvaroli, 1982). I'll use a coding system to show you how he read the first three sentences. The letter *d* above a word indicates that Matt defaulted on the word. That is, he needed to have the teacher decode it for him. The other miscues are substitutions, for example, *Sunday* for *study*.

       d   *prōve*   *d*   *Bleend*

Scientists wanted to prove that seals had excellent hearing. Blind seals were

          Sunday   *blid*   *especially*   *hear*

used in the study. The blind seals were trained to expect food when they heard

sounds.

     At the time of the recording, as you can see, Matt was basically a one-cued reader. He relied primarily on graphophonic cues and ignored the three cueing systems—semantic, syntactic, and schematic—he used when listening. As you might imagine, his comprehension of this selection was quite poor. And his memory for details or inferences related to this story was equally poor.

     Matt's one-cued reading strategy caused him to accept the nonsense word *prōve* (rhyming with *stove*) for the actual word *prove*. If he had been *listening* to this sentence instead of reading it, he probably would have stopped the speaker to say, "Prōve? What does *prōve* mean?" Instead, he went right on, using his graphophonic sight words to move rather swiftly through the morass.

     Plunging through the muddy marsh, he arrived at the word *Blind*. Not recognizing this word as a sight word, he again relied solely on "phonics" and came up with the nonsense word *Bleend*. So by this time Matt had created a group of scientists trying to *prōve* something about *bleend* seals. It's doubtful, however, that Matt was keen on understanding the text, since he next had the "bleend seals" being used "in the Sunday."

     Note that *Sunday* has four out of the five letters found in *study*, which demonstrates Matt's relatively great concern for the graphophonic cueing system and his lack of concern for context clues (semantic, syntactic, and schematic). Note also that when Matt arrived at the verb *expect*, he cheerfully substituted an adverb *(especially)*, creating nonsyntactic language that he would never use in speaking.

     We can see, then, that when someone reads as Matt reads, his comprehension is going to suffer, not only because of the wrong concept of reading ("reading is strictly decoding"), but also because of the wrong strategies for reading. Matt's main strategies fit his concept of reading perfectly: (1) defaulting (pausing long enough for the teacher to give him the word), (2) gratefully pronouncing any word that is a sight word, and (3) substituting words that are graphophonically similar but contextually off the mark. For all three strategies, Matt relies primarily on only one cueing system.

Let's use an analogy to help you emotionally grasp the situation that Matt and others like him are in. There are four cueing systems necessary for good reading, and "Matt readers" use only one. All right, to help you *feel* how meaningless (how "comprehensionless") it is to be a one-cued reader, I'd like you to become a "deaf" and one-eyed reader for a moment. You're going to use only one out of four of the stimulus avenues normally available to you. Just for fun, try reading the following sentence with only one eye open and without allowing yourself to hear any of the words that your one eye is passing over.

Are you ready? Here's the sentence:

High-quality pedagogical guides show pedagogues how to have neophytes engage in the use of all four cueing systems when perusing text and to cogitate at literal, inferential, evaluative, and inventive levels of thinking.

If you didn't "cheat," in either an auditory or a visual way, I doubt that you comprehended that sentence. If you now go back and use both eyes—and both "ears," so to speak—you'll do much better (especially if you use all four cueing systems).

All right, I'll admit it. Some people enjoy that analogy; some think it's quite silly. But you know what I'm driving at: If you want better reading comprehension from your students, one of the things you'll need to concentrate on is having them use all four cueing systems interactively. And now I would imagine your next question to be, "How do you get children to use all four cueing systems interactively?" I will gradually suggest some answers to this question throughout the rest of this chapter and book. For now, though, let me put them in a nutshell for you:

Getting students to use all four cueing systems interactively, and thus improving their reading comprehension, can be encouraged by:

1. Modeling this process out loud for them
2. Oral and silent cloze experiences
3. Study of new vocabulary in context
4. Fluent practice with easy text
5. Guided practice in predicting and confirming
6. Fluent practice with patterned books
7. Echo, choral, and repeated reading
8. Writing often and reading one's own writing
9. Enhancing students' schemata before they read

THE IMPORTANCE OF FLUENCY TO COMPREHENSION

The connection between reading comprehension and the use of all four cueing systems is probably *overly* clear to you by now. However, there's another connection that's equally important, and that is the connection between fluency and comprehension. Let's first look at the most obvious reason for this connection. Jill reads a 12-word sentence in 3 seconds flat. Not a world's record by any means, but a comfortable rate for a good reader of fiction in the third grade. On the other hand, Dennis (another third-grader) requires 24 seconds for the same sentence. By the time he finishes the twelfth word, he's forgotten the first. His comprehension suffers from sheer time-lag memory loss.

This is not to imply that fluency is a synonym for speed. To read fluently requires much more than speed. Think of what we mean, for example, when we make the statement, "She speaks fluent French." We don't mean that she necessarily speaks as rapidly as Joan Rivers. We just mean she can communicate with others with ease in the French language. Fluent reading is similar to the concept of fluent French. A fluent reader notices all four cueing systems, thus speeding up both his pronunciation and his understanding. A fluent reader reads not word by word but in natural-sounding phrases, just the way he would speak them. A fluent reader makes constant predictions about the next word coming and about the next event or thought coming. Thus, his eyes are leaping forward to the next words to confirm what his predictions have led him to expect. If he's reading out loud, the word being formed by his mouth is not controlled by his eyes. (Remember, they're leaping ahead to join with the brain in confirming predictions or in creating new predictions.) The word he's reading out loud is controlled by his brain's short-term memory.

So as you can see, fluency requires a complex interaction of the eyes and the brain. And it requires a complex interaction between the reader and author. Just as the goal of the fluent speaker is to communicate with the listener, the goal of the fluent reader is to communicate with the author. This often takes the form of "getting inside the author's head"—in a sense, speaking and thinking the way the author does. Such an act requires a strong awareness of the schemata triggered by the author, the phrases used, the particular vocabulary, and so on.

Richard L. Allington (1983) makes the very believable claim that fluency has not become a "major focus" of our reading programs. And yet, he points out, "a preponderance of empirical and clinical evidence supports the relationship of fluent oral reading and good overall reading ability."

Research by Collins (1982) seems to demonstrate that teachers themselves cause much of the problem by emphasizing decoding and accuracy too much—especially with poor readers. Evidently, the poorer the reader, the more likely he is to be placed in word-emphasis programs rather than fluency-emphasis programs. Thus the poor reader becomes less and less daring and less and less fluent. In addition, poor readers are often segregated from good readers and get to hear other poor readers as their chief models!

Fortunately, there are a number of research-based methods of improving both the fluency and the meaningfulness of children's reading. The rest of this chapter will therefore concentrate on these methods.

THE ROLE OF SCHEMATA IN FLUENT, MEANINGFUL READING

The first and most important method we'll discuss is that of enhancing children's schemata before they read. Nearly all thinking and communicating involves our various schemata. People are always getting confused in conversations because of a schema difference or two. Joe is talking about how great California is and Sam is saying, "It's the pits." Joe is responding to his schema about Disneyland. Sam is responding to his schema about the freeways. The same kind of confusion occurs in reading situations. The author presents an idea using her background and schema. The reader, unbeknownst to the author, does not have the *same* background and schema. Alas, both fluency and communication suffer. The teacher of reading needs to be alert for "schema deficiency" and "schema conflict," both serious problems for the reader. And these problems don't hover over children only in the upper grades; they begin much earlier. Take the following first-grade story, for example:

> Bill saw a box. It was big. He opened it. He got in. He sat down. Dan saw
> the box. He got in too. He sat down. They sat still. They were hiding. Susan
> was looking for them. She looked up. She looked down. She kept looking.
> She saw the box. She did not see them. Bill and Dan saw Susan. Then they
> laughed. She heard them. Then she found them.*

All right, so you had no trouble reading that exciting mystery. Now imagine that you have never, in your entire life, played or heard of hide-and-seek or anything similar to hide-and-seek. Go ahead. Read the story again, and try to experience the schema deficiency problem you would have.

Now I'm going to ask you to read it once more. But this time let's say you have a schema *conflict* rather than a schema deficiency. You see, when you were a kid, your big brother made you sit in a dark, stuffy box. Not only that, he covered the box and wouldn't let you out until your mother came home. All right, read it once more, please, and see what this schema conflict does to your communication with the author.

Finished? What was different? As you read it this last time, did you perhaps wonder why the boys in the box were laughing? (What could possibly be so funny about being inside a huge, dark box awaiting nothing but certain death by suffocation?) Well, you get my point. Before asking children to read a selection,

---

*Colin Dunkeld, Portland Informal Inventory, Form P, unpublished manuscript, School of Education, Portland State University, with permission from the author.

the teacher needs to ask himself, "What schemata do they need in order to understand it?" Even for the simple story about the two boys in a box, they need to have developed a schema about hide-and-seek. Since the author never even mentions this game, they will certainly need minitheories about its objective and its rules, or the point of the story will be lost on them. They'll also need a schema related to the size of boxes that allows them to imagine two children getting inside one.

What should the teacher tell them ahead of time? "Boys and girls, today you're going to read a story about three children playing hide-and-seek." Well, that would help them understand the story, all right, but it would also spoil the fun the author had in mind for the readers. And besides, the chances are quite good that they've already played hide-and-seek. A better approach, since the box is so important in the story, would be to talk about various sizes of boxes and what might fit inside a big one. "Could you fit a bicycle inside a big box? Could you fit a child? Two children?" Then you might get them interested in the story: "This story is about a big box. And it's also about a game some people like to play. After you're all through reading the story, I'll let you whisper to me what you think the game is."

The Relationship between Schemata and Inferential Thinking

Why do we need to worry so much about children's schematic backgrounds before asking them to read a selection? Because without adequate development of their schemata, they will stumble and falter instead of predicting and confirming with fluency. Furthermore, they'll read without meaning. But why does this happen, actually? *Because without the proper schemata, people find it difficult or impossible to make inferences as they read.* Let me give you an example of this. The text I'm going to ask you to read doesn't stimulate the schemata in your mind that you'll need in order to infer what's going on. Try it, and you'll see what I mean:

> This operation is really not that difficult. First you remove them from the room you've just used and take them into the other room. Next you remove the material you no longer want and place each one in the appropriate place. Don't worry if this sometimes seems difficult. In time you'll get used to all the possibilities that are available to you. After you're satisfied with the arrangement, just follow the directions on the front and you'll be finished for a while. Later, when you have a need for them again, you can use them directly or put them away and use them some other time. It's true that you have to repeat the operation many times in the course of living, but I'm sure you'll agree that it's worth it.

Did you understand the author's message? Could you predict what the next words and ideas were going to be? Did your fluency suffer as you kept returning to previous text to figure out the meaning? Not to worry. It's very normal. Most people find it extremely difficult to comprehend until I tell them to use their

schema related to washing dishes in the dishwasher. Then, when they read it again, it makes sense.

Going back to our hide-and-seek story, you can imagine how difficult it would be for a child to comprehend it if he had never played hide-and-seek, or if he had never developed a schema about boxes that included the possibility of hiding inside one. He could use every syntactic cue, every semantic cue, and every graphophonic cue available and still not understand the story. Without the appropriate schemata, he could not make the necessary inferences, and without inferences, there is no real reading (Carr, 1983; Dehn, 1984; Hansen & Pearson, 1980; Rumelhart, 1984; Smith, 1979).

Inferential Thought: Its Role in Fluent, Meaningful Reading

Studies indicate that inferences play a major role in reading comprehension. Research results also support the theory that the reader constructs inferences during reading to make the story coherent. (Carr, 1983, p. 520)

Not only do readers need to make one large inference related to what the story is about, but they also need to fill in "empty slots" with inferences as they read from sentence to sentence. Let me show you what I mean by using the familiar story "The Three Bears." When authors write stories, they don't tell you everything; they leave empty slots for your imagination to fill in. Even "The Three Bears" usually has one or two empty slots between each sentence. For example, between the following two sentences, we can find at least two:

> One morning the mommy bear put some hot cereal into three bowls—a great big bowl, a middle-sized bowl, and a wee little bowl.

> *Empty slot 1:* Where were the bowls? *Inference:* On the kitchen or dining room table.

> *Empty slot 2:* Who were they for? *Inference:* Daddy, mommy, and baby, in that order.

> The cereal was too hot to eat, so the three bears went for a walk in the forest.

In other words, when people read, they must read between the lines to understand the text. They must infer what the author didn't actually say. Such inferences are based on the reader's schemata, which in turn are based on the reader's background experiences. *The teacher who ignores this basic component of the reading act cannot hope to teach reading comprehension successfully.*

David Pearson has this to say about inferential reading: "We now view text as a sort of blueprint for meaning, a set of tracks or clues that the reader uses as s/he builds a model of what the text means. . . . In this new view, we recognize that . . . authors omit from their texts exactly those relationships and nuances they expect (and hope) readers can figure out for themselves" (1985, p. 726).

Put another way, if I might add to Pearson's words, reading is not a copy machine process. It's more like a weaving process. We don't make a copy of the print in our mind as we read. We interweave the author's words with the mini-theories developed through background experiences. And yet, in observations of elementary school classrooms, Durkin (1978–79, 1984) found that helping children develop the necessary background before they read an assigned selection was the one step teachers most consistently omitted. The reason? "It takes too much time."

Research on Inferential Reading

Research has borne out the importance of background knowledge in making inferences. But background can be enhanced by the teacher, and so can children's ability to read between the lines (applying their background as they make hypotheses about the author's message). Research tells us the following:

> Poor readers and very young readers have the most trouble reading inferentially (Holmes, 1983). This trouble is directly related to background deficiency. In fact, background knowledge "seems to account for text difficulty to a greater degree than . . . sentence length and word frequency" (Lipson, 1984).
>
> Very young readers have trouble reading many "basal readers" (the books they are most often given for reading instruction) because authors who write the stories are not allowed to use very many words. As a result, the words are not as precise as they should be and leave gaps that the beginning readers have to fill in with their own background. Thus, they "have to use more inferencing than older children—at a time when they are less equipped to infer than older children" (Beck, McKeown, & McCaslin, 1981).
>
> Children need much more than the experience of defining words before they read a selection. Equally important are discussions on why people behave in certain ways in certain situations. Comprehension of stories requires considerable understanding of human nature—emotions, customs, roles, goals, and ways of achieving those goals (Dehn, 1984). Jane Hansen (1981), for example, was successful in using this approach in a ten-week study with second-graders. After working with new vocabulary in each story to be read, she discussed three ideas important to the story, first in relation to the children's own experiences and then in relation to their predictions of what was going to happen in the story. For example, the main character in one story looked at his feet when he was embarrassed—an important clue to the reader. The children might have missed it without a discussion first of what people do when they feel embarrassed. The group who consistently had the benefit of this type of discussion each day raised their standardized reading score considerably more than did a control group; they also made greater improvements on tests of inferential thinking.
>
> Mere practice in answering inferential-type questions before, during, and after reading can improve your students' reading ability, whether the students are poor readers (Holmes, 1983) or average readers (Hansen & Pearson, 1980).
>
> Science and social studies should not be omitted from a busy schedule just to provide more time for "reading" instruction. These two areas of the curriculum are vital in developing children's backgrounds and schemata (Kellogg, 1971).
>
> Creative drama is an excellent medium for developing the schemata necessary for inferential thinking (Manna, 1984).

PREDICTABLE READING MATERIAL
FOR DEVELOPING FLUENCY

There's a certain kind of text that is ideal for teaching beginners to read fluently, with meaning, and with uncomplicated "inferencing." Text of this sort is often so simply written that fluent "reading" can occur even on the first day of first grade. This is why "patterned literature" is being used more and more in the first two grades and for older remedial readers.

Patterned literature usually comes in the form of picture books (although most picture books would not be considered patterned literature). In addition, basal reader ("Dick and Jane") publishers are now including many patterned stories in their series. Patterned stories that you may have already seen include the series written by Bill Martin, the most famous one being *Brown Bear, Brown Bear, What Do You See?* Here's a piece of that one:

> Brown bear, brown bear, what do you see?
> I see a red bird looking at me.
> Red bird, red bird, what do you see?
> I see a yellow duck looking at me.

And, of course, the next line can be easily predicted. This pattern is repeated more than a dozen times as Martin's book continues.

Predictable language can also be found in many Mother Goose rhymes:

> Jack Spratt could eat no fat,
> His wife could eat no lean,
> And so betwixt themselves,
> They licked the platter clean.

While it's true that such "rhymes" do not imitate natural, predictable speech, they have a rhythm, a pattern, and a plot that stick in the mind. It is easy for most children to remember some of them well enough to chant them with other children or to read along with the teacher or with other children.

Don't get the idea, though, that patterned literature usually has a rhyme. Far from it. Although Mother Goose books are one type of excellent text for beginning readers, limiting your use of patterned literature only to rhyming material would miss the point. What we want is text that is *predictable*, either from the standpoint of language patterns or from the standpoint of plot patterns (or both). And please don't get the idea that I'm referring to materials with predictable *spelling* patterns: "Pat sat on that mat. That mat is Pat's mat. That rat on Pat's mat is fat." What I'm talking about is predictable *language*. "That mat is Pat's mat" is *not* predictable language—no one talks that way, no literature is written that way.

Judith Viorst's *Alexander and the Terrible, Horrible, No Good, Very Bad Day* is an example of a patterned book with a highly predictable plot pattern and moderately predictable language patterns. Alexander, as you may recall, has one of those days when everything goes wrong. It was "one of those terrible, horrible, no good, very bad days." He doesn't get a window seat in the car, he doesn't get an easy question from the teacher, even his best friend doesn't want to play with him. Although the language is not the same from episode to episode, the language and sentence structures tend to be the same. Many of the words are repeated from episode to episode, especially his forlorn statement about his horrible day.

An excellent type of predictable text is a story written by a child himself, either with a group or individually. After all, there's nothing more predictable than one's own language. After a child has just written (or dictated) a story, it's pretty easy for her to read it. That's why the language experience approach works so well—an approach in which children dictate or write their own reading materials. (See Chapter 8 for samples of this.)

Beyond language experience stories, though, the most abundant source of predictable language is the library. For the teacher interested in fluency and the interactive approach to reading, there is no shortage of books that can be used. There are literally hundreds of patterned stories, in picture-book form, that can provide the predictability needed. I'll give you just a few more examples here, and you'll find many more in Appendix P. One of the favorites of children I've worked with, especially in the primary grades (1–3), is Rose Bonne's and Alan Mills's version of *I Know an Old Lady*. You remember this old-time jingle, don't you? Here's the first verse:

> I know an old lady who swallowed a fly.
> I don't know why she swallowed a fly.
> Perhaps she'll die.

And here's the third verse:

> I know an old lady who swallowed a bird.
> How absurd to swallow a bird.
> She swallowed a bird to catch the spider.
> That wriggled and jiggled and tickled inside her.
> She swallowed the spider to catch the fly.
> But I don't know why she swallowed a fly.
> Perhaps she'll die.

An example of a more subtle patterned book (with a more interesting plot) is one by Stephen Kellogg, called *Can I Keep Him?* In this book a little boy (with a vivid imagination) keeps bringing home a different kind of pet to show his mother. "Can I keep him?" he asks each time. And each time his mother gives him a new excuse, for example, "Your grandmother is allergic to cat fur." The story is touching and humorous, with insights into both children and mothers, and it contains words and sentence patterns that are similar throughout. It's a delightful book that children from first grade on up can enjoy reading "one more time."

So now that you know what I mean by "predictable materials" and "patterned books," we can move on to the advantages of using them. Remember that with the interactive approach, the student will be engaged in making hypotheses as she reads. Her procedure will be to predict what the author is going to say next and to sample enough of the print to confirm her predictions. The trick is to find those materials that cause the student to use this procedure without getting bogged down in decoding each word separately.

With predictable materials, the child, *from the very first day of school,* can learn that reading depends on other cues besides letters. She can learn intuitively that reading is very much like something she's been doing for years: *listening.* Whether a person listens or reads, she pays attention (without thinking about it) to the syntactic and semantic cues in the language, and to the schematic cues that reside in her mind. Just as we hypothesize when we listen, so do we hypothesize when we read. What is the speaker saying? What is the *author* saying? What does the speaker mean? What does the *author* mean?

Connie Bridge asks this question: "Is it possible for the novice reader to learn to read by reading?" (1979, p. 503). She justifies her question by saying, "It is only through practice in reading that children can learn to be efficient predictors of meaning and economical users of visual information (print)" (p. 504). And finally she answers her question this way: "When given structured language patterns it is possible, even from the beginning stages, for readers to use their predictive abilities. . . . They are role playing themselves as readers and thus have taken a giant step toward becoming successful readers" (p. 505).

> "Role playing themselves as successful readers"—that's a very important teaching strategy for those interested in the interactive approach (and for those using the complementary approach referred to as "whole language"). When children are asked to "sound out" each word as they read, they are *not* role playing as successful readers. *They are practicing poor reading.* A successful reader is a fluent reader, not a halting, stuttering, moronic-sounding reader, puffing and growling his way through pieces of language that might as well be Latin or Greek.

I've often wondered how we would like it as adults, if we were taken to, say, the Soviet Union, plunked down in a "little reading circle" with other frightened adults staring at us, and were made to "sound out" word by word a story written in Russian (with the Russian alphabet as well). I don't think we would think of ourselves as fluent, successful readers. I doubt that we would go home to our spouses, with joy shining from our faces, and say, "I can't wait to go back to school tomorrow."

"Fluency: The Neglected Reading Goal" is the title of a now-classic article in the February 1983 edition of *The Reading Teacher.* I hope you'll get a chance to find it in the library. In this article Richard L. Allington argues for predictable materials as an answer to a very prevalent problem in the schools: reading that is not fluent. That is, the reading is not smooth and expressive; nor does it show that the author is understood. You see, we are still convincing ourselves in some schools that when Clifford passes lots of miniature tests on even more miniature "subskills" (for example, "The student will be able to decode words that rhyme with the phonogram *ame*"), he is becoming a reader. Nothing could be further from the truth. Sooner or later, someone notices that Clifford can pass all the tests but his fluency is very poor. And, as Allington says, this diagnosis "often leads to further instruction in letters, sounds, or words in isolation" (1983, p. 557). Yet if we look at the research on this problem, we find that children who are guided into reading-for-fluency increase their reading *comprehension* considerably more than children who are taught to concentrate on word accuracy (Allington, 1983).

Suggestions for Using Patterned Books

The following is a list of ideas for using patterned books to develop fluent, natural reading with beginners. The same ideas have been used very successfully with older readers who need to change their concept of reading.

1. After reading the title of the book to them and showing them the pictures on the cover, ask them to predict what the book will be about.
2. After reading three or four pages to them, ask them what they think will happen next or what they think a certain character will say next.
3. Have children explain their reasons whenever they make predictions. For example, Why do you think that will happen? Why do you think those words will come next? Have you seen those words before in this book? Is that the kind of thing he would say? Why do you think so?
4. Follow each set of predictions and reasons with a chance for them to confirm or disconfirm their predictions.
5. Read the rest of the story to them and ask them to join in whenever they think they know the words.
6. On the second day read the story to them again, allowing them plenty of opportunities to join in and also some opportunities to say the next line before you read it.
7. Now use either a large wall chart or individual ditto booklets. Have them take turns or use their own booklets to point to the words as you read the story again.
8. On the third or fourth day, after they have had enough time following along, ask for volunteers to read parts of the story.
9. When they have learned the story well, let them take the booklets home (with their own illustrations if you wish) and read them to their parents.
10. Try having them write a similar story (with your guidance the first time you try this. See Chapter 8 for details.).

Selecting Your Patterned Books

Perhaps the most important step in using patterned books is that of *choosing the selection!* As Carol Louritzen suggests, having learned, no doubt, from her experience as a remedial reading teacher, "The choice of reading material and the method of presenting it are crucial to success" (1982, p. 457).

My own experience with patterned books reminds me that the *selection* must be the major source of motivation—rather than tokens, progress graphs, or scratch-'n-sniff stickers. Unless the selection sparks their interest, you'll find yourself engaged in orthodontia rather than teaching. If you find that the book doesn't excite them on the first reading, put it aside and try your next choice. Keep trying until you find one that produces a glow of excitement.

As you search for selections of this type, look for those with a definite rhythm, with repeated phrases or sentences, or at least with very similar sentence patterns (remembering that rhyme is not necessary). The sequence of events must have a pulling quality—one that makes you want to go on, for example, to see what else the Old Lady will swallow. The books I've listed in Appendix P have those qualities, but don't be limited by that list. There are hundreds more!

THE CLOZE TECHNIQUE FOR IMPROVING STRATEGIES AND FLUENCY

Let's now look at another major technique for encouraging "contextual fluency" (fluent reading for meaning). Although the "cloze technique" is often perceived as a testing procedure (one that I will describe in Chapter 11), it is a much more functional and useful technique than that—when used with discretion (Jongsma, 1980). The cloze technique is not difficult to use—it involves nothing more than leaving out words in a sentence or letters in a word. However, this technique does require careful judgment in order to achieve what you want it to accomplish.

A warning before we talk about it further. The cloze technique is not a panacea (any more than any one technique is). After exhaustive review of the research on cloze, Jongsma concluded that this procedure *can* be effective, but cloze activities need to be "carefully sequenced as to difficulty, length, or purpose" (1980, p. 21). Jongsma further warns us that the cloze procedure is most effective for instruction in reading comprehension, but least effective in vocabulary instruction.

Let me give you an example, then, of a carefully sequenced use of cloze in developing skill in reading comprehension:

Imagine that you're preparing a group of second-graders to read a story by Colin Dunkeld. It's about two boys building a playhouse, which eventually crashes to the ground. Here are some steps you might follow in using the cloze technique. Your goal will be to help your students understand, intuitively at first, "the four clues" available to them. The story begins this way:

Bob and Paul had been sawing and hammering all day.
They were building a playhouse.

Step A: Before you tell them what the story is about, and before they have a chance to read these sentences, write the first sentence on the board with blanks replacing *saw* and *hammer*. Then read it to them, saying "blank" and "blank" where the blanks are:

Bob and Paul had been _____ ing and _____ ing all day.

Step B: Now ask them for words that could fit in the blanks. Make a list of their suggestions. They might give you words like *fight, run,* and *sleep.* If they haven't already given you *pound, hammer, saw,* and *build,* add them to the list. (If they don't give you *any* words at first, just start listing some and have them add more as they feel confident.)

Step C: You can now intuitively build their "syntax sense" by asking them whether other words will work: "Will *happy* or *heavy* work in the first blank [where *hammer* will go]? Will *soon* or *silly* go in the second blank [where *saw* will go]?" Ask them to explain why not. ("They sound funny.")

Step D: Now bring in the schematic cueing system by telling them that the story is going to be about two boys who try to build a playhouse. Ask them to choose two /ing/ words from their list that will best fit the story they're going to read. *Have them use their own experiences to justify their choices.* This process can intuitively build their "schematic sense." That is, it can help them see the importance of bringing their prior knowledge to bear on comprehending what they are reading.

Step E: Put the second sentence of the story on the board, and read the two sentences with your students: "Bob and Paul had been *blanking* and *blanking* all day. They were building a playhouse." Ask them which words in the second sentence help them know what will go in the blanks. Have them circle *building* and *playhouse* and tell you why these words help. This can intuitively develop their "semantic sense" by helping them realize the importance of the author's words that surround the "target words."

Step F: To develop their "graphophonic sense," add letter clues to the blanks. (But when you do use graphophonic clues don't always use the first letter of the word.) For example,

Bob and Paul had been s___ ___ing and ___ ___mmering all day.

Ask them again to "guess" what the two words will be in the story.

Step G: Now let them confirm their predictions by reading part or all of the story.

This should give you some idea of the versatility of the *cloze* technique. The blanks that you use depend upon your good judgment. You'll have to ask yourself, What kinds of cues are these particular students ignoring or using the most? If they're using graphophonic cues too much, for example, save these cues for last. If they're using them too little, use them first.

Making the Intuitive Awareness a Conscious One

After you have conducted several lessons using the cloze technique to provide intuitive awareness of the four cueing systems, it is probably a good idea to make your students more conscious of the "four clues" available to them. Research indicates that conscious awareness can enhance reading comprehension and comprehension monitoring (Mosenthal, 1984).

To enhance their awareness, you will need to think of labels that seem to be understandable to the particular students you're working with. When developing syntactic sense, for example, you may want to talk about how some words (like *fight* and *sleep*) "fit" in a blank and some words (like *happy* or *desk*) do not—"because the language sounds funny." So one of the four clues might be brought to their attention with a question: "Does this word fit the way we speak our language?" And a label you might want to use for this cueing system might be the "Fit Your Language Clue."

For the schematic cueing system, you might use questions such as these: "What experiences have *you* had in your life [for example, building a playhouse] that would help you guess a word that fits in the blank? Does the word you're suggesting fit your experience?" And a label for this cueing system might be the "Fit Your Experience Clue."

For the semantic cueing system, we want the students to notice (among other things) the word clues offered by the author, such as *building* and *playhouse*. So your question might be, "What words does the author use that help you know what to fit in the blank?" And your label might be something like "Fit the Author Clue" or "Fit the Other Words Clue."

Finally for the graphophonic cueing system, we can simply ask, "What word fits the letters?" And the label could be "Fit the Letters Clue."

Using Cloze without Blanks

In a normal reading situation, of course, we don't have blanks to fill in. Instead, we have sentences in which one or more of the words are difficult. In Chapter 5 and later chapters, you will be shown classroom episodes in which teachers use the cloze technique without blanks. That is, instead of having a blank, the teacher will have the children *say* "blank" for any word that they're having trouble with. For example, Sandy might fluently substitute "blank" for "leopard" in this sentence: "With a growl the spotted leopard sprang from the tree onto the helpless animal below." When she finishes the sentence, she would then go back and figure out the word by using the four clues. By reading the sentence fluently, she will be more likely to deal with the difficult word in context rather than in isolation.

Research on Cloze Instruction

After summarizing several major studies on the cloze technique as a teaching strategy, Grant (1979) concluded that it was useful for teaching reading at any grade level. Gove (1975) found it useful even in first-grade classrooms. She felt that children at this age were significantly helped in understanding language better. (My guess is that the cloze technique causes students to intuitively examine the cueing systems of language.) Gomberg (1976) discovered that with careful deletion of words, the cloze procedure could be used with older children to help them comprehend the author's purpose. (In other words, she did *not* delete words that helped to *explain* the author's purpose, but she did delete words that, when filled in by the students, would demonstrate their understanding of the author's purpose.)

As I mentioned before, Jongsma (1980) examined numerous research studies and found that whereas cloze is not very effective with vocabulary development, it is often very effective in developing reading comprehension. This makes sense to me; the cloze technique doesn't really concentrate on vocabulary. Instead, it causes students to engage in the process of using all four cueing systems interactively (a process that seems to be a better "definition" of comprehension than, say, 80 percent on "comprehension questions"—see Chapter 11 for more on this).

Jongsma advises us further. Research shows, he says, that serial deletion (such as every fifth word) is effective in *testing* students but not very effective in *teaching* them. It's much better, he emphasizes, to delete according to your teaching purposes.

Proper Deletion of Words

Let me show you what I think both Jongsma and Gomberg are talking about. Suppose your teaching purpose is to get children to use the four cueing systems interactively. You decide to present them with a written paragraph with every fifth word deleted. In order for you to see the significance of this problem, I'll use a paragraph at a college level of understanding. By deleting every fifth word in this paragraph, you would end up deleting words that are really quite necessary for schemata stimulation. You also would end up deleting trivial signal words such as *a, that,* and *to.*

> Generally speaking, then, the _____ needs must be at _____ partially met before the _____ needs of self-actualization and _____ understanding will emerge. In _____ practical sense, this means _____ the teacher who ignores _____ lower needs will find _____ rather difficult to motivate _____ to learn something just _____ satisfy his intellectual curiosity _____ to satisfy his desire _____ become a more skilled _____ fulfilled person.

To activate students' schemata and to instigate their use of the four cueing systems more thoroughly, the following would be a better form of deletion:

> Generally speaking, then, the "lower" needs must be at least partially met before the _____ needs of self-actualization and intellectual understanding will emerge. In a practical sense, this means that the teacher who ignores Bobby's _____ needs will find it rather d __ __ __ __ __ __ __ __ to motivate him to learn something just to satisfy his _____ curiosity or to _____ his desire to become a more sk __ __ __ __d and fulfilled person.

As you probably discovered, the second set of deletions is more suitable for the teacher's purpose of stimulating the use of all four cueing systems. Perhaps the most important cueing system not to ignore when establishing your deletions is the schematic one. To increase the fluency of their reading, children need to be able to predict what is coming next. This is too difficult for some children if the words are deleted too soon. Take this deletion, for example: The man _____ into the swift flowing river. For an older student this would pose no problem. But for a younger one, or one having difficulty with reading, the blank comes too soon. For this kind of student you would want to start with a sentence like this: The man jumped into the swift flowing _____. Thus, you would provide enough clues to enable him to engage in fluent, interactive reading.

FLUENCY THROUGH EASY, CHORAL, ECHO, MODELED, AND REPEATED READING

We've talked about three ways of increasing the amount of fluent and interactive reading: building children's schemata for a selection of text, using predictable materials such as patterned books and children's own writing, and using the cloze technique. All of these procedures are excellent, but there are five others that you should add to your repertoire.

Easy Reading

Probably the most effective of all techniques is that of providing an abundant number of books that are easy to read. I'm going to talk about this in Chapter 9 on teaching reading through literature, but for now, let me just mention what research shows about this (which will be obvious to you)—namely, that having children read lots of easy books increases their fluency. Unfortunately, children in many classrooms are lucky to get as much as a half hour a week reading "extended text" (books, long stories, articles). And, as you know, at home most children spend 30 hours or more watching TV rather than reading. Well, enough of that for now. Let me just add a quote from S. Jay Samuels, a well-known researcher in education. Samuels wrote an article in the April 1988 edition of *The Reading Teacher* called "Decoding and automaticity: Helping poor readers become automatic at word recognition." Dr. Samuels has been arguing for many years that "the only way to become a fluent reader is by becoming automatic at decoding." But contrary to what some think he advocates today (lots of phonics), the main point of his article is this: "To develop fluent reading skills in poor readers, get them to read as many enjoyable, easy to read books as possible, so that they will become automatic at *contextual* reading." (The italics in that quote were mine, I'll confess, but otherwise it was all Samuels.)

Choral and Echo Reading

I'm quite sure that choral and echo reading have been around for hundreds of years, but research on these techniques has been sparse. Back in 1968, Mary Neville reported on her findings that both techniques were useful in increasing fluency and comprehension with early readers. Many teachers I've worked with also find that these techniques work well with older remedial readers. With choral reading, of course, the children read out loud together, sometimes breaking into small groups or even soloing on occasion. Any type of choral reading has the advantage of taking the pressure off the reader, since there's a sense of security in numbers—and also a chance to learn from others. Some teachers don't like working with large groups of children for choral reading, so instead they have a pair of children read out loud at the same time, thus providing each of them with a greater sense of security.

With echo reading the teacher or other leader reads a sentence or more, and the rest of the group repeats what has been read, using as close to the same intonation as possible. The advantage of this approach is that the children hear the correct words and intonation before they have to read it themselves. Echo reading is an excellent way of building confidence and fluency. Simply have the children repeat each sentence you read, following along both times with their own copy—first when you say it and then when they say it. Let them point with their fingers as they follow along. (More experienced readers can repeat an entire paragraph.) After the children have repeated a sentence as a group, allow the eager ones to repeat it solo.

Modeled Reading

For those who don't wish to try either echo or choral reading, an even simpler procedure can be used with moderate results. In Smith's study (1979), she found that after only six days a simple modeling tactic improved the children's oral reading rate and decreased their errors. What was this tactic? Merely reading aloud the first 100 words or so of each reading selection that she introduced.

Let me hasten to add that many modeling tactics are more complicated than this one, and I'll be talking a lot about these in the next chapter. More sophisticated modeling includes demonstrating how to use the four cueing systems, how to read for purpose, how to figure out the author's "deep structure," and so on. But the type of simpler modeling that I've been describing is still quite effective. Probably one of the reasons it works so well is the reason given by Allington: "Poor readers primarily hear other poor readers in their reading group and rarely have a fluent reading model to emulate. The teacher's modeling, which is probably accompanied by more emphasis on fluency . . . seems to produce positive change in oral reading" (1983, p. 560).

Repeated Readings

You really should try "repeated readings" as well, if you haven't already done so. With this technique the student or small group rereads a short, meaningful passage until reaching a high level of fluency—smooth, expressive language that sounds as though the author were doing the talking. When the student or small group has been reasonably successful, it's time to move on to a new selection. But it's a good idea to frequently send a copy home for the students to read to their parents.

Samuels (1979) reports that an experimental group who tried a similar technique as an adjunct to regular instruction made significantly greater gains in both comprehension and speed, compared to a control group who did not use the technique. There has been a considerable amount of experimentation with the repeated reading method. In an earlier study Dahl and Samuels (1974) found that this method produced higher achievement than a method that focused on developing automatic word recognition. To put it more starkly: A fluency emphasis won out over a word emphasis.

Not that I'm against occasional "word emphasis" instruction. In fact, I hope you won't be too shocked when you get to Chapters 6 and 7 and I start talking about the importance of vocabulary and phonics instruction. I'm merely pointing out to you here that fluency and interactive reading are better things to emphasize, over all, than vocabulary and phonics. You see, one of the problems is this: "A lack of fluency is mistakenly viewed as simply symptomatic of poor reading, suggesting that the poor reader is inefficient in word recognition or graphophonic analysis. . . . This interpretation . . . often leads to further instruction in letters, sounds, or words in isolation, in the mistaken belief that more attention to this area will result in improved reading" (Allington, 1983). On the contrary, it often leads to word-by-word reading and an attitude of "I'm a poor reader," and this we want to avoid at all costs.

In a more recent study, Dowhower (1987) found that repeated readings resulted in "significant improvement" in reading rate, accuracy, comprehension, and prosodic reading (reading in meaningful phrases) of second-graders. The average reading rate doubled, word recognition accuracy increased from 89 percent to 95 percent, and the percentage of comprehension questions answered correctly rose from 66 percent to 81 percent. And this was after practicing repeated readings with only six different stories. The encouraging thing here was Dowhower's other finding that the reading gains carried over to new but similar selections. That is, the kids read better even with selections on which they had not done repeated readings.

Koskinen and Blum (1987) have developed a very practical classroom strategy for using repeated readings. With most approaches the students are expected to use a timing device and to get their reading rate up to 100 words per minute, a process that becomes a little difficult for, say, second-graders. With Koskinen and Blum's plan no timing devices are needed. Children work in pairs in this manner:

1. Partners each choose a different 50- to 75-word selection from their instructional materials and read their selections silently to themselves.
2. One child reads to his partner three times. After each reading, he rates himself on an evaluation form. After the second and third time, both the reader and the listener orally describe the improvement the reader has made on the first reading. They also show this improvement on a simple evaluation form.
3. Now, after the third reading, the partners switch roles from reader to listener and vice versa.

This procedure, according to Koskinen and Blum, takes only a brief introduction and modeling before the students can use it without help from the teacher.

During the modeling phase the teacher shows the students what repeated reading is all about, how to select material that is easy enough to read, how to listen, and how to make positive comments. The teacher usually works with one small group at a time and provides supervised practice. The next time the students do it on their own.

The reader's evaluation form has the question, "How well did you read?" followed by smiling or frowning faces and the related words, *fantastic, good, fair, not so good, terrible.*

The listener's evaluation form (used after the second and third readings only) has the question, "How did your partner's reading get better? Smoother?

_____ Knew more words? _____ More expression? _____ Tell your partner one thing better about his or her reading."

The usual time for this procedure is about 15 to 20 minutes. Seems worth a try. What do you think?

SUMMARY OF MAIN IDEAS

☐ When teachers correct each "mistake" that children make as they read, even when their miscues are completely in line with the author's meaning, it can have a negative influence on children's growth in comprehension.

☐ To *teach* comprehension instead of merely testing memory, the teacher must frequently guide children before and during the time they engage in silent reading. Discussing a selection *only* after they have finished reading it is not nearly as effective.

☐ By using reading materials with predictable language, teachers can provide children with practice in fluent, meaningful reading, thus helping them to develop an accurate concept of the reading process.

☐ There are numerous ways of encouraging fluent interactive reading, such as easy reading, the cloze technique, choral reading, echo reading, teacher modeling, repeated readings, and commenting specifically on children's "speechlike," meaningful renditions of text.

☐ Schemata enhancement before children read an assigned story is necessary for good fluency and comprehension. Vocabulary discussion alone is insufficient.

☐ Inferential thinking is an essential ingredient of reading comprehension. To be a fluent reader, one has to be an inferential reader. Using schemata enhancement techniques is one way of providing children with practice in inferential reading.

APPLICATION EXPERIENCES FOR THE TEACHER EDUCATION CLASS

A. *What's Your Opinion?* Discuss why you agree or disagree with the following opinions. Use both the textbook and your own experiences to justify your own opinion.

1. Reading is much more a process than a product.
2. Teachers should not correct every reading error a child makes. This could lead to a wrong concept of reading.
3. The best time to ask questions of children is after they have finished reading a selection. Otherwise, continuity and comprehension will suffer.
4. Predictable materials may improve children's fluency, but they don't really help children read better. The children are not reading; they're just memorizing.
5. The cloze technique actually teaches children to make wild guesses rather than to use the four cueing systems.
6. It's impossible to read more than three sentences with understanding without relying on inferential thinking.
7. Reading comprehension is based to a large extent on factors like early literacy and language acquisition.
8. One-cued reading can be avoided.

B. *Miscue Analysis:* Study Christopher's miscues and decide what cueing systems are most important to him. What might his concept of reading be? What influences might have caused him to have this concept? What are some things you would do to help change his concept? (Circled words are omissions.)

Pete cut it down. They loaded it on ~~to~~ the roof of the car and drove home. When they *(loaned)*

got home Cathy's tree was too big to go through the door. They had to cut ~~about~~ a *(thruff)*

foot off the bottom.* *(of)* *(bottle)*

C. *Using the Cloze Technique:* With one or more partners, rewrite the previous story text as the author wrote it, but use blanks in order to encourage each of the four cueing systems. Compare your use of the cloze technique with others in the class. Explain why you put the blanks where you did.

D. Find several patterned picture books in the library and bring them to class. In a small group compare with others to determine which books you feel would be appropriate for (1) developing fluency, (2) providing opportunities for predicting and confirming, and (3) developing language.

---

*Text by Colin Dunkeld, Portland Informal Reading Inventory, Form P, Unpublished Manuscript, School of Education, Portland State University.

FIELD EXPERIENCES IN THE ELEMENTARY SCHOOL CLASSROOM

1. Use the cloze technique in the same way called for in Application Experience C. Either use the selection you already prepared or prepare another selection more appropriate for the children you are working with. For each blank have the children tell you why they wish to fill it in the way they do.

2. Select a patterned picture book and try out some of the procedures discussed on page 127. Discuss your results with your class.

3. Write a brief report on the "instructional constraints" on reading comprehension that you notice in the classroom in which you are assisting. If you were in charge of the class, which of these constraints might you reasonably change? Refer to pages 111–114 for assistance.

4. With a small group of children, compare these three techniques: repeated readings, choral reading, and echo reading.

REFERENCES AND SUGGESTED READING

Allington, L. (1983). Fluency: The neglected reading goal. *The Reading Teacher, 36,* 556–561.

Beck, I. L., McKeown, M. G., & McCaslin, E. S. (1981). Does reading make sense? Problems of early readers. *The Reading Teacher, 37,* 116–121.

Bridge, C. (1979). Predictable materials for beginning readers. *Language Arts, 56,* 503–507.

Carr, K. S. (1983). The importance of inference

skills in the primary grades. *The Reading Teacher, 36,* 518–522.

Collins, J. (1982). Discourse style, classroom interaction, and differential treatment. *Journal of Reading Behavior, 14,* 326–341.

Crafton, L. K. (1982). Comprehension before, during, and after reading. *The Reading Teacher, 36,* 293–297.

Dahl, P. R., & Samuels, S. J. (1974). A mastery based experimental program for teaching poor readers high speed word recognition skills. Unpublished paper, University of Minneapolis.

Dasch, A. (1983). Aligning basal reader instruction with cognitive stage theory. *The Reading Teacher, 36,* 428–434.

Dehn, N. (1984). An AI perspective on reading comprehension. In J. Flood (Ed.), *Understanding reading comprehension* (pp. 82–100). Newark, DE: International Reading Association.

Dowhower, S. L. (1987). Effects of repeated reading on second-grade transitional readers' fluency and comprehension. *Reading Research Quarterly 22,* 389–406.

Duffy, G. G., Roehler, L. R., & Mason, J. (1983). *Comprehension instruction: Perspectives and suggestions.* New York: Longman.

Durkin, D. (1978–79). Reading comprehension instruction. *Reading Research Quarterly, 14,* 495–527.

Durkin, D. (1984). Is there a match between what elementary teachers do and what basal manuals recommend? *The Reading Teacher, 37,* 734–744.

Farr, R., & Carey, R. F. (1986). *Reading: What can be measured?* Newark, DE: International Reading Association.

Farrar, M. T. (1983). Another look at oral questions for comprehension. *The Reading Teacher, 36,* 370–374.

Gomberg, A. W. (1976). Freeing children to take a chance. *The Reading Teacher, 29,* 455–457.

Gove, M. K. (1975). Using the cloze procedure in a first grade classroom. *The Reading Teacher, 29,* 36–38.

Grant, P. L. (1979). The cloze procedure as an instructional device. *Journal of Reading, 22,* 699–705.

Guthrie, J. T. (1983). Children's reason for success and reading. *The Reading Teacher, 36,* 293–297.

Hansen, J. (1981). An inferential comprehension strategy for use with primary grade children. *The Reading Teacher, 34,* 665–669.

Hansen, J., & Pearson, P. D. (1980). The effects of interference training and practice on young children's comprehension (Technical Report No. 66). Urbana: Center for the Study of Reading, University of Illinois.

Harste, J. C., & Carey, R. F. (1984). Classrooms, constraints and the language process. In J. Flood (Ed.), *Promoting reading comprehension* (pp. 30–47). Newark, DE: International Reading Association.

Holmes, B. C. (1983). A confirmation strategy for improving poor readers' ability to answer inferential questions. *The Reading Teacher, 37,* 144–148.

Jongsma, E. A. (1980). Cloze instruction research: A second look. Newark, DE: International Reading Association.

Kellogg, D. H. (1971). An investigation of the effect of the science curriculum . . . on gains in reading readiness. Unpublished dissertation, University of Oklahoma.

Koskinen, P. S., & Blum, I. H. (1987). Paired repeated reading: A classroom strategy for developing fluent reading. *The Reading Teacher, 40,* 70–75.

Lee, G. (1982). Playing about a story: Its impact on comprehension. *The Reading Teacher, 36,* 52–55.

Lipson, M. Y. (1984). Some unexpected issues in prior knowledge and comprehension. *The Reading Teacher, 37,* 760–764.

Louritzen, C. (1982). A modification of repeated readings for group instruction. *The Reading Teacher, 35,* 456–458.

Manna, A. L. (1984). Making language come alive through reading plays. *The Reading Teacher, 37,* 712–717.

Marshall, N. (1984). Discourse analysis as a guide for informal assessment of comprehension. In J. Flood (Ed.), *Promoting reading comprehension* (pp. 79–96). Newark, DE: International Reading Association.

Miller, G. M., & Mason, G. E. (1983). Dramatic

improvisation: Risk-free role playing for improving reading performance. *The Reading Teacher, 37,* 128–131.

Mosenthal, P. (1984). Reading comprehension research from a classroom perspective. In J. Flood (Ed.), *Promoting reading comprehension* (pp. 16–29). Newark, DE: International Reading Association.

Neville, M. H. (1968). Effects of oral and echoic responses in beginning reading. *Journal of Educational Psychology, 59,* 362–369.

Paris, S. G., & Lindauer, B. K. (1976). The role of inference in children's comprehension and memory for sentences. *Child Development, 8,* 217–227.

Pearson, P. D. (1985). Changing the face of reading comprehension instruction. *The Reading Teacher, 38,* 724–738.

Pikulski, J. J. (1983). Questions and answers. *The Reading Teacher, 37,* 111–112.

Rowe, M. B. (1978). Wait, wait, wait . . . *School Science and Mathematics, 78,* 207–216.

Rumelhart, D. E. (1984). Understanding understanding. In J. Flood (Ed.), *Understanding reading comprehension* (pp. 1–20). Newark, DE: International Reading Association.

Samuels, S. J. (1979). The method of repeated readings. *The Reading Teacher, 32,* 403–408.

Samuels, S. J. (1988). Decoding and automaticity: Helping poor readers become automatic at word recognition. *The Reading Teacher, 41,* 756–61.

Shake, M. C., & Allington, R. L. (1985). Where do teachers' questions come from? *The Reading Teacher, 38,* 432–439.

Silvaroli, N. J. (1982). *Classroom reading inventory,* 4th ed. Dubuque, IA: Wm. C. Brown.

Smith, F. (1979). *Reading without nonsense.* New York: Teachers College Press.

Swaby, B. (1982). Varying the ways you teach reading with basal stories. *The Reading Teacher, 35,* 676–680.

Tompkins, G. E., & Webeler, M. B. (1983). What will happen next? Using predictable books with young children. *The Reading Teacher, 36,* 498–502.

Wilson, C. R. (1983). Teaching reading comprehension by connecting the known to the new. *The Reading Teacher, 36,* 382–390.

Wittrock, M. C. (1983). Generative reading comprehension. Ginn Occasional Papers. Lexington: Ginn.

Comprehension: Developing the Thoughtful Inferential Reader

CHAPTER PREVIEW

In Chapter 4, I reminded you of the difference between testing comprehension and teaching comprehension. One of the ways we can actually teach comprehension is to arrange learning situations (such as cloze passages, patterned books, and repeated readings) that provide practice in fluent, meaningful, and languagelike reading. In this chapter, you and I will be discussing other approaches toward the development of children's skill in comprehending what they read. I'll ask you to examine four questioning strategies that will encourage thoughtful inferential reading. I'll also ask you to think about using writing activities that can lead to better reading comprehension. Above all, I'd like to show you the importance of *modeling* thoughtful inferential reading for your students.

Set yourself to understand whatever you see or read. To join thinking with reading is one of the first maxims.

—Isaac Taylor

Children will not demonstrate the ability to think if they do not believe that thinking in the particular circumstances is possible or permissible for them.

—Frank Smith

The learning process is simply a matter of progressing from cocksure ignorance to thoughtful uncertainty.

—Esar

READING AS A THOUGHTFUL ACT OF COMMUNICATION

Teaching children to read for meaning, with languagelike fluency, might be considered metaphorically the "first step." But where do we go from there? If reading is a communication act, then it's also bound to be a thinking act. I'm not referring to the miniature thoughts we have each time we predict what word is coming next—as important as these thoughts are. I'm referring more to the thinking required to determine the deeper meanings of an author: What's the big idea he's trying to get across in this article? What is she trying to make me feel about the main character in this story—and do I really care about that character? We do this kind of thinking, you know, when we converse with someone—especially someone we respect or care about, or someone we're eager to "get to know better" (translate: "I wonder if this person is worth having coffee with."). We do wonder what his main point is—and sometimes we try very hard to figure it out. And we do wonder what he's trying to make us feel about him (and again whether we really care).

When it comes to reading, though, we often forget that we're supposed to be communicating with someone. We've been so programmed by our school experiences that it may not occur to us to communicate with *this* kind of person—an author. After all, when we were in school, our goal was to "cover the pages." You know, count the pages, look at the clock, yearn for the minutes and words to zip by. Schools tend to do this, don't they? Train us for "getting things over with" rather than educate us for enjoying the process of learning. But not all schools and not all teachers. I'm sure you've known a few (or hopefully many) who have turned you on to learning. I know I have, and I'm very grateful to them. I'm particularly grateful to them for "making me think." I've learned that once this kind of thing becomes a habit, it becomes a very enjoyable pastime. (It might even help us survive; at least I suspect that it does.)

So what does all this have to do with reading instruction? Well, reading is, after all, a big part of schooling, and probably will always be so in spite of computers and television. (Text is about the most efficient, accessible, and inexpensive form of communication that humankind has come up with.) If ever there was an opportunity for teachers to have an impact on students' lives, it certainly exists through reading—the books we ask them to read, of course, but even more importantly, the ideas that we discuss with them before, while, and after they read. And if schooling is ever going to be more than mere training (often of the wrong type), then those who teach reading have a real opportunity—to promote thinking, to promote communication in depth.

QUESTION STRATEGY ONE: DIRECTED READING-THINKING ACTIVITY

How to help children think inferentially and to read between the lines is a major concern of the teacher who understands the interactive nature of reading. There are a variety of ways to improve children's inferential thinking, one of which we discussed in the last chapter—namely, the enhancement of their background schemata before they are asked to read. Another way is to experience a reading selection *with* them: probing their thoughts about what they're reading, asking questions that stimulate further thinking, encouraging their insights. In a moment we'll watch a teacher who is using a venerable method labeled by Stauffer (1975) as "Directed Reading-Thinking Activity" (DRTA). In this method of guiding children's reading, children are first asked to predict what each page or two is going to be about. Second, they're directed to read silently to check on their predictions. And third, they're asked to prove their interpretations of what the author said.

> In a nutshell, with the DRTA method the teacher asks, in a variety of ways, of course, "What do you think? . . . Why do you think so? . . . Can you prove it?"

Several studies have shown that the DRTA method results in higher levels of comprehension than those methods that only test the children's memory at the end of their reading. One probable reason for this success? The DRTA method recognizes that each child differs—something that a mere testing approach to comprehension does not. "Children differ not only in motivation, attitude, and purpose but in the ability to grasp, assimilate, retain, and use information as well" (Stauffer, 1975, p. 3). Because of these differences, teachers shouldn't expect all children to give the same answers to the same questions (such as the ones shown as examples in the teacher's manual). Teachers who use the DRTA method properly don't even ask the same question of each child. Their interaction with children is dynamic, rather than a static relationship based on expected answers listed in a teacher's guide. Let's watch a teacher and her second-graders engaged in a DRTA:

MAGIC DOORS*

Johnny's mother asked him to go to the big new store at the corner. His little brother Howie said, "I want to go too! I want to go too! I'll be good."

So Johnny took his little brother to the big new store. There were two big doors. One door had the word IN on it. The other door had the word OUT.

Johnny and Howie went to the IN door. Whish! The door opened all by itself! Howie said, "Look at that. It's magic!"

"You are silly!" said Johnny. "It isn't magic. The new doors work by electricity."

MRS. S: [before the children read] Look at the title of this story and tell us what you think the story is going to be about.

JACKIE: Maybe about some doors that open by magic when you say "Open Sesame," and inside the doors you find gold and jewelry and things like that.

MRS. S: That's an interesting idea, Jackie. What makes you say that?

JACKIE: Well, I remember this story my daddy read to me once, and that's what happened.

MRS. S: All right. Who has another idea?

BONNIE: I think it's going to be about some doors in a closet that lead into another land with witches and elves and things.

MRS. S: Well, that sounds possible. Why do you think your idea is right?

BONNIE: Umm, well, I heard a story like that once.

MRS. S: I'll bet you did. There's a story like that called "The Lion, the Witch, and the Wardrobe."

BONNIE: Yeah, maybe that's the one.

MRS. S: Turn the page and look at the picture on the next page. Maybe that will give you another idea of what this story is going to be about.

DAVID: Oooh, I know.

MRS. S: David?

DAVID: It's a picture of a supermarket. I'll bet the magic doors are, you know, those doors that open all by themselves.

MRS. S: Do you see anything else in the picture that makes you think that David is right?

SANDRA: There's a lady walking through one of the doors and she's not pushing on it or anything.

MRS. S: Yes, you did some careful looking, Sandra.

RONALD: Maybe she already pushed the door and it's just staying open for a while.

---

*Bank Street College of Education, *Uptown, Downtown*, rev. ed. (New York: Macmillan, 1972). Reprinted by permission of the publisher.

MRS. S: Yes, that's quite possible, Ronald. Well, why don't you all read the first two pages to yourself, and see if you can find out why the author called the story "Magic Doors."

MRS. S: [two minutes later] Were you right, Jackie? Are they going to find gold and jewelry behind those magic doors?

JACKIE: [shaking her head] No, but they'll find ice cream.

MRS. S: [laughing] How do you know?

JACKIE: Because those doors go inside a supermarket, and that's where we buy our ice cream.

MRS. S: You can tell it's going to be a supermarket by the picture. Is that how you knew?

JACKIE: Yes.

MRS. S: Can you find something the author tells you that makes you sure?

JACKIE: [looking] Oh, here it is. It says, "One door had the word IN on it. The other door had the word OUT."

MRS. S: Good. Can you find another clue from the author, Bonnie?

BONNIE: [long hesitation]

MRS. S: What about the first sentence. Why don't you read it to us.

BONNIE: [reading] "Johnny's mother asked him to go to the big new store at the corner."

MRS. S: Does that sentence give you an idea of where Johnny will be going?

BONNIE: [smiles] To the grocery store.

MRS. S: Why do you say that?

BONNIE: Because that's where my mother always wants me to go.

MRS. S: Good. You used your own experience to help you think about this, didn't you?

BONNIE: Yes.

MRS. S: Yes. Let's see . . . David? Why don't you tell us what the magic doors were.

DAVID: [proudly] Just what I said. They're doors that open by themselves.

MRS. S: You were sure right, David. But what really makes the doors open? Is it magic, Ronald?

RONALD: No. It's an electric motor or something.

MRS. S: Can you find a sentence that proves it?

RONALD: The last sentence says, "The new doors work by electricity."

MRS. S: But how in the world did you read that big word?

RONALD: [smiles] I thought it was *energy* the first time. But then I saw it was *electricity*.

MRS. S: How did you know it wasn't something like *electronically*?

RONALD: [says nothing and smiles]

MRS. S: Suppose I read the last sentence this way: "The new doors work by electronically."

RONALD: [laughs] That sounds funny!

MRS. S: You're right, it does. But how did you know it was *electricity* and not . . . *energy*?

RONALD: [shrugs] I don't know.

JACKIE: I know. Because you can see the word *city* at the end of it.

MRS. S: Good, Jackie. What else can you see that makes you sure it's *electricity* and not *energy*?

JACKIE: [studies page but makes no response]

MRS. S: What two letters does *electricity* start with?

JACKIE: It starts with *e-l.*

MRS. S: And what would *energy* start with?

JACKIE: With *e-n.*

MRS. S: Yes, that's right. So, David, do you agree with Ronnie? Do you think that *electricity* makes sense in that last sentence?

DAVID: [smiling] Sure. I know it's electricity. It's not magic.

MRS. S: [nods and smiles] So now before you read the next two pages, what do you think will happen to Johnny and Howie in the big new store?

As you watch Mrs. Stineberg, you notice that she doesn't constantly refer to her teacher's guide as she leads the children through the selection. Not that she hasn't studied it before the discussion; she has, in order to reread the story, the recommended questions, and the teaching suggestions. But she doesn't follow it slavishly as she works with the children. Instead she interacts with each child in such a way that she accomplishes several teaching objectives:

She gets the children to make hypotheses and predictions, to read silently to confirm or disconfirm them, and to prove their ideas—by reading orally, by remembering what they read, or by relating the text to their own experiences.

She keeps the children focused on reading as a thinking and communication act rather than strictly a decoding act.

She prepares them for the selection by enhancing their schemata. She does not omit the crucial "background step."

She responds to them humanly, with interest, rather than mechanically with prepackaged questions. Thus, she models reading as a learning experience rather than one of coming up with "right" answers for the teacher.

She encourages them to use intuitively all four cueing systems: schematic, syntactic, semantic, and graphophonic.

She guides them toward reading inferentially rather than merely literally. She considers filling in the author's "empty slots" more important than reading every single word, letter-perfect.

She teaches comprehension rather than merely testing memory.

DRTA Update

The DRTA (directed reading-thinking activity) approach to comprehension building has been around in various forms for many years. In the 1970s and early 1980s, researchers at the Center for the Study of Reading at the University of

Illinois came up with a new version of DRTA. Their version was a result of their attempt to determine the best way of getting children to think more inferentially as they read. According to Pearson (1985), certain practices proved to be the most helpful. Let me summarize them for you:

1. Ask children to make several predictions before the selection is read. For example, "What do you think this will be about?" "What will happen in this story?" "What might you learn from this article?"
2. Encourage children to use their prior knowledge to make their predictions, and *explain why it is important for them to do this.*
3. Follow a four-step sequence for each inference question (usually asked after the students have read a page or two):
    a. Ask the inferential question (a question that requires them to read between the lines).
    b. Determine the answer together (and model this process with them).
    c. Help them find clues in the text to support the inference. (Let them prove their answer.)
    d. SHOW THEM HOW TO MOVE FROM THE CLUES TO THE AN-SWER. (Don't assume they will necessarily make that transfer by themselves).
4. Move gradually from modeling this four-step process to guided practice and then on to independent practice.

Nessel (1987) has a somewhat different adaptation of the DRTA approach. Although she agrees with Pearson about the importance of encouraging children to use their prior knowledge, she warns teachers not to start a lesson in the following fashion: "Have you ever [done such and such]?" This, she claims (and I'll vouch for this from my own experience), will cause children to switch their interest from reading to the telling of anecdotes. (A similar thing happens with adults—have you noticed?) It's better, she advises, to use the following steps when discussing fiction:

1. Determine a few major "turning points" in a story.
2. Stop at each of these points and ask the children what they think will happen.
3. Let them give evidence for their predictions: "What have you experienced or read in this story that makes you think so?"
4. After they've read further, have them evaluate their earlier predictions and give their reasons for keeping or changing them.

As you probably noticed, the three DRTA approaches discussed in this section—Stauffer's, Pearson's, and Nessel's—have a lot in common. They all emphasize the importance of predictions before reading, the use of personal schemata or text information to justify predictions or statements, and the importance of having children get actively involved by proving their predictions or statements. It's no wonder that this type of strategy leads to greater involvement and comprehension.

QUESTION STRATEGY TWO:
INTERACTIVE-THINKING OPERATIONS (ITO)

Since teachers ask literal questions five times as often as inferential questions, it is not surprising that children are not as good at answering questions which require inferences as their developmental and cognitive potential would indicate. (McIntosh, 1985, pp. 758–759)

The complex skill we're calling *reading comprehension* is really quite similar to listening comprehension. When a good listener listens, he concentrates not so much on the sounds as on the word order (syntax) and the speaker's implied meanings (semantics). But in doing this, he must rely heavily on the schemata he has developed through past experiences. Yet reading comprehension is more difficult than listening comprehension. For one thing, the written symbols stand in the way, and for another thing, the listener gets to watch the speaker's facial expressions and body movements—something the reader is deprived of.

Tiny Subskills versus Broad Interacting Operations

Although we educators have been sensible enough *not* to create long lists of tiny subskills related to listening comprehension, we have not been able to resist the temptation with reading. The thinking goes something like this: Since reading is a difficult skill for children to learn, let's make it easier by breaking it into sub-skills. And let's break those into even tinier subskills. Then, as children master each of them, it will be like building a reading castle: With each new brick (sub-skill) the castle will get stronger and stronger; the reading will get better and better.

A nice thought, but alas, it doesn't work that way with reading any more than it would with listening or speaking. No parent I know attempts to teach his child oral language that way. In fact, that method doesn't even work with some-thing like tennis. You could have Steffi Graf or Boris Becker show your students how to hold the racquet, how to rotate the wrist, how to hold the ball for a serve, and so on. Then you could have them test the kids on how well they can do each of the dozens of so-called subskills. And finally, you could provide them with a court and watch them play. But don't expect much. They would need to play tennis to learn how to play tennis, just as they have to read books to learn how to read books. A list of subskills looks impressive in school-district curriculum guides and in publishers' scope and sequence charts, but its deceptive simplicity hides the fact that reading is a complex, interactive process.

Here's a list of four broad kinds of thinking operations with a partial list of fairly broad subskills listed under each:

    A. Literal-thinking operations
        1. Translating text into mental images
        2. Following the sequence of events, ideas, or cause and effect
        3. Recollecting significant details
    B. Inferential-thinking operations
        1. Making predictions
        2. Reading between the lines
        3. Recognizing main ideas
    C. Critical-thinking operations
        1. Distinguishing factual from nonfactual
        2. Detecting author bias
        3. Evaluating according to criteria
    D. Creative-thinking operations
        1. Inventing flexible alternatives to author's or character's ideas
        2. Applying prior knowledge to a new situation
        3. Translating ideas read about into an artistic medium

Now, there's nothing wrong with coming up with a list of broad thinking operations or processes like those listed above. Such a list, for example, can be very handy in helping a teacher decide whether she's asking too many of one type of question and too few of another. The sad part, though, is that this list is often subdivided into dozens of even smaller "skills" by school districts or basal reader publishers—skills such as "recognizing that a topic is not the main idea of a selection." Then, even worse, children are made to spend enormous amounts of time filling out worksheets and taking tests related to these isolated bits of information called *subskills*.

You see, there is very little—if any—evidence that reading is a set of tiny subskills (Downing, 1982). The subskills have been invented through logic, but they haven't been verified by experimental research. No one, to my knowledge, has been able to produce a list of subskills, teach them, and then demonstrate that this approach produces better readers than those students who "merely" spend their time reading whole text.

The important thing is not a list of subskills itself, but rather how such a list is used. Although it might be used as a guide for selecting workbooks and tests for children, the resulting teaching procedures have doubtful value. I have yet to find a body of research that demonstrates that isolated tests and workbook exercises on single isolated subskills will cause children to read better. On the other hand, there does seem to be evidence that when teachers teach comprehension in an integrated, interactive way, with an emphasis on inferential thinking and the interaction of the four cueing systems, comprehension can be improved (Baker & Brown, 1984; Carr, 1983; Hansen, 1984; Hansen & Pearson, 1980).

As Wilson (1983) points out, comprehension seems less a set of isolated subskills than a process of connecting text information to the information stored in the reader's head. For the reader to make this connection, he has to confront a set of problems, such as decoding a strangely spelled word like *pseudoephedrine*, or seeing a word like *home* in a verb slot rather than a noun slot, as in "'Home it!' the catcher screamed to the pitcher." If there *are* separate subskills involved in reading (and right now we really don't know), they're likely to be thinking or problem-solving operations that are constantly changing and interacting as we confront the text and try to make sense out of it.

The ITO Approach in Action

In the following episode, you'll see how a teacher can encourage through her questions the interaction of such problem-solving operations. This teacher is working with a small group of fourth-graders who are going to read a short article about a snowstorm that hit New York City. You'll want to read the article so you can see how she prepares them for it and guides them through it, teaching comprehension as she goes rather than merely testing later for memory:

In 1888 a terrible snowstorm hit New York City. Tall poles snapped, and electric wires fell into the street. People were killed by electric shock. Some were killed by the falling poles. And nearly a thousand died in the fires that broke out.

The mayor saw that he must do something to make his city a safe place to live. He asked electricians to put electric wires safely underground. Then the mayor sent men out to take down the wooden poles.

These electric wires were the beginning of America's amazing underground city in New York. Today the narrow streets and the sidewalks hide more than four million miles of wire. In some places there are so many wires and pipes that two fingers cannot be pushed between them.*

*From page 250 of "Air Pudding and Wind Sauce," *Keys to Reading* (Oklahoma City, OK: Economy Company, 1972), adapted from "Amazing Underground City," by Edward Hymoff (*Boy's Life*, August 1963).

TEACHER: [before the children read] Do you know what kinds of things you can find underneath the streets here in New York City?

BARBARA: Oh, I know. Subways!

TEACHER: That's right. Can anyone think of something else you might find underneath the streets? [Operation D$_2$]

DONALD: There are all kinds of pipes under the streets. I know, because my dad told me. And they're full of water.

JANET: [sheepishly] Somebody told me there's monsters under there.

TEACHER: Well, I hope that's not true.

BILL: Aren't there wires and things like that down there?

TEACHER: Yes, there are over four million miles of wire under our streets. That's enough wire to go around the world over 160 times!

KEN: Wow!

TEACHER: Do you know why that wire is there?

KEN: It's for sending messages?

BILL: Naw, it's for telephones.

TEACHER: What do you think it's for, Janet? [Operation B$_1$]

JANET: Electricity.

BARBARA: Yeah, electricity.

TEACHER: Well, I'll tell you what. I'd like you to find out why that wire was put down there in the first place. Read the article to yourself and then let's stop and talk about it.

TEACHER: [several moments later] Well, now you know why they put the wire under the streets. What do you think it looks like under the streets? Can you get a picture in your mind? [Operation A$_1$]

BILL: I think it looks like spaghetti.

TEACHER: [joins in the laughter] You may be right, Bill. What do you think it looks like, Barbara?

BARBARA: I don't know, but I know it doesn't look like spaghetti.

TEACHER: Who can find a sentence on this page that tells what it looks like? [Operation A$_3$]

KEN: Oh, I know. It's the last sentence. It says, "In some places there are so many wires and pipes that two fingers cannot be pushed between them."

TEACHER: Yes, and maybe that's why Bill said it must look like spaghetti down there. [Operation A$_1$]

BILL: Yeah, like a whole bunch of spaghetti all squished together.

TEACHER: Would it be like uncooked spaghetti that comes out of the box all straight, or would it be like cooked spaghetti that's all piled up on your plate? [Operation A$_1$]

JANET: Oh, I know. It would be like uncooked spaghetti when it comes out of the box.

TEACHER: [nodding] Why do you think so, Janet?

JANET: Because that's what they do with wires and pipes.

TEACHER: They lay them out straight?

JANET: Yes.

TEACHER: Have you seen people do it that way?

JANET: Yes, that's the way they do it. They don't bunch it all up like cooked spaghetti.

TEACHER: [laughing] I'm sure you're right. Has anyone else watched people put in wires and pipes anywhere?

BILL: Yeah, I have. My uncle does that kind of thing for a living. He puts wires in buildings.

TEACHER: He's an electrician?

BILL: Yeah.

TEACHER: All right. Now let me ask you something else. Did they take down the wooden poles before or after they put the wires under the street? [Operation A_2]

KEN: They took 'em down and then put the wires under the street.

TEACHER: Well, Ken, let's pretend you were the mayor of New York at that time. If you told them to take down the poles and then had them put the wires under the street, wouldn't you have people get angry with you? [Operation B_1]

KEN: [laughing] Oh yeah. They wouldn't have any electricity if I had 'em take down the poles first.

TEACHER: [smiling] So what do you think would be the *smart* thing to do, as mayor of New York? [Operation C_3]

KEN: I'd put the wires under the streets, and then when they're all fixed up and the lights and everything working, then I'd do it.

TEACHER: Do what, Ken?

KEN: Have 'em take down the poles.

TEACHER: That makes sense. What do you suppose they used all those poles for? Do you have an idea, Donald? (Operation D_2]

DONALD: I don't know. Maybe they built log cabins with them.

TEACHER: That's a good idea. Any other ideas?

BARBARA: Oh, I know! They could use them for firewood!

TEACHER: Another good idea. We only have a minute or two left. Why don't we see how many ideas for using those poles we can think of in that time? (Operation D_2]

Comprehension Worksheets versus Whole Text

The teacher in the previous episode did not provide a worksheet or two on each of the twelve operations listed on page 149. Instead, she helped her students practice using these thought processes as part of the act of reading whole text. As a result, her students applied the operations as they learned them—something that can occur only as whole text, rather than a worksheet, is being processed by the reader.

Now, suppose though, that she wanted to get them to understand more clearly the meaning of one of the thinking operations. Would she then want to use a worksheet on this "subskill"? Well, this may surprise you, but yes, she might. There are those occasions when a worksheet, done together by the teacher and students, might provide just the kind of explanation and practice needed by the students—to understand what the teacher wants them to look for in whole text. Let me quickly add a proviso, however: You might introduce an idea through a worksheet, or provide practice with one, but you can seldom teach reading with one. The teaching of reading needs to be primarily with whole text—simply because that's the nature of reading. A worksheet can act as a hand-out for your lesson, but it should seldom *be* your lesson. And once you've used it as a handout, you'll want to quickly get into applying the idea through guided reading of whole text.

Creating Inferential Questions

Now that you've seen how inferential thinking fits in with other thinking opera-tions, let me suggest ways of making up inferential questions as you are interact-ing with your students. I showed you in Chapter 4 how much of reading is an inferential process, and I showed you with "The Three Bears" story how each sentence in an author's text has an empty slot or two following it. Let's review that situation.

When we last saw the three bears, they were starting off for a walk in the forest. Let's look at the next few sentences and find the empty slots:

Then through the forest came Goldilocks, hot and tired.

Empty slots: Goldilocks is by herself. She's hot and tired because she's had a long walk in the forest. The forest must be pretty large. It's summer.

Possible inferential questions to ask children: Do you think Goldilocks was alone or with someone? What does the author say or not say that makes you think so? What do you remember from your own experiences that makes you think so? Why do you think Goldilocks was hot and tired? Was this summertime or wintertime? Was the forest large or small? What makes you think so?

She saw the three bears' house and went inside.

Empty slots: The door was unlocked. Goldilocks knew the three bears? Gol-dilocks was an habitual trespasser?

Possible inferential questions: Try making up your own.

All right. I'm sure you get the idea. Since the reader must read between the lines as well as "on the lines," the opportunity for inferential questions is endless. And aye, there's the rub: Not every inferential question is worth asking! It de-pends on your instructional purpose. If you want your students to pay more at-tention to the setting of a story, then asking questions that make them realize the time of year or the size of the forest would be important. If the plot of the story isn't really affected by Goldilock's trespassing, then an inferential question about this matter might be a waste of time. Again, it depends on what you hope the students will learn from the story.

INFERENTIAL THINKING—NOTICING MAIN IDEAS:
THE WRITE WAY

One type of inferential question often asked by teachers has to do with finding the main ideas in a passage. Do you remember those little thin booklets in school that you were supposed to "work on" when you were through with your other reading assignment? They were different colors, you know, with blue for the best readers and some kind of insipid color for the poorest readers. There were exactly ten questions at the end of each article so that percentages could be computed easily by the teacher. And one of the questions would ALWAYS ask you for the main idea.

So, being a good student, you would knuckle down and fill in the blank with something—anything that had worked in the past. For example, "The main idea of this story is this: People should be good to each other." Or maybe you'd dig up something from your training with the Girl Scouts or Boy Scouts. And usually it would work. You'd get your point for the "correct answer" and life could go on.

All right. So that was one way of "teaching" comprehension, I suppose. But you and I know that we were being *tested* on, rather than taught, comprehension. And we also know that *our* primary goal of working in those books was to get into the blue series before Molly Hockstadter did. If writing down irrelevant but cute little main ideas was the way to beat Molly, we'd do that with gusto.

What I'd like to do right now is to give you a different notion of "main idea." You see, there's a reason why teachers and educational publishers have become rabid about pulling main ideas out of children's heads. And the reason is as much historical as it is conscious. As Cunningham and Moore (1986) have reminded us, main ideas were not "where it was at" in the last century. Typically, teachers carried on "recitations" rather than discussions, and the purpose of those recitations was to glean every last fact out of the class. All facts and ideas were essentially considered equal, since the purpose of the recitations was *not* to develop ideas but to test students on what they remembered. (Sound familiar?)

So, you see, it is a relatively recent event in our country to emphasize something we call *main ideas*. The problem, though, is that we educators don't seem to agree on what they are. According to research (Duffelmeyer & Duffelmeyer, 1987; Cunningham & Moore, 1986), many educators seem to think that main ideas are nothing more than topics. If the selection is about how bears live in the woods, then the main idea *is* (drum roll please): "How bears live in the woods."

Cunningham and Moore found that if you look at teaching manuals or ask teachers, there are at least nine notions of what a main idea is. These include the following concepts of "main idea": gist, interpretation, key word, selective summary, theme, title, topic, topic issue, and topic sentence. "We concluded," they said, "that main idea has been used so many ways that giving it one more meaning would add to the confusion" (1986, p. 6). They also decided, "In the ideal main idea instructional program . . . students would be expected by the end of some grade . . . to produce each of the nine types of main idea responses" (p. 14).

You can probably predict my response to this approach. The image of Skinner's pigeons pecking away does come to mind. In fact, this is a very good example of the subskill method of attacking a problem. Don't get me wrong. I probably would have agreed with this approach twenty years ago. But now I see it as largely a waste of the learner's time. Let me suggest a different way of getting across the notion of "main idea." First, though: It's true that nonfiction authors often have main ideas they would like the reader to grasp. (You've noticed that I couldn't refrain from repeating my main ideas at the end of each chapter.) It's also likely, though, that *fiction* writers would just as soon not have their stories skinned and boiled down to a cute little theme or capsule interpretation (even though television "critics" do it all the time). My point (main idea), at this moment, is that a teacher's concern for main ideas ought to be reserved for nonfiction—specifically, informational or persuasive writings.

But *now* my point (main idea) is going to change to this: The writing way is probably the best way to teach children to recognize main ideas when they read such nonfiction. That is, teach them to *author* main ideas, and they will then recognize them in other authors' writings. The use of writing to teach reading has already been mentioned in Chapter 3. It will be discussed much more thoroughly in Chapter 8 and again in Chapter 12. For now, I'd just like to show you how to use writing to help students recognize main ideas.

Flood, Lapp, and Farnan (1986) describe a four-stage procedure for doing this that seems to work quite well. I'm going to modify it slightly to fit my own experience.

A Four-Stage Procedure

Stage one: First, you need to have your students (third grade and above) each select a topic. One of the best ways of doing this is through brainstorming. Have the whole class list (for one or two minutes only) the topics they would like to know more about, and write the choices on the board. Next have each child make an individual list (for four or five minutes) and then have him pick a first, second, and third choice from his list.

Stage two: Now get a commitment from each student on his topic. Then get them to individually brainstorm again for another three or four minutes, this time on things they already know about the topic (or think they know.)

Stage three: Next, have them individually brainstorm some questions they would like to get answered when they look for reading material. Give them a day or two to get more information before continuing the process, but you'll probably be most successful if you also take them once to the school library.

Stage four: Once they've gathered some facts and written some of them down, you're ready to demonstrate the concept of main idea. "Start simple," is a good motto here (although my high school English teacher would have said, "Start simply"!). Flood, Lapp, and Farnan (1986) recommend starting with a simple paragraph. And I agree, as long as you help your students move on to the idea that an entire article can also have a main idea. What you'll need to do is model a way for your students to write a paragraph with a main idea and supporting details.

1. First present them with several statements and ask them which statement is the main idea and which ones support this main idea. Here are some fictitious examples—for you, not your students:
   a. The University of Spillvania has 87 living Nobel Prize winners among its alumni.
   b. The University of Spillvania (U of S) has 78 living Pulitzer Prize winners among its alumni.
   c. The U of S is one of the world's great centers of learning.
   d. The average student at the University of Spillvania graduates with a 2.1 GPA (out of a possible 4.0).
   e. The U of S once claimed Chevy Chase as a student.
   f. The U of S has 37 internationally top-ranked departments, including theoretical physics, mathematics, foreign languages, and water skiing.
   g. Each year the U of S has hundreds of people from other countries applying for entrance into its famous departments of music, art, and drama.

2. Once they've picked the obvious main idea and supporting details, write a paragraph with them, such as this:

   The University of Spillvania is one of the world's great learning centers. Its living alumni include 87 winners of the Nobel Prize and 78 winners of the Pulitzer Prize. It has 37 top-ranked departments, including theoretical physics, mathematics, and foreign languages. From all over the world people compete for entrance into its famous departments of music, art, and drama.

   You'll probably want to show them that the main idea can come at the end of the paragraph as well as the beginning:

   The living alumni of the University of Spillvania include 87 winners of the Nobel Prize and 78 winners of the Pulitzer Prize. The U of S has 37 top-ranked departments, including theoretical physics, mathematics, and foreign languages. From all over the world people compete for entrance into its famous departments of music, art, and drama. The University of Spillvania is one of the world's great learning centers.

3. All right, now it's time to have them plot their own paragraph. They've accumulated numerous facts and ideas concerning their topic, so they'll have to pick a cluster of them that seem to hang together. Ask them to "find four or five that are all about the same thing." Let them work with a partner and have them talk it through with him or her. Then after the partners have completed their paragraphs, have another pair of partners critique their work.

4. Finally, give each group of four children several more paragraphs for them to examine. Ask them to see if they can agree on the main ideas

for each paragraph. Then let the entire class discuss the paragraphs and justify their decisions. You can expand on this approach by having them gradually develop more paragraphs related to their chosen topic and by having each produce a brief six- or seven-paragraph report. This will take some modeling on the teacher's part as well, especially to show them how to organize their paragraphs under one main idea.

The writing way to reading comprehension takes more effort and time, of course, than the usual "find the topic sentence" worksheet, but it does pay off according to research (Taylor & Berkowitz, 1980; Bauman, 1984).

QUESTION STRATEGY THREE: STORY GRAMMAR

I've given you two strategies for inventing your own questions when you're helping children comprehend what they read—the DRTA approach and the ITO (interactive-thinking operations) approach. Having your own strategies for inventing questions is important. For one thing, it's the only way to be spontaneous rather than keeping your nose in the teacher's guide. And for another thing, as Shake and Allington found, when some teachers *don't* rely on the guide, their questions focus on "trivial information or defining unfamiliar words" (1985, p. 437). Now let's look at a third strategy, that of using story grammar.

I mentioned earlier that we all carry around a set of schemata that help us know what type of text to expect as we read: story-type schema, information-type schema, persuasive-type, and so on. Once we know that a text is going to be a story, we employ a particular schema for that type of text, one that tells us that we're going to have a main character, place, and time, a plot with a series of problems and resolutions, and so on. As we read a story, then, we expect these elements to show up. This expectation, if fulfilled, helps us comprehend the story.

When an author writes a story, she normally follows an intuitive story grammar, a set of rules as to what the text must include to comprise a real story. There must be a setting, including a main character (Goldilocks in the forest). There must be an initiating event to get the story going and to cause some sort of conflict (the three bears go for a walk and leave the house unguarded). There must be a response by a main character (she sneaks into the bears' house). This response should lead to further problems or a conflict (she makes the bears very upset). There should be a resolution (Goldilocks manages to escape rather than being thrown in jail for trespassing). Usually there's some kind of theme (bears are only human after all, *or* look what happens when you leave your front door unlocked, *or* people really don't like others sleeping in their beds).

For the past several years, teachers and researchers have been attempting to teach story grammar to children with the idea that it would improve children's prediction power and therefore their reading comprehension (Dreher & Singer, 1980; Gordon & Braun, 1983; Rumelhart, 1984). But as the research results have come in, it has become apparent that merely explaining story grammar doesn't improve children's comprehension. Explaining the story grammar of a *particular* story might increase their understanding of it, but there seems to be little carry-over to other stories (Dreher & Singer, 1980; Marshall, 1984; Rand, 1983; Rumelhart, 1984).

Two indirect approaches to story grammar, however, may enhance children's ability to read stories with better comprehension. One approach is advocated by Muriel Rand: "having many experiences with well-formed stories" (1983, p. 381). In other words, children will develop better schemata for stories if they have many stories either read to them or given to them to read. My recommendation is that you read stories to them often, at all grade levels, preferably every day, and, as Carol Peterman recommended to you in Chapter 3, that you sometimes talk informally about the components of those stories: "Who's the most important person in this story? What problems does he have? What's going to happen? How will he feel if it happens?"

The other approach is to use story grammar as a framework for inventing the questions you ask children before, during, and after a story you have assigned them. Based on my own experiences and on suggestions by Sadow (1982) and Marshall (1984), I'd like to recommend using the following kinds of questions during a guided reading of a story:

Character: What kind of person is she? What makes you think so? Why do you think she did what she did in this situation?

Conflict: What problem does she now face? How do you think she will solve it?

Setting: Where is this taking place? When? If it happened at another place, would it make a difference? What about another time?

Attempts: What did she do first? What do you think she'll do next? Why did the first attempt fail?

Resolution: How was the problem finally solved?

Reaction: How did she feel about the way it was solved? What are some other ways it might have been solved? What do you think she will do now that the problem has been solved?

These questions provide a framework not only for helping students understand a particular story but also for reading other stories. The particular ones I've given you are merely samples, designed to demonstrate the use of story grammar for increasing thoughtful reading and comprehension. You might also like to use story grammar to help students write better stories. Just as you can use writing to teach the concept of "main idea," you can also use writing to make students more aware of the story grammar that authors follow.

Teaching Children to Ask the Questions

Should the teacher always be the one asking questions? Obviously not. Somehow the students need to be the ones who eventually are asking *themselves* the questions as they read. The teacher's role, it's true, is to stimulate thinking through her questions. But the teacher's role can also be one of showing children how to ask themselves questions. Nolte and Singer (1985) carried on an unusual study of the effects of story grammar instruction on fourth- and fifth-graders. Their study was unusual because they taught students to take over the responsibility for asking the questions. Here's the way they did it.

Ruth Nolte, a fifth-grade teacher at the time of the study, planned her approach with Harry Singer, an educational researcher at the University of California in Riverside. One of their research goals was to see whether training children to ask their own story grammar questions would result in comprehension superior to that of a control group who did not get this training. Their other goal was to see whether this training would transfer to brand new reading material. (After all, it's one thing to have your experimental students do better on the training material. But what happens when you give them something to read that wasn't part of the training?) So this was their procedure:

1. *On day one*, Nolte explained story grammar to the whole class and gave them a pep talk on the importance of asking yourself good questions when you read. Then she guided their silent reading of the first half of a story by modeling story grammar questions after every paragraph or two. For the last half of the 40-minute period, the students finished the story, asking their own story grammar questions as they read. Then the students took a 15-item, multiple-choice comprehension test.
2. *For each of the next three days*, Nolte guided the whole class through a new story, asking students questions that gave them practice in phrasing story grammar questions. For example, "What would you like to know about what happens next?" And a student's question in response might be, "How does she solve this new problem?" Students were encouraged to ask only those questions that were central to the story. Then, at the end of each session, the students took a comprehension test.
3. *For the next three days*, the students worked in groups of five or six each, with one of the students eliciting story grammar questions from the others in the group.
4. *For the next two days*, the students worked in pairs, and in the final two days of the study, they read by themselves, asking themselves the questions.

Now, what about the control group of fourth- and fifth-grade children? What training were they getting? Not much, as you'll see. Each day the teacher wrote difficult words on the board and pronounced them; then she asked a question about the story. The children read the story and took a comprehension test on it. (I have seen a similar form of comprehension teaching many times in my classroom observations—particularly with children in grades four and up.)

On the final day of the study, both control and experimental groups were given a brand new story, with thirty minutes to read it and take a test. The average score for the experimental group was 12.3. The average score for the control

group was 9.9. (It was estimated that a difference this great would occur by chance only once in 100 times.)

A nice little piece of action research, the kind I hope you'll enjoy doing yourself some day, if you haven't already. My point is not that this study was a highly scientific one, but rather that it is one showing that children *can* learn to ask their own comprehension questions. I confess, though, that I couldn't resist taking a further look at Nolte's and Singer's data: I found that on the last two days of their study—the days on which the experimental children were now asking their own questions as they read—the differences between the experimental and control students were these: 14.8 versus 9.4 and 12.0 versus 7.9. Not only did they learn to ask their own questions, but their comprehension increased considerably as well.

Asking Their Own Questions about Nonfiction

Teaching children how to ask story grammar questions works only with stories, of course. What about informational articles, instead? Hahn (1985) found that fifth- and sixth-grade remedial students could be taught to ask themselves questions while reading expository text. After the teacher modeled the question-asking several times, the students gradually learned to write their own questions and ask their peers for answers. They also learned that there are three places to find answers: (1) from the author's words, (2) from between the lines, and (3) from their own experiences.

One more example of children asking their own questions: Shoop (1986) tells of elementary school classrooms in which children suddenly become reporters. At an important part of the story, the teacher interrupts the oral reading of the story to let some children act as reporters and some act as characters in the story. The teacher models for the reporters as to how to ask good questions (ones that lead the character actors to interpret the major events). She also models for the characters as to how to stay in character and think on their feet. Shoop also cites several studies demonstrating that comprehension improves when students ask each other questions. If you'd like more details on this, see the March 1986 issue of *The Reading Teacher*.

MODELING: A NECESSARY INGREDIENT FOR IMPROVING COMPREHENSION

By now it may be clear that teacher modeling is necessary for real instruction on reading comprehension to occur. You've recently looked at how a teacher's modeling of a writing process can be helpful in teaching the concept of "main idea." You've also learned of teachers who model how to act as either a reporter or a story character in order to help children learn how to ask their own comprehension questions. Also, Hahn explained how a teacher had modeled the process of asking important questions about expository text. And before that, we watched Ruth Nolte model the process of asking story grammar questions.

Let me give you three more examples of modeling. You see, the modeling of the reading comprehension process needs to begin very early in a child's career as a reader (as Dr. Peterman explained in Chapter 3). Norris (1988) shows how a teacher can do this in a one-on-one situation with a very young child (or an older child who's really having trouble with the process of reading). The teacher or parent should be sitting side by side with a child while they look at a picture book together. The story might be similar to the one Norris described:

> Tony lived in a zoo. Tony was a lion.
> He was a friendly lion.
> "I need some hair for a nest," said a bird.
> "Take all you want," said Tony.

TEACHER: [points back and forth between a picture and the lion's name in print, modeling the process of using picture context combined with print] This is Tony.

CHILD: Tony.

TEACHER: [points to next sentence] This tells you where Tony lived.

CHILD: [no response].

TEACHER: [modeling more use of picture context] It looks like he lives in a place where there is a cage, and where people come to see lions and other animals.

CHILD: [no response]

TEACHER: [pointing to the word *zoo*] This tells you what kind of place that is.

CHILD: Zoo.

TEACHER: You're right! [pointing at entire sentence] It does look like Tony lived in a zoo.

Now let me describe a modeling technique used in a group situation rather than a one-on-one situation. Combs (1987) compared a control group with a group of kindergartners who were provided with modeled reading. There were four high-readiness, four average-readiness, and four low-readiness children placed in each of the two groups. The control group had stories read aloud to them each day in the normal way. The experimental group had the stories read aloud from a ''big book,'' one of those books that a large group can see while the teacher reads it to them. For the experimental children, the teacher first got them to think of past experiences related to the story. Then she read it aloud as if she were thinking about it, making predictions to herself, asking for their predictions, wondering aloud how she knew certain things, confirming ideas by rereading certain passages. Gradually as the days went on, she would have the children do more of the out-loud thinking.

At the end of the experiment the children were individually tested on their recall of a ''final'' story to see how many ''story elements'' they could remember. Two types of recall were measured: (1) free recall, without prompting from the teacher, and (2) probed recall, with questions from the teacher. Here are the average results of the comparisons between the control and experimental groups:

	Free Recall			Probed Recall		
	High	Ave.	Low	High	Ave.	Low
Experimental	94%	82%	71%	100%	93%	86%
Control	64%	44%	22%	77%	63%	43%

As you can see the low, average, and high children all did considerably better under the modeled reading situation.

Now let's move on to another type of modeling that needs to be done—this time with better comprehension *monitoring* as the teacher's goal rather than comprehension only.

Modeling Comprehension Monitoring

''Whew!'' you must be saying. ''There's an awful lot to think about when you're modeling comprehension.'' True. And to make matters even more challenging for you, you'll need to model the metacognitive process called *comprehension monitoring* as well.

I mentioned the process called *metacognition* back in Chapter 2, when discussing one of the differences between good and poor readers. *Megacognition* is a fancy (but accurate) word that researchers use when referring to "knowing about knowing" (Guthrie, 1983, p. 478).

We adults, of course, know exactly when we know something and when we don't. (Just kidding.) Well, let's put it this way: When we adults are reading, we would like to feel that we *understand* what we're reading. Or at least we would like to feel that if we don't understand what we're reading, we do know what to do about it. This kind of ability, though, develops slowly with children. Children in the primary grades (K–3), for instance, often can't explain why they're having trouble understanding something. By the time they reach the intermediate grades (4–6), however, good readers can begin to verbalize the problem—"I don't know what that word means," or "I've never heard about this stuff before," or "I don't know how to pronounce that word" (Baker & Brown, 1984). Poor readers, however, even in the intermediate grades, need considerable help in developing their metacognitive awareness.

Baker and Brown have been studying metacognition at the University of Illinois Center for the Study of Reading for many years. Their major concern has been to determine how well children "monitor" their own reading comprehension. Here's the way they define comprehension monitoring:

> "Comprehension monitoring entails keeping track of the success with which one's comprehension is proceeding, ensuring that the process continues smoothly, and taking remedial action if necessary" (1984, p. 22). In other words, when good readers know they don't understand something, they do something about it.

The major reason for Baker's and Brown's concern about comprehension monitoring is this: Teachers and researchers used to concentrate on children's memory *after* they have read rather than their comprehension *while* they read. Today's researchers have been trying to make it clear to us that reading comprehension is a *process* that can be actually observed only while it's going on. It's not a product that can be measured later by how many questions are answered correctly. So where does comprehension monitoring fit in? It's actually part of the process of comprehension. It's also outside that process—like a friend or a coach watching you read.

Comprehension monitoring is a process of assuring yourself while you read that you are communicating with the author. It involves certain monitoring activities like those that follow. *(Warning: Some of the monitoring questions I'll be using as examples are designed to keep you alert rather than inform you.)*

1. Making sure you know what your purposes are for reading a particular text. Unless a reader knows what he's looking for and why he wants it, reading becomes nothing more than allowing the eyes to scan the print.

> *Comprehension-monitoring questions for the teacher to model:*
> What's my purpose for reading this?
> Am I really reading this with my purpose in mind?
> (Do I even have the book right-side up?)

2. Modifying your reading rate and strategies to match your purpose. This is something that many elementary and high school students don't do. It may horrify you to know that many *university* students neither set their own purposes nor vary their reading rates (Baker & Brown, 1984).

> *Comprehension-monitoring questions to model:*
> Should I be scanning this for certain details rather than reading the whole thing?
> Should I just skim this quickly to get the general idea?
> Should I read this slowly to make sure I understand every detail?
> Should I follow the plot quickly, or should I slow down enough to understand the characters? Am I interested in both the plot and the characters or just the plot?
> Should I take notes, or highlight, or make marginal notes?
> Should I recite what I've learned at the end of each section?

3. Using your background and schemata to relate to what the author is talking about.

> *Comprehension-monitoring questions to model:*
> What experiences have I had that are like this?
> What do I already know about this topic?
> What would I like to know about this topic?
> (Does this person have any idea how incredibly wrong he is?)

4. Paying attention to the *sequence* of events, steps, or logic (depending on the type of text). Students aren't always aware that the order in which the information is coming is something to think about. Good comprehension often requires understanding the sequence of information.

> *Comprehension-monitoring questions to model:*
> Which step goes next?
> Why does this step follow the last one?
> Now that I know the first event, what do I think the next event will be?
> Does this statement really follow from the last statement? (Or is this author selling me a used car?)
> Can I picture the steps (or events) the author wants me to follow?

5. Going back and rereading something that wasn't clear the first time. Good readers tend to do this. Poor readers usually don't.

> *Comprehension-monitoring questions to model:*
> Did I really understand that paragraph?
> Did I get the main idea of that paragraph?
> Did I get the really important details in that paragraph?
> (Did my whole mind, one-fourth of my mind, or just my eyes cover that last page?)

6. Self-correcting words that don't fit the context. As you may recall, good readers do this often. Poor readers are often content to say any word that comes to mind—just to get through the passage.

> *Comprehension-monitoring questions to model:*
> Does that word really fit this sentence?
> Am I communicating with the author or making up my own story?
> Am I just making word-noises rather than reading?

7. Getting help with words that are crucial to understanding the author's message. Poor readers are less likely than good readers to do this (Baker & Brown, 1984).

> *Comprehension-monitoring questions to model:*
> Can I figure out this word by looking at the other words in the sentence?
> Does the author explain this word in another sentence?
> Should I take the time and effort to check this word in a dictionary?
> Should I ask Jake or Maria? One of them might know what it means.
> (Could this word possibly be included in any language known to humankind?)

You can see, then, that if reading comprehension includes these kinds of monitoring processes, there is considerable modeling to be done in the classroom. Metacognitive questions do not come naturally to many children as they read. If you demonstrate this process, however, by reading in front of children and asking yourself questions out loud, you'll be going a long way toward actually teaching comprehension rather than testing it.

Research demonstrates that the metacognitive process of comprehension monitoring can be taught, even to poor readers (Baker & Brown, 1984). To conclude this section, I'd like to show you one more example based on a study by Jane Hansen (1984, p. 587). Notice how the teacher in this example tries to make a group of poor readers in fourth grade conscious of part of the comprehension process so that they can use it with other selections. The ''part'' I'm referring to is that of bringing their own past experiences to bear on understanding what the author is describing. Studies consistently demonstrate that many children don't realize they're supposed to do this (Baker & Brown, 1984).

TEACHER: For many weeks now we've been doing something special before you read each new story. Do you remember what it is?

SALLY: Talking.

TEACHER: Yes. What special kind of talking?

JOHNNY: Comparing.

TEACHER: Yes, that's the word we've been using.

PHYLLIS: Ooh, I know. Comparing what's happened in our lives to what will happen in the story.

TEACHER: You're absolutely right. And why have we been doing this?

JAY: So we'd . . . so we'd get an idea of what the story's going to be about.

SALLY: To help us understand the story better.

TEACHER: Uh-huh.

PHYLLIS: So we'd remember it better.

TEACHER: Yes, those are all good reasons. Now, last time we met I had you imagine the kind of comparisons you would make if you were going to read about some children flying kites. Remember?

CHILDREN: Yes.

TEACHER: Well, today, let's imagine that you're going to read in your social studies book about some schools in Japan.

PHYLLIS: Oh good.

TEACHER: [smiling] Okay, what might you think about before you read and as you're reading? What *comparisons* would you make?

JOHNNY: I'd think about our class.

JAY: I'd think about this school, and about my old school too.

PHYLLIS: We could see if their school is like ours.

JOHNNY: It'd be different, I'll bet.

QUESTION STRATEGY FOUR: PROVIDING TIME TO THINK AND GROW

The three frameworks I've mentioned for asking questions—DRTA, ITO, and story grammar—are subject to potential misuse, unless the teacher has a clear idea of what the questioning is for. As John Pikulski says, "Unfortunately, most of the questions we ask in the name of comprehension do little to stimulate thought or to *teach* reading comprehension. Most tend to *test* children's memory for facts contained in the materials they have read" (1983, p. 111). Research backs him up on this (Durkin, 1978–79, 1984; Gambrell, 1980, 1983). It's almost as if the teacher says to himself, "I must test these kids on this story. Otherwise, what good has it been for them to read it?"

Comprehension should not be seen as a minute point in time (Johnny got 7 out of 10 questions right on that selection). It should be seen as a long-range process. Answering questions on one selection should not always lead to answering questions on the next selection, as if the children were working on an assembly line for producing answers. There's something very "right" about having children extend the comprehension of a topic by finding other books on the topic, or by changing a story into a play so that they can *feel* what the characters in the story felt, or by creating their own book of stories similar to the story they've just read, or merely by talking about experiences they've had that were similar to those of the main character. We who teach children must create time for this. *We should take the time to model the process of learning from reading*, otherwise we are modeling only the process of testing.

We encourage mass production of question answerers rather than thoughtful readers by the *way* we ask questions. Not only are most questions of the literal- rather than inferential-thinking type, but "American teachers allow an average of only one second of think-time" (Gambrell, 1980, p. 143) after they ask a question. If the child doesn't come up with an answer in that time, the teacher tends to ask another child or ask another question or repeat the original question. Furthermore, questions are often asked in a formal way (sometimes straight from the teacher's manual), thus causing some children to feel highly threatened.

Some teachers, however, have mastered the art of questioning. Knowing that a question can be perceived unconsciously as an instrument of power, they ask their questions as indirectly as possible. For instance, Mary Farrar (1983) suggests that instead of asking questions directly, we should use a more informal, indirect approach.

> *Direct:* What reason did the author have for giving the story this title?
>
> *Indirect:* Do you think the author had a special reason for giving the story this title?

Farrar also recommends taking the time to give children a hint when they are having trouble. As she puts it, we have traditionally had "the notion that the best questions are *demanding* as well as being clear, concise, and complete. This concept of teacher questions is mistaken, however, because it fails to account for the social aspects of language use" (p. 371). A good point, I think, and kids are no different from adults in this respect—they don't respond well under bright interrogation lights. Not that teachers intend to make the question period an interrogation; it's just that because teachers are so busy, there's a temptation to read the questions from the teacher's guide as if one *were* interrogating instead of teaching. (I've been guilty of yielding to the same temptation.)

Some teachers have not only mastered the art of questioning, but they've also mastered the art of providing time for children to think. Those who have trained themselves to wait for five seconds after asking a question receive these rewards for their patience: (1) Students give longer responses; (2) students give more correct responses; and (3) students take more risks and dare to speculate (Rowe, 1978).

Crafton makes this point: "We have to ask ourselves what intellectual purpose is served when students are asked to answer questions unique to one text. It's *using* the information learned from reading that counts" (1982, p. 296). In most respects I agree with her. Sharing what they are reading or have read should provide children with an opportunity for personal growth. If all they get to do is answer questions delivered in a testlike atmosphere, they have been deprived of a major value of reading—to learn more about the world and about themselves.

SUMMARY OF MAIN IDEAS

☐ Question strategies can be an effective means of teaching children to create inferences as they read.

☐ The DRTA (directed reading-thinking activity) method emphasizes three questions: What do you think? Why do you think so? Can you prove it?

☐ Predicting and schemata enhancement are necessary for DRTA or any other question strategy.

☐ To use the ITO (interactive thinking operations) method, the teacher must be familiar with various types of literal, inferential, critical, and creative thinking operations.

☐ The teacher can create inferential questions by looking for the empty slots in the author's text.

☐ Writing is a valuable tool in teaching the concept of "main idea."

☐ To use the story grammar strategy, the teacher must know the basic elements of a story.

☐ Children can be taught to ask their own comprehension questions as they read. This training can lead to higher comprehension.

☐ Modeling by the teacher is necessary for helping children improve their comprehension and comprehension monitoring.

☐ The most important question strategy of all is to allow time for thinking, extension of ideas, and enjoyment.

APPLICATION EXPERIENCES FOR THE TEACHER EDUCATION CLASS

A. *What's Your Opinion?* Discuss why you agree or disagree with the following opinions. Use both the textbook and your own experiences to justify your own opinion.

1. The story grammar strategy is a better question strategy than the DRTA strategy.

2. To create an inferential question, all the teacher has to do is read between the lines.

3. In an elementary school classroom, using question strategies is more important than modeling comprehension processes.

4. Writing paragraphs with main ideas can only teach children to write better. It has little or nothing to do with reading comprehension.

5. Metacognitive processes are too difficult for elementary school children. It's best to save instruction on these until high school.

6. There's really not enough time in the school day to spend on extending ideas obtained from basal reader selections.

B. *Miscue Analysis:* Study Connie's miscues and decide what prereading question strategies the teacher might have used to avoid the miscues she made.

One day in the park Pedro saw a policeman on a horse. It was a big horse with a long black tail. The horse stopped by Pedro.

C. With a partner or small group, study the teaching episode on pages 144–146, a comprehension lesson related to the story "The Magic Doors." Mrs. Stineberg asks these three DRTA questions in a variety of ways: What do you think? Why do you think so? Can you prove it? Find at least two examples of each type of question.

D. With a partner or small group, study the teaching episode starting on page 150, a comprehension lesson related to the passage from "Amazing Underground City." Think of three other questions the teacher might have asked that would have "tapped" three other thinking operations besides the ones she already encouraged. See page 149 and also Appendix L for assistance.

E. With a partner or small group, create a new lesson for modeling the writing of a paragraph with a main idea and supporting details. Instead of the University of Spillvania model (page 157), create facts and ideas that are more suitable to a particular grade level in the elementary school. Then create two sample paragraphs, one with the main idea as the first sentence and one with the main idea as the last sentence. After you have finished, have your paragraphs critiqued by other people in the class.

F. Team-prepare one member of your small group to read a three- or four-page passage to another small group. While the "teacher" is reading, she or he should model the metacognitive process of comprehension monitoring shown on pages 165–166. The "students" of the teacher should also critique the lesson after it's over. Make sure the passage you select is reasonably difficult.

FIELD EXPERIENCES IN THE ELEMENTARY SCHOOL CLASSROOM

A. Use the DRTA question technique with a small or large group of children. Be sure to enhance their schemata before having them begin to read.

B. Use the story grammar question technique with a small or large group of children. Be sure to enhance their schemata before having them begin to read.

C. Try out the ITO (interactive-thinking operations) technique, after first developing appropriate schemata with the children involved in your lesson.

D. Experiment with the "Time to Think and Grow" techniques.

E. Try modeling either a comprehension or a comprehension-monitoring process with a group of children.

F. Attempt a lesson on main ideas similar to the one described on pages 156–158.

REFERENCES AND SUGGESTED READING

Baker, L. & Brown, A. L. (1984). Cognitive monitoring in reading. In J. Flood (Ed.), *Understanding reading comprehension* (pp. 21–44). Newark, DE: International Reading Association.

Bauman, J. F. (1984). The effectiveness of a direct instruction paradigm for teaching main idea comprehension. *Reading Research Quarterly, 20,* 93–115.

Beck, I. L., McKeown, M. G., & McCaslin, E. S. (1981). Does reading make sense? Problems of early readers. *The Reading Teacher, 37,* 116–121.

Carr, K. S. (1983). The importance of inference skills in the primary grades. *The Reading Teacher, 36,* 518–522.

Crafton, L. K. (1982). Comprehension before, during, and after reading, *The Reading Teacher, 36,* 293–297.

Combs, M. (1987). Modeling the reading process with enlarged texts. *The Reading Teacher, 40,* 422–426.

Cunningham, J. W., & Moore, D. W. (1986). The confused world of main idea. In J. F. Baumann (Ed.), *Teaching main idea comprehension* (pp. 1–17). Newark, DE: International Reading Association.

Dehn, N. (1984). An AI perspective on reading comprehension. In J. Flood (Ed.), *Understanding reading comprehension* (pp. 82–100). Newark, DE: International Reading Association.

Downing, J. (1982). Reading—skill or skills? *The Reading Teacher, 35,* 534–537.

Dreher, M. J., & Singer, H. (1980). Story grammar instruction unnecessary for intermediate grade students. *The Reading Teacher, 34,* 261–272.

Duffelmeyer, F. A., & Duffelmeyer, B. B. (1987). Main idea questions on Informal Reading Inventories. *The Reading Teacher, 41,* 162–166.

Duffy, G. G., Roehler, L. R., & Mason, J. (1983). *Comprehension instruction: Perspectives and suggestions.* New York: Longman.

Duffy, G. G., Roehler, L. R., & Herrmann, B. A. (1988). Modeling mental processes helps poor readers become strategic readers. *The Reading Teacher, 41,* 762–767.

Durkin, D. (1978–79). Reading comprehension instruction. *Reading Research Quarterly, 14,* 495–527.

Farrar, M. T. (1983). Another look at oral questions for comprehension. *The Reading Teacher, 36,* 370–374.

Flood, J., Lapp, D., & Farnan, N. (1986). Writing and reading a main idea paragraph. *The Reading Teacher, 39,* 556–562.

Gambrell, L. B. (1980). Think-time: Implications for reading instruction. *The Reading Teacher, 34,* 143–146.

Gambrell, L. B. (1983). The occurrence of think-time during reading comprehension instruction. *Journal of Educational Research, 77,* no. 2, 77–80.

Gordon, C. J., & Braun, C. (1983). Using story schema as an aid to reading and writing. *The Reading Teacher, 37,* 116–121.

Guthrie, J. T. (1983). Children's reason for success and failure. *The Reading Teacher, 36,* 478–479.

Hahn, A. L. (1985). Teaching remedial students to be strategic readers and better comprehenders. *The Reading Teacher, 39,* 732–737.

Hansen, J. (1981). An inferential comprehension strategy for use with primary grade children. *The Reading Teacher, 34,* 665–669.

Hansen, J. (1984). Poor readers can draw inferences. *The Reading Teacher, 37,* 586–589.

Hansen, J., & Pearson, P. D. (1980). *The effects of inference training and practice on young children's comprehension* (Technical Report No. 166). Urbana: Center for the Study of Reading, University of Illinois.

Hoffman, J. V. (1987, January). Rethinking the role of oral reading in basal instruction. *Elementary School Journal, 87,* 367–374.

Holmes, B. C. (1983). A confirmation strategy for improving poor readers' ability to answer inferential questions. *The Reading Teacher, 37,* 144–148.

Lipson, M. Y. (1984). Some unexpected issues in prior knowledge and comprehension. *The Reading Teacher, 37,* 760–764.

Marshall, N. (1984). Discourse analysis as a guide for informal assessment of comprehension. In J. Flood (Ed.), *Promoting reading comprehension* (pp. 79–96). Newark, DE: International Reading Association.

McIntosh, M. E. (1985). What do practitioners need to know about current inference research? *The Reading Teacher, 38,* 755–761.

Mosenthal, P. (1984). Reading comprehension research from a classroom perspective. In J. Flood (Ed.), *Promoting reading comprehension* (pp. 16–29). Newark, DE: International Reading Association.

Nessel, D. (1987). The new face of comprehension instruction: A closer look at questions. *The Reading Teacher, 40,* 604–606.

Nolte, R. Y., & Singer, H. (1985). Active comprehension: Teaching a process of reading comprehension and its effects on reading achievement. *The Reading Teacher, 39,* 24–31.

Norris, J. A. (1988). Using communication strategies to enhance reading acquisition. *The Reading Teacher, 41,* 668–673.

Paris, S. G., & Lindauer, B. K. (1976). The role of inference in children's comprehension and memory for sentences. *Child Development, 8,* 217–227.

Pearson, P. D. (1985). Changing the face of reading comprehension instruction. *The Reading Teacher, 38,* 724–738.

Pikulski, J. J. (1983). Questions and answers. *The Reading Teacher, 37,* 111–112.

Rand, M. K. (1983). Story schema: Theory, research and practice. *The Reading Teacher, 37,* 337–382.

Rowe, M. B. (1978). Wait, wait, wait . . . *School Science and Mathematics, 78,* 207–216.

Rumelhart, D. E. (1984). Understanding understanding. In J. Flood (Ed.), *Understanding reading comprehension* (pp. 1–20). Newark, DE: International Reading Association.

Sadow, M. W. (1982). The use of story grammar in the design of questions. *The Reading Teacher, 35,* 518–523.

Shake, M. C., & Allington, R. L. (1985). Where do teachers' questions come from? *The Reading Teacher, 38,* 432–439.

Shoop, M. (1986). Inquest: A listening and reading comprehension strategy. *The Reading Teacher, 39,* 670–675.

Smith, F. (1979). *Reading without nonsense.* New York: Teachers College Press.

Stauffer, R. G. (1975). *Directing the reading-thinking process.* New York: Harper & Row.

Swaby, B. (1982). Varying the ways you teach reading with basal stories. *The Reading Teacher, 35,* 676–680.

Taylor, B. M., and Berkowitz, S. (1980). Facilitating children's comprehension of content material. In M. L. Kamil and A. J. Moe (Eds.), *Perspectives on reading research and instruction* (pp. 64–68). Twenty-ninth yearbook of the National Reading Conference. Washington, DC: National Reading Conference.

Wilson, C. R. (1983). Teaching reading comprehension by connecting the known to the new. *The Reading Teacher, 36,* 382–390.

Winograd, P. N., & Bridge, C. A. (1986). The comprehension of important information in written prose. In J. F. Bauman (Ed.), *Teaching main idea comprehension* (pp. 18–48). Newark, DE: International Reading Association.

Developing Your Students' Reading Vocabulary

━━━━━━━━━━━ **CHAPTER PREVIEW** ━━━━━━━━━━━

You may have wondered why I waited so long to get to the topic of vocabulary. It's the most important part of reading instruction, isn't it? Well, it is, if you believe that reading is a bottom-up, word-accumulation process. If, on the other hand, you believe that reading is either an interactive or a top-down process, then vocabulary accumulation is not quite as important as language accumulation (or experience accumulation, for that matter). To accumulate language, children have to learn cueing systems for creating their own sentences and meanings. They need to have an abundant amount of whole language experiences—either in the home or in the school. Simply learning vocabulary doesn't prepare them for the reading process.

Vocabulary does play a very important role in this process, nevertheless. Yet there are so many different ways of helping kids gain a reading vocabulary! It boggles the mind, as the cliché goes. What I've tried to do in this chapter is to present some of the major methods, and some of the philosophical differences as well. In a nutshell, you have two kinds of vocabulary to teach, both of them part of reading vocabulary—sight word vocabulary and meaning vocabulary. Furthermore, you have different philosophical stances to deal with, and these philosophical concerns seem to boil down to two types of methodology—direct teaching (including mastery learning) and indirect teaching (including whole language).

This chapter will show you more direct methods than indirect, but this is not meant to suggest that I'm more in favor of direct methods. It's just that I present many more indirect methods in Chapter 8 on the reading/writing connection. I, myself, refuse to take a purist position on this issue—some-times one method, sometimes another is needed.

Read on . . . and join the debate.

When [words] *are learned we see what we had not seen before.*
—John C. Condon

Every reader reads himself.
—Proust

I can read that word. It's McDonald's!
—Phyllip, age 4

TEACHERS AT WORK: DIRECT VERSUS INDIRECT VOCABULARY INSTRUCTION

Vocabulary is a term we generally use to describe the words used by a speaker or author and understood by a listener or reader. Perhaps the most crucial question you'll have to answer for yourself is whether to teach vocabulary directly or help children learn vocabulary indirectly. But before I talk with you about this issue, let me first ask you to read a short article showing two teachers in action, one using an indirect method, one using a direct one. I have deliberately chosen examples at opposite ends of the continuum to show you what the range of direct versus indirect teaching of reading and vocabulary can be.

I'm definitely not advocating one or the other of these approaches. What I'm advocating is that you think about where you might fit on this continuum. Is there somewhere in the middle range that you would like to be? If so, what aspects of each approach would you adopt and modify? Can you adopt part of both extremes without violating the main goals and instructional philosophies of both?

As you read the article and think about these questions, you might also want to ask yourself these: Which method allows more *possibilities* for learning vocabulary? What does teacher-centered versus learner-centered instruction have to do with vocabulary learning? Which of these approaches would I feel most *comfortable* using? Which of them would be most comfortable to most *children*?

A TALE OF TWO CLASSROOMS*

Recently, we visited and observed reading instruction in two 1st grade classrooms over the course of a year. Children in both classes had similar socioeconomic back-

*From "Learning to Read, Learning Community: Considerations of the Social Contexts for Literacy Instruction" by Timothy V. Rasinski and Sally Nathenson-Mejia in the December 1987 issue of *The Reading Teacher*. Abbreviated and reprinted with permission from the International Reading Association.

grounds; indeed, the schools were located in the same small community. The teachers, however, approached the academic performance goal of reading instruction in markedly different ways. Each was highly successful in meeting those goals. Standardized reading test scores were consistently above national norms in both classrooms.

The difference between the two methods of reading instruction lay not in their achievement of the academic performance goals but in the ways these two classrooms used reading instruction to foster or inhibit social learning and living in schools.

The Structured Classroom—A Sense of Order

The reading instruction that we identified as the structured or mastery learning classroom was well ordered. It was sparsely decorated with commercial teaching aids. One bulletin board was reserved for outstanding examples of students' writing. There was a list of activities the children could work on as they completed their assignments. These activities included "make a list of words that mean more than one" (plurals) and "put a column of words in a-b-c order" (alphabetize).

The children progressed at their own pace in reading and writing. The classroom was ability tracked; the teacher grouped the children according to test results into high, middle, and low reading groups. Reading group time began with the children reading through several long lists of words, repeating each word 3 times while pointing with their index fingers to hold their place on the word chart. The teacher would then give the children new word endings and, using flashcards, lead them through a routine of say the word, spell the word, sound the word, write the word, and say the word. She also had whole sentence strips for them to read.

The teacher's manner was quick and efficient. The children knew what to expect and what was expected of them. Most had no problem reading the words and sentences presented. Interestingly, when they did read aloud from books their reading tended to sound like their word list chanting.

The programmed rituals of this classroom did not lend themselves to a class-as-community spirit. Only twice during the school day did we see the children come together as a whole group. Once was for a few minutes at the beginning of the day to discuss class business and special events. The only other time was for bathroom breaks, but even this activity did not encourage a community spirit, since the children were silently lined up at arms length in the hall to await their turns. We never saw the teacher read a book to the group, nor did we see the children collaborating on group projects.

All work was individualized; there was never an end to the things that one could do—alone—at one's desk. The children did not confer with one another or make suggestions and evaluations of each other's work as in other classrooms we had visited. Though they did speak to one another, talk was very constrained. On several occasions the teacher even had the children set their folders on end on their desks to serve as isolators while they practiced their word lists.

Interactions in the reading group were always of the "teacher initiation–student response" type. Children rarely asked questions or spoke to one another and there was never discussion, only teacher cues or questions and student responses.

The only individual work shared with the whole group were the occasional exceptional papers the teacher pinned on the bulletin board behind her desk. However, since movement around the room was limited, few children were able to look at these displayed works.

The teacher in this classroom was definitely the center of all activities. The children depended upon her for all decisions, including what they should do when they had completed their workbook pages, when they could go to the bathroom (no exceptions), and when they could read a book. We watched helplessly as one young fellow held his arm in the air for nearly 10 minutes waiting to be recognized. He needed the teacher to tell him whether to complete 10 more workbook pages or move on to something else. Since she was with a reading group at the time, and he was not allowed to leave his seat, he waited . . . and waited. In this structured classroom the teacher was ultimately responsible for all decisions and the children seemed left with a sense of powerlessness.

Class assignments were drawn completely from textbook curricula. We saw none of the outside world creeping into this class—no parents, no theme units, no community representatives. Instead of a feeling of cooperation and community, there was a sense of competition. Each child was expected to complete a given amount of reading and writing work, and learn it well enough to pass a criterion referenced, timed test in order to move on to the next level. The children were not competing with each other, but with themselves. Even in competition the group spirit was missing.

The teacher in this class was a warm person interested in the well being of her students. However, to use philosopher Nel Noddings's term, her engrossment or focus was not with the children but with the curriculum. Following the established routine had priority over understanding the children's immediate reality. Her attitude was one of strict control and prompt interference with undesirable behavior. Negotiation was not a consideration in this classroom.

Curriculum and interpersonal relationships reflected an I-It orientation to learning. The teacher looked at the curriculum as an object to be taught to students who were considered objects to be molded. Following their teacher's example the students approached school materials, and the act of learning itself, as an object, not to be understood and used but to be ingested.

The Informal Classroom—A Sense of Community

The second classroom we observed maintained the same academic goals but went about achieving them in a manner that was diametrically opposed to the structured room. We identified this room as an informal learning classroom. It was actually a split classroom in that it contained 1st graders and kindergarten children.

Both classrooms had structure; however, the structure of the first was boxed-in, linear, and simplified so as to maintain one clear line of communication. The second classroom, on the other hand, provided a circular structure which embraced many lines of communication and multiple collaborative activities. In this informal classroom the children were essential contributors to the atmosphere of the class. Their paintings and drawings were mounted and displayed on all available wall space, along with their accompanying stories. The stories came from the children themselves, whether originally written, dictated, or a combination of the two.

Close scrutiny of the room layout revealed a deliberate and well thought out system. Each of the 4 corners was set up for a specific purpose: the sharing/story corner, the reading corner, the playhouse corner, and the art corner. The rest of the room was taken up with tables and chairs set up so that children could work in groups or alone. The room was carpeted and full of bookcases and cubby holes which helped to absorb the sound of the children working and talking.

Throughout the day the children were involved in personal and group interest activities. Reading, writing, constructing, and dramatizing were in progress simultaneously throughout the room. The teacher was continually conferring with her students individually and in small groups. She asked them to tell her about what they had drawn, read to her what they had written, and discuss ideas about what else they might do. Children had picked up on this model and were conferring in like manner with one another.

Opportunities for building a sense of community were numerous in this classroom. For instance, the group came together at various times of the day. They began the day on the floor in the sharing corner to discuss class business, special events, and ongoing projects. In direct contrast to the structured class, the children had learned to take responsibility for each other in small but meaningful ways. They made sure that each student had all the needed materials and information; when someone had been absent, the children reminded the teacher of what the student had missed. The children also did their own lunch count every day, taking care of all the paperwork themselves. In one instance, when the teacher was held up at a meeting, the 1st graders took it upon themselves to get the kindergartners into their coats and boots and lined up to go home at noon.

At least twice a day the group came together to listen to an adult read them a story. Most of the time their teacher had this honor, but sometimes a student teacher, a mother who had come to help, or another adult would read to them. The children freely shared their opinions, comments, reactions, and story analyses with each other. Differing opinions were treated with respect and everyone's point of view was valued.

Before going home for lunch and at the end of the day the group came together to share what they had been doing. Those who had completed work would talk about it to the group and ask for questions and comments. Responses to one another reflected the respect their teacher had for all of their work. The children emphasized aspects which they liked about each other's projects.

The entire group came together 4 times a day in order to share some of the important things and events in their lives. The sense of classroom family was nurtured in individual encounters with the teacher as well as through group sharings. The children's personal work was developed through negotiation and collaboration between the student and the teacher. The teacher helped to draw out and focus the students' ideas. She continually checked back on their progress and encouraged them to get feedback from other students as well.

Personal work was drawn from the larger community. The children's models for writing came from books, movies, class theme units, other classes in the school, and other children. The outside world was continually brought into the school: mothers came to make bread and chicken soup, books and movies on a wide variety of topics were shared in class, class themes were oriented around such topics as growing plants, flying things, measurings, and colors.

For example, during an entire month the school dedicated its activities to the books of Tomie dePaola. Community members who represented the lives portrayed in dePaola's stories were brought in to talk to the whole school. The author climaxed the festivities by spending a whole day at the school giving workshops and seeing what the children had done during the preceding month. Parents and community members participated in this special day.

Reading instruction in this classroom was not a particular entity which could be singled out for study. The school considered reading and writing to be integral parts of all aspects of learning and community. Children were exposed to a wide variety of books and involved in a variety of reading and writing experiences throughout their day.

Individual work was shared on a one-to-one basis with others in the class as well as in other parts of the school. The teacher would ask a child who had completed a project to either read it or talk about it to three other persons. This practice, along with the group sharing, helped to build a feeling of participation in each other's work and sharing in the pride of a job well done.

Not all work was done individually. Children grouped together to build with large play blocks, construct dioramas and murals, dramatize in the playhouse area, and read to each other. The feeling of working and playing cooperatively was very strong. The children had an investment in each other and cared about the group as a community. The teacher was an important influence in this respect; by her actions she made it clear that each child was important and that everyone had a responsibility to the group.

Well, you probably didn't expect to run into this much philosophy in a discussion of vocabulary instruction. However, philosophical decisions are often at the heart of instructional decisions—as you've already seen from our discussion of bottom-up versus top-down notions of reading instruction. I'm going to try not to bias your thinking about the article you just read. Instead, I'm going to urge you to discuss the issues raised in that article, either by completing Application Experience B, page 210, with your peers or simply by talking with others informally.

We've talked about whole language before, but what you've just seen is a whole language view versus a mastery learning view. Both views have gathered considerable respect from teachers and other educators. With mastery learning the educated adult makes most of the decisions—about what vocabulary or other information should be learned by students. Performance objectives are established for the students, tasks and tests are created, direct teaching or directed use of worksheets is begun, and each student's performance is frequently and specifically measured. This procedure is followed by remediation for those who need it.

With a whole language approach, the decisions are made as frequently by each child as they are by the teacher. The atmosphere is far more informal, and vocabulary and other information are learned through a variety of situations, many of which are chosen by the child. Opportunities for sharing ideas, reading, and writing are abundant, and individual progress is measured seldom by tests but often by improvement in amount of reading and writing, as well as by observed quality of reading and writing. I'll talk to you much more about these two approaches in later chapters, but this gives you the gist of the debate.

For now, let's move on to the next debate about vocabulary instruction, and that is, Just how important is vocabulary to reading comprehension?

COMPREHENSION: RELATED TO VOCABULARY?

Thorndike (not the same one who experimented with cats) gathered information in 15 countries on 100,000 students (1973). What he found agreed with the findings of many other researchers: There is a fairly high correlation between students' scores on vocabulary and comprehension. (Those who score high on one tend to score high on the other.) He concluded that his results showed "how completely reading performance is determined by word knowledge" (Mallett, 1977, p. 62).

Mezynski (1983), on the other hand, examined correlations in eight other studies and concluded that word knowledge does not directly facilitate comprehension. So why such a difference of opinion? Correlations between vocabulary scores and comprehension scores are nearly always high, aren't they? Yes, they are. But it's our interpretations of the high correlations that differ.

What we need to remember about correlations is that they do not point to cause and effect. They point only to some kind of nebulous association. Let's say we give a Latin test and a Cantonese test to students who have been studying these languages, and lo and behold, there's a high correlation of the scores. Those who score high on Latin tend to score high on Cantonese. Aha, this must mean that learning Latin well causes people to learn Cantonese well . . . right? Not very likely.

Latin and Cantonese have a very different linguistic base. The high correlation is an association rather than cause and effect. The association might be due to the relationship between language learning and verbal intelligence, or perhaps to the personality factor called persistence, or . . . who knows. Still, the fact remains. There is some kind of high relationship between vocabulary knowledge and reading comprehension. So why does it exist?

Anderson and Freebody (1981) tell us there are three views on this matter. The "instrumentalist position" is a very practical view: No matter how a reading vocabulary is obtained, it's the main *cause* of good comprehension. According to this position, we should teach vocabulary directly rather than expect children to pick up words incidentally through reading.

The "aptitude position," on the other hand, is that a good vocabulary is merely the reflection of a quick mind—a mind that soaks up words as a person reads. Therefore, teach vocabulary by providing children with plenty of opportunities to read. To help beginners and poor readers, however, you should also provide a great deal of drill on quick recognition of words.

The "knowledge position" is that good comprehension is not *caused* by good vocabulary; instead, both comprehension and vocabulary abilities are caused by abundant knowledge about one's environment and culture. A good vocabulary is a reflection of one's general knowledge. According to this position, attempting to have children acquire more vocabulary without the experiences and concepts to go with it is at best an inefficient operation. The best way to increase vocabulary, therefore, is to provide more experiences to talk and write about, thus developing more schemata. This in turn enables children to learn new meaningful words *during* their experiences and to retain those words for use during the reading act. For example, a teacher might bring to the classroom several objects that relate to baking muffins—a tablespoon, measuring cup, a muffin pan, muffin liners, shortening, an actual muffin, and so on. The children could then experience the production of muffins and learn a set of related words, such as *tablespoon, muffin, shortening,* and so on. They would use these words in writing or dictating about their experience and purposefully review them later by reading their own and others' writing.

I'm cautious about pushing one of these positions much more than the others. All three seem to have something to say for them. I would, however, add a fourth position for your consideration, one I'll call an "interactive position." The other three positions might overlook the importance of *all four* cueing systems working together to produce good comprehension. We don't comprehend a passage by adding up all the separate word meanings in the passage. We comprehend, as you've seen in the previous chapters, by hypothesizing, predicting, and confirming, with the four cueing systems interacting as we go.

Let's look at another example of the way vocabulary and comprehension are interdependent:

Jake was beating the batter happily. The muffins were going to be great!
Suddenly he smelled something. One of the *liners* was smoking. Quickly he

> grabbed a pair of *tongs* and threw the *smoldering* liner into the sink. He had left on the rear burner underneath the muffin pan!

I've italicized three words that are unfamiliar to Nancy, the reader of this passage. She can use the graphophonic cues to help her pronounce them, but she doesn't know their meanings. Suppose that when she first reads that one of the liners is smoking she imagines a *liner* to be some type of person who smokes ("One of the liners was smoking."). But then, when Jake throws the liner into the sink, she knows her hypothesis is wrong. At this point, let's say she tries out another schema related to her experiences of watching her mother baking muffins and other baked goods. She remembers the "paper things" her mother puts in muffin pans—things she only thought of before as "pretty." Now she has another hypothesis and tries it out by rereading some of the passage. This time her hypothesis is confirmed. The semantic and syntactic rules that the author provides (and that Nancy recognizes as easy words) help her realize that the *liners* must be "those paper things" and the *tongs* must be something to hold the liner so Jake won't get burned. And the word *smoldering?* It must mean about the same as *smoking.* Without an ample vocabulary (in this passage only three words were unknown), Nancy would have had a very hard time making use of the semantic and syntactic cues to help her determine what was happening in the passage. Without the schematic cues that she brought to the passage, however, all the reading vocabulary in the world wouldn't have helped her comprehend this passage. *Vocabulary and schemata must interact for comprehension to take place.*

Now let's return to Thorndike's study of 100,000 students in 15 countries. As I said, there was a fairly high correlation between vocabulary and comprehension scores, but despite the high correlation, vocabulary apparently accounts for only 50 percent of a person's comprehension ability.* That still leaves 50 percent that hasn't been accounted for. Some of this remaining 50 percent is probably due to chance factors, but I suspect that part of it is due to schematic factors. Words are important, but so are schemata. Comprehension is not simply a result of "knowing a whole lot of words." It's much more likely to be a result of a student's using all four cueing systems skillfully and interactively. This skillful use of the four systems depends on the development of both schemata and vocabulary.

VOCABULARY: HOW IS IT USED BY THE CUEING SYSTEMS?

In the previous section we saw how Nancy used her reading vocabulary to understand the semantic cues the author was giving her. Knowledge of the words *muffins, smelled, grabbed, threw, sink,* and *burner* helped her figure out the unknown words and comprehend the author's message. But how did her reading

---

*Computed by squaring the average correlation of 0.71 in Thorndike's study.

vocabulary help her notice the syntactic cues as well? Largely because she knew all of the "function words" the author used—these italicized words:

> Quicky he grabbed *a* pair *of* tongs *and* threw *the* smoldering liner *into the* sink.

If you're not already convinced that function words are an important part of one's vocabulary, try that sentence again without them:

> Quickly he grabbed pair tongs threw smoldering liner sink.

A bit harder to read that way, isn't it? (Especially if you hadn't already known what the message was.) Your reading vocabulary of function words helps you derive both syntactic and semantic cues but largely syntactic ones. The tiny function word *a* sends out a syntax clue that a noun or an adjective is coming. Therefore, you're not surprised when you get *a pair*. The function word *of* also signals that a noun is coming. Therefore, you expect something like a pair of tongs, or a pair of scissors, or a pair of asbestos gloves. So you see, your reading vocabulary of function words provides you with syntactic cues.

What about the graphophonic and schematic cues? Does your reading vocabulary help these systems as well? Yes. Knowing a word like *coin*, for instance, helps you to pronounce an unfamiliar word in print like *foin* (a thrust, as in fencing). And if *foin* were already part of your listening or speaking vocabulary, it would probably trigger the appropriate schema related to your fencing experiences, thus enabling you to understand this author:

> His foin was wide of the mark.

Your reading vocabulary, then, aids all four cueing systems: (1) the semantic system, by providing you with the pronunciation and meaning of many of the author's words; (2) the syntactic system, by delivering the pronunciation and meaning of function words that predict the type of word coming next; (3) the graphophonic cueing system, by reminding you of words with similar spelling patterns; and (4) the schematic system, by triggering schemata created by prior knowledge and experience.

"But what *is* a reading vocabulary?" I hear you saying. "Sounds like more than one thing to me." And you're right, of course. Now that you've seen this phrase used several times in context, it's time for me to define it for you (or make an attempt, at least):

> Reading vocabulary includes two types of words: (1) *sight vocabulary*, or those words that can be decoded and pronounced instantly, regardless of meaning; and (2) *meaning vocabulary*, or those words that help the reader in three ways—by providing syntactic cues through function words, by triggering schemata, and by providing semantic context clues.

TEACHING TOWARD AN ESSENTIAL SIGHT VOCABULARY

There are a lot of sight words out there—over 500,000 in some dictionaries, if one wanted to learn them all. But teachers need some way to select those that will make the most impact in the shortest amount of time. The sight words that seem worthy of special attention probably are these:

1. The words the child really *wants* to know by sight—especially when she wants to express herself in writing
2. Those that are most common to children's speaking vocabulary
3. Those most frequently encountered in print

First, why should we be concerned so much with those words that children really want to learn? I think you already know the answer. Self-chosen activities, such as digging for buried treasure instead of working an eight-to-five shift, always create more energy and enthusiasm (usually more learning).

Second, why should we reading teachers be so concerned about a child's speaking vocabulary? There, again, you can probably predict what I'm going to say. Decoding, especially at the initial stage of learning to read, involves the translation of print to speech (vocal or subvocal). If a word already occurs frequently in a child's speaking vocabulary, the decoding process will lead instantly to comprehension and to an increase in fluency. This greater fluency will in turn lead to quicker comprehension of sentences and longer passages.

For example, read the following sentence: *I want to give you this ring for your birthday.* All the words in that sentence are generally quite common to a school child's speaking vocabulary. Suppose we leave out the two most difficult words and assume that the rest are sight words.

I want to give you this _____ for your _____ .

We can see that a large proportion of the meaning of the sentence has already been established and that the tough job of decoding and comprehending has been reduced to only two words, both of which can be partially decoded by using the context clues the sight words provide.

As for the third criterion—frequency of the word in printed materials—its significance in the selection of those words that should have special attention is probably obvious. But what may not be obvious is how the classroom teacher can take on the herculean task of determining those words that are most frequently encountered in print, in addition to determining the most common words in children's speaking vocabularies. Fortunately, both of these jobs have already been done for you. Back in the 1930s, Dolch (1936) compiled a list of 220 "basic sight words," mainly by selecting "tool words" (words other than nouns) that were common to three very comprehensive lists developed in the 1920s. Along with the list of basic sight words, Dolch prepared a list of "95 common nouns" that were common to all three lists. The 220 basic sight words, he then discovered, comprised anywhere from 52 percent to 70 percent of all the words children generally encountered in their assigned reading materials. Thus, by learning these 220 words, the children would have more than half the battle won.

For many years these 220 basic sight words—and to a lesser extent, the 95 common nouns—have been important ingredients in reading programs for children. More recently, however, numerous specialists in the field of reading have developed more up-to-date lists of words for children to learn. As is to be expected, these word lists do not agree with each other (although there is remarkable consistency if one looks at only the first 100 high-frequency words in each list). On the one hand, I'm inclined to agree with Johnson that the list of basic sight words developed by Dolch "has perhaps outlived its usefulness" (1971, p. 30). On the other hand, those who have been using Dolch's basic list can rest assured that a large proportion of the words on his list have not gone out of style. In fact, none of them has gone out of style; it's just that some of them can no longer be considered to be words of high frequency.

About 75 percent of Dolch's 220 basic sight words can be found on the Johnson list, for example. Words such as *the, go,* and *of* are on both lists and are entitled to be called "basic" sight words. Words such as *clean, wash,* and *shall* appear only on Dolch's list and probably should be retired as basic sight words— as should most of Dolch's "ninety-five common nouns." Only about 30 percent of his nouns can be found on the Johnson list. Some of the words that were on Dolch's list of nouns, such as *cow, chicken, corn, duck, farm, farmer,* and *stock* are not to be found on the Johnson list. Instead, you find nouns like *people, world, city,* and *group.*

Which Words to Emphasize?

So which list should a teacher use? If Dolch's list is outdated, is Johnson's list (1971) a better one to use? Is Johns's list (1974)? How about Fry's (1980)? One could become as neurotic as one of Skinner's pigeons by trying to choose from among all the excellent lists that have been compiled.

It seems probable that the nature of today's reading instruction makes all the lists obsolete for some purposes. Dolch's list was popular at a time when the majority of teachers were using the "look-say method" of teaching reading. Words were presented over and over again until children knew the words "by sight." Consequently, visual memory was called upon more than phonics. Only after children had learned a large body of words by sight was phonics introduced. And often phonics was introduced in an incidental fashion, rather than as a systematic form of instruction.

Today, judging from examination of the most popular reading programs and from observations in classrooms, phonics is a major component of reading instruction (sometimes *too* major for those of us who view reading as an interactive process). Since about three-fourths of the words in high-frequency lists have regular (phonetic) spelling—words such as *hit* and *lunch*—children will normally encounter these words during phonics instruction. Consequently, it might seem better to concentrate on those high-frequency words that have irregular spellings, such as *any, friend,* and *thought.*

If the teacher concentrates only on irregular words, however, she will overlook an important fact: Three-fourths of the 100 *most frequent words* in the English language have regular spellings. Furthermore, these 100 words "make up about 50 percent of all written material" (Fry et al., 1984, p. 2). Amazing, isn't it? We have over a half-million words to communicate with, but half of everything we write and read depends on the hundred most frequent ones. (This count includes derivatives as well; for example, *ring, rings,* and *ringing* all count as one word in this list of 100 words.) Furthermore, the first 10 words make up 24 percent of all written material (Fry, 1980). These ten words could win any popularity contest:

the	of	and	a	to
in	is	you	that	it

Just try writing awhile without using one of them.

I'm going to recommend, then, that teachers concentrate on a combination of two lists when teaching a reading vocabulary. One is the first 100 words in the list developed by Elizabeth Sakiey and Edward Fry (1979). The Sakiey-Fry list was created from a much longer list (Carroll et al., 1971), produced by taking 500-word samples from 1,045 books in 12 subject areas in grades three through nine. Samples were also taken from library books and magazines.

The second list is one I developed several years ago to show teachers those high-frequency words that need to be learned through visual memory rather than phonics because of their irregular spelling. The 96 words in that list were chosen not only because they were irregular in spelling *(one, brought),* but also because they were found on at least two of eight lists already in existence. As a list, those 96 words represented oral vocabularies as well as written vocabularies, adults as well as children, lower-income neighborhoods as well as middle-income neighborhoods, and various geographic areas.

Table 6.1 shows the combination of the Sakiey-Fry list and the earlier May list. Because of the importance of these 165 words in children's ability to read and write with fluency, I'd like to suggest that you *concentrate* on teaching these words during the first two or three grades. I'd also like to recommend that you teach them through the visual memory techniques I'll describe in this chapter, rather than wait for the regular (phonetic) words on the list to be learned through phonics lessons. Naturally, children will be learning many other words during the first three grades, but these 165 words deserve special attention through games, patterned books, spelling lessons, and numerous writing experiences.

Patterned Books versus Basals

As you can see from Table 6.1, the essential sight vocabulary consists of words that most children already use in their listening and speaking vocabulary by the time they reach school age. Consequently, teachers need to concentrate on help-

TABLE 6.1
Essential sight vocabulary*

anything	give	great	Mrs.	says	very
and	at	when	about	time	than
a	could	group	night	should	want
because	do	have	nothing	some	water
in	be	can	out	has	first
again	does	head	of	something	was
is	this	use	then	look	called
almost	done	knew	brother	the	were
another	door	heard	on	sometimes	wanted
that	or	an	them	more	oil
always	buy	know	off	their	what
it	had	each	these	write	its
any	enough	light	one	they	where
are	four	only	long	who	thought
he	by	which	so	go	now
been	from	dog	other	there	father
for	but	she	her	see	down
both	friend	many	own	through	goes
brought	full	might	people	to	work
as	words	how	make	number	day
house	don't	money	put	together	you
with	not	if	like	no	did
city	live	mother	right	today	would
come	gone	Mr.	said	two	your
his	all	will	him	way	get
year	they're	school	our	there's	once
I	we	up	into	my	find
made	may	part			

*Teaching goal: to have children recognize these words through visual memory within one second, preferably by the end of second grade or not later than third. Good testing procedures require that these words be arranged, as they are, in random rather than alphabetical order. Have the child being tested read each row from left to right.

ing children recognize them by *sight* rather than dwelling on their meanings. Sight recognition should be within one second, so that the cueing systems that depend upon the essential vocabulary can interact quickly and the reading can be fluent. (Fluency, remember, is crucial for good comprehension.)

Basal readers can serve as one medium for teaching the essential vocabulary and other high-frequency words. Basal readers, as you probably know, are books of stories, plays, poems, and informational articles; they're facetiously called "Dick and Jane books." These books are designed to introduce a few new words in each selection; they also provide a great deal of repetition of the new words. A new word may be repeated as many as 20 to 30 times in the first selection that features it, and then repeated in later selections. Some children learn the words strictly from the practice provided by the basal reader. *Many children need more practice than this.*

One of the best forms of additional practice can be found in the predictable patterned books I mentioned in Chapter 4. Researchers (Bridge, Winograd, & Haley, 1983) have found that patterned books might work even better than basal readers in teaching sight words. My hunch is that children like the *rhythm* found in patterned books but not always found in basal readers. Perhaps this rhythm-pattern approach activates the right side of the brain, which in turn assists the left side of the brain to learn and store words. (For thousands of years the human race has known that rhythm and rhyme help people remember better.)

In the study by Bridge, Winograd, and Haley (1983), experimental and control groups of first-graders were taught the same 77 words, with the experimental group using patterned books and the control group using basal readers. Both control and experimental groups consisted of below-average learners. The teaching occurred for 25 minutes a day, five days a week, for only four weeks. Here are the results:

Groups	Pretest	Posttest	Gain
Patterned books	15	52	37 words
Basal readers	23	35	12 words

As you can see, the patterned-book group gained 37 words in four weeks; the basal-reader group gained only 12. The differences between the two groups on the *pretest* were not statistically significant, whereas on the posttest they were. But even more important is the effect the patterned books had on children's strategies and attitudes. Many of the children who had the benefit of using patterned books changed their strategy, from slowly sounding out each word to greater reliance on context clues. By skipping a hard word and reading on, many found they could then figure out the word. Furthermore, when asked how they felt about reading out loud in their reading group, this group was more positive than the basal-reader group. You might like to try the following procedures the teacher used in this study. (You will need more than one day.)

Steps for Teaching Sight Words with Patterned Books

1. The teacher selects enjoyable patterned books that emphasize the "target words." (In this study, four Bill Martin books were used: *Brown Bear, Brown Bear, What Do You See?; Fire! Fire! Said Mrs. McGuire; The Haunted House; and Up and Down the Escalator.* The other two books were by Bruno Munari: *Jimmy Has Lost His Cap, Where Can It Be?* and *The Elephant's Wish.*)

2. The teacher reads the book out loud.
3. The teacher reads the book again, with the children joining in whenever they can predict what comes next.
4. The children take turns with echo and choral reading.
5. The teacher reads the text from teacher-made charts with no picture clues. Then the children read with the teacher.
6. The children place matching sentence strips on charts. (The teacher has made charts so that a sentence strip can be taped under a sentence on the chart.)
7. The children later place matching *word* strips on charts, saying the word as they match it. (The teacher has the children match words in correct order the first time this is done and in random order later.)
8. The children and teacher chorally read the entire story.
9. The teacher places word strips in *random order* at the bottom of the chart. The children come up and match the strips to words in the story, saying each word as they match it to one in the story.
10. The only step I would add to this excellent set of procedures is to have the children *write* the target words as well as read them. Research shows that writing words "helps the child to commit them to his sight vocabulary" (Bond & Dykstra, 1967, p. 124).

One tricky part to using patterned books this way is finding books that contain the exact words you want to teach. Actually, though, this is less of a problem than you might imagine, since the Essential Sight Vocabulary is composed of such high-frequency words. Thus, most patterned books use many of the words from the list. However, there are times when you may want to create your own patterned stories in order to emphasize certain words. You can do this by adapting a patterned story that already exists. For instance, the following story is one I adapted from Bill Martin's *Brown Bear, Brown Bear, What Do You See?* It features 13 words from the Essential Sight Vocabulary, as well as three repetitions each of several two-word phrases: *hungry bird, stalking cat, barking dog,* and so on.

"Little Bug, Little Bug, What Do You Fear?"

Little bug, little bug, what do you fear?
A hungry bird might come for me. That's what I fear.
Hungry bird, hungry bird, what do you fear?
A stalking cat might come for me. That's what I fear.
Stalking cat, stalking cat, what do you fear?
A barking dog might come for me. That's what I fear.
Barking dog, barking dog, what do you fear?
A teasing child might come for me. That's what I fear.
Teasing child, teasing child, what do you fear?
My angry brother might come for me. That's what I fear.
Angry brother, angry brother, what do you fear?
A scary night might come for me. That's what I fear.
Scary night, scary night, what do you fear?

A friendly sun might come for me. That's what I fear.
Friendly sun, friendly sun, what do you fear?
NOTHING!

For older children, more difficult sight words can also be taught through patterned literature. Any selection that includes occasional rhythmic repetition will do, as long as the words are suitable for their level of education. Third- and fourth-graders, for example, like chanting the phrase so often used in the well-known book about Alexander: "I could tell it was going to be a horrible, terrible, no good, very bad day." By placing these words on the chalkboard before the oral reading begins and then pointing to the words as they chant, you can help the children quickly learn more difficult words like *terrible* and *horrible*.

Games versus Worksheets

Teachers often use games for teaching essential sight words, but there's always that fear that maybe the children aren't really learning anything important when they play games. "Aren't they just having fun?" one teacher asked me. And another asked, "Don't the games distract them from really learning?" Well, I can understand fears like this, because I've often had them myself. (The Puritan ethic is still strong enough in our society to make us feel guilty for enjoying ourselves too much.) Fortunately, research shows that the use of games to reinforce sight vocabulary can work quite well—in fact, even better than traditional workbooks or worksheets. One of the best studies on this was conducted by Dolores Dickerson (1982), who compared the effectiveness of games with worksheets, using 274 first-graders from 30 classrooms in a large urban school system. Those children who knew more than 25 percent of the sight words before the experiment began were eliminated from the study. After six weeks the results looked like this:

	Active Games		Passive Games		Worksheets	
	Boys	Girls	Boys	Girls	Boys	Girls
Pretest	4	4	4	3	2	3
Posttest	35	34	30	27	21	21
Gain	31	30	26	24	19	18
One week later	32	31	27	25	20	20

Those are pretty impressive differences. The passive-games approach brought about a 30 percent greater gain than the worksheet approach; the active-games approach, a 53 percent greater gain.

What made the difference? Well, the worksheets involved *one individual* in matching exercises and sentence completion exercises. The games, on the other hand, involved *two or more* individuals in a cooperative learning situation rather than an isolated situation. The games also necessitated abundant feedback of an instantaneous and highly specific type ("No, that's not *thought;* that's *through;* you have to go back a step.") The active games included Word Toss, Words in a Circle, See the Same, Word Point, and Stepword from *Teaching Slow Learners through Active Games* (Humphrey & Sullivan, 1970). Another active game was "a variation on the commercial game *Twister* from Milton Bradley. . . . Passive treatment games were Go Fish, Word Checkers, The Snoopy Game, Concentration, Word Rummy, and Word Dominoes" (Dickerson, 1982, p. 47). Other studies have shown that using games can be an effective instructional approach to teaching sight words (Hunter, 1975).

Dickerson's advice, however, might prove valuable to you: "Incorporating games into regular lessons and not as adjunct activities increases the value of the game, since its objective reinforces the lesson" (p. 49). I would also advise that you schedule any adjunct game playing so that each child can play a particular game only a few times before moving to another game. Children tend to keep returning to the same game again and again because of their familiarity and success with it, so the teacher needs some way to challenge them to gain greater breadth of practice. You may wish to use some kind of merit stickers or tokens for those games they have completed.

In the list of suggested readings at the end of this chapter, you'll find several books and articles that will give you ideas for games. Also take a look at Appendix A for many more games.

Direct Teaching of Sight Vocabulary

Some children may need very direct lessons on essential words they are having trouble learning. The following sample lesson involves spelling and writing the words. As I mentioned, having children *write* the words they are attempting to learn to read seems to aid their visual memory of the words.

> *Step 1:* Introduce the words in context. About two to five words is enough. If you introduce more, it will be difficult for the children to master them. (Normally you will be working with a small group of children, rather than the entire class. It is assumed that they have already learned how to write each letter of the alphabet.)
>
> **A.** Write sentences containing the words on the chalkboard, using a form of printing. Underline the particular words you will be emphasizing.
> "<u>Who</u> has my ball?" Jim asked. "I <u>want</u> it back."
> "<u>There</u> it is," Janet said. "<u>Your</u> coat is on top of it."
> **B.** Read the entire "story" to your students.
> **C.** Have the children echo-read each sentence the second time through.
> **D.** Write each word on the board, using lowercase letters.
> **E.** (Optional Step)* Point to one of the words, pronounce it, and ask a child to make up another sentence using the same word. Have a different child do the same with each word.
> **F.** Point to one of the words, pronounce it, and ask a child to spell it out loud. Have her pronounce it after she has spelled it. Have a different child do the same with each word.

---

*This step is advised only when the students may not understand the word.

Step 2: Have the children enhance their visual memory and auditory memory of the word.

A. Have them look at one of the words and spell it to themselves. (By having them spell the word out loud and to themselves, you are helping them enhance their auditory as well as visual memory of the letters in the word.)

B. Have them close their eyes and imagine themselves writing it on their paper.

C. Ask them to look at the board to see if they have it correct.

Step 3: Using the following order, ask them to write the same word from memory:

A. Have them look at the word again and spell it to themselves.

B. Cover the word on the chalkboard and ask them to write the word on their papers.

C. Uncover the word and ask them to check to see if they have it correct.

D. Check each child's paper to make sure she has the word correct.

Step 4: Repeat steps 2 and 3 for each of the underlined words.

Step 5: Have them practice recognizing the words in isolation.

A. With the words written on flashcards, expose each one for about one second to the group and ask them to say it out loud together.

B. Expose each one again to one child at a time.

Step 6: Repeat step 5 with the first letter of each word capitalized *(Who, There, Want, Your).*

Step 7: To ensure that positive transfer takes place, arrange for them to practice the words in context.

A. Go back to the sentences you put on the board at the beginning of the lesson and ask the children to read them without your help.

B. Have them search for the words in their basal reader or other reading material; give them page numbers.

Step 8: Distribute the practice with games and activities over several days and weeks. There are a variety of ways to make the practice sessions different each time. Here are examples of some "practice" sessions:

A. Play the number-line game.

    1. Draw a number line from zero to ten for each child who will play the game.

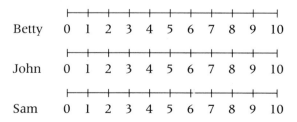

2. Prepare a stack of about 30 three-by-five cards, some with +1, some with +2, and some with +3 on them. Place them face down.

3. Flash a word card for one second to each child in turn, who must read the card to be permitted to draw a number off the top of the number stack. (She misses her chance if she cannot say it within three seconds after you've flashed the card.)

4. The child must then place an X above the correct number on the number line.

5. The first one to get to the 10 wins.

B. Before the children get to go somewhere—lunch, recess, home—they have to tell you the "password," which is simply a word on one of the flashcards.

Note: For children who are considered "slow" or "disabled" learners, these steps may be insufficient. Chapter 14 provides information and guidance on working with these children.

TEACHING TOWARD A MEANING VOCABULARY

We've been talking about teaching sight words from the Essential Sight Vocabulary. These words, however, are those that children already comprehend the moment they decode them. Let's talk, instead, about words they aren't sure of. As reading teachers, we have to help children *understand* words as well as pronounce them. But when is a word understood?

When Do We Know a Word?

Let's begin by talking about "nambol." I've given you only one of the four cueing systems you need to read this word. You can decode (translate from print to sound) the word *nambol* by using only graphophonic cues. You can see from the spelling patterns that there will be two distinct syllables when you pronounce the word: /nam/ and /bol/. You can also tell that *nam* will probably rhyme with *ham*.

So do you know this word now? Hardly. You have only an idea of what it sounds like. All right, then, let's introduce a bit of syntax. This time let's say "The nambol" instead of just "nambol." Now do you know the word better? Yes; by placing the word *the* in front of it, we've given *nambol* a position. It's no longer an isolated word. It's probably a nounlike word (The nambol is . . .) or maybe an adjective-type word (The nambol bogitt is . . .).

So now do you know the word? Only a little better. All right, let's introduce the semantic cueing system. We'll insert a word that adds meaning rather than mere position: The muddy nambol . . .

Do you know the word now? At this point, most readers are ready to make a hypothesis about its meaning. Why? Because the word *muddy* means *wet, squishy dirt.* But good readers don't think like a dictionary and stop with "wet, squishy dirt." Instead, they use their personal schemata about mud, such as

"found in a river," or "found all over the bodies of pigs," or "scraped from a little boy's clothes." It is this ability to combine all four cueing systems that enables good readers to *know* a word.

In actuality, good readers are open-minded about what they know. We may hypothesize that a nambol is a river, but as we read further, we may change our hypothesis. If we read "The muddy nambol licked . . ." we may quickly hypothesize that it's not a river; it's probably a creature of some sort. The word *licked* has given us more pieces of the puzzle. The syntactic position of the verb *licked* assures us that *nambol* is indeed a noun; the *-ed* at the end of *lick* has told us that an action has already taken place. Semantically speaking, we suspect that a nambol is a creature with a tongue. But schematically speaking, we also suspect from our past experiences that a nambol is a dog or cat—or something similar. Only when we read the complete sentence do we feel we *know*: "The muddy nambol licked its feet and purred."

The point I'm making here is that a word is seldom "known" in isolation. When words are used for communication, they are known or understood in *context*. Goodman (1983) demonstrated with 100 first-, second-, and third-graders that children can miss many words they attempt to read on a list, then turn around and read three-fourths of the missed words correctly in a story. When the children in Goodman's study had all four cueing systems available to them, they could read the words quite well! Other researchers have had the same results (Highes, 1977; Hudelson-Lopez, 1977; Pearson, 1978; Veatch et al., 1979).

So, going back to our original question, when do we know a word? From the standpoint of reading, one answer would be, when all four cueing systems lead us to its meaning in a particular passage. But my hunch is that you'd like a more definite answer. All right, let's look at the problem from a different angle. Suppose we ask ourselves how we might measure a reader's meaning vocabulary. Of course, we could do what is so often done—we could give her a multiple-choice test. For each word presented, there would be four alternative synonyms, and all she has to do is select the right synonym for each word. What could be simpler?

But what's wrong with this scene: a teacher teaching words in isolation, then testing them in isolation, without regard for context, without regard for communication as a goal? Picture another scene: a pet store, with an anxious proprietor, cracker in hand, trying to teach its newly acquired expensive parrot how to say as many words as possible. Do you see any similarities? Again, one has to ask the teacher, What's your goal? The reading process is an intelligent, active process of observing, predicting, and confirming, with a purpose in mind—not a passive one of mindlessly spouting words and synonyms for a cracker. When is a word known to a *reader?* When he or she uses that word in order to understand a particular message presented by a particular author in a particular passage.

Vocabulary versus Communication

The notion that a large vocabulary demonstrates superior intelligence still lingers on in our society. We are still apt to be impressed by those who use "big words," rather than by people who communicate simply, clearly, and thoughtfully. Such a notion about intelligence easily creeps into our thinking as we work with children. Our goal sometimes becomes one of increasing their vocabulary rather than increasing their ability to communicate. Unfortunately, our tendency to set the goal of a large vocabulary is encouraged by the fact that vocabulary growth is so much easier to measure than communication growth.

This is not to say that teachers shouldn't spend a considerable amount of time strengthening children's vocabularies; I only wish to urge teachers to use the concepts of cueing systems and communication as guides in determining how much time to spend on learning the meanings of particular words. Vocabulary is only part of the picture. One may understand every word in a message in the greatest detail and still not understand the message.

What Media to Use in Teaching Meaning Vocabulary: Using Dale's Cone of Experience

Back in 1946, Edgar Dale developed a useful model for teachers to use when planning vocabulary-building experiences (1969). This model, the "Cone of Experience," is shown in Figure 6.1. In essence, Dale's theory goes like this: Children learn at the deepest and most intense level through direct, purposeful experiences, the base of Dale's cone. They learn at the shallowest and least intense level through sheer verbal experiences, the tip of the cone. In between the base and the tip of the cone are vicarious (indirect) experiences that provide different depths and intensities of learning. Next to a direct experience of driving a car, for instance, the deepest and most intense experience would be that of a contrived

FIGURE 6.1
Dale's Cone of Experience. From AUDIOVISUAL METHODS IN TEACHING, Third Edition by Edgar Dale. Copyright 1946, 1954, © 1969 by Holt, Rinehart and Winston. Reprinted by permission of Holt, Rinehart and Winston.

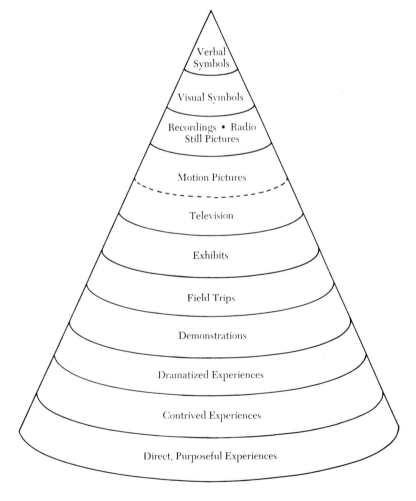

experience with a mock-up car, one that simulates a road, other cars, a crash, and so on.

In theory at least, the information we receive at the verbal level (including new words) often goes in one ear and out the other, sticking inside just long enough to use it for passing a test. Information we receive at the direct level of experience (such as the word *hot* the moment we touch a hot stove) tends to stay with us longer and to become a part of our readily available source of words or concepts.

Let's take the words *rozaga hunt* as an example. The best way to teach David about a rozaga hunt would be to take him on one. Let him get up with you in the middle of the night, carry one of the four-celled flashlights in one hand and the sharpened spear in the other, and stumble through the woods toward the swamp. Let him listen to the hurrumping of the bull frogs, the hooting of the owls, and that eerie low whistle of the rozaga. Let him shiver with fright as he unexpectedly comes face to face with one, its fangs and yellow eyes highlighting the swanlike neck covered with dark leathery scales, its snakelike tongue darting in and out of its mouth only three feet away from David's right arm. Let him hear your shout of warning and feel his tight-muscled arm jab the spear through the vital spot, right through the neck. Do you have any doubt that David will forget the word *rozaga?* (Be assured that there are no rozagas lurking about; the rozaga is a creature of the author's imagination.)

Assuming for a moment that the rozaga is a real animal, let's suppose you are teaching a social studies unit on the rozaga hunters of North Borneo. You are trying to show how these people have adapted to their environment, and since rozaga hunting is their chief means of survival, it is important that your students understand the words *rozaga hunt*. Since you plan to discuss these people on and off for the next few weeks, you want your students to make the words *rozaga hunt* part of their vocabulary. What should you do?

Obviously you can't provide them with the direct experience of rozaga hunting. So, looking at Dale's Cone of Experience, what would be the next best learning experience? A *contrived* experience might be out because of the time and expense (although taking apart and putting together a plaster model of a rozaga would be one type of contrived experience).

What about a dramatized experience of a rozaga hunt? This would be excellent after children have developed some simpler ideas of what a rozaga is and how a rozaga hunt is carried out. In fact, telling the students that they will eventually get to enact a rozaga hunt will spur most of them on to finding out more about one.

The next layers of the Cone of Experience suggest the use of demonstrations, field trips, and exhibits. Having someone (such as the teacher) who has seen a movie of a rozaga hunt provide a demonstration of the hunt would help the children get a deeper understanding of the concept. A field trip, in this case, would be impractical, unless you were able to take them to a museum showing exhibits related to the rozaga hunt. At an exhibit, they would be able to see the weapon and perhaps a stuffed rozaga close at hand.

A movie or a televised documentary, although not providing the close-at-hand experience of the exhibit, would provide the emotional impact that has so far been missing in your attempts to get them to understand a rozaga hunt. But if nothing else is available, perhaps you'll at least have some still pictures showing the rozaga and the hunters and perhaps a recording of someone describing an actual rozaga hunt.

As you can see, we've reached the top of the Cone of Experience with nothing left but visual symbols (such as diagrams or maps) and verbal symbols (words and definitions). You could simply write the word *rozaga* on the board and say, "A rozaga is an amphibian with dark leathery scales and a swanlike neck living in the swamps of North Borneo." That would take a lot less time than all the vicarious experiences we've been discussing. And there are times when that's all a word deserves. Other times a picture will do, or a quick discussion. But on all occasions when you truly want the children to make a word part of their meaning vocabulary, you'll want to think of how to back up the verbal experience with one or more nonverbal ones. The right medium for placing a word in children's meaning vocabulary depends on your purpose, on practical considerations, and on your estimation of the value of the word.

Using the Dictionary: A Useful Medium?

Must all words for a meaning vocabulary be developed through direct or vicarious experiences? What about the "good old dictionary," or just picking up new words in context as the child begins to read for recreation and information? An important point: To learn all words through direct or nearly direct experiences would require the nine lives of a cat. Many words must be added to one's reading vocabulary just through reading and discussion, looking up words in a dictionary, and through wide, thoughtful reading. And yet an understanding of dictionary definitions depends upon prior experiences—direct, vicarious, and verbal.

For instance, if you look up the word *excursion* in a dictionary, you may find as one meaning, "a short journey or trip." Now, having the children look up this word in a dictionary is a much quicker and more sensible way of getting them to discover its meaning than packing them up and taking them for an excursion—providing you're sure of two things: (1) the children have all experienced a journey or trip, and (2) they have all heard (and preferably spoken) the word *trip* or *journey* in this context. (If Bobbie has only heard the word *trip* in connection with drugs, she may be somewhat puzzled.)

One secret to success in teaching children to use a dictionary is to avoid assigning dictionary tasks that are too difficult. Too often children are asked to use dictionaries before they are ready to use them, and this leads to plenty of frustration for children and teachers alike.

Let's take the word *fatigue,* for example. Suppose you ask Henry to look up this word and tell the class how to pronounce it. What skills does he need to do this quickly and correctly? Assuming he knows where to find the dictionary (an assumption that could easily be erroneous), he should know first of all that since the word starts with *f*, he will need to open the dictionary somewhere in the first part of the book. If he opens it to words beginning with *g*, he must know that he should now go toward the front of the book rather than toward the back. As soon as he finds the *f* pages, he shouldn't look randomly for the word *fatigue*; he should head toward the first *f* pages, since the second letter in *fatigue* is *a*. To put it another way, he should know alphabetical order perfectly. As Henry continues his search, his eyes should be scanning only the top of each page rather than the whole page, since at the top he will find two guide words that indicate the first and last entries for the page.

Now that he's finally found the word, he should study the respelling in parentheses. In this case it's (fə/tēg'), rather than (fat'/ig/yū), which is what he thought it was going to be. Suppose he's thrown by the pronunciation of (fə), the first syllable. Then he should glance immediately to the bottom of the page at the ''Concise Pronunciation Key'' to find that (ə) is equal to *a*, as in *alone*. Now, by paying attention to the diacritical mark over the *e*, by noticing the syllabication and the accent mark, and by employing his phonics knowledge, he is ready to tell the class how to pronounce it.

You can see, then, what you've really asked Henry to do! In list form, to be able to decode a word ''simply'' through the use of a dictionary, he must be able to do these things:

1. Locate the appropriate section of the pages
2. Determine whether the first letter of the word is before or after the page he is reading
3. Determine whether the second letter of the word is before or after the page he is reading
4. Determine whether the third or possibly the fourth letter of the word is before or after the page he is reading
5. Locate the guide words (entry words) that ''enclose'' the word he's seeking
6. Locate and use the Concise Pronunciation Key, if necessary, to determine the pronunciation of each syllable
7. Use the diacritical marks to determine the pronunciation of certain graphemes (letters that stand for speech sounds)
8. Interpret syllabic division correctly
9. Interpret accent marks correctly
10. Employ his knowledge of phonics

But that's not all! Suppose you want Henry to find the *meaning* of the word as well? Then the poor kid has to go through each of the definitions (and some words have dozens) to find the one that matches the context of the sentence he's looking at. Perhaps it's clear, then, that before asking children to use dictionaries, it would be wise to teach them each of the operations involved in looking up a word. Appendix N offers suggestions you may wish to follow in doing this.

Instructional Principles for Teaching Meaning Vocabulary

Earlier we discussed when a child knows a word (that is, the word has become part of his or her meaning vocabulary). Now let's look at some instructional ideas that will help children learn more words—whether you decide to teach vocabulary directly or indirectly.

1. Help them associate new words with the schemata they've developed from prior knowledge. In this way they will not only understand the word better, but they will probably remember it longer also (Blachowicz, 1985). Here's an example of how a teacher can use this principle:

   AUTHOR: It's time to *impound* that dog. He's been tearing up the neighbor's flowers. He's been barking all day long and waking up everybody's baby within a forty mile radius. And he's been keeping me from getting a decent sleep! It's time for him to be locked up!

   TEACHER: [after paragraph has been read; questions interspersed with discussion with students] Can you tell from what you just read what happens when a dog is *impounded?* What else do you think happens? Would you like your dog to be impounded? Are there times when animals really should be impounded?

2. People can learn words well only when they are actively involved in the learning process (Carr & Wixson, 1986). Vocabulary instruction needs to be as learner-centered (rather than teacher-centered) as possible.

   AUTHOR: At the costume ball he wore a captain's uniform and a black mask. He claimed to everyone that this was his real uniform and that he was a soldier in the Foreign Legion on vacation. She could tell from the red socks he was wearing that he was not a soldier. He was clearly an *impostor.*

   TEACHER A: [learner-centered] Can you think of anyone that might be considered an impostor?

   TEACHER B: [teacher-centered] An impostor is someone who pretends to be someone he's not.

   TEACHER C: [learner- and teacher-centered] An impostor is someone who pretends to be someone he's not. Can you think of anyone that might be considered an impostor?

3. As vocabulary teachers, we must realize that not all words are equally learnable (Sorenson, 1985). Words differ in several ways—in concreteness, in relevance, and in syntax class. Here are three teachers thinking about the words they plan to teach.

   TEACHER A: Okay, the word *elephant* is very concrete. Just a picture will do, or a quick discussion of their prior knowledge of elephants. But this word *freedom* . . . hmmm. That's going to take more time . . .

more discussion—maybe even a bit of role playing. For some of the kids we'll have to develop a schema for the word.

TEACHER B: This selection has both the word *school* and the word *senate* in it. Now, *school* is highly relevant to my students' lives, but *senate?* Doubtful. I'll spend a second or two on school, just asking for a pronunciation. But I'll need a minute or two on *senate,* since this word is so important in the selection. I need some way to make it relevant to their own lives . . . perhaps by thinking with them about "rule makers" they know, and how they're selected. Our student council representative could probably help.

TEACHER C: All right, now, I've got three nouns and three prepositions on my vocabulary list for this selection. These nouns are pretty concrete, but the prepositions aren't. Prepositions are almost always harder for these second-graders than nouns are. I'll use pictures for the nouns, or maybe just a quick description if I don't have a picture for each of them. But for the prepositions? I'll probably have to dramatize those with them . . . have them do some pantomiming of someone looking *behind* something, *around* the room, and *beneath* something.

4. Teach most new words in context. This principle is so important let's spend the next section thinking about it.

Learning Meaning Vocabulary through Context

An educational researcher observed intensively in six different classrooms. This is what she found:

1. Vocabulary instruction before a selection was to be read did *not* include context 55 percent of the time. The "difficult" words coming up in the selection were treated in isolation without any context clues.
2. When context was used, it was usually only a single sentence, and this sentence was usually unrelated to the selection the students were about to read.
3. Most of the time vocabulary was taught orally. The words and sentences were not put in written form for the students to see.
4. Teacher *modeling* of the use of context was not observed once.
5. "The major vocabulary goal . . . was to develop discrete word meanings rather than to develop vocabulary related to the conceptual framework of the selection or [to develop] independent word learning strategies" (Blachowicz, 1987, p. 135).

Now, we might be tempted to cast aspersions on these teachers, but I suspect they were victims of goal confusion rather than stupidity or negligence, and goal confusion is something that we harried teachers suffer from more frequently than we'd like to admit to the public. In this case the goal confusion (what I should teach and why) also led to methods confusion—as it usually does. Not really understanding why vocabulary is taught in the first place led to not really knowing *how* to teach it.

We'll get back to that idea in a moment. For now let's stick with the idea of the importance of teaching vocabulary in context. By the time you've come this far in this book, you probably already know why you should teach words in context (to provide meaning, to provide practice in using the four cueing systems, and all that sort of good stuff). But there's an even greater issue buried within this one. I mentioned earlier in this chapter that one big issue is whether to teach vocabulary directly or indirectly. And now that we're thinking about context, we simply *have* to get back to that debate.

Let's suppose for a moment that you've decided to teach directly every single word that children need to learn while they're in school. Okay, fine. But what's your goal as a reading teacher? Are you just teaching vocabulary? Is your goal to enable your students to do well on TV word shows? Or do you hope that by teaching them vocabulary, you will enable them to comprehend the many things that they will be reading through the years?

All right. Now let's assume that your main goal and mine are the same—to help students become experts at comprehending what they read. In that case let's see what research tells us about the direct teaching of vocabulary. One important study (McKeown et al., 1985) showed that if you wanted direct vocabulary instruction to have any lasting effect on comprehension ability, you'd have to spend as much as 20 minutes per word (whether you tried to teach it in isolation or in context). You would also need up to 24 encounters with each word.

All right, by golly, we'll do it. We're determined to teach vocabulary directly. We'll put that much time into every word.

Or will we? Nagy and Herman (1987) determined that the size of the reading vocabulary children encounter in student reading materials between grades three and nine adds up to about 88,500 words. They further calculated that learning these through direct instruction would require teaching 12,600 words per year. *However,* if we teachers provided 20 minutes per word and up to 24 encounters, we would have to spend over 24 hours per day just teaching vocabulary.

Now, I know you're a superior teacher, and I'm pretty good myself, but I don't think we could accomplish that.

Nagy and Herman (1987) also cite studies demonstrating that the number of words that children learn through context during periods of sustained silent reading far outnumber the words that they learn from direct instruction. So it appears that we've finally come around to the most important reason for having children learn vocabulary through context: *It's the only way to get the job done, folks.*

You see, teaching vocabulary through context is not only a good way to emphasize reading as a meaningful process of communicating with someone else. It's not only an excellent way of teaching children how to use the four cueing systems. It's also the way for children to become *independent readers.* I realize that it's enjoyable playing the role of expert and passing on bits of knowledge to students, but 24 hours a day? And what do they do when they get out of school? How many years of their lives must they spend in class learning vocabulary directly?

Okay, enough of that. What I'm really leading to are my next two sections, one on teaching *some* words directly, and one on modeling the use of context clues.

Learning Meaning Vocabulary through Direct Instruction

There *are* times when you'll probably want to teach some words through direct instruction. When you're teaching a social studies or science unit, for example, there will be a few words that are labels for the most important concepts in the units. If you decide that these words are not going to be learned well or quickly enough through the context of reading or experimenting or observing, then direct teaching of the words may be the best solution. This is also true when you're assigning children to read a selection in a basal reader. Sometimes the author of the selection has simply not provided enough context for the word to become easily learned.

Studies by Stahl (1986) have convinced him of the importance of following three principles when you teach vocabulary directly:

Principle one: Give both context and definitions. Research shows that providing only definitions or synonyms seldom leads to improved comprehension. Providing several examples of the word correctly used in context, along with a quick definition or synonym, leads to better comprehension.

Principle two: Memory and comprehension are improved when information is processed at a deep level. The association technique, such as providing the students with a quick synonym for the target word, is the least effective teaching tactic (all by itself). *Application* of the association is more effective (such as asking the children to now think of an antonym or now fit the word in a cloze sentence). But deepest and most effective of all is generating a new product, such as a new sentence that truly uses the word in such a way that the meaning is clear, or a discussion with the children as to what this word has to do with their lives.

Principle three: Give multiple exposures to the word. Use either repetitions of the same material over time or preferably different contexts each time. One or two exposures do not lead to sufficient improvement in comprehension.

Modeling the Use of Context Clues

What I've been emphasizing is that direct teaching of vocabulary can be highly useful, but it's a limited form of vocabulary instruction. Because there are so many words in the English language, most vocabulary instruction must be carried on by the students themselves. And this is why it's important for teachers to model context analysis for them. This means perceiving the role of the teacher differently—not as a purveyor of knowledge bits but as an expert on learning processes.

Let me give you two examples. The first one shows a teacher using context clues flexibly, the way a normal, good reader does; the second one shows a teacher who can't get out of her role as purveyor of knowledge bits, even when she models. Instead of demonstrating a good *reader* in action, she demonstrates a *teacher* presenting rules.

MODELING . . . HELPS POOR READERS
BECOME STRATEGIC READERS*

To illustrate the difference between modeling mental processes and modeling steps, note that the teacher in the following lesson excerpt, while being explicit, also conveys a flexibility about the reasoning she does when using context clues.

T: I want to show you what I look at when I come across a word I don't know the meaning of. I'll talk out loud to show you how I figure it out.

[Teacher reads.] "The cocoa steamed fragrantly." Hmm. I've heard that word *fragrantly* before, but I don't really know what it means here. I know one of the words right before it though—*steamed.* I watched a pot of boiling water once and there was steam coming from it. That water was hot, so this must have something to do with the cocoa being hot. OK, the pan of hot cocoa is steaming on the stove. That means steam coming up and out, but that still doesn't explain what *fragrantly* means. Let me think again about the hot cocoa on the stove and try to use what I already know about cocoa as a clue. Hot cocoa bubbles, steams, and . . . smells! Hot cocoa smells good. "The cocoa steamed fragrantly." That means it smelled good!

[Teacher addresses the students.] Thinking about what I already know about hot cocoa helped me figure out what that word meant.

In contrast, note the following example from another teacher's context lesson. This teacher, like the one above, is very explicit. However, she is explicit about procedural steps, not about the reasoning used.

T: The first thing you do is try to guess from your own experience what the word is. Do you know what experience means? If you can predict what the word is, then fit the word into the sentence to see if it makes sense.

Second, if you can't guess, ask yourself this: Is the word defined in the passage? Look before and after the word. If it is, then see if the word makes sense.

Third, ask yourself this: Is there a synonym for the word before or after the

*"Modeling . . . Helps Poor Readers Become Strategic Readers." From an article by Gerald G. Duffy, Laura R. Roehler, and Beth Ann Hermann in the April 1988 issue of *The Reading Teacher*. Abbreviated and reprinted with permission from the International Reading Association.

word? Do you know what a synonym is? It's when the words have the same meaning, like *big* and *large*.

Fourth, ask yourself if you can guess what the word is by the general mood or feeling of the passage. Using these steps will help you predict what the word might mean and it's faster than going to a dictionary.

In contrast to the first teacher who conveyed a sense of flexibility in using context clues and background knowledge to figure out the meaning of an unknown word, this teacher tells the students to follow a set of steps. She does not communicate to students the flexibility which is essential in strategic reading.

Teaching the Use of Context Clues Prior to Assigned Reading

In a whole language program, which I will discuss a little in this chapter and much more in Chapter 8, very little if any of a child's reading is actually assigned. But in many classrooms reading *is* assigned. What can you do in the latter situation to encourage the use of context clues? Well, I've already discussed the use of modeling, both in this chapter and in Chapter 5. But you may sometimes wish to do some direct teaching as well.

Before you have children read an assigned selection, either in their basal readers or in a science or social studies text, you will normally want to discuss some of the difficult words they will encounter. Some teachers discuss far too many of them—and often because the teacher's manuals recommend too many. But a more serious error is teaching them words that they can understand by using context clues. A better practice is to show them *how to use context clues,* using those words as examples.

One simple way is to list those context-laden words on the board with the page numbers next to them. Then, for the first word, tell them to find it in the book they're about to read and to "see who can discover what it means by reading the words around it." If a child gets the correct meaning, have him explain his "secret method" of finding out what it means. Then do the same for each of the other words. (Don't forget to model out loud one of those words, yourself.)

On the occasions when students can't discover a secret method, you'll need to teach them a method, or explain the word's meaning with vicarious and verbal experiences, or help them use a dictionary or glossary. Here are some of the "secret methods" you may wish to teach:

"*Place*" clues: Here we try to get them to notice syntactic cues intuitively without getting into a formal discussion of syntax. For example, suppose they're about to read a selection that includes a sentence similar to the one we've already discussed: "The muddy *nambol* licked its paws and purred." Ask them questions like these: "Do you think *nambol* is an action word or a name of something? How can you tell? What would happen if we put *nambol* in a different position in the sentence?" (Try it: "The nambol muddy . . ." Also try presenting one word at a time as I did for you on pages 192–

194.) In addition, you might ask them to list words that could fit in *nambol's* place.)

"Memory" clues: Here we try to have them notice semantic cues that trigger schematic cues. Ask them, "What does the word *muddy* make you remember? Do you think *that* memory will help you figure out what *nambol* means? What about the word *licked?* What does *that* word remind you of? Will it help you decide what *nambol* means?"

"Double-comma" clues: Children usually enjoy searching for these. They're straightforward and easy to spot—even by the reluctant reader.

> The *gully,* a deep ditch, was full of water.

> The *galloon,* or braid, was made of silver thread.

"Definition" clues: These are usually easy and need very little demonstration by the teacher.

> "The kind of *poke* I'm talkin' about is a small bag."

> An *ophthalmologist* is a doctor who treats eye diseases.

"Mood" clues: These are much more difficult to use and may require several demonstrations by the teacher.

> The house was dark. The wind was howling through the cracks like ghosts. I was *terrified*.

> First he'd lost his best friend. Then he'd lost his bus fare. He was totally *depressed*.

"Building-block" clues: These are simply derivatives—words built by adding suffixes and other word parts to an original word.

> She *unwillingly* walked to school. *(willing) + (un) + (ly)*

> He was *unfastening* his seat belt.

"Interpreter" clues: These are clues derived from the reader's interpretations or inferences, and they are the most difficult to demonstrate.

> His *opponent* for the boxing match looked much stronger and bigger.

> He was so angry his face was *florid*.

By teaching many words through context analysis, teachers can provide children with long-range strategies for learning new words by themselves. And, of course, by concentrating more on context analysis, you will also be emphasizing reading as an interactive rather than a word-by-word process.

Learning Meaning Vocabulary through Mapping and Clustering

Two direct teaching procedures related to vocabulary development have become popular since the early 1980s. *Clustering* is a process of relating a target word to a set of synonyms or other associated words. *Mapping* is a process of visually displaying such associations.

Let's talk about mapping first. Perhaps the best way for you to understand or review the concept of semantic mapping is to complete the semantic map shown in Figure 6.2. Just fill in the blanks (in your mind).

When you've completed it, you can see that semantic mapping is a procedure for extending the meaning of a word by showing the categories of words that relate to it. Semantic mapping is based on the premise that everything we learn must be related to something else that we already understand. If I want to teach the meaning of the word *rozaga*, for instance, I may relate it to words such as *fangs, swan, leather, snake, hunting, spear,* and *swamp*.

The advantage of the semantic-mapping process is that it enables a child not only to visualize relationships, but to categorize them as well. Such categorization reinforces both the understanding of the word in question and the child's ability to perceive similarities and differences in the environment.

The steps one might use for semantic mapping with children are these:

1. Select a word you want them to understand in greater depth.
2. Provide direct and vicarious experiences related to the word.

FIGURE 6.2
Semantic map

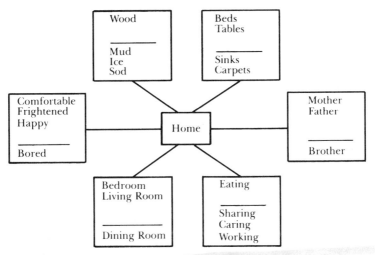

3. Have each child write down as many words as she can that she thinks have some relationship to the word.
4. Map and categorize the words together on the chalkboard.
5. Have the children create a title for each category.

A study by Stahl and Vancil (1986) demonstrated that when students are producing a semantic map, it is important for teachers to have a discussion with them during the process. This discussion should center upon the relationship among the words.

Blachowicz (1987) found many teachers reluctant to use either mapping or clustering because these approaches often didn't seem to apply to target words they were teaching before the children read in their basal readers. For example, words like *adopted, thermos,* and *recalled* don't lend themselves to such a process. This points out the need for teachers to be selective in their procedures for vocabulary development. Sometimes one procedure works well, sometimes another, depending upon the target word. Sometimes elaborate methods such as mapping are called for; sometimes it would be best to discuss quickly the children's prior knowledge and then move on to another word.

Some teachers I've talked to have the misconception that all mapping pertains only to vocabulary development, but this is not really true. Many of the articles about mapping in *The Reading Teacher,* for example, pertain to story mapping, which is a way of displaying the different elements of a story so that children understand it better. Story mapping *might* help in the building of vocabulary, but it often does very little in this regard.

Clustering, on the other hand, usually relates directly to vocabulary building. Marzano and Marzano (1988) define *cluster* as a set of words that relate to a single concept. The concept of coldness, for example, includes words like *cold, cool, frigid,* and *arctic.* It is their contention in their book, *A Cluster Approach to Elementary Vocabulary Instruction,* that by teaching a cluster rather than a single word, teachers help the students understand the target word better and retain it longer.

My own opinion on this? I'd like far more proof that the extra time is worth it in a busy classroom. At the same time, I see clustering as a way of adding *variety* to one's vocabulary teaching—something to use now and then for a concept that is both highly important and difficult to explain well through a direct *experience* or one of the vicarious layers of Dale's Cone of Experience.

TEACHING SIGHT AND MEANING VOCABULARY THROUGH WRITING

I don't want to steal my own thunder from Chapter 8, which is about the reading and writing connection. Yet I do want you to anticipate the possibility of several more ways of teaching vocabulary, using techniques that are not quite as direct as many I've mentioned here (although they are just as highly planned by the teacher). Let me just give you the flavor of this by mentioning one way of using writing to teach vocabulary.

Many years ago Sylvia Ashton-Warner discovered (or rediscovered) a way of motivating children in New Zealand to learn words rapidly. She called this the "key words" method, by which each child would accumulate his own word cards based on his own needs for words that were important to him (1963).

This method is being used today in many language experience programs and has been advocated for many years by Jeannete Veatch, a strong advocate of whole language instruction. We'll talk more about her ideas in Chapters 8 and 9, but for now let me summarize the steps that she and others recommend for developing a key word vocabulary (1979).

1. Each day the child tells his special word to his teacher.
2. The teacher prints the word on a large card, saying the letters as she writes.
3. The child traces the word with his finger, then talks briefly with the teacher about the word and why it's important to him.
4. The child is now reminded of possible things to do with the word, such as writing it on paper, drawing a related picture, writing it on the chalkboard, making sentences with several of his cards, and so on, depending on the child's wishes and the facilities in the classroom.
5. About every two or three days, the child brings his words to the teacher and reads them as quickly as he can. The words he can say within one or two seconds he gets to keep; the teacher keeps the others. (My own preference is to put a check mark on those he missed and give him a second or third try the next time; if he misses some the third time, he's probably not very interested in them.)
6. Gradually children engage in more and more writing, using their key words and any other words they have learned to write about their own lives.

Some teachers use other language experiences for developing vocabulary. Instead of using key words, children dictate a story to the teacher, who then duplicates the story and provides each child with a copy the next day. The child receives a word card for those words in the story she still remembers. These word cards are then used in much the same way as those developed through the key word approach—both for writing and for reading.

Chapter 8 will give you many more ideas on how to use other writing experiences, including journal writing, to teach reading. The important thing to know is that language experience approaches that emphasize reading materials created through children's own writing or dictation can be as effective as basal reader approaches. In Kelly's study (1975), for example, below-average third-graders who were given 15 weeks of instruction through language experiences gained 22 percent more sight words than a control group given instruction through basal readers. A more recent study by Gunderson and Shapiro (1987) found that no important high-frequency sight words were missing in the compositions of first-graders. In fact, the rank order list of vocabulary from compositions matched very well the list used by a basal reader program.

SUMMARY OF MAIN IDEAS

☐ Vocabulary is related to comprehension, but it is not the direct cause of comprehension. Vocabulary and comprehension interact as the reader searches for meaning through the use of the four cueing systems.

☐ Essential sight words are those that are high in frequency and often used in children's writing and speech. Children should learn them primarily through writing and through visual memory activities.

☐ Meaning vocabulary is learned best and most efficiently through context, but it can also be taught directly through mapping and clustering, and through the skillful use of Dale's Cone of Experience.

☐ The use of games and patterned books can be highly effective in teaching or reinforcing essential sight words.

☐ Our goal as reading teachers should be not to help children develop huge vocabularies of isolated words, but rather to help them learn how to unlock word meanings and messages in the context of whole text.

APPLICATION EXPERIENCES FOR THE TEACHER EDUCATION CLASS

A. *What's Your Opinion?* Discuss why you agree or disagree with the following opinions. Use both the textbook and your own experiences to justify your opinion.

1. A good reading vocabulary is all you need for good reading comprehension.

2. The aptitude position (page 180) makes more sense than the knowledge, instrumentalist, or interaction position.

3. Direct instruction in vocabulary is more efficient and effective than indirect instruction.

4. To teach essential sight vocabulary, teachers should rely on games and patterned books.

5. We know a word when we can select the correct synonym for it on a standardized test. This is what really counts.

6. According to Dale's Cone of Experience, it's very important to learn words first through direct, purposeful experiences.

7. Vocabulary instruction needs to be as learner-centered as possible.

B. *Analysis of Two Classrooms:* With a small group first decide on the three or four main issues that are raised in the article presented on pages 174–178, "A Tale of Two Classrooms." List these issues; then discuss them and decide where you stand on them at this point. Decide how effective you think your views will be in helping you teach vocabulary. Then compare your views with those of other small groups.

C. *Miscue Analysis:* Study Matt's miscues and decide how his reading vocabulary helped him use the cueing systems to comprehend the author's message. For example, what enabled him to self-correct his substitution of *swimming* for *sawing*? Was it just his use of graphophonic cues? (A large *C* means a self-correction.)

Bob and Paul had been [~~swimming~~] sawing and hammering all day. They were building a play house . . . [~~They~~] The boys finished the frame but they did not nail any boards across the [a] [~~flame~~] frame to make it strong. Instead, they [~~decided~~] started work on the roof.*

D. *Essential Reading Vocabulary:* With a partner or small group, make a list of the nouns from the Essential Sight Vocabulary in Table 6.1. Why are these nouns of such high frequency in our language? How might they be important to children in their writing?

E. *Planning for Teaching:* Decide with a small group how you might use some ideas in this chapter (including Dale's Cone of Experience) to help you enhance children's schemata before they read a selection about living on a farm in 1880. Three of the words in the story are *plow, oxen,* and *yoke.* You have allowed no more than ten minutes to prepare them for reading the selection. (You discover that one of the sentences in the selection is "Jake attached the yoke to one of the oxen, but the other ox started to move away.")

FIELD EXPERIENCES IN THE ELEMENTARY SCHOOL CLASSROOM

A. With two or more children, try out the direct lesson approach to teaching three or four sight words from the Essential Sight Vocabulary in Table 6.1.

B. Prepare two or more children for reading a selection from a basal reader, social studies textbook, or science textbook. Spend ten minutes on schemata enhancement and on vocabulary. Make sure you introduce at least two of the new words through context from the selection.

C. Use a patterned book to teach one or more children several sight words from the Essential Sight Vocabulary in Table 6.1. For a list of patterned books, see Appendix P.

---

*Colin Dunkeld, Portland Informal Reading Inventory, Form P. Unpublished manuscript, Portland State University, School of Education. Reprinted by permission of the author.

(Bring an extra patterned book or two in case the children don't care for the one you have chosen.)

D. Use one of the games in Appendix A to teach one or more children some of the sight words from the Essential Sight Vocabulary in Table 6.1. The first time or two you play the game, you should help the children with words they don't know, or you may wish to play the game after you've taught the words through direct lessons.

E. Teach a dictionary lesson as described in Appendix N.

F. Teach one or more words using a mapping or clustering technique.

REFERENCES AND SUGGESTED READING

Anderson, R. C., & Freebody, P. (1981). Vocabulary knowledge. In J. Flood (Ed.), *Comprehension and teaching: Research reviews* (pp. 77–117). Newark, DE: International Reading Association.

Aserlind, L., Jr. (1963). *An investigation of maternal factors related to the acquisition of verbal skills of infants in a culturally disadvantaged population.* Unpublished doctoral dissertation. University of Wisconsin.

Ashton-Warner, S. (1963). *Teacher.* New York: Simon & Schuster.

Ayers, J. B., & Mason, G. E. (1969). Differential effects of science—A process approach upon change in Metropolitan Readiness Test scores among kindergarten children. *The Reading Teacher, 22,* 435–439.

Barrett, T. C. (1965). The relationship between measures of prereading visual discrimination and first-grade reading achievement: A review of the literature. *Reading Research Quarterly, 2,* 51–76.

Bellack, A. A., & Davitz, J. R. (1963). The language of the classroom. Cooperative Research Project No. 1497. New York: Institute of Psychological Research, Teachers College, Columbia University.

Bethel, L. J. (1974). *Science inquiry and the development of classification and oral communication skills in innercity children.* Unpublished doctoral dissertation. University of Pennsylvania.

Blachowicz, C. (1985). Vocabulary development and reading: From research to instruction. *The Reading Teacher, 38,* 876–881.

Blachowicz, C. L. Z. (1987). Vocabulary instruction: What goes on in the classroom? *The Reading Teacher, 41,* 132–137.

Bond, G. L., & Dykstra, R, (1967). The cooperative research program in first-grade reading instruction. *Reading Research Quarterly, 2,* 5–142.

Bormuth, J., Carr, J., Manning, J., & Pearson, D. (1970). Children's comprehension of between- and within-sentence syntactic structures. *Journal of Educational Psychology, 61,* 349–357.

Braine, M. D. S. (1963). The ontology of English phrase structure: The first phase. *Language, 39,* 1–13.

Bridge, C. A., Winograd, P. N., & Haley, D. (1983). Using predictable materials vs. preprimers to teach beginning sight words. *The Reading Teacher, 36,* 884–891.

Brophy, J. E., & Good, T. L. (1970). Teachers' communication of differential expectations for children's classroom performance: Some behavioral data. *Journal of Educational Psychology, 61,* 365–374.

Carr, E., & Wixson, K. K. (1986). Guidelines for evaluating vocabulary instruction. *Journal of Reading, 29,* 588–595.

Carroll, J. B., Davies, P., & Richman, B. (1971). *The American Heritage word frequency book.* New York: Houghton-Mifflin.

Chomsky, C. (1969). *The acquisition of syntax in children from 5–10.* Cambridge: Massachusetts Institute of Technology.

Christensen, C. M. (1960). Relationship between pupil achievement, pupil affect-need, teacher warmth, and teacher permissiveness. *Journal of Educational Psychology, 51,* 169–174.

Clay, M. M. (1972). *Reading: The patterning of complex behavior.* Aukland, New Zealand: Heinemann.

Cunningham, P. (1982). Improving listening and reading comprehension. *The Reading Teacher, 35,* 486–488.

Dale, P. S. (1976). *Language development.* New York: Holt, Rinehart, & Winston.

deHirsch, K., Jansky, J., & Langford, W. S. (1966). *Predicting reading failure: A preliminary study.* New York: Harper & Row.

Deutsch, C. P. (1964). Auditory discrimination and learning: Social factors. *Merrill-Palmer Quarterly of Behavior and Development, 10,* 277–296.

Devine, T. G. (1978). Listening: What do we know after fifty years of research and theorizing? *Journal of Reading, 21,* 296–304.

Dickerson, D. P. (1982). A study of the use of games to reinforce sight vocabulary. *The Reading Teacher, 36,* 46–49.

Dolch, E. W. (1936). A basic sight vocabulary. *Elementary School Journal, 36,* 456–460.

Downing, J. (1973–74). The child's conception of "A Word." *Reading Research Quarterly, 9,* 568–582

Downing, J., & Thackray, D. (1971). *Reading readiness.* London: University of London Press.

Duffy, G. G., Roehler, L. R., & Herrmann, B. A. (1988). Modeling mental processes helps poor readers become strategic readers. *The Reading Teacher, 41,* 762–767.

Duncan, M. H. (1949). Home adjustment of stutterers versus nonstutterers. *Journal of Speech and Hearing Disorders, 14,* 255–259.

Durrell, D., & Murphy, H. (1962). Reading in grade one. *Journal of Education, 146,* 14–18.

Dykstra, R. (1966). Auditory discrimination abilities and beginning reading achievement. *Reading Research Quarterly, 1,* 5–34.

Ellis, D. W., & Preston, F. W. (1984). Enhancing beginning reading using wordless picture books in a cross-age tutoring program. *The Reading Teacher, 37,* 692–698.

Fagan, W. T. (1971). Transformations and comprehension. *The Reading Teacher, 25,* 169–172.

Fry, E. B. (1980). The new instant word list. *The Reading Teacher, 34,* 284–289.

Fry, E. B., Polk, J. K., & Fountoukidis, D. (1984). *The reading teacher's book of lists.* Englewood Cliffs: NJ: Prentice-Hall.

Gibbons, H. D. (1941). Reading and sentence elements. *Elementary English Review, 18,* 42–46.

Golden, M., Bridger, W. H., & Montare, A. (1974). Social class differences in the ability of young children to use verbal information to facilitate learning. *American Journal of Orthopsychiatry, 44,* 86–91.

Goodall, M. (1984). Can four year olds "read" words in the environment? *The Reading Teacher, 37,* 478–482.

Goodman, K. S. (1965). A linguistic study of cues and miscues in reading. *Elementary English, 42,* 639–643.

Gunderson, L., & Shapiro, J. (1987, spring). Some findings on whole language instruction *Reading-Canada-Lecture, 22–26,* as reported in the December 1987 issue of *The Reading Teacher,* p. 292.

Hare, V. C. (1984). What's in a word? A review of young children's difficulties with the construct "word." *The Reading Teacher, 37,* 360–364.

Harris, A. J., & Sipay, E. R. (1980). *How to increase reading ability.* New York: David McKay.

Hess, R., & Shipman, V. (1965). Early experience and the socialization of cognitive modes in children. *Child Development, 36,* 869–886.

Higgenbotham, D. C. (1961). *A study of the speech of kindergarten, first, and second grade children in audience situations with particular attention to maturation and learning as evidenced in content, form, and delivery.* Unpublished doctoral dissertation. Northwestern University.

Highes, M. A. (1977). *Word identification and comprehension in learning to read.* Unpublished doctoral dissertation, University of Toronto.

Hudelson-Lopez, S. (1977). Children's use of contextual clues in reading Spanish. *The Reading Teacher, 30,* 735–740.

Humphrey, J. H., & Sullivan, D. D. (1970). *Teach-*

ing slow learners through active games. Springfield, IL: Charles C. Thomas.

Hunter, D. L. (1975). Spoken and written word lists: A comparison. *The Reading Teacher, 29,* 250–253.

Hymes, J. L. (1968). Early reading is very risky business. In V. M. Howes & H. F. Darrow (Eds.), *Reading and the Elementary School Child* (pp. 153–157). New York: Macmillan.

Johnson, D. D. (1971). The Dolch list reexamined. *The Reading Teacher, 24,* 449–457.

Karnes, M. B., et al. (1968). An evaluation of two preschool programs for disadvantaged children. *Exceptional Children, 34,* 667–676.

Kellog, D. H. (1971). *An investigation of the effect of the science curriculum improvement study's first year unit, material objects, on gains in reading readiness.* Unpublished doctoral dissertation. University of Oklahoma.

Kelly, A. M. (1975). Sight vocabularies and experience stories. *Elementary English, 52,* 327–328.

King, E. M. (1964). Effects of different kinds of visual discrimination training on learning to read words. *Journal of Educational Psychology, 55,* 325–333.

Kinstler, D. B. (1961). Covert and overt maternal rejection in stuttering. *Journal of Speech and Hearing Disorders, 26,* 145–155.

Lippitt, R., & White, R. K. (1958). An experimental study of leadership and group life. In E. E. Maccoby et al. (Eds.), *Readings in Social Psychology.* New York: Holt, Rinehart & Winston.

Loban, W. (1963). *The language of elementary school children.* Urbana, IL: National Council of Teachers of English.

Lyon, R. (1977). Auditory-perceptual training: The state of the art. *Journal of Learning Disabilities, 10,* 564–572.

MacKinnon, A. R. (1959). *How do children learn to read?* New York: Copp Clark.

Mallett, J. J. (1977). *101 make-and-play reading games for the intermediate grades.* Englewood Cliffs, NJ: Center for Applied Research in Education.

Marzano, R. J., & Marzano, J. S. (1988). *A cluster approach to elementary vocabulary instruction.*

Newark, DE: International Reading Association.

McCarthy, D. (1954). Language development in children. In L. Carmichael (Ed.), *Manual of Child Psychology* (pp. 492–630). New York: Wiley.

McKeown, M., Beck, I., Omanson, R., & Pople, M. (1985). Some effects of the nature and frequency of vocabulary instruction on the knowledge and use of words. *Reading Research Quarterly, 20,* 522–535.

Menyuk, P. (1984). Language development and reading. In J. Flood (Ed.), *Understanding reading comprehension* (pp. 101–121). Newark, DE: International Reading Association.

Mezynski, K. (1983). Issues concerning the acquisition of knowledge: Effects of vocabulary training on reading comprehension. *Review of Educational Research, 53,* 253–279.

Mickish, V. (1974). Children's perception of written word boundaries. *Journal of Reading Behavior, 6,* 19–22.

Milner, E. (1951). A study of the relationship between reading readiness in grade one school children and patterns of parent-child interaction. *Child Development, 22,* 95–112.

Moll, K. L., & Darley, F. L. (1960). Attitudes of mothers of articulatory-impaired and speech-retarded children. *Journal of Speech and Hearing Disorders, 25,* 377–384.

Moncur, J. P. (1951). Environmental factors differentiating stuttering children from nonstuttering children. *Speech Monographs, 18,* 312–325.

Morrison, B. M. (1966). *The reactions of children to patterns of teaching behavior.* Unpublished doctoral dissertation, University of Michigan.

Nagy, W., & Herman, P. (1987). Breadth and depth of vocabulary knowledge: Implications for acquisition and instruction. In M. McKeown and M. Curtis (Eds.), *The nature of vocabulary acquisition.* Hillsday, NJ: Erlbaum.

Nelson, L. N. (1964). The effect of classroom interaction on pupil linguistic performance. *Dissertation Abstracts International, 25,* 789.

Noyce, R. N., & Christie, J. F. (1981). Using literature to develop children's grasp of syntax. *The Reading Teacher, 35,* 298–302.

Odegaard, J. M., & May, F. B. (1972). Creative grammar and the writing of third graders. *Elementary School Journal, 73,* 156–161.

Pavlak, S. A. (1973). *Reading comprehension—a critical analysis of selected factors affecting comprehension.* Unpublished doctoral dissertation, University of Pittsburgh.

Pearson, P. D. (1978). On bridging gaps and spanning chasms. *Curriculum Inquiry, 8,* 353–362.

Pearson, P. D. (1985). Changing the face of reading comprehension instruction. *The Reading Teacher, 38,* 724–738.

Rasinski, T. V., & Nathenson-Mejia, S. (1987). Learning to read, learning community: Considerations of the social contexts for literacy instruction. *The Reading Teacher, 41,* 261–265.

Reid, J. (1970). Sentence structure in reading. *Research in Education, 3,* 23–27.

Richek, M. (1976). Effect of sentence complexity on the reading comprehension of syntactic structures. *Journal of Educational Psychology, 68,* 800–806.

Ritz, W. C. (1969). *The effects of two instructional programs (Science—a process approach and the Frostig program for the development of visual perception) on the attainment of reading readiness, visual perception, and science process skills in kindergarten children.* Unpublished doctoral dissertation, State University of New York, Buffalo.

Robinson, H. A. (Ed.). (1977). *Reading and writing instruction in the United States: Historical trends.* Newark, DE: International Reading Association.

Rosenthal, R., & Jacobson, L. (1968). *Pygmalion in the classroom.* New York: Holt, Rinehart & Winston.

Ruddell, R. B. (1965). The effect of oral and written patterns of language structure on reading comprehension. *The Reading Teacher, 18,* 270–275.

Ryans, D. G. (1961). Some relationships between pupil behavior and certain teacher characteristics. *Journal of Educational Psychology, 52,* 82–90.

Sakiey, E., & Fry, E. B. (1979). *3,000 instant words.* Highland Park, NJ: Drier Educational Systems.

Saltz, R. (1973). Effects of part-time 'mothering' on IQ and SQ of young institutionalized children. *Child Development, 44,* 166–170.

Salus, P. H., & Salus, M. W. (1984). Word finding, word organizing, and reading. In J. Flood (Ed.), *Understanding reading comprehension* (pp. 122–139). Newark, DE: International Reading Association.

Searfoss, L. (1987). An interview with Jeanette Veatch. *Reading Psychology, 8*(2), 119–125.

Sivaroli, N. J., & Wheelock, W. H. (1966). An investigation of auditory discrimination training for beginning readers. *The Reading Teacher, 20,* 247–51.

Snow, R. E. (1969). Unfinished pygmalion. *Contemporary Psychology, 14,* 197–199.

Sorenson, N. (1985). Basal reading vocabulary instruction: A critique and suggestions. *The Reading Teacher, 39,* 80–85.

Stahl, S. A. (1986). Three principles of effective vocabulary instruction. *Journal of Reading, 29,* 662–668.

Stahl, S. A., & Vancil, S. J. (1986). Discussion is what makes semantic maps work in vocabulary instruction. *The Reading Teacher, 40,* 62–67.

Strickland, R. G. (1963). Implications of research in linguistics for elementary teachers. *Elementary English, 40,* 168–171.

Templin, M. C. (1957). *Certain language skills in children: Their development and interrelationships.* Minneapolis: University of Minnesota Press.

Thorndike, R. L. (1973). *Reading comprehension education of fifteen countries.* New York: Wiley.

Veatch, J., Sawricki, F., Elliott, G., Falke, E., & Blakey, J. (1979). *Key words to reading.* Columbus, OH: Merrill.

Watts, J. C., Halfargood, C., & Chan, I. (1974). Environment, experience and intellectual development of young children in home care. *Journal of Orthopsychiatry, 44,* 773–781.

Wepner, S. B. (1985). Linking logos with print for beginning reading success. *The Reading Teacher, 38,* 633–639.

Whitehurst, G. J, Novak, G., & Zorn, G. A. (1972). Delayed speech studied in the home. *Developmental Psychology, 7,* 169–177.

Wingert, R. C. (1969). Evaluation of a readiness training program. *The Reading Teacher, 22,* 325–328.

Zajonc, R. B., & Markus, G. B. (1975). Birth order and intellectual development. *Psychological Review, 82,* 74–88.

Zirkelbach, T. (1984). A personal view of early reading. *The Reading Teacher, 37,* 468–471.

Graphophonic Patterns: Those Necessary Cues and Confirmations

━━━━━ CHAPTER PREVIEW ━━━━━

In Chapter 6, we discussed vocabulary, one of the language tools children need for using the four cueing systems effectively and communicating with authors. In this chapter we're going to study the graphophonic cueing system—a tool that the other cueing systems require for (1) confirming those predictions made through context cues and (2) stimulating predictions that are then confirmed through context cues.

I'll show you that both direct and indirect ways of learning ''phonics'' can be employed, and I'll suggest to you that graphophonic analysis (decoding a word through its letters) is an intelligent, primarily right-brain process of recognizing patterns, rather than one of merely sounding out words letter by letter or memorizing verbal left-brain rules.

You will be given five ways to help children acquire those patterns, whether your teaching mode is direct or indirect. Two of these ways have an auditory emphasis, and three a visual emphasis. Then we'll see how children's knowledge of patterns can be applied to words with more than one syllable. We'll also look at an important but commonly underlearned part of the graphophonic cueing system, namely, punctuation. But most importantly, you will be encouraged to show children how to use graphophonic cues in the context of whole text.

*The emerging emphasis on larger meaning . . . does not usually deny
the use of phonics and sight words in reading. It tends, rather, to ask
how readers understand those clues so that the communication of ideas
between reader and writer can take place.*
—Roger Farr and Robert Carey

*All that phonics can be expected to do is help children get approximate
pronunciations of written words.*
—Richard C. Anderson et al.

*Huemuns spell wirds in a flitey, inkunsistent wae. This must make it
hard for yungstirs too lirn too rede.*
—Uncle Bogglestar

THE PLACE OF THE GRAPHOPHONIC CUEING SYSTEM IN INTERACTIVE READING

It wouldn't surprise me if researchers were to find that the most common phrase children hear as they're learning to read is "Sound it out." This three-word imperative sentence might not be as common in a child's life as "Drink your milk" or "Eat your spinach" or "Don't bother me," but it *is* delivered quite freely by a child's parents, relatives, and teachers. Yet it is probably one of the poorest pieces of advice ever passed on from one generation to the next.

There are several reasons that it's poor. First of all, if you give this advice often enough, it can profoundly affect a child's concept of reading—and therefore his strategies for reading. Imagine, for example, that Tyrone is reading this sentence: "The bicycle hit the hole and Dan went flying over the handlebars." He points to *flying* and asks you what this word is. If you say, "What word would make sense in that sentence?" you are telling Tyrone that *making sense* is what reading is all about. If instead you say, "Sound it out" you are telling him that *pronouncing words* is what reading is all about.

Second, by telling Tyrone to "sound it out," you are missing a chance to help him see that reading is an interactive process with *four* cueing systems rather than one. Why not encourage him to use one of the abundant schemata he has no doubt developed by this time in his life; for example, "Have you ever been riding a bike, Tyrone, and all of a sudden you hit a curb or a bump—or a hole in the street?" With this kind of question you'll probably be talking in a moment about the time he or one of his friends had a temporary catastrophe.

If you don't have time for informal chatting, you could just ask him more questions: "What happened when you hit it, Tyrone? What do you think is happening to Dan in this story? When you fell from your bike, was it a little bit like flying for a moment? Do you suppose that *flying* is the word in this sentence?

What sound does flying begin with? What letter stands for that sound? What happens when we take the *ing* off the word flying?'' And so on. By now, I'm sure you see how a teacher can encourage interactive predicting and confirming rather than the mechanical sounding out of letters.

And you can see how a teacher can encourage the use of graphophonic cues as an aid to predicting and confirming. As one remedial reading teacher said to me, "There's no sorrier sight than a poor reader who has become a slave to phonics. He's just *got* to sound it out, that's all there is to it—even though he could easily predict the word by using his intelligence and his past experiences."

THE GRAPHOPHONIC CUEING SYSTEM: WHAT IS IT?

Is the graphophonic cueing system (sometimes oversimplified with the term *phonics*) merely the process of sounding out words? No, it's much more sophisticated than that. Take the nonsense word *cibby*. When we come across a hard word like this, do we "sound out" each letter one at a time—first the sound of *c*, then the sound of *i*, then the sound of *b*, then the sound of *b*, again, then the sound of *y*—and then put all the sounds together? Well, if you've been *taught* to do that, you might. But good readers don't do it that way. Instead they look for letter *patterns*. As Glass and Burton (1973) found in their study, 85 percent of the decoding done by successful readers (second- and fifth-graders in their study) consists of recognizing *groups* of letters.

What patterns or groups do we notice in the word *cibby*? Some people will intuitively notice the *ci* pattern, indicating that the *c* probably has a soft sound as in *city*. Some will intuitively notice the double consonant letter *bb* in the middle of the word, indicating that the *i* sound will probably be short as in *kitty*. Some will intuitively notice the vowel-consonant pattern *ib*, indicating that the *i* sound will probably be short as in *it* or *fib*. And most will intuitively notice that the *y* comes at the end of a two-syllable word, indicating a long *e* sound as in *baby* or *daddy*.

For good readers, graphophonic analysis is *not* sounding out words letter by letter; it's a process of decoding new words by means of recognizing spelling patterns in known words. From our memory of *city*, for example, we can take the *ci* pattern and apply it to *cibby*. Or from our memory of *fib* we might take the *ib* and apply it to *cib*. Or from *tubby* we might take the *bb*. And so on. Eventually, as we learn to read, we get so good at this that we recognize spelling patterns by sight and do very little thinking about them. The patterns have become as easily recognized as sight words.

Certainly we do not sound out words like *knight*. Try it, and you'll see why this word, although once pronounced just the way it's spelled, has been simplified over time. What we do today, because the old spelling has remained, is to recognize the combinations *kn* and *ight* as in *knife, knee, right,* and *tight*. So basically what good readers do when they use the graphophonic cueing system is to (1) visually recognize known patterns of letters; (2) translate those patterns into the sounds they represent; and (3) blend the sounds together to form the correct pronunciation. This, as you can see, is not the same as "making a sound for each letter."

GRAPHOPHONIC PATTERNS AND THE BRAIN

> Quite apart from anything the teacher does . . . the student, being human, is a pattern-finder and a pattern maker. . . .
> —*David B. Bronson (1977, p. 453)*

As you know, the left and right sides of our brains perform different functions. The right side is generally responsible for pattern decoding and encoding (recognizing or producing a pattern). While the right side specializes in dealing with such nonverbal aspects of the individual's environment, the left side specializes in verbalizing about it (Hart, 1983; Smith, 1984). For an efficient reader, for example, it's my guess that the right side has the main responsibility for graphophonic and syntactic cues while the left has more responsibility for the semantic and schematic systems. This is only a guess, of course, since our knowledge of the brain is so limited—first by the difficulty of examining it while a person is using it and second by its incredible complexity.

At any rate, though, there seems to be little doubt that human beings have survived and evolved as pattern-seeking creatures (Hart, 1983; Smith, 1984). It is only wise, therefore, for a teacher to take advantage of this natural inclination when teaching reading. In earlier chapters we talked about children recognizing syntactic patterns as they read. We also discussed their use of schemata, which at first may be mere hypotheses but in time may become fairly rigid memory patterns that help them explain their world and what they read as they experience it. In much of this chapter, then, we'll look at ways of encouraging children to recognize graphophonic, right-brain patterns as they read.

DIRECT VERSUS INDIRECT INSTRUCTION: ROOM FOR BOTH?

You expected this section, didn't you? After all, we talked about the direct-versus-indirect controversy when we discussed *vocabulary* instruction. So here's that controversy again. You see, some teachers and educational writers are convinced that the English graphophonic cueing system is very tough. Therefore, they reason, it takes a lot of time and direct instruction for children to learn it. Others are convinced that learning the graphophonic system is no more difficult than learning to speak—maybe even easier. Therefore, they say, since we don't need direct instruction to learn speech, we don't need it to learn how to spell or how to decode print. Essentially, they proclaim, literacy is best gained indirectly through meaningful experience. Speech, spelling, and phonics are learned through use and feedback, use and feedback, more use and feedback.

Direct people say, "Uhh uhh! A few bright kids might learn the graphophonic system on their own. But the vast majority need lots of instruction—the more direct and explicit, the better."

Indirect people retort, "Nearly all children can learn the system on their own, given the right kind of whole language experiences—including plenty of personal journal writing and lots of feedback from the teacher."

Rod Maclean takes a direct point of view. He says (referring to the fact that phonics is used *relatively* little by mature readers), "It is useful to teach beginning readers a skill for which they will have little need as competent readers. . . . In many fields it is impossible to teach directly to novice learners the strategies used by experts. Learners [have to be] taught via an instructional representation. . . . Reading is like this and phonics becomes an instructional representation" (1988, pp. 514–515).

Maclean's analogy is interesting, but I doubt that it's appropriate. Reading is not a single cueing system, but phonics *is*. Reading, as you well know by now, is an interactive process. Therefore, if we want to use a more accurate instructional representative for novice learners, why not use *listening* instead. Listening is interactive and much more like reading than phonics is. Both listening and reading require real communication; both require that the communicators pay attention to syntax, to meaning, and to the background information required for understanding to take place.

What this means in practice is that teachers need to spend a considerable amount of time developing oral language experiences (listening and speaking) that lead to writing and thus to the *meaningful* use of the graphophonic system. This process will be explored much more thoroughly in Chapter 8 on the language experience approach and the relationship between writing and reading. For now, let me simply urge you to avoid the dichotomies that some educators get into about phonics—that it's either the answer to better reading or that it's the curse that causes poor reading; that it must be taught directly or that it should be taught only indirectly. Philosopher John Dewey (1933) once talked about this problem—the problem of educators polarizing their thinking: "It's either this or that. You can't have it both ways." Well, as Dewey patiently explained, you *can* have it both ways—and all the ways in between. It all depends on what you need at the moment with a particular child.

For decades, Patrick Groff has been one of the foremost advocates of direct phonics instruction. Yet what he's discovered, out in the classrooms, is that many teachers take direct teaching too seriously. They waste a lot of time teaching graphophonic patterns that children have already learned (either directly or indirectly). Few pretests, he says, are administered "before phonics instruction is given. More than likely all pupils . . . receive instruction in a particular aspect of phonics simply because that aspect appears as the next exercise in the workbook" (1986, p. 921). Furthermore, Groff says, teachers overteach phonics by assuming that it's an exact science. Phonics, he reminds us, provides a rough estimate of the sounds that letters represent. Take the word *from*, for example. Even second-graders, he found, could pronounce that word correctly after learning the sound of a short *o*. Even though it should be spelled *frum*, according to most dialects, f-r-o-m is close enough (especially if the word is in the context of a sentence).

Let me give you an example of what I think he means. If the child is reading, "The man took the stick away from the dog," she's going to pronounce *from* in such a way that it fits the context. Even if she doesn't know *from* as a sight word and has to sound out every single letter, she's still not likely to be satisfied with *from* rhyming exactly with *Tom*. She's going to use her pronunciation as a graphophonic clue that interacts with the other cueing systems. Thus she's more likely to pronounce it /frum/.

The point of all this is that "direct versus indirect" may not be the question at all. "Direct versus indirect" may be a symptom of our bipolar mode of thinking rather than a reflection of classroom reality. Classroom reality calls for doing what is necessary to get the job done with each individual child. Sometimes we need to be rather indirect, sometimes very direct, sometimes in between.

Learning Styles and Graphophonic Patterns

Now, whether you teach children through a direct systematic approach (such as one developed for a basal reader program) or through an indirect approach (such as a whole language program) or through an approach somewhere between, you'll need to be aware of how children do learn the graphophonic system. As we know, learning takes place in a variety of ways: Some children rely more on the auditory mode than other modes, some use visual modes more often, and some need kinesthetic and tactile stimuli to help the learning to take place. But we also have children who are what Carbo (1987) calls "whole to part learners." These children literally *require* whole text reading of high-interest, emotionally involving materials rather than workbook phonics exercises. These children seem unable to learn graphophonic patterns any other way. (I'll talk more about these kids when we get to Chapter 14.)

I'm going to show you five of the ways that children learn to recognize graphophonic patterns. By learning all five ways, you can individualize your instruction, using one or two methods with Jimmy, one or two other methods with Jenny, and so on. Or if you decide to teach "phonics" very directly and systematically, you can use more of an eclectic approach, combining auditory, visual, and kinesthetic-tactile approaches in each lesson.

LEARNING GRAPHOPHONIC PATTERNS THROUGH AN AUDITORY EMPHASIS

Some children seem to learn graphophonic patterns by relying more on auditory techniques than visual techniques. They're good at noticing auditory differences, such as those between the vowel sounds in *pen, pin,* and *pan.* They're the first ones to tell you excitedly, "Those three words all start with the same sound!" These children often teach phonics to themselves. Others are often *taught* phonics in this way, even though they may not *learn* phonics this way.

Two methods of teaching the graphophonic system favor auditory learners. One method is called the *analytic* method, the other, the *synthetic* method. The analytic method is more popular (Farr & Carey, 1986). I'll describe each method to you and show you a direct way of using them. Remember, though, that they can be used more indirectly as well, depending on the kind of program you are using—see Chapters 8 and 9.)

The Analytic Teaching Method

Suppose some of your students are having trouble decoding the digraph *sh,* as in *shell* or *dash.* (A digraph is a combination of two letters standing for one sound, such as the *th* in *thin* or the *oa* in *boat.* For other "phonics words" you don't understand from context clues, please refer to Table 7.3, "A Glossary of Graphophonic Terms.") Suppose, moreover, that you have already used an *sh* lesson in a basal reader teacher's guide, so you decide to make up another one for these children. Here are some planning steps you can follow to use the analytic method.

Planning Steps

1. Make a list of easy words that include the digraph *sh.* To have every list a teacher might conceivably need when teaching graphophonic analysis, you may some day want to order a copy of *The Reading Teacher's Book of Lists* (Fry, Polk, & Fountoukidis, 1984). In the meantime, words ending with *ash* would give you a start in your planning for this lesson: *cash, dash, gash, hash, lash, mash, crash,* and so on. Those ending with *ish* might also be listed—*dish, fish, wish*—as well as some beginning with *sh: shell, shut, should,* and *ship.*

2. Write one sentence for each word you plan to use in your lesson. Usually four or five words are enough, unless you decide to have one sentence for each child in the group. To provide more context, you can weave the sentences together to make a very short story, like this:

"I like <u>hash</u>," Dan said.
"I like <u>fish</u>," Nan said.
"What <u>should</u> we do?" Dan said.
"I know what we can do," <u>she</u> said. "Let's eat <u>fish</u> <u>hash</u>!"

Try to make the words in the sentences simple and meaningful to the children. The context words that surround the "target words" (underlined) should not be more difficult than the target words themselves. After you have put your story on butcher paper or the chalkboard, you're ready for the third planning step.

3. Find other *sh* words in their basal reader (or another book they use in common) and write down the pages on which the children can find the words later in whole text.
4. Plan a reading game or activity that will provide them with more practice.

Now that you've done your planning, here are some actual teaching steps:

Teaching Steps

1. Read the sentences out loud to the children, smoothly and informally, as if you were speaking to them.
2. Have them echo-read each sentence after you.
3. Have them say each target word together after you.
4. Have each child say one target word after you and then use it in a sentence.
5. Say all the target words to them again and ask them what letters are the same in each word.
*6. Ask them what sound is the same in each word. Have them make the sound with you.
*7. Ask them what sound they should think of when they see the letters *sh* together.
8. Return to the sentences and have the children first read them together and then individually read them.

---

*Strictly "implicit" programs avoid having children pronounce letter sounds in isolation. Instead, children are asked to notice that the words all have the same sound in them, and then they are asked to think of other words that include that sound.

As you can see, the analytic method starts with several target words imbedded in contextual sentences. It requires the children to analyze the target words to determine the common grapheme (such as *sh*) and the phoneme (such as /sh/) that the grapheme stands for. The children learn this grapheme-phoneme connection (letters and corresponding sounds) through discovery rather than through being told by the teacher ahead of time.

Phoneme: a distinctive speech sound that can contrast one word with another, for example, *hip, lip.*

Grapheme: one or more letters used to represent a phoneme.

Practice in using the analytic method. Make up either a quick "story" or four separate sentences designed to teach the *ea* digraph, as in the one-syllable words *beat, beak, seam, seal,* and so on. (Be sure to have no more than one *ea* word in each of your sentences; the other words in the sentence should provide context clues to meaning.) Now go through the teaching steps in your mind for teaching the *ea* digraph with the analytic method.

The Synthetic Teaching Method

Whereas the analytic phonics method has children break words down into grapheme-phoneme units, the approach referred to as "the synthetic method" has them build words up from grapheme-phoneme units. Basically, with the synthetic method, children learn first to decode letters in isolation and then learn how to put them together to make words. As I did with the analytic approach, I'll give you one type of sample lesson plan that uses the synthetic phonics method. (There are many other types).

Let's again suppose that some of your students are having trouble decoding the digraph *sh.* This time assume that you've already taught this grapheme through a language experience lesson (as shown in Chapter 8). In planning a lesson for these children, you would make a list of one-syllable words that include the grapheme *sh,* such as *shack, ash, bash, cash,* and so on. Now you're ready to begin your lesson using the synthetic approach. Here are some teaching steps you might follow:

Teaching Steps

1. Write *sh* on the board. Point to this digraph and tell the children "explicitly" what sound they are to make when they see it. (Refer to the letters as "standing for the /sh/ sound.")

2. Have the children make the /sh/ sound whenever you point to the letters. Make sure each person in the small group can say it.

3. Review the sounds related to the graphemes *a, b, h, m,* and *ck* in the same way, using steps 1 and 2.

4. Have each child write the digraph *sh*, first on the board and then on paper. Have them point to what they've written on the board and say the sound (not the letters).

5. Remind them how to blend sounds together by using a "reminder word" they already know, such as *mess*. Write it on the board and have them say it slowly: "mmmeeesss." Then have them say it fast: "mess."

6. Point to the isolated graphemes that you've put on the board (*sh, a, b, h, m, ck*). Tell them they "are now going to blend these together to make some words. Whenever I point to one of them, you make the right sound."

7. Point to three graphemes (from left to right) that will produce a word, such as *b, a,* and *sh*, and have them make the appropriate sounds as you point to them /b/ + /a/ + /sh/. Point to the sequence of three graphemes several times, each time faster than the previous time. Finally, tell them to "say it fast."

8. Write the word you've just produced, in this case, *bash*. Have each child "say it slowly" and then "say it fast." Then have them write it.

9. Do the same thing with other possible words: *hash, mash, shack*.

10. Finish the lesson by using some of the words in context with them; for example, "Do you like to eat *hash?*"

Maybe you've noticed from the sample lesson plan some advantages and disadvantages of the synthetic method. On the plus side, this method is much more explicit than the analytic method. Children are told what sound is associated with what letter or letter pair. They don't have to discover this association on their own as they do with the analytic method. And this seems to fit the learning style of some people (but definitely not all). Those who have trouble learning to decode through the analytic method often are able to learn to decode with the synthetic method (Bond & Dysktra, 1967; Weaver, 1978; Anderson, et al., 1985).

But we should look at the minus side as well. Unfortunately, by learning to decode letters in isolation, the child is not learning to use graphophonic analysis in the most efficient way. Many letters do not stand for sounds when they're all by themselves. They must be seen in a spelling pattern before they can be properly decoded. The letter *a*, for example, stands for a different phoneme in *can* and *cane*. It's the spelling pattern that makes the difference. In the word *can*, we see the VC (vowel-consonant) pattern, whereas in *cane*, we see the VCE (vowel-consonant-final *e*) pattern. Furthermore, the *c* in *cane* has a different sound from the *c* in *city*, because of the letters that follow the *c* in each case. In addition, many groups of letters in our written language have to be seen as patterns for correct decoding to take place, such as the *ight* in *night*, the *ai* in *wait*, and so on.

Furthermore, concentration on sounds in isolation may increase *some* children's difficulty in blending sounds. For example, if *b, a,* and *sh* are first presented as a whole word, the child learns the proper blending of sounds from the very beginning. If these same graphemes are sounded out separately, however, the child is actually trying to blend four phonemes, rather than three: /b/ + /u/ + /a/ + /sh/. The reason there are four phonemes here is that it is nearly impossible to produce most consonant sounds without an accompanying vowel sound.

Nonetheless, despite the disadvantages of the synthetic phonics method, research shows that it works reasonably well for some children (Anderson et al., 1985). Many teachers recommend it for children who are having trouble learning the analytic method. Reading teachers should become familiar with this method so that they can use it with any child who simply is not getting it any other way.

Rather than rely on either the analytic or synthetic method alone, however, I strongly urge you to combine one of these methods with one or more of the visual-emphasis methods I will describe. I also recommend that you combine either method with a language experience approach (see Chapter 8) so that children do not get the wrong idea of what reading really is. It's so easy for some children to learn the wrong thing—that reading is a process of making word-sounds rather than creating meaning.

Practice in using the synthetic method. Select four one-syllable words that contain the *ea* digraph. Using the synthetic method, plan a brief lesson around those four words, and go through the teaching steps in your mind. (Be sure to place the *ea* together on the chalkboard.)

LEARNING GRAPHOPHONIC PATTERNS THROUGH A VISUAL EMPHASIS

Now let's look at three methods that emphasize the visual rather than the auditory mode of learning. Whenever I've asked groups of people to indicate whether they prefer the visual or auditory mode of learning, most people choose the visual mode. Yet when I ask them to remember a telephone number that I write on the chalkboard and then erase, many people combine visual memory with auditory memory in one way or another. For instance, if I were to give you the number 847–5329, you might remember part of it visually and the other part by reciting it over and over to yourself.

Like adults, children too have preferences for the visual or auditory mode of learning certain things. Besides preferences, they also have learning-mode strengths and weaknesses. Some children's auditory memory may be quite weak when it comes to words or phonemes; for instance, they may have trouble thinking of rhyming words or coming up with words that begin with a particular phoneme you give them, such as the /m/ sound. Others may have trouble telling the difference between certain phonemes, such as the vowel sounds in *bed* and *bad;* their auditory *discrimination,* as well as their auditory memory, may be weak.

I'm not recommending that you teach each child according to his strongest perceptual mode. That idea has been tried many times in the history of education and found wanting. (For one thing, the mind/body is designed to use a variety of perceptual and memory modes, often in combination. For another thing, the complex act of reading is more of a conceptual process than a perceptual one.) What I *am* recommending is that you use more than one mode in your teaching. Since the analytic and synthetic methods rely more on the auditory than the visual mode, it seems advisable to supplement them with one or more of the methods that emphasize the visual mode. (And if you add writing to your lesson, you can engage the kinesthetic mode as well.)

Phonogram Method

For purposes of reading instruction, the following clusters of letters are called *phonograms: ack,* as in *back, sack,* and *pack; ip,* as in *hip, ship,* and *lip; ake,* as in *cake, make,* and *lake; ight,* as in *fight, night,* and *light.* These letter sets are extremely handy in teaching children how to use graphophonic cues. Why?

They have a reasonably consistent pronunciation from one word to the next (Jones, 1970; Wylie & Durrell, 1970; Groff, 1983).

They seem to be a kind of pattern that children notice naturally, even with little or no instruction (Cunningham, 1975–76).

Teaching children to read phonograms may allow teachers to move more quickly into teaching words of more than one syllable (Groff, 1971*b*). The word *hobbit,* for example, includes the familiar *ob* and *it* phonograms found in *job, rob, sob* and *bit, hit, sit.*

Suppose we've just used the analytic method to teach a group of children to decode the *sh* grapheme. Since the analytic method has an auditory emphasis, let's now switch to a visual emphasis by using the phonogram method. This may seem strange, since by now you may be convinced that the phonogram method merely uses rhyming words (which would involve *auditory* memory rather than visual.) This impression isn't quite true. With the phonogram method, the teacher *uses* rhyming words but does not *ask* for rhyming words. Instead, the teacher writes two words on the board, such as *bash,* and *cash,* and asks for more words that end with the same three letters: *a-s-h.* To make the experiences even more visual, this is how the teacher writes the words the children give her:

	V C C
b	a s h
c	a s h
d	a s h
l	a s h
sl	a s h
g	a s h
tr	a s h
r	a s h
h	a s h
thr	a s h

A vertical line separates the phonogram from the other letters, or the phonogram is underlined with different-colored chalk. This helps the children learn the phonogram by visual memory, just as if it were a sight word to be learned through abundant repetition. It also helps them see the vowel letter in a *pattern* rather than in isolation. In this case, for instance, the letter *a* is seen in a VCC pattern (vowel-consonant-consonant), indicating that the *a* probably has a short

TABLE 7.1
Phonograms with ten or more rhyming words

Short A:	VC:	ab, ad, ag, am, an, ap, at
Short A:	VCC:	ack, amp, and, ang, ank, ash
Long A:	VCE:	ace, ade, ake, ame, ane, ate, ave
Long A:	VVC:	ail, ain
Long A:		ay
Irregular A:		all, ar, are (dare), ark, aw
Short E:	VC:	ed, en, et
Short E:	VCC:	ell, end, ent, est
Long E:	VCE:	unusual pattern for long *e*
Long E:	VVC:	eak, eal, eam eat, eed, eep, eet
Irregular E:		ear (fear), ew (few)
Short I:	VC:	id, ig, im, in, ip, it
Short I:	VCC:	ick, ill, ing, ink, int
Long I:	VCE:	ice, ide, ime, ine, ive
Long I:		ight
Long I:		ind (find)
Short O:	VC:	ob, od, og, op, ot
Short O:	VCC:	ock, ong
Long O:	VCE:	oke, one, ope
Long O:		old, ow (low)
Diphthong O:		ow (cow)
Irregular O:		ore, orn
Short U:	VC:	ub, ug, um, un, ut
Short U:	VCC:	uck, uff, ump, ung, ush, unk
Long U:		none with ten

Other phonograms with five or more rhyming words:	aft, air, age, aid, air, alk, ance, ant, ape, art, ask, awn, ast, atch, ead (head), ean, eek, eel, een, eer, ess, ife, ift, ike, ile, ipe, ire, irt, isk, itch, ite, oat, ode, oil, ole, oll, olt, ook, ool, oom, oon, oop, oot, ort, ose, oss, ought, ound, ouse, out, owl, own (down), oy, ry (cry), ud, ude, udge, ull, umb, unch, unt, ur, ust.

Example: Phonogram *ab.* Rhyming words: cab, gab, jab, tab, crab, drab, grab, scab, slab, and stab.

sound. This visual presentation also helps children learn or review the initial consonant letters *b, c, d, l, g, r,* and *h* and the consonant clusters *sl, tr,* and *thr.* If the teacher wishes, he can also have them look at words like *crashing* and *smashing* so that they can see the value of the phonogram in multisyllable words. Table 7.1 shows a list of phonograms that will be valuable for your teaching

    Practice in using the phonogram method. Using Table 7.1, select two phonograms with a VCC pattern that will help you teach the short *a* sound. Plan a brief lesson using these phonograms, and go through the teaching steps in your mind.

Phonogram: For purposes of teaching reading, a phonogram is being defined as a combination of at least one vowel letter and at least one consonant letter at the end of a one-syllable rhyming word.

The Substitution Method

Again, suppose we've just taught some students by one of the auditory methods (analytic or synthetic) to decode the digraph *sh;* that is, to think of the /sh/ sound whenever they see the letters *s* and *h* together. This time, when we supplement the lesson with a visual approach, we'll use the substitution method instead of the phonogram method. To plan for this part of the lesson, we'll need to list several pairs of words on a chart or on the board. Each pair of words will show *minimal* contrast, such as *he* and *she.* In *The Reading Teacher's Book of Lists* (Fry, Polk, & Fountoukidis, 1984), I find a list of *sh* words that includes *she, shell, ship,* and *shot,* among many others. This is how I would pair these four words to use the substitution method:

he	she
sell	shell
hip	ship
hot	shot

And here's how you could use these pairs with your students. Moving your hand from left to right for each pair, you might say: "This word is *he,* and it's spelled *h-e.* But the word next to it is spelled *s-h-e.* What sound does *s-h* stand for? . . . That's right. So if this word is *he,* then what word is next to it? . . . Yes, if this word is *he,* then this word must be *she.*" Follow the same procedure for the other pairs in your list. *You* tell them the word on the left, *they* tell you the word on the right. Whenever they have trouble, show them the difference in the spellings of the two words.

When they seem to understand the procedure, you can introduce some more difficult *minimal contrasts,* such as those at the *end* of words:

hat	hash
fib	fish
track	trash
win	wish

When children have difficulty seeing the minimal contrast, you can also place the pairs vertically as well as horizontally, like this:

ha|t	fi|b	tra|ck	wi|n
ha|sh	fi|sh	tra|sh	wi|sh

Practice in using the substitution method. Just to make sure you understand the substitution method, let me ask you a question. If you wanted to teach the *st* cluster with the substitution method, which of the following pairs of words would show the *minimal contrast* in letters that you need to show?

mist	mast
stick	stack
fast	fan
mash	mast

Which pair did you choose?

The first pair would be useful for teaching the short *a,* since that's what you're contrasting with the short *i.* Do you see what I mean? The second pair would be useful for teaching the short *a* again. The third pair would be good for teaching the decoding of *n,* although if the pair had been reversed, it could have been used to teach *st.* Only the last pair is appropriate for teaching children to decode the *st* grapheme. ("If this word is *mash,* and the second word ends with *st* instead of *sh,* then what is this second word?")

The Vowel Pattern Method

Vowel letters are the most difficult to decode because vowel sounds can be spelled so many different ways. The long *e* sound, for example, can be spelled seventeen ways, as in *see, team, equal, he, key, Caesar, e'en, deceive, receipt, people, demesne, machine, field, debris, amoeba, quay, pity.* Fortunately, though, there are only two or three *common* ways for each vowel sound. For long *a* there are two: *made* (VCE) and *maid* (VVC); in *made* we have the (vowel + consonant + final *e*) pattern, more easily referred to as the VCE pattern. In *maid* we have the (vowel digraph + consonant) pattern, referred to as the VVC pattern.

To use letters to designate the vowel pattern, simply start with the first vowel letter and add the letters to the right, as we see in Table 7.2. (This works for all patterns except the CV pattern.)

TABLE 7.2
Words for teaching vowel patterns

	Short VC	Short VCC	Long VCE	Long VVC	Long CV
	in	ink	ape	eat	he
p	in	sink	cape	heat	she
	at	ill	ate	aid	go
c	at	pill	plate	paid	me
th	at	spill	note	mail	by
d	ot	blank	lake	soak	fly
c	up	dash	like	boat	try
ch	ip	bell	five	feet	no
	top	send	came	road	Hi
	not	lamp	rope	train	my
	bud	best	nine	green	be
	fun	sick	flame	jail	we
	bed	bang	time	beak	so
	sad	spring	poke	pain	pro
	spin	hint	bone	mean	sky
	pet	sock	kite	clean	spy

June Knafle (1978) found that children taught to recognize vowel patterns did better in reading words than those in a control group. This doesn't surprise me, since my university students and I have had similar results with children above second grade. What does surprise me is how few experimental studies have been done on this seemingly very effective method. Patrick Groff (1971*a*), because of his own research and research reviews (1971*b*), has been advocating the use of vowel patterns and phonograms since 1971, but few have taken up the call to examine its effectiveness in classroom situations.

A large part of the effectiveness of teaching vowel patterns depends, of course, on *how* you teach them. The methods I'm going to explain are those that my students and I have found to be the most enjoyable and productive. As you may have already noticed, when you teach phonograms you are already beginning to teach vowel patterns. When you use the *et* phonogram with words like *bet, let,* and *met,* you are already demonstrating the VC vowel pattern. All you have to do is incidentally place a VC above the column of words and mention that all the words end with a vowel letter followed by a consonant letter. (Children seem to like using the letters VC better than the words "vowel-consonant.") Thus by the time you use more *direct* teaching of the vowel patterns, the children will have already learned a great many phonograms and developed an idea of what the vowel patterns are.

Teaching Steps

1. Display on a chart or chalkboard the first eight words from the VC column in Table 7.2. Use a vertical rectangle to separate the phonograms from the initial consonant letters or digraphs. Write the letters VC above the rectangle.

2. Read the first eight words to the children and point out that each word ends with a vowel followed by a consonant. Tell them that "these words are all VC words." (Think of this as more a right-brain *intuitive* learning experience than one that takes a lot of left-brain verbal analysis.)

3. Hand each of the children five cards which have a word from each of the five columns (lower half). For example, you might hand Bernice these five: *top, send, came, road,* and *Hi.* Ask them to find the one card that is like the column on the board.

4. Have them all show you this card at the same time. Ask them to check their card to see if it ends with a vowel letter followed by a consonant letter. (If necessary, remind them what the vowel letters are.) Have them hold up their cards again. You should help those who have the wrong pattern find the right one.

5. When they all have the correct pattern, have them each try to read their word (with your help, if necessary) and place it on the chalkboard railing. As each one comes to the board, ask him what kind of word he has ("VC word"), and have him point first to the vowel letter and then to the final consonant letter.

6. Have the children play a game with the VC words. For example, you might play a game of concentration by having two cards for each of ten words in the VC column. This will give you four rows of five cards. For a more difficult game, use more of the words. (See Appendixes A and B for instructions on Pattern Concentration and other pattern games: Wild Things, Steal the Words, and Word Chase.)

7. Have them find VC words on designated pages of whole text that you have preselected.

After the children have thoroughly learned the VC pattern, you're ready to use the direct teaching approach with the VCC pattern. As soon as you think they're ready, you can have them work with both patterns at once. For example, instead of finding a VC word in their stack of five cards, they now find both a VC and a VCC card. If you wish to make this more challenging, you can give them more than five cards to deal with. After they have mastered the VC and VCC patterns, gradually teach them the VCE, VVC, and CV patterns, in that order. You'll find that the activities and games become increasingly interesting and challenging to them as they deal with more and more patterns.

Most second-graders we've worked with seem able to handle the first three patterns, but only if they've first had considerable experience with phonograms. Without numerous phonogram experiences (including incidental teaching of vowel patterns), it would be better to postpone *direct* teaching of the vowel pat-

terns. By the time children reach third grade, most can handle all five patterns, if introduced after previous ones have been mastered. Many children get into grades four through eight without really mastering the vowel patterns. This is unfortunate, since without this mastery their access to graphophonic cues is limited, which in turn limits their ability to confirm the predictions they make through syntactic, semantic, and schematic cues. As remedial reading teachers so often tell me, "They just don't *know* their vowel patterns."

Practice in using the vowel pattern method. Using Table 7.2, plan a lesson for teaching the VCE pattern as contrasted with the VC pattern. Go through the teaching steps in your mind.

Patterns versus Rules

Is it "better" for children to learn vowel patterns than rules such as these?

"When two vowels go walking, the first one does the talking."

"When there are two vowels, one of which is final *e*, the first vowel is long and the second is silent."

Experience and research (Cunningham, 1975–76; Glass & Burton, 1973) tell me "Yes." Learning graphophonic analysis, as I mentioned, seems to be largely a right-brain phenomenon that relies on a great many experiences in decoding words. In fact, *many children teach the vowel patterns to themselves, simply by reading and writing.*

If we can rely on what children tell us, they do not recite rules in their heads as they decode. They see clusters of letters that remind them of known words or known phonograms or known vowel patterns. Downing put it well: "Very young children perform wonders in manipulating . . . language, without anyone telling them the rules or their being able to describe them. . . . It is quite unnecessary for rule following behavior to be based on verbal formulation of the rule" (1969, p. 226).

Tovey (1980) demonstrated that Downing was correct. When Tovey administered a phonics test consisting of nonsense words to children in grades two through six, he found they did quite well in pronouncing the words correctly, with scores ranging from 55 percent to 83 percent. When they were asked to *verbalize* their phonics knowledge, however, very few of them were successful. A study by Rosso and Emans (1981) was even more revealing. They also gave children a phonics test, this one consisting of 14 words that represented 14 phonics rules. Each student was then asked to give a rule for the words he had pronounced correctly. An average of 75 percent of the children pronounced each of the words correctly, but an average of only 14 percent could explain the rule for their correct pronunciation.

So we see, then, that children can learn the patterns quite well in an intuitive, nonverbal, nonrulelike manner. But how reliable are the five patterns in predicting the correct pronunciation of words? The answer depends upon a very important concession. To treat these patterns as reliable, one must concede that it's necessary to teach children some major exceptions. The so-called "bossy *r*" is one of them. When this letter follows a vowel, both the rules and the patterns crumble. The word *car*, for instance, can't be placed in the VC column, indicating a short a. The short /a/ heard in *can* is very different from the /a/ heard in *car*. So when a child wants to put a word like *car* or *fur* or *her* in the VC column, just calmly put it in a new column called "the r column" and show her how the vowel sound differs for words that end in *r*. Words placed in the VC or VCC columns *must have a short vowel;* this means that words rhyming with *find* shouldn't be placed in the VCC column. Sorry, but the *ind* phonogram is a loner and a spoilsport.

Now let's look at a major exception in one of the long-vowel columns, namely, the renegade VVC column. In this column we find a fairly consistent long sound if we stick to the *ea, oa, ai,* and *ee* pairs, as in "Eat toad tails? EE!" But stay away from those inconsiderate pairs, *ei, ie, ou, oi,* and *oo.* To teach *oi, oo,* and *ou,* you'll need the phonogram method and these phonograms: *oil, ook, ool, oom, oon, oop, oot, out.* As for *ei* and *ie,* the few words that contain these strange digraphs should be learned as visual memory sight words or through regular spelling lessons—and through regular reading. (How many words with *ie* or *ei* can you think of that children really need, besides *friend, piece,* and *Leif Ericson?*) There is one other major exception in that VVC column. The *ea* digraph works just fine for the phonograms *eak, eal, eam, eat,* and *ean*—as in *leak, seal, seam, seat,* and *bean*—but don't count on the *ead* phonogram, as in *dead head.* It has a short sound and needs to be learned via the phonogram method, all by its nasty little self.

If at times you become a little discouraged with our crazy spelling (especially when a student points out inconsistencies like *bone, done,* and *gone*), rest assured that it's not as bad as it may seem. Just smile and remember that there's also *cone, drone, hone, phone, shone, stone, tone,* and *zone.* Look at it this way: About three-fourths of the time, our spelling is consistent with the way words sound (Bailey, 1967; Burmeister, 1968; Clymer, 1963; Emans, 1967; Greif, 1980). Wouldn't you rather have kids decode words with a three-out-of-four-chance for success than with only a random chance?

TEACHING GRAPHOPHONIC ANALYSIS WITH MULTISYLLABIC WORDS

One of the most important advantages of teaching phonograms and vowel patterns is the contribution they make toward determining the pronunciation of words with more than one syllable. In examining hundreds of miscue analyses on poor readers, I've often noticed the paralysis that sets in for these children whenever they reach "big words." Sometimes it's paralysis; other times it's a frantic display of bravado, throwing out any big word starting with the same letter:

The car was speeding down the boulevard. *bulletin*

And then there are times when the child invents a new word right on the spot, as when Brenda read *hillycopy* for "helicopter."

How can a knowledge of phonograms and vowel patterns help this situation? Let's assume for a moment that *rabbit, basket,* and *robin* are not part of Randy's sight vocabulary. One glance at *rabbit* and he's got the familiar phonogram *ab,* which children who have been taught phonograms will associate with *cab, grab,* and other *ab* words; he's also got the familiar phonogram *it,* which he will have associated with *bit, sit,* and many others. It's quite true that the second syllable in *rabbit* contains a schwa vowel sound rather than a short *i* sound, but research has shown that this is really not a problem. Wylie and Durell (1970), for example, have found that 95 percent of the phonograms in the words used in primary-grade books can be read intelligibly by ignoring the schwa sound and using a short or long vowel instead. Groff (1986) agrees.

Looking at the word *basket*, Randy will find not only the high-frequency phonogram *et*, but also the phonogram *ask*—one with considerably lower frequency. If Randy has learned vowel patterns, however, he can intuitively see that *basket* can be broken up mentally into two VC patterns, *bas* and *ket*; or it can be broken into a VCC pattern, *bask*, and a VC pattern, *et*. Either form of syllabication will work fine; the point is that with both phonogram and vowel-pattern knowledge, Randy has an excellent chance of decoding the word with minimal discomfort.

What about a harder word, like *robot* or *robin?* Using a rule once taught to me, I would divide *before* the consonant. It works with *robot* but not with *robin*. Whatever rule you might have learned, the fact is that dividing before the consonant letter works 50 percent of the time, and dividing after the consonant letter works 50 percent of the time (May, 1985). But more importantly, it's doubtful that children should be straddled with *any* syllabication rules. Instead of rules, they need strategies for finding recognizable clusters of letters in words; teaching them vowel patterns provides them with a strategy. With words like *robin* and *robot,* for example, we can encourage them to "try pronouncing the word both ways."

V C   C V   V C   C V

Try r o b/i n and r o/b i n. Try r o b/o t and r o/b o t.

Whichever sound "rings a bell" or seems right in context is the one to use. In other words, instead of teaching children syllabication rules, teach them to keep right on using the four cueing systems, but armed with knowledge of phonograms and vowel patterns.

If you want children to understand this concept more thoroughly, here's one way to demonstrate it. Have them read each word *out loud* both ways and then tell you which one sounds right in the sentence.

V C	C V	
m i n/ e r	m i/ n e r	The miner is in the pit digging coal.
V C	C V	
c e d/ a r	c e/ d a r	The blankets are in the cedar chest.
V C	C V	
C h i n/ a	C h i/ n a	China is a country in Asia.
V C	C V	
s t a p/ l e r	s t a/ p l e r	Use a stapler to put the pages together.

Making Syllabication a Context Strategy as Well

You probably recall that a dictionary presents two ways of dividing each word, first according to printing convention and then according to the need of the reader; for example, risk/y (ris′/kē) and drift/er (drif′/tər). It would be helpful for the reading teacher to look at word division in this same way—as two separate conventions. As a reading teacher, of course, you're concerned only with the decoding convention and not the printing convention.

You see, a secretary or printer divides words according to *printing* conventions and not according to what's helpful to the reader. For example, a printer would divide the word *hoping* this way: hop-ing. A reader who divides it mentally that way would come up with *hopping;* and, through contextual analysis, he would know that he had divided it the wrong way. If he then switches to ho-ping, he'll come up with a better pronunciation and the right meaning.

Syllabication, then, becomes a tool for the reader who is searching for meaning—searching for the message the author is presenting. Syllabication should not be a "busywork" exercise of merely drawing lines between syllables according to rules.

TEACHING GRAPHOPHONIC ANALYSIS IN THE CONTEXT OF WHOLE TEXT

Studies show that more time in classrooms is spent on isolated phonics lessons and practice than on any other aspect of reading instruction (Durkin, 1978–79). The fact that insufficient time is spent on comprehension is something we'll talk more about in Chapter 15. Right now, let's just say that *most practice time on graphophonic analysis needs to be carried on in the context of regular reading, guided by a skillful teacher.* This would be the best way to encourage interactive reading. If children spend most of their time on phonics lessons worksheets, they are simply not going to have enough time *applying* what they've supposedly learned from those lessons. No matter how well they score on phonics subskill tests, they are *not* demonstrating growth in actual reading.

Here is one example of a teacher's skillfully combining instruction in context and graphophonic analysis, helping children use all four cueing systems:

BENNY: [reading] The man aimed his rifle and shot the deer.
TEACHER: [for the benefit of the group] How did Benny know that last word was *deer* and not *desk?*
MARTHA: [laughing] Because *deer* doesn't end with *sk.*
TEACHER: Good, you noticed one of the clues. Now what's another clue? George, do you know why that last word couldn't be *desk?*
GEORGE: Because . . . uhh . . .
TEACHER: Why don't you try reading Benny's last sentence again, but this time use the word *desk* instead of *deer.*
GEORGE: The man . . . the man aimed his rifle and shot the *desk.* [laughs out loud] You can't shoot a desk.

MARTHA: Yes, you could. You could shoot a desk.

GEORGE: Yeah, but it would be silly, and . . . and besides this man's out in the woods. There wouldn't be any desk out in the woods!

TEACHER: All right. Good work, both of you. You paid attention to the letter clues, but you also paid attention to what the author *meant*. Lucilla, why don't you read the next page.

LUCILLA: When the man reached the dead deer, he looked at the an . . .

TEACHER: [after several seconds] Try that trick I showed you.

LUCILLA: With a blank?

TEACHER: Yes, the blank trick.

LUCILLA: When the man reached the dead deer, he looked at the blank and saw that he had killed a five-point buck. His family would eat well this winter.

TEACHER: Now go back to your blank and see if you can fill it in.

LUCILLA: [after a few seconds] Antelope?

TEACHER: Try it out.

LUCILLA: When the man reached the dead deer, he looked at the antelope and . . . Oh no, that wouldn't make sense.

TEACHER: [smiling encouragement] How about the last part of that sentence? What does it say after your blank?

LUCILLA: And saw that he'd killed a five-point buck.

TEACHER: Do you remember what we said a buck is?

LUCILLA: A male deer.

TEACHER: That's right. And what part of a male deer would have five points on it?

LUCILLA: Oh, I know. That thing on top of his head. His horns.

TEACHER: That's right, And those horns have a special name.

GWEN: I know what they are.

TEACHER: Lucilla, would you like Gwen to tell you what she thinks they are?

LUCILLA: [smiling] Yes.

GWEN: They're antlers.

LUCILLA: Oh yeah, antlers.

TEACHER: All right, Lucilla, try your sentence again, and fill in the blank.

LUCILLA: When the man reached the dead deer, he looked at the antlers and saw that he had killed a five-point buck.

TEACHER: Did it make sense this time?

LUCILLA: Yes.

TEACHER: So now your guess is a good one. But what should you check to make sure?

LUCILLA: Check the letters.

TEACHER: Right. How do we know that word is really *antlers*. Do you see any group of letters that you recognize?

LUCILLA: Oh, I see *a-n-t*.

TEACHER: Good. And how do you say that part of the word?

LUCILLA: Ant.

TEACHER: Yes, and what about the second part?

LUCILLA: Lers.

TEACHER: Fine. That was good checking. Now let's have Judd read the next page for us.

PUNCTUATION AS PART OF THE GRAPHOPHONIC CUEING SYSTEM

From the very beginning of instruction in reading, children need to learn that those little ink blots (punctuation marks), wiggly letters (italics), and other graphic signals help the reader know how to "say it the way the author would say it." Most of us adults forget how important those insignificant-looking graphic cues are.

Suppose someone asks you this question in a letter: "Are you going there?" Which one of these is probably meant by the question?

Are YOU going rather than someone else?

Are you GOING there or have you already been there?

Are you going THERE instead of somewhere else?

ARE you going there, or are you just bluffing?

It depends, of course, on which word the letter writer meant to stress. And your comprehension of the intent depends on which word you stress. If the writer meant for you to accent *there,* and you accented *you,* a serious misunderstanding could ensue. ("What does she mean, am *I* going? Doesn't she think I'm good enough to go?")

We've talked about how a person's reading comprehension is influenced by her understanding of words in a language context. Now we need to look at another component of the language comprehension process—the component often referred to as "expression." *Expression* is a general term that covers three specific signals: stress, pitch, and pause. Without the proper use of these three signals, it can be quite difficult for one person to comprehend another person's speech or writing. You've seen one example of this difficulty already. Now look at this one. A scribbled note from your friend says, "Come join us at the park buy some ice cream sandwiches and pop." Which of these did your friend probably mean?

Join them at the park but first buy some ice, cream, sandwiches, and pop.

Join them at the park but first buy some ice-cream sandwiches and some pop.

You decide that your friend meant the second alternative; you buy the stuff and drive to the park in your hot car. By the time you get there, the ice-cream sandwiches look like burnt toast floating in a puddle of milk. Your friend laughs hysterically and says, "I didn't want you to bring us anything. I just meant you could buy some ice cream, sandwiches, and pop for yourself—here—at the park!"

Quite likely you can think of other incidents when confusion arose over misplaced stress or pauses. During a conversation you have with another person, that person's intonation, gestures, and so on, usually provide the clues that are necessary for comprehension to occur. But when a person is reading what another has to say, she has to provide her own interpretation of what the stress, pitch, and pause patterns should be. And sometimes the reader makes the wrong interpretation, as in the case of the melted ice-cream sandwiches.

Teachers will sometimes say to children, "Read it with more expression, Susan!" or "Read it as if you were just talking to us, Ronny." In most cases this probably demonstrates the teacher's understanding of how important pitch, stress, and pauses are to good reading comprehension. But just telling children to "put more expression into it" is often not enough. Instead, they need to be shown why expression is important, what it sometimes "looks like" in print, and how one can determine the proper pitch, stress, and pauses that are necessary for reading with comprehension.

First task: Showing them why expression is important. This can be handled in a manner similar to the way I tried to show you why it is important. For instance, suppose you and the pupils come across this passage in a story from a basal reader:

Bill watched Jim throw the ball.

Bill called, "Hey! Show me how to throw, Jim."

By reading the second sentence out loud to the children in a variety of ways, you can help them see the relationship between expression and comprehension. Some of the ways this sentence can be read are as follows:

Bill called, "Hey! Show me how to *throw*, Jim."

Bill called, "Hey! Show *me* how to throw, Jim."

"Bill!" called Hey. "Show me how to throw *Jim*."

Bill called, "Hey! Show me *how* to throw, Jim?"

Bill called, "Hey! *Show* me how to throw Jim."

Bill called, "Hey! Show me how to throw *Jim*."

Just by reading this sentence in a variety of ways—and letting them try their hand at it—you can help them discover intuitively why pauses, pitch changes, and stress variations are important.

Second and third tasks: Showing them what symbols are used in print to indicate expression. Showing them how to determine the proper pitch, stress, and pauses. The need for printed symbols for stress, pitch, and pauses becomes evident to children during an experience like the one just described. The importance of commas seems obvious to them when they realize that without them *Jim* is thrown instead of the ball and *Bill* is called by *Hey* instead of calling "Hey!" himself. Likewise, they can see that a period, a question mark, and an exclamation point are not just simple stops like commas, but indicators of pitch changes as well.

With a language experience approach (described in Chapter 8), the teacher can casually show the children how to use punctuation and underlining as she takes dictation of their stories. Suppose one of the children dictates this, for instance:

> Bob said, "Did you take my hat?"

The teacher can show in a natural way how to separate the speaker's message from the actual speaker, and how to use capital letters, commas, quotation marks, and question marks. As the children read what they have dictated, the teacher helps them notice the graphic expression marks so that they can read the message in the way they, as the authors, intended the message to be read. This type of experience demonstrates vividly to children the importance of expression to reading comprehension. Sometimes, of course, stress is indicated by letters in italics or uppercase: "I want *you* to eat it. I've had ENOUGH!" But often a reader is expected to provide her own italics, as in the case of the following passage:

> Bill watched Jim teaching Harry how to throw.
>
> Bill called, "Hey! Show me how to throw, Jim."

In a case such as this, the child must learn to rely on context for a clue as to which word to stress. Since Bill has been watching Jim teach Harry how to throw, it is likely (but not certain) that Bill would say, "Hey! Show *me* how to throw, Jim."

In addition to the types of experiences with stress, pauses, and pitch I've described, the teacher can provide the children with photocopied stories that are completely lacking in punctuation and ask them to insert capital letters, periods, commas, question marks, and exclamation marks and to underline the word in each sentence that should be given the most stress. You may want to try this example yourself.

> I'll do it Roy shouted Terry you run back to town and get some copper wire clippers and some electricity tape tell them Roy sent you and tell them we'll be needing more copper wire soon.

Children can get excellent practice in reading with expression by reading plays to each other—or stories that have a lot of dialogue. Whatever practice materials are used, however, positive reinforcement should be given for meaningful expression and not just for interesting variations in pitch or stress. Some children can appear to be reading with magnificent expression, yet show through their answers to questions that they had very little idea of what they were reading. The goal of communicating with the author should always be paramount.

A GLOSSARY OF GRAPHOPHONIC TERMS

When teachers share ideas for teaching graphophonic analysis, they use certain terms—the jargon of the trade. These terms are used by authors of basal reader teacher's guides, by remedial reading teachers, by speech therapists, and by other people in the profession. You've already read many of these terms in context; you can review them in Table 7.3.

TABLE 7.3
A glossary of graphophonic terms

Sample Words	Letter Symbols	What to Call the Letters That Represent the Sounds	What to Call the Sounds	Sound Symbols
hat	a	Vowel letter	Short vowel sound	/a/
wait	ai	Vowel digraph	Long vowel sound	/ā/
hobby	y	Vowel letter	Long e sound	/ē/
yell	y	Consonant letter	Consonant sound	/y/
shake	sh	Consonant digraph	Consonant sound	/sh/
stop	st	Cluster or blend	Cluster or blend	/st/
boy or now	y or w	Consonant letter	Glide (if preceded by o)	/y/ or /w/
cow, boy	ow, oy	Diphthong	Diphthong (vowel sound + glide)	/ow/ or /oy/
out, oil	ou, oi			
pencil, about	i, a, e, u, o	Vowel letter	Schwa sound	/ə/

Note 1: If you see /sh/, say the *sound.* If you see *sh,* say the two letters.

Note 2: Linguists, speech therapists, and reading educators don't always agree on terms. For example, many linguists use the word *blend* to indicate a word produced by joining parts of other words, for example, *smoke* joined to *fog* yields *smog.* (Terms are often more historical than rational.)

SUMMARY OF MAIN IDEAS

☐ Phonics and reading are not the same thing. Graphophonic cues are only one of four types of cues used in the reading process. The teacher's overemphasis on phonics may cause reading problems.

☐ Although graphophonic analysis should be seen through the perspective of the total reading act, it *is* an important and sophisticated process, much more complex than sounding out letters one at a time.

☐ Whether the teacher uses a direct or an indirect way of teaching phonics is probably not as important as how flexible she is. Sometimes an indirect approach is called for, sometimes a direct way—it depends on the child and the circumstance.

☐ It is natural for children to look for patterns in their environment. By teaching children with the phonogram and vowel pattern methods, we may be able to enhance this natural inclination.

☐ The analytic and synthetic methods of teaching graphophonic analysis emphasize the auditory mode of learning more than the visual mode. They should be supplemented with methods that emphasize the visual mode, such as the phonogram, substitution, and vowel pattern methods.

☐ The only purpose of teaching syllabication strategies is to help children apply graphophonic analysis to the syllable units. Syllabication instruction can coincide with or follow instruction on phonograms, vowel patterns, and suffixes.

☐ Graphophonic analysis is probably more a right- than left-brain operation. This belief coincides with research showing that it is easier for children to learn graphophonic patterns intuitively than to learn phonic rules verbally.

☐ Practice in graphophonic analysis should be combined with context analysis more often than conducted in isolation.

APPLICATION EXPERIENCES FOR THE TEACHER EDUCATION CLASS

A. *What's Your Opinion?* Discuss why you agree or disagree with the following opinions. Use both the textbook and your own experiences.
1. When a child doesn't know a word, just tell him to sound it out.
2. Direct instruction in phonics is better than indirect instruction (through reading and writing).
3. A child should learn as many phonics rules as possible.
4. Children should have the opportunity to learn graphophonic analysis techniques with more than one method.
5. The synthetic method is superior to the analytic method.
6. The substitution method is superior to the phonogram method.
7. The nonsense word *cobanantopes* must be syllabicated like this in order to pronounce it: co/ban/ant/o/pes. There is no other way.
8. Phonic analysis should be combined with context analysis.

B. *Miscue Analysis:* Scotty is a third-grader. Analyze his miscues in this passage. Does he appear to be using graphophonic cues in a way that leads to comprehension? Does he need any particular help on graphophonic analysis? (A check means a long hesitation; a large C, a self-correction.)

Bob and Paul had [been sawing] *(been watching)* and hammering all day. They were building a play house . . . Mr. Kramer, who lived *(had)* next door, had *(he'd)* given them some lumber from an *(a)* old garage. He had also given them some bricks to make a solid *(sold)* floor.*

C. *Teaching Vowel Patterns:* Using Tables 7.1 and 7.2, decide on some of the phonograms you should probably teach before teaching children the difference between the VC and VCE patterns. How will you teach those phonograms?

D. Teach the VC and VCE patterns from Table 7.2, using peers as your students. (See "Teaching Steps" on page 234.)

E. Practice using the analytic method as suggested on page 225 with the *ea* digraph.

---

*Colin Dunkeld, Portland Informal Reading Inventory, Form P. Unpublished manuscript, Portland State University. Reprinted with permission from the author.

FIELD EXPERIENCES IN THE ELEMENTARY SCHOOL CLASSROOM

A. Using one auditory-emphasis and one visual-emphasis method, teach a consonant letter, digraph, or cluster. Discuss your procedures and results with at least one other person. (You will find a list of consonant letters, digraphs, and clusters in Appendix H.)

B. Teach three different phonograms related to the same vowel pattern from Table 7.1. Then play a game of Steal the Words with one or more children, using one-syllable words that have those three phonograms as endings. (See the directions for Steal the Words in Appendix A.)

C. Teach two different vowel patterns from Table 7.2, using children in grade four or up as your students. (See "Teaching Steps" on page 234.)

D. Guide children's reading of a selection, using the techniques described on pages 239–241. Teach the graphophonic clues in context.

REFERENCES AND SUGGESTED READING

Anderson, R. C., Hiebert, E. H., Scott, J. A., & Wilkinson, I. A. G. (1985). *Becoming a nation of readers: The report of the commission on reading.* Washington, DC: National Institute of Education.

Bailey, M. H. (1967). The utility of phonic generalizations in grade one through six. *The Reading Teacher, 20,* 413–418.

Bond, G. L., & Dykstra, R. (1967). The cooperative research program in first-grade reading instruction. *Reading Research Quarterly, 2,* 5–142.

Bronson, D. B. (1977). Towards a communication theory of teaching. *Teachers College Record, 78,* 447–456.

Burie, A. A., & Heltshe, M. A. (1975). *Reading with a smile: 90 reading games that work.* Washington, DC: Acropolis.

Burmeister, L. E. (1968). Usefulness of phonic generalizations. *The Reading Teacher, 21,* 349–356.

Carbo, M. (1987). Deprogramming reading failure: Giving unequal learners; an equal chance. *Phi Delta Kappan, 69,* 197–201.

Clymer, T. L. (1963). The utility of phonic generalizations in the primary grades. *The Reading Teacher, 26,* 252–258.

Cunningham, P. M. (1975–76). Investigating a synthesized theory of mediated word identification. *Reading Research Quarterly, 11,* 127–143.

Dewey, J. (1933). *Experience and education.*

Downing, J. (1969). How children think about reading. *The Reading Teacher, 23,* 217–230.

Durkin, D. (1978–79). What classroom observations reveal about reading comprehension instruction. *Reading Research Quarterly, 14,* 481–527.

Dykstra, R. (1968). Summary of the second-grade phase of the cooperative research program in primary reading instruction. *Reading Research Quarterly, 1,* 49–70.

Emans, R. (1967). The usefulness of phonic generalizations above the primary grades. *The Reading Teacher, 20,* 419–425.

Farr, R., & Carey, R. F. (1986). *Reading: What can be measured?* Newark, DE: International Reading Association.

Fry, E. B., Polk, J. K., & Fountoukidis, D. (1984). *The reading teacher's book of lists.* Englewood Cliffs, NJ: Prentice-Hall.

Glass, G. G., & Burton, E. H. (1973). How do they decode? Verbalizations and observed behaviors of successful decoders. *Education, 94,* 58–64.

Greif, I. P. (1980). A study of the pronunciation

of words ending in a vowel-consonant-final E pattern. *The Reading Teacher, 34,* 290–292.

Groff, P. (1971*a*). Dictionary syllabication—How useful? *Elementary School Journal, 72,* 107–117.

Groff, P. (1971*b*). *The syllable: Its nature and pedagogical usefulness.* Portland, OR: Northwest Regional Educational Laboratory.

Groff, P. (1983). A test of the utility of phonics rules. *Reading Psychology, 4,* 217–225.

Groff, P. (1986). The maturing of phonics instruction. *The Reading Teacher, 39,* 919–923.

Hart, L. A. (1983). *Human brain and human learning.* New York: Longman.

Jones, V. W. (1970). *Decoding and learning to read.* Portland, OR: Northwest Regional Laboratory.

Knafle, J. D. (1978). Word perception: Cues aiding structure detection. *Reading Research Quarterly, 8,* 502–523.

Maclean, R. (1988). Two paradoxes of phonics. *The Reading Teacher, 41,* 514–519.

Mallett, J. J. (1977). 101 make-and-play reading games for the intermediate grades. West Nyack, NY: Center for Applied Research in Education.

May, F. B. (1985). *A case for vowel pattern instruction.* Unpublished paper.

Rosso, B. R., & Emans, R. (1981). Children's use of phonic generalizations. *The Reading Teacher, 34,* 653–658.

Russell, D. H., et al. (1981). *Reading aids through the grades.* New York: Columbia University Teachers College.

Smith, A. (1984). *The mind.* New York: Viking.

Tovey, D. R. (1980). Children's grasp of phonics terms vs. sound-symbol relationships. *The Reading Teacher, 33,* 431–437.

Weaver, P. (1978). *Research within reach.* Newark, DE: International Reading Association.

Wylie, R. E., & Durrell, D. D. (1970). Teaching vowels through phonograms. *Elementary English, 47,* 787–791.

The Writing/Reading Connection:
Through Literature, Whole Language, and
Language Experience Approaches

━━━━━━━━━━━ CHAPTER PREVIEW ━━━━━━━━━━━

I've been hinting throughout the book that writing and reading should be taught together. Now, in this chapter, I'll explain why, and I'll also suggest several ways of doing this—through literature, through whole language programs, and through language experience approaches. *Literature*—especially patterned literature like rhymed poetry, patterned picture books, and detective stories—provides children with a comfortable model for writing, one they can imitate

while satisfying their own creative urges. As they produce their own sample of a literature genre, they can, in turn, experience abundant practice in whole text reading—of their own writing and the writing of their teacher and peers.

Whole language programs, more than any other type of instructional approach, provide a flexible, creative atmosphere in which to explore both writing and reading in a natural way. In these programs, subskill practice is held to a minimum, while practice in whole text writing and reading become the name of the game.

Language experience approaches, often dubbed LEA, are methods of combining the four language arts—speaking, listening, writing, and reading—into one instructional program. LEA is used in many whole language programs and can be used with basal reader programs and literature-based programs as well. Through group experience charts and personal stories, children can learn the interrelated processes of communication.

In our zeal to make it easy, we've made it hard. How? Primarily by breaking whole (natural) language up into bite-size, but abstract little pieces. It seemed so logical to think that little children could best learn simple little things. We took apart the language and turned it into words, syllables, and isolated sounds. Unfortunately, we also postponed its natural purpose—the communication of meaning—and turned it into a set of abstractions, unrelated to the needs and experiences of the children we sought to help.

—Ken Goodman

Human beings have a deep need to represent their experience through writing. We need to make our truths beautiful. . . . We write because we want to understand our lives.

—Lucy Calkins

Asking a working writer what he thinks about critics is like asking a lamppost how it feels about dogs.

—Christopher Hampton

POETRY IN THE WRITING/READING PROGRAM

Mrs. Friedman read several poems to her fourth-grade class that day. "It was just one of those poetry days," she said later. The sun hadn't been out for three days straight, Billie Jean had thrown up in the cloakroom, and Mrs. Friedman had forgotten to turn in her lunch count, thus getting a mild reprimand over the public address system. "If ever humorous poetry was called for," she said, "it was that day."

Shel Silverstein came to the rescue with his poem about Peggy Ann McKay, who was able to find sixteen chicken pox on her body, along with a sunken bellybutton and twenty-five other ailments that were sure to keep her from going to school. And there was his poem about the peanut butter sandwich that locked the jaws of a silly young king. And, of course, the one called "Stone Telling."

How do we tell if a window is open?
Just throw a stone at it.
Does it make a noise?
It doesn't?
Well, it was open.
Now let's try another
CRASH!
It wasn't!*

Among all the poems read that day was my own opinionated one, "Waffles Are Better," given in Figure 8.1. The students in Mrs. Friedman's class enjoyed this poem, and there was quite a discussion about the virtues of pancakes versus waffles. She realized, while the children were engaged in debate, that this poem would be a useful model for their own writing.

The next day, when things were running smoothly once more, Mrs. Friedman showed them the poem, now written on a large chart. She invited them to

FIGURE 8.1
Waffles Are Better

Some favor pancakes
Fried in a pan,
Then piled high,
Slathered in butter
Drowned in syrup!
But not I.

I favor waffles.
Waffles are something
You never fry.
You pour in the batter,
You put down the lid,
And my oh my!

You wait and you wait,
Your patience so thin,
Your hopes in the sky,
While the magic takes place,
While waffle elves work,
And eternity goes by.

You watch and you stare
Through mystical steam
At the little red eye.
"Will it ever go off?
Will it ever turn dark?"
You cry . . . then sigh.

But at last the aroma!
And the steam disappears.
The red light does die.
You open the lid
And the magic is done.
It's time to pry.

Out pops the disk
As gold as the sun,
As round as a pie.
On goes the butter
Like molten lava
From mountains high.

Then on with the syrup
Into valleys so deep
You try and you try
To fill every one . . .
And not miss a peak:
A feast for the eye!

Now gobble that moonscape,
Demolish that city,
Let no building lie.
You could have had pancakes
So flat and so smooth
And delicious—but why?

---

*"Stone Telling" from WHERE THE SIDEWALK ENDS by Shel Silverstein. Copyright © 1974 by Snake Eye Music, Inc. Reprinted by permission of Harper & Row, Publishers, Inc.

join her in a choral reading of the poem, with Mrs. Friedman reading every other verse by herself (to provide modeling) and the children reading the alternating verses as a group. Then she asked them to tell her how the poem had been written. Through skillful questioning, she helped them come up with these characteristics that she wrote on the chalkboard:

1. Two favorite things were compared.
2. Every third line rhymed.
3. The rhyming sound was the same throughout the poem.
4. One of the favorite things was shown to be better.
5. The rhythm throughout the poem was the same.

With these characteristics on the board, the children then attempted to write a similar poem as a group. Janet suggested that they compare eggs with bacon, but Kim thought they were too different and suggested chicken with steak. Nancy waved her hand wildly and said, "Oh, I know! Let's compare an ice-cream cone with a candy bar!" This idea met with approval from the entire class, but now they had a bigger problem to solve: Which one would they show to be better? The vote was close, but the ice-cream cone won. To diminish the candy lovers' disappointment, Mrs. Friedman told them they could write the parts of the poem in praise of the candy bar.

Now they had to select a rhyming sound that would be the same on every third line. Mrs. Friedman asked, "What are some words that rhyme?" and Dennis came up with *cat, bat,* and *sat.* The list of *"at* words" on the board grew from three to eighteen, and they decided they had enough. Mrs. Friedman wrote the first line and invited the candy-bar lovers to describe a candy bar in such a way that everyone in the room would want one.

"Some like candy bars," she wrote, and then waited for a response. "Filled with nuts and covered with chocolate," Robin said. The teacher wrote:

> Some like candy bars,
> Filled with nuts
> And covered with chocolate.

This version met with strenuous protest, since the third line didn't exactly end with the rhyming sound of /at/. Mrs. Friedman asked for another third line.

"Pat, pat, pat," Cindy said, smiling and patting her hand on her desk. Mrs. Friedman smiled back. "You mean as if someone were patting the nuts into the candy bar?" Cindy assured her that this was exactly what she had in mind!

The teacher changed the third line by drawing lightly through it and writing the new third line off to the side. In this way, she knew she wouldn't lose the contribution that had been made earlier about the candy bar being covered with chocolate. The poem now read:

> Some like candy bars,
> Filled with nuts.
> Pat, pat, pat.

Mrs. Friedman said, "Since we're putting all those nuts into the candy bar, perhaps we need a word that's stronger than *filled.*"

"Smashed," said David.

"Mooshed," Diane said.

"Crammed," Bobbie said.

And on through their poem they plunged and weaved and slashed, the teacher contributing a line now and then to keep them going, until thirty-five minutes later the tired poets rested. Their poem is shown in Figure 8.2.

THE WRITING/READING CONNECTION: RESEARCH AND THEORY

You've just seen an example of a teacher combining writing and reading instruction through the use of rhymed poetry. Why combine instruction in reading and writing? What are the advantages?

Much of the new emphasis on combining them comes from our knowledge of "early readers"—those who learn to read and write before they even enter school. Durkin (1966) studied early readers for six years in California and for three years in New York City. One of her conclusions was that the scribbling and writing these early achievers had done before starting formal schooling made an important contribution to their success in learning to read at an earlier age than

FIGURE 8.2   *Ice Cream Cones Are Better!*

Some like candy bars,
Filled with nuts
Pat, pat, pat.

Some like candy bars
Mooshed with cream,
Fat, fat, fat.

Most like candy bars
Smothered with chocolate,
Imagine that!

With so much sugar
It can sweeten up
The meanest brat.

But I like ice-cream cones,
So smooth and round
Not bumpy and flat.

You stand at the counter
With noses pressed to the glass,
You and Shelly and Nat.

And you wait and you wait
As she scoops it up,
Pat, pat, pat.

Finally yours is ready
And you take a secret nibble,
Feeling like a rat.

You know you should wait
For your friends to get theirs.
So you anxiously chat

About weather and school,
About cabbages and kings,
About zit, zoom, and zat.

And finally you've got them
Enclosed in your fists,
The ball and upside-down hat.

Only one more choice to make:
To lick, lip, or bite.
Oh, drat!

most children. One implication she made from her research was that writing and reading should be taught together.

Other researchers have come up with the same inference from their research (Chomsky, 1971; Graves, 1979; Hansen, 1987). Loban (1976), for instance, found in his thirteen-year study of children's development that children who did well in writing tended to do well in reading, and vice versa. Although this correlation does not demonstrate a cause-and-effect relationship between the two language processes, researchers strongly suspect that the two skills enhance each other's growth. Several other researchers have also found a significant relationship between children's reading achievement and the syntactic complexity of their writing (Evanechko, Ollila, & Armstrong, 1974; Evans, 1979; Lazdowski, 1976). This makes sense. When children learn to speak and write complex sentences, they are more capable of handling those kinds of sentences in a reading situation.

In his synthesis of research on the reading/writing connection, Holbrook found that "almost all studies that used writing activities specifically to improve reading comprehension or retention of information found significant gains" (1987, p. 216). In another synthesis of research results, Harp (1987) found that scores on the Stanford Reading Test were considerably higher for the first-, second-, and third-graders who were involved in an "authorship" program.

Although using writing and reading in combination can lead to greater reading achievement, Shanahan warns us that it's the combination that works, not one or the other: "Many teachers and curriculum designers seem to have assumed that reading and writing are so closely related that students would require only instruction in one or the other" (1988, p. 636). This, he advises, is simply not so.

Although writing can cause gains in reading *achievement*, it can have a powerful motivational effect as well. Dionisio (1983), for instance, found that teaching reading *through* writing was the best approach for her sixth-grade remedial readers who were "turned off to reading." By modeling both writing and revising behavior with the students and giving them plenty of opportunity to *read* each other's work (as well as their own), she was able to help them improve in their *reading* abilities—even without providing them with formal reading instruction. Graves and Murray (1980) had similar results with their writing programs for children.

These results are not too surprising, since the students' *motivation* to learn was greatly enhanced by the switch from the traditional reading emphasis to a writing emphasis. A writer (including a child writer) can feel almost godlike as he or she creates a title or a topic, a plot or an organization, a well-developed character or a well-developed argument. Maybe this is why most children, under certain teaching conditions, can learn to really enjoy writing in a school setting. (See Burrows, *They All Want to Write*, 1985, for examples of such enjoyment.) After all, a school setting seldom provides autonomy for children—especially for remedial readers. They are often pulled this way and that as teachers make their assignments and demands. The chance to make decisions and to take control comes rarely in many classrooms. Yet writing, with its numerous opportunities for decision making (What will *my* plot be? What will *my* main character be like?), can provide this chance.

The Commercialization of the Reading/Writing Concept

As you think about whether you're interested in trying a writing/reading form of instruction, you'll want to be aware of the commercialization of such programs that occurs in the "ed biz." These commercial reading/writing programs tend to be stilted and formalized. Unfortunately (or fortunately), writing does not lend itself to canned programs. Writing is a creative, spontaneous, and intuitive operation, one that requires a surprising degree of social interaction and instructional flexibility for learning to take place.

I should also mention that when you're interested in teaching reading through writing (and writing through reading), it's often a good idea to have the writing experiences precede the reading experiences. This approach is different from the way many of us in this country are used to thinking about teaching. We're used to thinking of reading being a sacred subject, taught all by itself, for its own sake. As Graves pointed out in his 1978 Ford Foundation Report:

> Although reading is valued in other countries, it is viewed more in the perspective of total communication. . . . Our anxiety about reading is a national neurosis. . . . Concern about reading is today such a political, economic, and social force in American education that an imbalance in forms of communication is guaranteed from the start of a child's schooling. (Graves, 1978, p. 3)

An Examination of Reading/Writing Theories

The strong movement in our country toward writing/reading instruction has been due to the work of dedicated teachers and theorists: Lucy Calkins, Carol Chomsky, Dolores Durkin, Ken Goodman, Donald Graves, Jane Hansen, and Donald Murry, to mention just a few. These people have intensely observed children learning to write, witnessed success that at least appears to be caused by the relationship between learning to write and learning to read, and theorized the causes of this relationship.

Let's examine the theories that writing/reading proponents have developed. Tierney and Pearson (1983), for instance, theorize that both writing and reading require planning, composing, and revising. Let me give you some examples of what I think they're saying. Good writers *plan*, but, as you already know, so do readers. Good readers plan their reading by doing two things ahead of time: (1) setting purposes and (2) thinking of prior knowledge related to the topic or setting. They also *compose* as they read. Although the words are there already, the reader must create the meaning of the passage—as well as creating predictions and hypotheses about upcoming words, ideas, and events. And finally, good readers also *revise* as they read. This revision takes place whenever a reader's hypothesis or prediction is not confirmed. Because of these three basic similarities between reading and writing—the planning, composing, and revising of language—we can theorize that practice in *written* composition will lead to improved reading "composition." Conversely, of course, reading can also lead to improved writing. This relationship might be called the "comprehension relationship" since both reader and writer, when they are composing, are concerned about meaning or understanding.

I would add a fourth dimension of similarity between writers and readers—simply that both writer and reader must think about their "communication partner." A writer must think about his audience if he's going to communicate well. A reader must think about the author in order to communicate with him: What's he trying to say? Is he biased? If so, is his bias supported with evidence? Is he trying to be funny or serious? Both communication partners, in other words, whether communicating through writing or reading, must size up their partners.

Shanahan (1988) has something to add to this idea about communication: In developing their reading/writing ability, he says (and I'm paraphrasing his idea), children learn not just a spelling, decoding association. They also sense a comprehension relationship: We read to understand or enjoy the author. We "author" to help others understand and enjoy. In addition, children learn a vocabulary relationship. They learn words through reading that they later use in writing. They learn words through writing that they later recognize when reading.

There are two other relationships I'd like to mention: (1) cueing systems and (2) language concept. When writing, we attempt to provide the appropriate graphophonic, semantic, and syntactic cues that will stimulate the reader's schematic cueing system. When reading, we activate our own schemata in order to connect with the author's semantic, syntactic, and graphophonic cues.

Now let's get into a very fundamental relationship, one that surpasses even the importance of the cueing systems: the language concept relationship. As you probably suspect, a child develops a concept of writing as well as a concept of reading. So far so good. The important thing for a teacher to realize, though, is that a child's concept of writing influences greatly his concept of reading. In fact, as he learns to write, he gradually learns what reading is all about.

Since writing is a more personal, more involving process, it is an excellent medium for understanding authors and the relationship between authors and readers. The child is continually writing and then trying to read her own writing (or having someone interpret what she just wrote, if she's using invented spelling). This process teaches her the meaning of reading—how it is connected to someone doing some writing, someone trying to communicate. When we separate reading and writing, as we often have done in the schools, we create an unnatural, nonlinguistic division.

TEACHING READING THROUGH THE WRITING OF PATTERNED BOOKS

One way of helping these relationships along is to engage children in the use of patterned literature. In Chapter 4, we discussed the use of patterned books to help children develop the concept of reading as a fluent process of predicting and confirming. Later we talked about using these books as media for teaching sight words and graphophonic patterns. In this chapter I'd like to show you another use for them. Let's see how a teacher in Vancouver, Washington, used a patterned book to teach reading and writing to three first-graders in her "learning disabled classroom." The teacher, Brenda Louthan, chose Steven Kellogg's book, *Can I Keep Him?* The main character is an imaginative boy who keeps telling his mother about a new animal he's found and asking her if he can keep it. The mother, of course, has an appropriate excuse for each one of her denials. Here's the way Mrs. Louthan describes her experience:

Day one: I read Kellogg's book to the children. I then read it again and asked them if they had noticed anything that had happened over and over in the story. They were able to see the pattern in which Arnold tries to bring home pet after pet and his mom always tells him, "No, dear. You can't keep him."

Day two: I read the book again and we made a list on the board of all the animals that Arnold had brought home. We went back through the book and checked to see if we had found all of them.

Day three: I read the book again and we made a list of all the other animals that Arnold *could* have brought home. They really enjoyed this and came up with a long list.

Day four: I read the book again and we made a list of all the reasons Arnold's mom gave him for not keeping the pets. We also looked closely at the illustrations this time, as they showed clearly what Arnold's mom was talking about.

Day five: At this time I told the three children to each choose one animal from our long list that they would like as a pet. They chose a hippo, a bald eagle, and a worm. We then made a list, for each animal, of reasons a mother might give for not keeping these pets.

Day six: I read the story again and we made a list of all the reasons Arnold gave his mom for keeping the animals. We then made a list for each of our three animals. We also made a list of all the places these animals might be found, and each child got to choose one for his animal.

Day seven: I read the book again and discussed the pattern of mother's replies to Arnold. We looked back to the list we had made on day five (reasons for not keeping animals) and chose three of them for each of our animals. We then put these reasons into sentences, using the pattern of the mother's words. We also chose our main character, who turned out to be a boy named Fred.

Day eight: I read Kellogg's book again and this time we discussed the pattern of Arnold's words. We then looked back at the list we had made on day six (containing reasons for keeping our animals) and chose three of those for each of our animals. We then put these reasons into sentences, using the pattern of Arnold's words and including where our animals had been found.

Day nine: On separate pages the children and I wrote out each sentence we had developed. We read these together and the children illustrated two pages each.

Day ten: We talked about the ending of the story where Arnold tries one more time to bring home a pet. There is only a picture of this event, so each of the children drew a picture of what animal they thought Fred might bring home. We then made a cover for our book, and each child drew a picture of one of our three animals on it.

Day eleven: We made photocopies of our book and then read it together. The children then colored the pictures and took the book back to their other rooms to share. They were really thrilled that they could write and read a book! I felt it was a very positive learning experience.

Suggestions for Writing Patterned Books

I have had the pleasure of working with hundreds of children and teachers in the creation of patterned books. Here are some of the things we have found to be important in the production of patterned books in the classroom:

1. Be sure to work only with a model book that the children show considerable enthusiasm toward!
2. Don't rush it. It usually takes five to ten days to do it well. Spend only twenty to thirty minutes a day on the process to avoid fatigue and increase excitement.
3. Several readings of the model book are necessary, but read for a different purpose each time. Brenda Louthan, you may have noticed, read the

book to her students eight times, but each time so they could make a new list or description. The children were not bored with that many readings, because they read on different days and because they had a specific goal for listening to it again. They knew they were writing a new book like Kellogg's book and that making lists and descriptions was necessary in this process.

4. Making lists related to the model book and then the new book helps children focus on descriptions, plot patterns, and language patterns in the model book. This listing also provides ample practice in meaningful writing and reading.

5. Be sure they each get a copy of the book to read to others—including parents. (Parents are generally very impressed.)

6. Provide encouragement to those individuals who decide to make their own "personal" new book (even though it might be quite similar to the group-made one).

Other Types of Literature to Use for Reading/Writing Programs

You've seen that literature can provide excellent models for children as they learn to write and read. By showing you examples of this learning through rhymed poetry and patterned books, I've only scratched the surface. Many types of literature, including wordless picture books (Cairney, 1987), can serve as models. One of my favorite experiences, for example, is inspiring children (from third grade on up) to write detective stories. (See Appendix I for a list of good model books.) Detective stories tend to have a definite pattern. So do myths, folk tales, tall tales, and (alas) love stories. All of them, when read in abundance before children try to write their own—and then in abundance as they share their own with others—become perfect models for their practice in connecting writing and reading.

WHOLE LANGUAGE APPROACHES TOWARD READING/WRITING INSTRUCTION

There are two other major writing/reading approaches I'd like to discuss with you: (1) whole language and (2) language experience. Both also use literature as one of their foundation stones, and both of them are based on some important notions about children and language. Let's talk about whole language first.

Facetiously, I should warn you that whole language is not a religion, although some people make it sound like one. At the same time, it *is* a philosophical set of beliefs about children and language (Altwerger, Edelsky, & Flores, 1987; Brountas, 1987; Goodman, 1986). I'll summarize these beliefs for you.

Ten Theses of Whole Language Advocates

1. As much as possible, *writing and reading* should be learned together (for reasons I've already given).

2. Writing and reading should be learned in *meaningful situations,* because our "real" use of language always occurs in meaningful situations. We talk and write outside of school in order to communicate, to express our needs, to persuade. Talking, writing, reading, and listening in school should imitate these kinds of meaningful communications. Thus, in a "whole language classroom," the teacher attempts to provide problems to solve or topics of interest to explore rather than having children spend much time on isolated subskill exercises. Social studies and science topics are highly appropriate. Furthermore, the problems or topics selected should have the potential to require a considerable amount of communication: talking, writing, listening, and reading.

3. Our language has *interacting cueing systems* (something I believe I mentioned before). Thus, whole language advocates try to provide practice mostly with whole text and whole composition rather than primarily with subskill exercises in phonics, punctuation, or other isolated language bits.

4. *Written language* is not merely a mirror image of spoken language. It's also a system of its own. We can learn language through this system just as we can through the oral language system. Although it's often helpful to have oral language precede written language, it doesn't always have to. The best example I can give of this is the way one of my friends pronounces certain words. She's an avid reader and learns all kinds of new words through her reading. Occasionally, though, she doesn't pronounce them correctly. One of these was the word *solder,* which she had never heard in an oral language context. She pronounced it so that it rhymed with *older,* even though it's supposed to rhyme with *odder.* In other words, we do learn vocabulary (although sometimes incorrectly) just from reading written language. We also learn sentence structures and grammatical concepts this way.

5. Language is best learned in a community setting. Therefore, the classroom should provide community interaction and *cooperative learning.* Working with a partner (or two or ten) can lead to increased communication skills, as well as social skills. Children should have frequent *writing conferences* not only with the teacher but also with a peer. Children should write for each other, not just for the teacher.

6. Whole language approaches require whole books—thus the need for a strong *literature program.* (See Chapter 9.)

7. For writing to flourish, it needs time. Just as professional writers need time for *writing each day,* so do children. (And, of course, such writing leads to reading their own manuscripts and those of others.)

8. *Teachers need to be writers.* By writing, yourself, and by sharing that writing with your students (including the troubles you had writing it), you

can model the process for them. Don't model a perfect product, though, that they'll be expected to follow. In a whole language classroom the teacher's way is not "best."

9. The teacher's major function is that of *benevolent responder*. The way we respond to young writers and readers should be the same as the way we respond to young speakers. When children are just learning to speak, "adults respond to the messages young children try to communicate, not to the errors they make in their attempts. . . . We respond to what we think they are trying to tell us" (Hansen, 1987, p. 13).

10. Writing is a *process* more than a product. It's a thoughtful, problem-solving process of selecting, rehearsing, composing, and reading. It's a process of finding one's own "voice" (Graves, 1983), one's own motivated desire to communicate. This process cannot develop unless teachers allow *choice*. Choice of books, choice of topics, choice of ways of expressing themselves—all are crucial ingredients of a successful reading/writing program.

Whole Language Programs in Action: Journal Writing

Perhaps the most common procedure used in whole language classrooms is that of journal writing. Journal writing occurs at all of the grade levels, but it is especially important during the first two or three years, when children are developing their literacy awareness. Journal writing is not assigned writing. The time is provided and children write what they wish to in their personal journals.

Can children be expected to write on the first day of first grade? Well, if you remember from my discussion in Chapter 4, we can expect them to "read" on the first day, provided the teacher uses some form of simple patterned material. Actual writing, though, rather than dictating, is asking too much for some of the children. Gunderson and Shapiro (1988) collected writing samples from two multiethnic first-grade classes for a year. They found that half of the children needed to dictate to the teacher. But the other half were able to write letter strings (BVTHGT) or an exotic concoction consisting of letter strings, conventionally spelled words, and invented spellings (*fite* for *fight*, *brd* for *bread*). Within four weeks, however, the "dictators" had gradually switched to invented spellings, spacing between words, and identifiable sentence strings.

How did this amazing transformation take place? Well, ask yourself how it might take place if you were suddenly placed in a foreign culture and you had to communicate in order to feel comfortable in that environment. Would you ask your neighbors how to say something? How to write it, perhaps? Would you pay very close attention to how "experts" spoke or wrote? Would you pay attention to any type of print in your new environment? (Whole language teachers call it *environmental print*.) Would you seek out someone who would *respond* to your attempts to use the language orally and in writing? These are the kinds of things that happen in a whole language classroom. Lots of interaction among the "members of the community." Lots of helping and caring, as modeled by the teacher—

very much like, say, a large family of six to ten children might do it (at least on television). Everyone helping one another get into the literacy club. Plenty of environmental print all around the room and school: "coats and jackets," "scissors," "What will we do today?" Time for journal writing every day. Time for a writing conference every day—either with the teacher or with a peer. Written and oral responses from a teacher or peer about each child's writing.

What were some other things that Gunderson and Shapiro (1988) discovered as they observed their particular sample of first-graders? (1) By using a simple computer program that rank-orders the frequency of words in students' writing, they noticed that these children did learn important high-frequency words, even though they were not exposed to the words through a basal reader program. (2) The children's invented spelling revealed their growth in awareness of phonic patterns as well.

Here's what another researcher had to say after observing journal writers for their first four years of school: "The most outstanding development at Springside during the four years of dedication to journal writing is the abundance of eager authors. Students write fluently and easily. They take risks with paper and pencil because they have years of experience in building confidence" (Kintisch, 1986).

Three other researchers analyzed the contents of journals written by 20 first-graders during their first school year. They found that the writing ranged widely: scribbling, random letters, descriptions of pictures, lists, informational "articles," imaginative stories, retelling of stories, you name it. "All of these first graders wrote in their journals from the very beginning of the year and did not seem to lose interest during the year. Most of them wrote several times a week and shared what they had written with their teacher and peers" (Manning, Manning, & Hughes, 1987).

Responding to Children's Journals

Perhaps the most difficult skill for some whole language teachers to develop is that of responding to what children write in their journals. There is a tendency to write evaluative comments instead of responding to the actual content of what the child has said. Sumitra Unia (1985, p. 68) gives us an example of this difference:

CHILD: I saw my mom. I want four a walk with my clase. I like my teacher. I saw some machines and they were picing up rokse. My friend came to My hose and we played dolls and It wass fun. I wore a dress today Im invited to melanie Birthday she is going to be 7.

EVALUATIVE COMMENT: You are doing your journal very nicely. I am very pleased.

CONTENT-ORIENTED COMMENT: Your dress is very pretty. I hope you have fun at Melanie's birthday party. Do you like wearing dresses? It is nice to be able to wear different kinds of clothes. I am glad I don't have to wear dresses to work all the time now. In cold or rainy weather, I prefer to wear pants. How about you?

The content-oriented comment provides motivation for practice in actual communication. The evaluative comment, when used exclusively, makes journal writing just another test.

Another skill for whole language teachers to develop is that of writing comments that are *not* contrived to teach or demand. The following examples are based on those provided by Unia (1985, p. 68):

CHILD: Dear cjch I am going to the contest and It's going to be fun. I want to the vair and it was fun. I want to the Falie to pike some apples and pirs. and then we want to a plaes to eat awer lunch and It was fun.

CONTRIVED RESPONSE: How many pears and apples did you pick at the fair? I would like you to tell me more about your weekend.

As Mrs. Unia points out (p. 68), this type of message from the teacher is merely an attempt to demonstrate the correct spelling of misspelled words. It also shows the teacher's dissatisfaction with the *amount* that the student produced.

So I guess what this means is that to get children to really communicate through a journal, you, the teacher, will need to avoid being teacher-and-judge for a while and simply communicate back with them. Too much teaching or evaluating at this point will dry up the children's enthusiasm and their real attempt to use language as a means of communication.

Does this mean that a teacher who uses journal writing responds to every child's every entry? Not at all. Probably no more than once a week for many teachers. Remember that children respond to each other's journal, for one thing. And for another thing, many of them don't actually want a response each time. Much communication that we do in journals and diaries, after all, is to ourselves.

Is journal writing only for children in early grades? Not at all. Journal writing is useful right through high school. By fourth grade or so, however, *some* teachers don't provide a daily time for personal writing, choosing instead to use two or three of the days each week for children to record what they're learning from social studies and science experiences.

Whole Language in Action: The Writing Conference

As I've already mentioned, writing conferences, either with the teacher or with a peer, are standard practice in many whole language classrooms. But what are writing conferences, anyway? They're probably not what most adults think of. For the teacher they're often only an informal way of moving from desk to desk, assisting Marcia and Jan, who seem to need help right away because they "can't get started," or commenting on Fred's topic about dinosaurs, or providing Amalia with positive feedback on the paper she gave her to read the night before. For the peer they're often only an informal way of responding to a friend's question, "Hey, man. How's this look to you?" (and not having the teacher interrupt him as he gives straightforward feedback on his friend's composition).

Sometimes, of course, teachers decide to schedule some of the conferences—either teacher-student meetings or peer meetings. This seems to work pretty well, too, as long as the content of the child's composition is the focus of the conference and the child's spelling and mechanics are discussed only in a peripheral way. If you would like to learn more about writing conferences, I recommend a book by Donald Graves entitled *Writing: Teachers and Children at Work*. I also suggest that you write for a catalog of interesting paperback books on writing and reading published by Heinemann Educational Books, 70 Court Street, Portsmouth, NH 03801.

Writing conferences are a way of cementing the community of literacy learners. They provide one avenue for communicating about children's real problems with—or enjoyment of—language.

LANGUAGE EXPERIENCE APPROACHES

While most elementary school teachers use basal readers (Dick and Jane) to teach reading, a growing number are using one of the language experience approaches—either as a substitute or as a supplement. Rather than rely upon basal readers as the sole medium of instruction, they rely as well (or instead) upon the language of their students. Children dictate or write their own reading selections and thereby learn in a practical way that reading is a form of communication and

that authors and readers are truly communicators. Teachers use the selections created by their students as instructional material for readiness, decoding, and comprehension experiences. They keep track of children's progress through a "skills-management system" or through careful observation.

Differences between LEA and Whole Language?

As you can already predict, the language experience approach (LEA) is a vital element of many whole language programs. Although language experience was once a set of beliefs about language and children, in the same way that whole language is today, the term *language experience* has come (through use and misuse) to mean more a *method of instruction* than a philosophy. In this sense it tends to be slightly more teacher-directed than those methods used in many whole language classrooms. For instance, a whole language teacher might rely more on daily journal writing or writing conferences (with the teacher or a peer), while a language experience teacher might rely more on group stories about common experiences. This difference between whole language and language experience teachers is more an historical and semantic difference than one that can be brought to sharp focus in an actual classroom. In today's classrooms I see whole language and language experience ideas merging and melding.

Students Who Can Learn from a Language Experience Approach

A variety of types and ages of students have been taught reading and writing successfully through a language experience approach. Many kindergarten teachers use LEA to get children ready for more formal instruction in first grade. Children in small or large groups dictate their ideas or experiences to the teacher, who immediately prints them, exactly as dictated, on the chalkboard or on tagboard charts. The teacher reads the ideas back to the children and then encourages them to "read" (say) the ideas with her, thus getting the kindergartners used to the idea that printed words can represent spoken words. A left-to-right reading orientation is developed; letter names are taught or reviewed; and visual and auditory discrimination are reinforced—all through the use of such "experience charts."

In first grade, such an approach is taken several steps further. Not only do children dictate their thoughts; they begin to write them as well. In addition, they learn from dictation and writing to recognize numerous words by sight, as well as common suffixes and graphophonic patterns. As the year progresses, they read not only their own and their peers' written accounts, but the stories and descriptions of adult authors as well. Library books, and even selections from basal readers, become opportunities to practice the communication skills they have gained through creating and reading their own stories, articles, and books.

Other first-grade teachers use a language experience approach right along with a basal reader program from the very first. For skill development, they rely on the basal program; for developing the concept of reading as communication, they rely on LEA.

In the later grades, LEA is used to enrich children's understanding gained through more formal reading instruction and through social studies, science, and other areas of the school curriculum. The children create charts, stories, magazines, newspapers, journals, and books as records of what they are learning, experiencing, and feeling. These materials also provide excellent reading opportunities.

Children who need remedial instruction, at any grade level, can be helped through LEA. This is especially true of those youngsters in grades three through twelve who have been "turned off" by too many previous experiences with completing worksheets and drilling on subskills. For many remedial readers, a language experience approach can provide a first glimpse into the real meaning of reading. Tyrone, for example, was a leader of a small "gang" of third-grade boys who hated "readin' and goin' to school." Their teacher asked me for help, so together we came up with a plan. At that particular time in my life I was driving a 240Z sports car, one that, alas, I had to give up later when my family grew. Anyway, according to plan, I drove to her school the next day and gave Tyrone's gang, one boy at a time, an exhilarating ride in my sports car. When we got back to her classroom, the teacher skillfully took dictation while the boys excitedly took turns telling her about their adventure. When their story was finished, they read it with the teacher several times and then proudly to the entire class. For the first time, reading made sense!

Tyrone's teacher duplicated their story so that they could take it home to read to their parents. She then formed a special writers group, appropriately called "Tyrone's Gang." This group of authors created numerous experience stories and gained reading skill through the use of their own compositions. By the end of third grade, they had become bona fide members of the literacy club.

What about children who don't speak Standard English? They, too, can be taught through a language experience approach. Through use of LEA, their own language is not denigrated but instead is used as the first building block toward learning to read. Since early reading is primarily a matter of translating print into speech, it is highly important that such print represent the way children normally speak. (This type of language experience approach is discussed in further detail in Chapter 14 and also in this chapter.)

Rationale of and Research Related to LEA

By now you could probably write your own rationale for the use of language experience approaches. LEA uses the child's present language. It does not rely on language created by adults. Thus, the translation of print back into speech (or subvocal thought) is natural, predictable, and meaningful. Furthermore, children quickly learn the most important concepts about the reading process: (1) Reading involves communication with a person who wrote down her thoughts; and (2) reading is *not* a subject in school, a torturous process of "sounding out" words or an endless conveyor belt of worksheets and workbook pages. In addition, a language experience approach does not separate the language arts into separate skill areas of reading, writing, speaking, and listening. All four avenues of language are used in combination to take advantage of children's natural desire to communicate and to use whole language.

A vast majority of the research studies on language experience approaches have demonstrated that LEA is as effective as basal reader programs and may even have special advantages (Hall, 1981). Perhaps the greatest fear educators and parents have about the use of a language experience approach is that children will not gain as much in vocabulary as will children who are taught through other approaches. Hall summarizes the research on vocabulary this way:

> A persistent criticism of language experience instruction is that students may not develop a satisfactory reading vocabulary, since the lack of vocabulary control and the lack of systematic repetition may be detrimental to learning. The research refutes this criticism. Language experience instruction presents learners with meaningful vocabulary, and a reading vocabulary is acquired by learners through the use of LEA. (Hall, 1978, pp. 27–28)

Others have been afraid that a language experience approach does not expose children to the graphophonic regularities in our language (such as the change in meaning and pronunciation between *can* and *cane* and the consistency in pronunciation of phonograms such as *ill, at,* and *ap*). In a study by Dzama (1975), however, it was discovered that the words used by first-graders in language experience programs provided ample examples for learning such regularities. Major studies as far back as the 1960s (Bond & Dykstra, 1967; Dykstra, 1968) have shown that LEA students tend to learn graphophonic decoding skill about as well as students in basal programs. Furthermore, Chomsky (1971) demonstrated, not surprisingly, that LEA students usually become better spellers than students taught in a basal program.

A Word of Caution (But Not a Wet Blanket)

If LEA works so well, why aren't the majority of elementary school teachers using it to teach reading? Probably for two reasons: (1) Because some teachers and principals fear public criticism for not using a more "systematic" basal program; and (2) because it takes more skill and effort to teach reading this way. With a language experience approach, the teacher must do much more of the daily planning. With a basal reader program, the teacher is given essentially a cookbook in the form of a teacher's guide.

Because LEA is such a useful approach, however, even back in the early 1970s teachers and principals were accepting it, at least as a supplementary procedure (Staton, 1974). Also, keep in mind that the rewards of teaching through LEA are often what many people go into teaching for—enthusiastic learners. If, however, you're not feeling up to using LEA as the major approach for your reading program, you may decide to use it as an auxiliary program.

PROCEDURES FOR CREATING GROUP EXPERIENCE CHARTS

Group experience charts may be created with the *entire* class on some occasions and with any grade—following a field trip to a farm, for example, or a nuclear energy plant. But to get every student involved, it is sometimes best to develop experience charts in smaller groups of ten or fewer. When you do this, however, don't put all your confident language users together in one group and your quiet ones in another. Children with low self-confidence seem to need the company of their more confident peers as language models.

Experience charts are created and used in roughly this order:

1. Developing interest about an experience or topic
2. Discussing the experience or topic
3. Dictating and writing the chart
4. Reading the chart
5. Using the chart to teach and learn words and language concepts

The length of time for each of these steps varies a great deal. Step 1, developing interest, may take five minutes, several hours, or no time at all, if it's an experience the children have had outside the classroom. Normally, however, steps 1–4 are completed during one "sitting" of twenty to forty minutes.

Developing Interest

LEA, like any other approach, can become dull and lifeless if the teacher doesn't concern himself with motivational principles. The experiences and topics selected by the teacher, and the procedures he uses in communicating about them, should (1) provide novelty, (2) meet basic needs of belonging and self-esteem, and (3) fit the appropriate level of difficulty for the children. (See Chapter 13 for more on these principles.) To be successful in using a language experience approach, it is extremely important for the teacher to plan (or capture) stimulating experiences and topics for children to talk and write about. Here are some samples at various grade levels:

A hamster in our classroom

Things we have lifted that are really heavy

What we bought with our class "millionaire fund"

What we plan to do at Disney World

What we would need to survive on a space trip

How we would have prevented the Revolutionary War

Stars: What we've learned about them

The experiment we did about air

Our Halloween party plans

Mike Mulligan and His Steam Shovel

Characteristics of Tolkien's Hobbit

This is just a tiny sample of the possibilities for experience stories. As you can see, most of them are not topics all by themselves but arise out of experiences that the teacher plans for the students to have (such as reading *The Hobbit* together). You may wish to examine the Peabody Language Development Kits by Dunn and Smith (1965, 1966, 1967), as well as Van Allen's *Language Experiences in Reading* (1974) and Hall's *Teaching Reading as a Language Experience* (1981). All contain numerous ideas for language experience activities. You'll also find more ideas in Appendix D.

Discussing the Experience or Topic

Some teachers get in a hurry when using LEA and have children start dictating or writing too soon. In most cases it works much better to have a careful discussion of the topic or experience before writing about it. Such a discussion usually gets the ideas flowing, as one thought stimulates another. Research by Torrance (1962) and Burrows (1985) shows that this type of verbal stimulation *before* composing can produce longer and more creative compositions than you would get by simply having the children write or dictate without discussion. Teachers often worry that a discussion will lead to everyone saying or writing the same thing when it comes time to dictate or write. Some of this "copycat" behavior will occur, it's true, but this is far better than having several children not communicate at all. Remember, the purpose in developing experience charts is to teach the communication skills of speaking, listening, writing, and reading rather than to produce "original" compositions. As with the whole language philosophy, process counts much more than product.

It would be difficult to emphasize this point too much, if one follows the original philosophy of LEA advocates like Stauffer (1980) or Van Allen (1974): The oral language experiences that children engage in are just as important for the development of writing/reading skills as the actual writing or reading itself. Oral language growth at any grade level is a major factor in producing greater growth in both reading and writing. In the case of experience charts (or personal stories), a good oral exchange usually leads to easy and natural dictation or writing, followed by easy and natural reading of the composition(s).

Actually, these two stages—developing interest and carrying on a discussion before story production—are usually inseparable. For example, the teacher can develop interest and at the same time start the discussion by asking an open-ended question about a caged animal she has brought in:

TEACHER: What do you think this hamster feels about your looking at him?

JERRY: I think he's happy.

TEACHER: Why, Jerry?

JERRY: Because he has someone to play with.

TEACHER: [nodding appreciatively] He doesn't seem very frightened, does he?

MONA: He's got long whiskers.

TEACHER: Yes, they're quite long. How long would you say they are? Are they as long as this pencil?

FRANK: [laughing] They're not that long. They're as long as . . . as long as my little finger.

TEACHER: Yes, I think you're right, Frank. What else do you notice about this little hamster . . . Stephen?

STEPHEN: He's got real sharp teeth.

TEACHER: How can you tell?

STEPHEN: Because . . . because they're pointed and because he can chew up those little round things real fast.

TEACHER: Yes, he can, can't he? Those little round things are called *pellets* and they're what he likes to eat. Do you know what they're made of?

STEPHEN: I don't know. Nuts maybe.

TEACHER: Well, in a way, you're right! They're made from the seeds of wheat and barley and other grains like that. Since nuts are a kind of seed, Stephen, you were right!

STEPHEN: [smiling] Yeah.

TEACHER: What do you think he'll do when we each hold him?

Dictating and Writing the Chart

After the discussion (and experience) have continued awhile, the teacher begins the dictation period by moving to a tagboard chart and asking something like this: "Who would like to begin today? We need a sentence at the top that will remind us what we've been doing just now . . . Julie?"

JULIE: We've been lookin' at a funny little hamster.

TEACHER: All right, let's write that down. I'll start way at the top and way over on the left side. I'll start with a capital letter. [She writes: We've been looking at a funny little hamster.] That's what Julie said: "We've been looking at a funny little hamster." Who would like to have the next turn . . . Stephen?

STEPHEN: He has real sharp pointed teeth.

The dictation continues until everyone has had a turn or until the group feels that the "story" is complete. Here's an example of what a finished chart in first or second grade might look like:

A Funny Little Hamster

Julie says: We've been looking at a funny little hamster.
Stephen says: He has real sharp pointed teeth.
Frank says: He has whiskers as long as my little finger.
Mona says: He lives in a wire cage, and he keeps looking at us.
Marilyn says: The funny little hamster runs races with himself.

David says: The funny little hamster ain't got a friend to live with.
Francis says: But we can be his friends. We'll feed him and give him water and play with him.

When taking dictation, the teacher usually avoids the temptation to edit the children's language. In other words, if a child says "ain't," the teacher writes *ain't*. She does not attempt to control the vocabulary or sentence structure or grammar in any way. The only modification she would make is in spelling; when a child mispronounces a word, she doesn't spell it according to the mispronunciation. The teacher spells it correctly and lets him read it any way he wishes later.

One reason the teacher avoids editing grammar, vocabulary, and sentence structure, of course, is to make sure the child perceives reading as a true communication process, rather than a process of pleasing adults. Teachers who edit anything other than spelling will find that children are less willing to volunteer their ideas. Since the teacher's use of standard spelling does not seem to inhibit children's communication, it is probably wise to avoid nonstandard spelling. Some children will take offense if they discover you've been misspelling words to allow for their peculiar way of pronouncing them.

Another reason the teacher avoids editing grammar, vocabulary, and sentence structure is that children tend to read their sentence as they have dictated it, rather than as the teacher has edited it. Thus, once their dictation has been edited, the important link between print and speech has been broken: They no longer read what they see, but what they once said. This in turn makes it more difficult for them to develop their awareness of sight words and graphophonic patterns. (You and I can talk later about working with children who speak in a nonstandard dialect.)

Reading the Chart

The chart that children create is read many times, both by the teacher and by the students, but each time in a slightly different way. Some teachers read the chart as they write it, word by word. Some wait until an entire sentence has been written and then read it back to the children. Some do both and then read the entire thing to the children after it has been completed. In any case, a successful teacher reads the text *to* the children before asking them to read it with her or to read it by themselves.

After reading the chart to the children, the teacher then asks them to read it with her. Next she calls on individuals to read one or more sentences by themselves, helping them as soon as they run into trouble. The important thing is that the reading experience is an enjoyable, successful one. (One way of assuring this success is to have each child read by herself only the sentence she dictated. Later, after the story has become more familiar, each student is asked to try other sentences.)

Using the Chart to Teach Words and Language Concepts

The day following the creation of a chart, the children are usually shown the tagboard version of the story and are presented with a dittoed personal copy as well. The teacher has also prepared a word card for each word in the story. These materials, along with others, are used for developing vocabulary, graphophonic awareness, or comprehension. Each of these will be discussed separately in later sections.

PROCEDURES FOR CREATING PERSONAL EXPERIENCE STORIES

While children are becoming familiar with the process of developing group experience charts, they are usually given opportunities to develop their own personal stories. At first these stories are dictated to the teacher or another person (teaching aide, parent, volunteer aide, teacher trainee, or older student from another room or school). Gradually, as children develop writing skill, the stories are written entirely by them.

Motivation for developing such personal stories arises from many sources. Often a small-group story or total-class story can lead to additional stories created by each child in the classroom. Following the group experience story on the hamster, for example, the teacher could have inspired children in small groups each to write a brief, separate story—one group writing about what the hamster eats, other groups writing about how it plays, how it sleeps, what its mouth and nose are like, what its eyes and ears are like, and so on. Or she might have inspired each child to write a brief adventure of "the funny little hamster."

Other possible motivations for writing personal stories might include these:

Journal writing (as in whole language classrooms)

A picture the child has drawn or painted while working in the art corner

A class discussion on a peculiar object the teacher has brought to school

A follow-up story after having a turn at show-and-tell

A special trip taken over a weekend or holiday

An illustration the child has made for a group experience chart

A show seen on television

A response to seeing a photograph of himself

A picture book read either by the teacher or by the child

A "big plan" for making something

A chance to contribute a page to a group-produced book

A response to something learned from a science or social studies unit

Essentially the same procedures used for developing group experience charts are used for personal stories. Interest is developed in creating the story; the topic is discussed with the teacher or another person; the story is dictated or written; the child reads his own story and listens to other people read it; and the teacher uses the story to provide practice in interactive reading and in recognizing sight words and graphophonic patterns.

TEACHING VOCABULARY IN AN LEA PROGRAM

Vocabulary development is a very personal process. The words that relate to a child's own experience, particularly when those experiences have been highlighted by either positive or negative emotions, are those that are learned and retained most easily (Olson & Pau, 1966; Veatch et al., 1979). Sylvia Ashton-Warner (1963), in her successful attempt to teach Maori children of New Zealand, found that one child who had great difficulty learning words such as *come* and *look,* could quite easily learn words like *knife* and *gaol (jail).*

Because of the personal nature of vocabulary building, teachers who use a language experience approach usually try to personalize the acquisition of vocabulary. To do this, the teacher asks each child to develop a personal "word bank." A word bank usually takes the form of small cards kept by the child in a small box or alphabetically on a large ring. A word is written for the child on a card whenever she demonstrates that she can read it. After the teacher passes out a dittoed copy of a group experience chart, for instance, children are asked to underline the words they know. If Barbara successfully reads her underlined words to the teacher, the teacher makes out a card for each word and gives them to her for her word bank. The same procedure of underlining and presenting word cards is also used for personal experience stories. Other words children learn, such as personal "key words" or those gained from noticing the environmental print the teacher has placed in the room, can also be added to their individual word banks.

The individual word banks have several major functions:

To serve as a record of the reading vocabulary of individual children (helpful to child, teacher, and parents)

To serve as references for creative writing and spelling

To provide reinforcement through repeated exposure to words

To serve as stimulus words for examples during skill instruction

To provide independent activities with word games, matching activities, and sentence building

To provide examples for group language study (Hall, 1981, p. 61)

The children keep the word banks at their desks to practice with each other, to match with the words in their dittoed stories, to use with their journal writing or personal stories, and to play games suggested by the teacher. They bring them to the small-group meetings to use as their own suggested examples of a grapho-

phonic pattern (such as words with a VC spelling pattern) and to help the group create "group word banks."

Group word banks are produced by both the small groups and the entire class. This type of word bank is designed to help children become more aware of word categories and sentence patterns. Examples of group word banks are Color Words, Action Words, Sound Words, Names of Animals, Homophones, and Feeling Words. This type of "bank" is often printed on large tagboard charts so the children can refer to them when they are composing. Sometimes the words are also printed on cards and placed in boxes so the children can use them for independent activities suggested by the teacher.

The words in the group word banks are accumulated gradually throughout the year. One way to begin them is to ask children in a small group to look through their personal word banks and find all the color words (or action words or whatever category the teacher wishes to emphasize). After the group word banks are printed on tagboard, they become a quick reference for various activities such as producing group stories, writing personal stories, or simply creating sentences. In creating sentences, a child can select, for example, an animal word and an action word: Dogs dig. The rest of the group then tries to alter and expand this basic sentence: The frisky young dogs dug deep holes all over the garden.

TEACHING DECODING AND COMPREHENSION THROUGH LEA

In addition to teaching vocabulary through children's writing and word banks, the teacher can also use these materials for teaching special lessons on graphophonic patterns, context clues, suffixes, and comprehension. Occasionally a teacher will feel that these materials are not providing enough practice; thus she may decide to use the teacher's guide to the basal readers the children would normally read at that particular grade level. In the teacher's guide, she'll find numerous ideas for lessons to supplement those based on children's group charts and personal stories.

When using a group chart, for example, the teacher conducts a miniature "phonics lesson" whenever she has the children notice how letters represent sounds and how spelling patterns determine sounds. For instance, the teacher may indicate three words in a story that all start with the letter *p*, then pronounce the three words with the children, and next ask the children what sound they hear at the beginning of each word. She may also find two words with the same final phonogram, such as *night* and *fight*. This could lead to a one-minute lesson on the *ight* phonogram. At some other time, she might point out the difference between the words *hat* and *hate* in a story, and how the VC pattern and VCE pattern predict different sounds. Having introduced a particular graphophonic pattern through a story, the teacher would later review this pattern, either by using later stories or occasionally by providing a lesson from a basal reader program.

It should be noted, however, that a great deal of graphophonic patterns, sight words, and suffixes are learned through the writing component of the LEA method. By using invented spelling on their first drafts, for example, children are automatically going through the process of learning the phonemic quality of our language. Then as they work on their final drafts for a book or a class magazine or just "a story to take home," they also learn the conventional spelling of words.

Children also learn derivatives through the writing process and by noticing compounds, contractions, roots, suffixes, and prefixes in their stories and word banks. Contrasts are made, for instance, between such words as *happy* and *unhappy, happy* and *happiness, fast* and *faster*. To learn context analysis, teachers block out words in a story and children predict the word or words that would fit in the blank. This activity is usually followed by a brief discussion of the clues that enabled them to make such good predictions.

A language experience approach provides a firm foundation for developing comprehension monitoring because of its total emphasis on meaning and communication. Once children catch on to the communication process between author and reader, they are *eager for meaning:* "That word doesn't make sense, Mrs. Bender." Or "That doesn't fit what we did at all!"

THE VARIETY OF LANGUAGE
EXPERIENCE APPROACHES

The LEA method is flexible and creative, and it does not require some kind of lock-step procedure day after day. One of the most heartening things I've witnessed in my observations of both British and American schools has been the variety of ways teachers have invented to apply both the whole language philosophy and the LEA method to their own particular classrooms.

Wright and Laminack (1982) describe an innovative practice in which a first-grade teacher used a language experience approach to teach his students about television commercials. The children learned a great many "commercial words" such as "fresh" and "product" and other favorites of advertisers. They also wrote many language experience charts to describe how they tested the advertiser's claims:

> We listened to a cat food commercial. They say that it is sealed in a pouch.
> . . . On TV when the man opens the pouch a voice says, "Fresh!" Cammie tried this at home. Her cat food did not say, "Fresh!"

> We put water into two small cups. Next, we put a Mounty paper towel in one cup and a plain paper towel in the other cup. . . . We could lift a cup with a wet Mounty. The plain paper towel fell apart.

> Z-soap will make you feel awake. Meredith tried Z-soap. She said that she did not feel any better. We did not see her jump up and down.

Mallon and Berglund (1984) describe a language experience approach that differs from the one I offered, both in sequence and in the amount of personal involvement. You may like this one better:

> *Day one:* A stimulus is introduced followed by discussion. The stimuli might include toys, books, trips, pictures, special events, or a retelling of a story. After discussion, a list of children's suggestions for stories are put on a chart.

> *Day two:* Yesterday's discussion is reviewed. Each child draws a picture of his idea and begins writing or dictating, depending on his skill.

> *Day three:* Each child reads her story to the teacher independently. The teacher underlines known words. Other students are finishing their stories and illustrations, reading their stories to each other, working in a center, or completing other work.

> *Day four:* Children read their stories to the teacher again—independently. The teacher underlines words again, including those already underlined, that the child knows. Some words now have two lines under them.

> *Day five:* This is skill development day. Children make cards for words that have been underlined twice. The children use these cards for lessons on graphophonic patterns, suffixes, or vocabulary. (Mallon & Berglund, 1984)

If you would like to see how one teacher taught reading through LEA for the first time, find the article by Allen and Laminack in the March 1982 issue of *The Reading Teacher.* This article excerpts Mr. Laminack's journal in which he describes his stumbling but very successful first year with an LEA program. If you're interested in trying the language experience approach, I think you'll find this seven-page article quite inspiring.

Lancaster (1982) got her second-graders to write three times a week by following Chomsky's advice (1971) to encourage children to use invented spelling. Gradually the calls for her help diminished, and most of the children's energy was put into getting down their thoughts. The longest stories they wrote were their retellings of favorite folk tales the teacher had read to them. As the program evolved, four principles or procedures seemed to emerge:

☐ Writing three times a week was just about right.
☐ A teacher-led discussion before the children wrote was very important.
☐ Having the teacher circulate around the room to encourage and help children with their *thoughts* (not spelling) was essential.
☐ The children's writing needed to be shared in some way—especially by reading it aloud to the class after lunch and by having the stories typed and made into a book.

Virginia Morrison (1983), a teacher in Saline, Michigan, put her microcomputer to good use in a language experience program. Rather than write her children's dictated stories on a chart or chalkboard, she used word processing software to take dictation. The child (or children) whose story was being dictated could watch his story unfold on the video screen. The story could be stored on a disk for future use and printed out whenever needed. Children could edit their own stories as they dictated them by asking the teacher to make the appropriate changes, or the stories could be edited at a later date after a discussion of ways to "make the story even better." The children's word banks could also be stored on disk and printed out whenever needed.

Gillet and Gentry (1983) have developed a controversial method of using an LEA to teach reading to children who speak a nonstandard dialect. First they have the children read their stories exactly as dictated until they can read them fluently in their own dialect. This enables them to make that necessary connection between speech and print, as well as helping them develop the concept of reading as communication. Then the teacher rewrites the story (out of the children's view) and presents it as "another story about the funny fruit." After the children have learned to read the second story, the teacher brings out the original story and helps each child to make his contribution longer and to "think of another way to say it." Finally the children learn to read the third story. Here's an example of an original story (about two kiwi fruit) and the two transformed stories.

Original Dictated Story

Mandy said, "They was in a bag—a lunch bag."
Kareem said, "They was some kind of fruits."

Tonya said, "Teacher say feel it."

Jerome said, "They was real squishy."

Teacher's Story

Mandy, Kareem, Tonya, and Jerome learned about some funny fruit. First we looked at a lunch bag. Second, we each felt the funny fruit. Then, we talked about the fruit. We tried to guess what the fruit was. Last, we wrote a story about the funny, squishy fruit.

Children's New Story

Mandy said, "First we looked at the lunch bag."

Kareem said, "There were some fruits in the bag."

Tonya said, "Our teacher said to put in your hand and feel around but don't tell what it is."

Jerome said, "The fruit felt squishy and sort of round."

What do you think of Gillet's and Gentry's method? Can you see some advantages? Disadvantages?

KEEPING TRACK OF STUDENTS' PROGRESS: WHOLE LANGUAGE VERSUS SUBSKILLS

Evaluation of children's progress in learning to read through LEA can be done either formally or informally depending upon your beliefs about reading and your district's policies. First, let me explain the formal way, one based on the belief that reading is learned primarily through the mastery of subskills. What you'll need to do if you have this type of situation is to rely on the "skill tests" provided by the district-adopted basal reader program and the "skill lessons" offered in the teacher's manual accompanying the basal program. Achievement and retention tests are administered throughout the year and records are kept on each child. Normally, a skills-management checklist (of subskills) is kept on each child, and this checklist is completed on the basis of both tests and classroom observations. Following the tests or observations, the children are provided with remedial learning experiences.

If, on the other hand, you and your district believe in at least experimenting with the whole language philosophy, you will rely not on subskill tests but on these things: (1) observations of children's reading, writing, and oral language behavior; (2) your own observation notebook; (3) records of books read; (4) records of books, stories, and articles written; and (5) a file of actual written work produced by each child.

Tests on graphophonic patterns, sight words, and other separate parts of the reading act are seldom used with a whole language program, since such testing implies that reading is a composite of separate skills rather than a process of dealing with whole language. Occasionally, "comprehension" tests might be used but only with whole articles or stories rather than the small bits of text often seen in standardized tests. Such comprehension tests can be administered in both a silent and an oral reading context.

An important form of evaluation often used in a whole language program is that of miscue analysis. In this type of evaluation, a teacher listens to a student read aloud and notes the types of miscues he makes. From noting these miscues, the teacher can tell a great deal about the student's concept and strategies of reading and how they might need to be changed. (There is considerably more on this evaluation method in Chapter 11.)

HANDLING THE LIMITATIONS OF LEA

Perhaps the greatest limitation of a language experience approach is inherent not in the approach itself but in the later transition to another approach. Some children who have started out learning to read "à la LEA" become frustrated after moving into a basal program. Their frustration is quite understandable and usually occurs when the teacher using a basal program does not provide ample time for writing creatively and for expressing oneself in group discussions. (It's quite similar to giving an adult a job, respecting her ideas and opinions for a year, giving her many choices for her own way of handling things, and then suddenly presenting her with a very autocratic boss who wants things done exactly his way.) As I've implied, this limitation is not as strong when the teacher using a more structured approach provides numerous opportunities for the children to express themselves in discussions and through writing.

A second major limitation is the resistance parents sometimes offer. Some parents become confused by a language experience approach and get the idea that children are "not really learning how to read—they're just memorizing little stories that they're making up. Why, my Johnny is finishing first grade and can't even sound out words yet." Such criticism is bound to be discouraging to teachers. Many teachers, though, avoid criticism by carefully explaining their instructional approach at the beginning of the school year—either in a letter to the parents or in a general meeting with them. This is followed up with newsletters that explain LEA in more detail.

Children are also asked to take home certain experience stories to read to their parents. The first stories selected for this honor are usually those that contain mostly words the child already has in his personal word bank. Furthermore, they are stories that do not contain nonstandard grammar. As the year progresses, however, and the parents seem to understand the program more thoroughly, the stories are selected with less scrutiny. Conferences are usually scheduled with parents of each child so that the teacher can show them the type of text their child can now read, the stories and articles he has written, the word bank he has developed, and, if used, any achievement and retention test results or any observation checklist that the teacher has used. With the help of their contented students, most teachers I've talked to have been able to transform parental resistance toward LEA into enthusiastic support for it.

SUMMARY OF MAIN IDEAS

☐ The writing and reading processes have much in common and should probably be developed at the same time, with writing experiences often coming immediately before reading experiences.

☐ Patterned books, rhyming poetry, and other forms of predictable literature can provide excellent models for children's composition. These compositions, in turn, serve as practice in reading whole text.

☐ Whole language programs are based on the philosophy that language (including writing and reading) should be learned in a natural, whole text, purposeful way. In place of subskill lessons, writing and reading are learned through the needs for communication and problem solving. Journal writing and writing conferences are usually important features of a whole language program.

☐ Language experience approaches are sometimes more direct and more group-oriented than whole language programs, but they too use a child's own language to teach him how to read. The four language arts are taught together, thus providing children with the opportunity to learn that reading is a communication process. Group experience charts and personal experience stories, along with individual and group word banks, provide the major instructional media. Graphophonic patterns and vocabulary are learned through writing and also through discussions and reading of children's own writing.

APPLICATION EXPERIENCES FOR THE TEACHER EDUCATION CLASS

A. *What's Your Opinion?* Use your own experiences as well as the textbook to help you defend your opinion:
1. Writing experiences can help children realize that reading is a communication process.
2. Writing involves the same cueing systems as reading does.
3. Mrs. Friedman, the teacher described on pages 250–253, was teaching poetry. She wasn't really teaching reading or writing.
4. Learning to write and read are essentially oral language experiences.
5. Teaching reading with a basal reader program designed by experts would be more effective than teaching reading through language experience approaches.
6. Having each child write or dictate his own stories makes more sense than having a small group dictate or write one together.
7. The LEA method of Gillet and Gentry (page 277) is the best way to work with children who speak a nonstandard dialect.
8. Whole language programs are truly different from LEA programs.

B. *Miscue Analysis:* Holly is in fourth grade. In what ways do you think her natural language differs from the author's? Rewrite the paragraph the way you think she might have written it in her own language. What does this tell you about the potential of whole language or LEA programs?

Next Saturday the whole family drove ~down~ to the forest. They found the ~a large~ ranger station and

bought a permit. ~It's close to~ It cost a dollar. The ranger had marked off a place ~a~ for ~where the could~ people to cut

trees.

C. *Teaching Decoding and Comprehension through LEA:* With a partner or small group examine the experience story "A Funny Little Hamster" on page 270. Make a list of specific things you might be able to teach through the use of this story. For example, could you teach a lesson on contractions? Which ones? Compare your list with lists made by others in the class.

D. *Using a Group Experience Chart:* Divide up the class into several groups and secretly give each group a different "Earth object," such as an eggbeater or a felt pen. The students are to imagine themselves as people from a faraway planet who are studying Earth. They should then write a report on the strange and mysterious object they have found. Each group should appoint one person as their teacher-recorder. Go through the five stages of development discussed on pages 268–272. Then share your reports with other groups.

If you prefer topics instead of mysterious objects, then here are some topics you may wish to use:

Here's how you make muddy gravel soup

Here's why applesauce can be dangerous to your health

Here's how to scratch your back, eat chocolate pudding, and read a textbook assignment at the same time

The monster who ate important belongings of college students

What students know about teachers

What teachers know about students

FIELD EXPERIENCES IN THE ELEMENTARY SCHOOL CLASSROOM

A. Help a few children develop a group experience chart. (What highly interesting, but brief, experience can you help them have first?)

B. Help a small group of children bind a book that they have created. Simple means of binding books are described in the books by Van Allen, Hall, and Dunn and Smith listed at the end of this chapter, and also in the free booklet called *Cover to Cover* published by the Encyclopaedia Britannica Press, 425 North Michigan Avenue, Chicago, IL 60611. Most libraries also have other books on this subject.

C. Come up with a writing experience of your own that you can turn into a reading experience for one or more children.

D. Use poetry or a patterned book to stimulate a group of children to write (and read). Be sure to look back at the chapter for suggestions (so that you can avoid pitfalls).

E. Try journal writing yourself. Then help one or more children try it. Allow time for sharing, for written comments, and for conferences.

REFERENCES AND SUGGESTED READING

Allen, E. G., & Laminack, L. L. (1982). Language experience reading—It's a natural! *The Reading Teacher, 35,* 708–714.

Altwerger, B., Edelsky, C., & Flores, B. M. (1987). Whole language: What's new? *The Reading Teacher, 41,* 144–145.

Ashton-Warner, S. (1963). *Teacher.* New York: Simon and Schuster.

Bond, G. L., & Dykstra, R. (1967). The cooperative program in first grade reading instruction. *Reading Research Quarterly, 2,* 5–142.

Brountas, M. (1987, November/December). Whole language really works. *Teaching K–8,* 57–60.

Burrows, A. (1985). *They all want to write.* Newark, DE: International Reading Association.

Cairney, T. H. (1987) Collaborative stories. *The Reading Teacher, 41,* 116–117.

Calkins, L. M. (1986). *The art of teaching writing.* Portsmouth, NH: Heinemann.

Chomsky, C. (1971). Write first, read later. *Childhood Education, 47,* 396–399.

Cramer, R. L. (1970). An investigation of first-grade spelling achievement. *Elementary English, 47,* 230–237.

Dionisio, M. (1983). Write? Isn't this reading class? *The Reading Teacher, 36,* 746–750.

Dunn, L. M., & Smith, J. O. (1965, 1966, 1967). Peabody language development kits, Levels I, II, III. Circle Pines, MN: American Guidance Service.

Durkin, D. (1966). *Children who read early: Two longitudinal studies.* New York: Teachers College Press.

Dykstra, R. (1968). Summary of the second-grade phase of the cooperative research program in primary reading instruction. *Reading Research Quarterly, 4,* 49–70.

Dzama, M. A. (1975). Comparing use of generalizations of phonics in LEA, basal vocabulary. *The Reading Teacher, 28,* 466–472.

Evanechko, P., Ollila, L., & Armstrong, R. (1974). An investigation of the relationship between children's performance in written language and their reading ability. *Research in the Teaching of English, 8,* 315–325.

Evans, R. V. (1979). The relationship between the reading and writing of syntactic structures. *Research in the teaching of English, 13,* 129–135.

Gillet, J. W., & Gentry, J. R. (1983). Bridges between nonstandard and standard English with extensions of dictated stories. *The Reading Teacher, 36,* 346–360.

Goodman, K. (1986). *What's whole in whole language?* Portsmouth, NH: Heinemann.

Graves, D. H. (1975). An examination of the writing processes of seven-year-old children. *Research in the Teaching of English, 9,* 227–241.

Graves, D. (1978). *Balance the basics: Let them write.* New York: Ford Foundation Report.

Graves, D. H. (1979). Research update: What children show us about revision. *Language Arts, 56,* 312–319.

Graves, D. (1980). Research update. A new look at writing. *Language Arts, 57,* 913–918.

Graves, D. H., & Murray, D. H. (1980). Revision in the writer's workshop and in the classroom. *Journal of Education, 162,* 38–56.

Graves, D. H. (1983). *Writing: Teachers and children at work.* Portsmouth, NH: Heinemann.

Gunderson, L., & Shapiro, J. (1988). Whole language instruction: Writing in first grade. *The Reading Teacher, 41,* 420–437.

Hall, M. A. (1978). *The language experience approach for teaching reading, a research perspective.* Newark, DE: International Reading Association.

Hall M. A. (1981). *Teaching reading as a language experience.* 3rd ed. Columbus, OH: Merrill.

Hansen, J. (1987). *When writers read.* Portsmouth, NH: Heinemann.

Hansen, J., Newkirk, T., & Graves, D. (1985). (Eds.) *Breaking ground: Teachers relate reading and writing in the elementary school.* Portsmouth, NH: Heinemann.

Harp, B. (1987). Why are your kids writing during reading time? *The Reading Teacher, 41,* 88–90.

Henderson, E. H., et al. (1972). An exploratory study of word acquisition among first-graders at midyear in a language experience approach. *Journal of Reading Behavior, 4,* 21–31.

Holbrook, H. T. (1987). Writing to learn in the social studies. *The Reading Teacher, 41,* 216–219.

Hoover, I. (1971). *Historical and Theoretical Development of a language experience approach to teaching reading in selected teacher education institutions.* Unpublished doctoral dissertation, University of Arizona.

Hubbard, R. (1985). Drawing parallels: Real writing, real reading. In J. Hansen, T. Newkirk, & D. Graves (Eds.), *Breaking ground: Teachers relate reading and writing in the elementary school.* Portsmouth, NH: Heinemann.

Indrisano, R. (1984). *Reading and writing revisited.* Occasional Paper No. 18. Columbus, OH: Ginn.

Jacobson, D. (1987). Working together for change. *Teachers Networking, 8*(1), 2.

Kintisch, L. S. (1986). Journal writing: Stages of development. *The Reading Teacher, 40,* 168–172.

Lancaster, W., Nelson, L., & Morris, D. (1982). Invented spellings in Room 112: A writing program for low-reading second graders. *The Reading Teacher, 35,* 906–911.

Lazdowski, W. F. (1976). *Determining reading grade levels from analysis of written composition.* Unpublished doctoral dissertation, New Mexico State University.

Loban, W. (1976). *Language development, kindergarten through grade twelve.* Urbana, IL: National Council of Teachers of English.

Mallon, B., & Berglund, R. (1984). The language experience approach to reading: Recurring questions and their answers. *The Reading Teacher, 37,* 867–873.

Manning, M., Manning, G., & Hughes, J. (1987). Journals in first grade: What children write. *The Reading Teacher, 41,* 311–315.

Martin, J. H. (1984, February). Writing to read—Challenging an age-old tradition. *Electronic Education, 3,* 21–22.

Morrison, V. B. (1983). Language experience reading with the microcomputer. *The Reading Teacher, 36,* 448–449.

Newman, J. M. (Ed.). (1985). *Whole language: Theory in use.* Portsmouth, NH: Heinemann.

Olson, D. R., & Pau, A. S. (1966). Emotionally loaded words and the acquisitions of a sight vocabulary. *Journal of Educational Psychology, 57,* 174–178.

Otto, W., & Askov, E. (1973). *Rationale and Guidelines.* The Wisconsin Design for Reading Skill Development, National Computer Systems.

Prescriptive reading inventory. (1972). New York: CTB/McGraw-Hill, 1972.

Shanahan, T. (1988). The reading-writing relationship: Seven instructional principles. *The Reading Teacher, 41,* 636–647.

Staton, J. (1974). *Initial reading practices in open education environments in the midprairie states.* Unpublished doctoral dissertation, Oklahoma State University.

Stauffer, R. G., & Hammond, W. D. (1967). The effectiveness of language arts and basal reader approaches to first grade reading instruction. *The Reading Teacher, 20,* 740–746.

Stauffer, R. G. (1980). *The language experience approach to the teaching of reading.* New York: Harper & Row.

Tierney, R. J., & Pearson, P. D. (1983). Toward a composing model of reading. *Language Arts, 60,* 568–580.

Torrance, E. P. (1962). Creative thinking of children. *Journal of Teacher Education, 13,* 448–460.

Unia, S. (1985). From sunny days to green onions: On journal writing. In J. Newman (Ed.), *Whole language theory in use.* Portsmouth, NH: Heinemann.

Van Allen, R. (1974). *Language experiences in reading:* Chicago: Encyclopaedia Britannica Press.

Veatch, J., et al. (1979). *Key words to reading.* Columbus, OH: Merrill.

Wright, J. P., & Laminack, L. (1982). First graders can be critical listeners and readers. *Language Arts, 59,* 133–137.

Literature Approaches to Reading Instruction

=========== **CHAPTER PREVIEW** ===========

You've seen what it's like when teachers use children's own writing as the major medium of reading instruction. In this chapter we'll look at children's literature—the stories, novels, poetry, biographies, and nonfiction books that are written for children by skillful, professional authors. How might the teacher use this awesome collection of writings for the purpose of teaching and inspiring reading?

First we'll look at the importance and usefulness of literature in any type of reading program—as the perfect substitute for those never-ending worksheets and workbooks, as a stimulus for inspired writing and further reading, and for its many other

virtues. Then we'll talk about the things teachers can do to encourage literature reading—by knowing children's literature and by providing time to read, chances to choose, a variety of books to choose from, and time to share.

Next we'll want to discuss the possibility of relying on children's literature as the main (or only) source of materials for reading instruction. Some teachers do this, you know. Their whole reading program revolves around literature in what I'm calling a "personalized literature program," or PLP. If you were to do this, how would you manage the individual conferences that go along with this program? How would you keep records? What would you do about vocabulary or phonics?

We'll take a hard look at those things called "readability formulas" and some ways of interpreting them. And then, for the chapter punch line, I'd like to suggest that you consider the possibility of combining your literature and writing programs.

Children's success as readers of "whole books" turns them first into their own press agents, "Hey, I can read this book all by myself!" and soon after into proud critics of their reading experiences, "This is the best book I ever read!"

—Bill Martin, Jr.

From the time they enter kindergarten until they graduate from high school, our students should find a high standard of thought and feeling at the heart of their English language arts education: great literature.

—Bill Honig

A reader is a person who decides what to read.

—Jane Hansen

Always read stuff that will make you look good if you die in the middle of it.

—P. J. O'Rourke

THE CONTRIBUTION OF LITERATURE TO ANY INSTRUCTIONAL APPROACH

As you already know, some teachers use basal readers as the main source of reading instruction material. Some use children's writing. Some use literature, often referred to in schools as "library books." Whichever medium of instruction you use, however, you'll probably want to include literature as an important ingredient of your reading/writing program. But what are the advantages of including literature?

A Superior Substitute for Worksheets

Richard C. Anderson and several other educators were asked by the Department of Education to study the American schools and make recommendations on improving reading instruction. Here are a few of their findings:

1. Up to 70 percent of the time set aside by elementary school teachers for reading instruction was actually spent on activities related to worksheets—explaining how to do them, doing them, checking them together, and so on. At best, only 12 percent of the reading instruction

time was spent on actual reading of text [although much of this text was not whole text but merely a paragraph or other text fragments].

2. It was not unusual for a child to complete 1,000 reading worksheets [or workbook pages] in a year's time.

3. The use of worksheets [or workbooks] did not lead to improvement in reading ability.

4. The more that whole text was read by children, the more their reading improved.

As a result of these findings, the commission recommended that children be provided in the school environment with at least two hours per week of uninterrupted silent reading of literature (Anderson, 1985). Such findings and recommendations are nothing new to those of us who have been in the profession for a while. Many of us have been complaining about the worksheet problem for years. At last, though, we have a U.S. commission report that people are paying attention to, and we're all "exceedingly glad." Imagine, 1,000 worksheets per year from kindergarten through eighth grade. Figuratively speaking, this has burdened most children in America with the weight of 18 reams of ditto paper on top of their brains (the brain weighing in at only 3 pounds) before they even reach high school. And this weight is just from reading alone. It doesn't include the worksheets from math, science, and other areas. Such brain-squashing feats, at least in principle, are finally going out of fashion.

Again, let me remind you that I'm not against all use of worksheets. I've seen very good teachers use them, but they use them infrequently, with discretion, and often as part of a teacher-guided lesson. What I am against is the use of worksheets as seatwork to keep most of the class busy while the teacher is working with one small group of children. The supposed purpose of such seatwork is to give the children "practice." It does give them practice, all right, but it's generally the wrong kind. As you already know, the best kind of practice is the reading of whole text. And as you're no doubt predicting, the reading of whole text can best be accomplished with a literature program.

Provision for Individual Differences

There was a time in educational writing when the term "individual differences" could be found in just about every paragraph. The term implies something teachers have always known—even back in the cave clan days of teaching children to catch fish with their bare hands and scare woolly-haired bears with fire: People learn at different speeds and in different ways. How easy that is to say! And yet how very difficult—under certain teaching conditions—to do anything about it! Basal reading programs, for example, sometimes allow for different speeds of learning, but none of them allows adequately for different *ways* of learning. Most teachers become adept at pacing the learning differently for different individuals, but few become adept at the far more difficult process of varying the learning style or content.

The problem of individual differences can be quite severe when it comes to reading instruction. We know, for instance, that teachers working in self-contained classrooms usually have students whose general reading abilities vary by several grade levels. A fifth-grade teacher may have to work with children whose reading-achievement grade-level scores range from 2.0 to 8.0. Even more important, each child's *specific* reading abilities may also vary by several grade levels. Let's compare Sally's scores with Virginia's as an example. Sally and Virginia both had a total reading ability score of 5.0. But here's how they scored on the specific subtests:

	Sally	*Virginia*
Vocabulary (isolated)	4.7	3.4
Vocabulary (in context)	5.1	5.1
Paragraph understanding (literal)	5.2	4.5
Paragraph understanding (interpretive)	2.7	5.9
Phonics knowledge	6.3	2.6
Phonics application	5.8	4.5
Morphemic analysis	3.5	7.8
Total score	5.0	5.0

In spite of such differences between Sally and Virginia, however, they would most likely be placed in the same reading group and assigned to the same basal reader. To make matters worse, Sally is crazy about animal stories—horse stories and dog stories in particular—and almost any stories dealing with the great outdoors. Virginia, on the other hand, doesn't care for this kind of story at all. Virginia likes stories of teenage romance, as well as realistic stories about racial strife and other social phenomena. As you can see, then, here's a chance for literature to come to the rescue—for both the teacher's and the child's benefit. Literature does provide for individual differences.

Opportunities for Personal Growth

Psychologists tell us that one of the chief ways in which people develop values, ambitions, and a self-concept is through emotional identification with another person—by imagining ourselves to be that person or by becoming like that person. Literature, particularly biographies and fiction, offer infinite opportunities for such identification. A single book, of course, is not likely to provide as powerful a model as, say, a likable teacher or an admired parent. Yet thinking about your own experience with books would probably cause you to remember the times that books made a difference in how you felt—about yourself, about human behavior, about beliefs you once held. Even if a book doesn't cause any permanent change in behavior, it can at least reinforce one's developing values or make a person question those values.

Motivated Practice of Interactive Reading

From either a subskill or an interactive point of view, trade books also provide motivated practice of whatever reading skills or reading concepts the teacher wants her students to acquire. The practice is "motivated" by the fact that children are reading books of their *own choice,* and if the books are the right choice, they are giving them pleasure.

Today, even first-graders can find series they will enjoy enough to motivate reading practice. One of these series is the *Beginning Books* series, including the first one in the series entitled *The Cat in the Hat* by Dr. Seuss. And for the true neophyte, there's the series called the *Beginning Beginner Books.* One of the books in this series—*Bears on Wheels* by Stan and Jan Berenstain—has only fourteen different words, and surprisingly enough it is usually fun for both children and adults to read. Another series is the *I Can Read* books, including *Frog and Toad Are Friends* and *Frog and Toad Together*—the first of which was a Caldecott Honor Book, and the second a Newbery Honor Book. There is also an *Early I Can Read* series, including the book on a favorite children's topic: *Dinosaur Time.* In addition, there are the *Giant First Start Readers,* including *Double Trouble* (34 different words), *Yummy Yummy* (37 different words), and *The Tooth Fairy* (49 different words). For an excellent list of easy nonseries books, see *Children's Choices* (Roser & Firth, 1983), International Reading Association, 800 Barksdale Road, Newark, DE 19711.

Enrichment of Other Curriculum Areas

Without using children's literature, it would be nearly impossible to achieve some of the objectives of the social studies and science programs. In the social studies area, for example, the teacher is usually trying to help children *identify* with the problems, values, and life styles of different people. Simply reading about these people in a textbook will not accomplish this aim. Social studies textbooks, because of their wide coverage, tend to be somewhat shallow and explanatory. It is difficult for children to identify with the people talked about in the textbook, and it's also difficult for them to find enough meaningful associations and examples. They need more learning in depth and more emotion. Films and other audiovisual media help a great deal, but literature—fictional, informational, and biographical—offers vital opportunities for emotional involvement in the lives of other people.

Models and Inspiration for Writing

As a model and inspiration for children's own writing, it is hard to beat literature. I've always had interesting and highly motivated writing occur in the classroom following the conclusion of books I've read aloud. Many teachers I've talked to have had the same experience. If the teacher has helped the children become

aware of an author's use of words, the personalities of the characters, and the subtleties of the plot, many children will be bursting with ideas for extending the story, changing its ending, or even writing a sequel. Similar enthusiasm often follows the conclusion of a book they have read by themselves—provided they've had a chance to discuss the book with a few others in the class.

Aesthetic Experiences

This leads us to another virtue of high-quality literature—the aesthetic experience provided by the book itself. Some of the best writing and graphic art today is found between the covers of a children's book. (And probably some of the worst as well, I'll admit.) Marguerite Henry's classic *King of the Wind*, to take just one example, is rich in beautiful prose, sensitive characterization, and subtlety of plot development. To read a book such as this is to achieve that intangible something called an *aesthetic experience*. One feels better for the experience, and perhaps that is enough justification for reading any book. Then, too, there is the aesthetic experience provided by the superb illustrations in many picture books and other children's books. New printing techniques have made it possible for artists to use freely and creatively any graphic media they wish. You've probably seen some of the books illustrated by Ezra Jack Keats, Symeon Shimin, Leo Lionni, Marcia Brown, and many others, and you probably know exactly what I'm talking about.

Two coveted awards have been associated with, and perhaps partly responsible for, the aesthetic quality of children's books. One is the John Newbery Medal, presented each year to "the author of the most distinguished contribution to American literature for children." The book whose author will receive the award is selected by a committee of the Children's Services Division of the American Library Association. This committee selects the book it considers to be the best one published the previous year, and also a number of Honor Books for that year. A list of the winners since 1922 may be found in Appendix J. It should be emphasized that not all of the award-winning books are enjoyed by children, and some of them are better read aloud by the teacher because of their difficulty.

The other highly coveted award is the Caldecott Medal, presented each year to "the artist of the most distinguished American picture book for children." The winning book and illustrator, along with several Honor Books, are selected by the same committee that selects the winner for the Newbery award. A list of the winners since 1938 may be found in Appendix J.

To limit one's selection of books to the winners and runners-up for the Caldecott or Newbery awards, however, is to make the error of attributing godlike power to the committee of human beings who make such awesome decisions each year. On the other hand, it is probably wise to read several of them to sharpen one's own awareness of the qualities that make certain books seem great and others mediocre.

Social Cohesion

Another value of literature is its contribution to social cohesion, the glue that makes us a society rather than a mere collection of unrelated individuals. I'll admit that some of our cohesion comes from watching the same television programs—particularly those like *David Letterman, Oprah Winfrey,* or *Saturday Night Live.* But schools have an equal opportunity (since young people spend so much time there). In the *Handbook for Planning an Effective Literature Program* developed for teachers in the California schools, author William Boly stresses the importance of literature in the development of social cohesion:

> The public schools are potentially one of the most meaningful forces for social cohesion. They are the modern equivalent of the village square—a form of identifying the shared ethos of our diverse and cosmopolitan society; a place where all our children can come together and discover what it is that unites us as a people. Well-taught literature is an essential part of that consensus building." (1987, p. 12)

Ethical Responsibility

Books, by themselves, can't really teach us right from wrong. But they *can* show us individuals struggling with the problems of meeting their own needs without infringing on the rights of others. They can make us realize what it means to think of others as well as ourselves.

Boly feels that the greatest value of literature is that of helping each young person become "ethically responsible." As he puts it:

> Literature asks the big questions such as: "What is the relationship of the individual to society? What gives meaning to a man's or woman's life?" In providing answers to these questions authors do not sermonize but rather show plausible characters grappling with the force of circumstance and the consequences of their own acts. (1987, p. 9)

WHAT TEACHERS CAN DO: KNOW CHILDREN'S LITERATURE

In many libraries, "juvenile" books account for at least one-half of the total circulation. This is a distinct rise from 1939, when juvenile circulations accounted for only one-third of the total (Huck, 1976). Part of this increase probably comes as the result of the vast growth in the publication of juveniles—from 852 new titles in 1940 to over 3,000 annually in recent years. Along with this quantitative growth has come an increase in the variety of children's books available. The ever-popular mysteries and fantasies must compete for shelf space with fictional stories of ever-increasing realism, with informational books on nearly every conceivable subject, and with a host of other types.

Teachers who wish to foster children's growth through reading should be aware of these various types of trade books so that they can participate in the process of helping the right child find the right book at the right time. But perhaps you're already aware of the various types. To test your awareness, try the matching exercise in Figure 9.1. See if you can "find" the type of books that "a child needs." Then check the answers at the end of the matching exercise.

If you got twelve or more correct, you should probably celebrate this event in some way, for these sixteen categories and their descriptions are slightly ambiguous and rely upon subtle distinctions. Some teenage romance stories, for instance, could be classified as realistic fiction; some science fiction could be classified as fantasy. Precisely how one decides to classify a particular book, of course, is not very important. What is important is that you become familiar, if you're not already, with the various types of books available for children at various age levels.

Joseph Leibowicz (1983), in his summary of research on children's reading interests, found that no single story structure is an exclusive favorite. Children have a wide range of interests, just as adults do. Greenlaw (1983), on the other hand, found that certain types of books are more consistent favorites than others. "Funny" books are a distinct favorite among primary-grade children, followed by Make-Believe, People, and Animals. Among intermediate-grade children, the most consistent favorite is the Adventure type of book, followed by Jokes and Humor, Informational, and Fantasy. Greenlaw's data are based on the choices of about 60,000 children all over the country between 1973 and 1979. It is quite conceivable that by, say, 1995, children's interest in various types of books will change. Greenlaw's research shows that such changes have taken place in the

The Type You Will Look for When . . .	A Child Needs or Wants a

g 1. Fictional book that portrays people coping with universal problems of life as these problems exist in modern times

h 2. Fictional story that concentrates on finding clues to discover why and how an incident took place

n 3. Book of short selections, most that describe the essence of something—sometimes in colorful language, sometimes in rhyming or rhythmic patterns of words

a 4. Book in which story is told or information given in two ways, both at the same time—one way is through words, the other is through numerous illustrations

m 5. Fictional story of an adolescent coping with universal problems of love

b 6. Book of legends, fables, tall tales, epics, myths, old fairy tales, or other traditional stories formerly handed down by word of mouth

o 7. Fictional story in which situations or characteristics, usually of a realistic nature, are exaggerated to the point of amusement

i 8. Fictional book in which an animal, such as a dog or horse, becomes a heroic figure in a realistic way

f 9. Fictional book based on principles or possibilities of nature, often involving future times, space travel, other worlds

d 10. Nonfictional book about a noteworthy person

c 11. Fictional story in which success in an athletic game is an important element of the conflict and is generally related to the "game of living"

p 12. Book of fictional stories written in drama format, nearly all dialogue

k 13. Nonfiction book that explains natural and social phenomena or suggests experiments, activities, or procedures

e 14. Fictional book emphasizing historical settings and usually historical characters or events

l 15. Fictional story involving danger, courage, and a struggle with the natural elements

j 16. Fictional story created in writing rather than handed down orally in which events are not only improbable but seem impossible, for example, talking animals, magic wands, tiny people, events conflicting with present scientific knowledge

a. picture book
b. book of folk tales
c. sports story
d. biography
e. historical fiction book
f. science fiction book
g. realistic fiction book
h. mystery story
i. animal story
j. fantasy
k. informational book
l. outdoor/adventure story
m. teenage romance story
n. book of poetry
o. humorous story
p. book of plays

Answers

1—g	2—h	3—n	4—a	5—m	6—b	7—o	8—i	9—f
10—d	11—c	12—p	13—k	14—e	15—l	16—j		

FIGURE 9.1
A matching exercise

past. On the other hand, the category of Funny has remained constant for many years among primary-grade children, and the Animals category has also remained in the top four.

For intermediate-grade children, the only category that has remained consistently popular through the years has been Adventure. Don't worry; this doesn't mean that children in grade four and up aren't interested in Funny books—they're just more selective. If you'd like a list of sure-fire Funny books for children of this age, here are some culled from a list prepared by John and Priscilla Bennett (1982). I chose from their list only those that *every* child in their small sample said were funny:

> ***Funny books for intermediate-grade children***
>
> *Bunnicula: A Rabbit-Tale of Mystery* by Deborah Howe
>
> *Fat Men from Space* by Daniel Manus Pinkwater
>
> *Help! I'm a Prisoner in the Library* by Eth Clifford
>
> *Jim Bridger's Alarm Clock and Other Tall Tales* by Sid Fleischman
>
> *Johnny May* by Robbie Branscum
>
> *Konrad* by Christine Nostlinger
>
> *The Mark of Conte* by Sonia Levitin
>
> *My Mother Is Not Married to My Father* by Jean Okimoto
>
> *Pippi on the Run* by Astrid Lindgren
>
> *Superfudge* by Judy Blume
>
> *Think about It. You Might Learn Something* by Robyn Supraner

Now let's return for a moment to the sixteen types of children's books described in Figure 9.1. Naturally, if you're teaching second-graders, you can forget about the teenage romance stories, but all the other types have been published for children of this age. Teachers in the intermediate grades will want to become familiar with all sixteen types—even the picture books, many of which have been published for children beyond the primary grades.

The best way to become truly familiar with children's books is not to rely just on reviews, but to read and enjoy the books themselves. (It's probably a good idea to keep a laminated card file on the books you have read—to jog your memory later and to hand to a child as your personal recommendation.) When you read children's books, you may want to follow these suggestions:

□ *Read books for a wide range of age levels.* Remember that children at any grade level vary tremendously in their reading abilities and interests. Carolyn Haywood's books (for example, *B Is for Betsy* and *Eddie and His Big Deals*) are excellent for the average reader in grades two and three. But some children at this grade level will be reading fourth- and fifth-grade books, such as *Henry Huggins* by Beverly Cleary or *Little House on the Prairie* by Laura Ingalls Wilder, while others will be reading simple picture books like *Where the Wild Things Are* by Maurice Sendak or *Millions of Cats* by Wanda Gag.

☐ *Read a variety of book types.* In this way you can be more helpful, even to the child who is looking for "a real good football story."

☐ *Read them with a sense of involvement from cover to cover.* Skimmed books are as bad as poorly digested meals. Only by reading books thoroughly and emotionally can you prepare yourself to share them honestly with children.

☐ *Start by reading several that many people consider to be of "good" quality.* Then when you come across poor-quality books, you will recognize them almost instantly; you will thus avoid wasting your own time and be able to recommend high-quality books to children. In the references at the end of this chapter, you'll find several sources that will help you decide which books are likely to be worthy of your time. Appendix I provides "Fifteen Categories of Literature for Children" that two of my colleagues and I selected. The California State Department of Education has an excellent list, called *Recommended Readings in Literature, Grades Kindergarten through Grade Eight* (1986). This can be purchased for a very small amount from Publications Sales, California State Department of Education, P.O. Box 271, Sacramento, CA 95802.

☐ *Read books that might meet the needs and interests of particular children in your classroom.* Helping children find just the right book is greatly enhanced by learning as much as you can about their interests. How? Through informal conversations, through observations, through children's writing, and through questionnaires. In this way, you can suggest books to children that are highly meaningful to them personally.

☐ *Stay in touch with sources of book reviews.* Excellent reviews can be obtained in textbooks on children's literature, such as Sutherland's, Huck's, or Norton's (see the references at the end of this chapter). *Hornbook Magazine,* available in most libraries, has extensive reviews of new books. Some of the basal reader publishers now have incorporated book reviews in their teacher's guides. *The Reading Teacher,* the monthly journal of the International Reading Association, publishes an annotated list each October of "Classroom Choices: Children's Trade Books." This list contains books selected primarily by children and includes annotations that tell how each book fits into the school curriculum. Also see Sam Sebesta's fabulous monthly column in the same journal called "Critically Speaking: Literature for Children."

WHAT TEACHERS CAN DO: PROVIDE TIME, BOOKS, CHOICES, AND SHARING

As Jane Hansen says (1987), readers need long blocks of uninterrupted time: time to choose books, time to think, time to interact with other readers, time to show their excitement. Notice that she says what *readers* need, not what children need. If you think about yourself as an adult reader, I think you'll agree that she's right. I, myself, am not too keen on being interrupted while I'm reading a novel. (I eventually get cranky about it.) And I really like to choose my own books, thank you, so don't plan on giving me one for Christmas. But I do like to share things I've chosen and read myself. (That's why I might be tempted to interrupt *you* if you were reading close by.)

In spite of the hustle and bustle of a modern classroom, it's often a better place in which to read than the home. At home, remember, reading must frequently compete with the omnipresent television set and its tempting tidbits of instant culture, instant mirth, and instant action.

Numerous studies have shown that the average elementary school child watches television for as many hours as he spends in school. Even in the 1970s this was the case. Long and Henderson (1973) studied the activities of fifth-graders when they were not in school. The average time per week spent reading was three hours; the average time per week with television was thirty hours.

This is not to say that all TV is bad for children's reading growth. When television is viewed for up to ten hours per week, it *can* be beneficial to a child's intellectual development, according to research (Boly, 1987). However, this same research demonstrated that those students who spent more time reading for pleasure and doing homework and less time watching TV scored higher on reading achievement tests. You can see the need for scheduling time in school for the reading of books.

Many teachers, of course, sincerely believe they offer their students enough time to read library books during the school day. But when they're pressed to define what they mean by "enough time," some of them answer like this: "I let them read all during the day. Whenever they get their assignments done, they're supposed to get out a library book and read quietly." What this generally means in practice is that the same five or six students who always get their assignments done early are doing about 90 percent of the reading. Most of the others either spend all their time on their assignments or, if they finish early, have so little time to read before the next assignment befalls them that they usually decide not to bother.

A first-year teacher wanted to know why his fifth-grade students didn't want to read. When he was asked how much time they had for "free reading," he said, "Well, whenever they finish their assignments—and sometimes I give them five or six minutes before lunch." It was suggested to him that he try something for two weeks: give his students three 30-minute periods a week for free reading. In two weeks time, he had changed his mind about most of his students: "It takes some of them quite a while to get started, but once they get going, I can't tear them away from their books."

The SSR Approach

Many years ago Fader and McNeil provided one answer to the time problem in *Hooked on Books: Program and Proof* (1968). In their book they recommended a timed approach in which during the first week, only five minutes a day is set aside for intensive silent reading. This time is gradually increased until the children are reading for thirty minutes or more a day. Fader and McNeil claimed considerable success, even with children who were reluctant to read. Their name for this approach was "Uninterrupted Sustained Silent Reading" (USSR), but for obvious reasons this has been changed over the years to the "SSR approach."

Research on SSR provides mixed reviews; however, as Spiegel (1983) points out, most researchers have tried the approach for only a month or two before administering achievement tests and closing up shop. (It's funny about our society. When a new football coach is hired, the fans usually give him two or three years to shape up the team. When a new idea is tried in a classroom, the teacher is expected to produce results in two months!) Donald Pfau (1966) had the right idea. He studied the effects of an SSR program for two years instead of two months. Children who engage in a long-range program of sustained silent reading, he found, do perform better on achievement tests than those who don't. The Commission on Education reported the same (Anderson, 1985).

Kaisen (1987) studied the effects of SSR as early as first grade and found that it seems to work as long as these conditions are met: (1) Teachers themselves read; (2) each child has several books with her; (3) wordless picture books are available; (4) books that have been read to them at home are available; and (5) preprimers are available.

As much as I want to encourage the use of an SSR program, though, I should caution you not to consider it a panacea. It's not a cure-all, but it can be a good supplement to a strong instructional program in interactive reading (such as the one described in Chapters 4 and 5). True, daily periods of library book reading are what children need, all right. But on the other hand, children who have not mastered the use of all four cueing systems *can* be practicing the wrong thing! For the child who is relying solely on graphophonic cues, the gift of thirty minutes of timed practice is a consignment to a half-hour in Hades.

Poor readers need a great deal of *guided* as well as independent reading. Some of this guided reading should be oral, some silent. In either case, the teacher should be directly involved in establishing purposes for reading and in showing the children the cues available to them, both from the author and from the readers' schematic backgrounds. Furthermore, poor readers need more help than other children in selecting interesting and *easy* books to read on their own. The practice they have on independent reading must be *successful*—just having them "read" is not enough. The child who is asked to "read" unsuccessfully for thirty minutes develops a neon sign that blinks on and off inside his head: WARNING: READING MAY BE HAZARDOUS TO YOUR HEALTH.

Moore, Jones, and Miller reviewed the research on SSR and other forms of "recreational reading" and came up with two conclusions: (1) "SSR [on the average] has a positive effect on student attitudes toward reading" and (2) "SSR has a positive effect on reading ability when combined with a regular program of reading instruction" (1980, p. 448). McCracken and McCracken (1978) investigated several SSR programs that were doing poorly and found these common characteristics:

The teacher did not read during the SSR period.

The troublemakers did not read during the SSR period.

A visiting adult or an aide did not read during the SSR period.

The SSR period was too long for the particular children involved.

There were not enough books available.

The teacher didn't want to give the program time to work.

And let me add two characteristics based on my own observations:

Many children were attempting to read at their frustration level rather than their independent level; the teacher had not helped them learn how to find interesting and easy books.

Many children had not been given sufficient modeling of the use of all four cueing systems.

Provide Choice

I've already mentioned how important it is for children to have a chance to make choices about what they will read. What this means in practice is having lots of books representing a variety of interests and many levels of difficulty. So where does the classroom teacher get all those books?

Of course, many schools today have their own libraries. If not, some teachers take their children to nearby municipal libraries. There, this "reading horde" (to the librarian's eyes) checks out a vast collection, which they then take to the classroom for a month-long classroom library. Not a bad system. I've seen it work very well in my own and other classrooms.

A large number of teachers encourage their students to purchase their own paperback books at a reasonable price from one of the Scholastic Book Clubs.* These books are relatively inexpensive and long lasting. Several publishers have come out with fairly large classroom collections of paperbacks designed for "individualized" or "literature" programs. Two examples are the Reading Spectrum published by Scholastic and the Pal Paperback Kits published by Xerox. If you'll look at Appendixes E and K, you'll find addresses for publishers. A letter to them will get you more mail than you've had for a month. School libraries, municipal libraries, county libraries, state libraries, book clubs, bookstores, publishers—a resourceful teacher can always find ways to provide students with a wide choice of literature.

In selecting your books, though, try to find a large quantity of easy books—those that are interesting to your students but a snap to read. Children (and adults) can easily become discouraged if one book after another offers them little

---

*For a list of Scholastic book collections write to Scholastic's Readers' Choice, 904 Sylvan Avenue, Englewood Cliffs, NJ 07632.

more than frustration. Teachers who make it a habit to read children's books themselves have little trouble offering children guidance in this respect. One of my secrets in using a literature approach was to take advantage of the marvelous incentive that's given to the teacher who uses a Scholastic Book Club: For every five books your students buy, you get a free one of your choice. Naturally, my choices were always from Scholastic's list of high-interest, low-vocabulary books.

The International Reading Association occasionally puts out an annotated list of high-interest, low-vocabulary books. One of theirs, called *Easy Reading* (1979) by Graves, Boettcher, and Ryder, describes a variety of book series and periodicals for "less able readers." You'll find another list, along with addresses, in Appendix E.

Provide Sharing Opportunities

Still another way to promote the reading of literature is to establish means for sharing books or reacting creatively to them. The unimaginative book report, it goes without saying, doesn't generally meet this need. A better approach—one that many teachers have found much more successful—is to encourage various types of sharing and creative projects following completion of a book. In Appendix F you'll find about seventy "Book Projects for Children and Teachers," which you can modify to fit the age level and interests of your particular students. All have been tested in classrooms and appear to be interesting and worthwhile to children.

Of course, the guidance the teacher offers is often the key factor in making the projects interesting and worthwhile. Simply passing out a list of projects is not very motivating. Probably the most effective form of guidance is that of reading children's books and carrying on some of the projects yourself. For instance, one of the oral projects suggested is to "put on a puppet play about one part of the book." You can imagine what an inspiration your sharing a book in this way could be for children to read "your" book or to share theirs in a similar fashion. Don't make your presentation so awe-inspiring, though, that they'll be afraid to emulate you. Use a simple cardboard stage and puppets that the children can easily make themselves.

Along with the more creative approaches, just chatting a bit about a book you have read will usually encourage many in the class to read the same one or to use this same form of project with another book. Besides guiding by showing, however, the teacher can occasionally meet with individuals for a few minutes to talk about books they have recently read and ways they may share them with others. (Incidentally, sometimes a child prefers simply to share his book with you alone.) Or you can have the children get together in small groups of three or four once every two weeks to talk about books they've been reading. If you structure this activity so that each child has around five minutes to talk and one person is the "chair," it generally works very well.

Although the children usually carry on oral, arts-and-crafts, and drama projects with great enthusiasm, some teachers report that they often greet the written projects at first with something less than spontaneous joy. This lack of enthusiasm usually occurs in classrooms where writing has not been taught as part of the reading/writing program and children are simply not used to writing. Here again, the teacher's leading the way can help immensely. A "class book" for written projects is generally a must. Here others may see the teacher's and children's written projects that have been "second-drafted" and donated. (Again, however, don't overawe them with your writing powers, or your writing will be the only one in the book.)

Use Extrinsic Motivators If You Have To

I know. Reading is its own intrinsic reward. And that's what we're aiming toward. Yet sometimes on the way . . . well, some kids need what they're used to—a token symbol of achievement. (You know, the way adults like their achievement plaques on their walls, their bowling trophies, their medals, their certificates.) We've already talked about using intrinsic forms of encouragement, such as finding them books that are easy enough, making a wide choice available, and providing avenues for sharing and reacting creatively. All of these are directly involved with the act of reading itself, and they *are* the most important motivators. But sometimes an additional extrinsic reward makes the literature program just that much more enjoyable to many kids. I'm not going to push this idea too hard (for fear that you might talk me out of it), but I am going to at least mention it. I've used it. Many successful teachers have used it, but we all seem to have a slight touch of GUILT about it. After all, our big G tells us, reading should be done only for personally desired information or pleasure.

Fine. But here goes.

One form of extrinsic reward is simply having the children keep a personal record of the books they read. By checking these records with the children every few weeks and by privately encouraging the quality, or variety, or, in some cases, the quantity of reading they have done, you can often spur children on to further reading. Some teachers like to add a bit of spice to the record keeping by providing small rectangles (about one-half inch by four inches) of colored paper that represent book spines. On each slip of paper the child writes the title and author of the book she has just finished; then she pastes the slip of paper on a photocopied "shelf" and places the photocopy in her folder or notebook.

Along with an individual record scheme such as the one just described, you may wish to keep a class record of "Books We Have Read." Note, however, that this does not refer to a competitive form of record such as a chart of names with so many stars after each name. Such a record may easily do more harm than good, since the slowest readers have no chance to win and many children will falsely claim to have read certain books just to win it. What I am referring to is a cooperative record similar to the thermometer graph so often used for community chest or blood bank drives. Or you may wish to construct a "class bookshelf," using different-colored paper for different types of books. You can have the children put the title and author on the front of the piece of paper and their name on the back. These "books" can then be "taken off the shelf" and returned in an envelope to each child at the end of the year. For some reason, whenever I've done this with children they seem to get a strong sense of community pride ("tribe pride") as they watch *their* bookshelf grow across the room.

Some teachers give symbolic tokens for books that children have simply read; some prefer to give them only for books shared through projects. Whatever tactic teachers use, though, they shouldn't defeat the purpose by becoming too serious or demanding about it. Encourage rather than nag, inspire rather than require, help them cooperate rather than compete—these should be the mottoes of a teacher who desires to foster the reading of literature for information and pleasure.

TEACHING READING IN A PERSONALIZED LITERATURE PROGRAM (PLP)

Some teachers choose to go all the way with library books and use them as the major instructional material for teaching reading. With this approach, the children do the actual selection of materials to read. To differentiate this approach from other literature programs or from other ways of individualizing reading instruction, I'm calling it the "personalized literature program," or PLP. The PLP is based on three principles espoused several decades ago by the child-development specialist Willard C. Olson. The three principles are (1) seeking, (2) self-selection, and (3) self-pacing. In essence, Olson was saying that children, by nature, are "seeking organisms" who are curious about their environment and want to learn about it. This learning is best motivated and maintained when children are given many opportunities to select their own stimuli and experiences and to explore at their own individual pace. Olson felt that these principles applied to the processes of learning to read, and thus he supported the PLP movement so fervently advocated by Jeanette Veatch and Walter Barbe and often referred to as "individualized reading."

Similar views of learning and reading were advocated before Olson by Piaget, Dewey, Froebel, Rousseau, and other educational philosophers. Today's educational philosophers—Ken Goodman, Frank Smith, and Lucy Calkins, just to name a few—also seem to agree with Olson's goal: Educators should provide children with opportunities to seek, to self-select, and to self-pace. The use of literature as the main medium of instruction offers one way of achieving this goal. (Later in this chapter, though, I'll suggest a combination of *two* media—literature and writing—as the most successful way.)

Research on PLPs

Research on personalized literature programs—as they existed in the 1960s and 1970s—had inconclusive results (Johnson, 1965; Macdonald et al., 1966; Safford, 1960; Thompson, 1975; Vite, 1961). Some teachers got excellent results; some didn't. In general it appeared that the success of a PLP depended upon the knowledge, skill, and enthusiasm of the teacher. The same thing is likely today: Those who are successful in using a PLP will need to be knowledgeable about the nature of reading and its place in the language arts, the various ways of teaching reading, the means of managing such a flexible program, and the ways of finding books that fit children's needs and interests. It is definitely not a program to enter casually or half-heartedly.

A more recent study by Eldredge and Butterfield (1986) did show that literature can make a difference in reading achievement. "The use of children's literature to teach children to read," they found, "had a positive effect upon students' achievement and attitudes toward reading—much greater than the traditional methods used."

PLP Skill Instruction: If You Have a Subskill View of Reading

How does one teach vocabulary or phonics in a personalized literature program? I gave you some ideas on this in Chapters 6 and 7, but I'd like to expand on those right now. How you teach vocabulary or phonics depends on your views of reading, language, and children. If you believe in the bottom-up, subskill view of reading and language—that children need to be taught language directly rather than acquiring it indirectly—you will probably want to use some type of SMS (skills management system).

An SMS provides the teacher with tests, instructional materials, and record-keeping devices. With an SMS, a teacher tests her students to see what "skill lessons" they need. She then divides the students into temporary groups in order to teach those lessons. And she keeps quantitative records of the children's test scores, using posttests and skill checklists.

Although a skills management system can be purchased separately from your regular reading program, many teachers who use an SMS rely on the testing, remediation, and record-keeping materials provided with a regular basal reader program. The teacher simply uses the skill lessons in the teacher's guides and the various tests and skill checklists provided by the publisher. The basal readers themselves then serve primarily as anthologies of stories that children may or may not read depending on their own desires, although basals are also used to teach comprehension and decoding during temporary skill group meetings.

Those using an SMS approach may teach some skills during an individual conference, but most of the skill instruction is carried on with small groups of children who have similar skill deficiencies. Mrs. Spiegal, for instance, may determine during an individual conference that Sandra needs help on decoding vowel patterns. Although she may spend a moment teaching one of those patterns, she will also make a record of Sandra's problem and make sure she later receives instruction along with other children who are having similar problems. (Occasionally, the teacher may decide the entire class needs instruction on the same skill.)

There are, of course, all sorts of ways to schedule these skill group meetings. One fifth-grade teacher, for example ("I have a compulsion to teach skills," she told me), schedules seventy-five minutes of individual conferences with her students three days a week and seventy-five minutes of small-group instruction two days a week. (On these two days she meets with three groups for about twenty-five minutes each.) Another teacher does it this way:

Monday: Individual conferences—50 minutes; skill group A—25 minutes

Tuesday: Individual conferences—50 minutes; skill group B—25 minutes

Wednesday: Individual conferences—30 minutes; skill group C—20 minutes; skill group D—20 minutes

Thursday: Individual conferences—30 minutes; skill group C—20 minutes; skill group D—20 minutes

Friday: Individual conferences—50 minutes; book sharing—25 minutes

In addition to this type of scheduled instruction (or instead of it), the teacher using a personalized literature program carries on spontaneous instruction during some of the individual conferences. Sometimes after a conference in which a particular decoding or comprehension concept has been discussed, a teacher will assign a practice worksheet for the child to take back to her desk.

Teachers using a PLP often have children keep track of the unfamiliar words they run across during their reading. One teacher, for example, has children make a bookmark for a new book. On the bookmark, the children write down each word that causes them trouble. Then during a scheduled individual conference, they talk about the words that are difficult to decode or understand.

Another teacher, who is concerned that children always learn words in context, has the children keep track of "hard words" by writing down on a sheet of paper the page number, the entire sentence, and the underlined word. Another teacher uses the bookmark idea but has the children write both the word and the page number. That way the child doesn't have to write the entire sentence (an onerous task when you're trying to read), but the teacher can have him find the word again during the conference and help him use the four cueing systems to discover the pronunciation and meaning. (Caution: If you're not careful, you'll spend your entire conference time on this. Instead, you might have the child select two of the words on his bookmark—"two that you really want to learn.")

PLP Skill Instruction: If You Have a Whole Language View

Suppose that you have a whole language view of reading rather than a subskill view. With a whole language view the key concern would be not what you can *teach* your students about decoding and comprehending, but how you can *respond* to their efforts to learn about these things. Remember, the whole language view calls for learning to read and write in a way that is similar to the way very young children learn to speak and listen—which is to experiment with language and see what kind of response they get from adults and peers. The idea here is that children essentially teach language skills to themselves.

What this would mean in a practical sense is that comprehension processes could be modeled in the same way that I described in Chapters 4 and 5. It would make little difference whether you use basal readers or literature for this purpose, provided there are multiple copies of the particular literature you're using—or provided you use "big books" that several children can see at the same time you're reading to them.

To teach vocabulary or phonic patterns, though, there are at least three approaches:

1. You can use the comprehension-modeling procedures just mentioned but include the graphophonic cueing system in your modeling. For example, in addition to modeling the processes of using schemata and making predictions, you could also model how you use the graphophonic cueing system along with the other three systems to predict or confirm the pronunciation and meaning of an unknown word in the text.

2. You can use the fairly direct language experience approach already described. To the whole language purist, a teacher-directed language experience approach—with its sequence of stimulating interest, discussing, writing, reading, and skill development—might miss the essence of the whole language view I just mentioned. Even though the writing ideas do come from the children, the teacher might do much more teaching than necessary and not enough responding to children's needs and interests. You might think of an LEA, then, as a *modified* whole language approach, one that uses more group teaching and teacher direction.

3. You can teach vocabulary and graphophonic patterns through a more informal approach of combining your literature and writing programs, a combination I've shown you already, but one I'll discuss further at the end of this chapter.

MANAGING INDIVIDUAL CONFERENCES

An essential ingredient of a personalized literature program is the individual conference. Many teachers shy away from "those things" because they're not used to one-on-one types of relationships with students. On the other hand, many teachers swear by them because of the possibilities for really knowing and assisting their young students.

The two most frequent questions about individual conferences are these:

☐ How long and how often should they be?
☐ What's supposed to happen during a conference?

Length and Frequency of a Conference

Unfortunately (or rather fortunately), there are no easy answers to these questions; the answers depend on your purpose for a particular conference with a particular child. You may decide to give Jerry two conferences a week for about fifteen minutes each; Patricia, one conference a week for about ten minutes; and Randy, one conference every two weeks for five to ten minutes. Jerry, you see, is so far behind the rest of the class in his reading strategies that you decide he needs a lot of individual help. Patricia is doing reasonably well in her reading

strategies and needs only a moderate amount of conferencing to build her confidence and broaden her reading interests. Randy, though, must have been born with a book in his hands. Your major purpose in meeting with him is to provide warm encouragement and show interest in what he has been learning about through his reading.

Some teachers, on the other hand, feel it's important to give each child the same number of conferences and about the same amount of time. Consequently they schedule each child for one conference a week for about ten minutes each. With thirty students, this adds up to 300 minutes per week or one hour per day.

Conferences for Gathering Information about Each Child

As to what happens during a conference, this, of course, varies widely with the different needs of the children, whether it's early in the school year or later. Early in the school year, the first few conferences are often used for administering informal reading inventories in order to determine the *nature* of the child's miscues (errors). This enables the teacher to determine what concepts of reading and what strategies of reading each child has developed.

Once the miscue analyses have been completed (see Chapter 11), or even before they've been completed, teachers often use the individual conferences to determine each child's skill in selecting her own library books. This is usually done by listening to her read out loud to see how difficult the book is that she has already selected, and to talk about her interests. These interests and other observations are recorded in a notebook or folder for further reference. This enables the teacher to help each child find appropriate books.

Conferences for Skill Development

Later conferences *can* be used for developing certain skills that you feel strongly about. My own feelings about this, though, from using a PLP with several groups of children, is that skill development in conferences should seldom take more than one-third of the conference time. Most of the time should normally be spent in *responding* to what the children are learning about. In other words, if you really want children to read for meaning, you must respond to meaning and not merely to their decoding mistakes. (Note that this is the same idea advocated for the writing part of your program.) Since I've already hit this issue pretty hard in Chapters 4 and 8, I won't go over it again. Conferences, to put it succinctly, have two major functions: (1) inspiration and (2) diagnosis. Inspire them to read even more. Determine strengths and weaknesses in their *reading concepts* and *reading strategies*. (See Chapters 4 and 11 for more on these two ideas.)

On the other hand, for teachers who use a skills management system in their literature program, conferences are often used as a time to reinforce a skill or a word that was taught to the child during a recent small-group skill lesson. These teachers usually feel the need to spend more time on vocabulary and phonics development. In fact, they may even tie the conferences directly in with their skill lessons by asking the children in each skill group to, "Look for an example in your library books of what you've learned today. Write down the page number, and show me the example during your next conference with me."

Conferences for Guided Interactive Reading

Whether you use a skills-oriented program, though, or a whole language one, an individual conference can be not only a good time for inspiration and diagnosis but also an excellent time to encourage interactive reading. You can do this simply by letting the child retell what he's read however he wishes, while showing enthusiasm for his way of retelling. Then you can have him read part of his book out loud to you.

His first selection should be one he has practiced for the occasion so that you can provide him with encouragement. The second selection should be one you select "magically" by simply giving him a page number at random. Whenever the child makes a self-correction, praise him specifically for coming up with a word that "makes more sense." Whenever he comes up with a substitution that doesn't make sense and is not self-corrected, wait until he has read the paragraph or page, then return to the uncorrected miscue. Read the sentence the same way the student read it, then ask *him* to find the word that didn't make sense. Talk informally about the things that are different between the "author's word" and his original substitution. For example, to help him see intuitively the importance of schemata, you might ask him to tell you what pictures he gets in his mind when he reads the author's word. Then ask him what pictures he gets when he uses the word he substituted.

Conferences for Building Teacher/Student Relationships

Conferences can be part of the very important process of building enthusiasm for school, for learning, and for reading. They are among the few times the child has the chance to relate to the teacher all by himself. As one teacher put it: "Through individual conferences, I've come to know each child quite well!"

Peer Conferences

But what about peer conferences? You'll remember that I encouraged these when it came to writing, and I'm encouraging you to consider them for reading. Once you've had several weeks to model good conferencing techniques, you can have children pair up for at least one peer conference per week. Or sometimes you can have them conference in small groups of three or four.

Enhancing Thinking Processes during a Conference

Like everything else in a school setting, conferences can also be used for developing thinking processes. In a conference, though, this should obviously be done in a very informal way. For more formal work in modeling and practicing thinking processes, you would normally be better off using a small group and talking about a book or story that they've all read.

Whenever you do ask questions, though, remember that questions that tap only literal thinking don't encourage higher-level thinking processes. If you always ask a child, "Who is the main character of this story?" or "What is this story about?" you are merely encouraging him to read for shallow details. If you want him to read with greater depth, try to vary the questions from conference to conference and use plenty of questions at the inferential, evaluative, and creative levels. Here are a few examples of open-ended questions at these levels for any book. (For more on questioning strategies, see Chapter 5.)

Inferential Questions

You say this story is about Jeff Roberts? Would you say that Jeff is struggling against another person, against himself, or against nature? Why do you think so? (Encourage her to think about all three.)

Can you tell me about something in this book that makes the title of the book a good one?

You've read about half the book now. What do you think is going to happen next?

Tell me, what did you need to picture in your mind before you could understand that sentence?

Critical-Thinking Questions

Is the story you're reading a real-life story or a make-believe story? What makes you think so?

Would you say this book (nonfiction) is full of facts or opinions? Can you give me an example of a fact that the author presents? Can you give me an example of an opinion?

Do you think this author is biased in any way? Or for younger children: How do you think the author feels about that? Do you think she likes it?

Do you think Jeff Roberts (the main character) did anything that showed he was strong (or fair, or kind, or smart, or devious)?

Creative-Thinking Questions

Jeff Roberts had a problem in this story. What was it? If you were Jeff Roberts, how would you solve that problem?

Do you have any problem in your life that is like the one Jeff Roberts had? How do you think you might solve that problem?

Now that you've finished this book, is there a special way you'd like to share it? Is there a book project you've never tried before? Do you have an idea for a book project no one has tried yet?

KEEPING RECORDS

Keeping records is a vital component of a personalized literature program, whether you use a skills approach or a whole language approach or something in between. Adequate records are necessary in order to know what help each child needs, what reading interests each one has, how much a child has read during the year, how deeply she is comprehending and thinking about what she reads, and what to tell parents during parent conferences. (Some parents may be worried, anyway, when they discover that basal readers and workbooks are not being used as they once were. Thus it is highly important to communicate with parents about the program and about their child's progress.)

A folder is usually kept for each child with such things (depending on your view of reading) as a checklist of skills, comments on his reading abilities, his test results, results of observing him in the library, samples of his responses on worksheets, notes on his reading interests, a list of new words he is mastering, how his reading has been influenced by his writing or vice versa, and a record of his actual writing and reading. Each child often keeps this last record herself. Each time that Janet reads a new book, for example, she fills in information on her Book Record Sheet, as shown in Figure 9.2.

READABILITY FORMULAS: HOW GOOD ARE THEY?

Another kind of record keeping that some teachers carry on is simply recording those books that are highly successful with the children or those that are easy enough for the slower readers. Sometimes, though, when you're trying to help children find books that are easy enough for them, you'll wish that you had some kind of quick and magical way of selecting those books. Well, many people have tried to find such a way (and found it's like looking for the fountain of youth).

There have been numerous formulas developed to "estimate" the reading levels of books, the easiest one being Edward Fry's formula (see Application Experience D, pages 315–316). Fry's formula has been used by teachers, authors, and publishers for many years and has often (unfortunately) been the "proof" of a

FIGURE 9.2
Book record sheet

Reading Record
Name: Janet Fromkin   Year: 1982–83

Author	Title	Pages Read	Rating 0–5	Project
Buck	The Big Wave	All	4	Oral #3
O'Dell	Islands of the Blue Dolphins	All	5	Drama #6
Jones	All about Tar	6	0	None
Baker	Walk the World's Rim	All	4	(My own idea)

book's appropriateness for a certain grade level. "This social studies book has a readability level of 3.1 on the Fry scale. Therefore, it's perfect for third-graders." Or, "This book about horses has a 2.2 readability level. It might be perfect for Mickey. He's in fourth grade, but he's only reading at about a second-grade level."

Well, let me warn you. Using a formula to find the exact readability level of a particular book for a particular child is like putting your hand on a child's forehead to determine exactly "what ails 'm." There have been many times when I've personally recommended a book to a child because "the formula" yielded a low readability level—only to find out later that the book was much too hard. Why? Because readability formulas don't take schemata level into account.

The problem with most readability formulas is that they're based only on sentence length and word difficulty. For example, with the Fry formula, you simply count the number of sentences and the number of syllables in three samples of 100 words each. If you count syllables to show how difficult a word is, however, what happens when one selection uses the three-syllable word *Saturday*, which every child understands, and another selection uses the three-syllable word *saturant*, which very few people would understand? And if you simply count the number of sentences in a passage, you get only a measure of sentence length. Yet look at these three equally "long" sentences:

> The boy sent his girl friend a letter.
>
> The swain dispatched his love object an epistle.
>
> To cherie baby he did post a missive.

Although each sentence has eight *words*, only the first one has the *language* that an elementary student would understand.

Let me demonstrate again by showing you what happens to two selections that have exactly the same number of sentences and syllables but require very different schemata for comprehension to take place. Both are rated by the Fry formula as "fifth-grade readability," but only Selection A, I'm sure you'll see, can be handled by a fifth-grader. Whereas Selection A talks about Arthur's earning some money, something even a fifth-grader can understand, Selection B talks about Arthur's crimping some limeys (recruiting some British sailors for a sailing voyage).

Selection A
(Fry's Readability Level:
Fifth Grade)

Arthur Finnington swung his thin legs out of bed and sat on the edge in a stupor. Suddenly he sat up straight.

"Hey, it's Saturday!" he said to himself. "My day for making some money!"

Selection B
(Fry's Readability Level:
Fifth Grade)

Arthur Finnington swung his lank legs out of bed and slumped on the edge in a stupor. He suddenly sat up straight.

To himself he moaned, "Jeze, Saturday. My day for crimping some limeys."

Absent-mindedly Arthur picked his clothes off the floor and began putting them on. His brain was sluggish from a good night's sleep, but he kept on trying to think anyway. He thought about last Saturday—a pretty good day selling homemade popsicles, but too much trouble trying to keep them from melting.
 	
    This time it had to be something *big*, he resolved.
	Absent-mindedly he plucked his togs from the earthen floor and covered his flimsy frame. His brain, sluggish from sleep, wanted to shut down, but willpower won out in the end. Arthur thought about Saturday last—a blimey good day crimping hard up journeymen, but too much trouble trying to keep them from leaving.
	
	    This time he had to find other types, he resolved.

Both of these selections have the same readability rating on the Fry scale, because both have the same number of sentences and syllables. But if they'd been rated by an experienced teacher, I'm sure she'd agree with me that Selection A would be about right for a fifth-grader to understand but Selection B would be much too difficult. Before advising a child on a book, then, I strongly urge you to check the "language load" and "schemata load" yourself rather than relying on a formula.

Yes, you say, but what about all those other formulas? Aren't they "better" than the Fry formula? A little, but none of them sufficiently takes schemata load into account. And what's worse, the different formulas don't give you consistent results. As Zakaluk and Samuels discovered, "The readability level . . . might be rated as most difficult by one . . . formula and least difficult by another. . . . The difficulty level of one . . . text was rated by one formula as the easiest of the nine texts surveyed and by another formula as the next to the hardest" (1988, pp. 123–124).

EASING INTO A PERSONALIZED LITERATURE PROGRAM

As you can see by now, a PLP can be an exciting and worthwhile form of reading instruction. At the same time, it requires a considerable amount of knowledge and management capability on the part of the teacher. If you lack confidence and enthusiasm, it's probably not the approach to take in your first year of teaching. Even if you've had a year or so under your belt, you may feel more comfortable easing into this type of program. Some teachers try it for the first time by having only the "top" group engaged in the program while the other groups continue in the basal reading program. Then, as the teacher gains experience, she has other groups gradually switch over to a PLP.

Another way to break into a PLP is to use it only one day per week at first, but with the entire class. As you develop skill in handling the program on a once-a-week basis, you can then increase the program to two days per week, and so on. This approach is more satisfying to teachers who don't wish to single out one group of children as "privileged." In either case, whether you break in with one group or with one day per week, some kind of gradual adjustment to a personalized literature program may be advisable.

A LITERATURE/WRITING APPROACH TO TEACHING READING

All right. I know you must suspect by now that I'm leading you down the rose-strewn path toward some kind of perfect program. But I'm not. The program that a teacher uses depends on so many factors, not the least of which is his or her personality. I have seen teachers *combine* literature and writing, however, and the results *can* be dynamite.

If you're interested in this approach, I recommend Jane Hansen's book, *When Writers Read* (1987). Hansen, as I've already shown you earlier, is an enthusiast for teaching reading through writing. In her work with the teaching of writing and literature, she discovered that both require the same ingredients. This is because both readers and writers need:

1. Large chunks of uninterrupted time (for reading, writing, or thinking)
2. Opportunities to make choices (topics, books, and procedures)
3. Time to share ideas with peers and adults (and to express their excitement about their reading, writing, and thinking)

Since I've already gone over these three ideas with you, I won't repeat myself. I just wanted you to see that they apply to both reading and writing. Instead, let's review a few ideas about the reading/writing connection that began back in Chapter 3. In that chapter Dr. Peterman described how children learn in a natural way to speak, write, and read—by experimenting and receiving feedback on their experiments. Early readers, she told us, tend to be early writers as well. And their parents tend to be people who encourage both processes by the way they *respond* to these early learners. Their children write and receive responses. And these responses are usually to the *content* of what they write. If the writing doesn't quite communicate what the children wanted to communicate, the children learn to change their writing a bit. These same children read and receive feedback (but not criticism) on their reading. If their reading doesn't quite make sense, they learn to modify their reading behavior. Through experimenting with language and receiving friendly response, they gradually move into the anteroom of the literacy club.

In Chapter 5, I showed you how writing could solve problems for more advanced readers, even with as difficult a problem as trying to figure out what a main idea is. By learning how to *write* a main idea, they can learn how to recognize a main idea in their reading.

In Chapters 6 and 7 we discussed the opportunity teachers have for teaching vocabulary and graphophonic patterns partly through the writing process. And in Chapter 8, we explored the many ways that writing and reading are similar processes and the many ways in which they can be taught together: through poetry, patterned books, journal writing, writing conferences, group experience charts, and personal experience stories.

As I implied back then, successful writing on interesting, self-chosen topics inspires children to read other authors' writing, including the writing of peers and professionals. At the same time, successful reading of interesting, self-chosen literature inspires children to write literature of their own. The writing/reading process is a reciprocal one—like a long, two-colored spiral staircase—that can gradually lead children toward the advanced information and pleasure available up in the main room of the literacy club.

SUMMARY OF MAIN IDEAS

☐ Many children today do not have enough opportunity outside of school to practice real reading. Teachers should provide that time during the school day.

☐ A personalized literature program (PLP) in which children read library books rather than basal readers can be an exciting and successful way to teach reading—requiring skill, knowledge, and management capability on the part of the teacher.

☐ Whether a teacher uses a literature program or any other instructional program in reading, encouraging the reading of library books is essential. It's easy for teachers to get so wrapped up in teaching isolated subskills that they forget to give their students practice in reading real books.

☐ To use any literature program, the teacher needs to know children's literature well, provide time for uninterrupted reading, allow children to make choices among a great variety of books, and encourage sharing of books through book projects, conferences, and peer interaction.

☐ Individual conferences between the teacher and students allow for many different types of communication and learning.

☐ Readability formulas need to be used and interpreted with considerable caution. They are not designed to take the schematic cueing system into account.

☐ A combination literature/writing program can be the most satisfying way of teaching reading for both teachers and students.

APPLICATION EXPERIENCES FOR THE TEACHER EDUCATION CLASS

A. *What's Your Opinion?* Use your own experiences as well as ideas from the textbook to help you defend your decisions. (Remember, these statements are designed not as true-or-false choices but as stimuli for your own thinking.)

1. A personalized literature program is better than either a whole language program or a language experience approach.

2. Kids are kids. We worry too much about how they differ from each other. When it comes to reading instruction, we should be more concerned about how similar they are.

3. The SSR approach is the way to go: It helps children get used to reading library books. Timing kids is probably even more important than allowing them choices.

4. It's smarter for a teacher to read aloud those books from the *Children's Choices* list than from Newbery or Caldecott award lists.

5. Reading and writing are similar or connected processes in at least twelve ways.

6. Giving so many reading choices to children is a mistake. Adults should assert their expertise and experience in the choice of books.

7. Book projects are really no better or worse than old-fashioned book reports.

B. *Miscue Analysis:* How can you tell from Steve's miscues that this first-grader already enjoys the process of reading (in spite of his eight miscues and the author's use of basal reader style for this story? How would this subject of Mary and Dog have been treated differently in a piece of children's literature? Rewrite this text for a group of children, making the language more natural—more like someone talking or more like a story someone is telling.

Mary has a dog. His name is Rex. He is little. He is brown. He likes to play. He likes to run. He runs fast. Mary follows him. Then he stops. He can do tricks. He sits up. He rolls over. He shakes hands. He can swim. He swims in the river.

C. *Simulation of an Individual Conference:* Carry on an individual conference with a partner about a book (preferably a children's book) she or he has just read or is in the process of reading. If your partner has not read one recently, use a movie or television show as a substitute. Discuss the events or ideas that were important in the book or movie. Then *informally* ask your partner a few of the questions from the inferential, critical, and creative questions on page 309. Also discuss one unusual word from the book or movie. Use Appendix F to determine together what kind of project would be suitable for sharing this book or movie. Keep notes on the conference. If you have time, switch roles with your partner.

D. *Determination of Readability:* Using any book you wish with a partner, determine its readability level in two ways:

1. Using a combination of three 100-word selections from different parts of the book, think about prior knowledge required for understanding to take place; then guess the *schematic* grade level (K–17, or kindergarten to graduate-school level).

2. Using the same three selections, compute the readability level using Fry's method and the graph in Figure 9.3.

Now compare your estimates obtained from methods 1 and 2. Report your findings to the rest of the class.

Fry's Method for Obtaining Readability

1. Select three 100-word passages near the beginning, middle, and end.

2. Count the total number of sentences in each 100-word passage (estimating to nearest tenth of a sentence). Average these three numbers.

3. Count the total number of syllables in each 100-word sample. Average the total number of syllables for the three samples.

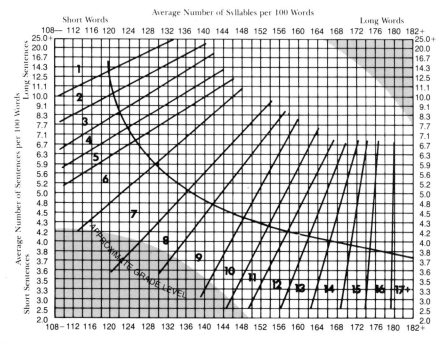

FIGURE 9.3

Fry's graph for estimating readability. (From Edward Fry, "A Readability Formula that Saves Time," *Journal of Reading* 11 [April 1968]: 513.)

4. Plot on the graph the average number of sentences per 100 words and the average number of syllables per 100 words. Most plot points fall near the heavy curved line. Diagonal lines mark off approximate grade-level areas.

For example,

		Sentences per 100 words	Syllables per 100 words
100-word sample	Page 5	9.1	122
100-word sample	Page 89	8.5	140
100-word sample	Page 160	7.0	129
		3)24.6	3)391
	Average	8.2	130

Readability level: fifth grade

FIELD EXPERIENCES IN THE ELEMENTARY SCHOOL CLASSROOM

A. Conduct an individual conference with one child related to a library book he has been reading. Use basically the same procedure described in Application Experience C on page 315. In addition, have him read a few paragraphs aloud. Note his miscues and try to determine his ability to use all four of the cueing systems. If possible, share your notes with another teacher who has been working with the same child.

B. Examine the school library to see whether it has developed any system for helping children find books at the right level of difficulty. If there is no system, think about a system that could be used. If there is no school library, find out what other ways teachers in the building help children get access to a variety of library books.

C. Plan your own way of combining a literature and writing experience, using any genre of literature that you prefer. Show your plans to a colleague before trying them out with children.

REFERENCES AND SUGGESTED READING

Arbuthnot, M. H. (1971). *Children's books too good to miss.* Ashtabula, OH: Western Reserve Press.

Barbe, W., & Abbott, J. (1975) *Personalized Reading Instruction.* New York: Parker.

Bennett, J. E., & Bennett, P. (1982). What's so funny? Action research and bibliography of humorous children's books—1975–80. *The Reading Teacher, 35,* 924–927.

Berglund, R. L., & Johns, J. L. (1983). A primer on uninterrupted sustained silent reading. *The Reading Teacher, 36,* 534–539.

Boly, W. (1987). *The handbook for planning an effective literature program.* Sacramento: California State Department of Education.

Chall, J. S. (1983). Readability and prose comprehension: Continuities and discontinuities. In J. Flood (Ed.), *Understanding reading comprehension* (pp. 233–246). Newark: DE: International Reading Association.

Criscuolo, N. P. (1976). Mags bags, peg sheds, crafty crannies and reading. *The Reading Teacher, 29,* 376–378.

Cullinan, B. E. (Ed.). (1987). *Children's literature in the reading program.* Newark, DE: International Reading Association.

Cunningham, P. (1983). The clip sheet: When is reading? *The Reading Teacher, 36,* 928–933.

Eldredge, J. L., & Butterfield, D. (1986). Alternatives to traditional reading instruction. *The Reading Teacher, 40,* 32–37.

Fader, D. N., & McNeil, E. B. (1968). *Hooked on Books: Program and Proof.* New York: Putnam.

Fountain Valley teacher support system in reading. (1971). Huntington Beach, CA: Richard L. Zweig Associates.

Graves, M. F., Boettcher, J. A., & Ryder, R. J. (1979). *Easy reading: Book series and periodicals for less able readers.* Newark, DE: International Reading Association.

Greenlaw, M. J. (1983). Reading interest research and children's choices. In N. Roser & M. Firth (Eds.), *Children's choices: Teaching with books children like* (pp. 90–92). Newark, DE: International Reading Association.

Hansen, J. (1987). *When writers read.* Portsmouth, NH: Heinemann.

Hickman, J. (1983). Classrooms that help children like books. In N. Roser & M. Firth (Eds.), *Children's choices: Teaching with books children like* (pp. 1–11). Newark, DE: International Reading Association.

Huck, C. S. (1976). *Children's literature in the elementary school.* New York: Holt, Rinehart, and Winston.

Hunt, L. (1970). The effect of self-selection, interest, and motivation upon independent, instructional, and frustration levels. *The Reading Teacher, 24,* 146–151, 158.

Individualized reading from Scholastic. Englewood Cliffs, NJ: Scholastic Book Services.

Johns, J. L., & Hunt, L. (1975). Motivating reading: Professional ideas. *The Reading Teacher, 28,* 617–619.

Johnson, R. H. (1965). Individualized and basal primary reading programs. *Elementary English, 42,* 902–904.

Kaisen, J. (1987). SSR/Booktime: Kindergarten and first grade sustained silent reading. *The Reading Teacher, 40,* 532–536.

Lapp, D. (Ed.). (1980). *Making reading possible through effective classroom management.* Newark, DE: International Reading Association.

Leibowicz, J. (1983). Children's reading interests. *The Reading Teacher, 37,* 184–187.

Long, B. H., & Henderson, E. H. (1973). Children's use of time: Some personal and social correlates. *Elementary School Journal, 73,* 193–199.

Macdonald, J. B., et al. (1966). Individual versus group instruction in first grade reading. *The Reading Teacher, 19,* 643–647.

McCracken, R. A., & McCracken, M. J. (1978). Modeling is the key to sustained silent reading. *The Reading Teacher, 31,* 406–408.

Moore, J. C., Jones, C. J., & Miller, D. C. (1980). What we know after a decade of sustained silent reading. *The Reading Teacher, 33,* 445–450.

Norton, D. E. (1987). *Through the eyes of a child: An introduction to children's literature* (2nd ed.). Columbus, OH: Merrill.

Otto, W., & Chester, R. D. (1976). *Objective based reading.* Reading, MA: Addison-Wesley.

Pfau, D. W. (1966). *An investigation of the effects of planned recreational reading programs in first and second grade.* Unpublished doctoral dissertation, State University of New York at Buffalo.

Prescriptive reading inventory. (1972). New York: CTB/McGraw-Hill.

Roser, N., & Firth, M. (Eds.). (1983). *Children's choices: Teaching with books children like.* Newark, DE: International Reading Association.

Sadoski, M. C. (1980). Ten years of uninterrupted sustained silent reading. *Reading Improvement, 17,* 153–156.

Safford, A. L. (1960). Evaluation of an individualized reading program. *The Reading Teacher, 13,* 266–270.

Schaudt, B. A. (1983). Another look at sustained silent reading. *The Reading Teacher, 36,* 934–936.

Sebesta, S. L. (1985). Literature for children. *The Reading Teacher, 39,* 94–99.

Spache, E. (1976). *Reading activities for child involvement.* Boston: Allyn & Bacon.

Spache, G. D. (1970). *Good reading for the disadvantaged reader.* Champaign, IL: Garrard.

Spache, G. D. (1974). *Good reading for poor readers.* Champaign, IL: Garrard.

Spiegel, D. L. (1983). *Reading for pleasure: Guidelines.* Newark, DE: International Reading Association.

Strazicich, M., & Hull, L. (1986). *Recommended readings in literature.* Sacramento: California State Department of Education.

Sutherland, Z. (1977). *Children and books.* Chicago: Scott, Foresman.

Taylor, F. D., et al. (1972). *Individualized reading instruction, games and activities.* Denver: Love Publishing Company.

Thompson, R. (1975). Individualized reading: A summary of research. *Educational Leadership, 33,* 57–63.

Veatch, J. (1966). *Reading in the elementary school.* New York: Ronald Press.

Vite, I. W. (1961). Individualized reading—the scoreboard on control studies. *Education, 81,* 285–290.

Wilson, P. J., & Abrahamson, R. F. (1988). What children's literature classics do children really enjoy? *The Reading Teacher, 41,* 406–411.

Zakaluk, B. L., & Samuels, S. J. (1988). Toward a new approach to predicting text comprehensibility. In B. L. Zakaluk & S. J. Samuels (Eds.), *Readability: Its past, present, and future.* Newark, DE: International Reading Association.

Basal Reader Programs: Uses and Misuses

Frank B. May and Carol L. Peterman

═══════ **CHAPTER PREVIEW** ═══════

Throughout this text you've seen teaching techniques and strategies that can be useful when presenting basal reader lessons. For example, in Chapter 5, you followed Mrs. Stineberg's use of the DRTA as she introduced the story *The Magic Doors*. She used this line of questioning as an alternative to questions presented in a teacher's guide. In Chapters 8 and 9, you learned about the language experience approach (LEA) and the personalized literature program (PLP) as supplements or alternatives to basal reader programs. In this chapter, our goals are (1) to help you decide how to most effectively use a teacher's guide when presenting basal reader lessons, and (2) to convince you to supplement basal reader programs with literature, language experience, and writing activities.

Being familiar with basal reader programs is essential because about four out of five teachers in the elementary grades use them; they are essentially a fact of life. You'll learn why basal reader programs are so prevalent and how teachers typically use them. Hopefully, you'll see some of the severe limitations of strict adherence to the teaching procedures that the basal authors intended primarily as suggestions from which teachers can pick and choose.

If you decide to use a basal reader program (or if your principal says you must use one), then you need to know how to identify a good one. Alternatively, if someone has already selected a mediocre one you must use, you need to know how to make it work for you and your students. Often, teachers can design spinoff lessons that are equally effective as, or more effective than, those presented in the teacher's guide. This makes sense simply because teachers are in a better position to judge their students' abilities and interests than are the publishers, who design a single program for students from Maine to California.

While you're reading this chapter, you might want to think about how basal reader programs, if used appropriately, can encourage the reading/writing connection and how they can be used in conjunction with other approaches. In fact, you'll be reading an excellent article by James Baumann (1984) who gives you concrete examples of "how to expand a basal reader program."

The observation that basal programs ''drive'' reading instruction is not to be taken lightly. These programs strongly influence how reading is taught in American schools and what students read. This influence is demonstrated by studies that have examined how time and instructional materials are used in classrooms. The estimates are that basal reading programs account for from 75 percent to 90 percent of what goes on during reading periods in elementary school classrooms.
—Richard Anderson et al. (1985, p. 35)

A GENERAL DESCRIPTION OF A BASAL READER PROGRAM

Because of the overwhelming prevalence of basal reader programs in elementary school classrooms in the United States, it's important for you to be aware of what basal readers are, what their typical components are, and what a typical lesson looks like. With this knowledge you'll be able to make informed decisions about how you'll implement these programs in your own classroom.

So just what are basal reader programs, and what kinds of materials do they include?

As a partial answer to those questions, let's see if the following anecdote accesses background knowledge from your own experiences with basal readers. The following represents a synthesis of experiences revealed to us by our college students:

I remember when I was in first grade. We used to sit in groups of seven or eight in little chairs forming a semicircle. The teacher had a big chart of words that we memorized and later read in our own little cloth-back books. I remember Dick and Jane, the mom and dad, and, of course, Spot, the dog. I often wondered why the people in the book talked the way they did—in short, little inane sentences—yet I liked the fact that I could read the words almost right away. I always felt sorry for the "black birds" who had to read the same stories over and over until they could read them out loud without any mistakes.

These "look-say" readers were popular in the 1940s and 1950s, since they allowed children to be successful right away by exposing them to a few high-frequency words (*the, you*), regularly spelled words (*Spot, stop*), and high-interest words (*mom, dad*) that would be read over and over again. Gradually, students were introduced to an increasing number of more difficult vocabulary items which were carefully monitored over several "readers" throughout the primary grades. Controlling the vocabulary seemed to be the essential criterion for helping students learn to read stories, articles, poems, and plays. Interestingly, this was the rationale behind the *McGuffey Eclectic Primer*, perhaps the first basal reader introduced in American schools in the 1880s (Smith, 1965).

You see, historically, learning to read was important so that children could read the Bible, religious verses, or moral lessons. In colonial times children memorized portions of *Pilgrim's Progress* or *The New England Primer*. The latter used "complex statements to teach the letters of the alphabet." For example, for the letter *F*, children learned to recite the following: "Foolishness is bound up in the heart of a child, but the rod of correction shall drive it far from him" (Mason and Au, 1986, p. 353).

However, with the introduction of the *McGuffey Readers*, children didn't have to memorize the text; they could actually decode the message, which was often of a patriotric or political flavor. At the beginning stages, the messages were simplified and included pronunciation keys for regularly spelled phonograms (commonly beginning with the consonant-vowel-consonant pattern, such as *man, ran, can*). These words were repeated over and over again until they became sight words (or words that children could identify immediately). Children could also begin to make connections between the letters and the sounds they represented, which made it possible for them to read unfamiliar words containing familiar letter arrangements. For example, if they knew *cat* and *man*, they would be able to decode *can*.

Today, publishers continue to control the vocabulary that children are expected to read by using readability formulas. As you know, these formulas take into account the number of words per sentence and the number of syllables per word, with the often questionable rationale that shorter sentences with shorter words are easier to read than longer sentences with multisyllabic words. But along with teaching children how to actually decode the text themselves, publishers expect teachers to teach children that reading is more than oral recitation. Children have to be able to understand what they're reading.

So today teachers tend to favor programs that include not only drill and practice on sight words but also comprehension instruction, vocabulary development, and decoding lessons dealing with phonics, context clues, and structural analysis (or use of prefixes and suffixes). They also favor programs that encourage supplementary language experience stories and the reading/writing connection. And not surprisingly, more and more teachers expect to see programs that help students use all four cueing systems rather than forcing them to focus on any one system.

Unfortunately, even though an increasing number of teachers are learning about the reading process as a constructive, problem-solving activity requiring the use of all four cueing systems, some publishers continue to publish programs that focus primarily on the graphophonic system to the exclusion of the others. Some programs neglect comprehension instruction, making the assumption that eloquent, prosodic oral reading is evidence enough of a student's ability to understand what he's "reading." What we're saying is that there's a wide range of basal reader programs on the market today, representing a variety of types and philosophies. Aukerman (1984) discovered that in addition to about 16 basal reader programs, there were 165 experimental programs being tried, all of which have been considered highly successful by those using them.

> "The greatest difference between programs is the way each program handles phonics. Some reading series begin by introducing one or two words a day with picture associations. This is known as the *look-say* or *sight word* method which the Scott, Foresman Company used in "Dick and Jane" readers. . . . Some reading programs start with phonics by teaching each letter, its name, and the sound it represents. . . . In some programs, children begin reading words composed of the letters already taught, but other programs teach all the letter-associated sounds prior to any significant reading. Procedures then emphasize the "sounding out" of words not recognized. . . . [Still another program] concentrates on teaching not just one sound for each letter, but all possible spellings for each sound" (Fields & Lee, 1987).

What this means, of course, is that you need to be able to select a program that's right for you and your students based on what you know about the reading process and your students' needs. Sounds like quite a challenge, doesn't it? So let us relieve some of your anxiety by making two points about the use of materials for teaching reading.

First, the selection of reading programs is often part of a democratic process among teachers within any given school district. Committees are formed and time is allotted to carefully consider the possibilities. State adoption guidelines and recommendations are provided. Often, school districts have created curriculum guides that identify specific reading goals for the various grade levels. The basal reader program can be and often is selected according to how closely its objectives match those identified in the district curriculum guides. And the reality of selection is that "although over a dozen well known basal reading programs are on the market, about 70 percent of American schools buy one or more of the five best-selling programs" (Anderson et al., 1985, pp. 35–36).

Second, it's the *teacher* who makes the difference in the use of published materials. The "First Grade Studies" and the "Second Grade Studies" of the 1960s showed that no matter what media teachers used (language experience stories, basal readers, phonics workbooks, whatever), children's reading achievement was about the same (Bond & Dykstra, 1967; Dykstra, 1968). It wasn't the materials that made the difference; *it was the teachers*. (For more on this topic, see Chall, 1967.) In other words, *good* teachers, who decide *how* and *when* to use the materials, will do a good job of teaching reading *in spite of* the limitations of the published materials. Our point? Selecting appropriate materials for your students is extremely important. However, what you do with the materials is even more important. So let's see what some of the published materials include.

COMPONENTS OF A BASAL READER PROGRAM

The range of instructional materials available to the teacher using a modern basal series is quite extensive. Listed below are just a few of them.

1. *Readers:* softbound and hardbound books of stories, poems, plays, lessons, and articles. Multiple copies of these are provided so that a group of children can use them at the same time.
2. *Teacher's guides:* manuals that contain precise lesson plans, review and enrichment activities, games, annotated lists of children's library books, scope and sequence charts for teaching skills, and other information.
3. *Practice books:* workbooks for reinforcing skills and concepts that have already been taught by means of the readers and the teacher's guides. These are consumable items often with perforated pages so that parents can see the "skills" covered over the course of the school year.
4. *Testing materials:* tests, inventories, and record-keeping devices that allow teachers to determine each child's reading level, strengths, and weaknesses, and to assess his progress as he moves through the program.
5. *Ditto masters:* for reproducing worksheets that help the teacher not only reinforce reading-skill development and provide extra practice for those who need it, but also provide enrichment experiences in spelling, writing, and other language skills. At adoption time, publishers will often promise teachers a set of these materials if they choose their series. The danger of these materials lies in the fact that they can become routinely used as independent seatwork. Children quickly lose interest when these materials are used in this way.

6. *Instructional aids:* charts, word cards, "big books" (large reproductions of readers at the lower levels), instructional games for reinforcing skills, and computer games and exercises.
7. *Supplementary paperback library books.*
8. *Dictionaries.*
9. *Cassettes and sound-filmstrips:* for children to use at classroom listening stations or for teachers to use with small and large groups. These cassettes and filmstrips are designed to reinforce earlier lessons and to provide enrichment experiences (such as listening to an author read her own book while the child reads along).

"An entire basal reading program would make a stack of books and papers four feet high" (Anderson et al., 1985).

These instructional materials are available for each reading *level*. For example, rather than producing one book for each of the eight grades in the elementary school, the authors and editors prepare instructional materials for about *fifteen* levels, ranging from readiness materials for kindergarten and first grade all the way up to literature and informational selections for seventh and eighth grades. Figure 10.1 illustrates a sample components chart from a leading basal reader program using this multilevel approach.

The idea behind the multilevel approach is to encourage teachers to instruct a class at various levels at the same time, rather than instruct all those in the same grade with the same book. Unfortunately, the children learn very quickly that *Glad to Meet You*, for example, is the first of two second-grade readers. How do they know? Because teachers tend to present *only* those levels associated with a second-grade curriculum. Their rationale: So that children who are behind will have a chance to catch up with their classmates and to make the third-grade teacher's job a little easier. In other words, multilevel materials are seldom used in a multilevel way.

For now, though, let's look at common lesson procedures found among most basal reader programs. After you're more familiar with a typical format, we'll look at ways of adapting (and perhaps ignoring) some of these procedures in order to promote an interactive approach to reading.

A TYPICAL BASAL READER LESSON

Most basal reader lessons follow a fairly similar format:

1. A number of new words are introduced before the children read a selection so that these words don't become stumbling blocks during their reading. Many series simply suggest that you write the words on the

	K	KorR	R	PP$^{1\text{-}3}$	P	1	2^1	2^2	3^1	3^2	4	5	6	7	8
LEVEL	1	2	3	4-6	7-8	9-10	11-12	13-14	15-16	17-18	19-24	25-30	31-36	37-42	43-48
Kindergarten Package	●	●													
Write-in Texts	●	●	●												
Students Texts					●	●	●	●	●	●	●	●	●	●	●
Teacher's Editions	●	●	●	●	●	●	●	●	●	●	●	●	●	●	●
PRACTICE MATERIALS															
Workbooks				●	●	●	●	●	●	●	●	●	●	●	●
Skills Practice Masters	●	●	●	●	●	●	●	●	●	●	●	●	●	●	●
Skills Practice Books		●	●	●	●	●	●	●	●	●	●	●	●		
Comprehension and Writing Masters				●	●	●	●	●	●	●	●	●	●	●	●
TESTING AND MANAGEMENT MATERIALS															
Readiness Test	●	●	●												
Initial Placement Inventory				●	●	●	●	●	●	●	●	●	●	●	●
Assessment Tests, Forms A and B	●	●	●	●	●	●	●	●	●	●	●	●	●	●	●
Testing/Management Resource Books		●			●			●		●	●	●	●	●	●
Achievement Tests					●			●		●	●	●	●	●	●
Student Profile Cards	●	●	●	●	●	●	●	●	●	●	●	●	●	●	●
Class Profile Cards	●	●	●	●	●	●	●	●	●	●	●	●	●	●	●
SUPPLEMENTARY MATERIALS															
Skill Development Charts				●	●	●	●	●	●	●	●	●	●		
Vocabulary Development Charts							●	●	●	●	●	●	●		
Solo Books	●	●	●	●	●	●	●	●	●	●	●	●	●		
Extras! For Reinforcement	●	●	●	●	●	●	●	●	●	●	●	●	●		
ABC Cards	●	●	●												
Phonic Picture Cards		●	●	●	●	●									
Word Cards		●	●	●	●	●									
Story Cards				●	●	●									
Read and Tell	●	●	●												
Pick 'n Play Packs	●	●	●												
Records/Cassettes				●	●	●	●	●	●	●	●	●	●		
Tutorial Program				●	●	●	●	●							
Parent Letters	●	●	●	●	●	●	●	●	●	●	●	●	●		

FIGURE 10.1

Components of a basal reader program. Reprinted with permission of Macmillan Publishing Company from FULL CIRCLE, Grade 3-2 (Series r: Macmillan Reading), Teacher's Edition, p. viii. Carl B. Smith and Virginia A. Arnold, Senior Authors. Copyright © 1986 Macmillan Publishing Company.

chalkboard, ask students to use them in sentences, or, with older students, have them look them up in the glossary and write sentences using these words.

2. After new words are introduced, the teacher "motivates" the children to read one or more pages silently. This is usually done through prereading discussion questions.

3. After the reading, teachers often ask children to "round-robin read" (having each student read a sentence or two in an around-the-circle fashion) in order to make sure they read the pages. This is supposed to help "guide" their reading and develop their comprehension. However, there are inherent flaws in this procedure which we'll talk about later.

4. The sequence of motivation, reading, and comprehension "teaching" is continued until the whole selection has been read.

5. A skill lesson is often taught on a different day. This lesson is one described in the teacher's guide and usually emphasizes a particular decoding or comprehension subskill, such as "reading the *ap* phonogram" or "recognizing details that support main ideas." The skill lesson is often followed by the explanation and completion of a workbook assignment. Very often these skill lessons are unrelated to those needed to read either the preceding or the subsequent story, and they often "flit" from one skill to another with seemingly no connection (Durkin, 1983).

6. Review lessons or enrichment experiences, described in the teacher's guide, usually occur on a different day. It's unfortunate that some teachers feel too rushed to allow time for these types of experiences—especially the enrichment type.

WHY MOST TEACHERS USE BASAL READER PROGRAMS

Studies within the last ten years or so have shown that not only do most teachers rely heavily on basal reader programs; they also follow the teacher's guides closely (Anderson, 1984; Durkin, 1984; Fisher et al., 1978; Mason & Osborn, 1982; Shannon, 1983). In fact, many of our students who have observed practicing teachers report that they've seen some teachers use every story, lesson, worksheet, and supplementary procedure that's provided. When asked why they do this, they often respond, "So that I can let the principal and the parents know that I've taught them everything I was supposed to teach them."

We're sure there are other reasons why teachers tend to overrely on basal reader programs and the extensive use of the teacher's guide. And we're sure their arguments sound pretty convincing. Take, for example, the fact that basal reader programs control the vocabulary in order for readers to make "continuous progress." Sounds like a pretty good rationale for using them, doesn't it? All right, except that those who advocate a language experience approach can say, "This is exactly what happens with LEA. The children control the vocabulary by using their own words!" Those who advocate a free-choice, library-books approach might say, "Children control the vocabulary by choosing books that are interesting and easy enough to enjoy." So you see, we're not really talking about vocabulary control; we're talking about who does the controlling—the children or the reading experts.

Perhaps another reason teachers rely so heavily on the teacher's guide is the sense of security it provides. For the teacher who wants to ensure that she's "taught everything she needs to teach," basal reader programs provide that security for at least three reasons.

First, these programs have a *logical organization*. The stories, poems, and articles are arranged in order of increasing difficulty. The vocabulary and skill lessons become increasingly more complex. Second, along with this logical organization comes an *organized sequence*. Teachers gain a sense of security because children move through a basal reader program sequentially from one selection to the next, one skill lesson to the next, one worksheet to the next, and one test to the next, according to the written sequence. The fact that the numerous basal reader publishers in the United States don't agree on the same sequence should be evidence enough of the somewhat arbitrary nature of this sequencing. By the way, programs such as language experience and personalized literature, which have no apparent sequence, seem to allow children to achieve as well as basal readers do (Bond & Dykstra, 1967; Britten, 1975).

A third reason teachers feel secure when using a basal reader program and the sequence provided by a strict adherence to the teacher's guide is that the skills are broken down into *manageable units*. Those interacting cueing systems we've been talking about are broken down into *hundreds* of decoding and comprehension situations that are labeled "subskills" and presented to children in hundreds of "skill lessons" and worksheets. With that many subskills represented in the teacher's guide, one could easily be impressed (and thankful) for the effort of the reading experts who have supposedly devised a way of simplifying the intricate process of teaching children how to read. If learning to read were only that simple, then teacher's guides would undoubtedly make life a lot easier.

Speaking of security, here's a confession from a former first-grade teacher:

> When I first started teaching, I had one year of education courses beyond a bachelor's degree in music. I felt very uncomfortable about teaching reading, especially in first-grade classrooms where it would seem to be of utmost importance to know what I was doing and why. As a result, I followed the teacher's guide fairly closely. As a substitute teacher, I was relieved when the teacher's "lesson plans" referred me to page so-and-so in the teacher's guide. And the reason this worked for me was that the elaborate, semiscripted procedures required little planning or preparation on my part.
>
> Yet these "cookbooks extraordinaire" worked for only so long. You see, when I was hired as a first-grade teacher, I continued to adhere quite rigidly to the author's suggestions. I figured that these books were written by people who knew what they were talking about. But the problem began when my

students (and myself, quite frankly) became rather bored with the same recipe for every lesson, every story. The stories began to lose their appeal, their flavor. The children even started to resist this diet altogether.

I decided that I needed to spice up my reading lessons. I noticed that, not surprisingly, children were still interested in library books or books they brought from home to share. So, like a good cook who uses a recipe as merely a guide, I stuck with the basic ingredients but gradually began to add a dash of drama, a sprinkle of suspense. Not only were my students enjoying reading again, but they were learning as a result of their reading.

So, for the beginning teacher, these cookbooks extraordinaire can be a godsend. But after a while, as you develop confidence from your experience, you'll begin to alter the recipes and create some of your own (Durkin, 1978–79; Shake & Allington, 1985). And it's amazing how fun teaching can be when you see children experiencing the pleasure of reading, especially when this pleasure stems from your own desire to make reading more than a subject that needs to be taught from 9:00 to noon.

LIMITATIONS OF BASAL READER PROGRAMS

There's nothing wrong with your using basal reader programs to teach reading as long as you control the materials and they don't control you. No one knows better than the teacher what reading experience the children need to have next. No teacher's guide. No written sequence. No principal. No superintendent. No reading expert from afar. Your sensitivity to the child and your own good judgment should be your major guides in the classroom. In fact, one well-known reading expert will tell you, "The responsibility of the truly *professional* person is to select from manual recommendations (a) only what will advance reading ability and (b) only what is needed by the particular group of students to whom the lesson will be directed. At any given time, therefore, what is suggested may be used, altered, shortened, lengthened, or skipped. What is important but *not* in the manual will have to be added by the teacher" (Durkin, 1983, p. 360).

Just so you'll remember how important you are in the decision-making process, let us remind you of some of the limitations of allowing the teacher's guide to run your reading program.

First of all, children can very quickly become bored with the whole process of learning to read. They learn to associate "school reading" with the reading circle, workbook pages, and listening to the stumbling, word-by-word reading of their classmates (Johns & Ellis, 1976; Wixson et al., 1984; and others). They don't see the connection between the "skills" they're expected to learn and how these will help them become better readers. Sometimes, these negative associations actually interfere with the child's desire to take part in anything having to do with "reading."

> From the observation journal of one of our practicum students:
> "The small group of students I am working with has been labeled
> "remedial readers" by their teacher. I feel like the teacher has
> given up on them and has turned them over to me (I guess she
> figures I can't do too much harm). Diane absolutely refuses to do
> anything with me if I even mention the word "reading." She is
> completely disenchanted with the prospect. Every once in a while
> I sneak in an activity that she actually enjoys—usually it starts
> with a discussion of something *she's* interested in. But the minute
> I ask her to read what she's written or tell her we're going to
> work on reading she crawls back into her shell."

Another limitation inherent in basal readers themselves is the language used. It's ironic really, because publishers control the language of basal readers in order to monitor the difficulty of the passages in order for children to be successful. Yet in reading books with controlled vocabulary, children are often exposed to "basal reader language" or "what someone once called the only language in print not spoken by any human" (Larrick, 1987, p. 186). This type of language doesn't allow children to rely on their oral language or to use the semantic and syntactic cueing systems. Let me give you an example of what Nancy Larrick calls "basal reader language" (contrasted with the more "familiar rhythm of everyday speech") in which the words tell "a ministory that builds its tiny plot from nothing to a ludicrous climax" (p. 186):

Basal Reader Language
Where Are Wheels?

Where are wheels?
Here are wheels.
Wheels are on a van.
Wheels are on a truck.
Wheels are on the go!

Verse from Karla Kushkin (1985)
There was a hog
who ate a dog
and then he ate
a grass-green frog
and then he was so full
he cried.
And then he lay down—
bang—and died.

Which type of passage would you rather read, day after day, without any choice? You see, in controlling vocabulary, skill sequence, and content so tightly, we can easily damage the desire between two individuals, reader and author, to communicate. Isn't the desire to read, to communicate, the purpose of our reading programs? If not, it definitely should be!

This brings to mind another limitation of the exclusive use of basal reader programs. Because they tend to be highly structured, basal reader programs don't lend themselves to spontaneous sessions involving listening, speaking, writing, or experiencing the ideas presented in print. Because most teachers are concerned

TABLE 10.1

Outcomes of teachers' overreliance on teacher's guides

Primary-Grade Level	Middle- and Upper-Grade Levels
Give too little time to new vocabulary and word practice	
Teach phonics in a way that is overly obscure and indirect	Forget that phonics was taught earlier, and encourage students to use glossaries and dictionaries for help with troublesome words
Provide decoding practice using words children can read	
Divide selections in readers into parts even though the division makes comprehension more, not less, difficult	
Give more attention to expressive oral reading than to comprehending text	Do more to help students locate information (for example, in dictionaries and encyclopedias) than to teach them how to understand it
Ask an excessive number of assessment questions	
Assign too many brief, written exercises without ever clarifying the connections between the exercises and real reading	

Source: Dolores Durkin, Teaching Them to Read (Boston: Allyn & Bacon, 1983), p. 359.

with content coverage and timelines (for example, a unit every week), they rarely choose to take time for spontaneous discussions where students and teachers interact with each other—listening, speaking, questioning, evaluating, or writing about ideas that are timely or personal. A story can inspire discussion about the children's own experiences and interactions with the world. An informational article can inspire a trip to the library or the neighborhood for more information. A poem can inspire a class collaboration collection. But these things won't happen if the teacher is overly concerned with content coverage and the skill sequence of the basal reader program.

What *will* happen, though, if you follow the teacher's guide too closely is something that Dolores Durkin (1981, 1983) has carefully researched and documented. She found that the misuse of the suggested procedures can result in the outcomes listed in Table 10.1. These outcomes are largely a result of the fact that basal reader programs are primarily subskill-oriented rather than focused on literature or writing approaches to literacy learning.

CRITERIA FOR GOOD BASAL READER PROGRAMS

In a later section you'll see what some innovative teachers do with basal reader lessons to make them more useful. First, though, let's consider that one of the things you can do is to select a quality program from the start. So let's talk about what makes a quality basal reader program, one that you can always improve by making judgments about its appropriate use.

To be competitive, publishers of basal reader programs must meet a number of standards that teachers, administrators, and sometimes even school board members demand. These standards have been studied by a number of researchers and teacher educators at the Center for the Study of Reading. They've examined basal reader programs, including their uses in school settings and adoption procedures and guidelines; and they've studied how to develop and improve basal reader programs through careful decision making (Dole, Rogers, & Osborn, 1986; Durkin, 1981; Osborn & Stein, 1986). In fact, Jean Osborn and her colleagues have spent a great deal of time actually working with school district personnel in order to show that basal reader programs can be used quite effectively if teachers are willing to put in the time and effort to select a series that best meets their district (as well as their own personal classroom) criteria. Some of their ideas are presented in the remainder of this section.

Obviously, the best way to select a basal reader series is to study it and work with it enough to know whether you'll feel comfortable implementing most of the suggestions provided by the teacher's guide. You should also be thinking about the "flexibility potential" which can be woven into the program.

> Personally, we would avoid programs that warn you to follow the sequence and format of the program "in order to ensure success."

Beyond these general guidelines, there are some specific questions you can ask yourself when examining basal reader series and the accompanying teacher's guide. You can use these questions, listed in Table 10.2, as a sort of checklist to compare the series you're actually considering. Oh, another thing: Don't forget to add items that are personal "bottom lines" you know about yourself. For example, we know that we couldn't use a series that didn't have interesting stories which included experiences our students could relate to.

As you can see, there's a lot to consider when selecting a basal reader program. Now, let's look more closely at these considerations.

TABLE 10.2
Questions to consider when selecting basal reader programs

I. Questions about the basal readers
   A. Are the selections interesting, varied, and well written?
      1. Do they include information and experiences that are appropriate and interesting for the children who will be reading them?
      2. Are at least some of the selections written by well-known authors?
      3. Do the selections represent a large variety of "genre"? (See Figure 9.1 for a list of literature categories.)
      4. Are the different sexes and cultural groups represented without stereotypes?
      5. Do the selections help children understand and appreciate different groups (multicultural, elderly, gifted, and handicapped)?
   B. Are the illustrations appealing, appropriate, and artful?
      1. Do the illustrations foster art appreciation through different techniques and styles?
      2. Do the illustrations realistically represent various cultural groups?
II. Questions about the teacher's guides
   A. Does the philosophy of the program reflect the view of reading as an interactive process?
      1. Does it show ways to develop the ability to use all four cueing systems? Or does it merely present subskills in isolation?
      2. Does it show ways to encourage inferential, critical, and creative thinking?
      3. Does it suggest ways to access students' background experiences, preview the type of text they'll be reading, and set a purpose for reading?
      4. Does it show how to teach reading in the context of all four language arts?
   B. Does the guide provide a variety of teaching suggestions that allow for appropriate, individualized instruction?
      1. Does it show how to use oral and silent reading experiences for a variety of instructional purposes?
      2. Does it provide ideas for working with gifted, handicapped, and "language different" students?
   C. Does the guide provide variety and allow flexibility in teaching concepts and skills?
      1. Do the scope and sequence of the program make sense to you?
      2. Does the guide suggest ways of teaching students how to *apply* concepts and skills to their independent reading?
      3. Are the number and type of new vocabulary items appropriate for your students? Are they presented in a variety of interesting ways that will motivate students to want to read the selection? Are there ample opportunities for students to practice these words before they'll encounter them in their reading?
      4. Does the guide provide suggestions for how to teach students to read and study content area texts?

A LOOK AT BASAL READERS
Appropriate and Interesting Selections

Undoubtedly, one of the goals of any reading program is to develop the reading ability of our students. But perhaps more importantly, we need to develop their *interest* in being able to read. And we need to develop their *desire to read*. Ultimately, we want them to *choose* reading for the purpose of gathering information, for pursuing vicarious adventures, for resolving problems in their lives . . . for simply passing the time during those long summer months. In order to do this, we need to provide them with suitable material during reading lessons. Hopefully, they'll see that learning to read has transfer value that's applicable to their personal lives beyond the parameters of the school day.

What kinds of materials are likely to fill the bill? Given what we've learned about schema theory, we would say that of utmost importance is the match between the reading material itself and the lives of the students. You can ask yourself if the selections contain episodes, experiences, or concepts that the children reading them are likely to have experienced. You can determine whether informational selections are relevant to content area guidelines for the grade level you're teaching. Good basal reader programs will even include items that are timely, although this means that the series will be dated according to the event (for example, the Olympics or the renovation of the Statue of Liberty).

Well-Known Authors

Most basal reader programs today include numerous selections by writers noted for their craftsmanship and creativity. For example, Scott, Foresman claims that students using the 1987 edition will:

> read both classical literature and the best of more contemporary authors. Many selections have won such awards as the Newbery, the Caldecott, the National Book Award, the Pulitzer Prize, and the Carnegie Medal. This list gives a small sample of the superb authors represented in the program:

Aesop	Robert Frost
Louisa May Alcott	The Brothers Grimm
Hans Christian Andersen	Alex Haley
Toni Cade Bambara	Virginia Hamilton
Pura Belpre	O. Henry
Ray Bradbury	Jamake Highwater
Gwendolyn Brooks	Russell Hoban
Anton Chekhov	Langston Hughes
John Ciardi	Washington Irving
Beverly Cleary	Joseph Krumgold
Jacques Cousteau	Randall Jarrell
Eleanor Farjeon	Martin Luther King, Jr.
Edna Ferber	Naoshi Koriyama
Anne Frank	Karla Kushkin

Madeleine L'Engle
Arnold Lobel
Jack London
Eve Merriam
A. A. Milne
Kazue Mizumura
Lilian Moore
Evaline Ness
Scott O'Dell
Philippa Pearce
Jack Prelutsky
Geraldo Rivera
Rosebud Yellow Robe
Carl Sandburg

Mari Sandoz
Dr. Seuss
Marjorie Weinman Sharmat
Shel Silverstein
Robert Louis Stevenson
J. R. R. Tolkien
Louis Untermeyer
Judith Viorst
E. B. White
Walt Whitman
Laura Ingalls Wilder
Jade Snow Wong
Richard Wright
W. B. Yeats

(Allington et al., 1987, p. T15)

Variety of Genre

Research has shown that most children have developed a fairly adequate "concept of story" by the time they enter elementary classrooms (see Chapter 3). But what is often lacking is their knowledge of the content and structure of informational text selections. Stories and informational texts obviously require different types of predicting and processing. And we know that "subject matter textbooks pose the biggest challenge for young readers being weaned from a diet of simple stories" (Anderson et al., 1985, p. 67). So it makes sense that textbook editors have begun to realize the importance of including a variety of text types in their basal reader programs. In quality programs you'll find not only good stories written by well-known authors, but also informational selections, poems, plays, excerpts from children's magazines, and sometimes even the work of students (see Figure 9.1 for a list of literature categories). Figure 10.2 shows that children today are exposed to good literature along with information about the author.

Diversity of Cultural Groups
Presented without Stereotypes

Fortunately, textbook editors today are more sensitive than in the past about the need to include a proportionate number of stories or selections about different cultural groups in a way that is nonbiased and without stereotypes. Even the different sexes are presented fairly objectively. This is quite an improvement over materials presented before the 1980s, which were found to be biased against women and girls (National Education Association, 1977). Materials before then tended to show men and boys in roles calling for courage, honesty, intelligence, and creativity, while women and girls, both in illustrations and in text, were portrayed as timid or unimportant—or they were not included at all (O'Donnel, 1974).

"My granddaughter," she said, "you have tried to hold back time. This cannot be done." The desert stretched yellow and brown away to the edge of the morning sky. "The sun comes up from the edge of earth in the morning. It returns to the edge of earth in the evening. Earth, from which good things come for the living creatures on it. Earth, to which all creatures finally go."

Annie picked up a handful of brown sand and pressed it against the palm of her hand. Slowly, she let it fall to earth. She understood many things.

The sun rose but it also set.

The cactus did not bloom forever. Petals dried and fell to earth.

She knew that she was a part of the earth and the things in it. She would always be a part of the earth, just as her grandmother had always been, just as her grandmother would always be, always and forever.

And Annie was breathless with the wonder of it.

They walked back to the hogan together, Annie and the Old One.

Annie picked up the old weaving stick.

"I am ready to weave," she said to her mother.

"I will use the stick that my grandmother has given me." She knelt at the loom.

She separated the warp strings and slipped the weaving stick in place, as her mother had done, as her grandmother had done.

She picked up a strand of gray wool and started to weave.

274

Author

This author has written many fine children's books under her pen name, Miska Miles, and under her real name, Patricia Miles Martin. She has been a teacher as well as an author of stories and poems. *Annie and the Old One,* winner of several book awards, was a Newbery Medal Honor Book.

275

FIGURE 10.2
Today's basal readers are using more children's literature, are telling more about authors, and are becoming more multicultural. From Houghton Mifflin Reading–Level J: *Journeys,* Teacher's Guide, p. 383. Text from ANNIE AND THE OLD ONE by Miska Miles. Text Copyright © 1971 by Miska Miles. By permission of Little, Brown and Company.

You'll even find interesting and informative stories and articles about the handicapped. In quality basal reader programs children are encouraged to understand how handicaps affect individuals as well as how handicapped individuals make important contributions to society. In one series, for example, students are encouraged to participate in the enrichment activity below, following their reading of a selection about a woman and her "hearing ear dog":

> Explain to students that hearing-impaired people like Jennifer can be helped in many ways. Special communication techniques such as lip-reading, sign language, and hearing aids may help them in their daily lives. Have small groups research and report on some of these techniques. If possible, ask a person who signs or a teacher of the hearing-impaired to speak to the class about the progress hearing-impaired people can make with help from hearing ear dogs like Cindy. (Fay et al., 1986, p. TG513)

Illustrations That Foster Art Appreciation

The illustrations in most basal reader programs today often include some that many of us would call "works of art." Such quality is partly the result of more sophisticated printing techniques, which allow artists to use nearly any technique and medium. It is also partly the result of better selection of artists by publishers. Many series, for instance, include illustrations by winners of the Caldecott Medal. Furthermore, to provide novelty from one story to the next, most publishers use hundreds of different illustrators, with their own particular styles and choices of media.

A LOOK AT TEACHER'S GUIDES
A Balance among the Four Cueing Systems

There have been periods of time in the history of basal readers when some of the cueing systems were considered more important than others. Visual memory of sight words was glorified during the "look-say" era; words were supposed to be learned as visual units, and graphophonic cues weren't given much significance. Even syntactic, semantic, and schematic cues weren't much help because of the stilted nature of the text.

Phonics was king during another era (and still is with a few of the basal reader series). This approach provides children with a more effective way to confirm predictions, but it causes many teachers and students to concentrate on word-by-word reading instead of interactive reading. During still another era, whole sentences (as opposed to words or letters) were considered to be the unit of instruction. This approach is likely to encourage interactive reading if children can discover the graphophonic system on their own. If not, however, they're left without an effective cueing system and might resort to "making up their own story" rather than communicating with the author.

As mentioned earlier, publishers today are promoting a better balance among the cueing systems, although different series vary according to their placement along the "meaning-versus-decoding" continuum. As an example of a "meaning emphasis" type of program, let's consider the Houghton Mifflin series. In each teacher's guide it appears that context analysis is emphasized slightly more than graphophonic analysis. In fact, the authors and editors state that through an emphasis on context, students learn to search for meaning while they read.

Even as early as Level A, when the relationship between sounds and letters is being introduced, students are required to pay attention to context clues. For example, in the sentence, "I helped Mom put the d _____ into the dishwasher," children have to tell why they should select *dishes* and why a word like *dentist* or *plates* is inappropriate. (With guidance the children realize that *dentist* doesn't make sense, and although *plates* makes sense, it doesn't fit graphophonically.)

In another series, the authors provide summary statements about their philosophy. They state that in the area of phonics, "sounds should be taught in words, not in isolation; decoding instruction should incorporate the powerful clues to word identification provided by context and word parts" and "from the beginning, students should learn that reading is more than decoding words, that comprehension of meaning is the purpose of reading" (Early et al., 1987, p. x).

Encouragement of Inferential, Critical, and Creative Thinking

Publishers were traditionally reluctant to put too many questions in the teacher's guides that asked for inferential or critical thinking—perhaps because so many teachers told them that such questions were too hard for children, perhaps for other reasons. If you look at teacher's guides of the past, you'll usually see that the questions were mainly of the "who did what" variety (Beck et al., 1979; Beck & McKeown, 1981; Beck, Omanson, & McKeown, 1982). But we've learned that basal reader lessons can and should include questions that probe the main components of the story and encourage inferential comprehension by accessing students' background knowledge about a topic or experience (Hansen & Pearson, 1983). See Chapters 3 and 4 for a review of these ideas.

As a way of preparing students to read a selection, most series today encourage the teacher to introduce relevant concepts and vocabulary items that might otherwise hinder comprehension. Next, it's usually suggested that the teacher prepare the students for reading. The Ginn series (Clymer et al., 1987) is especially good at suggesting ways of accessing students' background knowledge which will provide a focus for their reading as well as enhance inferential comprehension. The following is an excerpt from the teacher's guide (p. 185):

> **Preparing for Comprehension.** The most important preparation pupils can have for reading this selection is an understanding of and sympathy for Marcia's position as the new girl (at school). Ask pupils to recall what it was like to be in a particular situation for the first time, and have them share some of their memories. (It need not be a new school.) To help pupils remember such an occasion, you may want to ask such questions as these:
>
>> Has your family ever moved to a new town?
>> Have you ever gone to a playground, a party, or somewhere else where you didn't know anyone?
>> Can you remember how you felt?
>
> Allow pupils time to remember their experiences and to describe these to the group. Also ask them to think about the difference between how they felt in the beginning, when the experience or situation was new, and later, when they had become accustomed to the situation. To expand the discussion, have pupils who have moved tell something about where they have moved from. Have them tell what their old hometown was like and what things they missed when they moved.

In 1985 Scott, Foresman published a new basal reader series called *Focus*, designed for poor readers. What's interesting about this series is that contrary to what many people would expect, it doesn't assume that poor readers should spend *less* time on higher-thinking skills than good readers. Instead, the *Focus* program seems to assume that although inferential, critical, and creative thinking are more difficult than literal thinking, they're vital processes in communicating with the author, which can't be ignored regardless of ability. This gives readers the message that they can and should use their own background knowledge for thinking about the motives, plans, and actions of the characters they're reading about.

The following questions (with potential answers) are provided at the end of a selection about a fire at a neighborhood hall. Notice that these questions involve mostly inferential (interpretive), critical (evaluative), and creative thinking.

Checking Comprehension

1. The story never really says that the hall didn't burn all the way to the ground. How do we know it didn't? (The firefighters put the fire out quickly. The neighborhood hall will open soon. If the hall had burned down, it couldn't be opened soon.) (draws conclusions; interpretive)
2. What was the most important thing Ruth and Kathy did? (They thought before they ran to get help.) (details; literal/evaluative)
3. How do we know the Fire Chief liked what Ruth and Kathy did? (He came to their school to give them a reward and tell other children to act the same way in an emergency.) (draws conclusions; interpretive)
4. What would you do if you smelled smoke and saw a fire? (Answers will vary but should include the safety steps given in the story.) (creative) ["The Fire" in *Focus* (Glenview, IL: Scott, Foresman, 1985), p. 237]

Reading in the Context of Language Arts

Most basal reader programs *do* try to incorporate the other three language arts in their suggestions in the teacher's guides. At the end of each unit you'll usually find a section called "Enrichment Activities." These generally call for one of four kinds of experiences:

1. Relating what the children have read to another area of the curriculum, especially science or social studies
2. Discussions
3. Creative writing
4. Independent reading

For example, in Figure 10.3, following a comprehension check and skill lesson on main ideas, students are encouraged to discuss specific reasons for restoring an outdated library. A "brainstormed" list is written on the board. Then students are asked to explain their responses. Finally, students are encouraged to write a brief radio advertisement that synthesizes information gained through the reading, speaking, and listening activities.

Oral and Silent Reading Experiences

Many of today's basal reader series are designed to encourage teachers and children to put more emphasis on the communication aspects of reading. There's more emphasis, for example, on silent reading than on oral reading. This in itself communicates to the student that reading is a thinking, communicating process, rather than a mechanical, sounding-it-out process.

But even oral reading, in many of today's programs, is treated differently than when the emphasis was on the correct pronunciation of words (Heinrich,

FIGURE 10.3

Teacher's editions suggest speaking and listening activities. From *City Spaces*, Teacher's Edition, p. 120. Copyright © 1987 by Scott, Foresman and Company. By permission of the publisher.

Checking Comprehension and Skills

Thinking About What You've Read
• 1. What is the topic of this article?
2. Name three unique places in Boston. Do the same for San Antonio.
• 3. Reread the paragraph on page 111. Which of the following is the main idea of that paragraph?
  a. People come from all over the world to visit or live in Boston and San Antonio.
  b. Cities are interesting places.
• 4. What are two details you find on page 111?
5. Why do people restore buildings?
6. What do you think people in Boston might do today when they run out of growing room?
7. What do you think makes a city a special place to live?

Talking About What You've Read
  Pretend you live in a big city. The oldest building in town is the library. It is now too small to hold all the books, so some people want to tear it down. You will be asked to vote. Will you vote to keep it or tear it down? Why?

Writing About What You've Read
  Write a brief radio ad that will make other people feel the way you do about the future of the library.

• Comprehension Skill: Main idea and supporting details

Page 112 continued

Talking About What You've Read
Speaking and Listening
Have pupils read the paragraph on page 112. Have pupils name specific reasons for restoring the library. Record these reasons on the board. Also list reasons for tearing it down and replacing it with a new building. Have pupils explain the advantages of each decision.

Writing About What You've Read
Writing: A Radio Ad
Briefly review the ideas listed on the board from the foregoing discussion about restoring the library.

Before pupils begin to write, have them decide if they want to advertise to restore the building or to have a new one built. It might be fun to let the pupils vote to reach a decision, then write the radio ad to express their opinion.

If the *Vocabulary and Writing Book* is available, refer pupils to page 22 for the writing follow-up.

1976). Teachers are no longer encouraged to stop a child every time he makes a reading "error." If the child misreads a word in a way that indicates he is actually comprehending, the teacher is encouraged to ignore such "miscues." Again, the emphasis is on communication of the message rather than on the pronunciation of the exact wording.

Today, teacher's guides suggest that children be encouraged to read orally for a variety of purposes. In an actor-audience situation, for example, children are given time to practice what they'll read; those who aren't reading look at the "actor" rather than at their books. In this example, the silent reading is a way of effectively receiving the author's message before it is presented orally. The oral reading becomes a shared communication process—one that can entertain and inform others. And by having the "audience" look at the "actor" rather than silently following along in the book, the teacher ensures that the author's message is more likely to be received, since the potential for "subvocalization" is altogether eliminated (Sticht, 1984).

Let's briefly look at some suggestions in the teacher's guide *Glad to Meet You* (Clymer et al., 1987). Under the category "Discussing the Selection," teachers are given suggestions for summarizing the selection. One is to "ask pupils to find and read the sentences in the story that show how Jimmy felt about Madge's first trick" (p. 257). Another involves reading the story aloud as a play:

> This story is a favorite for reading aloud. Assign pupils to play the roles of the various characters. . . . Read the first page yourself as narrator so pupils can get accustomed to the shift in speakers. Then have pupils read the entire story. Allow as many pupils as possible an opportunity to read aloud. (p. 324)

In the *Focus* program, you'll find examples of imaginative oral reading which involve communication rather than word-by-word reading:

> Have pupils take turns rereading page 150 as though they were television reporters reporting the news. . . . Have [them] pretend to be the Fire Chief talking to the children in the school hall and . . . watch for the quotation marks showing the beginning and end of exactly what the Chief is saying. (pp. 235–236)

Experiences for Exceptional Students

As you already know, Scott, Foresman has a series specifically designed for the slow learner. However, other publishers are now beginning to include suggestions and guidelines for accommodating individual needs within their regular program. For example, Harcourt Brace Jovanovich (Early et al., 1987) includes a section entitled "Providing for Individual Differences," in which suggestions are given for reteaching, reinforcing, and extending various decoding and comprehension skills. Three levels of enrichment activities are included to accommodate the less advanced learner, the average, and the gifted. (See Figure 10.4.)

Students with severe learning disabilities and physical handicaps are generally forgotten in most basal reader programs. Occasionally, you'll come across a suggestion for working with the hearing-impaired. Since you're likely to be working with "mainstreamed children," you'll need to consider combining reading approaches, using supplementary materials and consulting resource personnel. For example, Payne, Polloway, Smith, and Payne (1981) offer suggestions for adapting basal readers for use with exceptional students.

Other programs are acknowledging the potential difficulty of "language different" students. This difficulty is a result of the students' having a *different* oral language base rather than a *deficit* in language development. In other words, we used to think of students who speak a second language as being deficient in terms of their ability to learn English. But today we simply acknowledge the difference in languages. In order to access these students' background experiences, and in order to understand differences in phonology between their language and English, basal reader programs are enlisting the help of bilingual authors and editors.

ENRICHMENT

Fine Arts: Art

(In order to provide for greater individualization, the following activities are coded *Easy, Average*, and *Challenging*.)

Illustrate the selection

EASY   Have students reread the selection "Nick Joins In." Then, have students draw a picture that shows how they think Nick felt when he rescued the ball from the roof.

AVERAGE   Have students reread the selection "Nick Joins In." Then, have students draw pictures that show how different characters felt at different parts of the story. Have students write a sentence from the story to describe each illustration.

CHALLENGING   What other special things do students think Nick could have done even though he was in a wheelchair? Have students make up an additional event for the story "Nick Joins In." Have students write this new part of the story and draw pictures to illustrate it.

Social Studies

Make your school even better

AVERAGE   Remind students that Nick went outside to play with his friends even though he used a wheelchair. **How could your school be made even better for students who use wheelchairs?** Have students think of improvements that could be made for students who use wheelchairs. List these improvements on the chalkboard and allow students to discuss them.

CHALLENGING   **Is your school a good school for students who need to use wheelchairs? Why or why not?** Have students write letters to the principal of your school that praise what is good about the school for students who have to use wheelchairs and suggest improvements where improvements might be made.

FIGURE 10.4
Examples of enrichment activities. From *Streamers*, Teacher's Edition, Part I, Level 6 (HBJ Reading Program), copyright © 1987 by Harcourt Brace Jovanovich, Inc.

The Riverside program (Fay et al., 1986), for example, lists a "Bilingual Materials" author. In this series, this person is responsible for providing suggestions for "Spanish Language Instruction" under the general category of "Meeting Special Needs." The following example comes from another series in which the emphasis is on the difference between the letter-sound associations in Spanish and English and how this affects the use of English phonics generalizations.

> **Language development: Spanish-English pronunciation** *quills* (p. 34) Point out that the double *l* in this word is pronounced with the single *l* sound in English. In Spanish the *ll* has the sound of a *y* (p. 28). (Allington et al., 1987)

Logical Scope and Sequence of Concepts and Skills

This criterion is difficult to evaluate because the scope and sequence of any basal reader program are often arbitrarily determined by the authors and editors. You see, by using a basal reader series, you can anticipate and monitor progress in the myriad of decoding and comprehension subskills to be introduced, "maintained," and tested. And this can obviously be one of the advantages of using a series provided you believe in reading as a subskill phenomenon. However, it can also be a drawback.

If students are being taught skills that are unrelated to the stories or texts they're reading, then they'll often miss the point of the instruction. They'll probably fail to transfer and apply this knowledge to new situations where it could have been employed.

So you'll need to see if there's at least *some* reasonable rationale for the order and inclusion of the reading subskills to be taught. You can check the front of the manual for the philosophy of the program to see if the series authors advocate a meaning emphasis or a decoding emphasis. You can determine whether the presentation of the skills bears out the stated emphasis and whether the order of presentation makes sense. For example, in Figure 10.5 you might ask why students receive instruction related to short stories beginning in kindergarten, yet instruction related to informational articles is postponed until fourth grade.

But in our opinion, the most important consideration is this: Does the lesson help students independently handle the selection they're about to read? Does the guide suggest ways of helping them see a purpose for this lesson? Does it encourage them to apply this lesson to their independent reading? If it doesn't, then you need to be prepared to do those things yourself.

Decoding Skills Taught as a Tool for Independent Reading

Quality basal reader series present lessons that promote independence in reading. For example, some series present selections that expect students to identify previously learned sight words. Other series present words from students' background experiences in a highly useful context. This allows them to integrate the use of all four cueing systems in order to identify the words. When students see that they can successfully and independently apply what you've taught them to their own reading, they're usually interested in learning even more about the reading process.

Notice in Figure 10.6 that the authors establish the goal for learning ("Today, we're going to learn how to use the other words in the sentence, or the context, to figure out which meaning is intended"); help students *apply* the skill to selected vocabulary; and explicitly discuss what to do when reading on their own.

Interesting, Varied, and Appropriate Presentation and Practice of New Vocabulary

One of the things you'll need to consider when selecting (and, of course, when using) a basal reader series is the way in which new vocabulary words are presented and practiced. You'll need to ask yourself if the number and type of vocabulary items seem appropriate for the children who'll be reading the selections. For example, are too many words merely exposed to the students rather than related to their background? After all, it often takes dozens of different exposures to a word before it can be identified in isolation by the average second-grader (Hargis et al., 1988).

Key
○ Exposure prior to major instruction
□ Instruction
▽ Review, reinforcement, extension
◇ Maintenance

T Tested in Quarter Test only
T Tested in Quarter Test and End-of-Book Test

	K	R	PP	Pr	1	2/1	2/2	3/1	3/2	4	5	6	7	8
Varies Reading Technique and Rate for Purpose and Content (*See* **Study Skills**)														
Demonstrates Oral Reading Ability														
Develops oral reading ability		□	▽	▽	▽	▽	▽	▽	▽	▽	▽	▽	▽	▽
Develops fluency as an aid to comprehension			□	▽	▽	▽	▽	▽	▽	▽	▽	▽	▽	▽
Literary Understanding and Appreciation														
Recognizes Story Elements														
Character	○	○	○	○	○	T	T	T	T	T	T	T	T	T
Setting	○	○	○	○	○	○	T	▽	T	T	T	T	T	T
Goal and outcome (*See also* Plot)	○	○	○	○	○	○	T	T	T	□			T	T
Plot (*See also* Goal and outcome)	○	○	○	○	○	○	○	○	○	T	T	T	T	T
Theme	○	○	○	○	○	○	○	○	○	○	T	T	T	T
Recognizes and Responds to Types of Literature														
Modern realistic fiction	○	○	○	○	○	○	○	○	○	T	T	T	T	T
Fantasy	○	○	○	○	○	○	○	○	○	□	□	□		◇
Traditional tales		○	○	○	○	○	○	○	○	□	□	□		
Folk tale		○		○	○	○	○	○	○	T	T		T	T
Fable			○	○	○	○	○	○		□				
Fairy tale				○	○			○			□	◇		
Myth						○				T	T	T	T	T
Tall tale						○		○	○	T	□	◇	◇	
Legend									○	T	T	T	◇	
Historical fiction						○	○	○	○	T	T	T	T	T
Science fiction								○	○	T	○	T	T	T
Short story													□	□
Poetry	□	□	□	□	□	□	□	○	□	□			□	T
Play				□	□	□	□	□	□	□			□	T
Nonfiction			○	○	○	○	○	○	□	□	□	□	□	□
Autobiography												□	□	□
Biography							○	○	○	T	□		T	T
Informational article			○	○	○	○	○	○	□	□	□	□	□	□
Essay													□	□
Speech												□	T	T
Newspaper article									□				T	
Journal, diary								○			□	□		□
Interview									□					□
Understands and Appreciates Literary Language														
Hyperbole											○	□	◇	□
Figures of speech														
Simile				○		○	○	T	□	T	T	T	T	□
Metaphor			○	○	○	○	○	T	□	T	T	T	T	□
Idiom				○	○	○	○	○	○	T	□	T	T	□
Personification				○	○	○	○	○	○	○	T	□	□	

FIGURE 10.5

An example of a scope and sequence for a reading program. From *City Spaces*, p. T33. Copyright © 1987 by Scott, Foresman and Company. By permission of the publisher.

1 Teaching the Skill Lessons

Objectives
*Uses context to determine appropriate word
  meaning: homographs **T**Ⓣ
Learns selection vocabulary: *case, lie, shock*
Identifies the stated main idea of a selection and
  details that support the main idea **T**Ⓣ

Materials
Charts 71-72
Workbook, pages 113-114
Masters, pages 113-114

Word Study Skill: Context

Teaching Homographs

Use Chart 71 or write the words on the board.

Chart 71

1. Matt started to <u>row</u> his boat toward
   the middle of the lake.
2. He saw all the ducklings swimming in
   a <u>row</u>, one behind the other.
3. We weighed the baby on the <u>scale</u>.
4. Tim practiced <u>scales</u> on the piano.
5. On a hot day, the dog will <u>lie</u> under
   the tree.
6. I know I should never tell a <u>lie</u>.
7. The man was in <u>shock</u> after the fire.
8. The corn was standing in <u>shocks</u> in
   the field.
9. Put the apples in the wooden <u>case</u>.
10. In this <u>case</u>, the runner was safe.

Explain the goal.
• As you read, you sometimes see words that have more
  than one meaning. Today we're going to learn how to
  use the other words in the sentence, or the context, to
  figure out which meaning is intended.

Use a known example—*row*.
Have pupils read sentence 1 on Chart 71 silently.
• The word *row* can mean "a line of people or things" or
  to "use oars to move a boat."
• By using the other words in the sentence, we can figure
  out that *row* in sentence 1 means "use oars to move a
  boat."
• What words in sentence 1 help us determine the correct
  meaning of *row*? *boat, lake*
• Now read sentence 2. What is the meaning of *row* in
  this sentence? "things in a line"
• What words helped you figure out the meaning? *ducklings swimming one behind the other*

Define homograph.
• A homograph is a word having the same spelling as
  another word, but a different meaning.

Use another known example—*scale*.
• Can you think of two meanings of the word *scale*?
  Allow pupils to answer.
• A scale can be an instrument you use to weigh some-
  thing, or a scale can be musical notes arranged in a
  certain order.
• Which meaning of the word do you see in sentence 3?
  an instrument to weigh something
• Which meaning do you see in sentence 4? musical
  notes

Practicing Homographs

Apply skill to selection vocabulary.
lie (319), **shock** (320), **case** (321) Use sentences 5-10
on Chart 71 or write them on the board. You may want to
write the definitions of each word on the board and have
pupils determine which is the appropriate meaning for
the way the word is used in the sentence.

Explain the meanings.
• To lie is to have one's body in a flat position along the
  ground or other surface. A lie is something said that is
  not true.
• A shock is a sudden, violent shake, blow, or crash. A
  shock is also a group of stalks of corn or bundles of
  grain set up on end together.
• A case is any special condition of a person or thing, or
  a case is a thing to hold or cover something.

Developing Independent Reading Strategies
• When you're reading on your own and you come to a
  word that has more than one meaning, use the other
  words in the sentence to determine the correct word
  meaning.

Further Practice
Workbook, page 113 (Homographs; see page 386)
Masters,   page 113 (Homographs; see page 387)

FIGURE 10.6

Teacher's guides promote independent reading strategies. From *City Spaces*,
Teacher's Edition, p. 374. Copyright © 1987 by Scott, Foresman and
Company. By permission of the publisher.

You'll want to see if the selection contains any vocabulary items that might be problematic yet aren't presented in the prereading list. Perhaps there are words that might be foreign to your particular group of students or students in your particular geographic location. Authors and editors can't account for problems such as the example of the difference between a grain elevator in the country and a high-rise elevator in the city.

Check to see if the same format for introducing the words is employed from selection to selection. If the procedure is always the same (for example, "Write the following words on the board"), it's understandable for students to become quite bored very early in the year. A good series will attempt to provide variety. Perhaps in one lesson, students are asked to look through the selection for unknown words. In another, the meanings of new words are compared and contrasted in graphic categories. In any case, the meaning and decoding elements are usually discussed and highlighted as to how they'll appear in the upcoming selection.

Presentation of Content Area Reading and Study Skills

Publishers of quality basal reader programs today make sure that the selections and related skill lessons reach beyond the framework of stories, plays, and poems. For example, the Ginn series includes a strand of subskills referred to as "Life and Study Skills." The stated goal is to help "pupils apply their reading skills to practical school and non-school contexts, such as textbooks, encyclopedias, directions and forms" (Clymer et al., 1987, p. T9). The series emphasizes comprehension and study strategies for learning about organizational features of content area texts such as social studies and science. For example, in one lesson students are directed to read about the structure of a social studies text and to notice that the title and pictures help them predict what the main focus will be. They're also asked what they already know about the subject; they are given a prereading question to help guide their reading; and they are directed to read the accompanying page.

Now that you've seen lots of examples of quality basal readers and teacher's guides, let's go over some of the decisions you'll still have to make even if you have a quality program to implement. We'll be discussing and reviewing ideas for teaching vocabulary, decoding, and comprehension. Organizational plans and skill management systems will be explained. But we want to focus specifically on decisions that help children see the connection between your reading lessons at school and the pleasure and satisfaction of reading for the various reasons found in their home environment. We also want to draw your attention to those decisions that help children see the connection between reading and writing—how their experience with oral language can help their written language development. We'll be drawing on some of the ideas from previous chapters on literature, language experience, and writing and how these can be used alongside your basal reader program.

> "While the basal-reader juggernaut rolls on, delivering truckloads
> of printed materials to schools and pulling in millions of dollars,
> more and more teachers are looking for effective ways to encour-
> age children's love of reading while they are developing reading
> skills" (Larrick, 1987, p. 187).

TEACHING VOCABULARY USING A BASAL READER PROGRAM

In Chapter 6, you were confronted with several issues about vocabulary instruction—mainly whether to follow a mastery approach or a whole language approach and whether to teach directly or indirectly. When you're using a basal
reader program, you're going to be tempted to use a mastery approach and teach
words directly. Why? Because this is how most of the teacher's guides are set up.

If you are already convinced that a mastery approach and direct teaching
are the best ways to handle any type of instruction, then you'll need to increase
the number of examples and exposures of each word listed in the teacher's guide.
As mentioned in Chapter 6, it can take up to twenty examples and exposures for
mastery to take place. If, on the other hand, you lean toward a whole language,
whole text way of teaching reading, you probably are wondering how in the
world you're going to teach according to your philosophy within a basal program
structure.

"It ain't easy," as the saying goes, but it can be done. First, be encouraged
by the research in Chapter 6 that demonstrated that to teach each word directly
and for mastery would require you to teach vocabulary over twenty-four hours
per day. Since you might not have that much time (some people don't), you may
want to choose carefully the number and quality of words that you do teach
directly. The basal manual will often suggest about six to twelve words for each
basal selection. To teach even six words for mastery, though, again according to
the research cited in Chapter 6, would require about two hours. You begin to see
the problem.

Now let's look at an alternative way of dealing with vocabulary, one that
fits your philosophy and the situation. What do we know about the development
of vocabulary? We know that in a natural environment, such as one in which
children learn speech, children learn words slowly over time. Parents seldom
teach words in a direct way, but rather indirectly through context. For example,
the word *hot* might be taught directly and learned on only one try (if the child
burns himself), but children pick up most words through hearing them and using
them several times in different situations: "We're going outside. See it outside the
window. It's raining outside." And so on.

Following the whole language notion that learning written language should
be nearly as natural as learning oral language, you would probably *not* want to
expect children to master vocabulary on their first try. (They won't anyway, in
spite of the assumption of authors of teacher manuals.) Instead, you'll probably

want to do one of two things that we discussed in Chapter 6—either (1) model context analysis of the words or (2) *introduce* the words in as meaningful a way as possible within the very short time that you have in a busy classroom.

In Chapters 5 and 6, you saw several demonstrations of teachers modeling the use of context clues. You also saw in Chapter 6 how to use Dale's Cone of Experience to guide you in making vocabulary instruction meaningful. Since we don't want to repeat too much of what was in those two chapters, we hope you'll look back at them if necessary to refresh your memory. We *will* repeat and elaborate, however, the four principles used in that chapter.

Principle one: Help them associate new words with the schemata they've developed from prior knowledge. Try to find out what several students already think about the word—particularly children from different cultural backgrounds. Help them connect the *text meaning* with *their* background. And if you want the associations to stick, you'll sometimes need more than a verbal treatment of the association. A visual treatment through pictures, objects, or a quick dramatization will usually enhance the association.

Principle two: As a vocabulary teacher, realize that not all words are equally learnable. Words differ in several ways, such as concreteness, relevance, and syntax class. Whereas *elephant* is relatively concrete, *freedom* is not. Whereas *school* is a relevant word for children, *senate* is not. Whereas many *nouns* are easy to demonstrate and relate to schemata, many *prepositions* are not. More time and energy must be spent on some of the listed words in the teacher's guide than others—a few seconds on some, a few minutes on others—especially if they're crucial to understanding the text.

Principle three: People can learn words well only when they are actively involved in the learning process. Vocabulary instruction needs to be as learner-centered as possible. The research cited in Chapter 6 demonstrated that teachers who rely on simply tossing out a synonym for each word are wasting their students' time. Children must be made actively involved in relating the word to their own set of meanings: through discussion with a group or partner, through needing the word to express themselves in writing, through speaking the word in a teacher-inspired dialogue, and through reading the word in another context before reading it in the required text.

Principle four: Teach most new words in context. This means context within the actual text rather than an oral rendition by the teacher or peer. Since this takes more time than most teachers normally spend on each word *suggested* in the manual, it means ignoring or giving very brief notice to many of the words on the list. It means providing quality instruction on a few words rather than quantity-type teaching. (This is hard for some teachers to do. As will be mentioned facetiously in Chapter 12, lists are horrible monsters that trap readers into looking at or using every single one on the list.) It also means going against tradition and having teachers and children use their basal readers rather than the chalkboard for much of the vocabulary instruction.

It can also mean *occasionally* having the children learn the new words through writing experiences before they read the new basal selection. One teacher, for example, wrote the following words on the chalkboard from her teacher's guide: *pendulum, weights, calm, emergency, steep, tailboard,* and *courage.* These words were discussed and related to children's schemata. Then she had the students predict what the upcoming basal selection would be about, using only the title of the selection ("The Baby in the Clock") and the list of words they had already discussed. Next she had them write their own story using the title and vocabulary list. The story that follows was written by Caitlin, an eight-year-old:

There was once a mischievous baby who got into everything. One day she saw the maid dusting the clock. Around 3:15 the maid's date asked her out. She forgot all about her work and left.

The baby's parents were napping so it was easy for the baby (whose name was Carol) to get into mischief. Carol found the clock door open and *calmly* crawled in. She closed the door behind her.

Carol climbed on to the *pendulum* with much *courage,* for it was swinging. She swung for a while, wondering how to get up the *steep* wall to the top where the *weights* were.

Then she spotted some pegs sticking into the back of the clock. She grabbed one and pulled herself up. She climbed almost to the top and would have made it but then tragedy struck.

One of the pegs was loose! Carol lost her balance and fell. (Luckily, the clock was only six feet tall.) She hit her head on the swinging *pendulum.* She thought it was an *emergency* but it wasn't. She climbed out of the clock ever so slowly. Carol crawled into her crib and fell asleep.

Her parents never suspected anything but they wondered how she got that bump on her head for the rest of their lives.

At the next meeting, the students were allowed to share their stories with the rest of the group. Interestingly, most had already read the story in their basal reader in order to see how it compared with the one they had written. So they had a stimulating discussion about the difference in meaning between the words used in their story versus the meaning in their readers. They also talked about their predictions about the basal reader story. Caitlin even told the teacher that she thought her story matched the title better than the one in the basal reader, since "it only had one thing about a baby in a clock."

TEACHING GRAPHOPHONIC ANALYSIS THROUGH A BASAL READER PROGRAM

As mentioned before, most basal programs today provide a heavy dose of "phonics" or graphophonic analysis. If you believe that this form of decoding needs direct teaching, and if you believe that the graphophonic cueing system needs much more instruction than the other cueing systems, the basal program's teacher's manual, along with the abundance of supplementary worksheets and workbooks, will make your dreams come true. Most units will have at least one lesson on a phonics subskill; you can be almost guaranteed of that.

If, on the other hand, you wish to lean more toward interactive reading practice (and toward a whole language, whole text view), you'll again have to adapt the basal materials to your philosophy. You may want to use a *portion* of the phonics lessons from the teacher's guide and a *portion* of the worksheets—but not nearly as many as are available to you. You'll also want to do these things:

1. Teach many of the graphophonic patterns through writing and spelling experiences. Whenever children are ready to do a final draft of a composition for a classbook, class magazine, or personal book, you'll have a perfect opportunity to do some brief instruction on "how to spell that word the way they do in newspapers and magazines." If you do use formal spelling tests, phonograms and vowel patterns are often emphasized in the spelling book. And if you create experience charts with the students, you can combine chart reading with brief lessons on phonic patterns.

2. When you do teach a basal program phonics lesson, be aware of which method is being used (see Chapter 7). If the method is highly auditory (analytic or synthetic), supplement your lesson with a visual approach as well, using the phonogram, substitution, or vowel pattern method. Then immediately have the children apply what they've learned by reading whole text and pointing out words that exemplify your lesson. Or have them write words in sentences that illustrate the point of your lesson.

3. Teach children how to use graphophonic patterns to unlock strange words while you are working on whole text together. See Chapters 5 and 7 for examples of teachers and pupils doing this.

4. Use the cloze technique to help students combine the graphophonic cueing system with the other three cueing systems. For example:

   Alfonso climbed out of the river and shook himself __ __ y.

   Demetri spread the mustard on the h __ m __ urg __ __.

5. Use one of the phonics games in Appendix B; then follow this with a whole text writing or reading experience that incorporates some or all of the words used in the game.

TEACHING SIGHT WORDS USING A BASAL READER PROGRAM

Well, here's where basal readers can shine. Remember from Chapter 6 that one way of teaching sight words is through basal readers. This is simply because basal authors purposely repeat certain words many times, especially in the early grades.

This repeated exposure, provided the children read the words correctly, helps them set the words to memory.

Does this mean, then, that basal reader programs should be used slavishly? Not at all. We're only saying that if children read the basal readers for pleasure, they will learn many sight words. So, you whole language enthusiasts, don't throw out the baby with the bath. Use the basal readers for excellent practice (provided the children can skip some of the selections they choose not to read).

Remember, though, that whereas basal readers may be effective in providing sight word practice, worksheets don't work as well for this purpose as games and patterned books do. Also remember, please, that games should be followed fairly soon with practice in reading those words in whole text.

One last thing to remember: Reading literature for pleasure or for information—literature that children have chosen for themselves—provides highly motivated practice in learning sight words. Need we say more?

TEACHING COMPREHENSION USING A BASAL READER PROGRAM

Regardless of the approach you decide to use, your top priority is showing students how to comprehend what they read. You can accomplish this in a number of ways, including reading to your students on a regular basis, modeling effective comprehension strategies, letting them see you read to yourself, and encouraging and motivating them to want to read. If they're motivated to read, they *will* read; and if they *are* reading, they *will* improve (Anderson, Wilson, & Fielding, 1988).

This sounds like common sense, right? Well, unfortunately, during reading instruction, children spend 70 percent of their time working independently, mostly completing worksheets. So it's not surprising to find that children choose reading for less than 1 percent of their free time (Anderson et al., 1985). We need to turn these figures around by showing children the value and pleasure of reading!

When children see the relationship between what they're reading and what they've experienced in their own lives, they read with greater interest. They're able to attend more closely to the text and engage in higher-level thinking strategies. They're reading with a vested interest in finding out what the story characters will do and how this compares with what they would have done (and perhaps with what they have done) in a similar situation. We can accomplish this by using some of the strategies discussed in earlier chapters.

For example, rather than using all of the questions listed in the teacher's guide, you should select those that focus on inferential, critical, or creative thinking. Creating "story grammar" questions helps students learn the structure of stories. Asking students to read orally to "prove their point" after reading is an effective way to check their comprehension. And don't forget the distinction made earlier in Chapter 4 between the process and the product of comprehension.

Merely asking questions will make the children believe that they should read to find the "one right answer" rather than to interact with the author (and with their own inner thoughts). We can teach children about the process of comprehension by relating the skills of comprehension to the selections they will actually be reading. You might want to reread Chapter 5 to think about other ideas for teaching comprehension using a basal reader program.

USING A SKILLS MANAGEMENT SYSTEM
WITH A BASAL READER PROGRAM

All basal reader publishers will provide teachers (at the school district's expense) with tests and record-keeping devices to accompany the teacher's guide. This set of materials is often referred to as a *skills management system*, or SMS. Most skills management systems have these components:

1. Placement tests for determining what book to provide each child for instructional purposes
2. A checklist for recording each child's test performances
3. A very brief test for each "subskill" taught in the program
4. Longer tests to check on retention of subskills

The placement tests are sometimes in the form of an individual informal reading inventory containing selections similar to those in the basal readers. The child reads these selections orally until the teacher notices that he is frustrated; then she stops the testing. (This procedure will be discussed more fully in Chapter 11.) The placement tests are sometimes in the form of a group test, similar to the multiple-choice tests university students know so well. The content of the group test is usually vocabulary and certain reading subskills considered important by the program's authors.

After children are placed, the teacher can begin the basal reader units. A unit usually consists of one or two lessons involving silent and oral reading of a selection in the reader, one or two skill lessons, and one or two opportunities for review or enrichment. (Unfortunately, the *poor* readers get the review and the good readers get the enrichment, even though the poor readers need motivation and real reading practice the most.) At the completion of the unit many teachers give a short test consisting of five to twenty items related to one or more subskills. Children who don't score high enough on this test usually receive extra instruction.

After several units are completed, a retention test is often administered and further instruction is provided for those who seem to need it. After scoring the retention test, the teacher usually records the scores on each child's checklist (see Figure 10.7). Some basal reader programs are designed for easy access to computers that will not only score the various tests but also print out a prescription for review lessons or practice worksheets.

B: BEARS

Date	FORM CSA	FORM B	TBRS
Word Recognition			12
1. Digraph *th* D1·7b	4		4
2. Following Directions CA1·1	4		4
* 3. Comma of Address C4·2a			
4. End Sounds *l, t* D1·7c	4		4
5. End Sounds *n, p* D1·7c	4		4
6. Letter Sounds & Context D1·7	3		4
7. Digraph *sh* D1·7b	4		4
8. Word Referents C3·1a	3		4
* 9. Exclamation Mark C4·1c			
10. Cluster *fr* D1·7d	3		4
11. Drawing Conclusions CA5·2	3		4
* 12. Clusters *lp, mp* D1·7e			
* 13. Intonation			
14. Predicting Outcomes CA6·2	2		4
15. Cluster *st* D1·7d, e	3		4
16. Noting Details CA2·1	2		4
17. Categorizing CA10·2	3		4
18. End Sounds *m, d, g* D1·7c	4		4

C: BALLOONS

Date	FORM CSA	FORM B	TBRS
Word Recognition			12
1. Noting Correct Sequence CA3·3	2		4
* 2. Contractions with *'s* D1·7f			
* 3. Sound Association for *x* D1·7c			
4. Plurals D1·7h	4		4
* 5. Verbs Ending with *s* D1·7g			
6. Clusters *sw, fl* D1·7d	2		4
7. Letter Sounds & Context D1·7	3		4
8. Cause-Effect Relationships CA7·2	2		4
9. Word Referents C3·1a	3		4
10. Main Idea CA4·2	2		4
11. Digraph *ch* D1·7b	4		4

D: BOATS

Date	FORM CSA	FORM B	TBRS
Word Recognition			12
1. Following Directions CA1·1	3		4
* 2. End Sounds *nt, nk* D1·7e			
* 3. Ending *ing* D1·7g			
4. Digraphs *th, sh, ch* D1·7b	4		4
5. Predicting Outcomes CA6·2	2		4
6. Sound Associations *c /s/* D1·7n	3		4
* 7. Ending *ed* D1·7g			
8. Noting Important Details CA2·1	3		4
9. Clusters *fl, sw, fr, pl* D1·7d	2		4
10. Multi-meaning Words C1·1c	2		4
11. Categorizing CA10·2	2		4
* 12. Reviewing Endings *s, ed, ing* D1·7g			
13. Word Referents C3·1a	3		4
14. Drawing Conclusions CA5·2	3		4

E: SUNSHINE

Magazine 1 Date	FORM CSA	FORM B	TBRS
Recognizing High-Frequency Words			12
1. Cause Effect Relationships CA7·1, 2	2		4
2. Short *a* Sound D1·7l	4		4
3. Long *a* Sound D1·7l	4		4
* 4. Quotation Marks, Comma CA4·8a			
5. Correct Sequence CA3·3	2		4
6. Doubling Consonants Before Endings D1·7j	4		4
7. Sound Associations for *y* D1·7l	2		4
8. Dropping Final *e* Before Endings D1·7j	4		4
Magazine 2 Date			
Recognizing High-Frequency Words			12
* 9. Contractions with *'s, n't, 'll* D1·7f			
10. Sound Associations for *oo* D1·7m	2		4
11. Compound Words D1·7o	2		4
12. Ending *er* D1·7g	2		4
13. Predicting Outcomes CA6·2	2		4
14. Short *e* Sound D1·7l	3		4
15. Long *e* Sound D1·7l	3		4
* 16. Intonation			
17. Sound Associations for *ai, ay* D1·7m	3		4
18. Drawing Conclusions CA5·2	2		4
Magazine 3 Date			
Recognizing High-Frequency Words			12
19. Short *i* Sound D1·7l	3		4
20. Long *i* Sound D1·7l	3		4
* 21. Sound Association for *kn/n* D1·7b			
22. Multi-meaning Words C1·1c	3		4
23. Main Idea CA4·2	2		4
24. Short and Long *a, e,* and *i* D1·7l	4		4

KEY

1. Digraph *th*   D1·7b

Skill Description → (1. Digraph *th*)

Skill Reference Number → (D1·7b)

Basic Reading Skill Lesson

FIGURE 10.7
A sample progress checklist for recording a child's scores (From ''Cumulative Individual Reading Record Folder'', Boston: Houghton Mifflin, 1981, p. 2.)

ORGANIZATIONAL PLANS FOR USING A BASAL READER PROGRAM

Teachers and administrators have developed numerous ways to allow for the variations among children, teachers, space, time, and materials when basal readers are used as the basic medium of reading instruction. It would be difficult to recommend one of these ways over any of the others, since their utility depends so much on the particular conditions of learning in a particular school. We'll simply describe them for you so that you can make an informed choice of plans best suited to your needs and the needs of the students in the particular situation you may find yourself.

The Self-Contained Plan

With the self-contained plan, each teacher divides her group of approximately thirty children into two to four (most often three) reading instruction groups that usually represent the "above-average," the "average," and the "below-average" students in the class. The teacher does this grouping after administering informal reading tests or looking at other information about each child's general reading ability. In a self-contained classroom, the same teacher teaches all the groups, which meet at different times of the day or week. While one group meets with the teacher, the other groups work on vocabulary and decoding skill assignments, reading enrichment activities (such as library book reading), or even work in another subject such as mathematics, art, or science. This seatwork, by the way, is an important area of decision making that you'll have to deal with; that is, "What do the other students do while I'm working with one group?" Of course, our response is an emphatic, "Let them read or write!"

> "It is important that seatwork offer opportunities to read, to compose, and to create" (Allington et al., 1987, p. 86).

The main advantage of teaching in a self-contained classroom is that throughout the entire year you have the opportunity to develop a good understanding of each child's reading ability—his strengths and his weaknesses—not only during "reading class" but during other subjects as well. In fact, this plan allows reading to be taught in the context of the other content areas, and it allows children to apply their developing reading skills to other parts of their school day. Hopefully, this will also transfer to their reading at home.

The main disadvantage can occur when the range of reading ability is so wide that you're unable to meet the needs of all your students. For instance, if the general reading range in your class is all the way from Level F to Level L, and you feel that you can handle only three groups, the children in Level L may have to work in materials below their abilities while those in Level F may be working at frustration level.

The Joplin Plan

The Joplin plan is sometimes referred to as the "cross-grades plan." Instead of one teacher working with three groups of children with varying levels of ability, the teachers in a school building all teach reading at the exact same time; each works with children who are reading at about the same level. At nine o'clock, say, a bell rings and all the children go to their reading teacher. For a few children this may mean staying in their homeroom, but for most children, it will mean going to another teacher for forty-five minutes or more. Mrs. Jeffreys may teach only Levels A and B; Miss Franklin may teach only Levels C and D; Mr. Chapman may teach only Level E (since so many children are reading at that level); Mr. Webster may teach Levels F, G, and H (because there are so few children reading at those levels), and so on, down the halls of the school building or within the first-grade wing, for example. There are many versions of the Joplin plan, but this gives you a rough idea of how it works.

The main advantage of the Joplin plan is that it drastically reduces the range of reading abilities each teacher has to face. The main disadvantage is the potential lack of transfer from reading instruction to actual reading of library books, magazines, and content area texts, such as social studies and science. Megan's reading teacher seldom has the opportunity to see that she practices, in actual reading situations, the skills she's been taught. Megan's homeroom teacher, unless she communicates extremely well with the reading teacher, is often not fully aware of Megan's reading strengths and weaknesses which might affect her success in reading materials related to other subjects. In addition this can be embarrassing at parent conference time—to admit not knowing some of Megan's accomplishments or shortcomings.

The Track Plan

The track plan can be used alongside either the Joplin plan or the self-contained plan. With this approach, the school district makes available to the teacher not just one basal reader series, but two or three (or in some cases an "advanced form" and an "easy form" of the same series). This approach increases the flexibility of grouping children. Let's take the extreme situation, for example, in which the teacher wishes to move a child back one or two levels from the one he was in at another school in another city that used the same basal reader series. In other words, she feels he has been pushed too fast and needs to gain skills he's missed along the way. Rather than have the child read exactly the same reader he has already read in another city (and complete the same worksheets, perhaps), she'll put him, along with a few other children, in another series that he hasn't seen before. As you can well imagine, there are numerous variations of the track system, depending upon the needs of the teachers and children.

The main advantage of the track system, as already mentioned, is the flexibility of grouping that such a system provides. The main disadvantage is that the teacher now has to become familiar with two or three series rather than one. This can be quite a burden, particularly to the beginning teacher; but wherever a particular school population is highly mobile, it may be one of the most reasonable solutions.

There are numerous other plans for organizing reading instruction, such as the variety of plans created through team-teaching situations. However, all of them attempt to provide greater individualization of instruction—some by more homogeneous grouping, some by providing greater choice of basal readers, and some by working with fewer children at one time.

THE USE OF LITERATURE, LANGUAGE EXPERIENCE, AND WRITING IN A BASAL READER PROGRAM

We hope we've convinced you that you need to play an active role in making decisions about how you use basal reader programs. We're hoping you'll consider combining the main approaches to teach reading that we've discussed so far: the personalized literature program (PLP), a reading/writing approach, and basal reader programs. By taking the best of each of these approaches, you'll find that you and your students will experience more satisfaction, more success, less boredom, and less anxiety than you might experience using only one of the approaches.

As we've mentioned, the basal reader program provides security for you, your principal, the parents, and often the children. It provides you with lessons and practice materials that you can adapt to your students' needs. It provides you with reading selections that can be used by several children at once—when you wish to guide them in the use of the four cueing systems and in the practice of inferential, critical, and creative thinking. As long as you realize that nothing horrible will happen to your students when you omit selections from the readers and lessons from the guides, you will be able to comfortably use other approaches along with your basal reader program.

Of course, this is the crux of the matter. Some teachers (and principals) are fearful of leaving one page unturned in the basal reader program. What a shame, for they have bought into the belief that basal readers and teacher's guides have been handed down from on high. That they are infallible. That they are "scientific." That when Michael misses one story, one worksheet, one lesson, he must make it up or "he'll get way behind." (On the contrary, Michael may have gotten ahead by lying in his sickbed reading a good book!)

But there's no point in pushing this point any further, as we believe we're talking about a personality consideration here. Some teachers have an adventurous personality that allows them to try out new ways and not be anxious about skipping basal lessons judged to be unnecessary (or even harmful). Some teachers, on the other hand, shy away from adventurous approaches. Those who are between adventurous and timid have to find their own middle ground.

Basal reader programs offer security and handy materials. But a whole language or language experience approach offers children something a basal reader program can't—the opportunity to learn to read naturally through their own language, the opportunity to learn how to write at the same time. And research shows, remember, that language experience approaches produce better spellers (Bond & Dykstra, 1967; Dykstra, 1968). The personalized literature program offers ample opportunities for children to practice *interactive reading* instead of mere worksheet completion. It also provides the perfect chance for teachers to get to know each child better through individual conferences to inspire them in a more personal way.

In March of 1984, James Baumann published an article in *The Reading Teacher* that we think you ought to read. It's entitled "How to Expand a Basal Reader Program," and it tells you one way to combine three major approaches. We're so convinced that you should read it that we've arranged to reprint it for you, so that you won't have to track it down in the library. Besides, we have the ulterior motive of encouraging you to read *The Reading Teacher* and to become aware of the publications offered to you by the International Reading Association. So here is Baumann's article. We hope it will persuade you to try combining various approaches in a way that works for you and your students.

HOW TO EXPAND A BASAL READER PROGRAM*

Consider the following scenario:

Ms. Murphy teaches a third grade class of 25 students. The school district has adopted a basal reader series that she is required to use. She has organized her class in three reading groups, the least capable, average, and most capable readers. Ms. Murphy writes separate daily lesson plans for each reading group and places this schedule on the chalkboard (Figure 1). She has introduced a reading kit and some

FIGURE 1
Daily schedule for Ms. Murphy's third grade reading class

Panthers [Slower Readers]	Tigers [Average Readers]	Lions [Better Readers]
Meet: Introduce "Mark and the Dinosaur."	Reread "The Friendly Fox" silently.	Do one story from the reading kits.
Finish reading silently then answer comprehension questions.	Meet: Discuss "The Friendly Fox." Skill review: Short vowels.	Finish book reports.
Work on sight word flash cards with your partner.	Complete short vowel work paper.	Meet: Discuss "Harriet Tubman" story from yesterday.

*James F. Baumann, in *The Reading Teacher*, March 1984. Reprinted with permission of James F. Baumann and the International Reading Association.

games, but all her lessons center around the basal reader—the heart of each lesson consists of reading and discussing a basal story or participating in a related skill development activity.

Although the specifics may vary, the structure of Ms. Murphy's reading class is typical of countless elementary classrooms. The teacher introduces the basal reader story; students engage in a directed reading activity; stories are discussed and comprehension is assessed; and skill instruction and reinforcement exercises follow.

These procedures represent a sensible use of basal readers that requires careful planning and skillful instruction. But with time the pattern becomes repetitious and tedium sets in. The efficiency of instruction diminishes.

A classroom teacher can liven up a basal reader program. Suggestions of three types will be discussed here: (1) Involve additional persons; (2) add elements of language experience and individualized reading; (3) involve students in a wide variety of language arts activities. Inspect Figure 2 while reading the following sections, because the sample class schedules demonstrate how Ms. Murphy has incorporated these elements in her basal program.

FIGURE 2

Three examples of daily schedules for Ms. Murphy's expanded basal program

Panthers [*Slower Readers*]	*Tigers* [*Average Readers*]	*Lions* [*Better Readers*]
Example 1		
Meet: Discuss "Alligator Story." Review sequence.	Silent reading of book you chose.	Go to the library with Ms. Smith to select a book.
Work with sixth grade tutors on oral reading and flash cards.	Meet: Rehearse "Mary the Marvelous Magician" play.	Silent reading. Tutors go and work with first graders.
Whole class vocabulary development activity: Homophones		
Example 2		
Write stories about yesterday's nature walk. Ms. Smith will help.	Work in classroom library kit.	Meet: Skill work: Distinguishing between fact and opinion.
Tape record your stories.	Meet: Plan next edition of the class newspaper.	Do workbook page 25. Silent reading of choice.
Meet with me individually: Read your story.	Work with editors on the paper.	
Whole class listening activity: Making mental pictures		
Example 3		
Whole class presents oral reports on nonfiction books		
Meet: Learn how to become kindergarten tutors.	Work with Ms. Smith constructing puppets for Wednesday's puppet play.	Go to library to work on "Famous Black Americans" reports.
Whole class watches TV program: "The Bird Book"		

READING HELPERS

One or more room parents, properly trained, can direct students in games or reading kits, accompany them to the school library and assist in book selection, conduct informal reading inventories, or guide students in plays or special projects. The classroom teacher is freed to work more intensively with groups or individuals giving special instruction, either corrective or for gifted readers who need more challenge.

A peer tutoring program also helps expand a basal reader program. Students from higher grades can assist the classroom teacher. For example, peer tutors from fifth or sixth grade could drill primary students on basic sight vocabulary or listen to them read orally. Students from a teacher's own class can tutor younger students. This experience, though primarily for the tutee, can also be motivating for the tutor, especially if the student is not a skillful reader: Success in being the teacher can stimulate confidence and self-concept.

Another option is to involve secondary students. Many high schools have co-op programs in which students participate in community activities. For example, students from early childhood classes in high schools may want to tutor in elementary classrooms. They tend to be enthusiastic, reliable, and competent.

It must be remembered, however, that the responsibility for training all tutors lies with the classroom teacher. Success depends upon appropriate training in specific tasks. Training may be time consuming, but the benefits are potentially great, for the added help is essential in making other modifications of the basal program, as described below.

LEA AND INDIVIDUALIZED READING

Reading educators frequently profess the benefits of a language experience approach (LEA) or individualized reading program [PLP] but fail to appreciate the problems involved in managing these methodologies when implemented in their entirety. A compromise is to retain the basal reader as the core of the reading program, but incorporate elements of language experience and individualized reading.

Struggling readers may profit from a limited but regular exposure to LEA reading and writing. Two or three times a week, the teacher may require this group to write experience stories and add new vocabulary words to their word banks.

Other groups of students may benefit from self-selection and individualized reading activities. For example, a group of capable readers may set aside the basal for a week or two, read children's books of their choice, and participate in student-teacher conferences and book-sharing activities. This gives them a break from daily basal instruction and exposes them to good children's literature.

LANGUAGE ART ACTIVITIES

A third way to expand a basal reading program is to involve students in varied language arts activities in the reading class. Good examples are creative writing and creative dramatics, large and small group listening and vocabulary development activities, and literary programs on educational TV and radio.

The groupings for these language arts activities can be different from the usual basal groupings, since they allow mixing students of varying reading ability. The advantage is that students have opportunity to learn from peers who are not in their regular basal groups.

One activity that promotes reading is a class or school-wide Author's Day on which all children come dressed as their favorite storybook character. Author's Day can involve parades of characters, contests for best costume, and book talks by the characters. (What could be more stimulating than a prepared oral reading from *The Cat in the Hat* by the Cat himself?)

Most of all, students need time to practice reading, for pitifully little time in reading class is devoted to actual reading. Teachers must realize that it is perfectly legitimate—and necessary—to have children sit and read books of their own choosing. A daily silent reading period is an appropriate component of any reading program.

Infusing LEA and individualized reading activities into a basal program is beneficial in several ways. Students have a change of pace; these activities promote positive attitudes toward reading; and the teacher has unique ways to teach vocabulary and comprehension skills. But because these activities are incorporated into a basal program, a teacher can remain confident that basic skills development is being adequately addressed. Note, however, that adding these elements is possible only with the help of room parents and peer tutors, who free the teacher to initiate and direct the new approaches.

CONCLUSIONS

As the daily class schedules (Figure 2) show, Ms. Murphy now has parent and student helpers and students are engaged in language experience, individualized reading, and other language arts activities. The basal reader remains the foundation, but students are now exposed to other activities designed to develop specific skills and to deepen interest and appreciation of reading.

It would not be prudent to attempt to incorporate all these features into a basal program at once. Instead, introduce them one at a time, over the course of a semester or school year. By expanding and augmenting a standard basal program, a teacher can liven up reading instruction and make the tasks of teaching and learning more enjoyable and effective for all.

SUMMARY OF MAIN IDEAS

☐ Basal reader programs (series) usually include hard-cover books of stories, poems, plays, and informative articles. They also include a spiral-bound teacher's guide containing skill lessons, lesson plans, and suggestions for enriching or reteaching certain skills presented with the reading selections. Publishers of the series often supply school districts with supplementary materials, mainly in the form of consumable workbooks and worksheets to reinforce the skills.

☐ Most basal reader lessons include a prereading lesson on vocabulary; a discussion to stimulate interest, access background knowledge, and establish a purpose for reading; an opportunity to read the selection; postreading discussion and comprehension checks; and a lesson on skills related to decoding or comprehension (but not necessarily those needed to read the preceding selection).

☐ Very often teachers rely heavily on the use of the teacher's guide that accompanies the basal reader program. They do so for a variety of reasons, including their lack of confidence or knowledge about how to teach reading, their belief that the program was designed by experts who "should know what they're talking about," pressure to use the materials purchased by the school district, and accountability to their public (including parents, principals, and school board members) to teach the "skills of reading." The structure provided by the program also makes it very easy for teachers to do little planning on their own; thus basal programs can make teaching reading "easy." Therefore, it seems that the overreliance seems to stem from the security they offer teachers, administrators, and parents rather than from their scientific validity or superiority over other approaches.

☐ Flaws in the exclusive use of any basal reader program include the fact that no single method or series can address what a particular group of students need or want to learn about language. Some programs focus primarily on one cueing system (in many cases, the graphophonic), thus limiting the students' abilities to (1) make accurate predictions about the intent of the author and the structure of the text, and (2) use their knowledge of oral language in decoding the written message.

☐ High-quality basal readers contain illustrations and content that represent different groups and genders without stereotyping them. The text is interesting and well written; the illustrations encourage an appreciation of artistic styles and media; and the selections represent a large variety of genre.

☐ High-quality teacher's guides show the teacher how to have children use all four cueing systems and think at inferential, critical, and creative levels. They also show how to use both oral and silent reading experiences for a variety of instructional purposes, how to teach reading in the context of the four language arts, and how to work with gifted, handicapped, and "language different" students.

☐ Your basal reader program should be thought of as a tool to be used selectively. Ultimately you need to decide how you're going to (1) organize and manage your program, (2) teach vocabulary, decoding, and comprehension using a teacher's guide, and (3) incorporate the use of basals with other approaches.

APPLICATION EXPERIENCES FOR THE TEACHER EDUCATION CLASS

A. *What's Your Opinion?* Use your own experiences as well as ideas in the textbook to justify your opinions.
   1. Basal reader programs allow teachers to monitor the skills children need in order to be good readers.
   2. With a basal reader program, teachers should feel secure in knowing that each child will be able to read at his level of ability.
   3. By using LEAs and PLPs, the teacher who uses a basal reader program can help children perceive reading as an enjoyable communication process.
   4. The Joplin plan is better than the self-contained plan in allowing for individual differences and encouraging interactive reading.
   5. It's important to present to students all of the suggested vocabulary items prior to their reading a selection. Otherwise their comprehension will be significantly hindered.
   6. It's more important to teach an established sequence of decoding skills than to select only those which are related to the selections that students will be reading.

B. *Evaluating Basal Reader Programs*

1. With one or more partners, evaluate an up-to-date basal reader series. Use the criteria in Table 10.2 for your evaluation. Or each group can concentrate on only one of the criteria. Report to the rest of the class on your findings.
2. Chapter 5 gave you several different strategies for producing questions that help children think more about what they've been reading. Evaluate the questions suggested in a basal reader teacher's guide. How well do they carry out those strategies? (You may want to divide into groups, with each group taking a different strategy discussed in Chapter 5.)
3. With a small group, compare a teacher's guide with a decoding emphasis to one with a meaning emphasis. What differences do you notice in terms of the criteria listed in this chapter? Report on these differences to the rest of the class.
4. Select a story from a basal reader program. After looking at the suggestions in the teacher's guide, decide how you might supplement the presentation using literature and writing activities.

FIELD EXPERIENCES IN THE ELEMENTARY SCHOOL CLASSROOM

A. Teach a lesson by exclusively using the teacher's guide to a basal reader program. In what ways did the guide limit you or your students? How would you modify the lesson the next time? How did the guide help you?

B. Try planning and teaching your own lesson related to a selection in a basal reader. Do not look at the teacher's guide until after you have taught the lesson. How was your lesson similar and different? What did you lose by creating your own? What did you gain?

C. Examine a lesson plan in a teacher's guide to a basal reader program. Then plan a way to teach the same skills or ideas through a language experience approach or with the library books your students are using. As an option, you may wish to plan a way to use all three approaches in combination.

REFERENCES AND SUGGESTED READING

Allington, R., et al. (1987). *Scott, Foresman reading: An American tradition*. Glenview, IL: Scott, Foresman.

Anderson, L. (1984). The environment of instruction: The function of seatwork in a commercially developed curriculum. In G. G. Duffy, L. R. Roehler, & J. Mason (Eds.), *Comprehension instruction: Perspectives and suggestions* (pp. 93–103). NY: Longman.

Anderson, R. C., Hiebert, E., Scott, J., & Wilkinson, I. (1985). *Becoming a nation of readers*. Urbana, IL: University of Illinois, Center for the Study of Reading.

Anderson, R. C., Osborn, J., & Tierney, R. J. (Eds.). (1984). Learning to read in American Schools: Basal readers and content texts. Hillsdale, NJ: Erlbaum.

Anderson, R. C., Wilson, P. T., & Fielding, L. (1988). Growth in reading and how children spend their time outside of school. *Reading Research Quarterly, 23*, 285–303.

Aukerman, R. C. (1984). *Approaches to beginning reading*. NY: Wiley.

Baumann, J. F. (1984). How to expand a basal reader program. *The Reading Teacher, 37*, 604–607.

Beck, I. L., McCaslin, E. S., & McKeown, M. G. (1981). Basal readers' purpose for story reading: Smoothly paving the road or setting up a detour? *Elementary School Journal, 81*, 156–161.

Beck, I. L., & McKeown, M. G. (1981). Developing questions that promote comprehension: The story map. *Language Arts, 58*(8), 913–918.

Beck, I. L., McKeown, M. G., McCaslin, E. S., & Burkes, A. M. (1979). *Instructional dimensions that may affect reading comprehension: Examples from two commercial reading programs.* Pittsburgh: University of Pittsburgh, Learning Research and Development Center.

Beck, I. L., Omanson, R. C., & McKeown, M. G. (1982). An instructional redesign of reading lessons: Effects on comprehension. *Reading Research Quarterly, 17*(4), 462–481.

Bond, G. L., & Dykstra, R. (1967). The cooperative research program in first grade reading instruction. *Reading Research Quarterly, 2*, 5–142.

Britten, G. E. (1975). Danger: State adopted texts may be hazardous to our future. *The Reading Teacher, 29*, 52–58.

Chall, J. (1967). *Learning to read: The great debate.* NY: McGraw-Hill.

Clymer, T., et al. (1978). *The Ginn reading program.* Lexington, MA: Ginn.

Cullinan, B. (Ed.). (1987). *Children's literature in the reading program.* Newark, DE: International Reading Association.

Dole, J., Rogers, T., & Osborn, J. (1986). *Improving basal reading programs: Report of the Adoption Guidelines project at the Center for the Study of Reading* (Reading Education Report No. 68). Urbana, IL: University of Illinois, Center for the Study of Reading.

Durkin, D. (1978–79). Reading comprehension instruction. *Reading Research Quarterly, 14*, 495–526.

Durkin, D. (1981). Reading comprehension instruction in five basal reader series. *Reading Research Quarterly, 16*(4), 515–544.

Durkin, D. (1983). *Teaching them to read.* Boston: Allyn & Bacon.

Durkin, D. (1984). Is there a match between what elementary teachers do and what basal reader manuals recommend? *The Reading Teacher 37*(8), 734–744.

Dykstra, R. (1968). Summary of the second-grade phase of the cooperative research program in primary reading instruction. *Reading Research Quarterly, 1*, 49–70.

Early, M., et al. (1987). *Harcourt Brace Jovanovich reading program.* Orlando, FL: Harcourt.

Fay, L., et al. (1986). *The Riverside reading program.* Chicago, IL: Riverside.

Fields, M. V., & Lee, D. (1987). *Let's begin reading right.* Columbus, OH: Merrill.

Fisher, C. W., Berliner, D., Filby, N., Marliave, R., Cohen, L., Dishaw, M., & Moore, J. (1978). *Teaching and learning in elementary schools: A summary of the beginning teacher evaluation study.* San Francisco: Far West Regional Laboratory for Educational Research and Development.

Hansen, J., & Pearson, P. D. (1983). An instructional study: Improving the inferential comprehension of fourth-grade good and poor readers. *Journal of Educational Psychology, 75*(6), 821–829.

Hargis, C. H., Terhaar-Yonkers, M., Williams, P. C., & Reed, M. T. (1988). Repetition requirements for word recognition. *The Journal of Reading, 31*(4), 320–327.

Heinrich, J. S. (1976). Elementary oral reading: Methods and materials. *The Reading Teacher, 30*, 10–15.

Johns, J., & Ellis, D. (1976). Reading: Children tell it like it is. *Reading World, 16*(2), pp. 115–118.

Kushkin, K. (1985). *Something sleeping in the hall.* NY: Harper.

Larrick, N. (1987). Illiteracy starts too soon. *Phi Delta Kappan, 69*(3), 184–189.

Mason, J., & Au, K. (1986). *Reading instruction for today.* Glenview, IL: Scott, Foresman.

Mason, J., & Osborn, J. (1982). *When do children begin ''reading to learn''?: A survey of classroom reading instruction practices in grades two through five* (Technical Report No. 261). Urbana: University of Illinois, Center for the Study of Reading.

National Educational Association. (1977). *Sex role stereotyping in the schools.* Washington, DC.

O'Donnel, H. (1974). Cultural bias: A many headed monster. *Elementary English, 51,* 81–109.

Osborn, J., & Stein, M. (1986). *Basal reading programs: Development, use, effectiveness, adoption, and more useful adoptions* (Reading Education Report No. 61). Urbana, IL: University of Illinois, Center for the Study of Reading.

Payne, J. S., Polloway, E. A., Smith, J. E., Jr., & Payne, R. A. (1981). *Strategies for teaching the mentally retarded* (2nd ed.). Columbus, OH: Merrill.

Shake, M. C., & Allington, R. C. (1985). Where do teacher's questions come from? *The Reading Teacher, 38,* 434–438.

Shannon, P. (1983). The use of commercial reading materials in American elementary schools. *Reading Research Quarterly, 19,* 68–85.

Smith, N. B. (1965). *American reading instruction.* Newark, DE: International Reading Association.

Sticht, T. G. (1984). Rate of comprehending by listening or reading. In J. Flood (Ed.). *Understanding reading comprehension* (pp. 140–160). Newark, DE: International Reading Association.

Wixson, K. K., et al. (1984). An interview for assessing students' perceptions of classroom reading tasks. *Reading Teacher, 37*(4), 346–352.

Diagnosis and Evaluation: Promoting Growth in Reading

━━━━━━━━━━━━━━━━━ **CHAPTER PREVIEW** ━━━━━━━━━━━━━━━━━

All of us teachers would like to know whether our teaching is effective. All of us who work with elementary school children would like to know whether our students are learning to read and write better—whether they are becoming literate human beings. This means that diagnosis of students' strengths and weaknesses is necessary. This means that evaluation is part of our role as teachers.

Just *how* we diagnose or evaluate is another matter. Should we simply engage in "kid watching," as Ken Goodman (1986) calls it? (And by the way, kid watching is not simple at all.) If so, what kind of watching should we do? Maybe we should give tests. If so, what kinds of tests should we administer?

In this chapter we'll discuss various ways of diagnosing and evaluating children and their reading progress. You'll see, I hope, that miscue analysis provides the most versatile procedure for the teacher, either for testing or for careful observing of children. You'll see how miscue analysis can be carried on during both reading and writing experiences. And you'll learn (or review) the procedures for administering, scoring, and interpreting informal reading inventories. We'll discuss some of the disadvantages of relying upon standardarized tests and of the strict use of evaluations by a child's previous teacher. We'll also look at the advantages and disadvantages of using the cloze technique. In all of this our goal will be to determine how effective teachers can promote growth through diagnosis.

Repeatedly asking questions about self, our instructional effectiveness, and our abilities to change helps us serve as models for students doing the same.

—Susan Glazer and Lyndon Searfoss

The limits of variation are really much wider than anyone would imagine.

—George Eliot

There is no such thing as ''best'' in a world of individuals.

—Hugh Prather

Behold the turtle: He only makes progress when he sticks his neck out.

—James Bryant Conant

CRITERIA FOR DIAGNOSTIC AND EVALUATION PROCEDURES

Sometimes when we observe or test our students, we teachers may lose sight of *why* we're doing this. In our hurry to place each child in the right book for reading instruction, or in our rush to "cure" a child of his reading difficulties, we may lose sight of the forest for the trees. We may begin to believe in the percentages and checklists we're producing more than we do in our intuitive understanding of the child. Or we may think that a child's sight word errors and graphophonic errors are more important than what she thinks reading is or what she uses as reading strategies.

The main reason this confusion occurs is that it's relatively easy to test children on their mastery of sight words or graphophonic patterns, or to compute the percentage of words they miss in a reading passage. Yet it takes much more skill and knowledge on the teacher's part to assess children on their ability to use the four cueing systems interactively, or on their awareness of reading as a communication process, or on the enjoyment they derive from reading. So because of this difficulty, it's terribly tempting for us educators to grab onto whatever "solid" test data we can get, even though these data are a measure of isolated subreading knowledge rather than a measure of the composite interactive reading process. (It would be a little like a zoologist studying a bee without paying attention to the bee hive.)

To help you keep these concerns in mind, here are a set of criteria that may help you decide which diagnostic or evaluation procedures to use. The diagnostic or evaluation procedures should

1. lead to better understanding of a child and not to labeling or only to placement.
2. treat each child as unique and not as a statistic.
3. increase a teacher's awareness of a child's concept of the reading process.
4. increase a teacher's understanding of a child's reading strategies.
5. help a teacher examine and determine a child's ability to read interactively.
6. increase a teacher's confidence in her ability to find instructional materials that are challenging but not too difficult for a child.

These six criteria lead to three practical concerns of the reading teacher:

1. How to determine and enhance children's attitudes toward reading
2. How to determine and strengthen their concepts and strategies of reading
3. How to assess their present levels of reading ability

ASSESSING AND ENHANCING ATTITUDES TOWARD READING

This topic is so important I've devoted another chapter entirely to it (see Chapter 13). All I want to say here is that research and common sense have made educators aware of the crucial role attitudes have in learning *anything*. This is certainly as true of reading as of anything else. When a student has developed a distaste of reading—or a distaste for learning the process of reading—the student's teacher is in deep trouble. At least temporarily he is, until he can determine a way around this distaste.

I say "a way around" because the teacher can't always assess attitudes or the causes of those attitudes. They may be much too deep for assessment. What often happens in these cases is that we rely more on "kid watching," intuitively trying one thing after another until we hit upon something that works.

Thirteen-year-old Kenny was a case in point. He'd been retained twice by the time I got him in sixth grade. And it wasn't until after Christmas that I was able to penetrate his wall of indifference and hostility toward reading. After watching me read aloud to the class every day, he eventually conceded that he'd been wrong at the beginning of the school year when he'd said that "reading's for sissies." And one day when I handed him a book on "How Things Work," he reluctantly leafed through it (while I pretended that I couldn't care less whether he read it or not). A half-hour later his nose was glued to the middle of the book so tightly he didn't budge when the rest of the class went to music. (And I wasn't about to make a federal case of his "disobedience" to the schedule.) Kenny was reading with real enjoyment.

ASSESSING AND STRENGTHENING CONCEPTS AND STRATEGIES

I've said or implied many times in this book, especially in Chapter 4, that what a teacher needs to determine about each child is what his reading concept and strategies are. She needs to find out what he thinks reading *is* and what strategies he uses for *getting through* a selection of text. When it comes to reading instruction, these two things are probably the most important kid-watching assessments. The reason for this is that reading concepts and strategies seem to determine the child's success more than nearly any other factor—more than vocabulary knowledge, more than graphophonic awareness, more than the massive doses of vitamin C he's been taking.

So how do we determine a child's reading concepts and strategies? Basically by listening to him read aloud and asking ourselves why he produces the miscues that he does. This is what is meant by the term "miscue analysis." Miscue analysis can help a teacher discover answers to questions like these: What strategies is Jimmy using to decode unfamiliar words? Is he guessing wildly or using context clues? Is he relying too much on graphophonic clues? Too little? Are some of his miscues a result of inadequate decoding skill, or simply a result of speaking a dialect different from the author's? Questions such as these are answered through analyzing the miscues a child makes during the time he is reading orally. Let's take Tommy as a case study.

Case Study One: Tommy

AUTHOR: Roy saw a little boat pull a big boat.
TOMMY: Roy was a little boat pulled by a big boat.

What you do when you carry on miscue analysis is simply to ask yourself why. Why did Tommy make his first miscue? Why did he make the next one? And so on. By answering these questions you'll often be able to learn about a child's reading strategies and his notion of what reading is. Once you've discovered his strategies for reading and his concept of reading, you probably will have come much farther toward helping him become a better reader.

If we take Tommy's miscues as an example, we can speculate that Tommy's concept of reading is probably that "reading is a meaningful process." Imagine Tommy defining it this way: "Reading is retelling a story in a way that makes sense." Since Tommy doesn't think it makes sense for a little boat to pull a big boat, he doesn't even see the way the author wrote the story. Therefore, he reads the sentence in a way that makes sense to him!

Now that we have a rough hypothesis for what Tommy's concept of reading is, let's see if we can discover his strategies for reading. Well, what's Tommy's first miscue? He sees the word *saw* as *was*, isn't that right? That tells us a little bit about his strategies. He predicts what words are coming next, for one thing. And that's a good strategy to have. But in this case he predicts *Roy was* instead of *Roy saw*.

Does he have a strategy for confirming his predictions? Does he glance at the first letter of the word he predicts, for instance, to see if it starts with the appropriate letter? Evidently not, for he goes right on reading. As a result, Tommy ends up with the idea that "Roy *was* a little boat." But this doesn't bother him, since after all, most people give their boat a name. So far, so good, as far as Tommy is concerned.

Now we come to the fifth word in the sentence. The author says, "Roy saw a little boat pull a big boat." But Tommy, remember, is talking about a little boat named *Roy*. Naturally, then, he wouldn't say, "Roy was a little boat pull a big boat." That simply doesn't make good grammatical sense. To make good sense, one would have to say, "Roy was a little boat pulled by a big boat." We now know a little bit more about Tommy's reading strategies. As far as he's concerned, a sentence should make sense both semantically and syntactically.

So what do we know from listening to Tommy read just one sentence? Well, actually we *know* very little, but we can begin to make some hypotheses that we can check as he continues to read. We can hypothesize that Tommy perceives reading as a form of communication and not just a process of "sounding out" words. We can also hypothesize that his strategies for reading include the strategy of "go for broke." That is, he goes for the big message and doesn't concern himself very much with the little clues. He ignores the little clue of the second word in the sentence starting with *s* instead of *w*. He ignores the little clue that there is no suffix *ed* at the end of *pull*. (And, as I discovered later, he ignores little clues like periods, question marks, and capital letters as well.)

As we continue listening to Tommy read, we discover that our hypotheses are probably correct. He consistently goes for the big message and ignores the little clues. We now have a better idea of how to help him improve his reading. We don't want to spoil his perception that reading is a form of communication, but we do want to increase the accuracy of his reading by encouraging him to confirm his predictions by paying attention to the first letter in a word (*s* instead of *w*), by paying attention to phonograms such as *aw (saw, jaw, paw),* by noticing whether a suffix is being used or not *(pull* vs. *pulled),* and by developing a better visual memory of important sight words like *was.*

Case Study Two: Sabina

AUTHOR: A beaver's home, called a lodge, always has a flooded lower room.
SABINA: A beautiful honey calls a loggid away his floor low room.

What do you think Sabina's concept of reading is? A search for the author's meaning? A recall of known words with letters similar to the author's? A process of getting through each sentence one word at a time? Probably the latter two hunches are more accurate than the first one. Sabina, at least with text at this level of difficulty, doesn't perceive reading as a meaningful process. It's basically a guess-and-semidecode operation. Reading, to Sabina, seems to be a series of word beads that have to be strung together until you reach one of those dots (periods) that tell you to stop.

What do you think Sabina's *strategies* are? How does she choose to get through a chunk of text? Does she rely on contextual clues (semantic, syntactic, and schematic)? Does she rely on graphophonic clues? If so, which ones? First letters? Phonograms? Suffixes? Do her predictions rely primarily on graphophonic clues or on context clues? Does she confirm her graphophonic-based predictions with context clues? Does she show comprehension monitoring by using self-corrections? By questioning what she's reading?

Sabina, it would appear, needs lots of guided practice with easier material. Lots of gentle, contextual questioning by the teacher: "Do you know what a *loggid* is, Sabina? . . . Since *loggid* doesn't make sense to you, how could you find out what word that really is? . . . If you look at the picture, can you tell me whether this story is about beautiful honey or about something else?"

Case Study Three: Maxine

AUTHOR: The man drove his auto up to his home and parked.
MAXINE: He drove his car to his house and parked.

What is Maxine's concept of reading? Why does she substitute *He* for *The man?* Doesn't this meaningful substitution actually show considerable comprehension on her part? And what about her substitutions of *car* for *auto* and *house* for *home?* Isn't reading a search for meaning as far as Maxine is concerned?

What about her strategies? She obviously relies on context, doesn't she? But does she really ignore graphophonic clues? Let's look at it from the standpoint of the way the eyes and brain work together. When a person is reading aloud well, she'll focus her eyes on words that are in advance of the ones she is actually saying out loud. Do you agree?

What this means, then, is this: "Since there is a distance between pronouncing words and visually taking in words, it seems likely the information picked up visually is briefly stored in the reader's memory. . . . The words fluent readers are pronouncing, then, are based on what is stored in memory rather than on the words visually seen" (Johnson & Kress, 1987).

Now you can see how Maxine's "errors" are related to her "good-reader policy" (sounds like an insurance term) of reading ahead of her voice. By reading ahead she assures both fluency and comprehension. This strategy demonstrates an active search for meaning. As she reads ahead, the words she sees are stored temporarily in her short-term memory. Then when she retrieves the words, her brain translates them into language that is more meaningful and natural to her: *He* for *The man, car* for *auto,* and *house* for *home.*

Again, we see how valuable miscue analysis is to the teacher of reading. With miscue analysis, several of the criteria for effective diagnosis and evaluation are met:

1. It leads to a better understanding of each child and not to labeling a child or to mere placement.
2. It treats each child as unique and not as a statistic.

3. It increases a teacher's awareness of each child's concepts and strategies of reading.

4. It helps a teacher examine and determine each child's ability to read interactively.

USING MISCUE ANALYSIS AS A KID-WATCHING PROCEDURE

One of the best kid-watching forms of diagnosis and evaluation, then, is miscue analysis. I'd like to emphasize this point a little more in this section. Whenever you have the opportunity to listen to a child read—whether you use a basal reader program, a language experience approach, a literature-based approach, or a whole language program—you can listen to his miscues and ask yourself why he's making them. In this way, as we did with Tommy, Sabina, and Maxine, you can find out more about his reading concepts and strategies, and thus his ability to read interactively. You will know, for instance, that Tommy needs more help in graphophonically confirming his predictions; that Sabina needs lots of context-oriented questions as she reads; and that Maxine needs to be left alone, with no corrections of "errors" please.

What this means, of course, is that your concern when listening to a child read should be for the process rather than the product. Be concerned not so much for a perfect performance that you create by correcting every mistake Lisa makes, but rather for the processes she uses to perform for you. Does her performance signify that she perceives reading as a process of sounding out each word correctly for you? Does her performance signify that she perceives reading as a task to rush through as fast as possible in spite of mistakes?

You may wish to stop a child sometimes when her rendition doesn't make any sense ("That sentence didn't make sense to me. Would you read it again, please?"). Often, however, the child will gain more if you just listen to her read, and carry on miscue analysis while you listen.

Suppose, for example, that Mrs. Franklin sees this: "The dog ran over to Sammy and barked and barked at him." But Kevin reads this: "Da dog wen' over to Sammy and bock and bock at him." Mrs. Franklin knows that Kevin's mother tongue is Black English rather than "Standard English." Therefore, she realizes that Kevin has performed a double translation—from print to Standard English to Black English—on the printed words *The* and *barked*. She also realizes that in substituting *went* for *ran* he has done little damage to his comprehension of the passage and simply used *went* because he had predicted that *went* would occur in that sentence slot. Mrs. Franklin decides not to stop Kevin.

On the other hand, suppose that Susan reads the same sentence like this: "Then Doug ran *other* to Sammy and *backed* and *backed* at her." Mrs. Franklin sees immediately that Susan is relying almost exclusively on minor graphophonic clues and is paying no attention to syntactic clues (*other* does not fit grammatically where *over* should be); or to semantic/schematic clues. (*Sammy* and *her* don't

match, and people seldom *back* at others.) Mrs. Franklin knows she has her work cut out for her. Susan needs to be taught to read for meaning rather than empty words. Mrs. Franklin knows this because she has carried on miscue analysis while Susan was reading.

She does not stop to correct Susan after each word that she reads incorrectly. She may not stop her at all at his point, preferring to wait until she has more time to work with her. Or if she does stop her, she stops her at the end of a sentence or paragraph to work with her on finding meaning clues.

THE IRI: DATA GATHERING FOR MISCUE AND LEVEL ANALYSIS

An occasional session of listening to a child read may not provide you with enough data on some children. In order to be sure of their concepts and strategies, you may decide to use an informal reading inventory (IRI). An IRI will not only provide you with plenty of data for this purpose; it will also help you in another way. Remember that we had one more criterion for evaluation and diagnostic procedures, namely, that these procedures should increase a teacher's confidence in her ability to find instructional materials that are challenging but not too difficult for a child. The IRI, as you may already know, provides you with data for miscue analysis at the same time that it helps you pinpoint different reading levels for each child: the level at which he can read *independently* without help from you, the level at which he probably should be *instructed* in reading, and the level at which reading materials would be too *frustrating.*

An informal reading inventory is simply a set of reading selections from easy to difficult that children can individually read aloud to the teacher—or silently in front of the teacher. For purposes of miscue analysis you'll need to have the child read the selection out loud and preferably use a tape recorder so that you'll have more time later to carefully analyze the miscues.

Informal reading inventories are available from nearly every basal reader publisher. IRIs usually start with a preprimer (early first-grade) selection and go up to at least an eighth-grade selection. After each one there are questions which you may choose to ask the child. Or you may wish to ask her to simply retell the story or tell you what she remembers about the topic. (You may even decide to skip this step after reading later in this chapter on ways of checking comprehension through miscue analysis.)

Using Informal Testing Conditions with an IRI

There are several things you can do when administering an IRI to encourage a relaxed atmosphere and to increase the accuracy of the test. These are some suggestions:

Make sure the child is seated in such a way that he is not distracted by your keeping track of his miscues.

Take a few moments to develop rapport by talking about his reading interests—his favorite book, the kinds of books he likes, when he likes to read, where he likes to read, and so on.

Explain the reason and nature of your examination, perhaps like this: "Billy, I'd like to hear you read for a while so I can decide what books might be enjoyable for you to read. Do the best you can, but don't worry if you make mistakes, because your mistakes will help me see how I can help you this year. After you read each story, we'll talk about it for a few minutes."

Don't give the IRI during recess or any other time the student can't devote full attention to it. (If the test is viewed as a punishment, your results will not be valid.)

Administer the IRI where the child can't see his peers without turning around.

Make sure he is near enough to enable you to hear or tape record miscues clearly.

Allow for a minimum of distractions and interruptions. Tell the rest of the class that you shouldn't be disturbed while you're working with "Johnny." Appoint a teaching assistant.

Make sure the lighting on the reading passages is excellent. This may have a significant effect on the level of the book in which you place the child.

Allow a *full five seconds* for the child to decode a word before pronouncing it for him. (Try not to "jump the gun.")

Keep the testing situation "light and breezy." A formal, overserious approach may reduce the validity of an IRI.

Administering an IRI

These suggestions for administering an informal reading are based on numerous articles by other reading educators, on my own experiences with children, and on the experience of the many teachers who have been kind enough to share their ideas with me.

1. *Where to begin:* Have the student begin reading two or three grade levels below the grade he's in. A fifth-grader would begin by reading a second- or third-grade selection; a third-grader would begin at the primer or first-grade level. Normally it's better to start too low than too high so that the student can feel more relaxed.

2. *Counting miscues:* Use tally marks on a pad in your lap to discretely record the number of miscues. Count omissions, insertions, repetitions, defaults, substitutions, and even self-corrections this time. (Later, if you decide to listen to the tape-recorded session and score the IRI, you should make quality rather than quantity judgments. This process of scoring will be discussed in a later section.) Traditionally we don't count punctuation errors, hesitations, or slow pronunciations. Here are samples of miscues to count during administration (but not necessarily during scoring):

Omission	(Then) she saw her mother coming.
Insertion	*In* ∧the forest was a big park.
Default	Child doesn't try the word. Teacher waits five seconds, then pronounces it, e.g., tea*d*cher.
Repetition	The boy went to̲ school.
Substitution (real word or nonsense word)	She worked with *them* him. He was a *taskammer* taskmaster.
Self-correction	He *was* s̲a̲w̲ his teacher.

3. *Pronouncing words for child:* When a child comes to a proper noun, such as a person's last name, pronounce it for her the first time she misses the word and also count it as a miscue. However, don't count it more than once in the same selection. Sometimes the same proper noun shows up repeatedly, and it seems to be invalid to count it more than once. Don't pronounce any other word unless the child has gone five full seconds without saying it.

4. *Dialect differences:* Don't count dialect differences (such as "chimley" for "chimney" or "I don't be going" for "I'm not going." If the child *talks* this way, it's not a reading error.

5. *Asking questions* (optional): Ask three to five literal questions and three to five inferential questions. Or ask the child to retell the story or to tell the important things he's learned. (Questions are almost always included in the commercial IRI that you will use, but you may want to modify them.)

Literal questions usually require the reader to:
a. Remember important details stated by the author
b. Remember the sequence of events
c. Translate written descriptions into oral ones (child's own words)

Inferential questions usually require the reader to:
a. Predict what's going to happen next (asked either at the end or half-way through a story)
b. Decide what caused what (if the author did not explicitly explain it)
c. Fill in information that an author has implied but not stated
d. Determine the most important ideas implied by the author

6. *When to stop:* Stop the testing when the child *finishes* a selection that has been obviously frustrating. This nearly always occurs by the time she has missed 15 percent of the words in the selection and 50 percent of the questions. To help you know when the child has reached this point, you may wish to compute the "stopping point" for each selection before she reads. You can obtain an objective stopping point by multiplying the total number of words in each selection by 0.15. For instance, if the total number of words is 140, the estimated stopping point would be 21 miscues.

   Another way to determine the stopping point is to decide subjectively whether the child has reached frustration. This is shown by such behavior as heavy sighs, extreme fidgeting, pained expressions, not understanding your questions at the end of a selection, or even the request, "Can we stop now?" In this case, even though she has not missed 15 percent of the words and 50 percent of the questions, stop the child at the end of the selection.

7. *Checking silent reading:* Some teachers feel it's important to test for silent reading ability as well. Therefore they use two forms of the IRI, one for

oral reading and one for silent reading. Because this adds to the time and fatigue involved, many teachers do not do this.

Using Miscue Analysis after an IRI

To carry on a systematic miscue analysis following an IRI, you'll need to code the miscues as you listen to the tape recording (with your copy of each reading selection in front of you to mark on). In the previous section, I showed you one way of coding the miscues. To code a substitution or mispronunciation (nonsense substitution), for instance, simply write the incorrect word or mispronunciation above the author's word. If the child then corrects this error, you can use a large C around the word and substitution combined.

Once you have coded the miscues, you need to look primarily at the defaults, substitutions, and self-corrections of substitutions. Research shows that these three are the most important miscues (Beebe, 1979–80; Goodman, 1969; Clay, 1968; D'Angelo, 1983). As you examine them, consider these questions:

1. Was this substitution caused by the child's prediction, and if so was the prediction a reasonable one?

   Example: The man ran fast. The man was scared.

2. Was the substitution caused by not confirming a context-based prediction with a graphophonic check?

   Example: He was frightened by a mad lion.

3. Was the substitution caused by not confirming a graphophonic-based prediction with a context check?

   Example: He was frightened by a mad lion.

4. Was this default caused by the word not fitting the child's schema or prior knowledge?

   Example: The lion plunged through the boscage.

5. Was the self-correction made probably because the substitution didn't fit the context? The graphophonic clues? Both context and graphophonic clues?

   Example: The man turned to see that the lion was nearly upon him.

You'll want to do this kind of miscue analysis for each selection, realizing as you do so that a child's major concept and strategy often change as the material gets too difficult. With the second-grade selection he may think of reading as a search for meaning, but with the fifth-grade selection he may think of reading as a meaningless decoding process. At the second-grade level his major strategy might be to confidently predict and confirm, comfortably using all four cueing systems. At the fifth-grade level, though, his major strategy for getting through the selection might be to use meaningless substitutions and to default a lot so that the teacher will give him the words. (The concept/strategy record in Figure 11.1 should be useful to you in recording your information about each child you decide to test.)

KID WATCHING FOR CONCEPTS AND STRATEGIES DURING WRITING EXPERIENCES

Determining a child's concepts and strategies of reading can also be done during writing activities. When Beverly is writing in her journal, for example, she delights in having her teacher write a note about the content of her journal entry; for example, "I like your idea about parties, Beverly. Do you think that birthday parties are a good idea for children *every* year?" Beverly also delights in trying to read her teacher's comments. Unlike some of her peers who ask for nearly every word, Beverly has concepts and strategies that are already fairly mature. She is already using known words to provide context for unknown words. Out loud, to an aide, she reads the teacher's comment this way: "I like your (something-whatever-that-is) about parties—I know it's *parties,* because that's one of my favorite words."

BEVERLY: [pointing to *idea*] But what's that word?
AIDE: Remember to say "blank."
BEVERLY: I like your blank about parties. Is it *story?* Story about parties?
AIDE: That's a good idea but *story* starts with *s.* This word starts with an *i.*
BEVERLY: I don't know a word that starts with *i.*
AIDE: Idea.
BEVERLY: [excited] Oh, that's what it is!

Thus, through observing Beverly's process of writing and her reading of her teacher's comments, her teacher and teacher aide determine that Beverly's concept of reading is that of searching for the meaning of the author. Her set of strategies already includes the use of a blank (or "something, whatever that is") as a place holder for an unknown word. This strategy in turn allows her to use context and graphophonic clues in concert.

DETERMINING CHILDREN'S READING LEVELS

I mentioned before that there are at least three practical assessment concerns for the reading teacher: (1) determining children's attitudes toward reading, (2) assessing their ability to read interactively by determining their concepts and strat-

Student _____ Grade _____ Date _____

Sample:

IRI level _P_: Concept *Reading is a decoding process.*

Coded example: Mary follows him.
                   d   *falls*

Strategy *Relies on letters to come up with familiar word.*

Coded example: He shakes hands.
                  shacks

IRI level ____: Concept _____

Coded example: _____

Strategy _____

Coded example: _____

IRI level ____: Concept _____

Coded example: _____

Strategy _____

Coded example: _____

IRI level ____: Concept _____

Coded example: _____

Strategy _____

Coded example: _____

IRI level ____: Concept _____

Coded example: _____

Strategy _____

Coded example: _____

Recommended level for instruction: _____

FIGURE 11.1

Estimates of major concept and strategy for each selection level egies, and (3) determining each child's *levels* of reading. Before we can talk about this final assessment problem, we'll need to discuss the meaning of "reading level."

The Concept of Reading Level

Suppose you were assigned to teach a group of thirty randomly selected fifth-graders. What range in reading levels (or abilities) would you expect to find? Would they all score at the fifth-grade level (between 5.0 and 5.9) on a reading achievement test? Obviously not, but how many in the class would you expect to score above or below the fifth-grade level? One or two? One-fourth of them? One-half? If you picked the last answer, you would probably come closest to being correct. Furthermore, the range of overall ability in reading may encompass the second- through eighth-grade levels.

What if you were assigned to a first-grade class instead? The range may not seem as great, but it would be just as important as the range among fifth-graders. A typical group of first-graders would contain children who are already reading at the first- or even second-grade level, some who are just beginning to read, and some who need considerable help in developing reading readiness skills.

It's probably obvious, then, that a reading teacher shouldn't use the same instructional material for every child in the room. One book would be all right for some of the children, boring and unchallenging to others, and terribly frustrating to still others. Yet this is exactly the way many teachers taught reading not too many decades ago. This is the way social studies, science, and other subjects are often taught today. This is exactly what many new reading programs today are advocating.

Some of today's newest reading programs insist that children should not be grouped for instruction, that grouping does more harm than good, and that ungrouped children will have more direct contact with the teacher and less time to waste on worksheets. All of these ideas are noble, worth considering, and possibly correct. Right now, however, the research comparing grouped and ungrouped students is meager, to say the least.

Frankly, whether you group your children for reading instruction may depend more on school district policy than on research evidence. All I can say is, the better you get to know each child, including his strengths and weaknesses, the more confidence you're going to feel about the help (or extra help) you give him.

Let's just assume for a moment that you're teaching in a district in which a determination of each child's best instructional level is encouraged rather than frowned upon. How are you going to make this decision about Beverly's best instructional level—that is, what materials would be most suitable for instructing her in reading? These are some of the sources of information teachers often use for this purpose:

☐ Recommendations from a previous teacher
☐ Standardized test scores

☐ Group administered tests developed by basal reader publishers
☐ Informal reading inventories
☐ Miscue analysis
☐ The cloze technique

Let's look at each source to determine its strengths and weaknesses.

Using Recommendations from a Previous Teacher

Many teachers place their students in instructional materials according to the recommendation of the previous teacher. If Mrs. Fisher, who taught Nancy in the second grade, recommends on Nancy's cumulative folder that she be placed in the 3_2 reader at the beginning of third grade, Miss Green, the third-grade teacher, often does just that. And, on the surface, this seems like the logical thing to do in many cases. Since Mrs. Fisher knows that Nancy has completed the 3_1 reader by the end of second grade, it seems only rational to recommend the 3_2 reader for third grade and for Miss Green to follow that recommendation.

There are several flaws, though, in this logical rationale. First, Mrs. Fisher may have done what many teachers have done in the past: She may have decided on Nancy's instructional level at the beginning of second grade and then not tested Nancy later in the year to see what level of achievement she had reached. Thus, all she really had Nancy do during the year was to follow along with the group in which she was placed. Since Nancy's group finished the 3_1 reader, Mrs. Fisher recommended that she begin third grade at the 3_2 level. In other words, she ignored Nancy's individual progress and simply treated her as a group member—exactly like all the other children in Nancy's group.

A second flaw in this simplistic transition from Mrs. Fisher to Miss Green is that of ignoring the three summer months, as if no reading growth or decline could have taken place during that time. As just one example of how fallacious this attitude is, Aasen (1959) used various devices to encourage children to read during the summer months, thus improving their reading grade by 0.7 year, in contrast to no improvement for a control group.

A third flaw in the Fisher-to-Green transfer is the assumption that a recommendation by a former teacher is based on hard objective data about a child's actual reading performance. A study by Brown and Sherbenou (1981) demonstrated that this is often not the case. Their study showed that a teacher's perception of a child's reading abilities may strongly relate to how much he likes the child's nonacademic behavior in the classroom. In contrast, the relationship to the child's actual performance on reading tests may be quite low. To put it another way, it seems quite possible that many teachers judge a child's actual reading ability more on the basis of the child's cooperativeness and other such traits than on decoding and comprehension abilities.

Haller and Waterman (1985) found that teachers use a variety of reasons for placing Johnny in group A, B, or C for reading instruction. Only 45 percent of the time was the teacher's decision based on reading ability. And when children were on the borderline between two groups (high versus average, or average

versus low) the decision was based on reading ability only 31 percent of the time. The other factors that sometimes weighed more heavily were general academic competence, work habits, behavior and personality, and home background.

What this means, in a practical sense, is that one should use the recommendation from the previous teacher as only one bit of information and only after determining the answer to three questions:

1. What actual procedures did the teacher use to arrive at his recommendation?
2. Do those procedures justify putting a great deal of faith in the recommendation?
3. What did the child do during the summer that might possibly make a difference in her reading development?

Using Standardized Tests

Another approach to determining each child's instructional level is that of relying upon standardized test scores. There is very little, if anything, to recommend this practice if the test scores are derived from group administered, rather than individually administered, tests. Let's talk about standardized tests for a moment, and at the same time I'll give you some reasons for discouraging you to use the usual group-test scores.

Standardized tests have several things in common. For one thing, they are designed to be administered in the same way to each child or group of children taking the test. Directions are read from a manual, the exact time for each subtest is supposedly the same from group to group, and the same sequence of subtests is followed.

For another thing, standardized tests are *norm referenced,* which means that the test publishers first administer the tests to groups of children called *norm groups,* who supposedly represent the rest of the population. The average scores for children at different grade levels become the norms. For example, if the norm group of fourth-graders gets an average score of 43 out of 60, the score of 43 then becomes a norm for all other fourth-graders who later take the test.

Another common feature of standardized tests is the manner in which raw scores are translated into standardized scores. These standardized scores usually take the form of percentiles, stanines, or grade equivalency scores. The type teachers most often use is the grade equivalent score. The grade equivalency score for a raw score of 43 out of 60 may be anywhere from 4.0 to 4.9, depending upon when the norm group took the test. Theoretically, if the norm group took the test during the first week of school, the grade equivalency score for 43 would be 4.0, indicating the very beginning of fourth grade. If the norm group took the test in the fifth month of school, the grade equivalent score for 43 would be 4.5.

In actual practice, test publishers seldom spend time and money assembling a different norm group each month to determine a grade equivalency score of 4.1, 4.2, 4.3, and so on. Instead they do a great deal of mathematical predicting (Baumann & Stevenson, 1982).

Misinterpretation of standardized scores. One of the worst problems of standardized tests is that their results are so often misinterpreted by teachers. For example, Frank Roberts, a fourth-grader, was administered a standardized test, along with his classmates, during the first week of school. He scored a total of 48 and received a grade equivalency score of 3.6. His teacher, Mr. Jackson, was concerned because Frank was "reading below grade level." Teachers and administrators often express such concern; there seems to be an assumption that every child should be reading at his grade level or higher. However, this assumption is based on the lack of realization of how the grade-level norm was originally obtained. It was obtained by getting the average score of the norm group at a particular time during the school year. Since *average score* means, roughly, "the score in the middle," 50 percent of the norm group had to score at or below the average score; 50 percent of the norm group had to score at or above the average score. Thus, if the norm group is representative of the total population, a teacher should theoretically expect half the children to score at or below "grade level" and half to score at or above grade level. Of course, it never works out this neatly, because a norm group can never come that close to representing every other group in the population. But the point should be clear, nevertheless: It is expecting much to much to have every child at or above grade level.

Other limitations of standardized reading tests. Standardized tests do have greater reliability than most other tests. That is, they do rank-order students from high to low pretty consistently from one form of the test to another. On the other hand, they have many weaknesses in practicality and validity:

They are so long (to increase their reliability) that they are usually administrated to groups instead of individuals. Thus the teacher is deprived of observing each child "in action."

They are usually timed, thus penalizing those who read well but slowly.

They often present conditions that are not typical of the reading act. For example, they ask children to respond to multiple-choice questions, which require recognition of the correct answer; reading, on the other hand, requires skill that is far more complex.

They frequently overrate a child's reading level, thus encouraging some teachers to place a child in a reader that is too difficult and frustrating.

Some children are good readers but poor test takers, particularly with standardized tests. Special forms are passed out, the right kind of pencil must be used, everyone in the room is sighing and moaning, the tension rises to fever pitch as the teacher looks at the clock and says, "Ready, begin." For some children, this kind of atmosphere is not conducive to clear thinking and careful reading.

The reading passages in standardized tests are usually quite short. A child who does well on short passages requiring little retention may not do as well on longer selections in basal readers and other materials.

The norm group quite likely will not truly represent the particular group of children you are instructing.

Standardized reading tests are often not accurate for those who are considerably below their grade level (Gunning, 1982). Let's look at a sixth-grade boy, for example, taking a sixth-grade test. This test may be designed in such a way that the lowest *possible* score would give him no less than a 3.2 grade equivalency. In reality, however, his level might be closer to, let's say, 1.8. Such an overestimate of his reading ability would cause a teacher to instruct him in materials that are much too difficult for him.

Standardized tests usually include twice as much informational text as basal readers, themselves, do. Thus, there's an overemphasis in the tests on text that is not that common in the most widely used instructional material (Flood & Lapp, 1987).

Group Administered Tests by Basal Reader Publishers

Some publishers of basal readers have developed norm-referenced tests similar to standardized reading tests. Because of this similarity, they suffer from some of the same validity problems. On the other hand, they tend to be slightly more valid than a regular standardized test, because the passages and words are similar to or the same as those used in the basal readers produced by the same publisher.

Other publishers develop criterion-referenced tests to use for placement of children in the readers. Rather than use a norm group, the publishing team has developed short, objective-style tests that sample the various "skills" taught through the basal reader program. On each short test, the child is expected to score at a minimum level to demonstrate his reading competence. This minimum level, often 80 percent, is called a *criterion*. By administering these short skill tests in the same order as the skills are presented in the basal reader program, and by adding the scores on these tests, the teacher arrives at a score that can then be converted into an estimate of the child's instructional reading level. Because these tests are group administered, however, they lack the validity that can be gained through individual administration. Also, because the tests are so short, they lack reliability. Furthermore, the nature of the objective-type tests, as well as their brevity, makes the testing situation quite different from the actual reading act.

Informal Reading Inventories

For placing children in instructional reading materials, informal reading inventories are quite popular among teachers (Johnson, Kress, & Pikulski, 1987). In one study, for example, (Harris & Lalik, 1987), 55 percent of the classroom teachers were using them to place children in basal readers. Of the 45 percent who were not using them, a large percentage were required to let the reading specialist place them (and a great many reading specialists use IRIs.)

Since we've already discussed IRIs, we needn't spend time on the administration of them. What we do need to talk about, though, is some ways of interpreting them. One way of interpreting them, of course, is through miscue analysis. If you look at Figure 11.1, you'll see that there is a space for indicating whether one of the passages appears to represent the child's instructional level. And some teachers are capable of doing this intuitively by simply examining the quality of the miscues. Are most of the miscues, for example, those that show a student using interactive reading? If so, then this selection represents at least instructional level, and perhaps even independent level. On the other hand, are most of the miscues showing a concept of reading as a meaningless operation? If so, then this selection probably represents frustration level—material at this grade level would probably be too hard for instructional purposes.

Other teachers, though, prefer some type of numerical score that will tell them what level each passage represents. Traditionally, teachers have relied on the exact percentages or some modification of those percentages devised by Emmett Betts (1946). Over the years these percentages have *approximated* those that follow:

Independent reading level:	98 percent of the words correct
	90 percent of the questions correct
Instructional reading level:	95 percent of the words correct
	60 percent of the questions correct

Frustrational reading level: below 90 percent of the words correct
below 50 percent of the questions correct

Thus, if Clifford were reading a selection from a fourth-grade basal reader and achieved a decoding score of 80 percent and a comprehension score of 80 percent, the teacher would probably conclude that fourth-grade reading material would be too difficult for instructional use. On the other hand, if he read a third-grade passage with a decoding score of 95 percent and a comprehension score of 70 percent, the teacher would probably place him in a third-grade basal reader for instruction.

So far this must seem terribly simple to you—and that's just the problem with it. It's a very simple way of looking at a process that is really quite complicated. We've been talking throughout this book about how reading involves four interacting processes, and now I'm showing you a testing device that relies primarily on the graphophonic process and largely ignores the three context processes (semantic, schematic, and syntactic). Although the traditional scoring procedure provides a decoding score, and thus an estimate of a child's ability to use graphophonic cues, it provides no real estimate of his ability to use context cues. You may wonder if the questions would provide such an estimate, but according to the research I'll describe in the next section, questions have several weaknesses. Clifford, for example, missed one out of every five words on his decoding score but managed to answer four out of five questions correctly. This kind of situation usually occurs under three conditions: (1) A child misses many of the words through default and the teacher tells him the words; (2) a child is bright enough to follow the general meaning of the selection because the teacher has provided him with most of the difficult words; and (3) a child can answer some of the questions because of his background of experiences rather than because of what he has read.

There are at least two ways out of this dilemma of using the traditional scoring methods. One is to avoid using the IRI altogether and to substitute the "cloze" or "maze" technique instead. The other way is to use a *qualitative* method instead of a quantitative method of scoring the IRI. Let's try the latter approach first.

Quality scoring of an IRI: What research tells us. As I mentioned in the previous section, reading educators have traditionally counted only the *quantity* of miscues in an IRI. I'm sure you would agree, however, that we should be concerned with the *quality* of our students' miscues, not just the quantity. But what does research tell us about miscues? Let's review this research.

Good readers (those who comprehend what they're reading) make many miscues that actually *enhance* comprehension—meaningful substitutions, omissions, insertions, and self-corrections (Beebe, 1978–79; Clay, 1968; D'Angelo, 1982). Our scoring of informal reading inventories should not penalize such positive reading behavior.

Poor readers do very little self-correcting; their substitutions are often not meaningful; and they frequently default on words by waiting for the teacher to pronounce them (D'Angelo, 1983; Goodman, 1969). These are "negative miscues." It doesn't make sense for our IRI scoring procedures to treat positive and negative miscues as equivalent—and as both negative. Nor does it make sense to place children in instructional materials on the basis of such a simplistic, quantity-type scoring procedure.

Counting whole-word omissions and insertions seldom adds significant information toward the decision as to which level is appropriate for instructing a student in reading (D'Angelo, 1983). Furthermore, both repetitions and hesitations are used primarily to allow time for readers to think (Goodman, 1969). Again, scoring procedures should not penalize positive miscues. Miscues that *consistently* provide reading educators with highly useful information are these:

> *Self-corrections* (usually showing that two or more of the cueing systems —syntactic, semantic, graphophonic, and schematic—are interacting)
>
> *Defaults* (showing that the student is afraid of attempting the word for fear of making a mistake, or that he is doing very little predicting, or that he does not recognize essential sight words, phonograms, vowel patterns, or suffixes)
>
> *Substitutions* (demonstrating comprehension when the miscue is relevant to the author's message or has the same meaning; demonstrating lack of comprehension *monitoring* when the miscue is a nonsense word, a word that doesn't fit the author's meaning, or a word of a different syntactic class). Substitutions also provide information about the reader's use of graphophonic cues. By examining the graphic similarity between the author's word and the reader's word, we can get some idea of how effectively she is noticing graphophonic patterns.

What about Questions? Their Use in Placing Children

Studies on comprehension questions indicate that they are often not reliable indicators of how well a child has understood a selection during an informal reading inventory (McKenna, 1983). One set of questions on a selection will place a child at the instructional level; another set of questions on the same selection will place her at the frustration or independent level. Furthermore, they are more likely to measure *memory*—of what she has read, of what the teacher pronounced, of answers to similar questions, or of prior knowledge. As research indicates, "in many cases the failure to perform well in the comprehension measures is the result of the failure to remember" (Johnson, Kress, & Pikulski, 1987, p. 54). And as Farr and Carey (1986) remind us, psychological studies show us that students can remember nonsense material without understanding a thing! Therefore, it does not seem advisable to base a child's instructional level solely on her responses to questions—even though we *call* these questions a measure of "comprehension."

A Quality Score That Is Simple and Practical

So what are we left with? If traditional quantitative scores don't fit our research knowledge about miscues, and if questions are often shabby indicators of comprehension, what should we use? Some say, "Don't use questions at all. Just have the child recall what he's read." Fine . . . But we're still measuring primarily memory rather than comprehension.

You're right. There is another way, and that's to study those miscues. Find out what they tell you about the child's concepts and strategies for each selection. But if you would like to have an actual score to use (let's say, for communicating with parents or principals—or just for your own security), I'll recommend one that's worked very well for my students and me.

I call it the poor reader score, or the PR score, and it's used like this. For each selection:

1. Count the number of miscues that show poor reader concepts or strategies. These most often (but not always) show up as defaults, as meaningless substitutions, and as nonsense substitutions (sometimes referred to as mispronunciations).

2. Divide the number of poor reader miscues by the number of words in the passage. Change this to a percent.

3. Consider a PR score of more than 5 percent to be an indication of a passage that is too difficult for the child. This passage, then, would represent frustration level rather than instructional level.

4. Consider a PR score of 1 percent or less to be an indication of a passage that is too easy for instruction and just right for independent reading. This passage, then, would represent the independent level rather than the instructional level.

5. Consider a PR score of from 2 percent up through 5 percent to be an indication of probable instructional level.

This method of scoring has been in a field-trial stage for several years and has been formally tested in the Portland Public Schools. Our results indicate that the PR score is both quicker and more accurate than quantitative scores and as accurate as more elaborate scoring systems. But again, let me urge you, whether or not you use a scoring system, to rely primarily on your careful examination of a child's oral reading miscues. This examination should allow your intuitive thinking, rather than a magical score, to help you make a wise decision. In fact, in time experienced teachers can do this without the use of a tape recorder.

Using the Cloze and Maze Techniques for Determining Instructional Levels

In previous chapters we've talked about using the cloze technique as an instructional device. Some teachers and researchers also use it as a group administered test for determining students' reading levels. Rather than administer an informal reading inventory to one child at a time, they give a large group of children the same selection to read *silently.* Usually this selection omits every fifth* word, and each student is to write down the exact word he thinks is missing. If he guesses at least 40 percent of the exact words missing, or 80 percent of the appropriate synonyms, the selection is considered representative of the instructional level for the child. Zintz (1972) recommends a more refined set of percentages:

Over 50 percent exact guesses = independent reading level

40 to 50 percent = instructional reading level

Fewer than 40 percent = frustration level

The cloze procedure has distinct advantages and disadvantages when compared to an IRI. Perhaps the major advantage is that it can be administered to a group rather than to one individual at a time. The children merely write in the missing words, and the teacher ignores misspellings when she scores each child's

---

*Sometimes the seventh or tenth word, depending upon the test maker.

inserted words. Another advantage is the way it emphasizes context cues more than graphophonic cues. On the other hand, it does not provide an easy way to carry on miscue analysis, which would allow you to ascertain reading strategies and reading concepts. Moreover, for this approach to be reliable, the selections must be several hundred words long. And, not least of all, scoring a cloze-type test can sometimes be horrendous, mainly because of children's handwriting and spelling when under stress.

To compensate for the scoring problem, some schools and school districts (New York, for example) have used a maze-type test instead of a cloze-type test. With the maze technique, children are given the usual blanks every so many words, but instead of writing in their word-guess, they select from multiple-choice responses. This is much more efficient, of course, but far less valid, since it requires more testlike behavior than actual reading behavior. Actual reading behavior requires one to predict the next word without the benefit of multiple-choice options.

Nevertheless, in spite of the disadvantages of cloze and maze techniques, they are a reasonably *efficient* way of quickly placing *intermediate grade* children in basal readers, and they work well for a "first-try-placement" procedure. When a child and instructional book don't seem to match, however (which you'll be able to determine in a week or two), I strongly recommend that you administer an informational reading inventory to that child and study the miscues at each level.

I'll end my discussion of cloze by presenting the opinions of some of the evaluation experts in the reading field:

> The cloze procedure has much to recommend it: it has been subjected to a substantial amount of research . . . and it can be used to evaluate large numbers of students in a relatively brief period of time. [It] cannot, however, yield the rich diagnostic information that can be derived from an IRI. (Johnson, Kress, & Pikulski, 1987, p. 7)

> Cloze performance correlates very highly with multiple choice test performance. . . . It provides roughly the same assessment as multiple choice tests. . . . Since we know there are problems with multiple choice tests [however], do we want to employ a device which correlates very highly with those tests? . . . To make decisions based on the use of cloze only is to make a less than informed choice. (Farr & Carey, 1986, pp. 36–37)

SUMMARY OF MAIN IDEAS

☐ The three most practical evaluation concerns of the reading teacher are to assess (1) children's attitudes toward reading, (2) their concepts and strategies of reading, and (3) their levels of reading. This can be done through informal testing and "kid watching."

☐ An excellent way of determining children's concepts and strategies of reading is to use miscue analysis.

☐ A child's concepts and strategies of reading can also be assessed through his writing and through his reading of the teacher's responses to his writing.

☐ A student's miscues on an informal reading inventory should be examined for quality rather than quantity.

☐ Children should learn to read with books that are not too difficult or too easy. This means that teachers who use basal readers need to place children in the correct basal, and that all reading teachers, no matter what medium of instruction they use, need to have a good idea of each child's instructional level.

☐ Recommendations from children's previous teachers should be only one source of information in making a decision as to instructional levels. There are many reasons for not relying exclusively on such recommendations.

☐ Standardized tests are norm referenced. They are valid only to the extent that the norm group represents your students. The group administered type is fairly accurate in comparing groups, but it is not accurate in comparing individual students. Teachers should *not* use group administered standardized test scores as the sole determiner of a child's placement in materials for instruction.

☐ Getting "every child up to grade level" is a goal that matches neither reality nor the meaning of "grade level." "Grade level" refers to an *average* score of a norm group. By definition, some children will be above and some below average.

☐ For children above the third grade, the "cloze" or "maze" technique can be used to provide rough first-time estimates of instructional levels.

APPLICATION EXPERIENCES FOR THE TEACHER EDUCATION CLASS

A. *What's Your Opinion?* Use the ideas in the textbook and your own experiences to justify your decision.
   1. Assessing students' reading concepts and strategies is more important than assessing their reading levels.
   2. Miscue analysis takes too much time for a busy teacher.
   3. Placing a child in instructional materials that are too hard to read is worse than placing her in materials that are too easy.
   4. Children should be placed in basal readers and reading groups according to their parents' wishes.
   5. The previous teacher has the best idea of a child's reading level. After all, she spent almost a year with that child.
   6. Standardized reading tests have the advantage of being scientifically developed and scored. They are an excellent indicator of each child's reading level and meet many criteria for helpful diagnosis and evaluation.
   7. Getting every child up to grade level is a goal that matches neither reality nor the meaning of "grade level."
   8. A child's miscues on an informal reading inventory should be examined for quality rather than quantity.

B. *Miscue Analysis and IRI:* Using Figure 11.2, determine, in four different ways, fifth-grader Victor's instructional level on the fourth-grade selection that he read.
   1. Determine whether this selection represents his instructional level. Use a quantitative way by subtracting his 22 miscues from the 182 words in the selection, then dividing this by 182. (Instructional level is about 92 to 98 percent words, 60 to 90 percent questions.)

Harriet Tubman never dreamed that she would become

famous. She had been born a slave and could neither read

nor write. When she was thirteen a slave boss struck her

on the head with a heavy iron weight. For the rest of her

life she carried an ugly scar.

She escaped from slavery and began helping others to

escape. People called her Moses because she would wait

outside a slave cabin and sing a little song, "Go down Moses."

It was a signal to get ready. She had come to help them

escape.

After a while she was so well known that the slave

owners offered a large reward for her capture. They offered

forty thousand dollars in gold for Harriet Tubman, whether

dead or alive.

One day she was sitting at a railroad station. Two men

walked by. She knew they were looking at her. She listened

carefully and overheard them talking about the reward. Quietly

she took out a book and pretended to read. They walked by

again and she heard one say, "That's not her. That can't be

Moses. Moses can't read."*

1. *Inferential:* (Asked after first paragraph) What is this going to be about? (I'm not sure. About a slave.)

2. *Literal:* Why did she have an ugly scar? (Her boss hit her.) What did he hit her with? (His pipe?)

3. *Inferential:* Did she help slaves or convicts to escape? (Slaves.) How do you know? (Because there were slave owners trying to catch her.)

4. *Literal:* How much was the reward for her capture? (Forty thousand dollars in gold.)

5. *Inferential:* Why did they offer so much money? (Because they were rich, I guess.) Any other reason? (They wanted to catch her real bad.)

6. *Literal:* What did she do to escape from the men who were looking for her? (She tried to look like she was reading.)

*Colin Dunkeld, Portland Informal Reading Inventory, Form P, Page 6, Unpublished Manuscript, Portland State University, School of Education.

FIGURE 11.2
Transcription of Victor's miscues

2. Determine whether this selection represents his instructional level in a combined quantitative/qualitative way. Use exactly the same method as in number 1, but this time don't count Victor's self-corrections (count only 20 miscues).

3. Determine whether this selection represents his instructional level by using only miscue analysis and your intuition.

4. Determine whether this selection represents his instructional level by using the "poor reader score." Count only those miscues that a poor reader would make, and divide this number by the total words of 182. (Instructional level is about 2 percent through 5 percent).

Now decide whether you think this selection represents Victor's frustration, instructional, or independent reading level.

FIELD EXPERIENCES IN THE ELEMENTARY SCHOOL CLASSROOM

A. Using a tape recorder, administer an informal reading inventory to an elementary student. Write a professional report, describing the following:
  1. Miscue data on three selections (similar to Figure 11.1)
  2. PR scores on the same three selections
  3. An assessment of the student's concepts of what reading is, using several miscues as examples
  4. An assessment of the student's reading strategies, using several miscues as examples
  5. An estimate of the student's instructional level, using both miscue data and PR scores as justification

B. Administer a phonics test to an elementary student, without the use of a tape recorder. Write a professional report describing your procedures, results, and conclusions. See Appendix H for sample phonics tests or use a phonics test provided by the classroom teacher.

C. Create a cloze test and administer it to three or more students. From a basal reader or other set of teaching materials find three selections of text, about 100 to 300 words each. One should be at the same grade level you are teaching, one a grade below, and one a grade above. Delete every fifth word, starting with the second sentence of each selection. Number the blanks that you create, and have the students number their paper and write a word for each blank you've created. Score and interpret your results, using the criteria on page 388. Write a professional report on your procedures, results, and conclusions.

REFERENCES AND SUGGESTED READING

Aasen, H. B. (1959). A summer's growth in reading. *Elementary School Journal, 60,* 70–74.

Baumann, J. F., & Stevenson, J. A. (1982). Understanding standardized reading achievement test scores. *The Reading Teacher, 35,* 648–654.

Beebe, M. J. (1979–80). The effect of different types of substitution miscues on reading. *Reading Research Quarterly, 15,* 324–336.

Betts, E. A. (1946). *Foundations of reading instruction.* New York: American Book Co.

Bond, G. L., & Dykstra, R. (1967). The cooperative research program in first-grade reading instruction. *Reading Research Quarterly, 2,* 5–142.

Bradley, J. M., & Ames, W. S. (1976). The influence of intrabook readability variation on oral reading performance. *Journal of Educational Research, 70,* 101–105.

Brown, L. L., & Sherbenou, R. J. (1981). A comparison of teacher perceptions of student reading ability, reading performance, and classroom behavior. *The Reading Teacher, 34,* 557–560.

Clay, M. (1968). A syntactic analysis of reading errors. *Journal of Verbal Learning and Verbal Behavior, 7,* 434–438.

D'Angelo, K. (1982). Correction behavior: Implications for reading instruction. *The Reading Teacher, 35,* 395–398.

D'Angelo, K. (1983). Insertion and omission miscues of good and poor readers. *The Reading Teacher, 36,* 778–782.

Dykstra, R. (1968). Summary of the second-grade phase of the cooperative research program in primary reading instruction. *Reading Research Quarterly, 1,* 49–70.

Ekwall, E. E., & English, J. (1971). *Use of the polygraph to determine elementary school students' frustration level.* Final Report, Project #OG078. Washington, DC: U.S. Dept. of Health, Education, and Welfare.

Elgart, D. B. (1978). Oral reading, silent reading, and listening comprehension: A comparative study. *Journal of Reading Behavior, 10,* 203–207.

Englert, C. S., & Semmel, M. I. (1981). The relationship of oral reading substitution miscues to comprehension. *The Reading Teacher, 35,* 273–280.

Farr, R., & Carey, R. F. (1986). *Reading: What can be measured?* Newark, DE: International Reading Association.

Flood, J., & Lapp, D. (1987). Types of writing in basal readers and assessment tests: An imperfect match. *The Reading Teacher, 40,* 880–883.

Goodman, K. (1986). *What's whole in whole language?* Portsmouth, NH: Heinemann.

Goodman, K. S. (1969). Analysis of oral reading miscues: Applied psycholinguistics. *Reading Research Quarterly, 5,* 9–30.

Gunning, T. G. (1982). Wrong level test: Wrong information. *The Reading Teacher, 35,* 902–905.

Haller, E. J., & Waterman, M. (1985). The criteria of group assignments. *The Reading Teacher, 38,* 772–781.

Harris, L. A., & Lalik, R. M. (1987). Teacher's use of informal reading inventories: An example of school constraints. *The Reading Teacher, 40,* 624–630.

Johnson, M. S., Kress, R. A., & Pikulski, J. J. (1987). *Informal reading inventories.* Newark, DE: International Reading Association.

Johnston, P. H. (1982). *Reading comprehension assessment: A cognitive basis.* Newark, DE: International Reading Association.

McKenna, M. C. (1983). Informal reading inventories: A review of the issues. *The Reading Teacher, 36,* 670–679.

Pikulski, J. J., & Shanahan, T. (Eds.). (1982). *Approaches to the informal evaluation of reading.* Newark, DE: International Reading Association.

Schwartz, J. I. (1977). Standardizing a reading test. *The Reading Teacher, 30,* 346–368.

Silvaroli, N. J. (1979). *Classroom reading inventory.* Minneapolis, MN: William C. Brown Company.

Zintz, M. V. (1972). *Corrective reading.* Minneapolis, MN: William C. Brown Company.

The Content Areas: Continued Growth in Reading and Study Skills

========== CHAPTER PREVIEW ==========

Between third grade and twelfth, a student is expected to read at least 30,000 pages from science textbooks, social studies textbooks, math textbooks, literary anthologies, laboratory manuals, and so on. Let's imagine that each one of those pages is a stepping stone placed across a wide lake. If we place those stepping stones three feet apart, a student could still reach the other side even if the lake were 17 miles wide!

That's a lot of reading! Yet it's just a 50-yard dash compared to what those marathoners have to read who continue on through college, graduate school, and a lifetime profession that requires daily reading to keep up to date. Becoming a better, more efficient, more flexible, and more reflective reader is a learning process that may end at

one's funeral, but certainly not at one's primary school graduation. This is why nearly every teacher becomes a reading teacher whether he wants to be or not. Nearly every subject that children and adults study today in our society must be partially learned through the process of reading.

Sometimes parents and teachers alike assume that once you teach a child the basic skills of reading, she should be able to read anything—a science text, a math text, whatever. Not so, of course. To take a simple illustration: Even something as easy to use as a telephone book requires special skills that need to be learned. Tammie may be able to read a sixth-grade basal reader, a library book about dinosaurs, and a long report on flying saucers that she wrote by herself, but still fail miserably in finding the telephone number of a good eye doctor whose office is not too far away.

Every type of reading material, as well as every content area, has its own peculiarities that have to be learned. Each content area has its own special vocabulary (and jargon), its own style of structuring sentences, its own logical organization, its own required reading speed, and its own assumptions about what experiences the reader has already had. In assuming what experiences the reader has encountered, the author can so often go wrong. Writers cannot know what experiences every reader has had, nor can they accurately guess what schemata readers have invented on the basis of their experiences. Thus, while helping children learn how to deal with this problem, teach-

ers need to understand why content area material is so much more difficult than experience stories, or basal reader stories, or most library books. They need to know how to develop children's schemata so that they can cope with such difficult materials, learn to read different materials at different rates, learn to skim or scan for just the right information and no more, and, especially, learn to read material aggressively for specific purposes.

Most adults would think it unwise to send a child on a long, difficult journey with only a map and no instruction on how to use a map. In the same way, it is unwise to send a child through the communication maze he is expected to get through during his life without first explaining to him some of the keys to the map.

Reading is not an end in itself; it is a means to . . . many ends.
—Arnold Davis

Most teachers would agree that the primary goal of education is to teach students how to learn on their own.
—Kenneth Graham and Alan Robinson

Content areas? I don't know what they are. . . . I don't even know what part of the school they're in.
—Ned, a fifth-grader

THE DIFFICULTIES OF CONTENT AREA READING

There are at least five reasons why kids have trouble reading textbooks in science, social studies, and other content areas. Once you understand those reasons, you can make a difference to your students in how successfully they read content area materials. The five reasons are these:

1. Expository style is a lot tougher to follow than the structure of stories.
2. The vocabulary is more abstract.
3. The sentence structure is more elaborate.
4. The nonnarrative paragraph structure requires a different language schema.

5. The imagery created by textbook writers is often lacking and needs to be filled in by the reader.

Let's talk about each one of these five difficulties and what teachers can do about them.

DIFFICULTY WITH EXPOSITORY STRUCTURES

Many educators today feel that the expository (explanatory) style of textbooks is the most serious obstacle to fluent and meaningful reading of content area materials. Even more of an obstacle than the difficult vocabulary in these materials!

For this reason they feel that teachers need to be much more concerned about explaining the nature of the expository form of writing, which differs so much from the story schema that children carry around in their heads. You see, in this country at least, students have consistently done better on the vocabulary part of the standardized tests than they've done on the so-called comprehension part—you know, the part in which they have to read short selections, then answer multiple-choice questions about them. To make the problem even more serious for kids, standardized tests usually have a much greater percentage of expository passages than basal reader programs do. Thus, kids have had much more practice with stories than they've had with informational text.

Fortunately, research shows us that children's skill in comprehending exposition can be strengthened when they are given knowledge of how authors use certain "structures" or ways of organizing and presenting information (Paratore & Indrisano, 1987). With this in mind, let me first explain more of the nature of expository structures. Then I'd like to show you some ways of teaching children to recognize and deal with the expository structures as they read social studies, science, and other content area materials.

More on the Nature of Children's Difficulties with Exposition

By the time they reach third grade, most children appear to be quite good at predicting what's going to happen next *in a story*. Their past experience provides them with a "top-level" schema about stories: There's going to be a setting, a main character, a conflict, and a resolution. When third-graders are confronted with reading *content area* materials, they lack the kind of top-level schema that has helped them understand stories.

There's a vast difference between story text and expository text. Expository (explanatory) passages usually give the reader no character to identify with, no setting, no conflict, no reaction to the conflict. Instead of leading the reader through a familiar and predictable structure, the writer instead tries to lead him through a mass of information, which must seem to a child like a jungle, full of strange and frightening animals. Instead of encountering a main character or two, he encounters a series of abstract *ideas*. Instead of watching a character face a conflict, the reader himself must face strange monsters such as comparisons, contrasts, cause and effect, or, most hideous of all, the nine-headed water serpents called "lists." No, the schema he has for *stories* can't protect him from the "monsters of exposition."

To put it another way, *content area* reading is a very different ballgame from reading fiction. The teacher can't expect children to move from reading stories to reading social studies and science textbooks without a great deal of guidance. True, more and more basal readers provide informational articles as well as stories, which helps the transition to some extent, but it doesn't seem to be enough. Many children have had several years of training in story schema by the time they reach third grade. It is unreasonable to think they will not need several years of training in expository schema. They will need to gradually learn how authors make comparisons and contrasts, show cause and effect, and develop main ideas through details.

Although we can often turn children loose to capture the butterflies called stories, we should not turn them loose with a butterfly net to capture the monsters of exposition. The teacher needs to provide much more guidance and protection, leading children through a textbook assignment step by step, showing them *how* to separate cause from effect, how to make visual images of lists, and so on. There needs to be much more talking and writing about *informational* things, not just story things; for example, "How can we compare these two things? How can we contrast these two things to show that they're different? What caused this to happen? Why?" Through *talking* about informational matters, and through *writing* informational passages themselves, children can get a better feel for the informational language they are expected to *read*.

The Major Expository Structures That Authors Use

To assist children with content area material, you'll need to recognize readily the main expository modes that authors use. I'll list them for you in the order of the difficulty that most children seem to have with them (Piccolo, 1987):

1. *Sequence:* The author is trying to tell the reader how to do or make something. I call it the "Do It My Way" structure.
2. *Enumeration:* The author lists things and usually tells a little about each one. My name? The "List Monster." (Notice how you're "trapped" by one right now! You feel almost compelled to keep going until you reach the bitter end of the thing.)
3. *Cause and effect:* The author presents one or more effects or results and provides the reader with one or more causes for them. The "How Come" structure.
4. *Description:* The author wants to tell you what something is or looks like. We authors sometimes do this in more detail than readers wish to receive.
5. *Problem/solution:* The author presents a problem or two, then gives you his or her solution to the whole mess.

6. *Comparison/contrast:* The author tells you how things are alike and different—usually more how they're alike because that's a lot easier for the author to remember.

Helping Your Students with Expository Structures

Whew! Now that you've made it through that enumeration structure ("The List"), I'm going to switch to a problem/solution passage. Ready? Here goes. The problem is this: You, the teacher, might know what these six expository structures are, but how do you get the students to recognize them? Well, they're not always easy to spot, especially when we authors sometimes make a slurry of the different structures—blending a problem/solution structure, for example, with a cause/effect structure. We don't do this, by the way, because authors are ornery people. It's just that in order to make things nonrepetitive and interesting—or in order to write the way we speak—we can't limit ourselves to only pure and unadulterated expository structures.

What this means for the teacher, then, is this (here come the solutions): (1) You'll need to find some fairly pure examples of the six types from your social studies and science textbooks so that your students (still neophytes in the literacy club) can see what you're talking about. (Don't worry, I won't insult you by doing this to *you*.) (2) You'll probably want to teach expository structures by showing them how to produce them in writing. The writing method tends to be more effective than merely explanations and examples (McGee & Richgels, 1985; Piccolo, 1987).

The Write Way to Teach Expository Structures

Figure 12.1 shows a type of "graphic organizer" that works well in helping children learn to write their own expository structures. Before you continue on with the text, see if you can write (at least in your mind) a simple paragraph, using this cause and effect structure.

All right, now you've seen how easy it is to write an expository paragraph by using a graphic organizer (given to you by someone else). Graphic organizers like this one are recommended by many educators, including Piccolo (1987) and McGee and Richgels (1985). The steps the three researchers have used with children, slightly modified to fit my own teaching experience, are these:

1. Find some rather pure examples of the expository structures you wish to teach (at least two examples of each).
2. Produce a graphic organizer for each.
3. Model the use of one of the graphic organizers by writing a paragraph or two with the group, using the organizer as the basis for information and format. For example:

Camels are still ridden by the people of the desert today. They are well suited for carrying people and heavy burdens for long distances in hot, dry places because

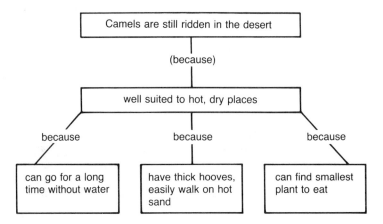

FIGURE 12.1
A sample graphic organizer for writing a cause and effect passage. (Reprinted by permission of *The Reading Teacher* from an article by McGee, L. M. & Richgels, D. J. in the April 1985 issue.

they can go for a long time without water. As a result of their thick hooves, camels can easily walk on the hot sand. Finally, camels can live off the desert because they are able to find even the smallest plant to eat hidden in the desert soil. (McGee and Richgels, 1985)

4. Now see if you and your students can make it even more interesting by making the first sentence a "real grabber"; for example, "You and I would travel by car across a desert, but not some people." You might also make it more interesting by adding some information based on the teacher's knowledge or the knowledge of the students—such as the fact that camels can carry water in their hump.

5. Show them the original passage that you used for making the graphic organizer. Have them compare it with the one they wrote. (Usually they'll say that theirs is more interesting.)

6. Label the type of expository structure or "explanation mode" that you've just used with them, and have a second sample of the structure for them to read and discuss.

7. Continue this process with the other structures, and through the next few weeks have them continue to apply what they've learned to new reading and writing situations.

8. Use the structures to help you think of prereading and guided reading questions. Here are some examples:

Cause/effect: Why do you think plants turn brown?

Comparison/contrast: How do evergreens differ from deciduous trees? How are they the same?

Problem/solution: If so many trees are being removed to make way for housing, what can people do to replenish the oxygen lost to the atmosphere?

Lists: Before you read this, let's make a list of those things that *you* think are necessary for the health of plants.

DIFFICULTY WITH VOCABULARY

Perhaps second in difficulty to expository structures is vocabulary. All the content areas have their own specialized vocabulary, sometimes referred to as "jargon." It's difficult to talk about the social studies, for instance, without referring to the word *culture,* or to talk about the natural sciences without using the word *energy.* In mathematics we speak of *sets* and *operations.* To comprehend what they read in the content areas, children must quickly face these types of specialized words and be able to pronounce and understand them.

What Teachers Can Do

In Chapter 6, we discussed how children need to acquire vocabulary through both nonverbal and verbal experiences. As you may recall, we examined the hypothetical case of children learning the phrase *rozaga hunt.* Using Dale's Cone of Experience as our model, we had David going on an actual rozaga hunt in order to get the deepest understanding of the phrase. Unfortunately, neither school districts nor teachers can afford to explain content area terms that well. They do have the rest of Dale's Cone, however, for inspiration. Vocabulary can be developed through contrived experiences, dramatizations, role playing, demonstrations, field trips, exhibits, television, films, recordings, pictures, dictionaries, and discussions related to the students' own experiences.

Naturally, you'll want to engage them in some of these vocabulary/concept experiences *before* they read so you can stimulate and develop their schemata—those hooks of the mind that grab and support new ideas your students confront as they read.

Another idea you may want to consider from Chapter 6 is semantic mapping (see page 206 for a sample). Semantic mapping can be used for any content area term that lends itself to categories. The word *government,* for instance, can inspire such categories as these:

Types of government: democratic, socialistic, communistic, autocratic, plutocratic, and so on

Government buildings: capitol, statehouse, legislative hall, county courthouse, city hall, and so on

Heads of state: presidents, kings, queens, prime ministers, and so on

Representative bodies: Senate, Congress, state representatives, city council, and so on

It's usually best to let the information come from the students at first. Then have them read in order to change or add to their group semantic map (or to their individually developed one).

Perhaps the most basic strategy most children need to learn for dealing with specialized words in content areas is *not* to ignore them. This tends to be a strong habit for some children by the time they reach the sixth grade—a habit that carries right on into adulthood. Their thinking, when you talk to them about it, seems to be something like this: "Oh, it's just a word we use a lot in science." If they can pronounce it, they are often content with that much success. Because of this attitude, it's particularly important for teachers to prepare children for reading a content area selection by discussing key words ahead of time. The word *energy*, for instance, may be placed on tagboard in sentences incorporating many context clues:

> The horse had enough *energy* to pull a heavy wagon.
>
> The chemical *energy* in a car battery is enough to run a starting motor.
>
> By turning on the toaster you can change electrical *energy* into heat *energy* and toast your bread.
>
> A doorknob changes muscle *energy* into mechanical *energy*.

Then, after they've read the sentences, have them discuss what they think energy is. After a brief discussion, have each child write down her own definition in one simple sentence. Then she can look up the word in a dictionary, glossary, or science book to see how close she came.

DIFFICULTY WITH SENTENCE STRUCTURES

As children are given more and more content area materials to read, the number of dependent (subordinate) clauses and phrases that they must face increases as well. Notice the dependent clauses and phrases (in italics) in the following sentences:

> Social studies: The Zambezi is a river in Southern Africa, *flowing about 1,650 miles southeast through Rhodesia and Mozambique to the Indian Ocean.*
>
> Science: Moisture and heat are two agents of chemical change *that can create compounds from two or more elements.*
>
> Mathematics: *Because of the commutative principle,* the order in which certain operations are performed will not change the result.

The greater number of subordinate clauses and phrases is just one of many types of alterations and expansions of sentence patterns that make content area reading more difficult than many basal reader stories or library books. Let me contrast the two styles for you:

> *Exposition:* Scientists all over the world are wondering why people believe in the bigfoot in spite of the lack of evidence for its existence.
>
> *Fiction:* "Why?" Tom said. "Why do so many people still believe in the bigfoot? There's hardly a scrap of evidence for their existence."

Sentences in expository text, as you can see, not only tend to be longer than sentences in fiction. They also tend to sound very different from the way people normally talk.

Understanding Sentence Structures

Odegaard and May (1972) and also Noyce and Christie (1981) found that when teachers helped their elementary school students become more familiar with written sentence structures, the children's writing not only became much longer; it also became more fluent and creative. In addition, they hypothesized that increased confidence in the use of sentence structures in oral and written language caused children to *read* with greater fluency and understanding. Their technique for developing greater fluency and confidence will probably work equally well with fiction and exposition (although to my knowledge no one has yet determined this with experimental research).

In a moment I'll describe the techniques that these teacher-researchers used for achieving such results. But first you will need to understand something about sentence structures. You already know about the importance of schemata and the importance of a sizable vocabulary. But a mature reader relies on more than schemata and vocabulary to understand text. Like the musician who reads musical phrases as well as notes and measures, the good reader reads not only letters and words, but sentences as well. José may know all the words in a sentence and still not be able to read it with comprehension. Why is this? Simply because the pattern of the words doesn't make sense to him; that is, he is not used to that particular order or arrangement of words.

Ted, for example, was quite capable of reading "He found the city there." When he was later confronted with the sentence, "There he found the city," however, he said it didn't make sense. He could read each word all right, but the sentence had no meaning for him. Not having spoken this pattern alteration before, his vocalization of the printed sentence provided him with no memory clues. It was "a silly sentence" as far as he was concerned. Research indicates that this boy's problem is not an isolated instance: Reading comprehension and sentence-structure understanding are significantly related.

Studies by Pavlak (1973), Reid (1970), and Ruddell (1965) all demonstrate that reading comprehension depends to a great extent on the similarity between the sentence patterns in the reading material and the sentence patterns children normally use in their oral language. For example, if Tommy is not used to using the passive voice in his speech, his comprehension will suffer when he is faced with a sentence like this one: "The town was flooded by the river." Since Tommy is used to using the active voice, he would have less trouble if the sentence were written, "The river flooded the town." Other studies by Gibbons (1941), MacKinnon (1959), and Strickland (1963) also show the strong relationship between sentence structure and reading comprehension.

Several researchers, in fact, have presented evidence that complex syntactic structures can interfere with children's reading comprehension (Bormuth et al., 1970; Fagan, 1971; Richek, 1976). One of these difficult patterns has a name more difficult than the pattern: the "subordinate sentence, tense shift, *if* clause structure." For example, *If you had a camel, you would ride it.* Another difficult syntax pattern is called the "relative clause without deletion structure," as in *The man who was driving the car was the king.* A third difficult pattern is called the "subordinate sentence, simultaneous structure," as in *When I came in, my brother yelled.*

The fact that reading comprehension depends on even more than vocabulary and schemata development makes it necessary for teachers to understand certain aspects of the structure of our language. Linguists have discovered, for example, that nearly all English sentences can be "generated" (created) by using or transforming a small number of basic sentence patterns. Six patterns that are common in materials written for elementary school children can be found in the following "historical account":

> The coyote was in the barn. The man came quickly. The man looked angry. The coyote was his enemy. The man shot the coyote. The man gave his wife the tail.

The six patterns are these:

Pattern	*Example Sentence*
1. Noun + *Be* verb + Prepositional phrase	The coyote was in the barn.
2. Noun + Intransitive verb + Adverb	The man came quickly.
3. Noun + Linking verb + Adjective	The man looked angry.
4. Noun + Linking verb + Noun	The coyote was his enemy.
5. Noun + Transitive verb + Noun	The man shot the coyote.
6. Noun + Transitive verb + Noun + Noun	The man gave his wife the tail.

Most children have listened to these patterns so often that they arrive at school already able to recognize them reasonably well. These patterns can be altered and expanded in countless ways, however, and this is where children may have trouble. If they are not accustomed to hearing particular alterations or expansions, many sentences may not make any sense to them in print.

Just hearing the pattern alterations or expansions on TV often doesn't seem to be enough. To make them part of their speaking and reading tools, children need to hear themselves utter the alterations and expansions and need to be reinforced or assisted by others. In a home in which verbal fluency is considered highly desirable, this type of assistance occurs quite often. The infant says, for example, "Daddy shoes," and the mother spontaneously replies, "Do you see daddy's shoes? I see his shoes, too." Thus the child learns in a natural way to refine and alter a basic sentence pattern. In a home in which verbal fluency is not considered highly desirable, such reinforcement and teaching seldom take place.

For many children, then, the teacher must provide oral language experiences that complement and supplement those received at home.

What Teachers Can Do

Much of the teaching related to comprehension of sentence patterns, alterations, and expansions can be integrated with regular instruction in reading or with the learning experiences the teacher instigates in her language arts program—even as early as first grade. Suppose, for example, that the teacher and children were reading a story from a first-grade basal reader and came to this passage:

Soon the storm came.

The people ran into their houses.

By asking the children to think of other ways to say each sentence, the teacher can help them become more aware of various patterns, alterations, and expansions of sentences. The first sentence, for instance, could be modified to read, "The storm came soon" or "The storm soon came"; or it could be expanded to say, "The terrible storm soon came." The second sentence could be changed to, "Into their houses the people ran" or "Into their houses ran the frightened people." The two sentences combined could read, "Because the storm was coming, the people ran into their houses." Once children get used to this procedure, such "incidental" learning need take no more than an additional minute in an occasional reading lesson. This same procedure can be used with upper-grade children, many of whom delight in creating and writing interesting alterations and expansions. Some common pattern alterations and expansions are given in Table 12.1.

More direct instruction can be incorporated into a reading/writing program—although direct instruction works better, I have found, when oral sentence modifying comes first, with reading and writing coming later:

Step 1: Introduce the children to a set of model sentences. Do this first orally by reading the model sentences to them. (Later, in the same lesson, you can present them in writing, provided they are reading at the first-grade level or above.) You might start with Pattern 5, shown below, since that seems to be the one with which most children are quite familiar:

The boy ate the apple.

The girl threw the apple.

The horse bit the apple.

The man smashed the apple.

Step 2: Have them "make up sentences that sound like these."* This should be done orally at this point. One or two written sentences might be required from the children at the end of the lesson, if you wish to evaluate how well each child comprehends the pattern (but go easy on this or you'll kill their interest). If a child states a sentence that doesn't fit the pattern, simply say something like this: "You're close, Jerry. You're almost in the pattern club, but not quite. Listen some more and then try again in a few minutes." In this way, all they have to think of at first are a simple subject and verb.

---

*Note: It's a good idea to accept other words for *The,* such as *A, His, Her, That.* It's also a good idea to accept other words for *apple.* But don't accept verbs that aren't in the past tense; just say, "I'll call on you again, after you've changed the third word in your sentence." Don't accept plural nouns.

TABLE 12.1
Some common pattern alterations and expansions of the sentence, "The man shot the coyote."

	Alterations	
1. present	The man shoots the coyote.	
2. future	The man will shoot the coyote.	
3. present perfect	The man has shot the coyote.	
4. past perfect	The man had shot the coyote.	
5. future perfect	The man will have shot the coyote.	
6. progressive	The man is shooting the coyote.	
7. infinitive	The man had to shoot the coyote.	
8. affirmative	The man did shoot the coyote.	
9. plural subject	A man shoots. Men shoot.	
10. passive	The coyote was shot by the man.	
11. pronoun	He shot him.	
12. Did?	Did the man shoot the coyote?	
13. negative	The man did not shoot the coyote.	
14. What?	What did the man shoot? The coyote?	
15. When?	When did the man shoot the coyote?	
16. There	A coyote is here. There is a coyote here.	
17. sequence	The man came quickly. Quickly the man came.	

	Expansions	
1. adjective	The angry man shot the coyote.	
2. prepositional phrase	The man with the gun shot the coyote in the head.	
3. adverb	The man shot the coyote quickly.	
4. compound subject	The man and the boy shot the coyote.	
5. compound predicate	The man shot and killed the coyote.	
6. relative clause	The man who had a gun shot the coyote.	
7. compound sentence	The coyote was here and the man came quickly.	
8. dependent clause	Because the coyote was his enemy, the man shot the coyote.	
9. *unless* clause	Unless the man shoots quickly, the coyote will get away.	
10. multiple expansion	If the man saw his enemy, the coyote, he would shoot it.	

Then you can have them modify the sentences they have created—first by changing *The* to words like *this, that, your, my, his, her,* and *a;* then by changing *apple* to words like *ball, rider, car,* and so on. ("That horse bit his rider.")

Step 3: After they are all in the pattern club, show them the model sentences in writing or read them to the children one at a time again. After each one, have them "listen to how I change it." For example:

The boy ate his apple. . . . The boy eats his apple.

The girl threw the ball. . . . The girl throws the ball.

After you've read two or three of these pairs of sentences, read them another one and challenge them to "change it in the same way." Like this:

TEACHER: The horse bit his rider.
CHILD: The horse bites his rider.

This part of the exercise, then, becomes an opportunity for children to get into a "new pattern club."

Step 4: After they are in the new pattern club, challenge them to get into one more pattern club. This time expand your pattern rather than alter it. Like this:

TEACHER: The boy ate his apple. . . . The hungry boy ate his apple.
TEACHER: The girl threw the ball. . . . The happy girl threw the ball.
TEACHER: The horse bit his rider.
CHILD: The angry horse bit his rider.
TEACHER: Good. You're in the club.

Noyce and Christie (1981) have expanded on the pattern club method by using children's literature for the modeling step. By selecting patterned books carefully, a teacher can provide the children with a greater variety of examples of the pattern as well as an enjoyable story. For example, since Noyce and Christie wished to teach the "subordinate sentence, tense shift, *if* clause structure" (*If you had a bicycle,* you would ride it), they chose the patterned book entitled *"You Look Ridiculous," Said the Rhinoceros to the Hippopotamus* by Bernard Waber to read to their students. (Having been told by the rhinoceros that she looks ridiculous, the hippo wanders around the jungle feeling sorry for herself. "If only I had handsome spots like the leopard, I wouldn't look ridiculous," she says after seeing the leopard.) They also chose the book entitled *If I Found a Wistful Unicorn* by Ann Ashford as another book for modeling the same syntactic structure.

After step (1), listening, the teachers had the children engage in (2) speaking activities such as the pattern club, (3) writing activities such as producing a book similar to one of the model books, and (4) reading activities such as reading on their own other books that have the same syntactic pattern. These are a few other books they recommend: *If All the Seas Were One Sea,* by Janina Domanska; *If I Had . . . ,* by Mercer Mayer; *If I Were a Toad,* by Diane Peterson; and *If You Were an Eel, How Would You Feel?* by Nina and Howard Simon.

Advanced Work in Sentence Structures

Obviously, *if* first- and second-grade teachers are doing this kind of thing, the job of introducing expository text in third grade will be a bit easier. But even if sentence structures have not been a subject of attention in the early grades, intermediate-grade teachers *can* do something about the problem. For one thing, they can still use the pattern club or patterned book approach to teaching structures. For another, they can modify those approaches to fit expository text. By examining the social studies or science textbook you are using, you'll be able to find sentence structures that need pattern club experiences to make them more understandable.

As an illustration of this, take the following sentences from a social studies textbook: "Unless Franklin got to the French on time, the money wouldn't be available. Unless the money became available, the soldiers would receive no supplies. Unless the supplies came soon, the soldiers would starve."

Establish a two-minute pattern club by showing them these three sentences and challenging them to come up with a similar sentence, "beginning with the word *unless.*" But first get in the club yourself by using one of your own, such as, "Unless my class understands this lesson, the principal will fire me." Note to grammar purists: This pattern is a little trickier than it appears. The subject of the dependent clause—"Unless my class understands this lesson"—is *class.* The subject of the independent clause—"the principal will fire me"—is *principal.* "Officially" speaking, the two subjects must be different for someone to get in the club. This, of course, would not be analyzed with the students. They would have to get it intuitively by listening to many sentences.

But you decide whether your group is ready for this exact an interpretation of the pattern—or whether you want to let them in the club just for using an "Unless" clause like this: "Unless I get an A in this class, I'll be in trouble with my dad." Either way, they'll get more exposure to this type of clause.

DIFFICULTY WITH PARAGRAPH STRUCTURES

Guthrie (1979), after reviewing results of experimental studies, concluded that a highly readable paragraph contains two features: (1) a topic sentence at the beginning of the paragraph, and (2) coherence among the sentences in a paragraph. However, many authors do not always write paragraphs with these two features. (Furthermore, such writing becomes rather dull.) The following are examples of paragraphs that are "easy" to read and "more difficult" to read.

> *Easy:* The skate is a strange looking fish. It's a flat fish with both eyes on top rather than one eye on each side of its head. As you look down on it, it appears a little like a diamond-shaped kite with a tail. The skate's tail looks as if it belongs to a snake rather than a fish.

> *More difficult:* As you look down on it, it appears a little like a diamond-shaped kite with a tail. Its tail looks as if it belongs to a snake rather than a fish. But it's a fish, all right. It's a flat fish with both eyes on top rather than one eye on each side of its head. And with those eyes it searches constantly for food. The skate is a strange looking fish.

Theoretically, the second paragraph is more difficult to read for two reasons: (1) You have to wait until the end of the paragraph to find out the main idea the author wishes to express, and (2) the fifth sentence does not relate directly to the topic sentence or to the rest of the sentences. Research (Dupuis, 1984) shows that

with this type of paragraph children find it more difficult to recall significant details. Yet one study (Donlan, 1980) found that in today's social studies textbooks, the topic sentence occurs as the first sentence of a paragraph only 13 percent of the time. In other words, in only one paragraph out of eight will you be likely to find the main idea by reading the first sentence.

What Teachers Can Do

Whether children *should* be taught to search for topic sentences is a moot point, since the research that justifies this activity is too sparse and inconclusive to give us any clear direction. Frankly, this has always seemed a rather mechanical, mindless way of looking for a main idea, anyway. Main ideas are seldom tucked neatly into one sentence. They are more dispersed throughout the entire paragraph or passage. Expecting to find the main idea in one sentence is like expecting to find the theme of an entire symphony in one measure.

As most teachers and researchers will probably admit, main ideas are *often* difficult for students to determine (Berryhill, 1984). My hunch is that this is *not* because authors refuse to encapsulate their main ideas into the first sentence in each paragraph; it's because the material children are reading is too difficult in the first place, and thus they have difficulty bringing their schemata to bear upon the task—reading becomes a consumption of words rather than ideas. In a study involving 7,000 students in grades four, seven, and ten, the reading materials required in both the language arts and the social studies were found to be above the students' grade level (Kirkwood & Wolfe, 1980). Every now and then, someone writes an article telling us that textbooks are getting easier. But when I actually look at those textbooks, I see the same kind of inherent difficulty—trying to cover too much material in too little space, thus depriving the student of the clues needed for schemata stimulation. I also find unnatural language with nice short sentences, easy but inexact and uncolorful words, and, of course, each paragraph beginning with a topic sentence.

UGHHHH! There's gotta be a better way!

My two points are these:

1. Even though research may show that children can read paragraphs more easily when the first sentence broadcasts the main ideas, most authors don't write that way (not if they have a natural bone in their body). And most people don't talk that way.

2. There are better ways to help children grasp paragraphs—through schemata enhancement, through vocabulary/concept development, through imagery development (which I'll discuss a little later), and through helping children find reading material at their level of interest and skill.

Finding Content Area Materials at the Right Level

Each child needs content area materials to read that interest *him*, that are challenging to *him*, but are not frustrating to *him*. Naturally these criteria can't be met when the teacher has every child "doing social studies" or "doing science" in the same textbook. Of course, there's nothing wrong in having every child use the same textbook for studying pictures, maps, and indexes, and for developing scanning and skimming skills. What may be wrong is to expect every child to be able to read the same book. A more successful approach is to have a variety of textbooks and trade books available, in the room or the library, that offer similar information at different reading levels.

This means in actual practice that teachers need to be willing to have children read for specific *purposes* rather than to cover specific pages. Rather than assignments of definite pages to read in a definite textbook, their assignments look more like this:

> "Where did Columbus get the idea that it would be safe to sail westward to reach the East Indies? What made him so sure of himself? Why did he want to make the journey? Was he trying to get rich, or do you think he had other plans? If you had been a sailor at that time, do you think you would have gone with him?"

With open-ended assignments like this, children are encouraged to read in a variety of sources and to look for sources within their reading capabilities.

Children's Literature Once More to the Rescue

Today's libraries are chock-full of trade books that can be used to supplement textbooks in the social, biological, and physical sciences. Books by Alvin and Virginia Silverstein, for example, can help children in grades three through six to a better understanding of humans and animals. Their series, *All About Them* and *Systems of the Body,* provide several books that are highly readable and informative. Another science author, Seymour Simon, has written more than fifty books designed to help young children understand, in everyday language, interesting facts and principles concerning the earth, space, and animals. His *Meet the Giant Snakes* and *Danger from Below: Earthquakes, Past, Present, and Future* are just two examples of the solid but easily digested ''food'' in this author's larder.

It would take several hundred pages to describe the thousands of trade books now available to elementary school teachers and students of the content areas. A good source for becoming aware of social studies trade books is the annual list, ''Notable Children's Trade Books in the Field of Social Studies.'' You can obtain this list by writing to Children's Book Council, 67 Irving Place, New York, New York 10003. These are a sampling of useful books in the biological, physical, and social sciences:

The Biological Sciences

Aliki, *The Long-Lost Coelacanth and Other Living Fossils*

Amon, *Reading, Writing, Chattering Chimps*

Bendick, *The Mystery of the Loch Ness Monster*

Cole, *A Frog's Body*

Dowden, *The Blossom on the Bough: A Book of Trees*

Graves, *What Is a California Sea Otter?*

Halmi, *Zoos of the World*

Levine, *Lisa and Her Soundless World*

McClung, *How Animals Hide*

Silverstein, *Exploring the Brain*

The Physical Sciences and Mathematics

Adler, *Magic House of Numbers*

Branley, *Color: From Rainbows to Lasers*

Freeman, *Gravity and the Astronauts*

James and Barkin, *The Simple Facts of Simple Machines*

Lauber, *Tapping Earth's Heat*

Maestro, *Oil: The Buried Treasure*

National Geographic, *How Things Work*

Navarra, *Earthquake*

Nixon, *Glaciers: Nature's Frozen Rivers*

Watson, *Binary Numbers*

The Social Sciences

Aliki, *Mummies Made in Egypt*

Baker, *Settlers and Strangers: Native Americans of the Desert Southwest and History as They Saw It*

Bales, *Chinatown Sunday: The Story of Lillian Der*

Bernheim, *In Africa*

Cartwright, *What's in a Map?*

Clarke, *The American Revolution 1775–83: A British View*

Erdoes, *The Native Americans*

Fisher, *The Factories*

Foster, *The World of William Penn*

Fritz, *The Double Life of Pocahontas*

Kurelek, *Lumberjack*

Macaulay, *Underground*

Meyer, *Eskimos: Growing Up in a Changing Culture*

Rau, *The People of New China*

Steele, *Westward Adventure: The True Stories of Six Pioneers*

Singer, *We All Come from Puerto Rico, Too*

Warren, *Pictorial History of Women in America*

Wolf, *In This Proud Land: The Story of a Mexican American Family*

DIFFICULTY WITH IMAGERY

When we read with comprehension, we have to create images in our minds: sights, sounds, smells, tactile sensations, muscular sensations, tastes. Reading in the content areas requires an enormous amount of intensive image making. With lightweight stories from basal readers or library books, image making becomes almost automatic, particularly when the child has been helped to find books and stories of the right difficulty. Furthermore, school-age children usually develop a story schema that helps them predict "what's going to happen next." With content area material, however, children are often expected to slow down and "figure out" just what picture or sensation in the mind the author wants the reader to make. Let's look at three sentences a second time to see the extent of image making that is required:

Social studies: The Zambezi is a river in Southern Africa, flowing about 1,650 miles southeast through Rhodesia and Mozambique to the Indian Ocean.

Science: Moisture and heat are two agents of chemical change that can create compounds from two or more elements.

Mathematics: Because of the commutative principle, the order in which certain operations are performed will not change the result.

Images, of course, are based on our own personal experiences and schemata. In the sentence about the Zambezi River, for example, we need to have had experiences similar to the following in order for understanding to take place:

1. Seeing rivers in reality or in pictures
2. Seeing Africa on a map or globe or journey
3. Using directions (N, S, E, W, SE) on a map
4. Hearing the word *flowing* when referring to liquid
5. Traveling for many miles and noticing how long it takes
6. Seeing oceans in reality or in pictures

Six Things Teachers Can Do

There are several ways of increasing student's imagery as they read content area materials:

1. Don't assign them material to read without schemata-building experiences prior to reading. This means in science that they usually should read the textbook *after* numerous first-hand observations and hands-on experimentation. It also means that you should give students opportunities to sketch their observations rather than only discuss them; then let them compare their sketches with pictures they find in encyclopedias and other books. In math this means dramatizing story problems. In social studies it means using discussions, pictures, films, video tapes, interviews, and artifacts before they read, and using dramatizations while they read or after they have read.

2. Use creative drama often. The ideas presented to children in social studies texts can often be made more visual and meaningful through creative dramatizations, as we see in this description of one teacher's use of creative drama in his fifth-grade social studies program:

> Mr. Novick and his pupils were studying European exploration of the Americas. The class was divided into five groups, one that chose to study Coronado, one to study Columbus, and so on. Each group was given help in finding information from library sources and the textbook. Each group then planned a skit to present the major ideas about the explorer. The plans were presented by each small group to Mr. Novick. Mr. Novick praised them for their work but asked questions to show them where they still needed to do more research. After further research, the groups modified the plans for their skits and again presented their ideas to Mr. Novick. If Mr. Novick approved their plans, they were free to rehearse their skits in earnest.
>
> After all five groups had their skits ready, they presented them in a theater-in-the-round fashion—skit in the middle of the room, audience in a cir-

cle. After each skit, the audience provided praise and specific suggestions for improvement. Further rehearsals prepared the groups for presenting the skits to another class.

Mr. Novick's approach was very well structured and certainly made the social studies reading more visual and real to the children. However, not all drama experiences related to the content areas need to be this elaborate. Once the children have become used to giving spontaneous skits, they can be invited at any time to dramatize something they've been reading. After one small group has tried it, another group can be asked to give *their* interpretation. Inviting another class into the room (or another group in a team-teaching situation) can be reserved for special occasions when the children have decided with you to polish a skit for a larger audience.

3. Through modeling and discussion, help your students realize that their ability to create images while they read is a major reason for their understanding or not understanding what they read. Model this for them, explaining the images you are creating as you read. Have them practice this often with a partner or two.

4. Help them realize what they *can* do when they can't come up with images for what they're reading. Model for them the use of prior experience, textbook pictures, maps, encyclopedias, and other visual sources such as graphs and tables. (See the later sections on study skills.)

5. Rely on cooperative education to partially solve this problem. Encourage your students to ask each other to provide images. Your students have diverse backgrounds, and what one child doesn't know from experience another child often does. By letting partners read content material together (a fluent reader with a less fluent one), you can provide more cooperative practice in image making. This is so much better than making kids sit at their desks helplessly moving their eyes over the pages, pretending that they're reading and longing for the bell to ring.

6. Engage children in writing that requires image making. Encourage descriptive writing by:
   a. Giving them a chance to informally imagine what you're reading to them, then briefly discussing what they "see."
   b. Reading children's writing and having the audience listen for good images; then commenting specifically on why the images are clear and interesting.
   c. Providing abundant images to write about. Objects and pictures you bring in. Cooperative experiences they can talk about, then write about. Journals of their own experiences and feelings. Vividly descriptive nonfiction books read to them—used as a basis for discussion followed by writing.
   d. Encouraging good readers to write clear, image-provoking minibooks for "next year's students." Then the following year these minibooks

can be recommended to children who are having trouble understanding the material in the content area textbooks.

Also Improve Imagery through Graphic Materials

When students see a graph or table in content area selections, they often say to themselves, "Oh boy! Now I have less to read." *And then they skip it.* I remember my own such joy as a student. But one day the textbook was so dull, I found myself trying to figure out a graph just to keep myself awake. It was on that day that I discovered a secret—that creating my own information from a graph or table was a lot more fun than reading page after page of text. Take the graph shown in Table 12.2, for example. See how much information you can create by examining it right now.

Do you see what I mean? Without reading a lot of text you can figure out for yourself that twice as many boys as girls have trouble when it comes to reading. (It's that little Y chromosome, you know.)

Maps can also be a fascinating way for children to gain information—witness the enthusiasm of children reading the map related to the journey of Bilbo Baggins in Tolkien's *Hobbit*. And so can diagrams and pictures, as shown by the eagerness displayed by children following diagrams for building model airplanes or studying pictures of dinosaurs.

If graphs, tables, maps, diagrams, and pictures can be so interesting, why are they often passed over with only the briefest glance? There are probably numerous reasons for this, including the possibility that they take more energy to read than simple exposition. But perhaps the biggest reason is that children have had too few opportunities to discover that reading them can be fairly easy and enjoyable. One way to bring about such a discovery is through having the children create graphs, maps, tables, diagrams, and informational pictures of their own. As a start you may wish to have them use simple information that you provide—such as average winter temperatures in various parts of the world, or

TABLE 12.2
Sex differences between the percentage of boys and girls reading one year or more below grade level*

Grade	Boys	Girls
2	10%	4%
3	15%	7%
4	24%	12%
5	26%	12%

*Adapted from Arthur W. Heilman, *Principles and Practices of Teaching Reading,* 4th ed. (Columbus, OH: Merrill, 1977), p. 74. Adapted with permission of the author and publisher.

other such statistical data found in almanacs. But as rapidly as possible, it's advisable to get them involved in gathering their own information and translating that information into graphic or tabular form. There are almost limitless possibilities for such projects—a graph comparing the number of children in fifth grade who prefer vanilla, chocolate, and strawberry ice cream; a map of the classroom, the school, or the neighborhood; a diagram of "my dream house" or "how to make a simple glider"; a table showing school enrollment during the past ten years; a mural giving a reasonably accurate interpretation of village life in the Middle Ages.

All of these projects can be displayed for other children to read and discuss. This provides some of the guided practice necessary for learning to appreciate and understand "visuals"—and through the construction of these visuals, they'll be able to discover for themselves the need for some type of scale or key on maps, graphs, diagrams, and informal pictures; the need for symbols such as color or special lines; and the need for accurate titles and labels.

STUDY SKILL ONE: METACOGNITIVE MONITORING OF CONTENT AREA READING

As I mentioned earlier, when we "good readers" read, we not only try to comprehend the text; we use metacognition to make *sure* we're comprehending it. Right now, for example, how do you know that you're understanding what you're reading? Can you tell when you're going too fast or slow? Do you have your "reading monitor" on so that you know when you've just read a sentence or paragraph—or entire page—without understanding "a bloody thing"? Do you know how to draw on your prior knowledge, on text pictures, diagrams, maps, or other visuals, to help you figure out the meaning of what you're reading? Are you quick at self-correcting when you've come up with a word substitution that doesn't make sense?

These are all part of the metacognitive process of comprehension monitoring. Some children do this well, some don't. Furthermore, such monitoring is much more difficult with content area materials than with fiction—for reasons I've already given you. In Chapters 4 and 5, I showed you how to model some of the metacognitive processes, and you may want to refer to those again. In this chapter I'll concentrate on the metacognitive process of "flexible reading" or reading at appropriate rates of speed.

Monitoring through Flexible Reading

Why do some kids read everything as if they're on a slow boat to China? Fiction, nonfiction, poetry, you name it, they'll read it with the same inflexible style and speed (McDonald, 1965). They seem to have no inner "comprehension monitor" urging them to speed up or slow down. We already know that this behavior is encouraged, or perhaps caused, by teachers who continually give them text that is too difficult and/or continually correct their words rather than their meaning. It's also encouraged by teachers who do not model interactive reading, showing them how to use all four cueing systems.

But perhaps most important of all, children who behave this way have simply had much too much practice reading without purpose. For years, Jimmy Miller, a slow reader, has been reading merely to please the teacher or to "get it done." He has little concept of what it means to communicate with an author because he's never learned that authors have much to say to him personally. His perception of reading is similar to that of Jack Jacob's perception of his painting job. Jack is a painter's apprentice and it's his job to scrape off the excess paint from the windows of the buildings his boss paints. He likes to start at the top and scrape off each window from left to right in the first row. Then he moves down to the second row and again scrapes off each window from left to right, and so on. In the same way, Jimmy Miller scrapes each word off the page and lets the letters fall to the floor.

If Jimmy had been offered some language experience approaches during his earlier years in school, and if he had been given numerous "directed reading-thinking activities" throughout his school years (as described in Chapter 5), perhaps he would not now be such a slow reader. He would understand that reading is a form of communicating (rather than merely getting a job done) and that one needs to read for specific purposes. Yet it is never too late for Jimmy to learn these two things. Language experience approaches and DRTA may be used at any level of education. In addition, one of the best long-range treatments is a steady diet of high-interest, low-vocabulary books—fiction or well-written informational accounts that sweep the reader along, causing him to devour books in large meaningful gulps rather than tiny meaningless nibbles.

The teacher also needs to remind Jimmy (and others) to change speed for different purposes. A good way to remind them is through analogies. Analogies can be useful metacognitive aids because they provide a visual or imaginative trigger to memory. Every child who enjoys back-seat driving in the family car, for example, is aware of the need for different driving speeds. One speed is fine for freeway and turnpike driving but extremely hazardous for mountain roads with snakelike curves. Once the teacher has helped children develop the capacity to read at different speeds, it then becomes a matter of explaining to them the virtue of reading different materials at different speeds and of helping them establish a *speed set* for each type of material.

For example, the teacher can compare the importance of reading flexibly to the importance of eating different types of food at different rates. Whereas butterscotch pudding (light fiction) can be gobbled with gusto, one needs to chew raw carrots (informational material) in a thoughtful manner. Otherwise, digestion (understanding) is seriously hindered. A person doesn't need to chew butterscotch pudding, and ought not to gobble raw carrots. These explanations should be supplemented with occasional reminders that help the children establish the proper set before they begin to read. If they are about to read informational material, for instance, they could be reminded that they will now be dealing with "raw carrots" rather than "butterscotch pudding."

An even more specific set can be established by discussing with them their purposes for reading a particular selection. If Donald's purpose is simply to find out what an authority has to say about a very specific topic, it is often a waste of his time to read an entire chapter or even entire pages. By using an index and by scanning until he finds a key word related to the topic, he not only saves himself a lot of time; he reads actively rather than passively—varying his rate of reading according to his purposes. This manner of reading is the type of mature behavior a teacher should encourage. And it *can* be learned (Spache & Spache, 1979).

Reading Content Area Material for a Purpose

The Jimmys and Jennies often need guidance in reading for a purpose. There is nothing more wasteful of a student's time and natural curiosity than to attack a reading assignment with no motivation to learn anything in particular. As you may guess, this nonmotivation can reach epidemic proportions by the time children reach the sixth or seventh grade.

There are many reasons for this nonmotivation, of course, depending on the particular child. But two of the most likely causes for such a poor attitude toward reading content area materials are: (1) assigning too many pages for one assignment (Smith & Johnson, 1980), and (2) assigning pages to read without helping children develop any sense of excitement about what they will gain from reading them.

As for the number of pages in one assignment, it's far better to assign too few pages than too many. Remember, you're developing *habits* and not just covering material. The best way to develop the habit of not completing a reading assignment is to assign so many pages that children experience fatigue and give up. Ask any high school teacher; she'll tell you of the numerous students who have *learned* that the best way to handle a long reading assignment is simply not to read it.

As for assigning pages without developing a sense of purpose and excitement, probably no one is more guilty of this than college professors—the very people who serve as the "last-stop" models for those who become elementary and high school teachers. But, alas, this gives us no excuse to get even and do the same to children. Instead, we can use a variety of "interest getters" to make sure that most of our students will want to read the assignment in content area materials.

Gaining Purpose through "Interest Getters"

Let's go back to the "directed teaching-reading activity" described in Chapter 5 for an example of creating motivation. The teacher wanted the children to read about the "Amazing Underground City" in New York; how the space under streets was filled with pipes and wires and other things, and how this underground city got started. She didn't say to the children, "For your social studies reading, I want you to read pages 257 to 265." Instead, she sparked their interest with an intriguing question: "Do you know what kinds of things you can find underneath the streets here in New York City?'' This led to some intelligent hypothesizing (pipes?) as well as to some imaginative guessing (monsters?). By the time they were through with their prereading discussion, the children were eager to read to find out two things: (1) What *is* under there? and (2) Was my guess right or not? In other words, the teacher used two types of "interest getters": first, sparking their curiosity about the unknown, and second, having them place their bets before the race begins (more mundanely known as "making predictions").

There are many other forms of "interest getters" you can try before asking children to read in content area materials. Here are just a few.

Believe it or not (before having them read an article about automobile manufacturing): "Do you think you could make your own car? . . . If you were going to make your own car, how many different kinds of parts do you think you'd have to put into it? . . . Did you know that to make a car today it takes 300 different kinds of parts . . . and not only that, those parts come from 56 countries! . . . As you read this article, see if you can find out what some of those different parts are and where they are made."

Battle of the ages (before reading about one or both of the paired topics):
   a. "Who do you think was braver—the crew of astronauts who went to the moon, or the crews of the Nina, Pinta, and Santa Maria?"
   b. "Whose discovery was more important to people: Pasteur's or Einstein's?"

Puzzle appeal (before reading an article that attempts to solve the puzzle):
   a. "How can the richest nation on earth have so many poor people?"
   b. "What do you think you would find if you looked under the streets of New York City?"

Picture appeal (have them look at the picture related to an article they're going to read): "What do you think is happening in this picture? . . . What else? . . . Why do you think this is happening? . . . Does it happen anywhere else, do you think? . . . Read this article and see if your ideas are correct."

Prove me wrong (present a stereotype or another type of false statement, then have them read in order to prove you wrong):
   a. The commutative property works for addition, subtraction, multiplication, and division.
   b. Solar energy won't be useful to us for another thousand years!
   c. All monkeys are alike!
   d. Our sun is the biggest star in the whole universe!

Best prediction (don't let children know which article or section they're going to read, just give them the title): "From hearing the title, I'd like you to write down three things you think the author will say. Put your name on this sheet, fold it up, and place it in this prediction box. After you're finished reading, we'll see whose prediction came closest."

Monitoring through Skimming and Scanning

Another way of increasing purpose, developing a more flexible reading rate, and fostering metacognitive processes is to teach your students how to skim and scan. Members of the literacy club usually don't have to read every word to get the information they want. They'd never be found reading the entire telephone book or even an entire page to find the name of someone they wished to call. They'd do something else called *scanning,* a basic tool of the literate reader (and one impossible to acquire for the child who has learned to read through a word-by-word, sound-it-out process).

Teaching how to scan. To teach children how to scan, you'll need to model the process in front of them. Display a page of text on an overhead projector and scan out loud for a small piece of information—a name, a date, or a place—demonstrating how to skip information that is irrelevant. Then give them a limited amount of time to find information in a fairly simple selection which they all are to "scan."

You'll need to model how to find three types of information through scanning, preferably in this order, helping them master one at a time:

Easiest type: Scanning for a bit of information that stands out in the text. "How long is the great white shark in the story you're about to read?"

More difficult: Scanning for an answer worded like the question.

AUTHOR: "The great white shark doesn't bother to circle its prey when it hunts."

QUESTION: "Does the great white shark circle its prey when it hunts or does it go straight for the kill?"

Difficult: Scanning for an answer that is worded differently from the question. "Do you think a great white shark is a cautious hunter or a fearless one? Find something on this page that either supports or doesn't support your opinion."

Teaching how to skim. While scanning is highly useful for finding specific facts, skimming has another function. Through skimming, one tries to get the gist of a story or article rather than find a specific answer to a specific question. We often use skimming to decide whether or not a library book is going to be a good one to check out.

Skimming is often used for previewing a selection before actually reading it. By reading the first paragraph, the subheadings, and the last paragraph, you are engaged in skimming. If the purpose, though, is to make sure a book has the kind of information or story one wants, many people extend their skimming by reading for several pages. In other words, they look for a rough idea of what the author is going to say. Sometimes they extend their skimming further by glancing through the index and table of contents. Some people skim this way simply to "pick up ideas" without having to read an entire book. (Bookstore proprietors will tell you that many people go into bookstores just for this purpose without ever buying a single book.)

To teach skimming you will again need to model the process, then follow up with an application experience and appropriate questions—asked just before they skim: "What is this book going to be about? What kind of information do you think there will be in this article that will be useful or interesting to you? Is this book fiction or nonfiction? Will this book give you information that you'll need for your report?"

Using the PQ3R Method as a Monitoring Scheme

To provide your students with a structured way of monitoring their comprehension, and to increase their retention, try PQ3R. You probably encountered PQ3R (or SQ3R) in your own former schooling. To refresh your memory, I'll summarize this method for you:

1. *Preview* (or *survey*) the first paragraph or two, the subheadings, and the last paragraph or two.
2. Change each subheading into a *question* before reading a section.
3. *Read* the section to answer the question.
4. *Recite* to yourself the answer to the question.
5. *Review* the entire selection by repeating steps 2 and 4 (*question* and *recite*) for each section.

The PQ3R method has had a good track record and seems to help many people comprehend and retain content area reading material better than when they use no system whatever (Spache & Spache, 1979). In fact, some of the basal reader series are now introducing this method in about fifth grade with selected informational articles. (It is not an appropriate method for fiction.)

The most effective means for introducing this approach is to have every child use the same book temporarily. You can give every child in the classroom a lower-grade social studies or science textbook for a few days. Rather than present the entire approach to the students in one session, it's best to introduce and practice one step at a time. Take two or three days to teach the preview step, for instance, before moving on to the question step. Before assigning them a few pages to read, have them use the preview step (first two paragraphs, subheadings, last two paragraphs). Then ask them questions like these: "What do you think this selection is going to be about? What else is it going to be about? What do you think the author will talk about first? What next? What we've just done is called a *preview*. Have you ever noticed how they use a preview on television—just before a movie or a show is going to start? Why do you think they do that? Why do you think it would be a good idea to preview something before you read it? Do you think it would get your mind ready for what the author is going to say to you?"

After they have learned the preview step well, introduce the question step. Go through an entire selection and show them how to change the subheadings

into questions. Then go back and ask them again how they would change the first subheading into a question. As soon as they agree on an appropriate question (or questions) for that section, have them read for the purpose of answering the question. After they have agreed on the best answer to the question, move on to the next subheading and try the method again. Be sure when you're practicing the PQ3R method that you work on it only ten or fifteen minutes per day, so they get the idea that it's a snappy method that *works* rather than an additional burden they're now going to have to put up with in school.

Once they've learned the preview and question steps well, you're ready to "prove" to them how well the entire PQ3R method works. Give them a very short assignment; ask them this time not only to preview, question, and read, but to recite to themselves after each section, and then go back and review each section. Promise them they'll do very well on a short test you'll give them when they're finished. (Be sure the questions you write for the test are directly related to the most obvious questions into which they will most likely change the subheadings.)

The PQ3R method will quickly fall into disuse unless you give them opportunities to practice it frequently. Whenever an informational article appears in a basal reader that a small group is using, for example, you can use the opportunity to reinforce their skill in the method.

STUDY SKILL TWO: LOCATING INFORMATION

To become adept at using content area materials, children need to learn how to locate precisely the information they want. The skill of locating information can be broken down like this:

1. Examining titles to determine appropriateness of books
2. Using a table of contents
3. Using an index
4. Using the glossary available in some books
5. Gaining information from appendixes
6. Finding appropriate visuals—maps, tables, graphs, pictures, and diagrams
7. Using the library card catalog
8. Using encyclopedias and other library reference books

Whereas most basal reader programs include useful exercises on many of the locational skills, these skills are usually mastered best through actual "research projects" in which children seek information in trade books, textbooks, encyclopedias, and other library references. Textbooks, though, such as those used for social studies or science, are often handy to use as raw material when the teacher wants to model locational skills with several students at the same time. Since several copies of a textbook are usually available, each child can look at the same example at the same time. Guided practice should not be limited to textbooks, however, as positive transfer is much more likely to take place when children also employ the locational skills with informational books and reference books they have found for themselves in the library.

As soon as children begin to use textbooks in science and social studies, they can begin to receive modeling and guided practice in "finding the secret treasures hidden within a book." Questions similar to the following are generally useful in helping children discover for themselves the utility of indexes, glossaries, illustrations, and so on. (To increase your own involvement and to gain a better understanding of the utility of such questions in aiding discovery, you can try answering these questions as they relate to the book you're reading right now.)

1. On what page can you find the beginning of an alphabetical list (called an *index*) of most of the things talked about in this book?
2. If you wanted to find out something in this book about how to increase children's reading speed, what topic would you look for in the index:

children's reading speed? rate of reading? how to increase children's reading speed? reading rate? reading speed? Try what *you* think may work and see which one is in the index.

3. On exactly what pages would you find information about children's reading speed?

4. On what page near the front of this book can you find a list of chapter titles?

5. On what page is there an appendix that might give you information about teaching dictionary use?

6. Between what pages is the chapter on "phonics"?

7. On what pages can you find suggestions for other books and articles to read on teaching phonics?

8. Looking only at the titles of articles suggested for additional reading on phonics, which one looks as if it may lead you to information on the so-called First Grade Studies. (Just indicate the author and date of the reference.)

9. If you were trying to find the library number of this book, which drawers would you look for in the card catalog? (Use letters.)

a. The _____ drawer if I knew the first author's name.

b. The _____ drawer if I knew the title.

c. The _____ drawer if I only knew the subject of the book.

10. On what page in this book is the word *phonogram* defined?

11. Between what pages is there an appendix describing numerous "book projects"?

12. If you wanted to find out something about "how to teach deaf children to read," which two encyclopedia volumes would be most likely to contain the information you want? H T D C R

In addition to discovery questions, a teacher can also get children actively involved as "library detectives." A "detective's badge" or similar token can be given to those children who "find all the clues" or "solve the mystery." In this kind of activity, children are usually given clue cards or a list of clues and sent to the library ("the place in which the crime took place") singly, in pairs, or in supervised groups. The following "clues," though facetious in this instance, are the types of clues you could use:

1. The kind of weapon used in the crime was a revolver used by the Barsimians in the War of Tulips. What was the name of the weapon?

2. The main suspect in this case was last seen in the city of Atlantis. In what country is this?

3. The main suspect has the same name (or alias) as the man who wrote *Call of the Tame.* What is the suspect's name?

4. The motive for the crime probably had something to do with narcotics. From what you can find out about narcotics, why do you think the money was stolen, and who else besides the main suspect do you think was responsible for this crime?

A simpler form of this activity involves "clues" that are more direct, though less imaginative. With this form no "crime" has been committed; the clues are simply research problems geared to specific locational skills. For example:

Find in the card catalog the author of *Call of the Tame.*

What book in this library tells about the War of Tulips? You'll find it in the subject catalog under one of these topics: War of Tulips, Wars, Battles, or Tulips.

Use an encyclopedia to find the name of the revolver used by the Barsimians in the War of Tulips.

Some teachers also create the need for practicing locational skills by requiring children to prepare an oral or written report. If you take certain precautions (see the 1985 edition of *They All Want to Write* by Burrows, Ferebee, Jackson, and Saunders), this is probably a worthwhile learning experience for most children. Requiring such a report, however, without first providing specific modeling in locating, comprehending, and recording information, and without providing specific guidance during the preparation of the reports, generally leads to frustration for the teacher and children alike. As always, testing is not teaching.

STUDY SKILL THREE: RECORDING INFORMATION

When children read content area selections, they may sometimes wish to go no further than locating the appropriate material and comprehending it. On certain occasions, though, such as preparing for a report or gathering data for a hobby, children will need to record some of the information. This process seems to be burdensome and cumbersome to many students, perhaps as a result of numerous unguided attempts, leading to a negative attitude and to practicing clumsy techniques. Many teachers, it appears, ask children to "take notes" on what they read without first providing the necessary modeling. As a result, the children usually copy informaiton verbatim rather than jot down its essence. It's not a rare phenomenon to see high school and college students continue this habit.

There are at least two useful approaches to the training. One is the traditional outlining approach, which calls for two steps: (1) teaching children the procedure by actually outlining portions of textbooks with them, and (2) having them apply the outlining procedure to note taking. For instance, take the previous portion of this chapter. The student who had received "training" in outlining might record the main ideas and important details like this:

    I. Locating information
        A. Specific skills related to use of
           1. Book titles
           2. Table of contents
           3. Index
           4. Glossary

      5. Appendixes
      6. Visuals—maps, tables, graphs, pictures, diagrams
      7. Card catalog
      8. Encyclopedias and other references
    B. Teaching techniques
      1. Basal reader exercises
      2. Social studies or science textbooks
        a. "Secret treasure" for children to discover
        b. Discovery questions leading to use of A.1–A.8
      3. Library detectives
        a. Detective's badge or other token
        b. Clues requiring use of A.1–A.8
      4. Preparation for reports
  II. Recording information
    A. . . .
    B. . . .

The outline approach, though, is appropriate only when students have a rather general assignment to learn all they can about a topic or to read certain pages in a text, or when they are preparing for a report on a general topic. It's probably more common in out-of-school situations, however, to read informational sources for a specific *purpose*—to find the answer to a burning question, to learn how to do a particular thing related to a hobby, and so on. When this is the case, note taking may be simply a matter of jotting down answers, rather than outlining a topic in logical arrangement.

Let's suppose, for instance, that you wished to read for the specific purpose of answering this question: How fast do high school students read? Using a graph provided by the author, your note taking may look like this:

    1. 9th grade—about 214 w.p.m.—average for informational material
    2. 10th grade—about 224 w.p.m.— "   "   "   "
    3. 11th grade—about 237 w.p.m.— "   "   "   "
    4. 12th grade—about 250 w.p.m.— "   "   "   "

To take an example closer to home, suppose you have to review for a test. You've heard through the grapevine that your instructor is going to make you "List ways of helping children learn the skills involved in locating information." (Let's hope this doesn't actually happen to you.) Instead of outlining what you've read on this, or covering three pages with yellow highlighter, you might take notes like these:

    1. Use discovery-type questions to guide them through these skills with social studies or science textbooks.
    2. Use exercises provided in basal reader program.
    3. Have children become library detectives; give "clues" requiring use of locational skills.
    4. Have them use locational skills in preparing reports.

These two approaches to note taking—the outlining technique and the specific-purpose technique—can be supplemented by the use of graphic organizers (charts that show relationships between ideas). For an example of graphic organizers, see Figure 12.1. For more ideas on graphic organizers, see the articles by McGee & Richgels (April 1985) and Piccolo (May 1987) in *The Reading Teacher*. All three approaches to note taking can be taught to a small proportion of children in the third grade, to many in fourth, and to the rest in fifth or sixth. It's doubtful, though, that such an important study skill should be reserved for high school. By that time the bad habits of copying verbatim and plagiarizing can be carved in stone.

SUMMARY OF MAIN IDEAS

☐ Since children and adults spend so much time reading informational, nonfiction, expository text, it's important that teachers prepare their students for this type of reading.

☐ Reading in the content areas has five difficulties associated with it: passage structure, vocabulary, sentence structure, paragraph structure, and imagery. There are specific things that teachers can do to help students with each of these difficulties.

☐ The metacognitive process of comprehension monitoring is often more difficult with content area materials than with fiction. Teachers can develop this form of monitoring by encouraging a flexible reading rate, by using "interest getters" and other methods of increasing students' purposes for reading, by teaching them how to skim and scan, and by modeling the use of the PQ3R method.

☐ Locating and recording information are two skills that need to be modeled by the teacher, followed by purposeful application with library books, multiple texts, and reference books at various levels of difficulty.

APPLICATION EXPERIENCES FOR THE TEACHER EDUCATION CLASS

A. *What's Your Opinion?* Use your own experiences as well as the textbook to help you justify your decision.
   1. Once you teach a child the basic skills of reading, she should be able to read anything—a science text, a math text, you name it.
   2. Children should learn to read standard textbooks rather than relying on library books.
   3. Peer-written or teacher-written booklets can be good substitutes for standard textbooks.
   4. Expository schema is not that much different from story schema.
   5. In this day and age, with copy machines everywhere, children really don't need to know how to take notes when they read.
   6. Scanning and skimming are very different processes.
   7. "Interest getters" may be fine for children up to fifth grade, but after that they really shouldn't be necessary.

B. *Miscue Analysis:* Why is Jennie having trouble reading this textbook selection?

The first [hunter/hundred] years in the history of the United States immigration had been, in general, a period free from all restrictions. America had become a refuge for the oppressed

of all lands.

C. *The PQ3R Method:* Use this method for a week or more with one of your college courses. Report to your education class on the effects you think this method is having on your retention of the materials you're supposed to be learning in that course.

D. *Preparing Students for Content Area Reading:* Divide the class into four groups: a math group, a natural science group, a physical science group, and a social studies group. Find two or three pages from a textbook pertaining to your content area. Then decide on the following:

1. What "interest getter" would you use to get students to want to read them?
2. For what two key words will you help students develop stronger images and associations? Precisely how will you do this? Plan the exact procedures you will use.
3. In what way can you use creative dramatics with students to help them understand the pages?
4. Try out your ideas with one of the other groups.

FIELD EXPERIENCES IN THE ELEMENTARY SCHOOL CLASSROOM

A. With one or more children, teach the first two levels of scanning skills described in this chapter. What different strategies did you have to use to help the children with the two different levels? What clues did you teach them to look for with the second type of scanning that were different from the clues you taught them to look for with the first type?

B. Plan and carry out a lesson based on Application Experience D. Try out your lesson with two or more children. Choose one of the children's textbooks for this activity.

C. With one or more children, create an "elevation map" of the classroom. Help them decide on an appropriate scale, such as "one inch is equal to one foot," or whatever is appropriate for the size paper you will use. Help them decide on an appropriate key to show the height of different objects in the room (for example, green could be used for objects less than 12 inches tall). What concepts about maps were you able to teach through this experience? Have them apply these concepts to reading other elevation maps?

D. Teach a small group of children how to use the PQ3R method.

E. Try rewriting a selection from a textbook that is too difficult for a particular group of children, or help an advanced group of readers rewrite it for other students.

F. Help a group of students understand math story problems through creative dramatics.

REFERENCES AND SUGGESTED READING

Askov, E. N., & Kamm, K. (1974). Map skills in the elementary school. *Elementary School Journal, 75,* 112–121.

Berryhill, P. (1984). Reading in the content area of social studies. In M. M. Dupuis (Ed.), *Reading in the content areas: Research for teachers* (pp. 66–74). Newark, DE: International Reading Association.

Beutler, S. A. (1988). Using writing to learn about astronomy. *The Reading Teacher, 41,* 412–417.

Bormuth, J., Carr, J., Manning, J., & Pearson, D. (1970). Children's comprehension of between- and within-sentence syntactic structures. *Journal of Educational Psychology, 61,* 349–357.

Braam, L. (1963). Developing and measuring flexibility in reading. *The Reading Teacher, 16,* 247–254.

Bruinsma, R. (1980). Should lip movements and subvocalization during silent reading be directly remediated? *The Reading Teacher, 34,* 293–396.

Davis, J. B. (1977). Improving reading and the teaching of science. *Clearing House, 50,* 390–392.

Donlan, D. (1980). Locating main ideas in history textbooks. *Journal of Reading, 24,* 135–140.

Dupuis, M. M. (Ed.). (1984). *Reading in the content areas: Research for teachers.* Newark, DE: International Reading Association.

Fagan, W. T. (1971). Transformations and comprehension. *The Reading Teacher, 25,* 169–172.

Fredericks, A. D. (1986). Mental imagery activities to improve comprehension. *The Reading Teacher, 40,* 78–81.

Gibbons, H. D. (1941). Reading and sentence elements. *Elementary English Review, 18,* 42–46.

Guthrie, J. T. (1979). Paragraph structure. *The Reading Teacher, 32,* 880–881.

Johnson, R. E. (1977). The reading level of elementary social studies textbooks is coming down. *The Reading Teacher, 30,* 901–905.

Kirkwood, K. F., & Wolfe, R. C. (1980). *Matching students and reading materials: A cloze procedure method for assessing the reading ability of students and the readability of textual material.* Toronto: Ontario Ministry of Education.

Luffey, J. I. (Ed.). (1972). *Reading in the content areas.* Newark, DE: International Reading Association.

MacKinnon, A. R. (1959). *How do children learn to read?* New York: Copp Clark.

Manzo, A. (1975). Guided reading procedure. *Journal of Reading, 18,* 287–291.

McDonald, A. S. (1965). Research for the classroom: Rate and flexibility. *Journal of Reading, 8,* 187–191.

McGee, L. M., & Richgels, D. J. (1985). Teaching expository text structure to elementary students. *The Reading Teacher, 38,* 739–748.

Meyer, B. J. F., & Freedle, R. (1979). *The effects of different discourse types on recall.* Princeton, N.J.: Educational Testing Service.

Moore, D. W., Readence, J. E., & Rickelman, R. J. (1982). *Prereading activities for content area reading and learning.* Newark, DE: International Reading Association.

Noyce, R. N., & Christie, J. F. (1981). Using literature to develop children's grasp of syntax. *The Reading Teacher, 35,* 298–302.

Odegaard, J. M., & May, F. B. (1972). Creative grammar and the writing of third graders. *Elementary School Journal, 73,* 156–161.

Paratore, J. R., & Indrisano, R. (1987). Intervention assessment of reading comprehension. *The Reading Teacher, 40,* 778–783.

Pavlak, S. A. (1973). *Reading comprehension—a critical analysis of selected factors affecting comprehension.* Unpublished doctoral dissertation, University of Pittsburgh.

Piccolo, J. A. (1987). Expository text structure: Teaching and learning strategies. *The Reading Teacher, 40,* 838–847.

Reid, J. (1970). Sentence structure in reading. *Research in Education, 3,* 23–27.

Richek, M. (1976). Effect of sentence complexity on the reading comprehension of syntactic structures. *Journal of Educational Psychology, 68,* 800–806.

Robinson, H. A. (1975). *Teaching reading and study strategies: The content areas.* Boston: Allyn & Bacon.

Ruddell, R. B. (1965). The effect of oral and written patterns of language structure on reading comprehension. *The Reading Teacher, 18,* 270–275.

Smith, R. J., & Johnson, D. D. (1980). *Teaching children to read.* Reading, MA: Addison-Wesley.

Spache, G. D., & Spache, E. B. (1979). *Reading in the elementary schools.* Boston: Allyn & Bacon.

Sticht, T. G. (1984). Rate of comprehending by listening or reading. In J. Flood (Ed.), *Understanding reading comprehension* (pp. 140–160). Newark, DE: International Reading Association.

Strickland, R. G. (1963). Implications of research in linguistics for elementary teachers. *Elementary English, 40,* 168–171.

Taylor, S. E., et al. (1960). *Grade level norms for the components of the fundamental reading skill.* Research Information Bulletin No. 3, Educational Development Laboratories.

Thomas, E. L., & Robinson, H. A. (1977). *Improving reading in every class.* Boston: Allyn & Bacon.

Tyo, J. (1980). An alternative for poor readers in social science. *Social Education, 44,* 309–310.

Uttero, D. A. (1988). Activating comprehension through cooperative learning. *The Reading Teacher, 41,* 390–395.

Fostering Positive Attitudes toward Reading

■ CHAPTER PREVIEW ■

Which of these goals do you think is more important for a teacher of reading?

To teach children how to read

To teach children to want to read

Not an easy question to answer, is it? But you may want to think of it this way: If you teach Roger how to read, but in the process, he learns to hate reading, what have you gained? Will he go to books on his own for information and pleasure? If not, then what have we lost? We've lost one important avenue toward Roger's success in life—toward his emotional maturity, his social awareness, his intellectual vigor, and maybe even toward his economic self-sufficiency.

But does reading instruction have anything to do with such broad concerns as emotional maturity, social awareness, intellectual vigor, and economic self-sufficiency? It can have, provided a teacher thinks of growth *through* reading as well as growth *in* reading as the ultimate goal of reading instruction. But growth through reading is possible only if children *want* to read about their social and natural environment and if they want to enjoy literature. If reading instruction is limited to workbook exercises and skill lessons, though, it's quite unlikely that such desires will flower in the classroom. Furthermore, it's quite unlikely that children will perceive reading as a process that involves pleasure as well as work.

Let's talk in this chapter, then, about ways to make sure that Roger's attitude toward reading is positive, that Marjorie's desire to learn to read better is strong, and that most of Pat's days of learning to read provide a sense of achievement and success and "growing up." The three approaches we'll concentrate on are (1) providing models, (2) providing motivation to learn, and (3) providing success through better retention. We'll also want to look at the important contributions that parents can make toward helping the teacher encourage positive attitudes toward reading.

The entire object of true education is to make people not merely do the right thing, but enjoy the right things.

—Ruskin

You can take a horse to water but you can't make him drink.

—Buffalo Bill's father

You can take a kid to the library but you can't make him check out the video you want to see.

—Bogglestar's friend

READING ATTITUDE: HOW IMPORTANT FOR READING ACHIEVEMENT?

Educational researchers have shown very little interest during the past decade in learning about the relationships between attitudes and achievements. In the third edition of the *Handbook of Research on Teaching,* for instance (Wittrock, 1986), less than a page and a half—out of 1,037 pages—was spent on this topic. The reason for this lack of interest? Probably the difficulty of measuring attitudes, although I'm not sure.

One researcher, however, thought reading was so important that he decided to ask children what their *attitude* toward reading was (Borton, 1985). Unfortunately, he didn't ask enough questions. An average of 86 percent of children in grades four through six, he found, feel it's very *important* to learn to read well. And this is encouraging, of course. But what we don't know is how many of those children had a positive attitude toward the *act* of reading. That is, did they *like* to read?

Evidently, many teachers do worry about whether or not kids like to read. In a study by Heathington and Alexander (1984), 101 teachers were asked to rank nine categories of reading instruction in order of importance. The category of "comprehension" came out on top, but right behind, even ahead of "phonics," was the category called "attitude." On the other hand, when they were asked to estimate the amount of time they spent on each of the nine categories, "comprehension" was first, "phonics" was second, and "attitude" was *eighth*. Something to think about.

I wish I could tell you that research "proves" teachers' beliefs that attitudes toward reading are highly important. Everyone who teaches reading knows that they are, but research doesn't often tell us which comes first—positive attitudes or positive achievement. Which causes which? Or is it impossible to tell? Some researchers (Puryear, 1975; Quandt & Selznick, 1984; Roswell, 1967) have found that children with negative attitudes toward reading tend to be those who have been unsuccessful at it. ("No surprise here," I'm sure you're saying.) Subjective observations from teachers also indicate, however, that those with negative attitudes tend to LEARN less than those with positive attitudes. (Again no surprise.) Three researchers (Neale, Gill, & Tismer, 1970) did find a significant correlation between children's attitudes toward reading and their reading achievement. But, remembering that correlations show only associations and not necessarily cause and effect, this still doesn't tell us whether positive attitudes lead to high achievement or high achievement leads to positive attitudes.

Newman (1982) got around this chicken-and-the-egg problem by doing a longitudinal study of twenty children. She studied a group of children who had scored *low* on the Metropolitan Readiness Test when they were about six years old. By ninth grade, though, these "low achievers" were now considered very *high* achievers in reading. In fact, they were much better readers than children who had scored *high* on reading readiness. So what made the difference between these slow-start-fast-finishers and their counterparts who showed so much promise but didn't do as well by ninth grade? According to Newman's findings, here is what made the difference:

Good models at home and school

A stimulating environment

Interest shown by parents and teachers

Good expectations expressed by parents and teachers

Encouragement to persevere

Low but positive pressure toward achievement

To put this succinctly, important adults spent time helping these high achievers develop positive attitudes toward reading! I have to conclude that positive attitudes *can* lead to positive achievement.

After examining the research on attitudes and reading, Alexander and Filler concluded that "a universal goal of reading instruction should be the fostering of positive attitudes toward reading" (1976, p. 34). After reviewing 110 research reports between 1900 and 1977 on reading achievement and reading attitudes, Davis (1978) concluded that teachers need to be aware of students' attitudes when planning instruction. She also concluded that careful planning can help learners develop positive attitudes.

PROVIDING MODELS

Observations and research consistently point to this: Children who want to learn to read better usually have adult models who like to read; children who feel the opposite about reading generally do not. Yet it is not unusual to find that parents want their children to be good readers but never crack a book in front of them. Nor is it unusual to find teachers who want their students to be good readers but never read for pleasure in front of them or talk about what they've read. (They're often so busy teaching reading they don't take time to read.)

At the risk of going off the deep end, let me throw out a hypothesis for you to consider: Teachers who spend as much time on the "modeling approach" toward teaching reading as they do on skill instruction will have greater success than those who spend all their time on skill instruction. Why I make such a statement is this: We humans are emotional as well as rational creatures. Most of us long to be inspired as well as instructed. Most of us, particularly as we grow up, want to imitate others whom we admire. Let me hasten to comment, though, that I'm not advocating that teachers use only themselves as models. Other people will also serve as inspiration, including children's own classmates. Let's talk, then, about how teachers can promote themselves, parents, other adults, and children's peers as models.

First, the teacher herself. Mrs. Weaver obviously believes in the "modeling approach." For one thing, she reads to her class every day, even though they're in the fourth grade. She selects her "read-aloud books" very carefully—some with male heroes and some with female heroines, but all with literary quality and "an exciting plot." She reads a chapter every day just before they go home. "That way," she says, "I can end each day on a positive note and they're eager to return to school the next morning." Mrs. Weaver doesn't have a "Hollywood voice," but she reads with enjoyment and with enough expression to display her excitement without overdramatizing. (She models good, involved reading without putting on a show that most kids can't imitate when reading to themselves.)

For another thing, Mrs. Weaver shares her own personal reading experiences with her class. Once or twice a week, during her students' daily "Newstime," she talks about something she has read in a newspaper, magazine, or book. Often she brings that newspaper, magazine, or book to hold up while she talks to them, "not necessarily to show them a picture, but just to show them that here's something I like to read when I'm home." Furthermore, when the children have their customary thirty minutes on Monday, Wednesday, and Friday for library books, she usually sits right up in the front of the class and reads a book of her own. "It's tempting," Mrs. Weaver says, "to use the time for planning and so on, but most of the time I can resist the temptation, because I know how important it is for children to watch me enjoy the process that I so fervently teach every day. Actually I feel hypocritical if I don't read in front of them."

Miss Weingardt uses herself as a model for her second-graders in much the same way. But she also tries to involve the parents in the modeling approach. In October, for her second "Teacher-to-Parent Newsletter" of the year, this is what she said:

> Dear Parents,
>
>   I do know how busy you are, so let me assure you that what I'm going to suggest will take no more than an average of five minutes a day. And it's

for a very worthy cause: your child. (I know that some of you are already doing the things I'm going to suggest, and to you let me just say thank you!)

From what we know about children, it appears that the good readers usually have parents who read themselves. These parents enjoy reading and like to share what they read with others. Their children evidently like to imitate them. Therefore, what I'm going to ask you to do (unless you already do it) is this:

1. Would you read silently something pleasurable to yourself—and in front of your child—at least once a week?
2. Would you read out loud something pleasurable to your child at least twice a week? (It doesn't have to be at bedtime; anytime will do: before the bus comes, right after supper, anytime.)
3. Would you make sure all television sets, radios, tape recorders, and stereos are turned off for at least one hour each evening, so that your child will be tempted to fill the time with pleasurable reading or creative play?

    If you will do these three things (or continue doing them), I feel confident you will be helping me to help your child.

Sincerely,
Marianne Weingardt

P.S. If you would like me to send you a list of good books to read aloud to your child, please sign below and return the bottom portion of this sheet through your child.

Yes, I would like you to send me a list of good "read-aloud books."

_____

Miss Weingardt decided this letter was so important that she sent it to each home by mail. "It cost me a few dollars postage," she said, "but my principal liked the idea so much, he's going to try to get some funds just for this purpose."

    In some schools the classroom teachers have the assistance of "special teachers" such as the physical education teacher, the music teacher, and the art teacher. These teachers are asked to mention occasionally (and casually) some information they have gotten from their own reading and to "soft-sell" the kinds of books and magazines they like. They are also asked to recommend specific children's books or magazines on sports, musicians, and artists. Even the principals get involved in some schools by visiting classrooms, talking about things they like to read, and recommending specific books for children. Schools fortunate enough to have librarians often set aside time for them to present "book chats" on new books that have arrived. In a few schools, the entire "community" gets involved, with the cook, janitor, nurse, secretary, principal, teachers, aides, and children all taking a twenty-minute "reading break" each day. In other schools, local celebrities are brought in to talk about topics of interest to children and to mention, without too much fanfare, the kinds of things they enjoy reading.

    Mr. Peterson is a fifth-grade teacher who likes to use "peer modeling" as well as adult modeling. Once a week the children in his class meet for forty minutes in "Book Clubs" of five or six children each. These clubs are not developed according to subject interest or already established friendships. Instead, membership is carefully planned by Mr. Peterson. "Each club," he says, "has two good readers, one or two average readers, and one or two poor readers. For the first twenty minutes they sit around the same table and just read whatever interests them. For the last twenty minutes, they tell each other a little bit about what they've been reading. It's quite simple really, but it seems to motivate all of them to do more reading—especially the average and poor readers, who are inspired by the good readers.''

Many other teachers, at all grade levels, use Mr. Peterson's approach. Some teachers also encourage book sharing and peer modeling by incorporating ''book projects'' into their reading programs. Two or three times a week, children get to sign up to ''sell'' their book through a dramatic skit, a brief reading, a television advertisement for the book, an advertising poster, and so on. When they complete their project, they tell where the book can be obtained and receive some type of ''book certificate'' or other symbol of accomplishment. Over 70 book projects are discussed in Appendix F. For other ways to use peers as models and as teachers, see Chapter 15.

MAKING PARENTS ACTIVE PARTNERS IN THE READING PROGRAM

Children's attitudes toward reading are certainly influenced by the degree of success they have in learning to read. But their attitudes must also be a consequence of their parents' behavior and interests. Several studies have shown that parent involvement in their children's education has a rather direct effect on reading achievement (Niedermeyer, 1970). In one study, for example (Shuck, Ulsh, & Platt, 1983), 150 students from grades three through five who were behind in reading by at least two grade levels were placed in a parent tutoring program. Trained parents worked with their children at home by helping them read a book, do homework, practice word lists, and play reading games. This experimental group of students ended the year with an average grade equivalent score in reading of 3.8 as contrasted to 2.8 for the control group that was not in the parent tutoring program.

John McKinney (1977) found that when 50 parents were trained to tutor their third-graders, the tutored children ended the year with an average score of 52 on a standardized reading test; the nontutored averaged a score of 37. Tutoring, though, is just one of many ways parents can get involved. Here are some others:

Have a special collection of books in the school library that children can borrow and take home for their parents to read with them. These should be carefully selected read-aloud books (Armstrong, 1981).

Use *The Read-Aloud Handbook* by Jim Trelease (1982) to help you select books for parents and children to read aloud (Penguin Books, 625 Madison Avenue, New York, NY, 10022).

Have a workshop for parents on the values and techniques of reading aloud with kids at home (Lautenschlager & Hertz, 1984).

Have a learning station in the classroom supervised by a parent; the parent can help children with basic sight words, skill lessons, writing language experience stories, and so on (Criscuolo, 1983).

Engage parents in producing a minilibrary of "thin books." These are made by cutting out interesting stories from old basals or other materials. The parents can then distribute them to the children, possibly read one aloud, and perhaps discuss them with children after the children have read them (Criscuolo, 1983).

If there is an extra room in the school building, arrange for parents to play educational reading and language games with the children during lunch periods and other times during the day. Arrange for the parents to check these games out to use with their own children at home (Criscuolo, 1983).

Recommend to parents special books and booklets developed by the International Reading Association (IRA) or the National Education Association. Four booklets I especially recommend from the IRA are these:

> *How Can I Help My Child Build Positive Attitudes Toward Reading?* by Susan Mandel Glazer, No. 879.
>
> *Why Read Aloud to Children?* by Julie M. T. Chan, No. 877.
>
> *How Can I Help My Child Get Ready to Read?* by Norma Rogers, No. 876.
>
> *How Can I Encourage my Primary-Grade Child to Read?* by Molly Kayes Ransbury, No. 875.

These four booklets may be purchased for about a dollar each and are available from the International Reading Association, P.O. Box 8139, 800 Barksdale Road, Newark, DE 19714.

From NEA I recommend these four books: *How to Prepare Your Child for School, Learning the Alphabet, How Letters Make Words,* and *Helping Your Child Read.* These books are designed so that parents can teach important concepts that will enable their children to achieve more readily at school. *Helping Your Child Read,* for example, has many stories for reading to children, with questions afterwards and picture cutouts for the child to paste in the book. The book encourages echo and choral reading and provides a list of poems and folk tales at the end. These four books are available for around $2 each and can be obtained from Avon Books, Department FP, 1790 Broadway, New York, NY 10019.

Start a summer reading program. Parents sign a pledge to get their children in the program, take them to the library during the summer, and talk about the books with their children. The children receive a certificate at the end of the program (Criscuolo, 1974).

Develop a workshop to teach parents how to make simple but effective reading games to use with their children (Criscuolo, 1974). See the references at the end of Chapters 6 and 7 for ideas. Also see Appendixes A and B.

Get more men to volunteer as reading models—fathers, principals, janitors, local businessmen, local athletes, physical education instructors. Get them to talk about a good book they recommend or how they use reading on their job or what reading has meant to them. According to a study by Downing and Thomson (1977), in some parts of North America there is a stereotype of reading as a feminine activity, which can influence some boys' attitudes. Downing and Thomson found that when children and adults were asked to decide whether the pictured activity of a person reading was more suitable for a boy or girl, the vast majority said, "For a girl."

PROVIDING MOTIVATION THROUGH THE USE OF LEARNING PRINCIPLES

Children's attitudes toward reading can be greatly influenced by how well teachers of reading employ basic psychological principles of motivation. These principles seem to be appropriate whether a person is teaching reading, mathematics, swimming, cooking, firefighting, janitoring, or even pick-pocketing (judging from Fagin's success with Oliver and his other boys). Let's look at four of these principles.

Principle One: Help Satisfy Their Basic Needs

According to Maslow's well-known "theory of motivation" (1970), human beings have basic types of needs: physiological comfort, physical and psychological safety, belonging and love, esteem from self and others, self-actualization, and knowledge and appreciation. The physiological needs for food, warmth, and sleep are generally dominant until they become at least partially satisfied. Once they're moderately satisfied, however, they give way to the need for safety (security, stability, and structure). Having moderately satisfied the physiological needs and the safety needs, human beings are then usually dominated by the need for belonging (love, companionship, friendship, and affection).

As each set of needs is reasonably satisfied, the next step in the hierarchy takes over—after love, the need for esteem (importance, success, self-respect, and recognition); after esteem, the need for self-actualization (self-fulfillment, satisfying one's potential, meeting one's self-ideal, and doing what one is fitted for); and finally, after (or as part of) self-actualization, the needs that relate most to schooling (knowledge, understanding, and appreciation). This hierarchy of needs is shown graphically in Figure 13.1.

Generally speaking, then, the "lower" needs must be at least partially met before the "higher" needs of self-actualization and intellectual understanding will emerge. In a practical sense, this means that the teacher who ignores Bobby's

FIGURE 13.1
The ladder of human needs

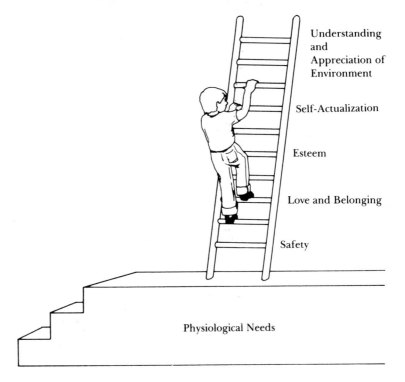

Understanding and Appreciation of Environment

Self-Actualization

Esteem

Love and Belonging

Safety

Physiological Needs

lower needs will find it rather difficult to motivate him to learn something just to satisfy his intellectual curiosity or to satisfy his desire to become a more skilled person. These so-called lower needs must be dealt with during the entire school day, of course, but even during a brief lesson a teacher who is conscious of them can be more successful than one who is ignorant of them.

Let's take, for example, the physiological needs of oxygen and exercise. Teachers may easily fall short of motivating children simply because they have failed to make sure that everyone has enough oxygen. Without a sufficient supply of oxygen, the brain becomes sluggish, curiosity dies, and boredom is the response to your frantic efforts to "teach them something." Making sure there is plenty of fresh air in your classroom is a help, of course, but it's often not enough. What some teachers have discovered is that some type of invigorating activity at periodic intervals throughout the day is essential to most children. Such activity, rather than interfering with learning, actually seems to enhance it.

This doesn't mean your classroom must be conducted like a three-ring circus. It does mean, though, that large-muscle movement should be encouraged frequently. Even if you do no more than ask them to touch their toes before they sit down for a reading lesson, you stand a better chance of getting their intellectual attention. And during the lesson you can get them up to the board occasionally or have them pantomime a word or sentence. (A few teachers behave as though their students were bodiless minds: Lavatory use is strictly scheduled, getting out of seats without permission is forbidden, and one intellectual activity follows another without any break for a physical activity.)

Which of these times would be best for having a session of dancing, rhythms, or dramatic play?

1. Just before recess so they can take their noise and excitement outside afterwards
2. Between two quiet intellectual sessions so they get the exercise they need
3. Right after recess because they'll be calmer then

Usually, it would be a good idea to use the dancing, rhythms, or dramatic play as an opportunity for plenty of movement—a chance for a physical break between two intellectual activities.

We've talked about a physiological need and how it can be met before and during your reading instruction. Now let's talk about the need for safety or security. This need can be met during your reading instruction in a number of ways— by providing each child with success, by accepting mistakes as natural allies of learning, and by assuring that instruction is carried on under reasonably orderly conditions. Obviously children are not going to feel secure if a lesson confronts them with a series of failures. To be motivated to engage in an intellectual exercise, they must experience success during that exercise. (More about success in a moment.) Nor will children feel secure if they perceive an intolerant attitude toward their mistakes. Nor will they feel secure if other children continually "misbehave" and things seem "out of control" to them.

Suppose you ask James to read aloud a page that he has prepared silently for a small group of children. At one point he reads, "The *tried* woman couldn't walk another step." What might be your best response?

1. "No James. You missed the second word in that sentence. Say it again."
2. To Melinda: "Good, Melinda! You corrected him on that second word. You're right. It should be *tired* and not *tried*."
3. "James, the second word in the sentence does look like *tried*, but since *tried* doesn't fit the meaning of the author, why don't you look at that second word again."

Which of those three responses would be most conducive to meeting James's needs for security, self-esteem, and belonging? Why do you think so? (If you like none of those three responses, how would you personally respond?)

Sarah is a second-grader with a minor articulation problem. Her teacher feels that Sarah is a "needy child." Sarah's need for love (affection, warmth, friendliness, and sense of belonging), like the need for security and the physiological needs, has to be considered throughout the school day. But even during a single lesson it can be partially met by letting her know that her teacher and peers are on her side in her efforts to learn to read. To meet both the need for security and the need for a sense of belonging, the teacher should vigorously discourage children from making fun of those who make mistakes. This effort is considerably easier, of course, if the teacher refrains from careless smiles and sarcastic remarks.

Instead of reading, "I see three cookies on the table," Sarah reads, "I see *free* cookies on the table." What would be the best response for the teacher to make?

1. "Sarah, let me help you make the *th* sound in the word *three*. Watch my mouth."
2. "Sarah, I've told you many times—the *th* digraph is not pronounced /f/."
3. "Free! I didn't know the cookies were free. Did you, boys and girls?"*

You can meet the need for esteem during a lesson by making children feel important to you and their peers. A child who is rarely called upon, for example, won't feel very important. Yet this can easily happen when the teacher hurries to "cover the material" or calls on only the brightest students so as to save himself the effort of teaching the slower ones. (This may happen especially when the teacher is tired or feeling "behind.")

Miss Black is developing a whole language program in which her second-grade children do a great deal of writing and also a lot of reading of literature and each other's writing. From something Samuel has written in his journal, she realizes that he is not feeling very important in the group. Which of these might be appropriate for Samuel?

---

*Responses like these are not fantasies; they are based on actual comments heard in classrooms.

1. Let him choose the book that the teacher will read to the class at the end of the day. If the children like it, tell them that Samuel selected it (if he hasn't already boasted about this).

2. Read an "anonymously written" story to the class written by Samuel (with his secret permission). After enhancing the excitement of this story with a "good rendition," ask the class to guess the real author. After three guesses say, "Will the real author stand up, please."

3. Announce to everyone in the room that Samuel has just written the "best story in the whole class."

One of these solutions violates principle one, of course. The other two don't. Perhaps you can think of an even better solution than those offered.

When teachers are aware of a child's physiological needs and her needs for security, belonging, and importance, the child is much more likely to be motivated toward self-actualization and intellectual understanding. The need for self-actualization, for most children, includes the desire to communicate better. Most children seem to perceive communication, including the act of reading, as "adult" and something they would like to be able to do as skillfully as adults do. Children who seem not to want to learn how to communicate better ("disadvantaged" children from all ethnic groups and economic strata) have frequently been unable to meet their "lower" needs. Attempts to motivate these children without taking their needs into account will often not succeed.

Principle Two: Teach at the Appropriate Level of Difficulty

Perhaps principle two is violated more often than any other principle of motivation. Most teachers learn quickly from experience that a learning task that is too easy for children will be boring, and one that is too hard will cause them to withdraw. This is easy enough to see, but what can you do about it? How can you select a learning task that will be just the right level of difficulty for each child?

Probably you can't. But to motivate children successfully, you have to try to come as close as possible to a task that will challenge them but not overly frustrate them. As an illustration, let's take Coach Cassidy, the track coach for Emerson High, working with a high jumper named Phil Peterson. Coach Cassidy puts the crossbar down fairly low the first time, so that Phil can clear it "with no sweat." Then he raises it slightly so that Phil has to expend a little more effort the next time. Then the coach raises it again—not so high that Phil misses and becomes frustrated, but just high enough to make him put a little more effort into the jump than he did the time before. This same gradual increase continues, making the task hard enough to be challenging but easy enough to be positively reinforcing: high enough to spur on the jumper to greater achievement, low enough to assure success. Success and difficulty go hand in hand to motivate the learner.

For the reading teacher, the task of finding the right level of difficulty is not as easy. A major step in the right direction is to teach diagnostically rather than with a shotgun approach. This means you must find out, through kid watching and informal testing procedures, approximately what level each child is reading on and what reading concepts and strategies he has. Having assessed the levels and problems of your students, you'll be able to teach them individually and to form small groups who need similar assistance.

But suppose the *lesson* you're teaching is obviously not at the right level: For some children it's too easy, and for some it's too hard. In this case, it's best to abbreviate your planned lesson and spend the extra time working with the children who are having trouble, while the rest move on to a follow-up activity or to reading in library books.

It's seldom advisable to ignore the difficulties some children may be having, thinking "they'll get it when they're older." Nothing is more dampening to motivation than to have one concept after another go by you and to fall farther behind. Nor is it advisable in your planning for the lesson to overlook its prerequisites. By carefully listing, mentally or on paper, and by teaching those prerequisite concepts first, you can avoid a serious motivation problem.

Halfway through a lesson on finding the root in words with an *-ed* suffix, you notice that Ronny understands it well and is looking quite bored. Which of these may be best to do?

1. Challenge him to find the root in some nonsense words such as *ruckled* or some hard words like *investigated*.
2. Do nothing special for him, as extra practice never hurt anyone.
3. Tell him that since he knows so much, perhaps he'd like to take over the lesson.

Principle Three: Provide Frequent and Specific Feedback

In brief, the procedure for following principle three is to help your students learn a small amount of information and follow this with a request for some type of response—answering a question orally, writing a response, circling something on the board, pointing to a place in their book. You then give the students feedback in the form of a nod or the correct answer to compare with their own, or whatever will inform them about the adequacy of their understanding.

Which type of written feedback on a child's daily journal would best meet principle three (and principle one as well)?

1. "Your writing during the past month, Judith, has been excellent!"
2. "What you said about donkeys, Judith, seems to be true. When I had my first ride on one, I had the same trouble getting him to move. Maybe this is why I enjoyed this story the most of all you've written. It sounds so true!"
3. "Your ideas may be fine, but your spelling makes them hard to read."

Principle Four: Add Novelty to Their Learning Experiences

This principle is perhaps so simple it needn't be discussed. But what about the children in some classrooms who daily suffer the tedium of teaching procedures and workbook formats that never vary? The novelty principle may be simple and obvious, but how often we teachers ignore it—although it's easy to understand why an overworked elementary school teacher may prefer the comfort of familiarity.

Following the novelty principle needn't be as time- and energy-consuming for the teacher as it sounds. Something as simple as having the children occasionally write on butcher paper with a felt pen instead of the usual chalkboard routine is often enough to cause a sharp rise in motivation. Or sitting on the floor instead of chairs. Or teaching a reading lesson in the afternoon instead of the morning. Or using sign language for part of the lesson. Or using a game for part of the lesson. Or giving a different piece of colored chalk to each child to use at the board: little things that take a bit of imagination but not much extra energy on the teacher's part.

On the other hand, I should point out that whole language programs or language experience approaches or personalized literature programs normally have considerable novelty built into them. Journal writing, for example, is highly personal, and therefore the chance for novelty is considerably better than it is with the filling in of worksheets. Choosing your own literature rather than reading what everyone else is reading in the basal reader has the potential for more novelty. What I'm suggesting, therefore, is that you build into your reading program, no matter what type it is, many opportunities for personal writing and personal selection of reading material.

If you'd like to remember these four principles of motivation you may want to make up some type of mnemonic (memory) device. Here's one that I like:

Novelty Needs Level Feedback.

By remembering that sentence, I can remember to think about novelty; concern myself with children's basic needs—especially for belonging and importance; teach at a level that is moderately challenging but not frustrating; and provide immediate and specific feedback whenever possible.

PROVIDING SUCCESS THROUGH BETTER RETENTION

The old adage that nothing succeeds like success applies to the development of reading skill as much as any other endeavor in life. The child who feels successful during the process of learning to read will generally have a positive attitude toward reading itself. The child who feels unsuccessful will often take out his frustration by misbehaving, refusing to read, and sabotaging the teacher's efforts to provide remedial instruction. The child-saboteur may even go to such lengths as to purposely do poorly on tests to prove that he's "too dumb to learn to read anyway, so why try."

For success to occur as she learns to read, a child must retain what she's learning long enough to practice it thoroughly in normal reading situations. If Millie learns several sight words during a reading lesson but then forgets them before she reads whole text that contains those words, her sense of success will not be enhanced.

It may be tempting for teachers to perceive success for a child in terms of how much praise or how many points he gets for performing noninteractive tasks, such as circling all the words that start with the /sh/ sound. Praise and worksheet points for isolated tasks may be necessary ingredients of success, but they're really only the peripheral measures. The real measure of success is whether the child, on his own, reading by himself, can holistically apply what he's learned from the teacher's modeling, can enjoy the process of reading, and can communicate effectively with an author; thus, the absolute necessity for him to retain concepts and insights gained during reading lessons.

Let's assume that by concerning yourself with their basic needs and by using the principles related to novelty, feedback, and difficulty, you have now sufficiently motivated your students—they are ready to learn certain concepts necessary to skilled reading. How should these be taught? Is there any way for children to experience them so that they understand them quickly and well—so well that they don't forget them in a few days? To answer this question, we must consider four additional principles of learning.

Principle Five: Teach for Mastery

Mastery learning has been receiving bad press ever since whole language programs have become popular. And probably deservedly so, since many mastery programs have been fanatically "pushed" and are overly behavioristic in format and philosophy. The concept of mastery learning, though, is ancient and useful—one that probably was conceived thousands of years ago in hunting and gathering societies. If one didn't master the knowledge of safe berries versus poisonous berries, for example, one didn't stay around long enough to complain about mastery learning.

Simply put, this principle means to teach with thoroughness and meaningfulness. It means to avoid covering information just for the sake of covering. Sometimes (but *not always*, please), it means that we set up specific performance objectives before teaching. That is, we think hard about (1) the things our students should be able to do as a result of a specific reading lesson; (2) the specific way we'll be able to tell whether they're learning from the lesson; and (3) how well they should be able to do the thing we want them to do as a result of the lesson.

Often, though, the mastery principle doesn't imply setting up performance objectives at all. It simply means that we try to make children's learning experiences clear and meaningful. Whole language advocates, for instance, feel that abundant practice with whole text reading and whole text writing provides plenty of opportunities for meaningful learning to take place. Through such opportunities, mastery of reading and writing processes occurs in a very natural way.

But why teach for mastery? Who cares whether children master what you teach them? Isn't it enough simply to introduce them to something and let them master it later if they wish? These are appealing questions that often arise when the teacher is getting discouraged and ready to give up on Betty and Tommy. Undoubtedly, there are some things that should only be introduced rather than mastered—things that lie in the realm of appreciation such as listening to symphonic music or having an enjoyable craft experience. But what about a basic skill, such as reading, that one is expected to acquire and use throughout life; a skill that if not acquired often causes one to think of herself as a failure? Here, it seems, we're talking about something that should be learned very well indeed.

What happens to Christina when she doesn't master what is taught in one lesson, and another, and still another? That's right, her accumulated failures begin to interfere with future learning. Furthermore, she gradually develops a habit of not learning and forms a picture of herself as a person who is incapable of learning.

Two of the following practices would be helpful in encouraging "learning for mastery." Which practice would not encourage learning for mastery?

1. Dividing the number of pages in a textbook by the number of school days and assigning that many pages each day
2. Basing the content of a lesson on the children's previous experiences and schemata
3. Comparing and contrasting the concept you're teaching with other concepts

Method 1, dividing the pages, is approximately the method used by some teachers—and understandably, too, if their basic goal is "coverage" rather than "mastery." Procedure 2, using previous experiences, uses positive transfer from prior knowledge to new learning, and therefore aids in the goal of mastery. Procedure 3, comparing and contrasting—that is, showing how the new concept is similar to and different from known concepts—is one of the best means of adding depth of meaning and assuring mastery.

Principle Six: Provide Massed Practice Followed by Distributed Practice

You may think this principle means simply to "give them lots of practice and review often." But as usual it's not as simple as that. If Glenda has learned a word with quite a bit of meaning, such as *mother* or her own name, she'll remember it with little or no practice. But for less meaningful words like *the, there, here,* and *come,* it is likely that she'll need massed practice at first, followed by distributed practice later. Provide frequent, closely spaced practice of only a few new words at first, while making sure the child is decoding the words correctly. Follow this with practice distributed over several days or weeks, with the space between practice periods getting longer and longer.

There is no magic formula for distribution of practice. It will depend on how meaningful the material is, how motivated the child is, and what problems the child is having in learning the material. The main points to remember in developing a practice schedule are these: (1) The student may need considerable guidance in the introductory session; (2) the practice sessions that immediately follow the introductory session should be brief, frequent, and closely spaced; and (3) the remaining practice sessions should be farther and farther apart.

Which of the following do you think is the best schedule of practice for learning how to relate new reading topics to prior knowledge and schemata?

1. During a thirty-minute lesson in which the teacher models "schemata referencing," then for ten minutes the following day with two or three topics, then for two minutes before lunch the following day, and occasionally throughout the year

2. During a thirty-minute modeling session, then for a ten-minute review a week later

3. During a five-minute modeling session, followed by a five-minute review once a week for the rest of the year

Principle Seven: Get Everyone Involved Each Step along the Way

If you want maximum learning to take place, try to get each child involved in each problem you pose and each question you ask, each step along the way.

Which of these approaches in Mr. Sanchez's class would get the greatest number of students involved?

1. "John, would you please go to the board and circle a word in the sentence that gives you an idea of what our target word in that sentence means?"

2. "Now, I'd like *someone* to go to the board and circle a word in the sentence that gives you an idea of what our target word in that sentence means."

3. "Whose turn is it to go to the board? Mary? Okay, you go to the board and circle a word in the sentence that gives you an idea of what our target word in that sentence means."

4. "Now, boys and girls, please watch while I circle a word in the sentence that gives me an idea of what our target word in that sentence means."

Approach 4 (". . . please watch while I circle . . . ") requires the responsibility of no one but the teacher, although he may hope that all the children will actually watch—and think about what they're watching. Unfortunately, this is often a vain hope. Very little challenge has been developed; all that the children have to do is tilt their heads in his direction, thus fooling Mr. Sanchez into thinking that learning is magically transferring from *his* lips to *their* brains.

Approach 1 ("John, would you please go . . . ") and approach 3 ("Whose turn is it to go . . . ") require the responsibility of only one child; the others are free to dream and scheme. The only approach likely to get them all involved is approach 2 (" . . . I'd like *someone* to go . . . "), since none of them is sure who's going to be called upon next. You can also try other approaches, such as everyone holding up a written answer at the same time, or everyone writing on the board at the same time.

Now let's try another situation. Which of these would encourage the most involvement? (*Hint:* One of these might work well for some children; one of these violates principle seven and is frequently used by college professors; one of these might work well for other children.)

1. Present a little bit of information, give them a problem or question, present a little more information, give them a problem or question, present a little more information.

2. Present all your information at once and then ask if there are any questions. Then say, "Well, if there are no questions, I assume you understand it perfectly."
3. Present a problem or question, give them a little bit of information, present another problem or question, give them a little more information, present another problem or question.

According to research (Pratton & Hales, 1986), active involvement significantly increases learning and retention. Why is this so? Let me speculate: For one thing, by getting a student personally involved, you've increased the amount of emotional impact of the instruction, and learning that takes place "with feeling" generally is retained longer. For another thing, the personal involvement results in the student's receiving a greater amount of feedback and also encouragement, if you've done a good job of teaching. Encouragement strengthens the desire to learn (Hicks & Driscoll, 1988); feedback provides the learners with a check on how well they are doing.

Principle Eight: Help Positive Transfer Occur

Positive transfer is the effect that previous learning has on helping a person learn something new. Teachers and researchers have discovered, however, that positive transfer often does not take place automatically. Rather, it takes place only when the learner perceives the similarity between one learning situation and a subsequent one. And frequently the similarity has to be drawn to the learner's attention by the teacher.

In which of the following situations would positive transfer most likely take place?

1. Learning to decode *cat,* followed soon by learning to decode *mouse*
2. A lesson on decoding the letter *b,* followed soon by a lesson on decoding the letter *d*
3. Learning to decode *cat,* followed soon by learning to decode *cats*
4. A lesson on decoding long *a* in a VCE pattern (*bake*), followed soon by a lesson in decoding long *i* in a VCE pattern (*bike*)

Very little positive transfer can take place in alternative 1, since it would be difficult for the learner to perceive any similarity between the *decoding* of *cat* and *mouse.* In alternative 2, the learner may perceive the similarity between the two learning situations but that's just the problem. Rather than positive transfer, you are more likely to have negative transfer. In fact, children often get *b* and *d* confused, especially if one is introduced before the other is learned quite well. (Once the two have become confused, however, about all you can do is to bring them together in the same lesson and show the learner how the two differ.)

In alternative 3, learning the word *cat* will probably help the child learn the word *cats,* particularly if she learns the word *cat* quite well before the word *cats* is introduced—and particularly if the teacher helps the child see what makes the two words similar and different. Alternative 4 (*bake, bike*) is also conducive to positive transfer, provided again that the long *a* in a VCE pattern is first mastered and provided that the teacher helps the child see the essential similarity between the two situations (that the VCE pattern generally makes both the *i* and the *a* represent long sounds).

Of course, there's one type of transfer the reading teacher wants more than any other: to have the children decode words they meet in books and on cereal boxes just the way they learned to decode them in a reading lesson. This is why most teachers try to provide practice in context during the course of a lesson. Reading whole passages, rich in context cues, not only provides vital practice in decoding the *words* in context; it also permits transfer from "skill lessons" to interactive reading. The teacher must keep these two ideas—contextual reading and interactive reading—constantly in mind if she wishes positive transfer of major importance to occur. If you make the practice during instruction similar to the long-range process you're trying to develop, positive transfer is more likely to take place.

To remember these four principles of "success through retention," you may want to make up another mnemonic device. One that works well for me is this:

Involved Masters Practice Transfer.

This sentence reminds me to get every learner involved in every step of the lesson; to teach for mastery rather than coverage; to use massed practice during the lesson and follow with distributed practice over the next few days and weeks; and to teach in such a way that positive rather than negative transfer occurs.

USING ATTITUDE AND INTEREST INVENTORIES

Some educators feel that teachers should use some kind of attitude inventory to determine each child's basic attitude toward reading. This is certainly not a bad idea if you're not sure, especially if you think the child would rather fill out an inventory than just talk it over with you. Most experienced teachers I've discussed this with have told me they prefer to get this particular information from observing a child and from talking with him. My own experience with children has generally been the same.

Nonetheless, if you want to be more objective about your judgments, Figure 13.2 is one form of attitude inventory that might be useful because of its brevity and simplicity. It was developed in 1976 by the Right to Read Office in Washington, D.C.

FIGURE 13.2
Reading interest/attitude
scale (Right to Read Office,
Washington, DC, 1976)

READING INTEREST/ATTITUDE SCALE

Right to Read Office, Washington, D.C., 1976

Date_____Grade____Name_____

Directions: Read each item slowly twice to
each child. Ask him or her to point to the
face which shows how he or she feels about
the *statement*. Circle the corresponding
symbol. Read each item with the same
inflection and intonation.

A
Strongly Agree
(Makes me feel good)

B
Undecided
(OK or don't know)

C
Strongly Disagree
(Makes me feel bad)

A B C 1. When I go to the store I like to buy books.
A B C 2. Reading is for learning but not for fun.
A B C 3. Books are fun to me.
A B C 4. I like to share books with friends.
A B C 5. Reading makes me happy.
A B C 6. I read some books more than once.
A B C 7. Most books are too long.
A B C 8. There are many books I hope to read.
A B C 9. Books make good presents.
A B C 10. I like to have books read to me.

For teachers in the elementary classroom, a more important type of inventory that provides specific help to the teacher seems to be an *interest* inventory. An interest inventory can tell you what kinds of books the child likes and what kinds of activities he engages in that he might also like to read and write about. To make an interest inventory about books, all we have to do is to borrow the ideas from Chapter 9. Make copies of the inventory in Figure 13.3 and read it to your students, one statement at a time, while they circle the appropriate number.

To make an interest inventory about activities the child enjoys, you can use a different format. For example:

1. What do you like to do in your free time?
2. Would you rather go to the science museum or the zoo?
3. Would you rather go to the library or to a music concert?
4. Would you rather write about an elf or about a spaceship?
5. What's your favorite TV show?
6. What do you like to do that you would like to share with friends?
7. What do you do best?

	A lot		A little		Not at all
1. I like to read about people that have real problems.	5	4	3	2	1
2. I like stories about finding clues and solving a mystery.	5	4	3	2	1
3. I like to read books of poems.	5	4	3	2	1
4. I like books with lots of pictures.	5	4	3	2	1
5. I like stories about people in love.	5	4	3	2	1
6. I like legends and tall tales.	5	4	3	2	1
7. I like funny stories.	5	4	3	2	1
8. I like books about animals.	5	4	3	2	1
9. I like make-believe stories about traveling in space.	5	4	3	2	1
10. I like books about important people.	5	4	3	2	1
11. I like sports stories.	5	4	3	2	1
12. I like to read plays.	5	4	3	2	1
13. I like science books.	5	4	3	2	1
14. I like stories about people of long ago.	5	4	3	2	1
15. I like adventure stories that take place outdoors.	5	4	3	2	1
16. I like fantasy stories about imaginary creatures and things that couldn't possibly happen.	5	4	3	2	1

FIGURE 13.3
Reading interest inventory

These are just a few ideas. You can easily make up your own and change them as your experiences dictate. The point is that you now have useful information to help children find books they will like, to help them write about things that really interest them, to help them feel a sense of belonging and importance, and to help them develop a positive attitude toward reading, writing, and school.

SUMMARY OF MAIN IDEAS

☐ A child's attitude toward reading can greatly affect his reading achievement.

☐ Parents can have a major influence on a child's attitude toward reading. They should be encouraged in a variety of ways to become involved in developing their children's reading abilities and attitudes.

☐ Success in reading growth may have as much to do with children's *models* as it does with the specific instruction they receive.

☐ Parents, teachers, and peers are all important models.

☐ Children's attitudes toward reading can be influenced by the principles of motivation a teacher follows or doesn't follow.

☐ Children's success in reading can be altered by the degree to which the teacher follows principles of retention.

☐ Interest inventories or conferences can provide teachers with specific insights about their students. These insights can guide teachers in helping children engage in appropriate reading and writing experiences.

APPLICATION EXPERIENCES FOR THE TEACHER EDUCATION CLASS

A. *What's Your Opinion?* Use your own background as well as what you've learned from the textbook to defend your decision.

1. Adults can sometimes be hypocritical with children about the importance of reading.
2. The most important models for children are teachers.
3. Encouraging parents to help teach children is a mistake. They'll abuse the power you give them and create more work for the teacher.
4. Reading out loud to kids just interferes with the time they have for reading by themselves.
5. Whether a child enjoys reading or not has a little to do with motivation principles but not with retention principles.
6. Don't worry about a kid's reading attitude. Just teach her how to read successfully and she'll have a good attitude.

B. *Learning Principles:* Examine the following case studies with a partner or small group and decide what to do in each case. Decide what learning principle or principles you used in making each decision.

1. *Case Study One:* During a lesson on the VCE pattern you discover that all but two of the children have not yet mastered the long and short sounds of the vowel letters. What should you do?

   a. Postpone your lesson on the VCE pattern and teach all the long and short sounds of the vowel letters.

   b. Have the two children do something else while you teach the rest of the group the long and short sounds of the vowel letters.

   c. Continue the lesson as best you can; otherwise you may never cover what you're expected to cover in a year's time.

2. *Case Study Two:* You are planning to show a film to your fourth-grade class to prepare them for some social studies reading they will be doing. Which of these procedures would be best?

   a. Show the film without stopping and give a test at the end of it.

   b. Stop the film once or twice, ask a question, have them write a brief answer, discuss the answer briefly before proceeding.

    c. Show the film without stopping, ask the children if they enjoyed it, tell them that maybe you'll show another film next week.

  3. *Case Study Three:* Suppose you have decided that Janice, a seven-year-old, needs to learn sixteen irregular words by sight. You provide her with a set of flashcards with the words printed on them and ask her to practice the words with a knowledgeable friend. How should she practice them for five or ten minutes a day so that she achieves mastery?

    a. Eight words the first day, eight more the second day, and all sixteen on the third day

    b. Four words the first day, the same four plus four more the second day, the same eight plus four more the third day, the same twelve plus four more the fourth day, all sixteen the fifth day, all sixteen three or four days later, only those she's having trouble with the next day, all sixteen the next day, all sixteen two weeks later

    c. All sixteen every day until she gets them all right

  4. *Case Study Four:* Which of these written comments by the teacher will probably lead to the greatest amount of learning?

    a. I like what you've written in your journal, Marianna.

    b. What you said about cats reminds me of my cat. He's also yellow like yours, but he likes cheese the best. I always knew that mice like cheese, but I didn't know that some cats like it.

    c. This is good, Marianna, but you might like to know that meat is spelled with an *e* and an *a* in the middle.

  5. *Other Case Studies:* Discuss the case studies in this chapter and decide how you would handle the situations described in such a way that learning principles are employed.

C. *Interest Inventories:* Add to the interest inventory shown in Figure 13.2. Select questions that will give you more insights into what the children would like to read and write about. Compare your questions with those of others in your class.

FIELD EXPERIENCES IN THE ELEMENTARY SCHOOL CLASSROOM

A. With one or more children, try out the attitude inventory shown in Figure 13.1. If possible, do this in an interview rather than passing it out as a checklist. This will give you more insights into why children feel the way they do about reading; use the interview questions as a foundation for a "frank discussion."

B. Find out the different ways the teacher you're working with uses the modeling approach toward improving children's attitudes toward reading. What are some other ways you can think of using the modeling approach?

C. What principles of learning does the teacher you're working with use to motivate the children and increase their retention? Precisely how does she do this? Are there some principles to which you would give greater attention?

D. Select three children and try to find out through observation and interview how much time they spend in one week reading just for their own pleasure or information. If possible, try to find out why the three children differ in the amount of personal reading they do at home and school.

E. Try out the interest inventory that you helped develop in your teacher education class.

REFERENCES AND SUGGESTED READING

Alexander, J., & Filler, R. (1976) *Attitudes and reading.* Newark, DE: International Reading Association.

Armstrong, M. K. (1981). Petunia and beyond: Literature for the kindergarten crowd. *The Reading Teacher, 35,* 192–195.

Borton, T. (1985). *The Weekly Reader national survey on education.* Middletown, CT: Field Publications.

Criscuolo, N. P. (1974). Parents: Active partners in the reading program. *Elementary English, 51,* 883–884.

Criscuolo, N. P. (1983). Meaningful parent involvement in reading. *The Reading Teacher, 36,* 446–447.

Cronbach, L. L. (1977). *Educational psychology.* New York: Harcourt, Brace, and World.

Davis, P. M. (1978). *An evaluation of journal published research on attitudes in reading, 1900–1977.* Unpublished doctoral dissertation. University of Tennessee.

Downing, J., & Thomson, D. (1977). Sex role stereotypes in learning to read. *Research in the Teaching of English, 11,* 149–155.

Glaser, R. (1969). Learning. In R. L. Ebel (Ed.), *Encyclopedia of Educational Research* (4th ed.) (pp. 706–733). New York: Macmillan.

Heathington, B. S., & Alexander, J. E. (1984). Do classroom teachers emphasize attitudes toward reading? *The Reading Teacher, 37,* 484–489.

Hicks, R., & Driscoll, A. (1988). Praise or encouragement? New insights into praise: Implications for early childhood teachers. *Young Children, 43,* 6–13.

Hunter, M. (1967). *Motivation theory for teachers.* El Segundo, CA: TIP Publications.

Hunter, M. (1967). *Reinforcement theory for teachers.* El Segundo, CA: TIP Publications.

Hunter, M. (1967). *Retention theory for teachers.* El Segundo, CA: TIP Publications.

Hunter, M. (1969). *Teach More—Faster!* El Segundo, CA: TIP Publications.

Klausmeier, H. J., & Davis, J. K. (1969). Transfer of learning. In R. L. Ebel (Ed.), *Encyclopedia of Educational Research* (4th ed.) (pp. 1483–1493). New York: Macmillan.

Klausmeier, H. J., & Goodwin, W. (1985). *Learning and human abilities, educational psychology.* New York: Harper & Row.

Lautenschlager, J., & Hertz, K. V. (1984). Inexpensive, worthwhile, educational—parents reading to children. *The Reading Teacher, 38,* 18–20.

Maslow, A. H. (1970). *Motivation and personality.* New York: Harper & Row.

May, F. B. (1969). An improved taxonomical instrument for attitude measurement. *College Student Survey, 2,* 31–35.

McKinney, J. A. (1977). *The development and implementation of a tutorial program for parents to improve the reading and mathematics achievement of their children.* (ERIC Document Reproduction Service, ED 113 703).

Neale, D. C., Gill, N., & Tismer, W. (1970). Relationship between attitudes toward school subjects and school achievement. *Journal of Educational Research, 63,* 232–237.

Newman, A. P. (1982). Twenty lives revisited—a summary of a longitudinal study. *The Reading Teacher, 35,* 814–818.

Niedermeyer, F. C. (1970). Parents teach kindergarten reading at home. *Elementary School Journal, 70,* 438–445.

Pratton, J., & Hales, L. W. (1986). The effects of active participation on student learning. *Journal of Educational Research, 79,* 210–215.

Puryear, C. (1975). *An investigation of the relationship between attitudes toward reading and reading achievement.* Unpublished doctoral dissertation. University of South Carolina.

Quandt, I., & Selznick, R. (1984). *Self-concept and reading*. Newark, DE: International Reading Association.

Roswell, C. G. (1967). *Change in attitude toward reading and its relationship to certain variables among children with reading difficulties*. Unpublished doctoral dissertation. George Peabody College for Teachers, Nashville.

Shuck, A., Ulsh, F., & Platt, J. S. (1983). Parents encourage pupils (PEP): An innercity parent involvement reading project. *The Reading Teacher, 36,* 524–528.

Trelease, J. (1982). *The read-aloud handbook*. New York: Penguin.

White, W. F. (1969). *Psychosocial principles applied to classroom teaching*. New York: McGraw-Hill.

Wittrock, M. C. (1986). *Handbook of research on teaching* (3rd ed.). New York: Macmillan.

Teaching Reading to C
with Special Nee

===================== **CHAPTER PREVIEW** =====================

We talked in Chapter 13 about increasing children's positive attitudes toward reading and reading instruction, but we left out a major influence on these attitudes—the degree to which the teacher relates to the special needs of gifted, second language, and handicapped children. In an average classroom in our country, nearly half the students belong to one of these three categories; when it comes to reading attitudes, the teacher's approach to these students is a major factor indeed.

In this chapter we'll discuss the nature of "advanced learners" who are at least mildly gifted and some ways to match your reading program to their needs. We'll also discuss ways of teaching children whose culture and language may differ from yours. We'll also examine means of helping two types of handicapped learners, the slow learner and the learning disabled. I have concentrated on these two types of handicapped students for two reasons: (1) They far outnumber children with emotional and dicaps, and (2) they have the handicaps that most elementary teachers are at least moderately pre-d to accommodate. At any rate, I hope at as you read this chapter, you rediscover

the need for teachers to be highly flexible in the materials and methods they use in working with a classroom of highly individual children.

Who's gifted? Who's disabled? Who's normal? These are questions that humans often concern themselves with. And never find answers. And why should they?

—Uncle Bogglestar

We need to look at the way that culture impacts the processing of information, the weighting, the prioritizing of experience and concepts. . . . The majority of kids that walk through your classroom door have a very distinct cultural style.

—Amalia Mesa-Bains

Zoologist Says Dog Yaps Make Sense

LONDON (EPI)—A zoologist from Oxherd University claims to have deciphered the yelps, snarls, and bays of canines. Dr. Feline, who has been studying dog "speech" for years, says that dogs communicate with each other by means of a very elaborate set of noises, which he has dubbed "fanguage."

After traveling through various parts of the world, Dr. Feline has come to the conclusion that there are at least 3000 different fanguages. Furthermore, he states, most dogs understand only one or two fanguages, resulting in a great deal of confusion, misunderstanding, and dog fights.

Not only are there a great variety of fanguages, but each fanguage has a number of "dogalects" (variations within a fanguage). A hound in one part of a large city, says Dr. Feline, may woof a dogalect which differs in many respects from the dogalect woofed in another part of the city. Curs from these two parts of the city can usually intercommunicate to some extent, but they find it either irritating or amusing. Dr. Feline has observed, moreover, that each canine acts as though his dogalect were superior to all other dogalects.

Dogalects differ not only among geographical regions, says Dr. Feline, but also between canine classes within a region. The upper-class dogs (consisting of pedigreed animals and those who strive to be like them) woof a different dogalect from the lower-class dogs (consisting of mutts, mongrels, and tramps). For example, the upper-class dogs in London will woof,

"Grrr rowlf urr yelp,"

whereas the lower-class dogs will woof,

"Grr rawlf orr yelp."

According to Dr. Feline, this slight difference is enough to cause
frothing of the mouth by upper-class and lower-class dogs alike.

—Frank May

DIVERSITY IN THE AMERICAN CLASSROOM

One of every six people in the United States does not use English as his or her first language (Bethell, 1976). One of nine people in the U.S. has a learning disability (Kirk et al., 1978). One of ten is at least mildly gifted or talented (Clark, 1983). One of seven is a slow learner (Kirk et al., 1978).

What do these approximate figures mean to the classroom teacher? It means that if you have a *typical* group of thirty children, you'll have five children who may not be proficient in English (and may not use it at home). It means you'll have three who are at least mildly gifted, three who are learning disabled to some degree, and four who are intellectually slow. Even allowing for overlap, nearly half your class will have special needs. These estimates vary considerably from classroom to classroom, and I don't cite these figures to frighten you. Yet I do want to remind you of the reality of human differences. These differences don't mean that a teacher must teach each child as a strange and isolated individual. After all, our similarities outnumber our differences. It does mean, though, that a teacher needs to be aware of differences and adjust her pace, methods, and materials. To make these adjustments, you'll need two kinds of information: (1) the nature of the differences, and (2) the methods and materials that can be tried with various individuals and groups. We'll begin our examination of differences by talking first about children who are considered at least mildly gifted. Remember, though, that there are many ways for children to be gifted: some with words, some with numbers, some with music, some with muscle coordination. Gifted children, like their so-called average classmates, vary enormously. We'll limit our discussion to children who are gifted in verbal intelligence.

ANNE MARIE: A GIFTED LEARNER

Although Anne Marie is only ten, she's in the sixth grade. Her vibrancy, easy laugh, and naturally tight-curled hair are just three of the things that make her stand out among her older classmates.

Her homeroom teacher, Mr. Jeremiah, likes her a lot. "She's such an eager learner," he says. Then he adds with a smile of admiration, "And a great softball pitcher as well." At times, though, she does annoy him with her sarcastic humor and her attempts to "reorganize the world, according to Anne Marie."

Anne Marie was born to loving and very bright parents. Added to this genetic inheritance was an early environment ready-made for such an eager and curiosity-driven disposition. Some people, of course, would have called her environment "impoverished"—no bustling city even close, a town of less than

3,000 souls, and a house in the country that provided no readily accessible neighbors or playmates. Except, that is, for her two slightly younger brothers and a much younger sister. These companions provided stimuli galore, a *Caddie Woodlawn* experience, the brothers outgoing and full of "I-dare-you-to's." And with her adventurous spirit she often *took* those dares and outdid her brothers in feats of "courage." They, in turn, with seldom a grudge, made her the unofficial leader of their four-member gang—her inventive imagination and organizational genius making her a shoo-in for the position. Her very young sister would have voted twice if there'd been an election; instead she became the perfect student for this natural-born teacher.

Anne Marie's parents and grandparents were avidly interested in their children's education. Yet they didn't rely on the local schools alone to provide it. Nor did they rely on the town library—especially since there was no town library. Instead, they filled the living room, dining room, and bedrooms with books of all sorts, books they could ill afford: twelve volumes from *My Book House* series, to take just one example. And they read these books with their children from the time Anne Marie could climb into the nearest adult lap.

But her parents didn't stop with books. Trips were important too. "Educational trips," her mother called them. To the fish hatchery, to the cheese factory, to the huge kitchens of the Welch's Grape Corporation. Her parents didn't use the word *schemata*, but they knew how to develop such things.

Books . . . educational trips . . . and people. Lots of people to help. When she was still two she was taught the alphabet by the adults and older children who often crowded the warm and friendly house. And she quickly learned her ABCs by heart—in order. She learned them verbally, that is. It took her until she was three to be able to write them—and to get *all* the letters correct. The main "one" she had trouble with was the "letter" *elemeno*. Somehow she'd convinced herself that L-M-N-O was a single letter, and this slowed her down a little.

By the age of four she could read several thin books by herself. Deprived of television and *Sesame Street*—her parents thought TV was a waste of time and money—she taught herself how to write words by pestering Mother, Dad, Gramma, and Grampa for instant feedback on her paper and pen attempts. Well before her fourth birthday she could write her first, middle, and last name.

Anne Marie had a lot she wanted to learn, and she waited to get into school like a puppy waits to be fed. There was no kindergarten in the school district budget, but through testing, and parent badgering, she was able to enter first grade shortly after her fifth birthday. During the next several years in school she often had to compensate for disillusionment; yet her active mind didn't allow her to dwell on disappointment or boredom. While the school work was often too easy, the group dynamics were always complicated and fascinating to her. Now it's especially so—now that she's with Mr. Jeremiah, who intrigues her with his amazing ways of getting the *rowdy* kids to behave.

In addition to watching a master teacher at work, she has another way of dealing with curricular disappointment. When the mobile library van comes to school, which it does every two weeks, Anne Marie very excitedly selects her six allotted books and dashes back to the classroom. There she proceeds to conceal one of them behind a social studies or science text and to gobble it whole. By the end of the two weeks she has read each of them at least three times.

Because of a federal regulation, Anne Marie was recently classified by her school district as talented and gifted—"my tag kid," as Mr. Jeremiah lovingly calls her.

WHAT WE PRESENTLY KNOW
ABOUT GIFTED LEARNERS

Most "intelligence tests" are designed so that the middle 50 percent of the population will achieve IQ scores of 90 to 110. The top 2 percent of the population will usually score above 131, and the bottom 2 percent below 69 (Clark, 1983). This means that about 10 percent will score around 120 or above. It's this figure of 120 (usually on *verbal* intelligence tests) that researchers have so often used in studying the effects of different "gifted child" programs in the schools (although Anne Marie's scores were always above 130).

All right, that gives us a very rough idea of what we mean by a "gifted learner" in a school setting—someone who verbal intelligence tests would place in the top 10 percent as far as *academic* potential is concerned.

Brain researchers claim that there are measurable *neurological* differences between gifted and "normal" individuals—such as faster movement between neurons which permits faster thinking (Thompson, Berger, & Berry, 1980); biochemically "richer" neurons that permit more complex thinking (Krech, 1969; Rosezweig, 1966); greater use of the prefrontal cortex, thus allowing for more foresight and more intuitive thinking (MacLean, 1978; Restak, 1979); more use of alpha wave activity, keeping the learner more relaxed, more capable of concentration and retention, and more likely to use the right and left sides of the brain in harmony (Lozanov, 1977; Martindale, 1976).

These brain differences, however, do not imply that heredity is the major factor in determining how advanced a student is. Numerous studies have shown that intelligence is also greatly influenced by environmental stimulation as well as by the child's inherited characteristics. Furthermore, IQ measures can change by 20 points or more depending upon the educational opportunities offered by the environment (Clark, 1983).

While high scores on intelligence tests and greater brain power are indicators of gifted-learner status, they are not the only indicators. Many, but not all, gifted learners are also highly creative as well. It is these children who probably suffer most in a school environment that encourages conformity and lock-step assignment production. These creative learners can perhaps be best identified through their personality characteristics. Research (Barron, 1962; Martindale, 1976) has shown that each of these children can be described with some of the following adjectives:

Autonomous: They make judgments without relying very much on the opinions of others. They have a high degree of self-confidence. They go against the crowd in the interest of trying to determine the truth.

Visionary: They desire change and perceive it as possible (when others may not). They feel that they are agents of change.

Goal-oriented: They have numerous ideas for keeping themselves occupied. They apply considerable effort toward projects that interest them.

Flexible: They show a high degree of adaptability in problem situations. They also use language flexibly and humorously.

Open: They demonstrate abundant curiosity and are reluctant to make judgments too quickly. They tolerate and seek new ideas and are willing to have closure or conclusion delayed.

Adventurous: They enjoy taking mild risks. They like to try new things. They enjoy the challenge of complex stimuli.

Unfortunately, some teachers perceive these characteristics differently:

Autonomous: This child is stubborn; conceited; can't follow directions.

Visionary: She's a rabble-rouser; daydreamer.

Goal-oriented: He can't apply himself to school work.

Flexible: This child is unprincipled; has an annoying sense of humor.

Open: She's always asking silly questions; can't make up her mind.

Adventurous: What a troublemaker he is; poor judgment.

As I mentioned, not all gifted learners are highly creative. Some may score high on intelligence tests but low on creativity tests. Furthermore, many teachers like to work with "high-IQ" children but not with high-creative children (Getzels & Jackson, 1960). One should not infer from this, though, that creativity and intelligence are unrelated. Some researchers (Getzels & Jackson, 1960) have tried to say that there is no relationship, but others have shown that the relationship is fairly strong (May & Ripple, 1962). Essentially, a certain degree of intelligence is necessary before creativity shows up on creativity tests. Those who score below 100 on verbal intelligence tests do not tend to do well on verbal creativity tests. When IQ scores rise above 115, however, intelligence no longer seems to determine how creative someone is (May & Ripple, 1962).

WORKING WITH GIFTED LEARNERS

Since the *creative* gifted learners seem to be the most difficult for teachers to work with, I'm going to concentrate on ways of working with them. Because these children tend to be *autonomous* in temperament, they usually thrive on opportunities to make "important" decisions that affect their lives. They welcome opportunities to choose their own books to read rather than being limited to the next story in the basal reader. They like to decide on book projects for sharing the books with others; to plan their own schedule of work; to present or write critical evaluations of books; and, in general, to guide their own ship whenever possible

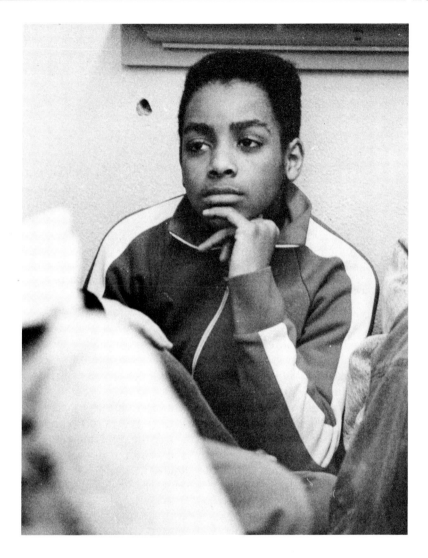

within the school setting. A PLP (personalized literature program) often works well with these children (see Chapter 9).

Since these children tend to be *visionary*, they usually enjoy reading about important change makers in our past and present; thus biographies should be a staple of their reading diet. Give them opportunities to talk and write about things that ought to be changed or improved in the world, in their classroom, in their private lives. The highly creative are fond of "make better" exercises and "what-if" exercises; for example, have them write about how they would improve such common things as pencils, chalkboards, shoes, and education. Then have them read their ideas aloud or read each other's ideas. Have them talk, write, and read about what-if situations: What if all boys had to prove they were men by cutting off their left little finger? What if we had such a severe shortage of sugar that only 100 pounds were available in our city for the next six months?

Because these children are usually *goal-oriented,* they tend to enjoy individual projects, particularly if they get to choose what they will work on. Have an index-card box on your desk with ideas for extra projects in it, such as creating a new spelling game, or writing a history of Jefferson School, or looking in an unabridged dictionary for the word that has the most meanings. They usually like book projects, particularly if they get a "ticket" or other token for each book they read and share through a book project. Have a different-colored ticket for each type of book (mystery, biography, and so on), and encourage them to read at least one of each type of book. (See Appendix F for book project ideas.) Don't forget to let them make up their own ideas for projects as well.

In addition to being autonomous, visionary, and goal-directed, high creatives tend to be flexible, open, and adventurous. Here are some ways to encourage these traits in your reading program:

Flexibility: Provide them with problem situations that require adaptability and more than one answer. For a language experience story, have them engage in an imaginary experience: lost in a huge city with no money—only a watch, a bag of lemons, and clothes—how to get home. Or try this one: stuck in a stalled elevator with your little brother who is crying—how to entertain him until help arrives—all you have in your pocket is a paper clip, a handkerchief, three pennies, and a pencil with no point. Don't forget to have them share their stories.

Also provide them with opportunities to use language flexibly. If they make a pun with your words, try enjoying it with them. (After that, if they do it too much for you, just ask them privately to write down the pun and save it for you to laugh at later.) And do help them play with words by recommending books by Fred Gwynne *(The King Who Rained; A Chocolate Moose for Dinner)* and Marvin Terban *(Eight Ate: A Feast of Homonym Riddles; In a Pickle and Other Funny Idioms; Too Hot to Hoot.)* See Helen Howell (1987) in the reference section of this chapter for more ideas.

Openness: Give them five minutes to list as many things as they can think of that they want to find out about. Have them use the "hot water" method when they make their list: The hot water of ideas is the only faucet turned on. "Don't turn on the cold water of criticism while the hot water is on or you'll just get lukewarm water. Write down every idea you have, no matter how silly it might seem." Then have them select the one they're most curious about. Develop a plan with them for locating reading material that will help them find out what they want to know.

Here's another idea for encouraging openness: Have two or more children read the same book and then compare their ideas about the book. Who was the most important character? How would they have done something different from the way the main character did it? Could this story have taken place in any other setting? If so, how would that setting have affected what happened in the story? Could the main character have been different in age or personality? If the children agree with each other too readily, the teacher should try disagreeing with them, gently challenging their ideas.

Adventurousness: Remember, these children often like to take risks, to try something new and even dangerous, and they often enjoy things that are complex. Recommend books such as *Island of the Blue Dolphins, Call it Courage, My Side of the Mountain,* and *The Hobbit.* Encourage them to try book projects that have never been tried by anyone else in the class. Help them use books as starting points for writing their own adventures and reading them to others. Let them use a tape recorder to add sound effects to their stories. Encourage them to write their own complex riddles, such as this one: "You throw away the outside and cook the inside. Then you eat the outside and throw away the inside. What is it?"* Have them try out the riddles on their friends. Plan a "dangerous" adventure with them, perhaps something they want to do on the playground that they've been afraid to do before. Then have them write or dictate an experience story describing their feelings as well as their adventure.

I would suggest, for high creative and other advanced learners, moving them out of a basal reader program as quickly as possible, either by having them move rapidly ahead in it or by omitting it entirely, depending upon the child's demonstrated abilities in reading and upon the policies of the school in which you're teaching. Generally speaking, these children need a strong alternate of a personalized literature program (Chapter 9) and a whole language program (Chapter 8). Certainly this type of child needs more stimulating writing and reading experiences than those normally provided by a basal reader program. If for some reason you feel they should go through the basal program, by all means use the enrichment experiences suggested at the end of each unit. Many of these experiences include the use of library books. You may particularly want them to consider books with gifted children as characters. Tway (1980) provides an annotated discussion of several such books in the January 1980 issue of *Language Arts,* another journal besides *The Reading Teacher* that you'll find useful in your teaching. For many ideas on helping gifted children, look also at the journal called *Gifted Child Quarterly.* Isaacs, for example, has a list of 100 classical ideas in the Summer 1973 edition. Also see *Creative Reading for Gifted Learners* (1985), edited by Michael Labuda, International Reading Association, 800 Barksdale Road, Box 8139, Newark, DE 19714.

VINCENT: A SECOND LANGUAGE LEARNER

When Vincent was seven years old, he spoke mostly Vietnamese and a little English at home. His father and mother were not born in the United States; they were born in Saigon. Vincent, first known as Rang, was born on a boat in the

---

*Corn on the cob.

South China Sea as he and his parents and twenty other adults escaped from reprisals of the North Vietnamese Army, hoping somehow to reach America across the enormously wide Pacific. All of them in the boat had sided with the United States and the South Vietnamese government and barely escaped with their lives for their "treason." By the time they were picked up by an American ship, three of his parents' friends had died of exposure.

Vincent's father had been vice president of a small bank in Saigon, but when he got to America, he couldn't speak any English and felt fortunate to find work with a Vietnam veteran—husband of a Vietnamese woman who had married the veteran while he was on duty. The work—painting cars—paid enough to provide the three of them with decent food and shelter. He was luckier than most. For the next four years, Vincent's father struggled to learn English and go to a school that taught automobile reconstruction—a trade he was told provided more jobs than did banking.

By the time little Vincent arrived at school, he had learned very little English. (His mother had stayed home to raise him and two younger sisters and had learned only a few English words; his father generally spoke Vietnamese at home.) His first-grade teacher, Mrs. Theophilus, was a loving soul. She liked his black hair and his "cleanliness," as she called it, but she had little idea of how to work with Vincent. Most of the time that year she let him draw or "do math," reasoning that he did learn numbers fast, especially with the use of manipulative aids, but his English would have to be learned "the way other immigrants had learned it—the hard way."

Vincent smiled a lot, and that helped a little. But the problem was that Mrs. Theophilus believed in "individual effort." And this meant every kid had to work by himself. No talking, except on the playground. And thus there was little opportunity for Vincent to learn English, except by listening to the teacher. I say *listening*, because he seldom spoke to the teacher for fear of making mistakes. And on the playground he suffered the same fear—plus the fear of not being able to play the games that the other children played.

By Christmas time, Vincent had learned a fairly large set of highly functional English words such as "Stop!," "bathroom," and "mine." But his inability to string words into sentences made it difficult for him to write or read. His inferiority complex worsened daily, but he bolstered himself by working hard at his drawing. If it hadn't been for the smiles he received for his "pictures," it would have been a very bad year indeed.

The next year Vincent was passed on into second grade, because of his age and obvious intelligence. There he was confronted with a different kind of teaching. Vera Rubanovick was his teacher and she placed him at a table with three other children, all of them highly verbal and friendly. On the very first day of class she explained why they were going to be taught in a "cooperative learning" way: so they could learn from each other, so they could work like a team, so they could provide "feedback" to each other, and so they could have a "multicultural experience." Vincent didn't know what *multicultural* meant, but Mrs. Rubanovick had placed the children in such a way that kids at each table were truly different from each other in one way or another. ("Not that that's very hard to do," she told her principal. "Kids *are* different—and whether the differences are cultural doesn't matter, as long as the children learn to respect and enjoy each other.")

For the first time Vincent was provided with actual instruction in reading English. The patterned books that Mrs. Rubanovick used every day helped a great deal. The repetition, rhythm, and humor made it much easier for Vincent to enjoy and hear the "music" of the language and not just the words. Daily writing in journals helped too, especially since the teacher often responded with short written notes. And especially since the three kids at his table would help him read the notes. And especially since these same three kids competed to have a chance to "teach Vincent."

There was no ESL (English as a Second Language) program, but Mrs. Rubanovick took the time to talk privately to Vincent in English, to "put words in his mouth" that he could repeat, to learn Vietnamese phrases from Vincent, and in general to be sensitive to his special needs. Second grade was a happy, growing year for him.

All of that took place in the 1970s. Now Vincent is a successful accountant in a large firm in Seattle. His success story was written by his brave parents, his indomitable spirit, his understanding teachers, and lots of friends who liked more than his pictures.

WHAT WE PRESENTLY KNOW ABOUT SECOND LANGUAGE LEARNERS

The birthrate in the United States has been relatively stable in recent years, but the population has been increasing—due mainly to the number of immigrants entering our country each year. This, along with the large number of second-generation children of immigrant families, causes many children in elementary school classrooms to differ from teachers in their cultural and linguistic backgrounds. It's these two forms of difference, culture and language, that we'll need to discuss now. Following this, we'll talk about what teachers can do to accommodate and cherish such differences.

Cultural Differences

"Majority-culture" (MAJ) children and teachers, a label I'm using only for purposes of discussion, are those who have adopted most of the values that cause the United States to be a mildly cohesive society. They also tend to use "Standard English" as their major means of communication. "Minority-culture" (MIN) children, again for purposes of discussion, are those who have *some* values that have been strongly held in another culture (past or present) and are not held by the majority of people in this country. These children also are in the process of learning Standard English as a second language or second dialect.

Most MAJ children are taught to look to the future, to set goals for the future, and to set small subgoals that will help them gradually reach their future goals. "Someday you'll be a successful businessman like your father. But that means you're going to have to do well in high school so you can get into college. And that means you'll have to learn to read and write very well. So you'd better GET THAT HOMEWORK DONE!!"

Although many "MIN kids" are taught the same thing, many are not. They—sometimes along with their parents—have had little experience with the type of success in which most school teachers believe. In fact, they may have experienced considerable failure as far as school-related tasks are concerned. They are therefore not used to the goal-setting approach that MAJ teachers advocate.

Another cultural difference is the way that people look at achievement. Most MAJ children are taught to achieve on an individual basis—to have the best batting average, to be the best speller, to win a gold medal (and to sob a bit if you get only a bronze). Many MIN children are not taught at home to achieve in such an individualistic way. In their homes a child's identity is more closely related to the family's identity. Achievement for the family (or extended family group, including certain friends) is more important than self-achievement. The welfare of siblings is considered extremely important, and the "good of the whole" is a family motto.

There are other cultural differences, of course, but those two should serve as examples. To continue itemizing cultural differences may run the risk of establishing even more false expectations for MIN children than already exist. MIN kids differ among themselves as much as MAJ kids do. The point I'm trying to make is that cultural differences do exist in the classroom, and these can affect the motivation each child brings into the learning environment. When one motivational approach doesn't work with a student, the temptation for some teachers is to consider that particular child lazy, or deprived, or in some other way inferior. I'm urging instead that teachers consider the possibility that cultural differences are interfering with the teaching-learning relationship.

Language and Dialect Differences

As mentioned earlier, at least one out of six people in the U.S. does not speak English in the home as his primary language. On top of this, many people who do speak English as their primary language don't speak the dialect called "Standard English." We have all kinds of labels for these MIN kids. For those who don't use Standard English, we have labels such as "Black English speakers" or "Pidgin English speakers" or what-have-you. For those who use English as their second language, many educators and government officials now use the label "Limited English Proficient." I don't use it personally because it hurts my tongue and my sensitivity toward the beauty of our language. It also offends my notion of people in general and of non-Anglo speakers in the specific: They are not limited.

There are a great variety of people in this world using English today. It *is* the international language. If we had to label all of the different English-speaking peoples, we would need a special glossary just to handle the communication problems this would raise. The fact of the matter is that these people are not speaking limited English; they're speaking *their* English. What we usually mean by "limited" is that they are not using the Anglo-English dialect. Or if we want to get even more precise, people often get upset if MIN kids are not using Standard English (which semi-facetiously means the English spoken by midwesterners with a degree from the University of Chicago).

Perhaps you already read the "news" report at the beginning of this chapter, in which I jokingly compared dogs and people. This news report is partly true—the differences in dialects (and dogalects, of course) do cause "frothing of the mouth." We'll be talking about things teachers can do to reduce this problem. But right now, let's look a little further into what the word *dialect* means. Which *one* of the following sentences is definitely not grammatical? Which one is grammatical but offensive to your ear?

1. John threw his dog some meat.
2. John throwed his dog some meat.
3. John some meat his dog threw.

You're right. Number 3 doesn't fit the grammar rules of English (whatever those unconscious rules actually are). It doesn't communicate very clearly what happened. On the other hand, dialects 1 and 2 do communicate clearly what happened. It's just that "throwed" is offensive to some people's ears (and may even cause frothing of the mouth). By the same token, a child who says "He be goin' " and the child who says "He is going"' can communicate quite well with each other, but their dialect differences may cause them to feel superior or inferior to each other.

Dialect Defined

Most people know what is meant by a language, but what is a dialect? To the person who speaks it, it's the "mother tongue." To the person who speaks the same language but a different dialect, it's "sloppy speech," or "jibberish," or "lower-class speech," or "hoity-toity talk."

A dialect is a variation of a language. It differs from other variations in three ways. First, it differs *phonologically;* that is, it differs in the way people produce phonemes or in the particular phonemes used. For example, in some parts of the deep South, native speakers may say /fee-ish/ for *fish,* using a long *e* sound before the short *i* sound. People in the North, who use the short *i* sound, find this minor difference quite amusing (although linguists say that the southern dialect comes closer to the English of the British Isles in colonial days).

Second, it differs *grammatically.* That is, it may differ in the way verb tense, negation, number, and other structural changes are signaled. For instance, someone speaking African American English may say, "From now on, I don't be play-ing," whereas someone speaking Standard English (or Anglo English) might say, "From now on, I'm not going to play."

Third, it differs *lexically*. That is, the actual words or vocabulary may differ. Someone speaking African American English may say, "Please carry me home," while someone speaking Anglo English might say, "Please take me home." Someone in *America* may ask where the *restroom* is. Someone in *England* might get very confused and ask you why you need to rest. You're supposed to ask where the *toilet* is. Someone in *New England*, by the way (especially if he's up in Maine), may refer to the toilet as the "flush."

Dialect differences do not indicate sloppy speech, as some people claim. They are systematic variations of a common language. If you listen to two people speaking African American English, for instance, the differences between "Black" and "White" dialects are consistent. If a person whose mother tongue is African American English is speaking to a person whose mother tongue is Standard En-glish, there may be a tendency for the person speaking African American English (particularly a child) to switch back and forth between "Black" and "White" dialects. This is especially true in a situation where speakers of African American are made to feel that their dialect is inferior.

WORKING WITH SECOND LANGUAGE LEARNERS

Now let's go back and look at each of the differences between MAJ and MIN kids and see what these might mean for the teacher of reading and writing. We'll look first at the cultural differences and then at the language differences.

Cultural Differences and Instructional Procedures

I mentioned that MAJ kids are often taught in the home to set goals for the future (for example, preparing for college) and to set subgoals along the way to their larger goals (for example, getting good grades each day). MIN kids, I said, may not be easily motivated this way. They may not see any value in either the long-range or the short-term goals. *If* this is the case (and it most certainly *isn't* with all minority children), and *if* you feel the need to help either a MAJ kid or a MIN kid set goals, then you may want to try a particular type of "behavioral manage-ment technique."

I'm not too crazy about that term, but what I mean by it is this: You pri-vately establish a short-range goal with the child in question, for example, par-ticipating actively in each reading lesson for the next week, and agreeing on the precise reward he'll receive for his successful performance (his own paperback book, a chance to use a special ball at recess, whatever *he* wants that you're willing to provide). It sounds a bit mercenary and crass, but many teachers swear by this motivational procedure. The rewards must be highly specific and relatively quick in coming. No promises of a field trip next month, or moving up to the next grade, or getting a job when he grows up.

I also said that most MAJ children are taught to achieve primarily on an individual basis and many MIN children are not. What's more, to some MIN kids, achieving individually might be perceived as unfair to the group they belong to.

The solution to this problem is to rely more on cooperative learning, something we've talked about several times before. Research shows that it works quite well (Glasser, 1986), and as William Glasser says, "Except for tradition, I don't know why schools use so little cooperative learning. . . . Students still sit and work alone, and are continually told to keep quiet and keep their eyes on their work" (Brandt, 1988, pp. 40–41). Throughout this book I've given you examples of cooperative learning, and I hope that if you need reminders of how to use this approach, you'll turn to the index and look up those pages on this topic. Or, if you don't do that, I hope you'll let your students at least occasionally work with a partner or a team.

You see, some children, MAJ or MIN, are used to working with others, and they perceive the process of achieving as a *group* process. For them the learning process is better in a cooperative learning setting, working with the teacher and other students rather than working by themselves. For them, learning proceeds more rapidly when peers work together, or when older students help younger ones, or when the teacher works with small groups who help each other. Here are some "for instances": Lawrence (1975) described the successful use of sixth-graders to help first-graders learn to read after she had first trained the sixth-graders in the language experience approach. Himmelsteib (1975) had ninth-graders act as buddies to third-graders in selecting library books and playing reading games. Boraks and Allen (1977) developed a more elaborate plan in which college students taught fourth- and fifth-graders to tutor each other in an inner-city school. The children were taught tutoring behavior such as promoting positive response patterns, keeping others on task, explaining the objectives, giving praise, and helping others verify their own responses. Breiling (1976) describes a program in which parents are trained by teachers to work with their own children—how to encourage their children, how to use reading games, and how to have the children read to them for ten minutes a day. Improvement in enthusiasm as well as sight vocabulary has been the reported result of this program.

In addition to the two cultural differences that I've mentioned, there are, of course, many more. Yet the classroom teacher shouldn't go crazy trying to determine all those differences. Instead, there are a few basic approaches that need to be explored:

> If there isn't a direct relationship between the text and the experience of the culturally diverse child, then it's up to the teacher, prior to the reading of the text, to draw an analogous relationship between something in the child's life and what will occur in the text.
>
> *Amalia Mesa-Bains*
> *San Francisco Schools*

Expose kids to many different kinds of learning experiences: writing, acting things out, and so on. This will help you allow for cultural differences. Plan your lessons so that a variety of learning styles are possible. But even more important, examine your own values. Appreciation of diversity requires that you check yourself out first. Multicultural bulletin boards won't do it.

Susan Arroyo
Portland Public Schools

In addition to these basic notions, perhaps the most important thing to remember is that all children differ from each other in interesting and sometimes marvelous ways. Through cooperative learning, through literature from all over the world, through sharing each other's written thoughts, through a willingness to discuss controversial issues, these differences can be learned, appreciated, and valued.

Language Differences and Instructional Procedures

I'd like to emphasize three instructional requirements here:

- ☐ The importance of a learning/teaching attitude on the part of the teacher
- ☐ The need for distinguishing between reading errors and dialect differences
- ☐ The necessity for a balance among three approaches—ESL, melting pot, and native vernacular

Several studies (Burg, 1975; Davison & Lang, 1960; Rosenthal & Jacobson, 1968) have shown that the teacher's attitude may be the most important factor in determining how well many MIN children learn to read. This problem of attitude occurs all over the world. Children on the border between Brazil and Uruguay, for example, speak a dialect that is quite dissimilar from the dialect used in the schools. Eloisa (1975) says that these border children are typically way behind the other children in the schools. The problem, she says, is the teachers. Many of them refuse to treat the border dialect as a valid language with long roots in history and through which its users "can express their full personalities."

I hope you'll agree with me that all languages and dialects can be equally beautiful and useful. If you do have this attitude, I think it will be much easier for you to work with children who differ from you in culture, language, or dialect. Teachers who feel that their language, dialect, or culture is superior to those of their students are likely to have considerable difficulty teaching them to read.

You will become a more successful teacher if you become a student too. If you try to learn as much as you can of the language and the customs of the person you will be teaching, both you and your student will have more success in learning a new language and new customs. (Johnson, 1975)

So the learning/teaching attitude of the teacher is one important element of instructing second language learners. A second element is that of recognizing the differences between a student's reading errors and her dialect differences. For instance, in the following passage, which miscues would you consider to be Beverly's reading errors and which are dialect differences?

He asked his brother to take him home. His brother said he was going home.
(handwritten annotations: ast, brutha, carry, brutha, he goin', real)

soon.

You're right. When Beverly read this to me, I considered her "miscues" to be dialect differences and didn't think of them as reading errors. When she transformed Standard English into African American, she was, in effect, performing a double translation, first from written Standard English into oral Standard English, then from oral Standard English into oral African American English—an intelligent job of interactive reading. Beverly, I felt, needed no reading instruction at this level.

A third element is that of achieving a balance among the three most common approaches toward working with students whose language or dialect differs from the teacher's.

The Melting Pot Approach

With this approach you "simply" teach the child to read in Standard English, hoping she'll pick up enough understanding of Standard English speech through normal interactions with peers and teachers in the classrooms and on the playground—as well as through picture books, television, and various contacts with Standard English speakers. This has been the main approach used in U.S. schools for over 200 years. Yet the fact that this approach alone often fails is borne out by several reports (Saville & Troike, 1971; Thonis, 1976; U.S. Commission on Civil Rights, 1975).

The ESL Approach

A second approach is the *English-as-a-second-language-approach*. With this approach, children are taught to speak in Standard English before or during the time they are expected to learn to read in Standard English. This approach has the theoretical virtue of building a child's language naturally from the oral skills of listening and speaking to the written skills of reading and writing. It also has the theoretical virtue of not labeling a child's language or dialect as "incorrect," seeking instead to teach Standard English as a second dialect or language—one that is necessary for all citizens to know in order to become "successful," both socially and financially.

There is a tendency, however, for some who advocate and use this method to look at those who do not speak Standard English as "handicapped." They often propose that Standard English be taught as soon as possible so that the "handicapped students" can function properly in a regular classroom (Donoghue, 1971). By using strictly this approach, we'd be trying to drown out the children's earlier means of communicating by saturating them with Standard English. Instead of building upon the preschool language learning of these children, we'd ignore that learning and start all over again.

On the other hand, the ESL approach can be, and often is, a much more humane one than the melting-pot-only approach—especially with children who speak little English at all. But for those who merely speak a nonstandard dialect, the use of an ESL program is questionable. With respect to African American–speaking students who have been put through an ESL program, the evidence is not very encouraging. Studies (Cagney, 1977; Eisenberg et al., 1968; Hall & Turner, 1974; Peisach, 1965; Weener, 1969) indicate that the problem some of these students experience in learning to read is not in their inability to speak Standard English—or even to understand it. In Cagney's study (1977), for instance, a group of first-graders who were fluent speakers of African American and whose home language was African American were exposed to a set of language experience stories written by other children. Half the stories were written in standard dialect, and half were written in an African American dialect. They were read to the children by a teacher who was fluent in both "Standard" and "Black" English. The children were then asked questions about the stories designed to test their comprehension. On the average, the children made significantly more correct responses to questions about the stories written in Standard English than to questions about the stories written in African American.

In other words, it would appear that most children who speak African American as their native language have been sufficiently exposed to Standard

English (via television and other sources) to understand it, even though they may not be fluent speakers of Standard English. The assumption that they must learn to speak Standard English fluently before they can learn to read it is probably erroneous.

With respect to children dependent on another language, there appears to be no evidence they would benefit from learning to speak Standard English *fluently* any more than children who speak African American. It is likely that they need abundant *exposure* to Standard English before they are expected to read it well, but fluent *speech* in Standard English is probably not necessary.

But an ESL program can't do the job alone. In many schools those children classified as LEP (Limited English Proficient) "receive special English language instruction from a resource teacher for only a few hours per week. The rest of their . . . language instruction comes from the regular classroom teacher" (Hough, Nurss, & Enright, 1986, p. 510). This means that the regular classroom teacher needs to adjust her teaching techniques to this condition. Here are some suggestions for handling this situation:

1. Read stories aloud at least once a day. In addition, have same-age or older peers read aloud as well. When you, yourself, do it, sometimes use "big books" that allow everyone to see the words and pictures.
2. Have children work in pairs and/or small groups whenever possible. (See *cooperative learning* in the index.) If they're having trouble working in groups, teach them how to do it, and encourage those groups that do it well. To learn a language, children need practice in using it!
3. Use patterned books often for both reading and writing experiences. See Appendix P.
4. Expect minimal verbal response at first. After responding has become a consistently successful process for the children, gradually increase the amount of thinking and the length of response requested (a form of "scaffolding").
5. Use drama and pantomime to increase awareness of Standard English meanings.

The Native Vernacular Approach

A third approach is the *native vernacular approach*. With this approach, second language children are first taught to read and write in their mother tongue, whether it be Puerto Rican Spanish, Cantonese Chinese, Sioux, or some other language. While they are learning to read and write in their native vernacular, they are exposed to Standard English through working with Standard English–speaking children in such activities as art, music, and physical education. Sometime before the end of third grade, they are given instruction in reading English as a second language.

The native vernacular approach has strong appeal to those who feel that a child's culture and vernacular should be respected and utilized in instructional programs. The teacher can start where each child is with respect to language development. Rather than start over, he can have the child reading as soon as MAJ children are, thus avoiding the stigma and devastation of failure.

Unfortunately, this type of program has serious drawbacks. The most serious drawback, of course, is that of resources, since this program requires skilled teachers or aides who can communicate in Spanish, Vietnamese, Chinese, and so on. It also requires instructional materials written in the various languages and dialects.

The problem of finding suitable instructional materials can be handled partly through a language experience approach to reading instruction. According to Hall (1972), this approach is particularly appropriate for use with second language children because it makes it possible to have reading materials that match both their experiences and their language patterns. As you already know, reading comprehension is enchanced by the similarity between the patterns of language used by the reader and the author. Since with the language experience approach children read what they have written or dictated, this similarity is assured. Again though, as Kanani Chong of the San Francisco Schools reminds me, it's very difficult to find adults who not only speak children's language but also can *teach*.

Besides language experience charts or stories, a supply of bilingual materials is gradually being developed, such as the Miami Linguistic Reader Series published by D. C. Heath. This series for English and Spanish languages is designed to teach Spanish-speaking children not only to read Standard English, but to pronounce it with precision. Several other publishers also have developed or are developing bilingual materials.

It should be pointed out, however, that publication of African American materials has tended to elicit quite negative reactions from both "whites" and "blacks" in the community. African American parents have been particularly incensed, because they feel their children need to learn the Standard English that will allow them to "get ahead" in our society.

The problem of finding suitable teachers may diminish as more universities train people to work in bilingual settings. Admittedly the greatest demand for these teachers is in population centers where second language children are concentrated. It is a rare school district that hires bilingual teachers when only a few second language children are present in the schools.

Most likely, a bilingual approach requires school settings in which teachers have extra training and motivation. So far, however, we have few assurances based on experimental research. Most of the present arguments for the bilingual approach are based on logic, politics, subjective observations, and humanitarian concern. Yet a concerted effort must be made to assist second language children, and the bilingual approach is a promising one at this point. As Nila Smith explains:

> There is a rapidly growing philosophy in regard to dialects and the teaching of reading which is widely advocated by many well-known linguists. These linguists differ somewhat in regard to details, but fundamentally all of them agree to (1) accept the child's dialect as his native language; (2) provide him opportunities to read in his own dialect as a precedent to or along with reading in Standard English; and (3)

combine teacher guidance, appropriate materials, teacher and peer associations to aid him in acquiring ability to speak and read with increasing fluency in Standard English as a second language while maintaining his native language. (Smith, 1975, p. 139)

RALPH: A "DISABLED" LEARNER

Ralph is a nine-year-old boy who wears many invisible labels. He's been called a "nonreader," a "dyslexic," a "disabled reader," and a host of other things. Ralph has straight blond hair, blue eyes, and a smile that would melt all but the sternest of teachers. His above-average intelligence is demonstrated daily by his witty remarks and his ingenious ways of getting into trouble. Until recently he was considered hopeless by his regular classroom teachers and by his former "Chapter One" teacher.

Although he is almost ten, he is only in the third grade, since he was held back a year. Until Miss Burnette came along, he was the number-one troublemaker in the school. Miss Burnette is the new third-grade teacher at Jefferson Elementary School, and Ralph is in love with her—as much as a nine-year-old boy can be in love with a twenty-five-year-old woman.

"Ralph has been a hyperactive child since birth," according to his mother. "He's always been more interested in fiddling with things or getting into mischief than in looking at books or talking to people. Even when he's watching TV, which is quite a lot, he's got his hands fiddling with things or he's climbing on something, or he's pestering someone. He's not like his sister at all. She's much quieter and likes to read. She's been saying real words since she was one year old, but Ralph—Ralph didn't say his first word until he was past two. And he's always talked so fast and mushylike I still have trouble understanding him at times."

Ralph is not a typical disabled learner, because there is no such thing as a typical disabled learner. Ralph's particular symptoms have caused him to be labeled by his teachers and parents as "dyslexic," a label that doesn't help him much, since it simply refers to a child who shows difficulty in learning to read (despite average or above-average intelligence and despite a variety of normal instructional strategies employed by his teachers). Ralph not only reads very poorly; he also spells atrociously, writes illegibly, speaks haltingly with weak enunciation, and performs awkwardly in physical education class. Some might say that Ralph is "discombobulated." Others would say he has "specific language disabilities," or "specific learning disabilities" (as if these longer labels somehow come closer to the truth).

WHAT WE PRESENTLY KNOW
ABOUT DISABLED LEARNERS

A disabled learner by definition does not have a low intelligence quotient. By definition (and these definitions are necessary in order to decide which schools get government funds), a disabled learner is average or above in intelligence, but his ability to perform school tasks such as reading and writing is well below what is expected of him. By definition, then, Ralph is a "disabled learner" rather than a so-called "slow learner." By definition, a slow learner is one whose IQ is "well below average."

The approximate proportion of so-called slow learners in the general school population is 16 percent (Kirk et al., 1978). Out of this total of slow learners, about 87 percent are considered "borderline children," with IQs ranging from roughly 70 to 85 percent. The other 13 percent of the slow learners (about 2 percent of the general school population) are generally classified as "retarded" and are often placed in highly specialized learning environments. In this chapter we'll talk only about slow learners who are considered "borderline," since these children experience much of their total instruction from regular classroom teachers.

The approximate number of so-called disabled learners in the general school population is more difficult to discover; some say 6 percent, some say 15 percent, some say higher. The problem is one of definition. If we were to agree, for instance, that over one-fourth of those children who speak Standard English in the home have problems learning to read, how many of those children will we say have trouble because of a learning disability, and how many because of a low intelligence quotient? If we arbitrarily say that 85 is a low IQ, then we could say that all children who have difficulty learning to read whose IQs are above 85 will be classified as "disabled" rather than "slow." If, on the other hand, we arbitrarily say that 95 is a low IQ, then we will come up with a lower number of disabled readers and a higher number of slow readers. You can see then what an arbitrary and sometimes meaningless distinction is made between groups of children who are having trouble learning to read.

The Nature of Ralph's Learning Disabilities

To explain the disabled reader's situation a little better, we'll continue to use Ralph as an example. In October Ralph's grade equivalent score on a standardized reading-achievement test was 2.1, although the norm was 4.2. On a standardized diagnostic inventory, his reading score was 1.5. Both standardized scores, as low as they were, estimated his reading performance at too high a level (see Chapter 11 as to why). On an informal reading inventory, for instance, he reached frustration level while reading a preprimer passage.

On weekly spelling tests Ralph was getting three or four out of fifteen correct, until Miss Burnette decided to give him only six words a week. Now he sometimes gets five or six correct. In mathematics he often surprises his teacher with his understanding of operations and with his reasoning ability, but he usually makes so many "silly" mistakes on his computations that he scores poorly on assignments and tests. "In science," Miss Burnette says, "Ralph is a whiz—as long as he can experiment with things instead of read about them." In creative writing he shows a mild degree of inventiveness, though he has to translate his illegible handwriting for his teacher.

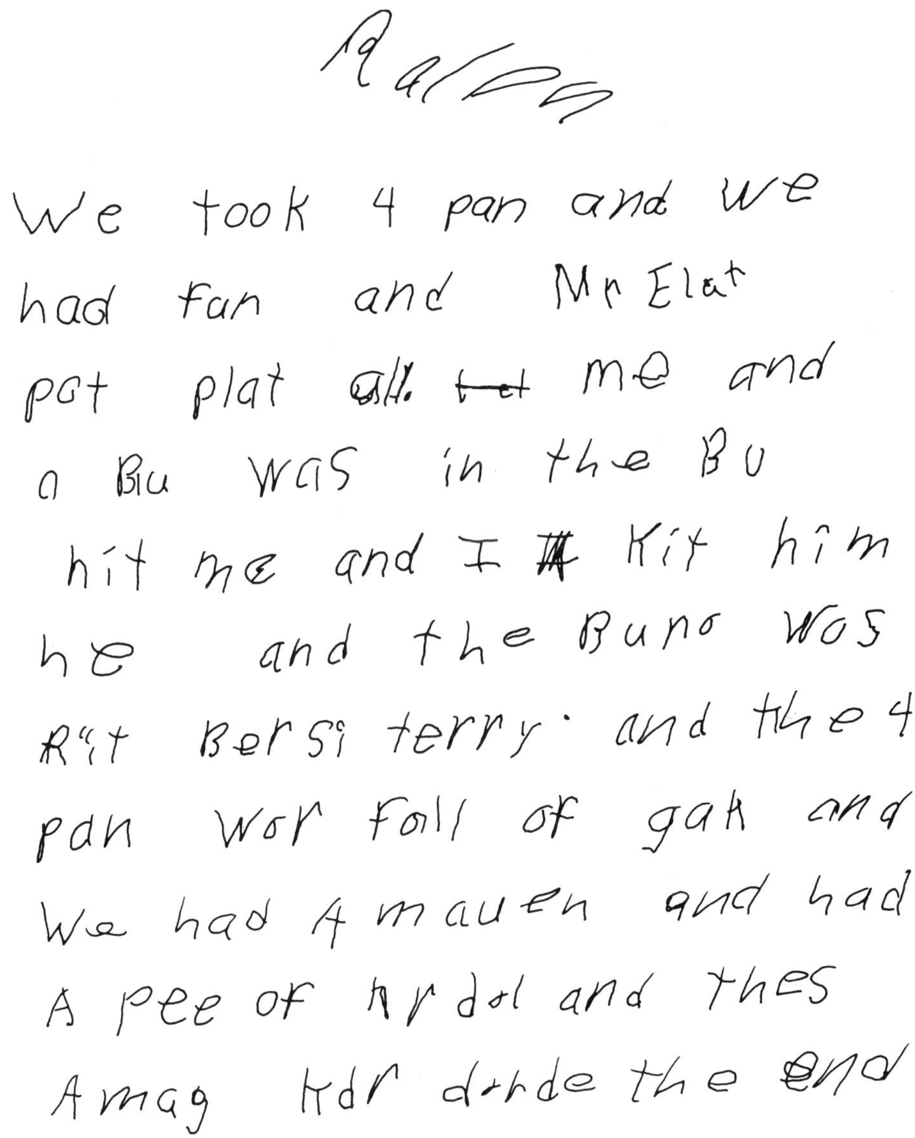

Ralph

We took 4 pan and We
had fan and Mr Elat
pot plat all. me and
a Bu was in the Bu
hit me and I Kit him
he and the Buno Wos
Rit Bersi terry. and the 4c
pan wor foll of gah and
We had 4 mauen and had
A pee of hrdol and thes
Amag hdr drhde the end

FIGURE 14.1
A language experience story created by Ralph.

Figure 14.1 shows a sample of Ralph's writing in response to a field trip he took with several other children who work with Ms. Benjamin, the new Chapter One teacher. These children went to Ms. Benjamin's basement darkroom to develop photographs she had taken of them. Her friend, Mr. Eliot, had built the darkroom for her with black plastic. Ralph's story should be translated as follows:

> We took four pans and we had fun and Mr. Eliot put plastic all over me and a boogie monster was in the black. The boogie monster he hit me and I

kicked him and the boogie monster was right beside Terry. The four pans were full of junk and we had a machine and we had a piece of cardboard and there's a magic trick that put it on the cardboard. The end.

Here's how one group of children, all Chapter One students, described the same field trip.

How We Made Our Pictures by Group 7

Ms. Benjamin took our pictures. Then she opened the film can in the darkroom. She took the film out of the can and wound it on the reel. Then she put it in the tank. Then we put the developer in the tank. We put the cover on the tank and shook it for seven minutes. We took the cap off and poured it out. We then poured in the stop-bath. We shook it for three minutes. Then we poured it out. We took the reel out of the tank and washed all the chemicals out. We hung it up to dry.

Then we went over to Ms. Benjamin's house on Friday afternoon. We went downstairs in the cellar to the darkroom. First we took off our coats and put them on a table. Then we went into the darkroom and found all these chemicals. We took the pictures out of a bag and put them in the enlarger. Then Ms. Benjamin took out the paper and put it in the enlarger. Ms. Benjamin cleaned the pictures. We timed them in the enlarger for four seconds. Then we put the picture in Mike's developer. Then we put it in Sandy's stop-bath. Sandy put it in Betty's fixer.

We went upstairs and had milk, peanut butter, and crackers. We put the pictures in the dryer. When the pictures were dry, we went back to school.

As seen in Figure 14.1, Ralph not only has difficulty with the mechanics of writing but also has difficulty expressing himself. His teachers feel that most of the problem comes from his inability to concentrate, especially when he is asked to write. Concentrating on the details of developing photographs, for example, may have been an arduous task, though he carried out his part with a reasonable degree of seriousness. When it came time to record his experience in writing, though, the additional concentration that it required seemed to be too much for him, and he resorted to a tale of a "boogie monster." In addition to the problem of concentration, Ralph may also have had difficulty perceiving and understanding the language used while developing the photographs. This would have resulted in a foggy memory of the experience.

Ralph's difficulty appears to be one of intake. The messages coming in from the language environment seem to be weak and distorted. It's as if his nerves are like garden hoses that someone is standing on, partially obstructing the flow to the brain. This analogy is merely figurative, of course. Exactly what causes this intake problem is not known.

In November, Ms. Benjamin administered the *Slingerland Screening Tests for Identifying Children with Specific Language Disability* (1971). This battery of tests seemed to "prove" to her that Ralph's reading problem was due to poor visual and auditory memory. I mentioned to her, however, that a person with severe learning blocks usually does poorly on *any* formal test. The anxiety is so great that they can't concentrate! One could give Ralph a formal test on baseball stars (something he knew a great deal about) and he'd do poorly on it.

She remembered that he *"was* kind of uptight" during the test. Nevertheless, we were both unhappy about the extent of his inability to concentrate on either visual or auditory signals. This showed up the most when he had to *write* the words rather than select them from among four alternatives. Let's take visual memory, for example: He was shown the word *thundering* on a card for a few seconds, then told to write it himself after the card was taken away. He wrote *t-h-u-e-n-d-r-o-n-b.* For a six-year-old, this isn't bad. For a nine-year-old, it's well below what would be expected. Now take auditory memory: He was read this sentence: "He saw this first girl." He wrote: *He scr ther gur feir.*

Several studies cited by Klasen (1972) show that Ralph is not alone. Here are some of the symptoms of severe reading blocks that are often noticed (although a single child seldom has all of these symptoms combined, like Ralph has):

Poor coordination: Ralph, for example, can't jump rope or catch a ball.

Lack of fine-motor control: He has great difficulty forming manuscript letters. He does much better with cursive, since he can move from one letter to the next without removing his pencil from the paper.

Directional confusion: Ralph, nearly ten, still reverses, inverts, and transposes letters and words. For example:
  reversals: *b* for *d, d* for *b, q* for *p, p* for *q, saw* for *was, was* for *saw*
  inversions: *u* for *n, n* for *u, p* for *b, b* for *p*
  transpositions: *neihgbor* for *neighbor,* s-p-r-t for s-t-p-r-
When he draws a circle, he sometimes draws it in a clockwise direction and sometimes in a counterclockwise direction.

Speech jitters: Ralph's stuttering is quite mild, but he seems to be struggling to put his thoughts into words, resulting in words and syllables that seem jumbled; his enunciation is very weak, making it hard for others to understand him.

Visual and auditory perceptual confusion: Ralph often (*though not always*) shows this confusion when tested on either his discrimination or memory abilities. This confusion is inconsistent (on and off).

Concentration problems: Ralph is quite hyperactive, which in itself causes concentration problems. He often complains that words are confusing to him. In addition, he shows unwillingness to concentrate. (Concentration in the past may have led to even more failure.)

Klasen, back in 1972, thought that such symptoms were due to neurological damage. The chances for such causation, however, are probably no better than 50–50. There are numerous other possibilities, such as emotional disturbance (Manzo, 1987), conceptual confusion about the nature of the reading process

(Otto, 1986), poor teaching (Carbo, 1987), fear of failure (Johnston, 1985), and sundry other reasons (Smith, 1979).

The Inaccuracy of the Dyslexia Label

The term *dyslexia*, although a short and once-popular term, is an inaccurate label for the condition we are discussing in this chapter. The original meaning of the word was simply "the inability to read." One dictionary definition of the word is "an impairment of the ability to read due to a brain defect" (Stein, 1973). However, this may be highly inaccurate and does not capture the nature of the malady that Ralph and other children like him experience.

From a practical standpoint, what teachers generally notice are inabilities in reading, spelling, handwriting, speaking, and certain activities related to physical education—in roughly that order. The title of Clarke's book *Can't Read, Can't Write, Can't Talk Too Good Either* (1974) is perhaps the most sensible, down-to-earth definition.

Because of the confusion surrounding the word *dyslexia*, many researchers and teachers now refer to this condition as *learning disabled*. But no label comes close to describing the difficulties these youngsters experience. In fact, labels probably do more harm than good in some cases. Educators may be making the same mistake that psychiatrists used to make by attempting to categorize disturbed people as manic depressives, hebephrenic schizophrenics, paranoics, and so on. Once people had been classified, the tendency was to treat everyone in the same category the same way and ignore individual differences. There is considerable danger that we will fall into the same trap.

There is also considerable danger in overusing the labels *dyslexic* or *learning disabled* to apply to anyone who is having trouble learning to read. Unfortunately, once children are so labeled, they are sometimes forgotten or rushed off to a specialist without first examining one's own teaching methods and one's way of relating to the particular child.

Allington presents several cogent arguments against the use of labeling:

Most of the labels simply do not have a single commonly accepted definition. For example, what is a *hyperactive* child? Is it one who disrupts the classroom? Is it the "normal," restless, active boy? Is a child *dyslexic* just because he reverses the *b* and the *d*? Many children do this for the first two grades.

Labels provide no useful information. Rather than label a child, it might be far better to determine the specific skills that are deficient and make plans for remediation.

Labels are often a feeble attempt to define the cause of the ailment (e.g., Poor Ralph can't spell because he has dyslexia). Knowing the causes is really not that useful in applying treatment anyway.

Assigning labels is beyond the professional skill of most teachers.

Labeling children only shifts the burden of failure to them. Perhaps a better label under which academic underachievers might be placed is *teaching disabled*. This term more adequately describes the situation. We are not faced with children who *cannot* learn, but with children who need instruction somewhat different from that provided in regular classrooms. These children can learn; it is the teaching that needs modification. (Allington, 1975, p. 367)

Harris and Hodges, editors of *The Dictionary of Reading and Related Terms* (1981), feel that the term *dyslexia* "has lost any real value for educators." It's better, they say, for the teacher to keep records of specific reading difficulties and to apply teaching strategies that relate directly to those difficulties, "not apply a label which may create misleading assumptions" (1981, p. 95). I wholeheartedly agree.

Classroom Determination of Children with Reading/Writing Blocks

Whatever the reasons for a child's difficulty with reading or writing, it's still important for the teacher to identify those children and provide them with extra help (or to change the type of instruction entirely). The earlier the difficulty is detected, the easier it is to treat (Jordan, 1977; Slingerland, 1970). But how do you determine when a child's block is severe enough to warrant special instruction (from either classroom or special teachers)?

This decision is truly arbitrary, although it can be a reasonably intelligent one. There are no standardized tests of reading disability to help you, and it's doubtful that such norm-based tests would be useful for such an individual problem. Slingerland (1970) and Jordan (1977) have developed diagnostic tests for reading and language disabilities that can be administered by specialized teachers; however, both are quite time-consuming. For the classroom teacher I recommend the checklists in Appendix O and the RAD test in Appendix G.

INSTRUCTIONAL NEEDS COMMON TO SLOW, DISABLED, AND SECOND LANGUAGE LEARNERS

I'm not going to present a separate section on instructing learning disabled children, partly because I'll be doing quite a bit on that in this section, and partly because "disabled" children differ among each other as much as they differ from second language learners. What I'm going to suggest to you in this part of the chapter are some general ideas that will help you think about what you might need for Ralph or for anyone else who might be having trouble learning to read or write. You see, children with this kind of obstacle have several things in common. They're generally in the minority in a particular classroom or in a particular school. And they *feel* their minority status. They often experience a damaged self-concept. They are nearly always in a position of having to learn something through the medium of a written language that they perceive as confusing (and perhaps meaningless). They can easily feel left out, abandoned. Therefore, both instruction and the classroom atmosphere need to compensate for these special feelings and learning blocks.

Help Improve Their Self-Concepts

Wattenburg and Clifford (1964) found that measures of children's self-concepts were better at predicting their reading achievement than the usual intelligence and readiness tests. But perhaps we don't need research reports to prove the obvious. It is readily apparent that people's conceptions of themselves influence and direct their behavior. If Janice feels she's a lousy cook, she's not likely to try hard at being a good cook, for fear of encountering more dismal failures. In fact, her negative self-concept in this case will probably influence her cooking behavior in such a way that she does burn the roast and lump the gravy. Similarly, if Sammy develops a concept of himself as a lousy reader, his chances for success are greatly reduced.

> Research conducted in the areas of self-concept and the role of teacher expectations as they correspond to academic achievement shows them to be interrelated. Poor achievement leads to a lowered self-image which results in continued poor achievement. (Clarke, 1974, p. 361)

How can teachers help their special children improve their self-concepts? Quandt and Selznick, in *Self-Concept and Reading* (1984), offer several suggestions:

1. Encourage children to encourage each other. Praise specifically for this behavior.
2. Whenever possible, avoid comparisons with other students. Help children see that they are valued not for their reading status but for their status as interesting and worthwhile human beings.
3. Use another basis for grouping children besides reading *ability*. Have reading *interest* groups as well that meet once a week for sharing.
4. Keep showing them their progress. Have an occasional individual conference with each child.
5. Help each child become a "junior expert" on something.
6. Change instructional approaches when one is not working. Don't expect the child to adjust to your approach.
7. Give them opportunities to demonstrate to others what they have learned rather than rushing on to the next skill.
8. Find materials easy enough for the child to feel success with.
9. Explain to parents the nature of self-concept and the value of parental encouragement.

Another way to improve self-concept is through providing models that children can emulate. One reason that some children perceive themselves as non-readers is that the people they identify with do not read. In a study by Nichols (1977), for instance, she found that none of the fathers of a group of "nonreading" African American boys used reading in his daily activities to any appreciable extent. Furthermore, the fathers placed a low value on reading. In addition, Nichols found census figures showing that for the top five occupations engaged in by African American men in this particular region, not one required reading or clerical skills. Nichols did discover, however, that many of the African American men in this region were highly skilled storytellers and that the boys gained status through imitating these men. In fact, many of the boys were superb storytellers by the age of ten. She suggests that the language experience approach be used with students in this kind of situation so that their stories can be captured in print and then used to inspire reading.

In addition to language experience stories, Nichols suggests that men in the community who use reading in their work be brought in for short visits with the children. Others suggest that various adults be brought in to read to children, that biographies of famous minority people be read, and that their pictures be hung on the school walls for inspiration. In general, providing identification figures for children is an important way to help them improve their self-concepts.

Use a Multisensory Approach

One way to help children who are having trouble learning to deal with a written language is to employ as many of the senses as possible. Whether a child is a second language, slow, or disabled learner, a multisensory approach can make the learning process easier. For example, when Miss Burnette wants Ralph to learn the letter *b*, she shows him the letter in print and says the letter to him. She

then reminds him how to make the *b* on the chalkboard, using large movements, starting the letter at the top and producing it with one motion, without taking her chalk off the board. She then traces the letter and says it simultaneously. Next she has Ralph look at the letter and say it. Following this, he is expected to look at it, say it, and trace it with his hand simultaneously. Then he writes it on the board, using the full swing of his arm. He then traces it and says it simultaneously. Then he moves to his desk and writes it two or three times on his paper, saying it each time he writes it. And finally he circles any *b* he finds on a worksheet. A similar approach is used for learning sight words such as *the, there,* or *off.*

Chapter 13 emphasized the need for massed practice followed by distributed practice. If ever this principle were needed, it's in teaching kids with learning obstacles. Furthermore, not only should the massed practice (such as the lesson on *b* just described) be multisensory, but the distributed practice as well. Before Ralph goes to see Ms. Benjamin, he is shown the letter *b* by Miss Burnette; he says it ten times as she traces it on his back. When he arrives at Ms. Benjamin's door he hands her a note from Miss Burnette explaining what he has recently learned. Ms. Benjamin asks him to read the letter *b,* trace it, and say it. Not only does he trace the letter in the air; he traces it on fine sandpaper or felt or wet paint. The same is true of words. He writes the word *there* (for his two teachers) with chalk, with felt pen, with finger paint, with a wooden stylus on a "magic-erase" wax tablet. The correct sequence of letters in each word is accented again and again—visually, auditorily, kinesthetically, and tactually.

Every conceivable device for keeping the multisensory approach from becoming drudgery must be used—novelty in writing tools, novelty in writing surfaces, novelty in praise, games as rewards for good work. The multisensory approach is sometimes slow and painstaking, but it needn't be painful. Children, especially hyperactive ones, enjoy getting out of their seats to write words, trace them, circle them, find them, and manipulate them.

Spelling and reading need to go hand in hand during many of the learning experiences. Research demonstrates a strong interrelationship and interdependence between spelling and word-recognition skills (Carbo, 1981). Ms. Benjamin often has Ralph shout not only the words, but the letters as well (on the playground). Spelling races, however, are never used since precision rather than speed is what children need to sharpen the images of what they receive.

Listening and reading should also go hand in hand whenever possible. The teacher should often read to the children while they follow along silently with their own copies. This procedure can be modified by using listening tapes in a reading or listening center. There is evidence that this approach, when combined with other multisensory experiences, can lead to significant progress in reading. Marie Carbo (1981) found that *some* of the children she worked with increased their reading scores by one and one-half years in just three months through the use of homemade "talking books." Carbo recommends making your own listening tapes to go along with easy-to-read books, because she has found that the commercial tapes are often too fast for children who are having trouble learning to read. She also suggests providing many clear clues for turning pages and for looking at pictures and reminding the children to put their fingers under the words as they hear them being read.

In the November 1987 issue of *Phi Delta Kappan,* the same Marie Carbo discusses the need for ''giving unequal learners an equal chance.'' In her words: ''Many poor readers are predominantly global, tactile, and kinesthetic learners'' (1987, p. 198). By *global* she means that these children often learn better when they can progress from the whole to the part (just the opposite of most ''phonics'' programs). Thus, she recommends the following teaching strategies for them (I've added my two-cents-worth to some of them). Have global readers:

1. Read whole text selections that inspire high interest and high emotional involvement. [A funny or exciting patterned book is a good example.]
2. Join you and others in choral reading. [Have a peer point to the words.]
3. Write or dictate stories. [Have them read the story immediately after writing or dictating it.]
4. Listen to story tapes. [Short snappy 5- to 7-minute ones; remember to remind them to follow the words with their fingers.]
5. Listen to the teacher or a peer read aloud [every day] while they follow along [either with your copy or with their own].
6. Combine the repeated reading technique [Chapter 4] with the story tapes.

Here's what Carbo recommends for emphasizing the tactile and kinesthetic learning modes: (1) computers, (2) typewriters, (3) active games, (4) drawing, (5) writing, (6) pantomime, (7) verbal drama, (8) puppets, and (9) following written directions for making things.

Note: By now I'm sure you see that good teaching, the kind you should use with *all* kids, is just what is needed by those children with special obstacles to learning.

Another note: See the very inspiring *Turnabout Children* (1986) by Mary MacCracken.

Note three: A significant multisensory experience can be provided through the use of patterned books—particularly if you and the children not only read them but write your own together. They seem to be a very natural medium of instruction for second language learners and for others with special learning obstacles. Be sure to check Appendix P for examples.

And still another note: Other types of easy literature are also effective with special learners (Schumaker & Schumaker, 1988).

Make Reading Meaningful through
LEA and Whole Language

From the very first dictated story, the blind child realizes, if he did not already know from home experience, that oral language can be *saved* in the form of Braille. Braille immediately has a *use* for him and learning to read and write it is not a chore detached from any purpose, but rather a discovery of how to help order his world of experiences. (Curry, 1975, p. 274)

I hope this analogy between a blind child and the special learners we're talking about is clear. All children who are learning to read, whether blind, sighted, second language, average, gifted, slow, or disabled, need to feel that the process is meaningful. One of the best ways to bring meaning into the process is through language experience approaches. Nothing is more meaningful to a child than his own experiences, his own way of looking at those experiences, his own way of expressing himself. By capitalizing on events that occur in the classroom, on the playground, and in and out of school, the teacher can help children develop their own reading materials—materials that make sense. This may mean tape recording their stories and finding someone to type them in two languages, but it could well be worth it for your own success in teaching them to read.

Ralph is particularly fond of using the tape recorder to dictate his stories, having someone transcribe them, and then reading them the next day. Like most children, Ralph seems genuinely thrilled to see his own creations "in print," and he invariably gets great pleasure out of reading them to others. Had the same stories been written by someone else and given to him to read, he would not have been able to read them. But because he has written them himself and because they are based on his own direct or imaginary experiences, he can read them with considerable skill (relative to his normal reading). Of course, much of this reading is based on memory, rather than on precise decoding. Nevertheless, Ralph is receiving excellent practice on the type of mature reading that we eventually want him to master. Even more important for Ralph now, reading is a meaningful act; it makes sense to him.

Meaningful Writing

It would be difficult to emphasize too much the importance of the *writing* process for adding meaning to the instruction of children with learning obstacles. Wong-Kam and Au (1988) make writing the prime ingredient of a program for helping these readers. The first step, they believe, is to bring them into the "community of readers and writers" by letting them experience the pleasure of writing. What this means, as you LEA experts know, is dictating to peers, aides, parents, or teachers, then gradually moving from reading their own dictation to writing and reading their own compositions, to reading professional authors.

Journal writing, as mentioned in Chapter 8, can also be highly meaningful to these children. Some children with obstacles to language learning seem to need to learn language as a young child does—but not with the reading materials of a young child! Instead, they can write in a journal each day, using invented spelling and getting written feedback from the teacher. This way, second language learners—along with children who use "non-standard English" and along with "learning disabled" students—have the chance to gradually develop awareness of conventional spelling, of conventional pronunciation, and of conventional syntax—all of which leads to a better chance of reading and understanding professional writers of English.

Meaningful "Phonics"

In addition to the whole language approach that Wong-Kam and Au (1988) suggest for readers in trouble, they also recommend supplementary work with phonograms—the kind of work I recommended to you back in Chapter 7, in which games are played with one-syllable words that have the same phonogram. Gradually the children are shown how to attack larger words through the use of phonograms, vowel patterns, and suffixes.

In addition, remember that graphophonic patterns can be pleasurably and meaningfully learned through journal writing, LEA charts, and both guided and "free" reading of whole text.

Make Reading a Personal Affair

As mentioned earlier, many so-called "problem readers" feel left out or even abandoned. Their sense of belonging is weak because of numerous failures to communicate with people, to achieve lasting friendships, and to achieve in the way their peers are achieving. Perhaps even more than children who are achieving at normal levels, they need someone who cares for them and is concerned enough to give them the extra time it takes to help them learn to read and write— someone who will help them stop feeling so inferior.

Their bad luck (in being a "problem reader" in the first place) often is exacerbated in school. For, according to research (Miller & Hering, 1975), it appears that most teachers prefer teaching the better readers. Even without research studies, casual observation in classrooms demonstrates that some teachers have far less patience with poor readers than with good ones. And because of this, the children who need the most help are often those who get the least.

In fact, this may be the most serious problem of all for children like Ralph— simply not getting enough help of the right kind when they need it. As a result, their self-concept deteriorates; they withdraw rather than risk further failure, and learning to read becomes a meaningless, senseless, impersonal, and chaotic experience.

A relatively "new" approach that hit the American shores in the mid-1980s may be one answer to this problem. It's called the Reading Recovery Program and was developed by Marie Clay in New Zealand. After about three months of daily thirty-minute tutoring, almost all of the children in this program in New Zealand caught up with their peers. Three years later they continued to make progress at average rates (Clay, 1982). Studies in Ohio (Pinnell, Short, & Young, 1986) have confirmed the effectiveness of the reading recovery approach.

But why is this approach so effective? Let's see what it *is* first, and then do some "wild and abandoned" guessing together. Trained adult tutors spend the first ten lessons (each thirty minutes long) informally getting to know the child, observing his reading and writing behaviors, and reading to and with the child (modeling fluent and expressive reading). The child reads many easy books to develop fluency and self-confidence. He also writes his own "book" each time. He learns how to predict through the use of syntax, through pictures, and through the examination of graphophonic patterns. Lessons 11 through 60 (if it takes that long) follow a fairly definite sequence (Boehnlein, 1987). The child:

1. Builds fluency by rereading some of his formerly read books (all of which are short and thin).
2. Orally rereads yesterday's new book while the teacher observes his miscues.
3. Identifies movable plastic letters on a magnetic board.
4. Writes his own sentence or story; gets help on sound/letter relationships.
5. Edits his story.
6. Reads a new book, guided by the teacher/tutor's emphasis on meaning, prediction, confirmation, and self-correction.
7. Reads the new book again independently.

All right, now that you know what the method is, why do you think it works? Do you see some familiar ideas in this list? These people are doing things rather masterfully, aren't they: an emphasis on fluency rather than mere words (Chapter 4); lots of easy books (Chapter 9); lots of writing (Chapter 8); learning graphophonic patterns through the use of whole text (Chapter 7); an emphasis on meaning, prediction, and confirmation strategies, as well as self-monitoring (Chapters 4 and 5); making reading a personal affair (Chapter 14).

I cite these now-familiar ideas to convince you (as if you really needed any convincing) that you needn't run out and purchase some commercialized version of THE READING RECOVERY PROGRAM IN YOUR VERY OWN CLASSROOM (Get It While It's Hot!). I'm sure you *know* how to develop your "very own" reading recovery program.

One of the things that should encourage you in this regard is the knowledge that the particular reading recovery program designed by Marie Clay does *not* use teacher's guides. The teacher/tutor is required to make up her own lessons as she goes, depending on what she observes each student doing as he reads and writes. The fact that teachers can do this so successfully should give you hope—if you didn't have it before.

Miss Burnette and Ms. Benjamin weren't afraid to try their own ideas with Ralph. After his first successfully written experience story, Ralph read it with ease to his reading teacher, Ms. Benjamin. He was so thrilled by his success and the praise he received, he spruced up his courage and asked his regular classroom teacher, Miss Burnette, if he could read it to the class.

He read it beautifully. And the children—even those who had laughed at him before—were stunned. Spontaneously, without any signal from the teacher, they clapped loud and long. Some even slapped him on the back and told him what a good reader he was. Ralph was welcomed into the literacy club at last.

Ralph hasn't been the same since. He now considers himself a reader. And with the help of caring, affectionate teachers, someday he'll be just that.

SUMMARY OF MAIN IDEAS

☐ To be successful with gifted and creative children, teachers need to respect and accommodate their autonomous, visionary, goal-oriented, flexible, open, and adventurous characteristics.

☐ Successful teachers appreciate each child's culture, language, and dialect, and they communicate this appreciation. They are learners as well as instructors.

☐ Multicultural education ought to be one of the goals of the reading/writing teacher.

☐ Many of the procedures used for second language, disabled, and gifted children are those used by good teachers for all children.

☐ Second language, disabled, and slow learners (like so many average and advanced learners) need multisensory learning experiences. They also need to perceive reading as a meaningful, communicative experience. And perhaps even more than other children, they need to experience reading instruction as a personal, friendly interaction with an affectionate, caring teacher.

☐ Whenever possible, use a child's own language or dialect as a temporary teaching medium; treat Standard English as another useful language rather than the "only" language.

☐ Avoid thinking of children as labels such as "dyslexics" or "slow learners" and think of them as individuals with specific strengths, problems, and instructional needs.

APPLICATION EXPERIENCES FOR THE TEACHER EDUCATION CLASS

A. *What's Your Opinion?* Use textbook ideas and your own ideas based on personal and professional experiences to defend your decision.

1. It doesn't really hurt gifted students to have to complete reading lessons on concepts they've already learned. This way they solidify their knowledge and also pick up things they might have forgotten.
2. Creative children are usually problem kids. There's not much a teacher can do but get out of their way.
3. When a child reads Standard English with an African American dialect, Spanish dialect, or other nonstandard dialect, it's a sign of a reading deficiency.
4. Cultural differences should be an important factor in determining a teacher's methods for reading instruction.
5. The ESL approach is better than the native vernacular approach.
6. A learning disabled reader is "dyslexic," and there's not much a teacher can do about it.

B. *Miscue Analysis:* The following is an example of Ralph's miscues on a preprimer selection (a *d* means default; the teacher pronounced the word):*

Boys and girls run down~~the~~ s~~t~~reet. *to* *d*

Run in, run~~out.~~ *to on*

Run up ~~and~~ down. *for*

Run up and down the street.

Two ~~girls~~ run. *get go*

Three boys run. *Trees*

What strategies is Ralph (a "learning disabled" child) using?

C. *Looking at Prejudices:* Discuss with three or four others any prejudices you may have had (or still have) toward people who speak a dialect or language different from your own. Discuss how you have overcome these prejudices or how you might overcome them as a teacher.

D. *Views from Practicing Teachers:* Arrange for teachers who are working with gifted, handicapped, and second language children to talk with your class. Ask them to discuss some of the children they're working with and the instructional procedures they use.

FIELD EXPERIENCES IN THE ELEMENTARY SCHOOL CLASSROOM

A. Using the procedures you learned in Chapter 11, carry on miscue analysis with a child whose mother tongue is not Standard English. Which of his miscues are truly reading errors; which are dialect translations? What recommendations would you make for providing reading instruction to this child?

B. Be a "student" to one of the MIN children in the school. Learn some of his dialect or language. Try to learn about some of his cultural behavior and values that differ from yours. Find ways to show your appreciation for his instruction.

C. Using the "Observation Checklist" in Appendix O, over a period of several days observe a child who has been classified as a disabled learner. If possible, do the same with a child who has been classified as a slow learner. What similarities and differences do you notice? Are these differences due to different *types* of children or simply to different individuals? What evidence do you have for your conclusions?

*Bank Street College of Education. "Lunch on a Boat," in *Around the City* (New York: Macmillan, 1965). Reprinted with permission from the publisher.

D. With a child who is considered a gifted student, informally discuss a library book that both of you have read. See what you can discover about his schemata related to the book. What effect do these schemata have on his interpretation of the book? How are these schemata enhanced or changed by reading library books?

REFERENCES AND SUGGESTED READING

Allington, R. I. (1975). Sticks and stones . . . but will names never hurt them? *The Reading Teacher, 28,* 364–369.

Barron, F. (1962). The psychology of imagination. In S. J. Parnes & H. F. Harding (Eds.), *A source book for creative thinking* (pp. 227–237). New York: Charles Scribner's Sons.

Bethell, T. (1976, May 26). Becoming an American. *Newsweek,* p. 13.

Boehnlein, M. (1987). Reading intervention for high-risk first-graders. *Educational Leadership, 44,* 32–37.

Boraks, N., & Allen, A. R. (1977). A program to enhance peer tutoring. *The Reading Teacher, 30,* 479–484.

Brandt, R. (1988, March). On students' needs and team learning: A conversation with William Glasser. *Educational Leadership,* 38–44.

Breiling, A. (1976). Using parents as teaching partners. *The Reading Teacher, 30,* 187–192.

Burg, L. A. (1975). Affective teaching—Neglected practice in innercity schools? *The Reading Teacher, 28,* 360–363.

Cagney, M. A. (1977). Children's ability to understand Standard English and Black dialect. *The Reading Teacher, 30,* 607–610.

Carbo, M. (1981). Making books talk to children. *The Reading Teacher, 35,* 186–189.

Carbo, M. (1987). Deprogramming reading failure: Giving unequal learners an equal chance. *Phi Delta Kappan, 69,* 197–202.

Carbo, M. (1988). The evidence supporting reading styles: A response to Stahl. *Phi Delta Kappan, 70,* 323–327.

Ching, D. C. (1976). *Reading and the bilingual child.* Newark, DE: International Reading Association.

Clark, B. (1983). *Growing up gifted.* (2nd ed.) Columbus, OH: Merrill.

Clarke, L. (1974). *Can't read, can't write, can't talk too good either: How to recognize and overcome dyslexia in your child.* Baltimore: Penguin.

Clay, M. M. (1976). Early childhood and cultural diversity in New Zealand. *The Reading Teacher, 29,* 333–342.

Clay, M. M. (1982). Reading recovery: A follow-up study. In *Observing young readers: Selected papers by Marie M. Clay.* Exeter, NH: Heinemann.

Curry, R. G. (1975). Using LEA to teach blind children to read. *The Reading Teacher, 29,* 272–279.

Davison, H., & Lang, G. (1960). Children's perceptions of their teachers' feelings toward them related to self-perception, school achievement, and behavior. *Journal of Experimental Education, 29,* 107–118.

Donoghue, M. R. (1971). *The child and the English language arts.* Minneapolis: William C. Brown.

Eisenberg, L., et al. (1968). Class and race effects on the intelligibility of monosyllables. *Child Development,* 1077–1079.

Eloisa, M. G. D. (1975). Frontier dialect: A challenge to education. *The Reading Teacher, 28,* 653–658.

Feeley, J. (1970). Teaching non-English-speaking first graders to read. *Elementary English,* 199–208.

Getzels, J. W., & Jackson, P. W. (1960). *The gifted student.* Cooperative Research Monograph No. 2. Washington: U.S. Department of Health, Education, and Welfare.

Glasser, W. (1986). *Control Theory in the classroom.* New York: Harper & Row.

Hall, M. (1972). *The language experience approach for the culturally disadvantaged.* Newark, DE: International Reading Association.

Hall, V. C., & Turner, R. R. (1974). The validity of the "different language explanation" for poor scholastic performance by Black students. *Review of Educational Research, 44,* 69–81.

Harris, T. L., & Hodges, R. E. (Eds.) (1981). *The dictionary of reading and related terms.* Newark, DE: International Reading Association.

Himmelsteib, C. (1975). Buddies read in library program. *The Reading Teacher, 30,* 32–35.

Hough, R. A., Nurss, J. R., & Enright, D. S. (1986). Story reading with limited English speaking children in the regular classroom. *The Reading Teacher, 39,* 510–514.

Howell, H. (1987). Language, literature, and vocabulary development for gifted students. *The Reading Teacher, 41,* 500–504.

Isaacs, A. F. (1973). What to do when you discover a child is gifted and interested in language; or one hundred ways to tickle your fancy with language and linguistics. *Gifted Child Quarterly, 17,* 144–149.

Johnson, L. (1975). Bilingual bicultural education: A two-way street. *The Reading Teacher, 29,* 231–239.

Johnston, P. (1985, May). *Harvard Educational Review,* 165–175.

Jordan, D. R. (1977). *Dyslexia in the classroom.* Columbus, OH: Merrill.

Kaplan, R. B. (1969). On a note of protest (in a minor key). *College English, 30,* 386–389.

Kirk, S. A., et al. (1978). *Teaching reading to slow and disabled learners.* Boston: Houghton, Mifflin.

Klasen, E. (1972). *The syndrome of specific dyslexia.* Baltimore: University Park Press.

Krech, D. (1969). Psychoneurobiochemeducation. *Phi Delta Kappan, 50,* 370–375.

Lawrence, D. (1975). Sparta revisited. *The Reading Teacher, 28,* 464–465.

Lozanov, G. (1977). A general theory of suggestion in the communications process and the activation of the total reserves of the learner's personality. *Suggestopaedia-Canada, 1,* 1–4.

MacCracken, M. (1986). *Turnabout children: Overcoming dyslexia and other learning disabilities.* Boston: Little, Brown.

MacLean, P. (1978). A mind of three minds: Educating the triune brain. In J. Chall & A. Mirsky (Eds.), *Education and the brain.* Chicago: University of Chicago Press.

Manzo, A. V. (1987). Psychologically induced dyslexia and learning disabilities. *The Reading Teacher, 40,* 408–413.

Martindale, C. (1976). What makes creative people different. *Psychology Today, 9* (2), 44–50.

May, F. B., & Ripple, R. E. (1962). Caution in comparing creativity and IQ. *Psychological Reports, 10,* 229–230.

Miller, H. B., & Hering, S. (1975). Teacher's ratings—Which reading group is number one? *The Reading Teacher, 28,* 389–391.

Niaden, N. (1976). Ratio of boys to girls among disabled readers. *The Reading Teacher, 29,* 439–442.

Nichols, P. C. (1977). A sociolinguistic perspective on reading and Black children. *Language Arts, 54,* 150–157.

Otto, W. (1986). Peter Johnston we salute you. *Journal of Reading, 29,* 700–703.

Peisach, E. C. (1965). Children's comprehension of teacher and peer speech. *Child Development, 36,* 467–480.

Pinnell, G., Short, K., Lyons, C. A., & Young, P. (1986). The reading recovery project in Columbus, Ohio: Volume II. Technical Report. Columbus, OH: The Ohio State University.

Quandt, I., & Selznick, R. (1984). *Self-concept and reading.* Newark, DE: International Reading Association.

Restak, K. (1979). *The brain: The last frontier.* New York: Doubleday.

Rosenthal, R., & Jacobson, L. (1968). *Pygmalion in the classroom.* New York: Holt, Rinehart, & Winston.

Rosezweig, M. (1966). Environmental complexity, cerebral change and behavior. *American Psychologist, 21,* 321–332.

Ruddell, R. B. (1965). The effect of oral and written patterns of language structure and reading comprehension. *The Reading Teacher, 18,* 273.

Saville, M. R., & Troike, R. C. (1971). *A handbook of bilingual education.* Teaching English to speakers of other languages. Newark, DE: International Reading Association.

Schumaker, M. P., & Schumaker, R. C. (1988). 3000 paper cranes: Children's literature for remedial readers. *The Reading Teacher, 41,* 544–549.

Slingerland, B. H. (1970). *Slingerland screening tests for identifying children with specific language disability.* Cambridge: Educators Publishing Service.

Slingerland, B. H. (1971). *A multi-sensory approach to language arts for specific language disability children, a guide for primary teachers.* Cambridge: Educators Publishing Service.

Smith, F. (1979). *Reading without nonsense.* New York: Teachers College Press.

Smith, L. B. (1976). They found a golden ladder . . . Stories by children. *The Reading Teacher, 29,* 541–545.

Smith, N. B. (1975). Cultural dialects: Current problems and solutions. *The Reading Teacher, 29,* 137–141.

Stein, J. (Ed.). (1973). *The Random House dictionary of the English language.* New York: Random House.

Thompson, R., Berger, T., & Berry, S. (1980). An introduction to the anatomy, physiology, and chemistry of the brain. In M. Wittrock (Ed.), *The brain and psychology.* New York: Academic Press.

Thonis, E. W. (1976). *Literacy for America's Spanish-speaking children.* Newark, DE: International Reading Association.

Torrance, E. P. (1962). Guiding creative talent. Englewood Cliffs, NJ: Prentice-Hall.

Tway, E. (1980). The gifted child in literature. *Language Arts, 57,* 14–20.

U.S. Commission on Civil Rights. (1975). *A better chance to learn: Bilingual-biculture education* (Clearing House Publication #51). Washington, DC.

Wattenburg, W. W., & Clifford, C. (1964). Relation of self-concept to beginning achievement in reading. *Child Development, 35,* 461–467.

Weener, P. D. (1969). Social dialect differences and the recall of verbal messages. *Journal of Educational Psychology, 60,* 194–199.

Wilson, M. (1981). A review of recent research on the integration of reading and writing. *The Reading Teacher, 34,* 896–901.

Wong-Kam, J. A., & Au, K. H. (1988). Improving a fourth grader's reading and writing: Three principles. *The Reading Teacher, 41,* 768–772.

Managing Time, Resources, and Behavior to Meet Your Literacy Instruction Goals: A Review and a Prophecy

━━━━━━━━━━━━━━ CHAPTER PREVIEW ━━━━━━━━━━━━━━

We've come a long way together, you and I. All the way from a visit with those philosophers from Zania in Chapter 1 to this chapter—a visit with the future. We'll attempt to predict the future by looking at the changes that will probably happen (and are happening) in the way classroom teachers manage their literacy programs. Looking into the future can be difficult for both the author and the reader, because it is sometimes discouraging to compare the future to the present, and great patience is called for. But looking ahead can be exciting too, as we see the possibilities for teachers to take

greater responsibility for creative planning, teaching, and managing.

The way a teacher manages his or her instructional program greatly influences how well children learn to read. Research shows us that, but it doesn't show us exactly *how* teachers should allocate their instructional time and *what* resources they should utilize the most. Only teachers and administrators, using thoughtful judgments, can make these decisions. Their judgments will depend today and tomorrow on how we perceive the reading process. If we perceive it one way, we will allocate most instructional and practice time to isolated subskill practice. If we perceive it another way, we will have children spend more time on integrated interactive practice. The viewpoints and decisions of teachers and administrators will continue to make an enormous impact on what children learn in school. The challenges that face us all—teachers, administrators, and teacher educators—are both impressive and inspiring.

Management's responsibility to employees begins and ends with creating an environment for individual opportunity.
—Richard S. Sloma

There is no doubt that reading instruction must focus on reading improvement. But reading instruction, whenever possible, must give children opportunities to work cooperatively.
—Timothy Rasinski and Sally Nathenson-Mejia

The second way to use time more productively is to initiate concurrent actions so that many more programs are completed in the same time. Getting six elephants pregnant at the same time will not reduce the gestation period to one-sixth the usual time, but it will produce six times as many elephants in the same period of time.
—Richard S. Sloma

THE NEED FOR GOOD MANAGERS IN THE CLASSROOM

Good teachers are generally good managers, and there's a lot of good teachers out there. But alas, poor teachers are generally poor managers, and there's a lot of poor teachers out there. Berliner and his colleagues (1981) studied a large number of teachers and found that the poor ones had very little idea of how to manage a classroom. This lack of knowledge and ability resulted in miserable efficiency and low achievement. To put it bluntly, the children who were in these classrooms wasted hundreds of hours of good growing time. And as the saying goes, a mind is a terrible thing to waste.

I don't cite this information to scare you out of teaching. Not at all. I only want to motivate you to make use of your natural management skills or—if management seems foreign to you—to read and take courses on classroom management. What I have to say in this chapter and what I've said in other chapters about management will hopefully be of use to you, but I doubt that one can ever learn too much about this topic. Your own continued reading and your willingness to experiment (in order to find out what works for you) may very well be crucial to your success.

Perhaps the best advice I can give you in this book on reading is to read. Read something each month from a professional journal. In this way the biases you develop about handling your classroom can be influenced by the preferences of others. As you've already determined, I, myself, do not "speak" to you without bias. The research reports, articles, and books I've sifted through, at the risk of poor vision and library mildew, have all pushed me (at too slow a rate) toward an interactive view of reading and a whole text view of reading instruction. My experiences with children and teachers through the years are also responsible—perhaps even more than research reports—for biasing me. If you don't agree with the views I've accumulated, I really won't feel as bad as you might think, because I know everyone has to find meaning in his or her own way. I only hope you'll keep your mind open to what your experiences teach you and that you'll continue to *read* throughout your teaching career. And please, let some of your reading be other than those "how to" articles in teacher magazines that are overloaded with commercial advertisements for this set of stickers and that set of worksheets. Some of that kind of reading can be useful, I'll admit, but what about articles that can have even greater, longer-lasting use to you and your students? I've mentioned magazines, or "journals," that can have a real impact on your goals and procedures, such as *The Reading Teacher* and *Language Arts;* now I'm going to give you addresses and zip codes in case you wish to have these journals come to your doorstep instead of reading them in libraries.

The Reading Teacher	*Language Arts*
International Reading Association	National Council for Teachers of
800 Barksdale Road	English
P.O. Box 8139	111 Kenyon Road
Newark, DE 19714	Urbana, IL 61801

Lest you fear that the articles in these journals deal only with large-scale issues, let me assure you that they're also full of very specific suggestions for your teaching. *The Reading Teacher,* for example, has an entire section in each issue called "The CLASSROOM Reading Teacher," consisting of creative ideas sent in by teachers. And most of the articles, no matter how large in scope, also relate the ideas to actual classroom teaching. I'm going to pick randomly one of the issues off my shelf right now and give you a small sample of the articles in it:*

"The missing ingredients: Time on task, direct instruction, and writing"

"Modeling mental processes helps poor readers become strategic readers"

"Improving a fourth grader's reading and writing: Three principles"

"From the mystery spot to the thoughtful spot: The instruction of metacognitive strategies"

"Expository writing program: Making connections between reading and writing"

"The classroom reading teacher—practical teaching ideas"

---

*April 1988.

Have I convinced you yet? *The good classroom manager needs to keep up-to-date by reading professional journals.*

AN "EASY" MANAGEMENT PROBLEM TO START WITH: ALLOTTING TIME FOR ORAL AND SILENT READING

All right, here we go with our first management problem. It seems simple enough, but it sure causes a lot of debate among teachers:

> "Kids should read orally. How else am I going to tell how well they're doing?"
>
> "That's silly. No adults read orally anymore. Kids need to practice real reading—silent reading."
>
> "Well, okay, you two don't have to get so . . ."

See what I mean? What's kind of bothersome about this is that it represents a type of thinking that gets in the way of thinking. A famous philosopher once called this form of thinking "hypergeneralization," and maybe the term still fits. With hypergeneralization, Dan argues for A, Jan argues for B, and neither person sees the truth—that sometimes A is great; sometimes B is just fine.

A better thing to argue about would be, *When* do I want my students to practice the reading process silently, and when do I want them to practice it orally? Unfortunately some teachers have already made a decision on the "when" issue. Both research and casual observation show us two favorite forms of reading instruction in the elementary schools. One is to have the children meet the teacher in small groups and take turns reading out loud, called the "round-robin approach." The other popular form, with children above third grade, is to assign a selection for children to read silently and have the children write answers to questions the teacher has written on the chalkboard. An observer in the schools often sees this form of "instruction" carried on right up through twelfth grade.

Obviously we need a more goal-oriented approach toward this managerial decision. There are different advantages to gain from silent and oral reading. When teachers decide on the form according to its advantages rather than according to tradition, I'm sure you'll agree that this provides a "plus" for both the teacher and the students.

Oral Reading

Let's start with oral reading. When would it be advantageous to use this form? I should first point out that there's good reason for this form to be somewhat more dominant in the primary than in the later grades. As Taylor and Connor (1982) point out, beginning readers seem to need more immediate feedback on their reading than do older children; a greater need to hear themselves speak the words; and more opportunity to read "like big people do" (Those children who have been read to think that reading is an out-loud kind of thing).

This does not mean, though, that young children should experience oral reading only. On the contrary. From the very first month of school, children should have chances to read silently on their own—guided sentence by sentence, if necessary, with a question or comment from the teacher: "So what did Bill do with the pencil? Have you ever used a pencil that didn't have to be sharpened? Here's the kind of pencil that Bill is using. Can someone show us how to get the lead to come out?" In this way they can be gradually introduced into the world of reading the way most people use it in everyday life, and they can read for meaning rather than only for correct pronunciation.

Going back to oral reading, though, a second advantage is that it does give teachers an opportunity to carry on miscue analysis. As I mentioned in Chapter 11, miscue analysis is one of the best ways to determine a child's concept of reading and his main strategies for reading, whether his concern is mainly for meaning or for letter-by-letter translation from print to sound. This particular advantage of oral reading is true at all levels and is especially necessary now and then with problem readers.

A third advantage of oral reading experiences is that of providing a chance for children to prove a point they've made during a discussion following silent reading of a selection. This, in turn, provides teachers with a chance to teach literal, inferential, critical, and creative thinking operations that are necessary in the reading process (see Chapter 5).

A fourth advantage of oral reading is the opportunity it provides to practice reading with expression—to use different pitches and pauses and to stress particular words the way the reader thinks "the author might have said it." This kind of expressive reading emphasizes the concepts of "reading as communication," "reading as sharing language and ideas," and "reading as entertaining or informing." It can also help develop a habit of reading for comprehension. Echo and choral reading, as mentioned in earlier chapters, are excellent for this type of oral reading. It is also effective to have children practice a portion of text silently and then read it to other children who have closed their books. And don't forget to have them read plays, or read dialogue in stories by taking roles and skipping the *he said* and *she said* parts. And what about having children share out loud part of a library book they're reading—right there in the instructional group? Just have a different person share each time you meet (but make sure she has a chance to practice first).

I guess my only admonition about oral reading is this: Don't bore children by having them read a selection silently and then, in round-robin fashion, read it orally. Use oral reading for one or more of its *advantages,* not for punishment. (Believe me, *you* would consider it punishment if you had to go through this procedure.) Oral reading should follow silent reading when children are engaged in a directed reading-thinking activity (DRTA) (Chapter 5) or when they're entertaining or informing others, but not as a way to check their reading errors after they've read it silently. If you're going to check their reading *strategies* (how much they rely on each of the cueing systems), it is generally better to omit the silent reading. In this way you can see how they attack something *new*. (I'll mention again, however, that during miscue analysis in small groups, the children should

be discouraged from correcting each other's *words*. After the child has finished a sentence or larger portion, read it the same way he did and ask him to correct *you* so that *you* make sense.)

Silent Reading

The ability to read well silently, of course, is what most people need in our society. There are relatively few opportunities to read orally. Furthermore, as I mentioned, silent reading provides an even better opportunity to read for meaning than does oral reading. This is because during oral reading children (and teachers) can so easily get lost in the *sounds* of words. With silent reading, the teacher can guide the children with specific purposes for reading each sentence or paragraph or page, and then sit back and not even think about how well they're pronouncing the words as they read to themselves. She can concentrate on helping the children arrive at the author's meaning!

Silent reading also gives children that wonderful opportunity to keep their miscues to themselves and to search for their own understanding (or at least for the answer to the teacher's question). When children are asked to read silently under the teacher's direction, they don't have to impress anyone with their fluency or their ability to pronounce each word. They can let their eyes drift ahead or behind, they can stutter and stammer inside their heads and mumble to their hearts content, *and no one cares!* Can you imagine what bliss this must be for some children? With silent reading, children are allowed to read as adults do—predicting, confirming, changing their hypotheses as they go, skipping a word here and there, throwing in a word now and then, self-correcting their miscues, even substituting words as long as the text still makes sense. *In silent reading, children can communicate with an author instead of an audience.*

MANAGEMENT DECISION TWO: COOPERATIVE VERSUS INDIVIDUAL LEARNING

For a time during the 1960s and 1970s, it was fashionable to have children work on reading, mathematics, and spelling on their own, on the theory that each child has his own learning pace and style and shouldn't be held back or frustrated by a group of peers. This practice made good sense to some people, and there are still some who argue vehemently for "individualized learning." Results from an extensive research project, the "Beginning Teacher Evaluation Study," however, put a damper on others' enthusiasm. The BTE Study found that working alone for a large percentage of time was not conducive to learning; that group instruction, large or small, produced better results than instructing a child through "individualized materials" such as worksheets and programmed booklets (Mc-Donald, 1976).

Why the advantage of group instruction? For one thing, having the learning experience directed by a teacher, rather than a booklet or worksheet, increases the "engagement rate"—the amount of time children stay on task. In fact, in the BTE Study the *conscious* nonattendance to a task averaged 16 percent of the time when children worked alone and only 5 percent of the time when they worked in groups with the teacher (Pearson, 1984).

Not that merely getting children together with a teacher makes the only difference; it also depends on what teachers *do* with children in those groups. As I mentioned earlier, teachers who are warm but task-oriented seem to help children achieve the most. Yet even task orientation isn't enough. Naturally, the more closely the learning tasks simulate real reading, the more difference they make in helping the learner increase reading achievement. Many teachers, for example, ask inferential comprehension questions, but it takes specific instruction in inferential thinking to make a major difference for children on reading achievement tests (Pearson, 1984). In other words, taking the time to *show* children, with actual text rather than an isolated worksheet, how to fill the author's invisible slots between the lines, how to predict what's going to happen next, how to tell cause from effect, and how to tell the author's main ideas, is what pays off.

Cooperative Learning Does Work

Working with the teacher is one kind of cooperative learning, but as you've already heard many times before, working with peers can work very well too. In the previous chapters I've cited studies that indicate the value of having peers work together. And later on I'll cite several more studies showing the value of peer tutoring, a highly useful form of cooperative learning. In a nutshell, kids really can help each other learn.

The trick is to get them to work *well* together. And you'll have to experiment on this one to see what works well for you. There are several things to keep in mind, though, as you're managing your groups of peers. These ideas come from my own experience as an elementary school teacher, from my reading, and from the ideas of teachers I've worked with:

1. It's a good idea to cooperatively develop a set of standards for group work. However, some teachers like to let things "go to pot" for a while before they establish standards. Children, these teachers feel, have to see the *need* for standards before they can wholeheartedly develop them with you (just as adults need to see the need for a law before they obey it). Once kids see this need, they can talk with you about what's been going wrong, how they'd like things to be, and how they could make them be that way. This development of group standards is an important part of cooperative learning.

2. Don't rely, though, merely on a written set of standards that you put on the wall. Go ahead and put them up, but do spend time whenever necessary to discuss the old problems that haven't been solved, the new problems that have come up while they've been working in groups, and the new solutions that you agree upon. If you just scold them for not following the "rules," you're not really engaging in cooperative education. Getting them to make up and follow rules that *you* want is "manipulative" rather than "cooperative" education.

3. At the same time, you *are* their leader, their model, their arbiter, their facilitator—and their boss, if you wish. As educational leader you really do need to take charge of who sits with whom. And here's where you can mix the group according to your goals for their learning. Mixing them heterogeneously has the advantage of allowing skilled readers and writers to be readily available to give assistance to those with less skill. It also has the advantage of providing models of good reading and writing.

Other Grouping Procedures

An additional way to group children for learning together is to use what is called "flexible grouping," something I mentioned in Chapter 9. With flexible grouping, you temporarily put a group of children together for specific instruction on a very specific problem the children have in common, such as those children who need cloze-type experiences in order to improve their predicting abilities. Such groups are formed and then dropped as the problem is alleviated.

And, of course, many teachers still group children for reading instruction according to what basal reader they've been placed in. There's nothing terribly wrong with this, provided you also place these kids in other groups as well—

groups that are *not* homogeneous in reading ability. Poor readers also need to work with good readers. Poor writers also need to work with good writers. Poor readers or writers also need groups in which they can *shine*—such as temporary hobby groups, or science groups, or math groups. They need to be noted as an expert on something now and then.

Anthropologists have been telling us for decades that human beings are social, cooperative creatures. Most of us are not like male bears, frogs, or fiddler crabs, which spend most of their lives alone. Ashley Montague tried to explain this back in 1950. In his book, *On Being Human,* he cites several examples of how cooperation among animals is quite common: White mice who live with groups grow stronger and faster than they do in isolation. Chimpanzees often pass food to each other through cage bars. Even goldfish survive better in groups, and humans generally can't maintain mental health without feeling that they're a member of *some* group, no matter how small. (In fact, Montague contended that since human relations are so important to people's health, it ought to be taught in school as the "fourth R.") You may have seen the articles in popular magazines telling how monkeys can learn more and faster when they're taught along with at least one other monkey. Some say this is because the monkeys enjoy the competition, but anthropologists might point out that even competition is a form of cooperation, since it helps both monkeys meet their needs.

If we want to develop "people" as well as "readers," perhaps we should heed this advice a second time:

> Children will find it difficult to learn citizenship and cooperation when the teacher turns the classroom community into a classroom of isolated individuals each seeking his or her own personal gain, often at the expense of others. . . . There is no doubt that reading instruction must focus on reading improvement. But reading instruction, whenever possible, must give children opportunities to work cooperatively." (Rasinski & Nathenson-Mejia, 1987, p. 633)

MANAGEMENT DECISION THREE: HOW TO USE PEER AND ADULT AIDES

In Chapter 13, I explained some of the ways that parents and other adults can act as tutors, both at home and at school. With tactful training, however, they can make excellent volunteer aides as well. Jack Cassidy, a former school district reading supervisor, found that senior citizens are good tutors, makers of instructional materials, and classroom aides. He mentions others who might also be called upon: "Groups often overlooked as volunteers are women . . . with grown children, men who do not frequent senior centers but may be involved in local clubs, and homebound persons who might help construct instructional materials" (Cassidy, 1981, p. 290).

If you'd like more information for you and your volunteer aides, write for the booklet, *Handbook for the Volunteer Tutor,* edited by Sidney Rausch and Joseph Sanacore, International Reading Association, 800 Barksdale Road, P.O. Box 8139,

Newark, DE 19714. Another book on this topic is Edward Robbins's *Tutor Handbook,* available from the Government Printing Office, Washington, DC.

Most of the teachers I talk to sing praises for their volunteer aides. As Beth DeVogele, a special reading teacher, said: "One success story I've had throughout my teaching career is the utilization of the volunteer tutor. Today is a time of larger numbers in the classroom, greater demands for individual needs, and record numbers of children with emotional and learning difficulties. The teacher can't possibly meet the demands placed on her. Salaried aides are often not feasible because of financial stress. We need to seek out capable willing volunteers. They *are* in existence, but they need to feel and *be* essential if they're going to work well with you."

I mentioned in Chapter 13 that volunteer aides can be used to supervise reading centers, an often vital function. They can also be extremely important in guiding and tutoring children who need your help *right now* when you're trying to work with reading groups. In addition, they can help you find and display appropriate library books and various materials related to science, social studies, and other units. When children need special help in learning sight words and graphophonic patterns, a volunteer aide can make the difference between success and failure.

Using Peer Tutors

When America became an urban instead of rural society, and one-room, multi-graded schoolhouses gave way to classrooms of children all the same age, we lost an important teaching concept. The concept was this: *Teaching teaches the teacher.* You probably developed this notion yourself somewhere along the way—that when you teach someone younger or less skilled, you're the one who learns the most. Research verifies your experience. Nevi (1983) presents several studies showing that tutors improve as much as or more than tutees. Allen (1976) examined more than 80 research reports and concluded that tutoring can lead to higher reading scores for both tutees and tutors. In fact, he found that all types of tutors can be effective: adult tutors, older-age students, students with behavioral problems, low achievers tutoring younger children, tutors of the opposite sex, untrained tutors, and trained tutors. He also found that no one method of training seemed to be definitely superior. Perhaps Ashley Montague was right: Human beings *are* cooperative creatures.

Allen and Feldman had previously studied a group of low-achieving fifth-graders. These children alternated between studying alone and teaching a third-grade tutee. When they were in the role of tutors, their reading test scores were higher than when they studied alone. Allen and Feldman explain the difference this way: "A substantial amount of empirical data demonstrates that role enactment does produce behavioral and attitudinal changes in the person enacting the role. . . . It is necessary for a teacher to adopt a completely different point of view from that taken by a student" (1973, p. 1). Thus, they explain, when children play the role of teacher, and look at the material to be taught, it takes on a different and more understandable organization. Furthermore, assuming the role of teacher gives some children a feeling of importance they've been missing.

For fear that I've given the impression that only the tutor gains from tutoring, let me cite a few more studies showing specific effects on those tutored. King (1982) trained seventh-graders to assist third-graders with SRA comprehension labs, to make and use flashcards with them, to play educational games with them, to read to them, and to listen to them read. The tutors also learned to discuss what the third-graders read and to ask them questions at various levels of thinking. After eight weeks of tutoring, forty minutes a day, the experimental third-graders were compared with a control group and a "placebo group." With the placebo group the tutors talked, played, and worked on art projects with the third-graders. The control group was merely supervised in a forty-minute study period each day and worked by themselves. (Children were randomly assigned to the three different third-grade groups.) The results after only eight weeks were as follows:

Tutees (experimental)	4.6 grade equivalency score
Placebo group	3.3 grade equivalency score
Control group	3.1 grade equivalency score

No, you're not seeing a misprint. In this particular case, perhaps because of the excellent and enthusiastic training received by the tutors, there is a one-and-one-half year difference between the tutored children and the children who worked alone. King cites several similar studies that demonstrate the same effect, including one showing that learning disabled children from special classrooms can benefit from in-class tutoring when they are mainstreamed into regular classrooms for reading instruction.

The city of Marshall, Minnesota, developed a system of peer tutoring on school buses. MacDermot (1982) reports that in this school system, fourth- and fifth-graders acted as tutors to second- and third-graders. The tutors received five hours of training and were shown how to use tutoring packets. These packets contained short review lessons with five activities for each target skill. The packets were placed where the tutors could get them without disturbing teachers or classes. When a tutor felt that his pupil had learned a particular skill, he recorded this and put the pupil's folder in a box labeled "Ready for Testing." A teacher then administered a test to the second- or third-grader and gave the results to the tutor to pass on to the tutee. The outcome of this program? Improved test scores for the tutees and positive attitudes for the tutors, tutees, parents, and teachers, all at a very low cost.

Lehr (1984) summarizes the research on peer teaching this way:

Peer teaching is especially valuable in reading.

Peer teaching often leads to higher performance in reading skills, writing mechanics, and sight words.

Many types of activities seem to be effective: flashcards, word lists, worksheets, games, dictating spelling words, studying for a quiz or assignment together, simply discussing ideas already introduced by the teacher.

Tutor training can help avoid tutors damaging tutees' self-concepts; it can also help teach tutors how to give directions, confirm correct responses, apply nonpunitive corrections, praise, gather and replace materials, measure and record performance, allocate time, and monitor progress.

Hiebert (1980) cites several studies that agree with the results reported so far. Moreover, she also cites studies showing that children who learn to read before school age have usually been taught by older brothers or sisters. Evidently, we humans are "natural-born teachers." Put someone younger (or at least innocent-looking) in our path and we can't resist teaching him something. It's too bad that many teachers don't take advantage of this natural compulsion. In fact, though, Hiebert cites studies showing that many teachers do their best to *prevent* peer interaction. In other words, some teachers are so concerned that children *will* help each other with their work, they neglect to capitalize on the benefits that can come from their tutoring each other.

Since research shows that a great deal of wasted learning time occurs when children must wait around to ask the teacher a question (Hiebert, 1980, p. 879),

it certainly behooves classroom teachers to plan ways to provide structured tutoring experiences instead. It also behooves them to arrange for cross-graded tutoring experiences to occur as well, since these experiences benefit both tutors and tutees. However, let me urge those who are considering such interaction among peers to consider materials in addition to flashcards, games, and worksheets for the tutoring media—namely, books. As King's study showed, having the tutor read to her pupil and having her listen to her pupil read were also effective. Children who require tutoring need more practice in interactive reading, and this is where training will be crucial; your tutors may need to be trained to help their tutees read for *meaning* and to look for context clues as well as graphophonic clues. When tutors themselves have already been taught this way, it will be natural for them to follow suit.

MANAGEMENT DECISION FOUR: HOW TO SCHEDULE TIME ACCORDING TO GOALS

Sometimes I get discouraged. There's so much knowledge about effective teaching of reading and writing that never gets applied in the classroom. I'm not *thoroughly* discouraged, mind you, just mildly. In fact, my discouragement is probably nothing more than childish impatience, for I know that over the next few decades changes will gradually take place, just as they always have. As we communicate with each other in this last chapter, then, let's both keep in mind that change is bound to take place and that both of us will probably be involved in causing changes to occur.

One of the changes we can hope for is that more teachers will allot instructional time according to *goals* rather than available materials. What researchers see too often in elementary school classrooms is teachers' letting materials dictate what happens next. Suppose, for example, that the next lesson in the teacher's guide is "what is meant by the terms *short vowel sound* and *long vowel sound.*" Yet suppose the teacher has observed that a particular group of seven children is still reading word by word, without predicting ahead, without noticing the same kind of syntactic and semantic cues they notice when they listen. What management decisions, according to the research I've just cited, will most teachers make? Most will decide to push ahead in the teacher's guide, to teach the lesson on the terms *short vowel sound* and *long vowel sound,* to assign the worksheets that "teach these terms," and to assume that word-by-word reading will go away in time anyway.

This is sad, for the vast majority of teachers are conscientious, concerned people who *want* to help their students become highly successful readers. But for a variety of reasons, most of them "go by the book." Poor training? Often. Personal timidity? Certainly sometimes. Lack of encouragement from administrators? Unfortunately often. Many school systems do not encourage teachers to develop management skills that would allow them to make more reasonable decisions. Too often, instead, teachers are encouraged to let the teacher's guide and other materials determine both the goals and the time allotments. True, some schools grams essentially imposed on teachers that allow very little flexible planning on the teacher's part. So you see, the change we're talking about involves not only teachers like you and teacher educators like me, but principals, reading coordinators, superintendents, and curriculum coordinators as well.

Managing Time for Reading and Writing Whole Text

Of course, as you already know, teachers' beliefs about what is important to learn greatly influence the way they manage the time available for reading instruction (Berliner, 1981). If you believe that reading is a composite skill consisting of "handtoes and handtoes of subskills" (as Philosopher Omega did in Chapter 1), you'll set up teaching goals that match that belief. More importantly, you'll be inclined toward allotting lots of time for subskill lessons and worksheets. If, on the other hand, you believe that reading is an interactive process between reader and author and among the four cueing systems, you'll want to manage your instructional time to include guided silent reading, modeled metacognitive processes, library book reading, and so on. Furthermore, you'll probably welcome research studies that show that increasing the amount of time children spend with whole text that is *easy enough* leads to higher scores on achievement tests, greater retention rates, and more positive attitudes toward school (Berliner, 1981).

During the 1960s, Jeanne Chall (1967) wrote a book entitled *Learning to Read: The Great Debate,* in which she examined the perpetual debate among reading educators as to whether to emphasize "phonics," or whole words, or meaning, or something else. Every classroom manager is intimately involved in this debate whether she realizes it or not. But when you get right down to it, the great debate for the classroom teacher, involved each day in making managerial decisions, is not whole word versus phonics, decoding versus comprehension, or subskills versus interactive reading. The debate is consciously or unconsciously one of whether to have the children practice reading skills in an isolated fashion (using worksheets and similar assignments) or to have them practice reading skills in an integrated, interactive fashion (using whole text reading and writing).

The Mason and Durkin studies indicate clearly which side of the debate most teachers have been on, as judged by the actual amount of time allotted to explaining, distributing, and correcting worksheets. It's not that they've always *wished* to be on this side of the debate. When you ask teachers what they're most concerned about, they invariably put comprehension at the top—and when asked, they'll put "reading attitudes" very high on the list as well (see Chapter 13 for research on this). But what people are most concerned about and what they do about it are not always the same thing, as most dieters will tell you.

The problem is threefold. For one thing, many teachers don't know *how* to actually teach reading as an interactive process (but you do, of course). For another thing, many teachers don't know how to *schedule* for interactive-type instruction. It's so much easier, they think, to schedule for subskill instruction: Just divide the number of pages and workbooks by the number of days in the school year, right? (I'll show you a better way in a minute.) And for a third thing, many teachers fear that the principal (or curriculum director) *won't let them* teach toward interactive reading: "I have to use the subskill materials they give me to teach with."

The "They Won't Let Me" Problem: Let's tackle this problem first, since solving it could solve a very basic need for the teacher: *not* to be frightened of being innovative. Here are some things that some teachers have done to alleviate this problem:

1. Use the materials assigned to your grade according to the sequence of particular children's needs for them rather than to a sequence preset by publishers. This will give you a lot more time for teaching interactive reading. As I mentioned earlier, no research has been reported that justifies a tight sequence dictated by page numbers in teacher's guides. Nor does any research demonstrate that skipping numerous pages in prescribed materials causes a decrease in reading achievement.
2. Better yet, follow the school system's curriculum guide more than you follow the publishers' teaching guides. The curriculum guides are usually more liberal and liberating in that they specify objectives and sample procedures rather than specific pages a publisher has produced.
3. Still better yet, talk to the principal and/or curriculum director about your goals and proposed teaching processes (strategies). Most of "them" are willing to listen and will encourage you to experiment (if not with the whole class, then with the advanced students; if not for the whole week, then for part of the week; if not for the whole year, then for a pilot study of one month).

The "How to Teach" Problem: In order to teach toward your goal of interactive reading, you'll need to think about the instructional processes or strategies that you need in order to inspire and teach this kind of reading. As you've seen in previous chapters (and this is your chance to review those chapters without turning more than one or two pages), interactive reading tends to be learned by children when teachers use the following processes:

A. Provide plenty of guided silent reading.
   1. Use questioning strategies that employ DRTA, story schema, interactive processes, and metacognitive monitoring.
   2. Enhance children's schemata before they read.
   3. Teach certain words before they read.
   4. Use interest getters—especially before they read content area material.
B. Guide their oral reading for specific purposes.
   1. Use miscue analysis to determine each student's concepts of reading and strategies for moving through text.
   2. Allow students to confirm their predictions through oral reading.

3. Encourage fluency through oral reading of easy patterned books and other literature.
4. Urge children to share literature passages with others.
C. Model reading strategies for your students.
   1. Show them how you personally use four cueing systems in order to read interactively, especially how you use your own schemata based on direct and vicarious experiences.
   2. Demonstrate how you personally predict and confirm plot events, character behavior, exposition structures, and word meanings.
   3. Demonstrate metacognitive monitoring. Show them what *you* do when you're confronted with the undeniable fact that you've just plowed right through some print that you didn't understand any better than a baby understands why his bottle is lost at the foot of the crib.
D. Model writing processes for your students (remembering that through the act of writing they can understand interactive reading better).
   1. Show them how you, yourself, create different types of exposition or stories. This can often be done along with a group experience of writing something together.
   2. Demonstrate how you plan your composition before you write it. (But make your demonstration simple please.)
   3. Explain your process of producing a rough draft by quickly getting down your ideas. Also explain how you, the linguistic expert, sometimes use invented spelling.
   4. Show how you go about editing your own manuscript for better clarity, interest value, imagery, spelling, punctuation, and coffee stains.
E. Guide their writing processes (with primary interest in the content of what they're trying to *communicate*).
   1. Provide informal conferences for idea development, either with yourself or with peers.
   2. Respond orally and in writing to their attempts to communicate.
   3. Encourage peer sharing and editing.
F. Provide encouragement of and time for nonguided reading of literature.
   1. Let them prepare and share book projects.
   2. Arrange for teacher and peer conferences on books.
G. Provide supplementary decoding instruction.
   1. Use observations of children reading out loud, as well as special tests on sight words and graphophonic patterns (see Table 6.1 and Appendix H).
   2. For those children who need them, provide special direct-instruction lessons, using one method that emphasizes the auditory mode and one method that emphasizes the visual mode. Provide tactile and kinesthetic activities for those who need them.

3. Use sight word and graphophonic pattern games—especially active ones—for those children who need extra practice (see Appendixes A and B).

4. Provide opportunities to learn sight words and graphophonic patterns through journals and through language experience charts and stories.

5. Provide opportunities to learn sight words and graphophonic patterns through the content areas.

The Scheduling Problem: Modeling, encouraging, and practicing interactive reading can all be arranged. But you'll have to schedule for it. Unless you specifically allot time for teaching interactive reading, you may find yourself falling back on assigning pages and worksheets. Or equally poor, you might fall back on having the kids do little more than "free reading" with little or no instruction from you. This is what happened to the so-called "individualized reading programs" of the 1960s.

If you have decided that interactive reading is a major goal of your reading instruction, and if you agree with the processes I've just listed for teaching interactive reading, you now have the job of allotting enough time to put those instructional processes into action. At first, this time allotment will take a little extra effort, but gradually it will become second nature for you to allow time for the various ways of developing interactive readers.

Figure 15.1 shows a weekly schedule sheet that should prove useful to you. By filling this out each week for a few months, you can get yourself into an "interactive groove." After that, perhaps all you'll need to do is tape one of these sheets on your classroom closet door for a gentle reminder. At first when you look at Figure 15.1 you might think, "My God, how could I possibly do all that in one week!" Let me assure you, first of all, that many teachers do accomplish much of this each week. Second, you don't have to accomplish *all* of it; some weeks you'll skip some of the processes. Third, once you've modeled the reading strategies and writing processes a few times, you don't have to keep modeling them every week. Fourth, there really are enough minutes each week to carry on these instructional processes—even if you use basal readers for your major source of text. (Of course, if you insist on doing every single page in every basal reader and every single page of the workbooks, and so on—well, then you may have a problem, if you know what I mean.) Try the schedule sheet; you'll find that it helps you plan not only next week but several weeks to come.

MANAGEMENT DECISION FIVE:
HOW TO USE TV AND COMPUTERS

While peer tutors and volunteer aides can be of great benefit to the teacher, two other resources have promise: television and the computer. Television was of limited use in classrooms during the 1960s and 1970s, since everyone had to drop what they were doing to watch a program scheduled by a local television station.

Week of _____ Teacher _____

Time available for literacy instruction (normal week)

Combined Time for All Kids

Daily reading period: 5 days @ 60 minutes   300 minutes

Daily writing period: 5 days @ 50 minutes   250 "

Science or social studies: 5 days @ 40 minutes   200 "

    Total minutes per week   750 minutes

1. Guiding silent reading (combined time for this week)
   - Schemata enhancement: reading period   _____ minutes
   - Schemata enhancement: social studies or science   _____ "
   - Vocabulary development: reading   _____ "
   - Vocabulary development: social studies or science   _____ "
   - Comprehension enhancement: DRTA, story schema, etc.   _____ "
   - Interest getters in content areas   _____ "
   - Actual reading time of whole text (rdg + sci + ss)   _____

2. Guiding oral reading (combined time)
   - For miscue analysis/checking concepts and strategies   _____ "
   - For student confirming of predictions   _____ "
   - Reading with fluency and expression   _____ "
   - Sharing portions of literature   _____ "
   - Actual reading time of whole text (rdg + sci + ss)   _____ "

3. Modeling reading strategies (combined time)
   - Interactive reading with four cueing systems   _____ "
   - Predicting and confirming plot events   _____ "
   - Predicting and confirming words and meanings   _____ "
   - Exposition schema: types of structures   _____ "
   - Metacognitive monitoring of comprehension   _____ "
   - Special guided practice following modeling   _____

4. Modeling writing processes (combined time)
   - Creating different types of exposition or stories   _____ "
   - Planning a composition before writing   _____ "
   - Rough drafting: fluent encoding of ideas   _____ "
   - Rough drafting: fluent use of invented spelling   _____ "
   - Editing for final draft   _____ "
   - Special guided practice following modeling   _____ "

5. Guiding writing processes (combined time)
   - Informal conferences for idea development   _____ "
   - Oral and written responses to compositions   _____ "
   - Assisting peer sharing conferences   _____ "
   - Assisting peer editing conferences   _____ "
   - Conferencing final processing for "publication"   _____ "

6. Nonguided reading of literature (teacher too)   _____ "
   - Preparing and sharing book projects (teacher too)   _____ "
   - Individual literature conferences   _____ "

7. Supplementary decoding instruction   _____ "
   - Total time for this week   _____ minutes

FIGURE 15.1

Scheduling of process-oriented instruction

Today, however, the courts have ruled in favor of noncommercial copying of television programs, thus freeing teachers to create videocassettes for instruction. In the near future, the VCR (videocassette recorder) could easily become one of the teacher's best friends.*

Even today, the teacher with access to a VCR is fortunate; the videocassette is an incredibly easy way to bring the outside world into the classroom. A cassette can't beat a direct experience, perhaps, but it can often make the pages of science and social studies textbooks, as well as basal readers, come alive. Interactive reading can't occur unless the reader brings schemata to the page, and video recordings, *before* reading, can provide the background experience necessary for developing schemata.

So when you're despairing because of the four hours a day of television viewing your students engage in, remember—there's a nugget of gold inside that large mass of mud and rock. The trick is to learn what's available from television that you can use in your classroom. If you're not now a habitual viewer of public television, you might want to make the minimum contribution they request so you can receive the monthly guide, *Dial,* that will come to your home at least a week before the programs are aired, enabling you to anticipate your need for a VCR. Regular programs (those your children favor) can also be used to your advantage in teaching reading, since transcripts of both PBS and commercial programs are often available. You can use transcripts of children's favorite programs like a play, with children taking turns reading parts. The teacher can use transcripts of informational programs to create reading charts or dittos (based on small segments of a program) to read and discuss after children view the videotape. The reading charts or dittos can be based on the exact words from a transcript or made simpler by paraphrasing. The charts, dittos, or actual transcripts can be used as part of an activity for children to engage in while the teacher works with reading groups, or they can be used as a class activity under the teacher's direction. To obtain transcripts, write for the particular program from the specific network:

ABC, 7 West 66th Street, New York, NY 10023

CBS, 51 West 52nd Street, New York, NY 10019

NBC, 30 Rockefeller Plaza, New York, NY 10027

PBS, 475 L'Enfant Plaza S.W., Washington, DC 20024

Using Computers and Word Processors

Another resource available for direct instruction or learning centers is a "personal computer," especially one equipped for word processing. Personal computers

---

*It's a good idea to obtain written permission from the broadcasting company if you plan to use the teacher-made videotape more than twice and also after ten days of the original broadcast. Otherwise, you may be violating the "fair use" guidelines developed in the U.S. in 1981 by film and TV associations.

were a novelty in schools not too long ago, but by 1984, there was one available for every 92 students in the United States (Hassett, 1984). By 1999, we should see that ratio greatly reduced. It may well be a rare classroom that does not have one. At any rate, "powerful microcomputers are now resident in many schools. . . . Traditional textbook publishers, along with commercial software houses and some nonprofit organizations, have begun to produce reading lessons based on a variety of instructional paradigms. Instructional tools—word processors, spelling checks, and management systems—have assumed a stage center position in the educational software market and in the software inventories of many schools" (Mason et al., 1983, p.vii).

When you consider two facts, that (1) children enjoy operating computers, and that (2) the main process involved in *operating* computer programs is the reading process, you can see why I have some enthusiasm for installing a computer in every classroom, especially when the initial research on the effect of computer use is so positive (Mason et al., 1983). And especially when you consider how well a computer's word processing capabilities allow a child to manipulate and generate language. How relatively easy it is for children to produce sentences, rearrange them, change them, add to them, and in general to create their own reading material. How painless it is for children to spend hours with computer games and simulations and not even realize how much effort they're putting into *reading*. And how relatively painless it is for teachers and aides to take dictation from children eager to tell their story and thereby create more reading text.

I certainly don't want to give you the impression that most of the computer games and simulations produced for schools are excellent; they're not. If you get a chance to read some of the software reviews in the computer journals, you'll discover that you have to be *very* selective. Before purchasing or recommending purchase of a game, simulation, or other software item, I strongly recommend that you check one of these journals for a review of the program:

The Reading Teacher (section called "The Printout")

Educational Computer Magazine

Compute

Classroom Computer Learning

Computers, Reading and Language Arts

Classroom Computer News

Creative Computing

Personal Computing

Journal of Educational Technology Systems

The biggest flaw in many programs is that they imitate worksheets; students merely plug in answers and get feedback. These are not the kinds of programs that turn children into more avid readers. Programs that interest them are games and simulations that involve some kind of goal, such as reaching an important destination, accumulating wealth, getting rid of bad guys, finding the treasure, solving a puzzle as quickly as possible, and so on. Especially challenging are programs that require children to solve problems and make decisions.

Mason (1983) brings up another use for personal computers in the classroom that allows a computer to act as a nonthreatening teacher. The program, CADPP (Computer Assisted Diagnostic Prescriptive Program in Reading and Mathematics) permits a teacher to program specific prescriptions, which are then presented by the computer to a student who has completed a test (for example, "Do page 19 in Booklet D"). According to Mason, students perceive the test corrections as well as the prescriptions that follow as less threatening than those presented by a teacher. This is particularly true for children who already think of themselves as poor readers.

Mason also recommends programs that put the child in a position of superiority over the computer—programs, for example, that require the student to tutor the computer. The program *Animal* is one of these. In this game the computer tries to guess what animal the student has in mind by asking the student questions. Whenever the computer fails to guess the animal, it requests that the student type in a new question and answer that will help it determine the correct animal. For instance, if the student notices that the computer has not asked anything about ears, she types in a question and answer that will help this poor ignorant computer learn that the animal she has in mind has long ears. As the game goes on, the computer guesses more animals, and the student *reads and responds* to dozens of questions—and *writes* dozens of questions.

Many programs also require the student to proofread and get rid of "bugs" before the computer will give the student what he wants. This often leads to improved spelling as well as reading (Mason, 1983), but it also leads to a feeling of triumph when the student finds bugs. "This joy in accomplishment is so profound that it often shocks teachers who had thought nothing in school could excite these children" (Mason, 1983, p. 506).

A program that won an Award of Merit from the Association for Media and Technology in Education is called "The Puzzler." As Casey (1987) describes it, "The beauty of the program is its departure from the old, 'one right answer only' philosophy. Answers . . . are solicited with a goal of justification, not correctness. . . . It is probably one of the best programs around for teachers who are looking for methods to help them model and teach comprehension skills as opposed to only testing comprehension" (1987, p. 800). If you're interested in a brochure describing this program, write to Sunburst Communications, 39 Washington Avenue, Pleasantville, NY 10570.

With the right software, you can also use a personal computer as an aid to your record-keeping system. If you choose to do so, your computer can be programmed to test students on their mastery of certain fundamentals, such as sight vocabulary, phonograms, or vowel patterns. It can also be programmed to maintain student files, to update their records, to list prescriptions for students, and even to generate reports for parents and administrators. For more information, write to Random House Management Systems, School Division, 201 East 50th Street, New York, NY 10022.

Most basal reader publishers now produce similar management systems, as well as numerous reading games that coincide with their basal reader programs. Remember, though, to make sure your school district is purchasing true games or simulations and not dull worksheet-style programs that are merely labeled "games." And don't restrict yourself to "reading" programs; take a look, also, at social studies and science programs, which usually offer more interactive reading and practice in inferential thinking than many reading programs.

MANAGEMENT DECISION SIX: WHAT TO DO ABOUT BEHAVIORAL PROBLEMS

All right now, you've got everything under control, right? You've carefully allocated your instructional time to match your concept of reading and your specific goals for a group of children. You've scheduled your time to allow for integrated interactive reading. You've arranged for children to choose books for themselves and to produce their own reading material through writing or dictation. You've even decided how you're going to handle the basal reader program you're expected to use. You know just how you're going to group your children for different kinds of experiences. And on paper, it looks just great.

There's only one problem: Children don't always behave the way you want them to. Well, I could take the easy way out and recommend that you take some type of "behavioral management" course—and I do recommend that—but in the meantime, let me give you some tips that have worked for a lot of teachers I've worked with.

Although I hate the term "behavioral management," people do need some kind of motivation. So before you despair because of certain children's behavior and immediately try "behavioral management," you might ask yourself whether you've been violating any of the motivation principles I reminded you of in Chapter 13: Novelty . . . Needs . . . Level . . . Feedback. Are the children acting up because of the lack of new stimuli—new materials, new approaches, something new and different in the routine? I'm reminded of stage actors who often must repeat the same lines day after day for months on end. Even for these professionals, a director finds it necessary to introduce a surprise in the routine now and then—a new line, a change in costume, a new song—anything to keep the actors from dying of boredom.

Are the children misbehaving because their basic needs for oxygen, importance, and belonging are being ignored? When was the last time you opened a window, touched your toes with them (well, maybe your ankles), found a way to make James feel important, or helped Ginny find a friend? Are some children sullen because the work you're asking them to do is too easy and "babyish"; too difficult or confusing the way you've been presenting it; not at "the right height for the high jump"? Do some children need more readiness experiences for what you're trying to teach? Do some children need a peer tutor or more help from a volunteer aide? And what about feedback? Does it occur every few seconds? Or does it come too late, way after the children have forgotten what they were doing in the first place?

> Quite often, children don't need a teacher with "behavioral management" principles; they need a teacher with *learning* management principles.

The four motivation principles are crucial to successful management of an elementary school classroom. And so are the four retention principles; violation of these also can lead to children's misbehavior. (Do you recall them? Involved . . . Masters . . . Practice . . . Transfer?) Are you constantly on the lookout for ways to involve each child in each step of the learning process? Thinking of ways of keeping Joyce from drifting away into noninvolvement? Do you sometimes get each child to jot down his answer before calling on someone? Or sometimes have them tell a partner before telling the rest of the group? Or are you rushing your lessons and letting only a few energetic children do all the thinking? Are you teaching for mastery of concepts or coverage of pages? Are you increasing mastery through adding meaning to your lessons, relating new ideas to old ones, new words to schemata?

Do you sometimes assume that teaching is the same thing as learning? "I taught it to them last week, so they should have learned it." Or do you review and check the very next day, and a week later as well? How much time are you allotting for positive transfer of concepts? Are they really getting enough practice *applying* what you teach them? Do you *help* them make the necessary application of a "skill lesson" to interactive reading? Basically, do you help them feel successful (through principles of retention) so they want to learn more?

"All right," you say, "I've tried every single one of those ideas on motivation and retention, and I'm still having trouble with Jimmy and Cleo." If you really have tried those principles for more than a few days, *then* you may want to try one more set of management principles:

1. *Help the misbehaving child understand exactly what behavior you want.* When I was first a classroom teacher, I spent a good deal of time telling my "discipline problems" what not to do: "Don't sharpen your pencil when I'm talking! Stop poking her! Stop talking! No eating in the classroom! Quit that humming!" It often never occurred to me to tell the offending child exactly what I wanted him to do during a lesson. Only gradually did I learn to say pleasantly but firmly: "You are here to learn, and I *want* you to learn. When I'm teaching you, Jimmy, I want you to do three things. I want you to sit up straight. I want you to keep your eyes on me or on the chalkboard. And I want you to try to answer every question. Now you tell me the three things I want you to do." This leads us to the second principle.

2. *Encourage the behavior you desire.* Having made it clear to Jimmy what behavior I considered "learning behavior," at least in a lesson situation, I then needed some way to help him achieve success. So I needed to make him feel successful, important, or liked whenever he accommodated me with "learning style behavior." If I said something like, "I really like the way Jimmy is sitting up straight with his eyes on me and waiting to answer *every* question," it usually worked. Not only did it reward Jimmy, it encouraged the laggards to get ready too. (But you know all this. You've seen it many times, haven't you? I hope so.)

3. *If possible, ignore misbehavior that is brand new to a child.* Suppose that talking to her neighbor during a reading lesson is a new type of behavior for Cleo, or one that occurs very infrequently. What would be the best thing to do when you see it occur?

Pretend you don't even notice it, while, at the same time, you praise others for listening so well.

Nip it in the bud. Let her know immediately that she is misbehaving. That way, the habit will never get started.

After she sees you looking at her, ignore her completely.

It might be tempting to select the second alternative and nip it in the bud. With negative responses of this sort you might be able to suppress her behavior temporarily, but you may not eliminate it. In fact, for some children, the attention you give them by scolding is a form of *positive reinforcement.* By scolding, you put them in the spotlight and perhaps even give them a bit of prestige.

If you chose the third alternative, you may be in for trouble, because essentially you're saying that even though you saw her misbehaving, it doesn't really matter to you. The first alternative is probably the best response—*if the behavior is new or very infrequent.* By ignoring the behavior and praising others, you can provide the opportunity for her behavior to go unrewarded.

4. *Use a negative response when positive responses fail to get the desired result, but be aware of possible side effects.* Let's say that Cleo doesn't care whether you praise others for listening, that she gives you no opportunity for rewarding her in any way, and that your ignoring her seems to encourage her to talk louder and louder and to generally disrupt your instruction. What should you do?

Send her to the principal who is trained to handle problems like this.

Tell her that since she's missed part of the lesson by talking, she'll have to stay in for part of the recess to learn what she missed.

Warn her to stop talking or she'll be in trouble.

The first procedure is a way of telling the child that she's too much for you to handle. Sometimes one has to admit defeat like this, but obviously it's not solving your problem very well, particularly since Cleo is missing a lesson she needs. The third procedure may suppress the undesired behavior, but the warning is so vague it may have an undesirable side effect. Instead of paying attention to the rest of your lesson, she may spend several minutes wondering just what kind of trouble she might be in if she talks to her neighbor again.

The second procedure, or something like it, would clearly indicate not only what behavior you *don't* want but also what behavior you *do* want. In addition, it signals to her that the more she misses of the lesson, the more she'll miss a chance to talk to her friends during recess. Of course, it may also have the undesirable side effect of making her think of you as an "old meanie," the type of side effect that often occurs with a negative response. However, during the first few minutes of recess, you can cancel out some of this by briefly and kindly explaining to her what behavior is important during a lesson, by asking her to listen carefully while you briefly check her comprehension of the previous lesson, by praising her for correctly answering your questions, and by sending her out for the rest of recess *immediately* after reviewing the lesson—don't spoil the effect by scolding her once more before dismissing her. The approach advocated for Cleo is not the approach to use with all children who interrupt a lesson by talking to their neighbors. It is merely one illustration of how a negative response can be used, if necessary.

5. *Distribute your praise.* Unfortunately, permanent behavior change seldom occurs during the course of a single lesson or other type of interaction between child and teacher. It takes time and distributed encouragement. To help Cleo's behavior become more permanent, which should you do?

Praise her every time she pays attention in all future lessons.

Keep praise to a minimum and keep her in for recess whenever she talks to her neighbor.

Praise her frequently at first but gradually diminish your praise.

Continual praise (the first alternative) is too much of a good thing and may make the child dependent on you. What you want, eventually, is to have the learning of communication skills become its own reward or at least to have Cleo learning without constantly needing your emotional support. The second alternative (minimum reward and maximum punishment) will convince her you're an "old meanie" and may destroy her desire to relate to you and learn from you.

The third alternative (praise that is frequent at first but gradually diminished) is more likely to succeed in the long run. By giving frequent praise at first, you will help to "set" the behavior you desire. Often, a smile, a friendly nod, or a quiet "Good thinking, Cleo" is sufficient. By gradually diminishing your praise, you will probably strengthen her desire for praise, her urge to learn from you in order to receive it, and eventually her chance to be rewarded just by learning itself.

SUMMARY OF MAIN IDEAS AND ONE MORE ATTEMPT TO PREDICT THE FUTURE

☐ Classroom management, involving decisions about time allotment, group work versus individual work, peer tutors and adult aides, utilization of computers, television, and other resources, and the control of misbehavior, will continue to have a major impact on reading achievement.

☐ As teaching becomes ever more complex, teachers will be increasingly better trained as managers of time, people, and resources.

☐ While the average teacher today allocates time more often according to available materials than to definite goals, this situation will most likely change as teachers and administrators learn more about the complex interactive nature of the reading process. Simplistic views of the past and debates over phonics versus meaning will gradually fade as reading educators continue to grow in sophistication.

☐ The "great debate" for the near future, when it comes to practical decisions in the classroom, will not be phonics versus meaning but whether to have children spend most of their practice time with worksheets and arbitrary subskills or most of their practice time with real text in an interactive fashion.

☐ A greater number of teachers will learn how to allocate time for silent versus oral reading according to the specific values of each. Round-robin reading and testing of comprehension will give way to thoughtful modeling of comprehension, practice in integrating the four cueing systems, and sharing written materials to provide information and pleasure.

☐ The VCR and the computer will become two of the teacher's best friends.

☐ Managing behavioral problems will become less of a nagging headache as teachers become more sophisticated in "learning management" through learning principles. There will gradually be less confusion in schools between teaching and learning.

☐ Since research continually shows that teachers are more important than instructional materials, teachers will slowly gain more control over the instructional program, especially as they demonstrate both management ability and knowledge of the reading process. The tyranny of "teacher proof" materials will eventually become a quaint cultural and historical artifact, and teachers and children will become freer to interact as human beings.

REFERENCES AND SUGGESTED READING

Allen, V. L. (1976). Research on children tutoring children: A critical review. *Review of Educational Research, 46,* 355–386.

Allen, V. L., & Feldman, R. S. (1973). Learning through tutoring: Low achieving children as tutors. *Journal of Experimental Education, 42,* 1–5.

Allington, R. L. (1980). Poor readers don't get to read much in reading groups. *Language Arts, 57,* 872–876.

Becker, G. J. (1973). *Television and the classroom reading program.* Newark, DE: International Reading Association.

Berliner, D. C. (1981). Academic learning time and reading achievement. In J. T. Guthrie (Ed.), *Comprehension and teaching: Research reviews* (pp. 203–226). Newark, DE: International Reading Association.

Casey, J. M. (1987). The puzzler. *The Reading Teacher, 40,* 800–801.

Cassidy, J. (1981). Grey power in the reading program—a direction for the eighties. *The Reading Teacher, 35,* 287–291.

Chall, J. S. (1967). *Learning to read: The great debate.* New York: McGraw-Hill.

Durkin, D. (1979). What classroom observations reveal about reading comprehension instruction. *Reading Research Quarterly, 14,* 481–533.

Gaskins, R. W. (1988). The missing ingredients: Time on task, direct instruction, and writing. *The Reading Teacher, 41,* 750–755.

Guzzetti, B. J., & Marzano, R. J. (1984). Correlates of effective reading instruction. *The Reading Teacher, 37,* 754–758.

Hassett, J. (1984). Computers in the classroom. *Psychology Today, 18,* September, 22–28.

Hiebert, E. H. (1980). Peers as reading teacher. *Language Arts, 57,* 877–881.

Judd, D. H. (1981). *Partners in education: Instructional uses of the microcomputer.* Chicago: Follett.

Judd, D. H. (1982). Word processing in the classroom: Is it really practical? *Educational Computer Magazine, 2,* May–June, 18–19.

King, R. T. (1982). Learning from a PAL. *The Reading Teacher, 35,* 682–685.

Lehr, F. (1984). Peer teaching. *The Reading Teacher, 37,* 636–639.

MacDermot, H. G. (1982). Bus tutoring. *The Reading Teacher, 35,* 481.

Mason, G. E. (1983). The computer in the reading clinic. *The Reading Teacher, 36,* 504–507.

Mason, G. E., Blanchard, J. S., & Daniel, D. B. (1983). *Computer applications in reading.* Newark, DE: International Reading Association.

Mason, J. M. (1983). An examination of reading instruction in third and fourth grades. *The Reading Teacher, 36,* 906–913.

McDonald, F. I. (1976). *Beginning teacher evaluation study, Phase II summary.* Princeton, NJ: Educational Testing Service.

Montague, A. (1950). *On being human.* New York: Henry Scribner.

Nevi, C. N. (1983). Cross-age tutoring: Why does it help the tutors? *The Reading Teacher, 36,* 892–898.

Pearson, P. D. (1984). A context for instructional research on reading comprehension. In J. Flood (Ed.), *Promoting reading comprehension.* Newark, DE: International Reading Association.

Rausch, S., & Sanacore, J., (Eds.) (1985). *Handbook for the volunteer tutor.* Newark, DE: International Reading Association.

Rasinski, T. V., & Nathenson-Mejia, S. (1987). Learning to read, learning community: Considerations of the social contexts for literacy instruction. *The Reading Teacher, 41,* 261–265.

Robbins, E. L. (1971). *Tutor handbook.* Washington, DC: National Reading Center.

Singer, H., McNeil, J. D., & Furse, L. L. (1984). Relationship between curriculum scope and reading achievement in elementary schools. *The Reading Teacher, 37,* 608–612.

Taylor, N. E., & Connor, U. (1982). Silent vs. oral reading: The rational instructional use of both processes. *The Reading Teacher, 35,* 440–443.

Appendixes

APPENDIX A MORE GAMES FOR LEARNING WORDS

Word Chase

Materials: Game board (see Figure A.1); place markers such as plastic cars or buttons; one die. Home spaces should be four different colors (same four colors as markers). You may wish to write the sight words on strips about ¾" by 1½". Glue clear plastic holders on the game board and insert the strips. This allows you to change the sight words whenever you wish. (Or make a new game board from a file holder.)

Object of game: First person to get from his home space all around the board and back to home space wins.

Procedures: (two to four may play)

1. Players roll die to see who goes first. Highest number goes first.
2. Each person rolls die and moves number of spaces indicated.
3. When person lands on a space, he must read word out loud.
4. If a player doesn't read word correctly (as decided by other players), he must move back to where he was.

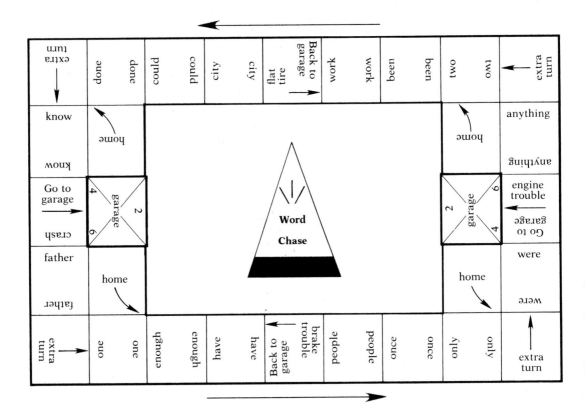

FIGURE A.1
Word Chase game board

5. Second person on same space bumps first person's marker all the way back to home space.
6. After going all the way around, player must roll the exact number on the die to get back into home space and win.
7. Must roll a 2, 4, or 6 to get out of the garages.

Word Toss

Materials: Four boards, each about 1″ by 6″ by 30″; twelve 2″ to 3″ nails; three rubber or plastic rings (see Figure A.2).
    Procedures: (best for two to four players)

1. Each person tosses three rings. Person with highest score goes first.
2. Leader shows a word with flashcard (about two seconds).
3. If player reads word correctly, he gets to throw three rings.
4. Leader keeps score with tally marks.
5. Whoever has most points at end of ten minutes (or some other designated time) is the winner.

Steal the Words

Materials: 64 cards* with 16 different high-frequency irregular words printed on them. Each word is printed twice on four different cards, once right-side up and once upside down (see Figure A.3).
    Object of game: Person with biggest pile of cards at end of game wins.
    Procedures: (two to four may play)

1. Draw a card to see who goes first. Person who draws word with most letters deals cards.
2. After shuffling cards, dealer gives four cards face down to each person.

FIGURE A.2
Word Toss playing board

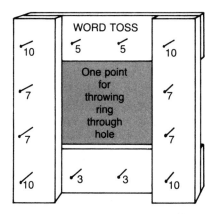

---

*Business cards work well, especially if sprayed with plastic or hair spray after words are printed. Check spray for running with one of the cards.

FIGURE A.3
Steal the Words game cards

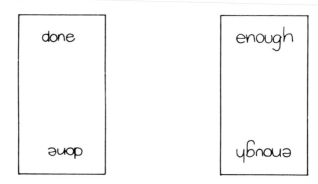

3. Dealer then places row of four cards face up in middle of playing area.
4. Person to left of dealer goes first.
5. If player has card that is the same as a card in the middle of playing area, she picks it up and places both cards face up in a pile close to her. (This forms the pile of words that others may later steal.) Before picking it up, however, she must read word to satisfaction of other players. If there are two cards in the middle that match one in a player's hand, she may pick up only one of them.
6. If player does not have a card that is the same as one in the middle, she must place one of her cards in the middle, thus adding to the selection in the middle.
7. If a player has a card that is the same as the top card of another player's pile, she must first read the word on the card out loud and then say STEAL THE WORDS as she takes the other player's entire pile and places it on top of her own.
8. A person may steal a pile of words only at the time of that person's regular turn!
9. After all players have used up their four cards, the dealer deals out four more cards to each; this time, however, the dealer does *not* place any more in the middle of the playing area.
10. Dealer places extra cards in center during her final deal.
11. When the final cards have been dealt and played, the game is over.
12. Last person to take a card with her card gets all the rest of the cards in the middle.

Word Checkers

Materials: Inexpensive or homemade checkerboard; set of checkers; paper labels slightly smaller than the squares on the checkerboard. Print a different word on each label—twice—so that each player can see the word right-side up.

Object of game: First person to get all of the other person's checkers wins; or the person who has the most checkers at the end of a designated time, such as ten minutes.

Procedures: Two people may play. Follow same procedures as with regular checkers, except:

1. Before person can move his checker, he must say the word or words that are on his path, including the word he finally lands on.
2. When a person cannot decode (pronounce) a word correctly, he loses his turn.

Boggle

A game that combines spelling and decoding; 16 lettered cubes. Purchase from Warren's Educational Supplies, 7715 Garvey Avenue, Rosemead, CA 91770.

Context Clues Game

A game that develops vocabularies through the use of context clues. Purchase from Lakeshore Curriculum Materials, 2695 E. Dominguez Street, P.O. Box 6261, Carson, CA 90749.

APPENDIX B MORE GAMES FOR LEARNING GRAPHOPHONIC PATTERNS

e-Boat Adventure

Materials: Game board (see Figure B.1); place markers such as buttons or tiny boats; one die.

Object of game: First one to get onto the Isle of *e* wins the game.

Procedures: (best for two to four players)

1. Roll die to see who goes first. Highest number goes first.
2. Each person rolls die and moves number of spaces indicated.

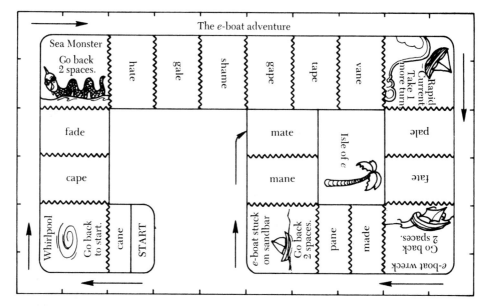

FIGURE B.1
e-Boat Adventure game board

3. When player lands on a word, she must read the word out loud as it is, then cover up the final *e* and read it out loud again (for example, *tape, tap*).

4. If player doesn't read word correctly both ways (and in the correct order), player must move back to where she was. (Other players decide.)

5. *Optional:* Player must say patterns as well; for example, "VCE, tape; VC, tap."

6. It is all right to have more than one *e*-boat on a space.

7. To land on the Isle of *e*, player must roll the exact number on the die.

Value of game: Practice in decoding VC and VCE words.

Adaptations of game: Use other VC-VCE contrasts such as *pine-pin, bite-bit,* and *ripe-rip;* or *rode-rod, ride-rid,* and *hope-hop.*

Wild Things

Materials: Deck of 58 cards with each card containing a one-syllable word. Each word should be an unambiguous example of one of the five major vowel patterns. You will need ten words for each of these patterns (see Table 7.2): VC, VCE, VCC, VVC, and CV. You will also need eight "wild thing" cards. (Do not use any word that ends in *r*.) See Figure B.2.

Object: First one to get rid of cards wins.

Procedures:

1. Deal five cards to each player face down.

2. Place rest of deck face down in center of the table.

3. Turn top card face up on the side of the deck to form discard pile.

4. Person to left of dealer begins play.

5. Each player plays (discards) or draws only one card; then it's the next person's turn.

6. In order to play, the player must be able to discard one card *(VC, VCC, VVC, VCE, or CV)*. Player must read pattern and word out loud to the approval of other

FIGURE B.2
Wild Things game cards

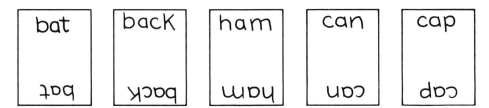

FIGURE B.3
Phonograms as Wild Things game cards

players or lose turn. Example: If *hunt* is top card on discard pile, player must discard a VCC word like *mask* and say, ''VCC, mask.''

7. If player does not have a word that follows suit, he may play a card having a word beginning with the same first letter as the top card on discard pile. This now changes the suit. Example: If *hunt* was down and next player discarded *ham*, next player must play a VC word or another *h* word; he must also call out the pattern he has used and the word.

8. A player may change suit anytime by playing a wild card and calling out the suit he wishes to change to. Example: Plays wild card and says, ''I want to change it to VCE words.''

9. If player does not have a playable card, he must draw *one* card from deck and *lose turn*. He may not play again until his next turn.

Value of game: Discriminating among five vowel patterns.

Adaptations of game: Use the five *r* patterns as suits: *ar, er, ir, ur,* and *or.* The player not only reads the word but calls out the pattern as well. Another adaptation is the use of phonograms as suits, such as *at, ack, am, an,* and *ap.* See Figure B.3.

APPENDIX C SOURCES OF MATERIALS AND INFORMATION ON BILINGUAL AND BICULTURAL PROGRAMS

International Reading Association
Executive Secretary
800 Barksdale Road
Newark, DE 19714

English as a Second Language Program
Center for Applied Linguistics
1717 Massachusetts Ave. N.W.
Washington, DC 20036

National Association for Bilingual
  Education
University of Texas at San Antonio
4242 Piedras Drive East
San Antonio, TX 78285

Teachers of English to Speakers of Other
  Languages (TESOL)
Executive Secretary
School of Languages and Linguistics
Georgetown University
Washington, DC 20007

Executive Secretary
National Council of Teachers of English
1111 Kenyon Road
Urbana, IL 61801

Bilingual-Bicultural Office
State Department of Public Instruction
Capital of your state, Your state

APPENDIX D MORE IDEAS FOR LANGUAGE EXPERIENCE STORIES AND OTHER TYPES OF WRITING

1. Have the children see how long they can make this sentence: "The bear chased the girl." They may change the sentence or the words in any way they wish. After they have made the sentence as long as they wish, they may also add more sentences.

2. Ask them to think of ideas for making the classroom more attractive.

3. Ask pupils to choose one picture (from a large set of pictures) to tell or write a story about. Give them a day or two to think about their idea. Then have them come one at a time to a quiet corner to tell you the story (or to tell it into a tape recorder). Let the child hold the picture while telling the story.

4. Find pictures that tell a story, for example, a crying child who is obviously lost. Have children tell or write (or both) what is happening now, what happened just before the picture, and what is going to happen after the picture.

5. Make a "touch book" with a different texture on each page: sandpaper, wax paper, silky fabric, and so on. Number each page and pass around the book. When a child has a turn with the book, she is to write down the page number and also at least five words that describe how the material feels. The child then hands in the paper to the teacher and passes on the book. (This is an excellent activity for a learning center.) Some children may need help from a large chart of "touch words" to select words for their own lists.

6. Ask pupils to make up one or two sentences that describe you, the teacher. Have fun reading them aloud, while at the same time discussing the kinds of words and phrases that can be used to describe a person's appearance and personality. Have the children use suggestions from your discussion to develop a paragraph about themselves.

7. Have the children make up a story or just tell about their own drawings or paintings. Take dictation during the telling or use a tape recorder. Or have them write up their story after telling it.

8. Develop a class story based on an event that occurs during the school day, such as an unusual fire drill or an animal that gets into the room. The teacher takes dictation from the class.

9. Read two or three Dr. Seuss books to the children and discuss the imaginary animals he created. Have them create their own imaginary animals on paper and tell or write about them.

10. Have the children close their eyes and imagine an imaginary character, such as a strange animal or funny person. Have them describe their characters one at a time and help weave them together into a story as they describe them. You may either stop here or write the characters' names on the board and have the children make up a story about them. They may use part of the story already created if they wish.

11. Have some of the children bring in toys to explain to the others. Have them pretend they are toy manufacturers and, together, think of ways to improve the toys. Accept even their wildest impossible ideas; in fact, encourage such ideas. If you wish, you can then have them write a story about a toymaker and how he tried to make the "best toy in the world."

12. Have children read each other's palms. Encourage them to tell exactly what adventures their partners will have, exactly how they will make their fortune, and so on.

13. Each person writes a detailed description of a character from a familiar story—one they've all read in class, favorite bedtime stories, and so on. Then each person reads her description and the rest of the class guesses who was described.

14. Make up "balloon adventures" about a helium-filled balloon and its travels around the world. An effective "starter" is to bring such a balloon to school and release it.

15. Have the children get in groups of four or five. Put several words on the chalk-board that might suggest a story, such as *sailboat, waves, rocks,* and *beach.* Each person in a group starts a story and then passes it on to another person in his group until the teacher says "time." When each person has added something to each of the stories, have the children read the stories to see how similar and different they are.

16. Give each child a newspaper funny with the words cut out. Have them write their own dialogue.

17. Have a class puppet who talks to the children every day. Have him tell about an adventure he had (the teacher had), about something he saw one of them doing that he didn't think was such a good idea, about how proud he is of them, and so on. Let the children make up adventures for him.

18. After practicing with some What-if questions (such as, "What if all the trees in the world were cut down?"), have them write their own What-if story.

19. After a period of spontaneous drama, have them write up the story they created.

20. Write a title on the board, such as "The Danger Zone" or "Flying Is for the Birds." Have each person write three sentences as a beginning of a story. Then have them put their names on their papers, fold the papers in half twice, and put them in a large box. They will then blindly pick one from the box and finish the story. Finally they will hand the story to the person who began the story, so that all may see how their story turned out.

21. Give each child five 3" by 5" index cards or other small pieces of paper. Have them write WHO, WHEN, WHAT, WHERE, and WHY on the five cards. After WHO they are to write the name and description of a character they have created. After WHAT they should tell something the character did. After WHEN and WHERE they should tell the time and place of the action. After WHY they should explain why the character did what he or she did (the motive).

    For example: WHO, Bill Robertson, a jeweler, age 40, tired-looking, graying hair, nail biter; WHAT, stole some of his own jewelry; WHEN, during a summer day when no customers were in the store; WHERE, in his own jewelry store in Chicago in a run-down shopping area; WHY, he wanted to claim he was robbed and collect the insurance money so he could send his daughter to college.

    Have the children put the cards in separate boxes: a WHO box, a WHAT box, a WHEN box, a WHY box, and a WHERE box. Mix the contents in the boxes and let the children each select five new cards—one from each box. They are to use their new cards, but only the ones that help them think of a story.

22. Have them create a story from a single Where sentence. Give each child a sentence on a piece of paper, for example, "I went to the circus," or "I went to a

farm," or "I went to a grocery store." It is all right if several children have the same sentence, but they should all begin with "I went to. . . ."

Show them how to create a "story" from a sentence. Put this sentence on the board: "I went to the new shopping mall." Under the sentence write the words *when, who, what, why*. Then show them how to ask questions that will help them describe their trip. For instance: When did you go? Whom did you see or go with? What did you do there? Why did you do these things?

23. Have them create a story from a single Who sentence. This is similar to 22. Work with Who sentences such as, "I saw Mrs. Twilliger, that lady who sells strange things." Ask questions about where, when, what, and why. For example: Where did you see Mrs. Twilliger? When did you see her? What was she doing when you saw her? Why was she doing it?

24. Have them create a story from a single What sentence, for example, "He was dropping cotton balls from an airplane." Ask who, when, where, and why questions.

25. Have them create a story from a single When sentence, for example, "It was on a dark, foggy night at the beginning of summer vacation." Ask where, who, what, and why questions.

26. Have them create a story from a single Why sentence, for example, "She was tired of having those kids tramp across her lawn and pick her flowers." Ask who, where, what, and when questions.

27. Have them create new adventures for their favorite cartoon characters such as Snoopy and Charlie Brown. This is especially good shortly after they have seen a Charlie Brown TV special.

28. Have them create new adventures for their favorite TV character.

29. Have them create a newspaper story about a game they have played on the playground. Be sure to have them include the who, what, when, and where in their story, and the why, if it's appropriate.

30. Have the children make up Crazy Titles and put them in a grab box for other children to pick from blindly. An example of a Crazy Title would be: "The Lion Who Ran the People Zoo" or "The Girl Who Walked Backwards."

APPENDIX E SOURCES OF HIGH-INTEREST, LOW-VOCABULARY BOOKS FOR CHILDREN

Publisher	Title	Reading Grade Level*	Interest Grade Level
Addison-Wesley Publishing Reading, MA 01867	Checkered Flag Series	2–4	6–12
	The Morgan Bay Mysteries	2–4	4–11
Children's Press 5440 N. Cumberland Avenue Chicago, IL 60656	True Book Series	2–3	3–6
Field Publications 245 Long Hill Rd. Middletown, CT 06457	Know Your World	3–5	4–8

Franklin Watts, Inc. 387 Park Ave. S. New York, NY 10016	Let's Find Out Series	2–4	5–6
Garrard Publishing 1607 N. Market Street Champaign, IL 61820	American Folktales	3–4	2–6
Merrill BasicSkills 936 Eastwind Drive Westerville, OH 43081	Focus on Reading	2–6	7–12
Reader's Digest Services Educational Division Pleasantville, NY 10570	Reading Skill Builders	1–4	2–5
Santillana Publishing 257 Union Street Northvale, NJ 07647	I Want to Be Series	2–4	4–6
Scholastic 730 Broadway New York, NY 10003	Action Libraries	2–3	4–8

*Reading level estimated by formula. Books should also be checked for schemata level.

APPENDIX F BOOK PROJECTS FOR CHILDREN AND TEACHERS*

Oral Projects

1. Try to interest others in a book you have read by reading an interesting part to the class. Practice before you read to them.
2. Read an exciting part to the class. Stop reading right in the middle of the action. Practice before you read to them.
3. Tell about one character in the book. Tell why he is such an interesting person. Make the others in the class want to know more about him.
4. Show on a globe or map how you would get from your home to where the story took place. Tell how you would travel there. Then tell something about this place. Tell a little bit about why the place was important to the story. Make the others in the class wish they could go there.
5. Pretend you are one of the characters in the book. Describe yourself and tell one or two things you do in the story. If others have already read the book, ask them to guess who you are.
6. Find an important object in the book you just read. Show it to the class and have them guess what it is and why it might be important in the story. Give them a few hints, but don't tell them too much.

---

*For modeling by the teacher and/or selection from a file card.

7. Play "Twenty Questions" with the class. Have them think of the object or person you have in mind that was important in the story. First tell them whether it is "animal, vegetable, or mineral." Then allow them 20 yes/no questions. After the game give them some hints as to why the object or person was important, but don't tell them too much.

8. Tell the class some interesting facts you learned about a country you read about. Then ask them three or four questions to see what facts they can remember.

9. Tell how you would have done something differently from the way a person in the story did it.

10. Prepare and present a TV commercial for your book. Try to interest others in "buying" your book.

11. Read to the class two or three poems from a book of poems you have read. Be sure to practice several times before you do this. You may wish to use the tape recorder for practicing.

12. Find someone else who has read the same book of poetry. Together, read two or three poems to the class. You might try different arrangements, as with a song; for example, one person could read the first verse, the other person could read the second verse, and both could read the third verse together.

13. See if you can recite from memory a favorite poem from a poetry book you have just read.

14. Dress up as a character in the book and tell about yourself or about one of the adventures you had.

15. After reading a book of folk tales, see if you can learn one of the stories well enough to tell it to the class.

16. Look up an author in _The Junior Book of Authors_ or _More Junior Authors_ (in the reference section of the library). Tell the class a few interesting things about him or her.

17. Make up another adventure for one of the characters. Tell the adventure to the class.

18. Make up a new ending for the book. Tell your ending to the class after you first tell a little bit about the beginning and the middle. Don't tell them the real ending, though.

19. Have a panel discussion about a book that three or four of you have read. Tell how you agree and disagree about some of the characters or about part of the story.

20. Tell about an adventure you had that was similar to one a character in the book had.

21. Meet in small groups to chat about books you have read.

Drama Projects

1. Pantomime a scene from your book. Have the class guess what you were doing. Tell them only enough to get them interested in the book.

2. Plan so that you and a friend read the same book, then prepare and present a skit about part of the book. You may have to make up some of your own dialogue, or you can say what the characters said in the book.

3. Tape record a skit based on the book. You may have to make up some of your own dialogue and make your voice sound like several different people. Play the tape recording to the class.

4. Put on a puppet play about one part of the book.

5. Play "Meet the Author." Find someone who has read the same book. One person pretends to be the author and the other interviews him. The interviewer asks questions about the book, about the author's life (if you can find information about his life), and so on.

6. Pretend you are the author of the book and are trying to get someone to publish it. Tell the "publishing staff" (your class) why it would be a good book to publish. Let them ask you questions.

7. Play charades with the class. Act out each word of the title. See how long it takes the class to guess the title.

8. If several others have read this book, pantomime a scene from the book *by yourself.* Then ask the class to guess the *title* of the book. See if they can also guess the author.

9. Pretend you are a character in the book you have read. Find someone who will pretend he is a character in a different book. In front of the class, carry on a conversation between the two characters. You might tell each other about some of your adventures or about some of the people you know (those who were described in the books).

10. Put on a play by yourself in which you play two or three parts. Make name cards for each character. Each time you switch parts, hold up one of the cards.

11. Find some dolls you can use to represent characters in your book. Put on a doll play about one part of your book.

12. Put on a play with one or two others. Have the class guess the title and author of the book.

Written Projects

1. Write a magazine advertisement for the book you have read. Put the ad on the bulletin board. Be sure to tell where the book can be found and a few things about why it's a "marvelous" book.

2. Write a letter to a friend and try to persuade her to read the book.

3. Make up a new table of contents for your book. Use your imagination to invent chapter titles that would interest someone else in reading the book.

4. Read two or three chapters of the book. Then write down what you think will happen in the next chapter. Then write briefly about how close your guess was.

5. Make a brief outline of your book. For example:

Tom Sawyer
  I. Tom plays, fights, and hides
    A. Tom tricks Aunt Polly
    B. Siddy gets Tom in trouble
    C. Tom fights with a new boy
    D. Tom returns home late at night
  II. The glorious whitewasher

6. Write about something that happened in the book in the same way a newspaper reporter would describe it. A reporter tries to answer these questions: Who? What? When? Where? Why? Don't forget to make up a snappy headline for your newspaper article.

7. Write a pretend letter to a character in the book. Tell the character how his or her life is the same as or different from yours.
8. Write a real letter to the author of the book. Send the letter in care of the publisher.
9. Make a short diary for one of the characters in the book. Describe three or four days as if you were the person in the book.
10. Pretend you are one of the characters in the book. Write a letter to another character in the book.
11. Add another chapter to the book. Tell what happened next, or what adventure was left out.
12. Write an ending to the book that is quite different from the one the author wrote.
13. Write about *two* books you have read about the same topic. Tell how the books are similar and different.
14. See how good your memory is. Describe the important details in one chapter. Draw a line under your description, then reread that chapter. Write down any important details you left out.
15. Write about an adventure you had that was like an adventure a character in the book had. Tell how the two adventures were alike and different.
16. Read in an encyclopedia or in another factual book about a person, place, or thing described in your book. Write down some of the things you learned this way that you did *not* learn from the book itself.
17. Try to make a list from memory of all the characters in the book. List both their first and last names. Draw a line under your list. Now skim through the book to see if you remembered all of them. Write down any you didn't remember. How good was your memory for names?
18. Write about the character in the story that you would most like to have for a friend. Tell why he or she would be a good friend. Also write about the character that you would *not* like to have for a friend. Tell why.
19. Write about how you would have solved a problem differently from the way a character in the book did.
20. Pick two characters from the story. Write about how they were alike and how they were different.
21. Make a list of words or phrases in the story that helped you almost be able to see or hear or smell or feel or taste something described in the story.
22. Write a poem that tells about one adventure in the book.

Arts and Crafts Projects

1. Make clothes for a doll to match a character in the book. Display it for the rest of the class to see. Make sure you put a card by it with the name of the book, the author, and your name.
2. Make an object that is important in the book you just read. Have the class guess what it is and why it might be important in the story. Give them a few hints, but don't tell them for sure.
3. Make a flannel board or bulletin board display about your book.
4. Make a comic strip about one of the scenes in your book. Put it on the bulletin board.

5. Make a diorama (a small stage) that describes a scene in the book. Use a cardboard box for the stage. Make the objects and people in your scene out of clay, cardboard, pipe cleaners, papier-mâché, or any other material.
6. Make a mobile representing five or six characters in the book.
7. If the book doesn't have a book jacket, make one for it. Be sure to put a picture on it and all the necessary information. A manila folder might be good to use.
8. Make a "movie" of one scene in your book. Use a long piece of butcher paper. After you draw a sequence of several pictures, roll the butcher paper. Then ask two people to unroll it as you describe the scene to the class.
9. Make a picture of one scene in the book. Put it on the bulletin board. Below it put the title and author and two or three questions about the scene. Try using crayon, chalk, or charcoal.
10. Same as 9. Use tempera, watercolor, or acrylic.
11. Same as 9. Use collage materials: bits of paper, cloth, or other materials.
12. Study the illustrations in the book. What techniques did the artist use? See if you can illustrate a part of the book that was not illustrated. Try to use some of the same techniques the artist did. Put your illustration on the bulletin board. Be sure to name the illustrator that you imitated.
13. Make a time line of the story showing main events rather than dates. Draw pictures to illustrate the main events.
14. Read half or more of the book. Then draw three pictures to show three different ways the book might end. Put them on the bulletin board, along with a card giving the title, author, your name, and "Three Ideas on How this Book Might End."
15. Make a scrapbook of things related to the book. Be sure to label what you put in your scrapbook.
16. Make a map to show where the characters went in the story.

Demonstration Projects

1. Demonstrate a science principle you learned from your book by performing an experiment in front of the class.
2. Show the class how to make something you learned to make from reading your book.
3. Show the class how to do something you learned to do from reading your book.

APPENDIX G   THE RAD TEST—RAPID ASSESSMENT OF A DISABLED READER

Directions for Group Administration

Note: This test is not a diagnostic test. Its purpose is to provide you with a means of quickly determining which children in a group *may* have a "specific language disability." The test is designed for second grade and up.

Part A: Visual-Kinesthetic Memory
Directions: Print the following words or letters at least 1½ inches high with heavy black felt pen on white cardboard about 3" by 8":

1. bad		6. hobby	
2. your		7. eighty	
3. top		8. minnow	
4. nuts		9. whenever	
5. JKBF		10. stumbles	

Show each card one at a time in the order given. (Do not print the number on the card. Just say the number as you show it.) Expose the card for about ten seconds while the students hold their pencils high over their heads.

After you have turned the card over, count five more seconds and say, "Write word number one." The children are then to write the word next to the number one on their sheet of paper. Give them about fifteen seconds to write the word; then ask them to raise their pencils above their heads again.

Repeat this procedure for each of the ten words. Do not show a word again after you have turned over the card.

Part B: Auditory Memory and Visual Discrimination
Directions: Have the following words and letters ready to read to the students:

11. quick		16. mommy	
12. fyqt		17. thought	
13. saw		18. surround	
14. bdec		19. running	
15. bubbles		20. everyone	

Say each word or series of letters. Say each one twice. While you are saying each one, the students should have their paper turned over. After you have said a word or series of letters twice, count five seconds and say, "Turn over your paper and find the words or letters in row one. Draw a circle around the word or letters I just said."

Allow about ten seconds for them to circle a word or series of letters. Then say, "Put your pencil down and turn over your paper. Listen for the next word or letters."

Repeat this procedure for each of the ten words or series of letters. Do not say a word or series of letters more than twice.

RAD Test

Student's Name _____ Grade _____

Teacher's Name _____ Date _____

Part A:

1. _____		6. _____	
2. _____		7. _____	
3. _____		8. _____	
4. _____		9. _____	
5. _____		10. _____	

Part B:

11.	puick	qnick	quick	pnick	kciuq
12.	fypt	tqyf	ftyq	fyqt	tyqf
13.	was	saw	sam	mas	zaw
14.	dceb	dbce	bedc	peqc	bdec
15.	buddles	dubbles	selbbub	bubbles	bnbbles
16.	mommy	wowwy	ymmom	mymmo	mowwy

17.	thought	tghuoht	thought	thuoght	thuohgt
18.	snrronud	surround	dnuorrs	sunnourd	surruond
19.	nurring	runners	running	gninnur	rurring
20.	evyerone	oneevery	evenyoue	everyone	evenyone

Directions for Scoring RAD Test

To derive a score from this test, simply add the number of correct items in the twenty-item test. Now compare the papers in the bottom third of the group with those in the top third. Disabled learners will usually stand out. This is not a precise assessment, but it gives you a way to determine quickly which children need closer observation.

Now use Appendix O. Do the test results coincide with your observations on the Observation Checklist in Appendix O? If so, you have candidates for special instruction, as described in Chapter 14.

APPENDIX H   PHONICS TESTS

Phonics Test One: The BAF Test

The BAF Test uses nonsense words and is not suitable for children who have not yet succeeded at the primer level or above. It consists of two parts and must be administered individually. Normally this test would be given to children above grade two who are considered "remedial readers." You have permission to enlarge and reproduce it.

Part I: Consonant Letters, Digraphs, and Clusters
The children should be encouraged to try decoding each nonsense word without your help. If they miss one, simply circle it and have them continue. Be sure to pronounce the first one for them /băf/ and have them pronounce it correctly before they continue. It is also a good idea to correct the second one if they miss it (*caf* is pronounced /kăf/). Consider a word wrong only if the target letter, digraph, or blend is wrong. For example, for 1c in Part I, *daf* is correct. So is *dap*, but not *paf*, since the target letter is *d*.

Name of Student _____

Directions to be read or told to the student:

"These words are nonsense words. They are not real words. I'd like you to think about what sounds the letters stand for; then read each word out loud without my help. Don't try to go fast; read the list slowly. If you have any trouble with a word, I'll just circle it and you can go on to the next one. The first word is /băf/. Now you say it. . . . All right, now go on to the rest of the words in row 1."

A	B	C	D	E	F	G
Consonant Letters						
1. baf	caf	daf	faf	gaf	haf	jaf
2. kaf	laf	maf	naf	paf	raf	saf
3. taf	vaf	waf	yaf	zaf	baf	bax

	A	B	C	D	E	F	G	H
Consonant Digraphs								
4.	chaf	phaf	shaf	thaf	whaf	fack	fang	fank
Consonant Clusters								
5.	blaf	braf	claf	craf	draf	dwaf	flaf	fraf
6.	glaf	graf	fand	plaf	praf	quaf	scaf	scraf
7.	skaf	slaf	smaf	snaf	spaf	splaf	spraf	squaf
8.	staf	straf	swaf	thraf	traf	twaf		

Part II: Vowel Letters, Vowel Digraphs, and Vowel Clusters
(For those whose instructional level is at least Primer)

This part of the inventory should also be administered individually. You will need to enlarge and reproduce a copy of this test for each child. The children should be encouraged to try decoding each nonsense word without your help. If they miss one, simply circle it and have them continue. Be sure to pronounce the first one for them /băf/ and have them pronounce it correctly before they continue.

Directions to be read or told to the student:
"These words are nonsense words. They are not real words. I'd like you to think about what sounds the letters stand for; then read each word out loud without any help. Don't try to go fast; read the list slowly. If you have any trouble with a word, I'll circle it and you can go on to the next one. The first word is /băf/. Now you say it. . . . All right, now go on to the rest of the words in row 1."

	A	B	C	D	E	F	G
1.	baf	bafe	barp	baif	bawf		
2.	bef	befe	berf	beaf			
3.	bof	bofe	borf	boaf	bouf	boif	boof
4.	bif	bife	birf				
5.	buf	bufe	burf				

Phonics Test Two: The Phonogram Phonics Test

This test will give you an idea of how well a student can recognize patterns of letters at the end of one-syllable words or at the end of syllables in multisyllable words.

High-Frequency Phonogram Test

Name of Student _____   Grade _____

zab	zack	zace	zail	zay	zall	zed	zell	zeak
zear	zid	zick	zice	zight	zob	zock	zoke	zold
zout	zorn	zore	zub	zuck	zy	zad	zamp	zade
zain	zar	zen	zeal	zew	zend	zig	zill	zide
zag	zand	zake	zark	zaw	zam	zame	zang	zash
zan	zank	zet	zim	zent	zeam	zing	zime	zod
zong	zone	zud	zump	zunt	zap	zate	zest	zat
zane	zug	zeat	zin	zish	zint	zeep	zatch	zeed
zog	zum	zip	zink	zone	zope	zun	zut	zive
zot	zuff	zunk	zeet	zung	zow	zown	zab	zack

1. Read the first two words to your student and explain that most of these words are not real words. Tell the student you want to find out how well he knows the sounds that the letters stand for.

2. Have him read the entire first row across the top of the page without help. Tell him to say "I don't know" whenever necessary.

3. Circle each one that he misses, using another copy for recording.

4. This test is recommended for grade 3 and up.

APPENDIX I FIFTEEN CATEGORIES OF LITERATURE FOR CHILDREN*

Realism

Author	*Title*
Blume, Judy	*Are You There, God? It's Me, Margaret*
Bonham, Frank	*Durango Street*
Brooks, Bruce	*The Moves Make the Man*
Buck, Pearl	*The Big Wave*
Burch, Robert	*Queenie Peavy*
Byars, Betsy	*The Pinballs*
DeClements, Barthe	*Nothing's Fair in Fifth Grade*
DeJong, Meindert	*The House of Sixty Fathers*
Guy, Rosa	*The Friends*
Hinton, S. E.	*Tex*
Howard, Ellen	*Circle of Giving*
Myers, Walter Dean	*Motown and Didi*
Paterson, Katharine	*Bridge to Terabithia*
Sebestyen, Ouida	*Words by Heart*
Taylor, Mildred	*Roll of Thunder, Hear My Cry*
Voigt, Cynthia	*Homecoming*
Yep, Laurence	*Dragonwings*

Fantasy

Author	*Title*
Alexander, Lloyd	*The Book of Three*
Babbit, Natalie	*Tuck Everlasting*
Banks, Lynn Reid	*The Indian in the Cupboard*
Baum, L. Frank	*The Wizard of Oz*
Butterworth, Oliver	*The Enormous Egg*
Carroll, Lewis	*Alice in Wonderland*
Collodi, Carlo	*Pinocchio*
Cooper, Susan	*The Dark Is Rising*
Dahl, Roald	*Charlie and the Chocolate Factory*
Grahame, Kenneth	*The Wind in the Willows*
Howe, Deborah and James	*Bunnicula*

*Compiled by Doris A. Kimmel, Eric A. Kimmel, and Frank B. May

Lawson, Robert   *Rabbit Hill*
Lewis, C. S.   *The Lion, the Witch and the Wardrobe*
Norton, Mary   *The Borrowers*
O'Brien, Robert C.   *Mrs. Frisby and the Rats of NIMH*
Pinkwater, D. Manus   *Lizard Music*
Tolkien, J. R. R.   *The Hobbit*
Travers, P. L.   *Mary Poppins*

Information

Author	*Title*
Cobb, Vicki	*Bet You Can*
Gibbons, Gail	*The Milk Makers*
Heller, Ruth	*Chickens Aren't the Only Ones*
Hollings, H. C.	*Paddle to the Sea*
Kramer, Stephen	*How to Think like a Scientist*
Macaulay, David	*The Way Things Work*
Macaulay, David	*Cathedral*
Simon, Seymoou	*Saturn*
Stevenson, Carla	*The Birth of Sunset's Kittens*
Tunis, Edwin	*Frontier Living*

Mystery

Author	*Title*
Avi	*Wolf Rider*
Bawden, Nina	*The Witch's Daughter*
Bellairs, John	*The House with the Clock in Its Walls*
Duncan, Lois	*Summer of Fear*
Howe, James	*Howliday Inn*
Konigsburg, E. L.	*From the Mixed-Up Files of Mrs. Basil E. Frankweiler*
Pullman, Philip	*The Ruby in the Smoke*
Raskin, Ellen	*The Westing Game*
Roberts, Willo Davis	*The View from the Cherry Tree*
Snyder, Zilpha Keatley	*The Egypt Game*
Sobol, Donald	*Encyclopedia Brown*

Animals

Author	*Title*
Burnford, Sheila	*The Incredible Journey*
DeJong, Meindert	*Along Came a Dog*
Gardiner, John	*Stone Fox*
Gipson, Frederick B.	*Old Yeller*
Henry, Marguerite	*King of the Wind*
Henry, Marguerite	*Misty of Chincoteague*

Kjelgaard, Jim	*Big Red*
London, Jack	*Call of the Wild*
Morey, Walt	*Kavik the Wolf Dog*
Mowat, Farley	*Owls in the Family*
North, Sterling	*Rascal*
Rawlings, Marjorie	*The Yearling*
Rawls, Wilson	*Where the Red Fern Grows*
Salten, Felix	*Bambi*
Sewell, Anna	*Black Beauty*

Science Fiction

Author	*Title*
Bradbury, Ray	*Dandelion Wine*
Cameron, Eleanor	*The Wonderful Flight to the Mushroom Planet*
Christopher, John	*The White Mountains*
Heinlein, Robert	*Tunnel in the Sky*
L'Engle, Madeleine	*A Wrinkle in Time*
Le Guin, Ursula K.	*A Wizard of Earthsea*
McCaffrey, Anne	*Dragonsong*

Humor

Author	*Title*
Avi	*The S.O.R. Losers*
Cameron, Ann	*The Stories Julian Tells*
Cleary, Beverly	*Ramona the Pest*
Fitzgerald, John D.	*The Great Brain*
Gilson, Jamie	*Thirteen Ways to Sink a Sub*
Haywood, Carolyn	*''B'' Is for Betsy*
Lowry, Lois	*Anastasia Krupnick*
MacDonald, Betty	*Mrs. Piggle-Wiggle*
McCloskey, Robert	*Homer Price*
Robertson, Keith	*Henry Reed, Inc.*
Rockwell, Thomas	*How to Eat Fried Worms*

Poetry

Author	*Title*
Ciardi, John	*The Monster Den*
Cole, William	*Beastly Boys and Ghastly Girls*
Field, Eugene	*Songs of Childhood*
Fisher, Aileen	*Like Nothing at All*
Giovanni, Nikki	*Spin a Soft Black Song*
Lewis, Richard	*In a Spring Garden*
Livingston, Myra Cohn	*Space Songs*
Merriam, Eve	*It Doesn't Always Have to Rhyme*

Milne, A. A.	*The World of Christopher Robin*
Peterson, Isabel J.	*The First Book of Poetry*
Prelutsky, Jack	*Nightmares*
Prelutsky, Jack	*Random House Book of Poetry*
Sandburg, Carl	*Rainbows Are Made*
Silverstein, Shel	*Where the Sidewalk Ends*
Stevenson, Robert Lewis	*A Child's Garden of Verses*
Worth, Valerie	*All the Small Poems*

Outdoor Adventure

Author	*Title*
Corbin, William	*A Dog Worth Stealing*
George, Jean C.	*Julie of the Wolves*
George, Jean C.	*My Side of the Mountain*
Hyde, Dayton O.	*The Major, the Poacher, and the Wonderful One-Trout River*
Morey, Walt	*Gentle Ben*
O'Dell, Scott	*Island of the Blue Dolphins*
Paulsen, Gary	*Dogsong*
Paulsen, Gary	*Hatchet*
Sperry, Armstrong	*Call It Courage*
Wyss, Johann	*The Swiss Family Robinson*

Biography

Author	*Title*
Adler, David A.	*Our Golda: The Story of Golda Meir*
Daugherty, James	*Daniel Boone*
Forbes, Esther	*America's Paul Revere*
Fritz, Jean	*Homesick*
Fritz, Jean	*Will You Sign Here, John Hancock?*
Hamilton, Virginia	*Anthony Burns, Fugitive Slave*
Hautzig, Esther	*The Endless Steppe*
Kherdian, David	*The Road from Home*
Latham, Jean Lee	*Carry On, Mr. Bowditch*
Singer, Isaac Bashevis	*A Day of Pleasure*
Sterling, Dorothy	*Freedom Train: The Story of Harriet Tubman*
Yates, Elizabeth	*Amos Fortune, Free Man*

Historical Fiction

Author	*Title*
Alcott, Louisa May	*Little Women*
Coerr, Eleanor	*The Josefina Story Quilt*
Collier, James Lincoln	*My Brother Sam Is Dead*

Conrad, Pam	*Prairie Songs*
Dalgliesh, Alice	*The Courage of Sarah Noble*
Forbes, Esther	*Johnny Tremain*
Lasky, Kathryn	*Beyond the Divide*
MacLachlan, Patricia	*Sarah, Plain and Tall*
O'Dell, Scott	*The King's Fifth*
Pyle, Howard	*Otto of the Silver Hand*
Speare, Elizabeth	*The Witch of Blackbird Pond*
Stevenson, Robert Louis	*Treasure Island*
Sutcliff, Rosemary	*Warrior Scarlet*
Twain, Mark	*The Adventures of Tom Sawyer*
Wilder, Laura Ingalls	*The Little House in the Big Woods*

Folk Tales and Myths

Author	*Title*
Aardema, Verna	*Tales for the Third Ear*
Asbjornsen, Peter Christian, and Moe, Jorgen E.	*East of the Sun and West of the Moon*
Baylor, Byrd	*And It Is Still That Way*
Chase, Richard	*Grandfather Tales*
Courlander, Harold	*The Cow-Tail Switch*
d'Aulaire, Edgar and Ingri Parin	*The Book of Greek Myths*
d'Aulaire, Edgar and Ingri Parin	*Norse Gods and Giants*
Erdoes, Richard	*The Sound of Flutes*
The Brothers Grimm	*Grimm's Fairy Tales*
Hamilton, Virginia	*In the Beginning*
Hamilton, Virginia	*The People Could Fly*
Jacobs, Joseph	*English Fairy Tales*
Rounds, Glen	*Ol' Paul, The Mighty Logger*
Singer, Isaac Bashevis	*Zlateh the Goat*
Wolkstein, Diane	*The Magic Orange Tree*

Picture Books

Author	*Title*
Brown, Marcia	*Stone Soup*
Brown, Margaret Wise	*Goodnight Moon*
Burton, Virginia Lee	*Mike Mulligan and His Steam Shovel*
Cooney, Barbara	*Miss Rumphius*
de Paola, Tomie	*Strega Nona*
Gag, Wanda	*Millions of Cats*
Keats, Ezra Jack	*The Snowy Day*
Kellogg, Steven	*The Day Jimmy's Boa Ate the Wash*
McCloskey, Robert	*Make Way for Ducklings*
Peet, Bill	*The Wingdingdilly*
Sendak, Maurice	*Where the Wild Things Are*

Dr. Seuss	*Horton Hatches the Egg*
Spier, Peter	*People*
Stevens, Janet	*Anansi and the Moss-Covered Rock*
Viorst, Judith	*Alexander and the Terrible, Horrible, No Good, Very Bad Day*

Sports

Author	Title
Christopher, Matt	*Look Who's Playing First Base*
Liss, Howard	*Giant Book of Strange But True Sports Stories*
Lord, Beman	*The Trouble with Francis*
Parish, Peggy	*Play Ball, Amelia Bedelia*
Slote, Alfred	*Matt Gargan's Boy*
Towne, Mary	*First Serve*
Tunis, John	*The Kid from Tomkinsville*

Plays

Author	Title
Bradley, Virginia	*Is There an Actor in the House?*
Burack, A. S., ed.	*100 Plays for Children*
Durrell, Donald D., and Crossley, B. Alice	*Thirty Plays for Classroom Reading*
Jennings, Coleman A. and Harris, Aurand	*Plays Children Love*
Kamerman, Sylvia E.	*Children's Plays from Favorite Stories*
Kamerman, Sylvia E.	*Dramatized Folk Tales of the World*
Miller, Helen Louise	*Short Plays for Children*

APPENDIX J NEWBERY AND CALDECOTT AWARD BOOKS

Newbery Books

Year	Title	Author
1922	*The Story of Mankind*	van Loon
1923	*The Voyages of Dr. Dolittle*	Lofting
1924	*The Dark Frigate*	Hawes
1925	*Tales from Silver Lands*	Finger
1926	*Shen of the Sea*	Christmas
1927	*Smoky the Cowhorse*	James
1928	*Gay Neck*	Mujkerji
1929	*Hitty, Her First Hundred Years*	Field
1930	*The Trumpeter of Krakow*	Kelly
1931	*The Cat Who Went to Heaven*	Coatsworth
1932	*Waterless Mountain*	Armer
1933	*Young Fu of the Upper Yangtze*	Lewis

1934	*Invincible Louisa: Anniversary Edition*	Meigs
1935	*Dobry*	Shannon
1936	*Caddie Woodlawn*	Brink
1937	*Roller Skates*	Sawyer
1938	*The White Stag*	Seredy
1939	*Thimble Summer*	Enright
1940	*Daniel Boone*	Daugherty
1941	*Call It Courage*	Sperry
1942	*Matchlock Gun*	Edmonds
1943	*Adam of the Road*	Gray
1944	*Johnny Tremain*	Forbes
1945	*Rabbitt Hill*	Lawson
1946	*Strawberry Girl*	Lenski
1947	*Miss Hickory*	Bailey
1948	*The Twenty-One Balloons*	du Bois
1949	*King of the Wind*	Henry
1950	*The Door in the Wall*	de Angeli
1951	*Amos Fortune, Free Man*	Yates
1952	*Ginger Pye*	Estes
1953	*The Secret of the Andes*	Clark
1954	*And Now Miguel*	Krumgold
1955	*The Wheel on the School*	de Jong
1956	*Carry On, Mr. Bowditch*	Latham
1957	*Miracles on Maple Hill*	Sorensen
1958	*Rifles for Waitie*	Keith
1959	*Witch of Blackbird Pond*	Speare
1960	*Onion John*	Krumgold
1961	*Island of the Blue Dolphins*	O'Dell
1962	*Bronze Bow*	Speare
1963	*A Wrinkle in Time*	L'Engle
1964	*It's Like This, Cat*	Neville
1965	*Shadow of a Bull*	Wojciechowska
1966	*I, Juan De Pareja*	de Trevino
1967	*Up a Road Slowly*	Hunt
1968	*From the Mixed-up Files of Mrs. Basil E. Frankweiler*	Konigsburg
1969	*The High King*	Alexander
1970	*Sounder*	Armstrong
1971	*Summer of the Swans*	Byars
1972	*Mrs. Frisby and the Rats of NIMH*	O'Brien
1973	*Julie of the Wolves*	George
1974	*The Slave Dancer*	Fox
1975	*M. C. Higgins, The Great*	Hamilton
1976	*The Grey King*	Cooper
1977	*Roll of Thunder, Hear My Cry*	Taylor
1978	*Bridge to Terabithia*	Paterson
1979	*The Westing Game*	Raskin
1980	*A Gathering of Days: A New England Girl's Journal, 1830–1832*	Blos
1981	*Jacob Have I Loved*	Paterson

1982	*William Blake's Inn*	Willard & Provenson
1983	*Dear Mr. Henshaw*	Cleary
1984	*Dicey's Song*	Voigt
1985	*Hero and the Crown*	McKinley
1986	*Sarah, Plain and Tall*	MacLachlan
1987	*The Whipping Boy*	Fleischman, S.
1988	*Lincoln: A Photobiography*	Freedman
1989	*Joyful Noises*	Fleischman, P.

Caldecott Books

Year	*Title*	*Author*
1938	*Animals of the Bible*	Lathrop
1939	*Mei Li*	Handforth
1940	*Abraham Lincoln*	d'Aulaire
1941	*They Were Strong and Good*	Lawson
1942	*Make Way for Ducklings*	McCloskey
1943	*Little House*	Burton
1944	*Many Moons*	Thurber & Slobodkin
1945	*Prayer for a Child*	Field & Jones
1946	*Rooster Crown*	Petersham
1947	*Little Island*	MacDonald & Weisgard
1948	*White Snow, Bright Snow*	Tresselt & Duvoisin
1949	*Big Snow*	Hader
1950	*Song of the Swallows*	Politi
1951	*The Egg Tree*	Milhous
1952	*Finder Keepers*	Nicolas
1953	*The Biggest Bear*	Ward
1954	*Madeline's Rescue*	Bemelmans
1955	*Cinderella*	Brown
1956	*Frog Went A-Courtin'*	Langstaff & Rojankovsky
1957	*A Tree Is Nice*	Udry & Simont
1958	*Time of Wonder*	McCloskey
1959	*Chanticleer and the Fox*	Cooney
1960	*Nine Days to Christmas*	Ets & Labastida
1961	*Baboushka and the Three Kings*	Robbins
1962	*Once a Mouse*	Brown
1963	*The Snowy Day*	Keats
1964	*Where the Wild Things Are*	Sendak
1965	*May I Bring a Friend?*	de Regniers
1966	*Always Room for One More*	Leadhas & Hogrogian
1967	*Sam Bangs & Moonshine*	News
1968	*Drummer Hoff*	Emberley
1969	*Fool of the World and the Flying Ship*	Ransome
1970	*Sylvester and the Magic Pebble*	Steig
1971	*A Story, a Story*	Haley
1972	*One Fine Day*	Hogrogian
1973	*The Funny Little Woman*	Mosel

1974	*Duffy and the Devil*	Zemach
1975	*Arrow to the Sun*	McDermott
1976	*Why Mosquitoes Buzz in People's Ears*	Aardema
1977	*Ashanti to Zulu: African Traditions*	Musgrove
1978	*Noah's Ark*	Spier
1979	*The Girl Who Loved Wild Horses*	Goble
1980	*The Ox-Cart Man*	Hall and Cooney
1981	*Fables*	Lobel
1982	*Jumanji*	Van Allsburg
1983	*Shadow*	Brown
1984	*The Glorious Flight*	Provenson
1985	*Saint George and the Dragon*	Hodges & Human
1986	*Polar Express*	Van Allsburg
1987	*Hey Al*	Yorinks & Egielski
1988	*Owl Moon*	Yolen & Schoenherr
1989	*Song and Dance Man*	Ackerman & Gammell

APPENDIX K BASAL READER PUBLISHERS

Addison-Wesley Publishing Company, Route 128, Reading MA 01867
Allyn & Bacon, 160 Gould Street, Needham Heights, MA 02194
Economy Company, 1901 North Walnut, P.O. Box 25308, Oklahoma City, OK 73125
Harcourt Brace Jovanovich, Inc., 6277 Sea Harbor Drive, Orlando, FL 32821
Harper & Row, Publishers, Inc., 10 East 53rd Street, New York, NY 10022
Holt, Rinehart and Winston, 1627 Woodland Avenue, Austin, TX 78741
Houghton Mifflin Company, One Beacon Street, Boston, MA 02108
Laidlaw Educational Publishers, Thatcher and Madison, River Forest, IL 60305
Macmillan Company, 866 Third Avenue, New York, NY 10022
Merrill Publishing Company, 936 Eastwind Drive, Westerville, OH 43081
Open Court Publishing Company, 315 Fifth Street, Peru, IL 61354
Riverside Publishing Company, 8420 Bryn Mawr Avenue, Chicago, IL 60631
Scott, Foresman and Company, 1900 East Lake Avenue, Glenview, IL 60025
Silver Burdett & Ginn, 250 James Street, Morristown, NJ 07960

APPENDIX L COMPREHENSION PRACTICE ACTIVITIES

These activities are designed to be used during interactive reading experiences or to be followed by interactive applications.

Practice in Developing Images or Associations

1. When reading a story aloud to children, occasionally have them close their eyes and picture what you're reading. Once in a while you may wish to pause to discuss their "pictures" or to write a descriptive word or phrase on the board.
2. Have them first read a passage silently and then draw a picture of what they see "in their heads."

3. Ask the children first to read a passage silently and then tell what they "saw."
4. Have them first read a passage silently and then tell what personal experiences it made them remember.
5. Arrange for them first to read a passage silently and then pantomime what they "saw."
6. Have one child read a passage aloud while other children pantomime the picture they "see."

Practice in Following a Sequence

1. Have the children work in pairs. Each member of the pair should read silently the same set of directions. Then one person should attempt to follow the directions while the other person judges whether he followed the directions correctly.
2. Provide children with directions for making things—paper airplanes, paper costumes for dolls, cookies, and so on. Have them work in pairs so they can check each other's comprehension of the directions.
3. Have them read a story, then decide in what order to place pictures depicting events in the story.
4. Ask them to read a story, then tell it to or act it out for some other children.
5. Provide a child with a set of directions for a game, then have her explain the game in sequence to some other children.
6. Ask the children to read informative passages about sequential occurrences, such as the water cycle or the cycle of life for a butterfly, then explain the cycle to some other children or depict the cycle in a sequential drawing.

Practice in Finding Important Details

1. Help the children change a story into a brief newspaper report. Help them write it as a reporter does, telling who, what, where, and when. The same activity can be used for an historical event described in a social studies book.
2. Help the children change a story into a telegram of twenty-five words or less. Show them how to include only the most important details. You can use the same activity for an historical event described in a social studies book.
3. After they have decided on the main idea for a passage, have them find or remember details that support their decision.
4. Ask them to scan a reading selection from a basal reader, social studies book, or science text to find highly factual information. This is best done orally in small groups, with the first child to find it reading the answer.
5. Develop their appreciation for literary devices by having them read aloud some sentences, phrases, or words that "help paint a picture for the reader."

Practice in Drawing Inferences

This thinking process can be practiced even on reading passages as simple as this:

One hot day Roy went on a boat ride.
He went with his teacher and his school friends.

To give children practice at *literal thinking*, the teacher might simply ask, "What kind of day was it when Roy went on a boat ride?" But to give children practice at *inferential thinking*, the teacher could ask, "What season of the year do you think it is—winter, summer, spring, or fall?" To answer this question, they would have to make inferences based on the words *hot, teacher*, and *school*. Robert may say "summer" because of the word *hot*. Jill may say, "No, it can't be summer because Roy is going with his teacher and school friends." Frank may then say, "I'll bet it's either spring or fall." All three children will be engaged in inferential thinking. The teacher has helped them communicate with the author rather than merely absorbing the author's words.

Practice in Determining Main Ideas

Try reading the following selection and then choose the title that best describes what the author has told you.

> In 1888 a terrible snowstorm hit New York City. Tall poles snapped, and electric wires fell into the street. People were killed by electric shock. Some were killed by the falling poles. And nearly a thousand died in the fires that broke out.
>
> The mayor saw that he must do something to make his city a safe place to live. He asked electricians to put electric wires safely underground. Then the mayor sent men out to take down the wooden poles.
>
> These electric wires were the beginning of America's amazing underground city in New York. Today the narrow streets and the sidewalks hide more than four million miles of wire. In some places there are so many wires and pipes that two fingers cannot be pushed between them.*

1. A terrible snowstorm
2. How some people were killed
3. Putting wires underground
4. How an amazing underground city began

Since the first three ideas all lead up to the fourth one, perhaps you would agree that number 4 is the best title. This type of exercise gives children specific practice in determining main ideas. Other types of experiences include these:

1. After they have read a selection, ask them questions such as these:
   "What do you think the author was trying to tell you?"
   "What was this story really about?"
   "Was there one big idea the author was talking about?"
   "If you were the author, what is the one thing you'd want the readers to remember from this article more than anything else?"
2. After they have read a story or an article, have them "capture the big idea" with a two-line or four-line verse. You'll need to do this together, and also provide them with the first line. Here's an example for "Goldilocks and the Three Bears":

Goldilocks bothered the bears.
She even broke one of their chairs.

---

*From page 250 of "Air Pudding and Wind Sauce," *Keys to Reading* (Oklahoma City, OK: Economy Company, 1972), adapted from "Amazing Underground City," by Edward Hymoff (*Boys' Life,* August 1963).

But she'll never do that again.
Not even now and then.

3. After older children have read a story, let them decide on the "basic theme": (a) people against nature; (b) people against people; or (c) people against themselves.

4. After they have read a selection, have them decide whether the title "tells what the story was really about." Or you might ask them if it "tells what the author was really trying to say." Then have them create a "better" title—one that describes better what the author was talking about.

Practice in Recognizing Details that Support Main Ideas

Let's look again at the article on New York City's amazing underground city (page 557). Mr. Hymoff, the author of this article, didn't simply tell the reader, "Now I'm going to tell how an amazing underground city began." Instead he chose to present as many details as he thought necessary to illustrate and lead up to this idea. To help children realize what the author has done, the teacher will often need to have children "reconstruct" the author's purpose and procedures. You can do this with questions like these:

1. Why do you think this article is called "Amazing Underground City"?
2. What can you find in this article that seems to be "amazing"?
3. Was the author, Mr. Hymoff, trying to just tell about the underground city, or was he trying to tell you how this underground city began? Or was he doing both? What can you find in the article to prove your point?
4. Mr. Hymoff tells us that in 1888 a terrible snowstorm hit New York City. Can you find anything in the first paragraph that would explain why he used the word "terrible"?
5. How did the amazing underground city begin?

Practice in Predicting

1. After they have read part of a story, have them guess what is going to happen next.
2. Let them draw or pantomime what's coming next, after they have read a certain portion of a story.
3. Have them continue the story in writing; then read the rest of the story and discuss how their endings differed.
4. Have older children read a dittoed portion of a newspaper editorial or other passage presenting an argument; then have them discuss what they think the author would have said next. Then read the rest of the editorial to them so that they can see how well they predicted. (You can do the same thing with an informative passage rather than an argumentive one.)

Practice in Understanding Cause and Effect

Cause-and-effect relationships are the nuclei of many stories and articles. Event B happens because of Event A; Event F occurs because of the personality of Character D; and so on. Unless children recognize such relationships, their understanding of an article or story will have little depth. In "The Amazing Underground City," for example, they would not really understand why the "mayor saw that he must do something to make his city a safe place to live" unless they connect this with the electric wires falling into the street.

The teacher's role is again one of asking thoughtful questions—this time questions that encourage children to notice the cause-and-effect relationships, such as these:

1. Why did the mayor see that he must do something to make his city a safe place to live?
2. What caused the electric wires to fall into the street in the first place?
3. Why did so many people die in the snowstorm of 1888?
4. Why did the mayor have the electricians put the wires under the ground?
5. What kind of person do you think the mayor was? Do you think this had anything to do with what he decided to do after the storm of 1888?

Practice in Distinguishing between the Factual and Nonfactual

This form of critical thinking can be practiced through at least eight types of activities:

1. Distinguishing between literal and figurative expressions
2. Distinguishing between real-life stories and fantasies
3. Distinguishing between real-life stories and satire
4. Distinguishing between factual statements and opinions
5. Recognizing differences between observations an author is making and inferences she is making
6. Recognizing differences between observations an author is making and judgments he is making
7. Detecting an author's bias and how this influences her statements
8. Deciding on the author's competence and how this may influence the accuracy of his statements.

Here are some corresponding sample learning activities for the critical-thinking activities:

1. Discuss the meaning of figurative phrases such as "shouting my head off" or "pulling my leg." Have the children think of others they have heard. Have them picture in their heads or on paper "what the words seem to mean and what they really mean." The same type of thing can be done with metaphors you and the children discover in descriptive passages. For example, in the sentence "John flew down the hallway to his classroom," what does *flew* seem to mean and really mean? (Other examples: Bill didn't get the *point* of my poem. That book is hard to *swallow*. I *plowed* right through my homework.)
2. After they've read a fanciful story in their basal readers or library books, ask them whether it was a "real-life" story or a "make-believe" one. Have them explain their answers.
3. Read aloud to the children *The Enormous Egg* by Oliver Butterworth. This book includes satire that most children in third through sixth grades will enjoy and understand. Ask them to discover how the author satirizes ("makes fun of" or "pokes fun at") advertisers, politicians, and others. Another book useful for this type of experience is Merrill's *The Pushcart War*. Discuss how Jean Merrill creates

imaginary characters and situations that are very like real people and real situations. Help them understand that authors sometimes do this to avoid criticizing people directly.

4. Show them how to tell the difference between factual statements and opinions. Use these nonsense statements as illustrations:

   a. A snurtzle has two eyes and three fleb pads. (factual)

   b. Snurtzles are very good at swinking. (opinion)

   c. A snurtzle can swink 50 gallons a day. (factual)

   d. It is clear that snurtzles are always flumptuous. (opinion)

   Ask them what makes them sure that statements (b) and (d) are opinions. Then present them with a list of actual statements and have them decide which statements seem factual and which seem to be opinions. Have them justify their answers. (*Note:* For this type of exercise, a "factual" statement is not necessarily a "truthful" statement.) Then have them look for factual statements and opinions in their basal readers, library books, or social studies textbooks.

5. Have them learn to distinguish between observations and inferences by discussing two-part statements such as these:

   Noticing: Jimmy Smith took the milk out of Mrs. Jones's refrigerator. (observation)

   Guessing: Jimmy *stole* the milk. (inference)

   Noticing: Jimmy Smith took the milk out of Mrs. Jones's refrigerator. (observation)

   Guessing: Mrs. Jones asked Jimmy to keep her milk while she was on vacation. (inference)

6. Have them learn to distinguish between observations and judgments by discussing three-part statements such as these:

   Noticing: Jimmy Smith took the milk out of Mrs. Jones's refrigerator. (observation)

   Guessing: Jimmy *stole* the milk. (inference)

   Judging: Jimmy is a *thief.* (judgment)

   Noticing: Jimmy Smith took the milk out of Mrs. Jones's refrigerator.

   Guessing: Mrs. Jones asked Jimmy to keep her milk while she was on vacation.

   Judging: Jimmy is a nice kid.

   After they complete exercises such as these, have them look for examples of when the author is "noticing, guessing, or judging" in their basal readers, library books, or social studies book.

7. Have the children study magazine ads with the intention of detecting these three propaganda tricks:

   a. *Expert appeal:* "Four out of five doctors recommend No-Ache Aspirin."

   b. *Winner appeal:* "More people buy Shuvvy than any other car."

   c. *Star appeal:* "Hefty Breakneck, star tackle for the Podunk Tigers, uses Left Tackle Deodorant. Shouldn't you?"

   Ask them why the advertisers use these tricks. Have them talk about the times they have used these tricks in their own lives. For instance:

Expert appeal: "If you don't believe me, just ask my mother."

Winner appeal: "But Mom, all the kids are wearing Squishtight Jeans."

Star appeal: "Frankie Hackshaw is in sixth grade and he wears 'em."

Ask them whether authors may sometimes use tricks like these to get them to believe something or do something. If possible, demonstrate this technique through the use of a basal reader, library book, or social studies text.

8. Have the children compare information in two science books or encyclopedias, one published recently and one published several decades ago; have them see how many disagreements they can find about topics such as Mars or atoms. Show them where to find the copyright date in books. Discuss the importance of currency for *some* information.

Practice in Creative Thinking

1. Ask the children, before or during the reading of a story, to imagine how they might solve the main character's problem. Then, when they have finished the story, have them discuss or write about how they might have solved the problem in a different way.

2. Have them discuss how the main character's problem was similar to one they have right now. Encourage them to tell how they might solve those personal problems. At a later date, encourage them to tell how they actually did solve them.

3. Encourage them to share their feelings about stories or books through drama, poetry, painting, and other media. For instance, a child can pretend she's one of the characters in the story; she can describe herself and tell about one or two things she did in the story. Two children who have read the same book may enjoy dramatizing a scene from the book. Another child may decide to make a diorama (a small stage) describing a scene in his book. (For other ideas, see Appendix F.)

4. Give them time to construct things (castles, dragons, rockets, and so on) they have read about.

5. Let them share their favorite passages from stories by reading aloud to each other. Give them practice time and assistance so that the experience will be a positive one for both the audience and the readers. Encourage them to give their own original interpretation to the reading.

APPENDIX M   EXAMPLES OF SIX COMMON SENTENCE PATTERNS FOR SYNTAX DEVELOPMENT

Pattern 1

Here are some examples of Pattern 1 (read them aloud, if possible):

Noun + Be verb + Prepositional phrase

The girl was inside the house.

My friend was outside the car.

The bear was in the zoo.

Bob was behind the door.

The doctor was in the hospital.

His doctor was under the table.

A nurse was near the bed.

The flebonk was in the malps.

Now you make up two or three.

Pattern 2

Here are examples of Pattern 2 (read them aloud, if possible):

Noun + Intransitive verb + (Adverb)*

The boy walked slowly.

The boy walked.

Susan walked.

That girl played under the house.

This girl played in the park.

My mother worked in the morning.

The giant spoke grumpily.

That flebonk lived in the malps.

Now it's your turn. Make one of them nonsensible if you can.

Pattern 3

These are examples of Pattern 3:

Noun + Linking verb + Adjective

The candy seemed sweet.

That candy was sweet.

His shirt looked dirty.

Notes: An adverb is not always needed. Also, a prepositional phrase may be used instead of an adverb.

Your dress was pretty.

The monkey seemed clever.

That child was cruel.

Alice appeared snobbish.

The flebonk was masty.

That flebonk smelled yucky.

My flebonk tasted delicious.

Pattern 4

Here are examples of Pattern 4:

Noun + Linking verb + Noun

The dog was his friend.

The dog became his friend.

The dog remained his friend.

Bob was a snob.

That girl became my sweetheart.

Her brother remained a fink.

Your costume was a scream.

My flebonk became a skiddle.

His skiddle remained a nurgle.

Pattern 5

These are examples of Pattern 5:

Noun + Transitive verb + Noun

The monkey climbed the ladder.

My father drove a car.

This motor ran the pulley.

Jim owned this place.

The train jumped the track.

Your sister liked my brother.

Her flebonk zagged his delbur.

His delbur zagged a flurtop.

Pattern 6

Here are examples of Pattern 6:

Noun + Transitive verb + Noun + Noun

The woman gave her dog a bone.

The woman fed her son a steak.

My father spared the beggar a dime.

The king granted Columbus an audience.

The club awarded Felix a prize.

Mr. Jones offered Mother a hand.

My uncle left my sister a fortune.

APPENDIX N   A SAMPLE LESSON ON DICTIONARY GUIDE WORDS

Say something like this to your students:

"Now that you've learned how to alphabetize, you're ready to learn how to use guide words. Let's look at some guide words in your dictionary. At the top of page 216 are the words *fast* and *fatten.* Can you find them? These are the guide words for page 216. These two words tell you that all the words on this page begin with the letters *f-a.* Can you tell me why I know that's true? Can you prove it to me?"

"These two guide words tell you that some of the words on this page start with *f-a-s* and some of them start with *f-a-t.* Can you prove this to me?"

"These two guide words tell you that none of the words on this page starts with *f-a-s-s.* How do I know that? Can you prove this to me?"

"These two guide words tell you that none of the words on this page starts with *f-a-t-u.* How do I know that? Can you prove this to me?"

Write *father, fatal, fashion,* and *favor* on the board. Then ask:

"Would you expect to find the word *father* on this page? Why? Prove it. Would you expect to find the word *fatal?* Why? Prove it. Would you expect to find the word *fashion?* Why not? Can you prove it? Would you expect to find the word *favor?* Why not? Can you prove it?"

"What guide words do you find on page 285? What things do these two guide words tell you? Do you see the word I've just written on the chalkboard? Would you expect to find this word on this page? Prove it. What guide words do you find on page 95? What things do these two guide words tell you? Without looking at the page, tell me one word that you think will be there. Tell me one word you're sure will not be there."

"On this worksheet is a list of words. After each word, I'd like you to write the two guide words you find in the dictionary on the page where the word appears. Let's do the first one together."

APPENDIX O OBSERVATION CHECKLIST FOR READING AND LANGUAGE DISABILITIES*

General Behavior

_____ 1. Shows average or above-average intelligence in some way; for example, does well in science reasoning or mathematical reasoning, shows sense of humor, or has ingenious ways of getting into trouble
_____ 2. Often has trouble expressing himself/herself
_____ 3. Often shows poor eye-hand coordination
_____ 4. Appears nervous or anxious in many situations
_____ 5. Tends to get frustrated easily
_____ 6. Withdraws when things get too difficult
_____ 7. Has far "too much" energy (or sometimes far too little)
_____ 8. Has trouble concentrating
_____ 9. Has trouble remembering directions, names, or other details
_____ 10. Has trouble making lasting friendships

Reading Behavior

_____ 1. Standardized reading achievement score: at least one year below grade level in grades two and three, and two years below in later grades
_____ 2. Standardized individual diagnostic score: at least one year below grade level in grades two and three, and two years below in later grades
_____ 3. Informal reading inventory: at least one year below grade level in grades two and three, and two years below in later grades
_____ 4. BAF Test: 40-percent error in grades three and above (see Appendix H)
_____ 5. Essential Sight Words: 40-percent error in grades three and above
_____ 6. Has considerable trouble concentrating on reading task even when working directly with teacher
_____ 7. Frequently guesses wildly at words rather than using word analysis skills
_____ 8. Forgets words shortly after learning to read them
_____ 9. Asks teacher to decode words rather than using word analysis skills
_____ 10. Transposes letters or words or syllables while reading
_____ 11. Loses place in reading passage easily
_____ 12. Often does not seem to know the meaning of what he or she has read
_____ 13. Usually a word-by-word reader
_____ 14. Makes many errors on worksheets; more wrong than right

Writing Behavior

_____ 1. Does very poorly on spelling tests, usually getting more words wrong than right
_____ 2. Creative writing has 40 percent or more of the words spelled wrong
_____ 3. Transposes words, letters, or syllables

*Student should display several of these in each category to be considered "disabled." See also the RAD Test in Appendix G.

_____ 4. Reverses letters such as *b* and *d, p* and *q*
_____ 5. Inverts letters such as *n* and *u* or *p* and *b*
_____ 6. Usually guesses at spelling rather than noticing graphophonic patterns
_____ 7. Forgets how to spell a word shortly after learning it
_____ 8. Has considerable trouble concentrating on learning how to spell words
_____ 9. Does not remember how to spell common prefixes or suffixes
_____ 10. Substitutes one suffix for another
_____ 11. Draws circles inconsistently counterclockwise and clockwise
_____ 12. Has considerable difficulty drawing a circle that is round and connected
_____ 13. Usually makes letters with one stroke if possible; lifting pencil tends to cause confusion
_____ 14. Writes as little as possible
_____ 15. Writing that requires memory of sequence and details is quite difficult
_____ 16. Writing is very laborious
_____ 17. Uses personal abbreviations for long difficult words
_____ 18. Has particular trouble with letter size and shape but also shows inconsistent spacing, alignment, and slant

APPENDIX P TWO HUNDRED PATTERNED BOOKS FOR TEACHING WRITING AND READING

Adams, Pam. *This Old Man*
Alain. *One, Two, Three, Going to Sea*
Aliki. *Go Tell Aunt Rhody*
Aliki. *Hush Little Baby*
Aliki. *My Five Senses*
Asch, Frank. *Monkey Face*
Balian, Lorna. *The Animal*
Balian, Lorna. *Where in the World Is Henry?*
Barohas, Sarah E. *I Was Walking Down the Road*
Barrett, Judi. *Animals Should Definitely Not Wear Clothing*
Barton, Byron. *Building a House*
Barton, Byron. *Buzz, Buzz, Buzz*
Baskin, Leonard. *Hosie's Alphabet*
Battaglia, Aurelius. *Old Mother Hubbard*
Baum, Arline, and Joseph Baum. *One Bright Monday Morning*
Baylor, Byrd. *Everybody Needs a Rock*
Becker, John. *Seven Little Rabbits*
Beckman, Kaj. *Lisa Cannot Sleep*
Bellah, Malanie. *A First Book of Sounds*
Berenstain, Stanley, and Janice Berenstain. *The B Book*
Bonne, Rose, and Alan Mills. *I Know an Old Lady*
Brand, Oscar. *When I First Came to This Land*
Brandenberg, Franz. *I Once Knew a Man*
Briggs, Raymond. *Jim and the Beanstalk*
Brooke, Leslie. *Johnny Crow's Garden*
Brown, Marcia. *The Three Billy Goats Gruff*

Brown, Margaret Wise. *A Child's Good Night Book*
Brown, Margaret Wise. *Do You Know What I'll Do?*
Brown, Margaret Wise. *Four Fur Feet*
Brown, Margaret Wise. *The Friendly Book*
Brown, Margaret Wise. *Goodnight Moon*
Brown, Margaret Wise. *Home for a Bunny*
Brown, Margaret Wise. *The Important Book*
Brown, Margaret Wise. *Where Have You Been?*
Burningham, John. *Mr. Gumpy's Outing*
Cameron, Polly. *I Can't Said the Ant*
Carle, Eric. *The Grouchy Ladybug*
Carle, Eric. *The Mixed Up Chameleon*
Carle, Eric. *The Very Hungry Caterpillar*
Charlip, Remy. *Fortunately*
Charlip, Remy. *What Good Luck!*
Cook, Bernadine. *The Little Fish that Got Away*
de Paola, Tomie. *If It's My Brother*
de Regniers, Beatrice Schenk. *Catch a Little Fox*
de Regniers, Beatrice Schenk. *The Day Everybody Cried*
de Regniers, Beatrice Schenk. *How Joe the Bear and Sam the Mouse Got Together*
de Regniers, Beatrice Schenk. *The Little Book*
de Regniers, Beatrice Schenk. *May I Bring a Friend?*
de Regniers, Beatrice Schenk. *Willy O'Dwyer Jumped in the Fire*
Domanska, Janina. *If All the Seas Were One Sea*
Duff, Maggie. *Jonny and His Drum*
Duff, Maggie. *Rum Pum Pum*
Edens, Cooper. *Caretakers of Wonder*
Einsel, Walter. *Did You Ever See?*
Emberley, Barbara. *Drummer Hoff*
Emberley, Barbara. *Simon's Song*
Emberley, Barbara, and Ed Emberley. *One Wide River to Cross*
Emberley, Ed. *Klippity Klop*
Ets, Marie Hall. *Elephant in a Well*
Ets, Marie Hall. *Play with Me*
Flack, Marjorie. *Ask Mr. Bear*
Galdone, Paul. *Henny Penny*
Galdone, Paul. *The Little Red Hen*
Galdone, Paul. *The Three Bears*
Galdone, Paul. *The Three Billy Goats Gruff*
Galdone, Paul. *The Three Little Pigs*
Ginsburg, Mirra. *The Chick and the Duckling*
Greenburg, Polly. *Oh Lord, I Wish I Was a Buzzard*
Gwynne, Fred. *The King Who Rained*
Higgins, Don. *Papa's Going to Buy Me a Mockingbird*
Hoffman, Hilde. *The Green Grass Grows All Around*
Hutchins, Pat. *Good-Night Owl*
Hutchins, Pat. *Rosie's Walk*
Hutchins, Pat. *Titch*
Ipcar, Dahlov. *I Love my Anteater with an A*

Joslin, Sesyle. *What Do You Do, Dear?*
Joslin, Sesyle. *What Do You Say, Dear?*
Joyce, Irma. *Never Talk to Strangers*
Katz, Bobbie. *Nothing but a Dog*
Keats, Ezra Jack. *Over in the Meadow*
Kellogg, Steven. *Can I Keep Him?*
Kellogg, Steven. *The Mysterious Tadpole*
Kent, Jack. *The Fat Cat*
Klein, Lenore. *Brave Daniel*
Kraus, Robert. *Good Night Little ABC*
Kraus, Robert. *Whose Mouse Are You?*
Krauss, Ruth. *Bears*
Krauss, Ruth. *A Hole Is to Dig*
Langstaff, John. *Frog Went A-Courtin'*
Langstaff, John. *Gather My Gold Together: Four Songs for Four Seasons*
Langstaff, John. *Oh, A-Hunting We Will Go*
Langstaff, John. *Over in the Meadow*
Laurence, Ester. *We're Off to Catch a Dragon*
Lexau, Joan. *Crocodile and Hen*
Lobel, Anita. *King Rooster, Queen Hen*
Lobel, Arnold. *A Treeful of Pigs*
Mack, Stan. *10 Bears in My Bed*
Mars, W. T. *The Old Woman and Her Pig*
Martin, Bill. *Brown Bear, Brown Bear*
Martin, Bill. *Fire! Fire! Said Mrs. McGuire*
Martin, Bill. *Freedom Books*
Martin, Bill. *A Ghost Story*
Martin, Bill. *The Haunted House*
Martin, Bill. *Instant Readers*
Martin, Bill. *Little Owl Series*
Martin, Bill. *Monday, Monday, I Like Monday*
Martin, Bill. *Sounds of Language*
Martin, Bill. *Wise Owl Series*
Martin, Bill. *Young Owl Series*
Mayer, Mercer. *If I Had . . .*
Mayer, Mercer. *Just for You*
Mayer, Mercer. *What Do You Do with a Kangaroo?*
McGovern, Ann. *Too Much Noise*
Memling, Carl. *Riddles, Riddles from A to Z*
Memling, Carl. *Ten Little Animals*
Mizumura, Kazue. *If I Were a Cricket*
Moffett, Martha. *A Flower Pot Is Not a Hat*
Nodset, Joan. *Who Took the Farmer's Hat?*
O'Neill, Mary. *Hailstones and Halibut Bones*
Patrick, Gloria. *A Bug in a Jug*
Peppe, Rodney. *The House that Jack Built*
Petersham, Maud, and Miska Petersham. *The Rooster Crows: A Book of American Rhymes and Jingles*
Pinkwater, Daniel. *The Big Orange Splot*

Polushkin, Maria. *Mother, Mother, I Want Another*
Preston, Edna Mitchell. *Where Did My Mother Go?*
Quackenbush, Robert. *Poems for Counting*
Quackenbush, Robert. *She'll Be Comin' Round the Mountain*
Quackenbush, Robert. *Skip to My Lou*
Raskin, Ellen. *Spectacles*
Rokoff, Sandra. *Here Is a Cat*
Rossetti, Christina. *What Is Pink?*
Scheer, Julian, and Marvin Bileck. *Rain Makes Applesauce*
Scheer, Julian, and Marvin Bileck. *Upside Down Day*
Schulz, Charles. *You're My Best Friend Because*
Sendak, Maurice. *Chicken Soup with Rice*
Sendak, Maurice. *Where the Wild Things Are*
Seuss, Dr. *Dr. Seuss's ABC*
Sharmat, Marjorie. *The Terrible Eater*
Shaw, Charles B. *It Looked Like Spilt Milk*
Shulevitz, Uri. *One Monday Morning*
Skaar, Grace. *What Do the Animals Say?*
Sonneborn, Ruth A. *Someone Is Eating the Sun*
Spier, Peter. *The Fox Went Out on a Chilly Night*
Stover, JoAnn. *If Everybody Did*
Tolstoy, Alexei. *The Great Big Enormous Turnip*
Viorst, Judith. *Alexander and the Terrible, Horrible, No Good, Very Bad Day*
Viorst, Judith. *I Used to Be Rich Last Sunday*
Viorst, Judith. *If I Were in Charge of the World*
Viorst, Judith. *I'll Fix Anthony*
Waber, Bernard. *Dear Hildegarde*
Watson, Clyde. *Father Fox's Pennyrhymes*
Welber, Robert. *Goodbye, Hello*
Wildsmith, Brian. *Brian Wildsmith's ABC*
Wildsmith, Brian. *The Twelve Days of Christmas*
Wildsmith, Brian. *What the Moon Saw*
Withers, Carl. *A Rocket In My Pocket*
Wolkstein, Diane. *The Visit*
Wondriska, William. *All the Animals Were Angry*
Wright, H. R. *A Maker of Boxes*
Zaid, Barry. *Chicken Little*
Zemach, Harve. *The Judge*
Zemach, Margot. *Hush, Little Baby*
Zemach, Margot. *The Teeny Tiny Woman*
Zolotow, Charlotte. *Do You Know What I'll Do?*

Index

About the Author

Frank May is the author of four books for preservice and inservice teachers on writing and reading instruction. He received his doctorate at the University of Wisconsin–Madison, his master's at the University of Chicago, and his bachelor's at Antioch College in Yellow Springs, Ohio.

He is now a professor of education at Portland State University in Portland, Oregon, and was previously professor of education at the University of Puget Sound in Tacoma, Washington State University in Pullman, the University of North Carolina at Greensboro, and the University of Wisconsin–Madison.

The author's classroom teaching positions have included all of the grades from one to twelve and a variety of locations in the United States: Pelham, New Hampshire; New York City; Greensboro, North Carolina; Dayton, Ohio; Chicago, Illinois; and Pullman, Washington. He has been actively involved for many years in planning and implementing research on reading and writing instruction. As a result of this research he has created several instructional processes and has invented a practical qualitative scoring system for informal reading inventories.

589

Dr. May lives in Portland with Dr. Amy Driscoll, his writing and teaching colleague, his wife and best friend. Together they have six grown children.

Frank May's other name is Brad Eliot, a name that he uses for writing novels, short stories, and poetry.